D1356622

The Perceptual World

The Perceptual World

K. von FIEANDT

Huntutie 24A, 00950 Helsinki 95
Finland

I. K. MOUSTGAARD

University of Copenhagen, Copenhagen
Denmark

1977

ACADEMIC PRESS

London   New York   San Francisco
A Subsidiary of Harcourt Brace Jovanovich, Publishers

ACADEMIC PRESS INC. (LONDON) LTD.
24–28 Oval Road,
London NW1

United States Edition published by
ACADEMIC PRESS INC.
111 Fifth Avenue
New York, New York 10003

Library of Congress Catalog Card Number: 76–016991
ISBN: 0 12 725050 6

PRINTED IN GREAT BRITAIN BY
ROBERT MACLEHOSE AND CO. LTD.
PRINTERS TO THE UNIVERSITY OF GLASGOW

Preface

To produce an advanced, comprehensive, up-to-date text on all aspects of perception might appear—if not directly hazardous—at least highly ambitious. Although the number of books on perception has steadily increased, no book has been published dealing with the historical and theoretical classical European tradition and the outstanding achievements of contemporary Anglo-Saxon research. Most contemporary works on perception have been specialized. Here an attempt is made to show how the problems of the specialist fields and their possible solution, are interconnected.

This approach to the subject has obviously produced difficulties. Furthermore the authors have hoped to make available to contemporary Anglo-Saxon students the distinctive flavour of European psychology and to interest European students, at both undergraduate and graduate level, in recent developments in Anglo-Saxon research. Yet at the same time this book addresses itself to a scholarly awareness of psychological investigation and research. Primarily the present text has been planned and structured for the purposes of the student, as explained in an introductory chapter.

An introductory text which addresses itself to the beginner and contains a deeper orientation in the origins of contemporary perceptual experimentation is by no means controversial. But review of the deeper analysis of perceptual events is also needed for more advanced readers.

Both authors have had a joint interest in what might be called the "Scandinavian tradition" in perceptual psychology. Originally founded by A. Lehmann in Copenhagen this tradition was further carried on by E. Rubin (Copenhagen), D. Katz (Stockholm) and E. Kaila (Helsinki). Within this tradition, the authors—unlike other introductory texts—provide an historical introduction. The problems of psychophysics and perceptual experimentation, which developed out of philosophical and medical traditions in nineteenth and twentieth century Europe, have accordingly been examined. The authors believe that such an historical understanding is a necessary condition to appreciating contemporary accounts fully.

Such an approach has obvious problems. Firstly, the dimensions of the field of research have grown so tremendously that the ability of one individual to master all the available information is questioned. Secondly, research in neuropsychology and sensory physiology especially is so revolutionary that "facts" which today seem the last word in scientific accuracy have to be radically amended in the light of new research.

We have been lucky in this respect in finding three contributors, Dr. J. Mollon (Cambridge), Professor V. Sarris (Frankfurt a.m.) and Professor R. O. Viitamäki (Helsinki), each of whom provides an excellent addition to the text. Dr. Mollon has written chapters 3 and 4 on the neuronal and sensorial basis of perception, Professor Sarris chapter 2 on psychophysics and Professor Viitamäki chapter 21 on perception and personality.

Professor von Fieandt's book, The World of Perception (The Dorsey Press, Ill., U.S.A.), provided the basis for the present text. But important developments in perceptual research made it necessary to add seven completely new chapters. Almost all the original seventeen chapters have been extensively rewritten. Only chapter 22, on perception of pictorial art, has maintained its original shape. Relatively few contributions had been published meantime on this intricate field.

The present work will attract teachers at universities and institutes of technology who may want to pick out appropriate chapters, or use the text as complementary source material, or as additional reading to other course material.

Without aid from the following funds and foundations we would not have been able to complete our editorial task. Ministry of Education in Finland; Research Council for the Humanities in the Academy of Finland; The Finnish Cultural Foundation; Societas Scientiarum Fennica; The Niilo Helander Foundation; The Orion Foundation for Medical Research; The Sandoz Foundation, Switzerland.

Last but not least we want to thank all our friends and colleagues at our respective universities for their unselfish interest, advice and support at all stages of our time-consuming work.

Kai von Fieandt, Helsinki
I. K. Moustgaard, Copenhagen
31 January 1976

Contents

Part Four Personal Determinants and Appearances of the
Perceptual World

1 | Introduction

The aim of this book is to give graduate students a general introduction to methods and theories within the field of perceptual psychology. To this end the book provides the reader with ordinary textbook material on the sensory neurophysiological level running from peripheral and relatively simple mechanisms to superimposed central systems and processes. At the same time, in its most substantial parts, the book aims at giving the student an introduction to problems of psychophysics and perceptual experimentation, showing the connecting paths along which study in this field originated in Europe and America.

On the European continent perceptual research for a long time constituted the substantial part of academic experimental psychology. At the time of its origins this new science inherited most of its problems (concerning stimulus-experience relationships) from nineteenth century philosophy, and its methods from human physiology. The first great pioneers in Europe, Weber, Fechner and Wundt, originally worked as medical doctors or physiologists who regarded psychology as a kind of "psychophysics of perception". Perception and learning have always been the fields of psychology most concerned with biologically oriented philosophy. The medical schooling of the pioneers augmented the interest in perceptual problems. New developing fields of psychology borrowed their methods mainly from the study of perception.

In America, on the other hand, interest in the field of perception was evoked in connection with problems of learning and development. Admittedly, there was the influential laboratory at Cornell, founded in 1895 by Titchener who brought over the perceptually oriented tradition from

Germany. Yet the school of functionalism with its emphasis on learning had already originated in Chicago. Within a decade the behaviouristic trends and the corresponding new method—the recording of overt human reactions—dominated the way of reasoning among American scholars in psychology. It is not purely a matter of chance that behaviouristic interest in perception began with an interest in *perceptual learning*.

The traditional "gap"—if such a strong expression is justified at all— between European and American points of view has gradually been bridged. The strong advances inside the field of sensory physiology have contributed to improved methods and fresh perspectives of investigation. In this situation of progress and revolution an up to date effort is needed at actually combining original and still significant European material with the new technically sophisticated scope of investigation.

This kind of synthetic or unifying mode of presentation clearly presupposes three fundamental elements of our science to be analysed and investigated. We list them here as *psychophysics*, *neurophysiology* and *phenomenology*. Each of them plays an important role in structuring the study of perception. What these roles imply in detail shall be taken up for consideration in the relevant context of this presentation.

The Psychophysical Tradition

The origin of experimental psychology dates back to the last decades of the nineteenth century. In 1860 Fechner published his "Elements of Psychophysics" (translated into English in 1966) which pointed out a new way of measuring and scaling mental acts and entities. When the first experimental laboratory of psychology was founded in Leipzig in 1879 by Wilhelm Wundt, its goals and functions were based on a research programme initiated by Weber and Fechner which they called *psychophysics*.

In the following words Fechner (1966, p. 7), clearly expresses the aims of psychophysics: "Psychophysics should be understood here as an exact theory of the functionally dependent relations of body and soul or, more generally, of the material and the mental, of the physical and the psychological worlds." Physical material processes which accompany or occur in reaction to mental activity are to be called psychophysical processes— "Psychophysics must on the one hand be based upon psychology, on the other hand it promises to give psychology a mathematical foundation" (Fechner 1966, p. 10). This pioneer experimental psychologist also made a distinction between "outer" and "inner" psychophysics: "From physics outer psychophysics borrows its methodology; inner psychophysics leans more on physiology and anatomy." We shall return to this distinction in our text.

The research methods which were developed within the frame of this programme found their first and most frequent application in the measurements called threshold determination. It is interesting to follow the origin and the elaboration of the threshold concept, and how the definition of different thresholds influenced the directions in experimental research. A more detailed survey on the development of psychophysics and on the present state of investigations in it will be given in chapter 2.

Sensory Physiology and the Study of Perception

As pointed out in the previous section Fechner made a distinction between "inner" and "outer" psychophysics. What belonged to outer psychophysics represented for him primarily methodology, in the form applied within the science of physics. The first mentioned approach, the "inner" one, however, borrows its data from physiology and anatomy. Even in this respect Fechner was a child of his time. An increasing interest in physiology had started all over in Europe around the 1850's. As a reaction against the loose speculative philosophy around problems of the human mind, more empirical evidence for the conditions of mental functions and procedures were strongly demanded. As a culmination point in this historical development stands the monumental work of v. Helmholtz whose brilliant spirit covered several fields of physics and physiology. His "Physiological Optics" was in fact also a text in perceptual psychology. Hering with his good phenomenological schooling complemented his great colleague in his ability for astonishingly careful and fine description of experimental situations. Wundt, former assistant of v. Helmholtz, brought the overestimation of these "inner" fields to his laboratory of experimental psychology in his choice of biological problems as much as in his enthusiasm for physical and medical equipment.

Many theories in the history of psychophysics have rested on some convictions about the nature of relevant physiological mechanisms. Much of this work has been influenced by the pioneering research of Hartline and Ratliff (1957) and others in vision (Ratliff 1962, 1965). The new methods based on microelectrodes which have been implanted on the level of receptor cells, on receptive afferent fibres and on connecting neurons in the midbrain ganglia as well as single units of the cortex have uncovered hitherto completely unfamiliar kinds of neuronal processes. By means of these improved methods it could, for example, be shown that each receptor element has both excitatory effects directed toward the higher-order nuclei and also lateral inhibitory connections to cells at the same neural level. With appropriately applied electrodes even "higher up" in afferent neuronal systems (Granit 1962, Svaetichin and McNichol 1958, De Valois

1965, 1972, Hubel and Wiesel 1959, 1960, 1961, 1962, 1965, 1968, Lettvin *et al.* 1959, etc.) these alternating on-off mechanisms have been shown to exist on the level of the geniculate bodies and even the visual cortex.

Research on sensory processes has occupied a predominant focus of interest, first centred around the *visual* system and then covering more and more of traditional classes of our senses. It is a fascinating approach which implies the replacement of "unknown, mysterious black boxes" by modern neurophysiological models of explanation.

Phenomenological Analysis of Perception

One speaks of a phenomenological approach to perception whenever the experimenter has focused his interest on the adequate description of the so-called *phenomena* or *experiences* (to use an imperfect translation for this complex term).

In our earlier list phenomenology was the third of the three fundamental parts in the study of perception. It is the description primarily applied during the era of early psychophysics and even later in the 1920's and 1930's by investigators who preferred direct observations of perceptual events instead of registering and recording reactions in terms of numerical scales. Yet phenomenological description has proved necessary even as a mode of exploration when planning and preparing most advantageous experimental situations. The main interest of the phenomenologist is to observe the phenomena in any form they may take, and to describe them in a truthful manner.

Phenomenologists are primarily interested in the individual "perceptual worlds" of the perceivers rather than in a physical description of a mutual "objective world". According to Rubin (1947) it is not until a *physical picture of the world* has been invented that one can speak about these alternative descriptions. Members of primitive tribes, or preschool children in our culture, would not understand the difference between the two ways of looking at our behavioural world—the physical and the phenomenological— as indicated by the inner circle and the enclosing ring in Fig. 1.1.

An unsophisticated person experiences the whole surrounding world phenomenologically. To him, things exist in the way they appear, he has no doubt whatsoever concerning the existence of a real world, which is mutually shared by other individuals too. Even a sophisticated adult to some extent retains this world of immediate experiences. The sun "rises" and "sets" in our perceptual world. Around this world (the inner enclosed field in Fig. 1.1) a more highly developed man constructs a conventional world view based on information about "inanimate nature". This physical picture of the world (outer circle in the diagram) has arisen as a result of educational tradition and forces itself on our way of describing mental events. The strict natural sciences, according to Rubin, restrict themselves to investigations of this second-order construction of environmental phenomena. They cannot satisfy our desire to understand the world of our direct experience. Thus a systematic phenomenal description can be considered one of the tasks of psychology.

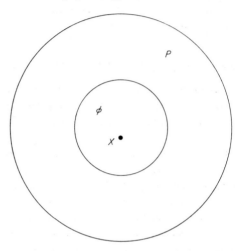

Fig. 1.1 Developmental stages in the perceived world (Rubin). An unsophisticated individual (a pre-school child) experiences the whole surrounding world in a phenomenal way (ϕ). Around it he constructs a physical picture of the world (P) as a result of sophistication. (From v. Fieandt, 1966 p. 5.)

The best illustrations of such a methodological approach can be found in the way some of the famous classical perceptualists, e.g. Hering, Rubin, Michotte, were working when they came upon their most striking new observations on our visual achievements. The empirical method followed by Hering throughout his book "Outlines of a Theory of the Light Sense" (transl. 1964) did not consist in gathering evidence from a series of systematic experiments. He invited the reader to carry out demonstrations, and the visual events he wanted to explain could only be caught by careful descriptions.

For example, when introducing his presentation of brightness and colour contrast phenomena (Hering 1920, pp. 115–129), he invites the reader to look at "a small piece of grey paper" when placed alternately on a white and on a black surrounding background (for chromatic impressions, alternately on a green and a yellow background). When discussing the contrast conditions he goes out from this presupposed evidence of the brightness and colour phenomena attained by means of direct observation.

For a closer explanation of the nature of the contrast phenomena, see chapter 6, pp. 187–189.

Content and Scope

The first nine chapters deal with fairly traditional psychophysical and neurophysiological problems of the senses in general and their receptors, of colour and light vision, and of auditory, olfactory, gustatory and soma-esthetical perception. Chapters 10 to 19 include the phenomenologically most important parts of the book. The concluding section, chapters 20 to 23, concentrates on man as a perceptual acting totality, and on the influences this total personality has on what will be perceived, especially experiences of pictorial art. Chapter 23 gives a summary of the main fundamental principles of perceptual functioning and of their epistemological implications.

Chapters 2 to 9 on the other hand are ordered in two subgroups of equal size, with 2 to 5 dealing with basic problems common to all modalities, and 6 to 9 concentrating on different senses and problems of their interaction.

Given these four levels (parts I–IV) of presentation it cannot be avoided that modality-specific processes, events and experiences have to be taken up for discussion several times but in still more complicated frames of reference. For example, the discussion of the perception of sound comes first in chapter 7, but higher achievements of audition (e.g. auditory distance, localization and auditory patterns) will not—strongly cognitive-oriented as they are—be taken up until chapter 17. The skin receptors are first touched upon in chapter 5, the perception of touch, vibration and temperature is discussed in chapter 8, and tactual complex shapes and patterns are dealt with in chapter 18.

The authors find this progression from peripheral and less conceptual events to more central connections a natural way of presentation. It only needs be kept in mind that the same sense modalities are discussed at several successive levels, within frameworks of increasing emphasis on central fields of psychology as a science of its own. The main principles arrived at, for instance in chapters 11, 12, 13 and 14 should be applied when later discussing other modalities in chapters 16, 17 and 18.

Why Perceptual Psychology?

Perceptual psychology has often been thought of as a field of its own, as something which must be regarded as strongly theoretical and very abstract. Yet the student observes without difficulty that some perceptual problems unavoidably lead to important statements and consequences within most branches of psychology.

There are *three main reasons* for studying perceptual psychology. (1) Perceptual events occur whenever there is behaviour. The very results of experimental perceptual research have convinced psychologists about the rich complexity of the background factors and conditions to what we pick up from our stimulus environment. More and more influential variables have been demonstrated.

(2) Perceptual research still offers an advantageous starting point and basis for theory construction within the total field of psychology. Even the analysis of social phenomena began with the aid of concepts taken over from the perceptual psychologists. This general applicability of perceptual concepts and methods holds true, even at the present time.

(3) Perceptual psychology shows an ever increasing amount of direct practical applications. Our perceptions determine to an astonishing extent how we behave in our everyday environment and in our social interactions.

Practical Applications of Perceptual Psychology

(1) *Ergonomics* is a systematic attempt at promoting our working conditions, e.g. at finding out more convenient and more efficient ways to handle our tools, to adapt ourselves to changing and demanding requirements of our job environments. It goes without saying that the study of perception is of prime importance for quite a lot of ergonomic applications.

Studies in visual performance play a substantial role for constructors of telescopes, scanning and steering devices, e.g. in ships, motor-vehicles and airplanes. Hearing conditions are important for everybody working with mass communication media (broadcasting, television, etc.). Even smell, taste and the cutaneous senses have gained more and more importance as indispensable aids to professional experts in different branches of food industries. The mass production of cooled "ready-made dishes" has given rise to several categories of "food tasters and smellers". Undoubtedly perceptual psychology might have something to offer these professionals, who want to know what is taking place in our organism and our behaviour when reacting to various kinds of food stimuli.

(2) How much our *traffic organisations* and the *driving safety on the highway systems* have improved from perceptual psychology is a well known fact. Imagine what the signal lights, the traffic signs, the judgments of speed—when encountering oncoming traffic—would look like had we not taken into account the most fundamental achievements of perceptual psychology (Näätänen and Summala, 1976).

(3) Along with the growing interest in *developmental psychology* new

experimental methods have been applied to newborn children, in order to investigate the development of visual perception. Fantz (1963) was interested in preference reactions of babies to stimulus objects differing in shapes. The subjects (from 4 days to 6 month old babies) lay on their backs and the time they spent looking at the stimuli was electronically registered. Fantz's experiments unmistakably prove that a child begins to visually interact with its environment at a very early stage of development.

Bower (1964) working with another method was able to demonstrate that after 50 to 60 days, newborn babies reacted adequately to the real form of objects, and that they were able at that age to recognize a triangle among other figures presented.

(4) The *differential psychology* is interested in individual differences of human behaviour. Even here it ought to be observed that these differences show up in *standardized perceptual situations*. It must not be forgotten that test situations, common psychodiagnostic praxis, are actually perceptual situations. So were the tests of the pioneer differential psychologist, F. Galton, who had his subjects visualize their breakfast table on the day of investigation.

Eysenck in particular started from differences of his observers in several perceptual achievements, when he constructed a system of normal and deviant "dimensions of personality". When he distinguished among different kinds of patients he made use of quite a few experiments, some of which were clearly perceptual in their nature. How several neurotic diseases, e.g. hysteria, may provoke visual, auditory, tactual and olfactory symptoms is a well known observation.

The Concept of "Perception" Precisely Defined

As mentioned above, the concept of perception as applied in this presentation comes close to the classical expression of the word. Early psychologists in the nineteenth century used to make a distinction between what they called "sensation" on the one hand and "perception" on the other. "Sensation" was thought of as some locally and specifically determined procedure in the receptive system of the organism, whereas "perception" referred to what was centrally picked up from the "sensory material". The opinion of the irrelevance of this distinction (see Gibson 1950, p. 15) is nowadays shared by most psychologists. Here the term "perception" will be preferred, despite its ambiguity. Such a term probably makes it easier to consider the alternatives of "objective" or "subjective", or better of "external" and "internal" determinants of our experienced life space (including ourself and our surrounding world). One of the trends within this field of research shows itself in the ever strengthening emphasis on the "subjective", i.e. the "projective" role of the perceiving organism. Four levels of investigation may preferably be discriminated:

1. Interest in primordial (sensorial) stimulation determinants (chapters 2 to 5 in the present text)
2. Interest in organizational determinants (chapters 6 to 9)
3. Interest in higher achievements of perception (motivation, selection, omission, completion, patterning, anticipation, see chapters 10 to 19)
4. Interest in social variables, e.g. of man in interaction with his environment (social perception, perception of art, etc. chapters 20 to 22).

Outlook and Plan of the Book

The processes of perception must be considered as some of the most vital conditions of adequate human actions. This book represents an action-oriented approach to the problems of perceptual psychology, stratified, as it were, from findings on the peripheral level all the way up to the most centrally focused contributions. The authors therefore have used as their scientific sources, material and results from the various psychological schools. In part I we rely on investigations in psychophysics, neurophysiology and neuropsychology. In the chapters grouped in parts II and III we complete these fields with phenomenological research and semantic descriptions which must be regarded as necessary conditions for a successful planning of experimental situations. In part IV we move further in the direction marked out by studies in personality and social interaction among "ordinary" and "deviant" individuals. The meanings of all these scientific terms will be explained and demonstrated during the presentation.

Part One

The Basis of Sensation:
Structures and Functions

2 | Basic Issues in Psychophysics

1. Scope and Relevance of Psychophysics

Introduction

Psychophysics is concerned with the experimental foundation of quantitative relationships between physical ("objective") and mental ("subjective") events in organisms. While a physical event is commonly termed as the *Stimulus* (S), a mental (psychical) event ("experience")—which is considered to be causally related to a physical event—is inferred from a behavioural *Response* (R), that is from an organism's individual reaction to a stimulus. When Fechner published his famous programmatic work (see chapter 1 pp. 2–3) "Elemente der Psychophysik" in 1860 he differentiated between the so called "outer" and "inner" psychophysics with respect to the human's response to stimulation. Modern psychophysiology corresponds to Fechner's inner psychophysics whereas the quantitative relationships between physical stimulation and a subject's verbal report characterize Fechner's better known outer psychophysics. In both cases, however, the lawful *sensory* or, should we say, *perceptual* reactions to physical stimuli are of main interest.

The psychophysical tradition started in Germany in the nineteenth century with the contributions of such eminent people as Weber, Fechner, Müller, and Urban. Basic interest in psychophysics was renewed, after the Second World War, expecially in the USA by S. S. Stevens and his research group at Harvard University and in Sweden by G. Ekman and his co-workers at the University of Stockholm.

The fact that psychology as an experimental science is largely built on both historical and modern developments in psychophysics is reflected by the notion that the history of experimental psychology is closely related to the history of psychophysics. The general importance of psychophysics for whole psychology stems from two main interrelated points:

(1) First, by means of psychophysics some basic experimental *methodology* has been introduced to psychology. In fact, nearly all genuine types of *measurement* in psychology are based on psychophysical methods. Since in any science, method represents the crucial tool of substantial research, the particular relevance of psychophysics for psychology becomes self evident.

(2) Much important research in quite different areas of *psychological content* (neuropsychology, social psychology, differential psychology, etc.) grew out of psychophysics. This historical fact is easy to understand because each successful scientific work is, in general, based on an efficacious methodology.

General Source Work in Psychophysics

Since the whole of psychology, in a broad sense, deals with behavioural responses to outer and inner stimulation, it becomes clear that "psychophysics" encompasses many different areas of scientific interest insofar as quantitative S–R laws are concerned. Consequently, there should be small surprise that there does not exist any cohesive experimental and theoretical unity in psychophysics. As there are nowadays many valuable monographs on both general and specific topics in psychophysics, this chapter is devoted to a rough overview of the most important issues in psychophysics. In other words, only the basic ideas of perceptual psychophysics will be considered here without going into any technical details. However, the interested student of psychophysics is urged to turn to the following representative works.

Whereas E. G. Boring's (1942) "Sensation and Perception in the History of Experimental Psychology" serves as an important *historical* introduction to the research aims and problems of psychophysics, there are well known *systematic* introductions to modern psychophysics, e.g. by Stevens (1951), Galanter (1962), Garner and Creelman (1967), Engen (1971a, 1971b), Ekman (1972), or Watson (1973). In all these works problems of psychophysical measurements are stressed. This emphasis on *scaling* holds particularly for the highly readable books of Guilford (1954), Torgerson (1963), Coombs (1964), and Gulliksen and Messick (1960). Beside these works the volumes of, e.g. Corso (1967), D'Amato (1970), Klix (1971), or Carterette and Friedman (1973, 1974) serve as excellent examples of how to treat psychophysical methodology systematically both from a scaling (measurement) and a psychological content point of view. The contributions of Jung (1961, 1967, 1973), Rosenblith (1961), Rosner (1962), Neff (1965, 1967), or Thompson (1967) are especially devoted to the sensory and *neurophysiological* aspects of psychophysics. Finally, methodological treatises, devoted rather to the *logical foundation* of psychophysics, have been offered by, e.g. Bischof (1966), Junge (1966), Savage (1970), Krantz *et al.* (1971), and Falmagne (1973).

Beside the broad area of general psychology, fields of application of modern psychophysics are, especially, *social psychology* (e.g. Thurstone, 1947; Sherif and Sherif,1969 ; Stevens, 1966b, 1972), *differential psychology*, including psychometrics, i.e. mental testing (e.g. Mosier, 1940, 1941; Gulliksen, 1950), *comparative psychology* (e.g. Stebbins, 1970; Blough and Lipsitt, 1971), and some branches of *applied psychology* like, e.g. engineering and environmental psychology (Chapanis *et al.*, 1949; Morgan *et al.*, 1963; Kryter, 1970; McCormick, 1970; Proshansky *et al.*, 1970; Glass and Singer, 1972). No claim is made here to deal with these interesting extensions of psychophysical knowledge to applied experimental work.

2. From Weber's Law to Fechner's Scaling Principle

Some basic problems in contemporary psychophysics may be neatly recognized by means of considering Weber's (1834) and Fechner's (1860) most influential contributions to psychology. It is illustrative to realize, just in the beginning of this paragraph, that both Weber's and Fechner's empirical "laws" do no hold in any general sense. Nevertheless they are still important firstly because they have been investigated on the basis of experimental *methods* and, secondly, they clearly reflect the fact, that, at least in psychology, there do not exist general quantitative laws which are experimentally correct for all time.

Weber's Weight-lifting Experimentation (1834)
Weber's experimental studies tried to answer the question of how to state a law of "just noticeable differences" (j.n.d.) between any possible pair of two different physical stimuli. In other words, Weber tried to establish a law which predicts a specific *difference threshold* (differential threshold; relative threshold) for any stimulus magnitude with a given sensory modality. Such a difference threshold (j.n.d.) corresponds to the minimal change in physical magnitude which can be detected as such by the perceiver. In his studies Weber relied on weight-lifting experimentation using the so-called *method of pair comparison* (from *n* different stimuli there are $n(n-1)/2$ possible pairs of stimuli to be compared with each other according to the judgmental alternatives "less", "more", or "equal").

Since Fechner's own pioneer work is based on Weber's findings, it may be of some interest to have Fechner quote a summary of Weber's historical experiments:

Weber makes a distinction between two modes of experimentation, one that involves only the sense of touch through the pressure of heavier and lighter weights on the hand resting on a table, the other where at the same time muscular sensation plays a role in lifting of weights, as when hand and weight are both raised. Now, regardless of whether a weight of 32 oz or 32 dr [drams] is employed as the heavier weight, in both modes of experimentation the just noticeable difference relative to the lesser weight remains practically the same. It amounted on the average for four persons and for both types of weight to 10·1 (ounces or drams) for the first kind and 3·0 for the second kind of experimentation, practically the same in both types of experiments. (Fechner, 1966, p. 115.)

This basic finding implies that the physical value of differential thresholds is directly proportional to stimulus intensity. That is, according to Weber,

[1] $\Delta S = k . S,$

where

S = any physical reference stimulus,

ΔS = the stimulus difference which corresponds to the experiential "just noticeable difference" (j.n.d.), and

k = an empirical constant the value of which has to be estimated for each sense modality separately.

This constant value k may be computed by means of a simple rearrangement of equation [1]:

[1a] $k = \Delta S/S.$ (Weber's law)

Example: If the reference stimulus S consists of a weight of 40 grams and the weight which is experienced to be just noticeably heavier happens to be at 41 grams, then $\Delta S = 41 - 40 = 1$; from this it follows that $k = 1/40 = 0·025$. If a reference stimulus of, say, $S = 400$ grams is used, the just noticeably heavier weight is expected to be of 410 grams if Weber's law holds, etc.

Table 2.1 shows some constant value k for *different* perceptual continua (Boring, *et al.*, 1948).
According to this table it appears, for example, that the discrimination capacity (sensitivity) for pitch is rather high ($k = 0·003$) as compared with the olfactory system ($k = 0·350$) in the human perceptual judgment. Furthermore, when choosing any specific value of a reference stimulus S_x (e.g. 1500 Hz for pitch)[1] and using the respective constant k, one can

1. Hz = an abbreviation for the so-called Hertz's unit, see chapter 7 p. 210.

Table 2.1. Weber ratios k for some perceptual continua (From Boring *et al.*, 1948)

Continuum	k
Pitch	0·003
Visual area	0·010
Brightness	0·016
Heaviness	0·019
Visual Length	0·025
Loudness	0·088
Pressure on palm	0·140
Taste	0·250
Smell	0·350

easily compute the stimulus value S_{x+1}, which is judged to be just noticeably "more" in magnitude than S_x according to the following equation:

[2] $$S_{x+1} = S_x(1 + k), \qquad (S_{x+1} > S_x)$$

which follows from Weber's basic equation [1].

The possibility of computing such a threshold is the main practical advantage of Weber's formula. This also allows the calculation of the total number n of j.n.d. steps for a stimulus range of a given sensory modality as follows (Woodworth and Schlosberg, 1955):

Let S_0 denote the primary reference stimulus and $S_1 = S_0(1 + k)$ the just noticeably higher stimulus value (Equation 2). In order to find the next j.n.d. stimulus value S_2 with, S_1 as reference stimulus, one simply uses the expression $S_2 = S_1(1 + k) = S_0(1 + k)^2$. It is easy to generalize this relation to the case of the next threshold values $S_3, S_4, \ldots S_n$:

[2a] $$S_n = S_0(1 + k)^n,$$

whereas n means the number of j.n.d. steps between the stimuli values S_0 and S_n. By means of this formula one may compute the number of just noticeable differences between any given range, for example of the pitch values $S = 1,000$ Hz and $S_n = 10,000$ Hz. Solving equation [2a] for n and using $k = 0.003$ from Table 2.1 one gets $n = 769$ pitch steps being noticeably different from each other. Generalizing this idea to all sensory modalities one may think of computing all possible numbers of j.n.d. steps which lie for a given modality between its *absolute threshold* S_0 (minimum noticeable stimulus magnitude) and its *upper threshold* S_n ("maximum perceptible", lat., i.e. the boundary above which increasing the magnitude of stimulation produces pain for an intensity dimension like light energy, etc. or no sensation at all for an extensive dimension like pitch).

Such computations would give us a comparative impression of sensory "richness" of differentiation for different modalities. However, this procedure presupposes that k remains *constant* over the entire stimulus range of a dimension. But this is empirically not the case. Both near the absolute and the upper thresholds the k values have generally been found to be higher than expected. To put this general empirical finding in other terms: according to Weber's "law" there should be found a parallel of the empirical k values when $k = \Delta S/S$ (ordinate) is plotted against S (abscissa); in contrast to this prediction, however, the empirical k values follow rather a positive quadratic trend (U shaped) for most perceptual continua. Weber's formula [1a] works fairly well only in the middle region of a given modality. As an example, Fig. 2.1 contains an illustrative set of data bearing on this point (sensitivity of saltness).

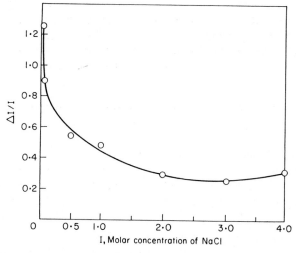

Fig. 2.1 Differential sensitivity $k(=\Delta I/I)$ for salt as a function of the molar concentration of the standard solution (I). The symbol I stands for "intensity" of stimulation (S). Instead of being constant the Weber ratio k appears to be variable with the reference solution I. (From Holway and Hurvich, 1937.)

For "Molar concentration" see p. 257.

One might well argue, therefore, that Weber's "law" should be termed more correctly an empirical *principle* (or "rule of thumb"). However, more interesting than the question of terminology is, in this connection, the notion of at least three important aspects of Weber's general finding:

(1) Weber has experimentally found a sensitivity "index" for a given modality at hand (weight-lifting) by means of introducing an important psychophysical *method* (pair comparison) which in itself has been of great value for later psychophysical work. This sensitivity index k appears to hold at least for the middle region of most perceptual continua.

(2) A quantitative principle of psychological *relativity* has been proven experimentally. This principle of relativity states that the numerical value of any just noticeable difference is not constant but varies relative to the magnitude of the respective reference stimulus. The generality of this finding is valid not only for the human perceptual judgment but also, apparently, for the animal's perceptual behaviour. Therefore, this principle of psychological relativity has some general significance for the organism's perceptual behaviour.

(3) Fechner's own psychophysical work, which was devoted to answering another psychological question, was based rather directly on Weber's principle both mathematically and empirically. This linkage between two different concepts is not only of a special historical interest but also of a general heuristic value since each experimental science tries to combine empirical findings and generalizations hitherto unrelated to higher-order principles. In the case of Weber's and Fechner's work, many scholars have believed that such a theoretical aim has been reached in the psychology of perception.

In order to understand this last implication (3) more fully, Fechner's psychophysical measurement will be described next.

Fechner's Basic Principle of Measurement (1860)

Fechner's basic aim was to find a generalized quantitative law of S–R relationships in psychophysics. The way in which he developed his well known S–R formula (*Fundamentalformel*) may be graphically demonstrated by means of formula [2a]. For better illustration a simple example of a j.n.d. scale is chosen here which has been mathematically constructed by Lewis (1960) from a set of data for pitch judgments of stimuli varying between about 30 and 12·000 Hz (Fig. 2.2). This curve shows the number of j.n.d. steps (ordinate) as a function of tonal frequency (abscissa) and represents a S–R relationship.

Fechner's main *assumption* was that each j.n.d. step (ordinate) is psychologically identical with a "unit" of sensation. This means, for example, it is assumed that the difference of, e.g. $200 - 100 = 100$ j.n.d. steps is not only numerically but *psychologically* equivalent to the difference of, say, $500 - 400 = 100$ steps in the upper region of the ordinate (see Fig. 2.2). There are, at least, three problems with this postulate:

(1) The psychological basis for this assumption has not been shown to be valid. That does not mean that the specific *S–R* relationship is an artefact in itself. It does mean, however, that the ordinate N (Fig. 2.2) does not necessarily reflect psychological *units* which would be invariant under different psychophysical methods to be used.

(2) Fechner uses Weber's formula [1a] and hypothesizes that an infinitesimal stimulus increment δS corresponds to an infinitesimal sensation increment δR so that the expression $k = \Delta S/S$ is replaced by $\delta R = c \cdot \delta S/S$, whereas c stands for an (theoretically unimportant) empirical constant.

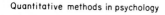

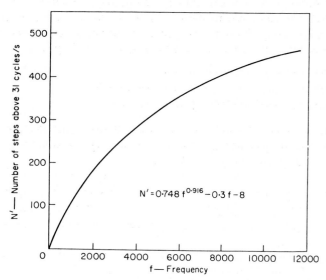

Fig. 2.2 Number of just noticeable differences, i.e. j.n.d. steps (ordinate) as a function of frequency in Hz (abscissa). This psychophysical function for the pitch of pure tones has been derived from the integration of Fechner's basic formula (*Fundamentalformel*). (From Lewis, 1960).

By means of mathematical integration Fechner gets the equation (*measurement formula*) of his "law":

[3] $R = K + c \cdot \log S,$ (*Fechner's law*)

whereas K means another (theoretically unimportant) empirical constant value. This equation implies that there is a linear relationship between $\log S$ and R values with intercept K and steepness c for different sense modalities.

Now, one has to remember that Weber's theoretically important value k is *not* an empirical constant over the entire range of a continuum. Therefore, Fechner's mathematical derivation of his "measurement formula" rests, at least, on a weak empirical basis.

(3) The S–R relationship is not invariant when different psychophysical

methods of perceptual judgment are used (see below). In this sense Fechner's formula lacks empirical generalizability.

Because of all these difficulties Fechner's law has been sharply criticized by many scholars. However, the scientifically more important features of Fechner's work are as follows:

(1) In order to find a general psychophysical principle, Fechner has investigated several sense modalities (weight, light, sound, temperature) rather *systematically*. By doing this he made use of at least three different psychophysical *methods* which soon became very well known:

(a) *method of limits* (Grenzmethode)
(b) *method of constant errors* (Konstanzmethode)
(c) *production method* (Herstellungsmethode)

the technical details of which are described almost in any modern elementary textbook of psychology (for an elementary introduction to these methods see, e.g. Manning and Rosenstock, 1968).

(2) By means of Fechner's work *psychophysics* has become an integral part both in perceptual psychology and in psychological measurement technology. New psychophysical techniques were also developed, especially after the Second World War, which have been inspired at least indirectly by Fechner's own scientific programme (see p. 27).

(3) Psychological measurement is based on psychophysical scaling principles. Though Fechner's own principle cannot be judged universally valid, some of his own measurement techniques have been successfully used in *applied* areas. This holds, at least, for the application of *specific S–R* relations. This means that Fechnerian psychophysics has been of pragmatic value, too.

3. General Assumptions of Contemporary Psychophysics

A Graphical Scheme of Psychophysical Processing

Contemporary psychophysical theory assumes rather generally that each Stimulus-Response relationship may be schematized by the consideration of three intercorrelated continua. These are the *Judgement* continuum (J), the *Physiological, Subjective,* or *Inferred* continuum (P), and the *Stimulus* dimension (S) as shown in Fig. 2.3. In this scheme there are graphically represented, as an example, four hypothetical discriminal dispersions on the continuum P corresponding to the four stimuli S_a, S_L, S_b, and S_c whereas the stimulus S_L defines some limen, e.g. the absolute threshold. The graphical model clarifies the basic assumption of the natural fluctuation of the perceiver's sensitivity to the stimuli $S_a, \ldots, S_c$, according to Thurstone (1927) who was the first to develop such an explicit probability model of psychophysical decision making. Because of simplicity all of these model's statistical frequency distributions are assumed to be normal and with equal variance around their means. The statistical character of the model reflects the fact that any psychophysical method makes use of several trials (sometimes more than 100 trials per stimulus) in order to establish reliable data on the $\mathcal{J}$ continuum.

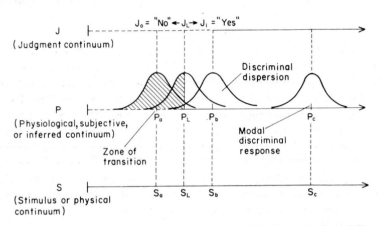

Fig. 2.3 Schematic arrangement of three conceptual continua S, P and $\mathcal{J}$ underlying contemporary psychophysical theory. For explanation see text. (From Corso, 1967.)

The scheme itself does not specify in which way these stimuli (S) are presented, nor by means of which method the behavioural measures $(\mathcal{J})$ are gained, nor what kinds of limens are to be investigated. However, it generally tells us that:

(1) the S, P, and $\mathcal{J}$ continua increase altogether in magnitude (intensity or extensity) from left to right,

(2) perfect monotonic intercorrelations between these continua are to be assumed, and

(3) there are transition zones of *probable* reactions (e.g. $\mathcal{J}_0 =$ "No"; i.e. for example: "I did not perceive S_L", etc.) to different physical stimuli (e.g. S_a, etc.).

The graphical model is general enough to encompass the basic psychophysical questions to be studied under various methods of stimulation (S) and different techniques of gaining perceptual measures $(\mathcal{J})$ for diverse kinds of sensory mechanisms (P). It permits study of Weber's and Fechner's questions as well as investigating those psychophysical problems which have been raised and developed later. Furthermore, it is based on the general assumption of statistical probabilities for the organism's response system as stated above.

A Formalized Model of General Psychophysics

According to classical thinking in psychology, psychophysics deals with the behavioural responses (R) to sensory inputs (S). Consequently, quantitative relationships between these events have been written in the general form:

[3a] $$R = F(S),$$

which says that R has been investigated as being a simple monotonic function F of the stimulus S. This was Fechner's own starting point.

The S–R model of psychology has been refuted more and more during the last decades because of its simplistic nature. In the meantime *Gestalt* psychology's great influence on the study of perception and cognition demands much more complex models of psychophysical processing. Strictly speaking, the assumption of investigating single S–R relationships is no longer based on the historical premise that psychologically relevant "stimuli" and "responses" are isolated events as "matters of fact". It is granted now that each psychological stimulation is, indeed, a compound of different aspects of the sensory input. The same holds, by analogy, for the response. It is only the very act of the measuring procedure itself which allows the psychophysicist to isolate somewhat artificially differential aspects of the stimulus and the response (Gibson, 1959, 1960). It is only in this sense that the following formalized *model* of general psychophysics (Graham, 1950) is conceptualized here as an economical working tool for studying single S–R relationships. To put this basic idea in other words, the isolated psychophysical relationships are abstract in nature as is true for any symbolized relationship. This notion by no means implies a general critique of psychophysical methods, since each experimental science deals with empirical laws which are and ought to be abstract in some way.

The general model of psychophysics reads as follows:

[4] $$R = f(a, b, c \ldots, \quad m \ldots t, \quad \ldots y, z, \ldots),$$

whereas the Response R is conceived to be a function f of the following variables:

$a, b, c, \ldots$ = quantitative values of different aspects of a molar stimulus S,

m = frequency of stimulation,

t = length of time of stimulation,

$y, z, \ldots$ = organismic factors, etc.

Typically, psychophysical experiments deal with the investigation of S–R relationships of the kind

[4a] $$R = F_1(a, b, c, \ldots),$$

which means that the other variables in Equation [4] are held constant. For conceptualizing a special S–R relationship, Equation [4a] should perhaps be written more correctly as

[4b] $$R = F_2(a, z_1),$$

where the symbol z_1 is conceived to reflect the special experimental procedure (e.g. psychophysical method, test instruction, etc.) under the *assumption* of other factors being kept constant throughout the psychophysical experiment at hand.

Other formal relationships may be deduced from Equation [4] as for example a simple psychophysical *equation of learning* which might be expressed as follows:

[4c] $$R = f_1(m),$$

where this equation shows the learning response R as being dependent on the frequency (m) of stimulation, only.

The symbol R is a generalized response indicator which might be further specified as, e.g. $R_A, R_B, \ldots$ according to the specific reactions to be provoked by the experimenter (see Garner *et al.*, 1956).

The model may be considered as an extension of the classical S–O–R model in psychology for the case of perceptual psychophysics where O stands for the "organism's" general influence on the behavioural response system. The model appears to be of some important heuristic value, though at first it may appear to be totally vague without having any specific meaning at all. However, the model facilitates the understanding of both the classical and the modern conceptualizations of specific psychophysical relationships. For example, it may help the scholar of perception to understand that different psychophysical methods may involve different perceptual functions. Also, it helps to recall that all classical and modern "laws" of psychophysics reflect only single abstract relations of a compound sensory, perceptual and cognitive functioning.

4. Some Problems and Methods of Psychophysics

Main Research Problems

According to Galanter (1962) psychophysics is concerned with four main areas of interest:

(1) *The detection problem.* The detection problem is, mainly, a problem of "absolute threshold". Below this threshold no sensory response is possible because of too weak a stimulation. Operationally, the absolute threshold can be defined, for example, as that statistical value at which the probability of stating "I've noticed the stimulus" is equal to the probability of stating "I've not noticed the stimulus" (see Fig. 2.3). The absolute threshold is often termed as the point of "psychological zero". Accordingly, the term "subliminal stimulation" refers to a stimulus the magnitude of which is less than the stimulus energy for the absolute threshold. Though much important experimental work has been done both with subliminal stimulation and absolute thresholds there is still some controversy as to the existence of subliminal perception (Dixon, 1971).

(2) *The recognition problem.* While the detection problem can be phrased as the question "Is there *anything* there?", the recognition problem can be stated as, "What is there?". This problem, therefore, is related to rather complex perceptual aspects of "recognition" as contrasted to the concept of absolute threshold which, by definition, is related to the hypothetical construct of a "sensory" processing.[2] An important book on *recognition* has been written by Neisser (1967). It shows that "recognition" is one key concept of perceptual (and sensory) and cognitive psychology.

(3) *The discrimination problem.* This problem might be phrased as *"Weber's problem"* in honour of the German physiologist E. H. Weber (1834) who as mentioned, p. 15 was concerned with the question of how big a difference between two physical stimuli must be in order to distinguish them ("just noticeable difference"). Contemporary psychophysics has other solutions at hand than had Weber (Green and Swets, 1966).

(4) *The scaling problem.* This problem might be phrased as *"Fechner's problem"* in honour of G. T. Fechner (1860) since he was the first to try to measure specific $S-R$ relationships according to a general psychophysical principle. Contemporary psychophysics has new proposals at hand to Fechner's problem (see below).

By giving detailed empirical answers to these main problem areas the study of the basic question as to the quantitative relation between the "objective" (physical) and the "subjective" (personal) world becomes prolific. The layman normally does not reflect about these fundamental problems of how to get experiential knowledge from the "outer" world, because to him the phenomenal facts appear to be rather self evident.

2. A strict differentiation between "sensation", on the one hand, and "perception", on the other hand is not scientifically meaningful as Gestalt psychology has convincingly shown (see, e.g., Boring, 1942; Corso, 1967). Nevertheless, such a distinction may be of some practical help for, e.g. the neuropsychologist when he tries to describe his particular interests in "psychophysics".

Therefore, sometimes it is not very easy to convince the layman of the importance for psychology to try and solve these fundamental questions of psychophysics. Though these problems still have not been fully answered by contemporary psychology, there does exist, nevertheless, a wealthy body of knowledge about many specific experimental details.

Some Psychophysical Methods

One general result of psychophysical research has been the development of many different psychophysical *methods*. There is now ample evidence that the psychophysical methodology had a great impact on the methodical development of psychology (see the references in the section above). In Table 2.2 some of the more well known techniques have been put together (Stevens, 1951, p. 43.) Most of them are described in detail in the work, for example, of Torgerson (1963). Four of these methods, which are briefly characterized in the table, may be called "classical" since Weber used the method of "paired comparison" (No. 3) while Fechner invented the three techniques No. 1, 2 and 4 (see p. 21). It is important to note, in this connection, that Stevens himself quite correctly states that ". . . there is no reason to suppose that these (psychophysical methods), or any others, are better or worse than what may be devised by tomorrow's genius" (Stevens, 1951, p. 43). It is simply that different methods are used for different problems at hand. This quotation shows not only that the listing of seven methods is rather arbitrary but also that Stevens' own psychophysical methods developed a couple of years later, may be judged according to the same line of evaluation.

Recently, Watson (1973, p. 279) has published a summary of psychophysical methods which looks very similar to Stevens' overview. Watson's table is based, however, on an additional distinction between "sensory capability" (the measurement of the sensitivity and resolving power of an organism) and "response proclivities" (the measurement of characteristic responses to particular stimulation, when the stimuli are clearly discriminable from each other). Still another possibility of summarizing contemporary psychophysical methods would be to categorize them in respect to the four main areas of interest in psychophysics, according to Galanter (see above).

5. Some "Indirect" and "Direct" Methods of Psychophysical Scaling

Basically, the scaling methods in psychophysics are classified within two types, i.e. the "indirect" and "direct" methods. This distinction stems from a methodological assumption that some methods allow the construction of psychological interval measurements only by means of "indirect" scaling

Table 2.2. Some methods of psychophysics (From Stevens, 1951)

Some Methods of Psychophysics			
Method	Brief Characterization	Usual Statistical Index	Problems to Which Most Applicable
1. Adjustment (average error)	Observer adjusts stimulus until it is subjectively equal to or in some desired relation to a criterion.	Average of settings (average error of settings measures precision).	Absolute threshold Equality Equal intervals Equal ratios
2. Minimal change (limits)	Experimenter varies stimulus upward and/or downward. Observer signals its apparent relation to a criterion.	Average value of stimulus at transition point of observer's judgment.	All thresholds Equality
3. Paired comparison	Stimuli are presented in pairs. Each stimulus is paired with each other stimulus. The observer indicates which of each pair is greater in respect of a given attribute.	Proportion of judgments calling one stimulus greater than another. (These proportions are sometimes translated into scale values via the assumption of a normal distribution of judgments.)	Order Equal intervals (under "distribution" assumption)
4. Constant stimuli	Several comparison stimuli are paired at random with a fixed standard. Observer says whether each comparison is greater or less than the standard. (A special case of paired comparisons.)	Size of difference limen equals stimulus distance between 50- and 75- per cent points on psychometric function.	All thresholds Equality Equal intervals Equal ratios
5. Quantal	Various fixed increments are added to a standard, with no time interval between. Each increment is added serveral times in succession. Observer indicates apparent presence or absence of the increment.	Size of sensory quantum equals distance between intercepts of rectilinear psychometric function.	Differential thresholds
6. Order of merit	Group of stimuli, presented simultaneously, are set in apparent rank order by the observer.	Average or median rank assigned by observers.	Order
7. Rating scale (single stimuli)	Each of a set of stimuli is given an "absolute" rating in terms of some attribute. Rating may be numerical or descriptive.	Average or median rating assigned by observers.	Order Equal intervals Stimulus rating

procedures, whereas others lead to psychologically meaningful units in a rather "direct", i.e. straightforward way of scale construction.

An "Indirect" Scaling Technique: The Method of Pair Comparison

The method of pair comparison has already been used by Weber (1834) for estimating threshold values (see above). By means of using pair comparison data in a quantitatively more sophisticated way than Weber, the construction of a *S–R scale*—instead of a simple threshold value—becomes possible as Thurstone (1927) has shown. This procedure presupposes, however, the validity of one of Thurstone's scaling models, by means of which the raw data from the pair comparison procedure (rank order type) are converted "indirectly" into normalized scale values (interval type).

For the psychophysical judgments $\mathcal{J}_i$ and $\mathcal{J}_k$ between any pair of, altogether, $n(n-1)/2$ possible comparisons there are assumed statistical response distributions being correlated with the respective discriminability distributions on continuum P (see Fig. 2.3, p. 22). In order to gain meaningful scale units the establishment of the psychological distance,

[5] $$D_{ik} = \mathcal{J}_i - \mathcal{J}_k,$$

between all pairwise mean response values $\mathcal{J}_i$ and $\mathcal{J}_k$ is important. For this aim the normalized standard deviations of the responses, i.e.

[6] $$z_{ik} = D_{ik}/s_{ik},$$

have to be considered whereas the standard deviation of a difference between two correlated measures i and k is mathematically defined as

[7] $$s_{ik} = \sqrt{s_i^2 + s_k^2 - 2r_{ik}s_i s_k}.$$

The symbols of this equation have the following meaning:

s_{ik} = standard deviation of a difference between the normal variables i and k,

s_i, s_k = the single standard deviations of the normal variables i and k, and

r_{ik} = the product-moment correlation coefficient for the variables i and k.

The reader who is unfamiliar both with psychophysical scaling and test theory is urged to consult one of the classical textbooks of test construction and test theory in order to understand the basic mathematics of Equation [7] (see, e.g. Gulliksen, 1950; Guilford, 1954; Lord and Novick, 1968). At any rate, the use of this very formula in the realm of psychophysical scaling underlines, once again, the close formal relations between psychophysical scaling and test construction.

For in both cases the establishment of the psychological *distance* between the reactions to "test" stimuli is of main methodological interest.

Solving Equation [6] for distance D_{ik} and considering Formula [7], one gets Thurstone's (1927) well known general expression of his "law of comparative judgment":

[8] $$D_{ik} = z_{ik}\sqrt{s_i^2 + s_k^2 - r_{ik}s_i s_k}.$$ (*Thurstone's law*)

This basic equation is simplified by means of several assumptions (Thurstone's Case V):

(a) the distribution of individual differences is normal,
(b) the standard deviations are all the same $(s_i = s_k)$,
(c) the correlation between any two test variables is zero $(r_{ik} = 0)$.

In this case Equation [8] is *reduced* $(D_{ik} \rightarrow D_{ik}^*)$ to the simple expression

[8a] $$D_{ik}^* = R_i - R_k = z_{ik}s\sqrt{2}$$

which, again, may be *reduced* $(D_{ik}^* \rightarrow d_{ik})$ to the simple relation

[8b] $$d_{ik} = R_i - R_k = z_{ik}$$ (*Thurstone's Case V*)

if one considers $s\sqrt{2}$ as the unit of measurement.

In practice, then, the Thurstonian scaling procedure simply requires first the estimation of the statistical mean proportion of the comparative judgments (e.g., "louder", "brighter", "heavier", etc.) for n psychological stimuli, and secondly, the transformation of these values into z_{ik} scores, simply by using a z *table*. The pair comparison method is the most prominent example of how to use "indirect" scaling principles. The basic character of *indirect* measurement is easily understandable when one realizes that simple pair comparison data are *transformed* into psychological measurements by the use of Thurstone's mathematical model. However, its main disadvantage is the introduction of strong, i.e. rather artificial assumptions, though recently some workers have tried to rely on less rigid premises (see e.g. David, 1963; Sjöberg, 1975). The main advantages of this measurement procedure are:

(1) One gets statistically reliable *S–R* relationships which serve well in many fields of application.
(2) The intercorrelations between these *S–R* relationships (pair comparison) and those being established by means of other psychophysical techniques

are generally rather high though such correlations are seldom linear but only monotonic in character (see, e.g. Ekman, 1962). The latter finding suggests that the aim of valid "interval" scaling, in the sense of establishing *equal units*, has not been gained so far by this and/or any other scaling method.

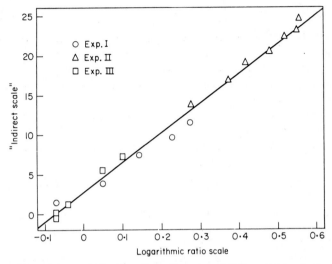

Fig. 2.4 A Comparison of "indirect" (ordinate) and "direct" (abscissa) scaling of aesthetic value for different handwritings (Ekman and Künnapas, 1962). As the data from three sub-experiments (I, II, III) show, there is a linear relationship only between the *logarithmic* values of magnitude estimation and the untransformed "indirect" scale values. This serves as an illustration for the basic nature of non-linear relationship between indirect and direct measurements. (From Ekman, 1972).

An experimental comparison of the measurement of aesthetic value by indirect and direct methods (see below) may serve as an illustrative example (Ekman and Künnapas, 1962). As Fig. 2.4 shows, there does exist a monotonic but not a linear relationship of the scale values for the aesthetic impressions of several handwritings (stimuli to be scaled). According to this example, which demonstrates consistent results of three sub-experiments I, II, and III, instead of a linear function there exists a logarithmic relation between the scale values from the direct method (magnitude estimation values at the abscissa) and from the indirect scaling technique (ordinate). (3) The psychophysical procedure itself is very simple. Even children and animals may be trained to give such behavioural responses of the "less—equal—more" type of reaction. This method has, therefore, the virtue of a very general applicability. Naturally, this is not the case of many other psychophysical scaling techniques.

There are other "indirect" methods of interest like the *"method of successive categories"*, the "method of triads", etc. which are described in length by, e.g. Torgerson (1963).

Two *"Direct"* Scaling Techniques: The Rating Scale v. the Method of Magnitude Estimation

In the last 20 years much basic psychophysical research has been concerned with the comparison of two "direct" scaling procedures, namely the *method of single stimuli* (rating scale) and the *method* of *magnitude estimation*. Whereas the rating scale technique is still very popular because of its simple and ubiquitous applicability in all fields of psychology, the method of magnitude estimation, which has been developed by S. S. Stevens (see, e.g. 1957), is of highest theoretical importance since, mostly by use of this very technique, Stevens and his scholars have created a wealthy body of knowledge which they call the *"new psychophysics"* (Marks 1974). Whereas the rating scale is a well known method even for the layman because of its common practical usage and, therefore, high face validity (see, e.g. the credit-point scales being used in schools, etc.), Stevens' technique is less well known and its psychological validity might not be so obvious to the layman so far. It should be also noted, that, at first sight, the use of rating scale procedures appears to corroborate the classical Fechnerian model while the magnitude estimation scale values are much more in line with Stevens' own general psychophysical model. Therefore, after a very brief description of the magnitude estimation procedure and Stevens' new psychophysical "law", some comparative data of validation are presented here in order to point to the still active rival interest in both rating scale and magnitude estimation measurements.

The *magnitude estimation* technique allows the observer to judge directly the subjective magnitude of a particular stimulus, in *reference* to a *standard* stimulus which is the same during the course of experimentation. In most experimental cases the standard's physical value corresponds to the *middle* of the comparative stimuli series. The perceiving subject is instructed to give judgmental responses in numerical units of subjective magnitude being informed that the standard stimulus has the size "10" (or, e.g. "100") and that he is free to assign any number to the stimuli to be judged ("comparative stimuli"), according to subjective *ratios*. If, for example, a comparative stimulus is experienced as being "half" in size as compared to the standard ("10"), the observer shall give the numerical response "5"; if another comparative stimulus is experienced as being "five times" larger in size than the standard "10", he shall give the answer "50", and so on. The subjective "calibrations" may be chosen by the subject himself.

Therefore the observer is free to choose any number insofar he is giving *ratio* judgments.

As Stevens has shown the data obtained by this procedure are described very well by power functions, of the general form,

[9] $R = Q \cdot S^n,$ (*Stevens' power law*)

where

$n =$ the empirical exponent which is assumed to be constant for a given modality but to vary characteristically from one modality to another,

$Q =$ an empirical constant which is, theoretically, of minor importance.

Equation [9] is a special case of Graham's (1950) general physical model (Equation 4). This relation is suggested (Stevens and Galanter, 1957; Stevens, 1961) to hold both for the so called *prothetic* continua, that is for those perceptual dimensions for which psychophysical judgments answer the question of "*how much*" (intensity), for example, heaviness of weights, brightness of lights, etc. and for the so-called *metathetic continua*, that is for those perceptual dimensions for which psychophysical judgments answer the question of "what kind" or "where" (quality or extensity),—length of lines, pitch of frequencies, etc. In other words, Stevens' "new psychophysics" encompasses altogether at least three methodical ingredients:

(1) a *method*, i.e. the magnitude estimation technique,
(2) a *perceptual theory*, i.e. the distinction between "prothetic" and "metathetic" continua which is made on psychophysiological grounds, and
(3) *a mathematical function*, i.e. the power law Equation [9] for fitting and predicting psychophysical data.

Stevens' basic power function [9] may be easily transformed, by taking logarithms on both sides, into

[9a] $\log R = P + n \cdot \log S,$

where, graphically, $P = \log Q$ means the *intercept* and n the *slope* in the example of a log S (abscissa) v. log R (ordinate) diagram. In Fig. 2.5 a magnitude scale of brightness serves as an illustration for the application of Equation [9a]. Since both the abscissa (luminance in decibels)[3] and the

3. In order to make it easier to compare facts in vision with those in hearing Stevens and Galanter (1957, p. 395) have proposed to state luminance in decibels re 10^{-10} lambert using a decibel-scale (see chapter 7 p. 215) with the reference level at 10^{-10} lambert Luminance is defined physically in footlamberts.

1 millilambert (mL) $= 0.929$ footlambert (ftL) $= 3.183$ candles per square m (c/m^2).

ordinate (magnitude estimations) are scaled in *log units*, the compuntional
work of estimating the intercept *P* and the slope *n* is straightforward
(Lewis, 1960).

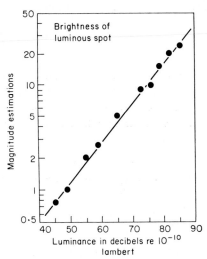

Fig. 2.5 Brightness of luminous spot as a function of luminance in decibels. The
magnitude estimation data, which are displayed in double logarithmic coordinates,
show a linear relationship thus supporting Stevens' *power-function* principle.
(From Stevens and Galanter, 1957, Fig. 11 p. 396.)

One of Stevens' most important contributions to psychophysics is the
systematic experimentation with so many different perceptual dimensions.
Since Ekman's school did follow Stevens' interest in large-scale psychophysical work there has been created a large body of new experimental
knowledge during the last years. As Table 2.3 shows, some representative
exponents *n* have been established for prothetic continua (Stevens, 1961).
According to Stevens, it appears that the magnitude of the exponents can
be interpreted in psychophysiological terms. This claim is illustrated by
displaying some magnitude data graphically on double logarithmic coordinates (Fig. 2.6) as this has been already demonstrated for brightness
(Fig. 2.5). The data of Fig. 2.6 were obtained by Stevens' (1961) *"method
of cross modality matching"*; these psychophysical data were obtained from
subjects just by "matching" the subjective *force of handgrip* proportionally
to the stimuli of various criterion modalities, such as electric shock or
warmth. The aim of this procedure was to have the magnitude scale values
less dependent on the subjects' numerical estimates. Instead of "force of
handgrip", any other intensity dimension could of course have been used.
Of particular interest is, also, that the exponents *n*, as having been computed

for each dimension from such cross modality experiments, have nearly the same numerical values as those which are estimated from simple magnitude scaling. Stevens (1961) has tried to show that this general finding is in line both mathematically and psychologically with his own premises. According to Stevens, such data serve as an important check on the validity (internal consistency) of the *new psychophysics*.

Table 2.3. Exponents (slopes) of the power functions relating psychological magnitude estimations to stimulus intensity (From Stevens, 1961)

Continuum	Exponent	Stimulus Conditions
Loudness	0·6	Binaural
Loudness	0·54	Monaural
Brightness	0·33	5° target—dark-adapted eye
Brightness	0·5	Point source—dark-adapted eye
Lightness	1·2	Reflectance of grey papers
Smell	0·55	Coffee odour
Smell	0·6	Heptane
Taste	0·8	Saccharine
Taste	1·3	Sucrose
Taste	1·3	Salt
Temperature	1·0	Cold—on arm
Temperature	1·6	Warmth—on arm
Vibration	0·95	60 Hz—on finger
Vibration	0·6	250 Hz—on finger
Duration	1·1	White-noise stimulus
Repetition rate	1·0	Light, sound, touch, and shock
Finger span	1·3	Thickness of wood blocks
Pressure on palm	1·1	Static force on skin
Heaviness	1·45	Lifted weights
Force of handgrip	1·7	Precision hand dynamometers
Autophonic level	1·1	Sound pressure of vocalization
Electric shock	3·5	60 Hz, through fingers

Stevens has gained further evidence for the general validity of his psychophysical theory from different sources of inquiry. As an example of the neuropsychological implications, Ekman (1972) quotes a recent study from Borg *et al.* (1968) which deals with both the psychophysical and neural responses to gustatory stimuli. As Fig. 2.7 shows both the psycho-physical (crosses) and neural (points) reactions have been displayed in double logarithmic coordinates as a function of stimulus concentration (abscissa). The data sets are not only best described by linear functions just fitting Stevens' power law model very well again but also the slope of both lines is almost the same ($n = 0.50$). This interesting finding suggests a close substantial psychophysiological "correlation" between both kinds of

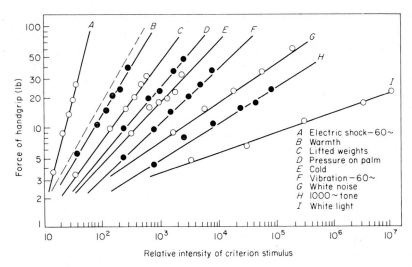

Fig. 2.6 Slopes (exponents) of Stevens' power functions for nine perceptual continua (*A*, *B*, . . . , *I*). The functions have been obtained by instructing the perceiver to match each stimulus with the corresponding intensity of handgrip (method of cross modality matching). (From Stevens, 1961).

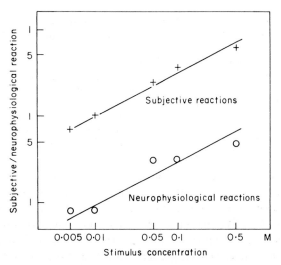

Fig. 2.7 Subjective (crosses) and neurophysiological (points) reactions as a function of stimulus concentration (intensity of gustatory stimulation). The parallel lines suggest a close psychophysiological correlation, which appears to be in agreement with Stevens' basic postulate for so-called *prothetic* perceptual continua (Borg *et al.* 1968). In spite of its convincing character these data should be best taken, however, as suggesting demonstrations but not as a proving evidence. (From Ekman, 1972).

measurements as this is demanded by the general model of psycho-physics (see Fig. 2.3). In passing, it should be added, however, that this finding does not have the quality of a direct "proof" on Stevens' psycho-physiological implications since it may well be that this "correlative" evidence is not related to Stevens' basic claims in such a direct way (see Thompson, 1967; Poulton, 1968).

As a further criterion of validity it has been shown that the magnitude estimation data are rather *context-free* (see chapter 23 p. 612), as compared, for example, to ratings. This is nicely illustrated in a comparative study cited by Galanter (1962). Two different stimulus spacings of, say, sound

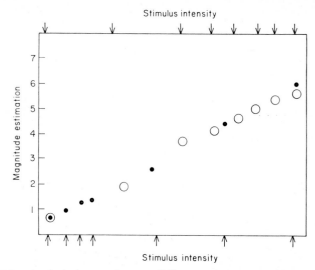

Fig. 2.8a Magnitude judgment for two different spacings (schematic diagram). A demonstration of *context-free* scaling by means of Stevens' method of magnitude estimation. (From Galanter, 1962).

were investigated both with magnitude judgments (Fig. 2.8a) and with category judgments (Fig. 2.8b), whereas the arrows point to one of the spacing conditions (the stimuli are more closely packed at the lower end of the scale, in this case). According to this illustration the magnitude esti-mations are invariant against different spacing conditions whereas just the opposite holds for category judgments; in other words the category scale appears to be severely "distorted" if the stimuli context is varied by spacing. Since a valid scaling procedure is expected to represent *invariant* relations of quantitative reactions to one and the same stimuli, it appears, accord-ing to Stevens, Galanter and others, that magnitude estimations are indeed valid as compared with category judgments (ratings). In this connection it is also interesting to note that category data seldom follow a straight line but rather a curvilinear function when plotted in double logarithmic coordinates. This implies that there is a nonlinear functional relationship between magnitude estimation values (abscissa) and category measurements (ordinate). In the review paper of Stevens and Galanter (1957) the general experimental finding points, in fact, to this nonlinear

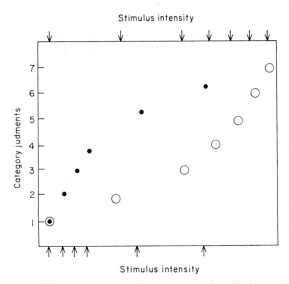

Fig. 2.8b Category judgments for two different spacings (schematic diagram). A demonstration of *context effects* in psychophysical judgment. There still is some controversy about the question if these context effects reflect semantic characteristics of the category scale, only, or perceptual alterations, or an interaction of both semantic and perceptual processing. (From Galanter, 1962).

relationship (see, also, Galanter and Messick, 1961; Sellin and Wolfgang, 1964). In view of the positive evidence for the *new psychophysics'* implications Stevens has been inclined to argue against the validity of category scale values. According to his notion ratings reflect rather "semantic" aspects of the category scaling procedure itself but not the "sensory" qualities of differential stimulation.

At this point, it should be noted that recently Stevens' general conclusions have been criticized by many workers on both theoretical and experimental grounds (see, e.g. Poulton, 1968; Savage, 1970; Watson, 1973; Anderson, 1974). Firstly, Stevens' *S–R* functions are not as invariant as the above figures indicate. There are a variety of conditions under which the general *form* of the *S–R* curves and the *exponents n* are *altered*, but no reasonable "sensory" explanation may be given for this (Poulton, 1968).

Secondly, the category scales do not *necessarily* reflect only the semantic usage of verbal labels. Thirdly, the validity criteria of both the method of magnitude estimation and the so-called power law lack some basic experimental and theoretical consistency (Anderson, 1974, p. 289 f.) At any rate, there is still much actual controversy about the whole approach of the new psychophysics.

However, in order to give a further demonstration of the great applicability of Stevens' work, an example of scaling *social value* may be of interest. Stevens (1959a) describes a study of the relation between the amount of US dollars (abscissa) and its respective subjective value (ordinata). As Fig. 2.9 shows, the results are, apparently, in line with a power law

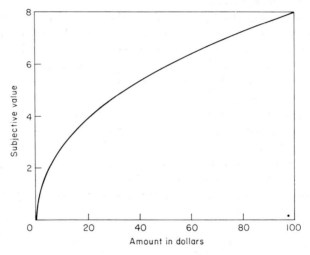

Fig. 2.9 Magnitude judgment as a function of the amount of US dollars. This *S–R* relationship of social value obeys Stevens' general psychophysical principle, too (power function). The data have been obtained by Galanter. (From Ekman, 1972).

function as to be expected by Stevens' psychophysical reasoning. Interestingly enough, however, this figure contains data which are not based on "sensory" mechanisms in contrast to Stevens' starting-point when interpreting his so-called "power law" psychophysiologically. This means that the magnitude estimation procedure is not only of scope and relevance, but also that some of Stevens' basic psychological assumptions may be well considered as *ad hoc*. Recently, a lucid comparative discussion from the standpoint of information theory has been given by the famous Finnish physiologist, Y. Reenpää (1973). The interested reader is referred to this article which has been published in German.

Take, for example, the following question: If the rating scale procedure had resulted in a data trend being rather different from the curve as depicted in this figure (Fig. 2.9)—a rather plausible assumption (see, e.g., Sellin and Wolfgang, 1964; Stevens, 1966b)—on which general rational psychophysical basis, then, should the magnitude estimation plot to be "preferred" to the category scaling? In this connection it may be of some interest to remind the reader of one of Stevens' own earlier statements as to the equal importance of methods for different questions (see p. 26).

There are other critical points of Stevens' new psychophysics which have been summarized by Watson (1973, p. 283 f.). The interested reader is referred to that article.

Intrasubjective Relationships
According to Ekman (1972), the so called "intrasubjective relationships" refer to R–R relations. No physical stimuli values (S) are needed in this case. Nevertheless, some classical and modern psychophysical methods can be successfully applied to this type of problem. As an example, the judgment of "similarity" between objects may be considered here (Eisler and Ekman, 1959; Künnapas and Künnapas, 1973).

According to Ekman, the *similarity* between different pitch stimuli for example, may be investigated from two different methodological points of view. In one experimental study seven frequencies of 200–12,800 Hz were chosen and scaled by means of, e.g. the magnitude estimation procedure. From this a similarity model was developed in which the value of predicted similarity (s_{ij}) is a function of the respective pair of magnitude scale values (R_i and R_j), namely,

[10]
$$s_{ij} = \frac{R_i}{(R_i + R_j)/2}, \quad (R_i \leqslant R_j).$$

This model simply states that, given the subjective R_i and R_j values, one can predict the psychological *similarity* between any of two stimuli i and j. Now, additionally, these test stimuli have been scaled according to their direct "similarity" values. Therefore such an additional experiment gives direct similarity judgments which are to be compared with the theoretical s_{ij} values as being predicted by Equation [10]. In Fig. 2.10 the relationship between predicted (abscissa) and empirical (ordinate) similarity data is depicted for pitch (circles), darkness (quadrats), and areas (triangles). There is a very close agreement between predicted and empirically established values for all three continua.

Though Equation [10] has been slightly modified rather recently by Künnapas and Künnapas (1973), it shows that it might become very useful to consider problems of scaling from an R–R standpoint as well (see also

Sjöberg, 1975). As Ekman (1972) says it may well be that some most important intrasubjective "laws" will be discovered by this attack, which is rather similar to the general approach of *psychometrics*.

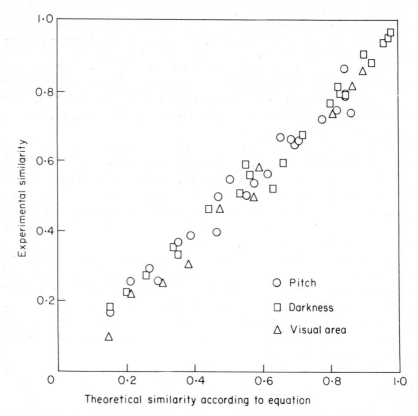

Fig. 2.10 A case of intrasubjective psychophysics: Empirical similarity judgment (ordinata) and theoretical "similarity" values for three different perceptual continua (pitch, darkness, visual area). The data are in close agreement with Eisler and Ekman's (1959) similarity model (see equation [10].) (From Ekman, 1972).

6. Recent Developments in Psychophysics

A careful consideration of the latest contributions to psychophysical theorizing is beyond the scope of this chapter. However, the interested reader should become familiar with the following recent developments in psychophysics.

One of the main features of modern psychophysics has been the enlargement of scope from unidimensional to *multidimensional psychophysics*.

Multidimensional scaling, the mathematics of which is similar to factor analysis, is treated in length for example, by Torgerson (1963). The important works on different theories and developments of this rather technical topic have been summarized in the recent two volumes on "Multidimensional Scaling", edited by R. N. Shephard and co-workers (1972). In contrast to the unidimensional approach, multivariate scaling models postulate two or more judgmental continua J (see Fig. 2.3) which are mathematically independent. Space does not allow us to go into any detail of these scaling procedures. The interested reader should know, at least, that the mathematical background for the understanding and application of these methods is much higher than for the application of classical psychophysical procedures.

The latter notion also holds for another interesting contribution to modern psychophysics, i.e. *signal detection theory* (see, e.g. Green and Swets, 1966). A valuable introductory textbook of signal detection theory has been written by McNichol (1972). A demonstration of a genuine application of this theory in human perceptual and cognitive function is given, e.g. by J. Mackworth (1970). For a short orientation the reader may consult Corso (1967). Signal detection theory rests, basically, on a probabilistic decision-making model for the "threshold" concept (see P continuum in Fig. 2.3). One of its main psychological assumptions is that psychophysical threshold data are influenced by the perceiver's differential "sets" when judging stimuli. Therefore, the separation between the observer's "sensitivity" (signal) and his personal variable "criteria" (noise) for giving psychophysical judgments (signal and noise) is the general aim of this promising approach.

Finally, Helson's (1964) *adaptation-level theory* deserves a special note since this contribution illustrates a further trend in psychophysics rather well, namely:

(1) Classical *S–R* psychology in psychophysics no longer serves as the general conceptual theoretical framework; i.e. the *relativity* of perceptual judgments is now granted by most research workers (Anderson, 1975).

(2) There is a growing methodological interest in combining the development and testing of both measurement and psychological theorizing altogether (see, especially, Anderson, 1974; see also McNichol and Pennington, 1973; Wilkening *et al.* 1972; Abresch and Sarris, 1975; Sarris and Heineken, 1976.) This means that a scaling theory should be linked to questions of psychological content.

Adaptation-level (AL) theory, which is based on a mathematical model, predicts that psychophysical judgments of stimuli are a monotonic function of its "background" (anchor) value. The organism's general perceptual behaviour is assumed to "adapt" to such background stimulation ("frame of reference"). For example, if a series of frequencies (e.g. 250, 275, 300, 325, and 350 Hz tones) is judged by use of a bipolar category scale (1 = very,

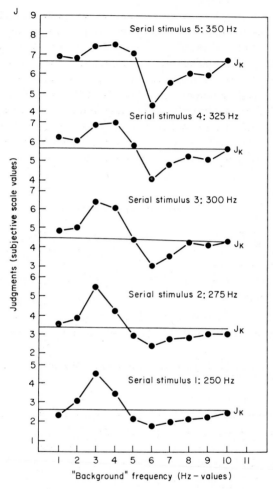

Fig. 2.11 A case of psychological relativity of perceptual judgments: The effectiveness of different "background" frequencies (abscissa) on psychological judgment (ordinate). The data show contrast-effect curves for five pitch stimuli (Sarris 1971; 1974). For explanation see text.

very low; ..., 5 = middle; ..., 9 = very, very high) the *relative* effects of a variable remote background is of main interest for AL theory (Appley, 1971). Whereas Helson was content to investigate only a small range of different background conditions, Sarris and his co-workers have been interested to "measure" these context effects in perceptual judgments rather systematically (Sarris, 1967, 1968, 1971; Wilkening et al. 1972; Abresch and Sarris, 1975).

As an example, Fig. 2.11 shows the effects of remote frequency anchors (abscissa) on pitch judgments (ordinate) with a wide range of anchors 25–10,000 Hz). Only the middle portion of each curve to a single stimulus (250, ..., 350 Hz) exhibits the familiar monotonic background effects; but as the anchor ("frame of reference") is extended in either direction, its effects are reduced, gradually, to zero (Sarris, 1971, 1974, 1976). This finding, which is in contrast to usual assumptions on "contrast" effects in psychophysics, has been replicated for several perceptual modalities by means of diverse psychophysical methods (Sarris, 1971). A brief evaluation of these experiments is given by Johnson (1972).

7. Concluding Remarks

Because of the mass of technical literature of psychophysical research work during the last few years it is easy to lose sight of the main problems still to be solved in this heterogeneous field of experimental psychology. Therefore, it is worthwhile to recognize the following main areas of developments in future psychophysics:

(1) There are still such basic problems of perceptual measurements in psychophysical theory with which Fechner has already dealt. It is interesting to remember in this connection, that Luce's (1972) somewhat provocative question: "What sort of measurement is psychophysical measurement?" is still under debate.

(2) Much further concern will be on problems of uni- v. multi-dimensional scaling in future research. This problem area will, hopefully, link the fields of perceptual and cognitive psychology, as well as the methodological topics of classical scaling and psychometrics, close together.

(3) Scaling methodology and psychological theory will have to be developed more and more within specific content fields of interest. The isolation of "measurements" from questions of psychological content will probably be reduced by means of new quantitative models in perceptual psychology.

(4) Much applied work in psychophysics has been published in the last years (see p. 15). This development may be taken as an indicator of growing methodological importance of psychophysics to whole psychology. However, one needs more data.

Finally, it seems that the fields of "perception" and "psychophysics" are becoming more closely related to each other, in as much that there are, and will be, better methodological answers to the above main problem areas than two or more decades ago. It may be considered an interesting symptom of scientific progress that in the fairly new journal *Perception and Psychophysics* one can detect more and more important experimental contributions to the present and future demands of perceptual psychophysics.

3 | Neurons and Neural Codes

The Neuron

The nerve cell, or *neuron*, is the basic anatomical unit of the nervous system; but it is protean in the forms it assumes and we shall see that it may not always be the basic functional unit.

The neuron of the textbooks is divided into three parts that reflect its functions of gathering, collating, and transmitting information (Fig. 3.1): *the dendrites*, which receive signals from other neurons, the *soma*, or cell

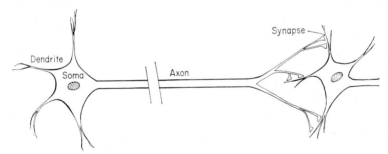

Fig. 3.1 A textbook neuron.

body, and the *axon*, which may be more than a metre in length and along which are carried nerve impulses, or *action potentials*. At its end the axon usually divides into a number of branches, which form junctions on the dendrites and cell bodies of other neurons. At these junctions, which are called *synapses*, the arrival of action potentials causes the release of packages of a *transmitter substance*. A particular synapse is either excitatory or inhibitory: the transmitter that it releases either increases or decreases the probability that the second neuron will respond with an action potential. In the resting state there is a difference in electrical potential between the inside and the outside of the recipient neuron, the inside being 60–90 millivolts negative relative to the outside, and the transmitter, by changing the permeability of the second cell's membrane to charged particles called *ions*, either reduces or increases this difference in potential. The depolarization, or reduction of the difference in voltage, that is produced at an excitatory synapse is called an *excitatory postsynaptic potential* (EPSP); the *hyperpolarization*, or increase in potential difference, that is produced at an inhibitory synapse, is called an *inhibitory postsynaptic potential* (IPSP). A single neuron may receive hundreds, sometimes tens of thousands, of synapses. It is thought (Eccles, 1973) that excitatory synapses are normally on dendrites and inhibitory synapses normally on cell bodies. At any instant the EPSP's and IPSP's sum algebraically to determine whether the cell will respond: if the net depolarization exceeds a certain threshold an action potential will be initiated near the point where the axon leaves the soma.

The action potential is unlike the graded potentials that gave rise to it: it is very brief, it is of fixed size and it is self-propagating. The membrane of the axon briefly becomes permeable to positively-charged sodium (Na^+) ions: the latter flow inwards and the internal charge typically reverses in sign, passing transiently from its resting value of -70 mv to $+20$ mv. A slightly slower, outward flux of positively-charged potassium ions (K^+), which pass through distinct channels in the membrane, soon restores the original polarization. Some axons are enclosed in an insulating *myelin sheath* which is interrupted regularly by *nodes of Ranvier*: here the depolarization leaps from node to node and the speed of conduction is increased.

Many sensory neurons correspond well with the classical description of the nerve cell, but the reader should be prepared to come across fundamental departures from the received pattern. Let us examine briefly a few of these variations.

(i) Neurons with axons shorter than 1 mm may not respond with action potentials. Of the six main types of nerve cell in the retina of the eye (see Fig. 3.2 and chapter 5 p. 101) the rods and cones, the bipolar cells and the horizontal cells respond only with graded potentials; and only the ganglion cells, the long axons of which form the optic nerve, respond with a train of action potentials. In the case of amacrine cells one or two spikes may be seen superimposed on a transient but graded depolarization.[1] These findings are well established for the retinae of amphibians, but graded potentials have also been recorded intracellularly in horizontal cells in the cat (Steinberg

1. The nature of the signals of amacrine cells is not yet clear. For discussion and references see Werblin (1974).

and Schmidt, 1970). It is an open question how common such neurons are elsewhere in the central nervous system.[2]

(ii) Not all synaptic transmission is chemical. Kaneko (1971) has shown direct electrical coupling of horizontal cells in the retina of the dogfish. Electrical connexions of this kind are thought to be associated with the *gap junctions*, or *tight junctions*, that have been described by anatomists and

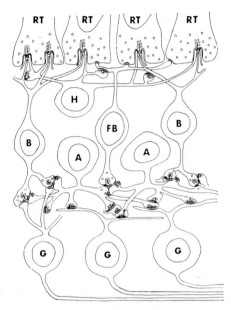

Fig. 3.2 A diagram to show the types of neuron and the synaptic arrangements found in vertebrate retinae. At the top of the figure are the receptor terminals (*RT*) and at the bottom are the ganglion cells (*G*), the long axons of which constitute the optic nerve. The receptors and the ganglion cells are connected, directly or indirectly, by bipolar cells (*B, FB*). Notice the laterally extending horizontal cells (*H*) and the axon-less amacrine cells (*A*). (From Dowling, 1970.)

at which the membranes of two cells are separated by as little as two nanometres.[3] Gap junctions have been found in the primate retina (Dowling and Boycott, 1966).

(iii) Often there is no clear distinction between the receptive ("postsynaptic") and transmissive ("presynaptic") parts of a neuron. An important

2. The discrete and unvarying action potential seems to have evolved as a device for transmitting neural signals over a distance. Since nerves have a very much higher resistance than does, say, copper wire, their signals must be regularly amplified. If information were transmitted by varying the size of the depolarization, any slight error in amplification might be rapidly multiplied. (For discussion, see Rushton, 1961b.)

3. 1 nanometre $= 10^{-9}$ m.

example is found in the phenomenon of *presynaptic inhibition* (Fig. 3.3A). Here the axon of the presynaptic inhibitory fibre (I) forms a synapse on the terminal of a second axon (E) and acts by depressing the output of excitatory transmitter at the second synapse rather than by opposing the post-synaptic action of that transmitter.

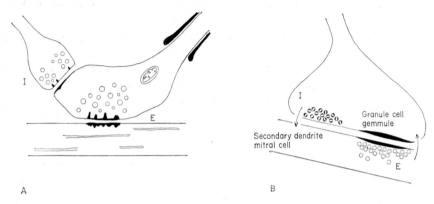

Fig. 3.3   A.   Presynaptic inhibition.
          B.   A reciprocal synapse in the olfactory lobe.

Impulses in the presynaptic fibre *depolarize* the terminal of the second axon. The size of action potentials in the latter is thereby reduced and the output of transmitter substance is in turn diminished.

A neuron may lack either a clearly-defined axon or clearly-defined dendrites. Thus the *granule* cells of the olfactory bulb[4] and the amacrine cells[5] of the retina are without axons: postsynaptic and presynaptic sites are intermingled on their dendrites.

(iv) It may be necessary to revise more radically the concept of a neuron and to question whether a nerve cell always does act as a single, integrated unit. Between the granule and mitral cells (chapter 5 p. 129) of the olfactory bulb (Shepherd, 1970; 1972; Rall, 1970) and between the amacrine and bipolar cells (chapter 5 pp. 103–106) of the retina (Dowling and Boycott, 1966) are found *reciprocal synapses*: two opposed synapses are found side by side and it is supposed that the granule and amacrine dendrites are providing immediate inhibitory feedback on to the mitral and bipolar cells respectively (Fig. 3.3B). It is possible that such *dendrodendritic* interactions may be quite local and that different parts of the inhibitory neuron may act independently. There may be cases where the cell body

4. The olfactory bulbs lie beneath the frontal lobes of the brain and receive the sensory nerves from the nose. (See chapter 5.)
5. "Amacrine" means literally "lacking a long fibre".

serves primarily a metabolic function and the physiologist who records only from the soma may gain a misleading or incomplete impression of the role of the cell. It is possible that the nervous system can economize by having one nutritive unit sustain more than one functional unit.

An instance where the parts of a neuron almost certainly do not speak to each other is provided by one of the types of horizontal cell found in the mammalian retina (Kolb, 1974). The dendrites of such a cell contact only cones (v. infra) whereas the axon terminals form an elaborately branched structure (the *terminal arborization*) that contacts only rods. These two parts of the cell are connected by a long and extremely slender axon that does not transmit action potentials and is thought to be incapable of transmitting graded potentials. That the cell body and the terminal arborization are indeed physiologically independent is suggested by the finding of Nelson *et al.*, (1975) that the two parts have different spectral sensitivities: when the retina was stimulated with red or blue flashes and electrophysiological recordings were made either from the cell bodies or from the terminal arborization of such cells in the cat, the terminal arborization, which draws its main input from rods, showed a proportionately greater sensitivity to blue light as would be expected. (See chapter 5.)

For a fuller discussion of the modifications that must be made to the neuron doctrine the book by Shepherd (1974) is recommended.

Receptors

To be regarded as specialized types of nerve cells are the *receptor cells* that are found at the first stage of any sensory system. The receptor can be defined as a neuron in which the generator potential is produced not by synaptic action but by particular environmental stimuli such as pressure, heat or light. The production of an electrical potential in response to stimulation is called *transduction*. Since most neurons respond to a chemical stimulus, transduction is not a peculiar property of receptors: an analogy can be drawn between the properties of the membrane of a receptor cell and those of the postsynaptic membrane of other neurons.

Some receptors, such as the hair cells of the ear (see Fig. 3.4A and chapter 5) and the rods of the retina (Fig. 3.4B), lack recognizable dendrites or axons and respond only with graded potentials that act directly upon the synaptic junctions. Other receptors, typically those found in the skin, muscles, joints and viscera of vertebrates (see chapter 5 p. 142), have long axon-like processes and the initial generator-potential gives rise to action potentials. A particularly well-studied example is the *Pacinian corpuscle* (Fig. 3.4C), a large pressure-receptor found throughout the body. Loewenstein and his collaborators have suggested that generator potentials and action potentials arise at distinct sites within this receptor cell (Loewenstein, 1970). The cell is surrounded by a granular mass called the *core* and the latter is in turn enclosed in concentric layers or lamellae, which rather resemble the coats of an onion. By removing both the lamellae and the core (some 99·9 per cent of

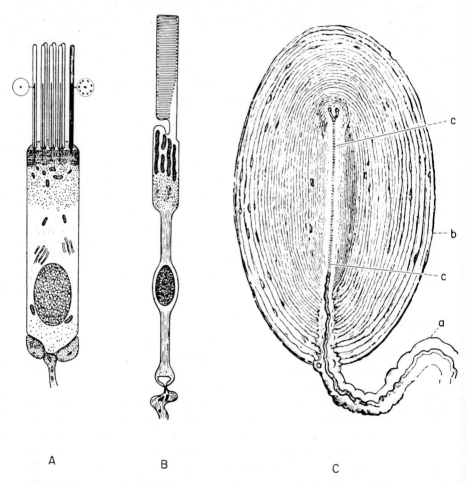

A   B   C

Fig. 3.4 Auditory (A), visual (B) and pressure (C) receptors. The Pacinian corpuscle (C) has a long axon-like fibre; the hair cells of the ear (A) and the rods of the retina (B) lack such a fibre.

the entire corpuscle) Loewenstein was able to stimulate, or to damage, selectively different parts of the receptor cell. Local pressure at different points on the exposed ending of the receptor cell produces graded potentials that are independent of one another, whereas action potentials are produced at the first node of Ranvier when the summed generator-potential exceeds a threshold. Since local distortion of the membrane of the nerve-ending produces only local increases in the conductance of the membrane, the total generator current increases with the area of membrane excited.

The visual receptors of vertebrates, the rods and cones, (Fig. 3.2) are unusual in that they respond to illumination with a hyperpolarization rather than a depolarization: the inside of the cell membrane becomes more negative (cf. chapter 5 pp. 104–106). The hyperpolarization is associated with an increase in the resistance of the membrane (Baylor and Fuortes, 1970) and it has been suggested that a transmitter is continuously released in darkness and is interrupted or decreased in illumination (Fuortes, 1971; Baylor and O'Bryan 1971).

Sensory Codes

Neurons transmit information. They also transmit action potentials. The reader is asked to distinguish carefully these two modes of discourse as we come now to discuss the ways in which the external world is represented in our sensory systems. We should also here anticipate later sections and mention that the chain of neurons that lies between a receptor and the brain is no longer regarded as a passive transmitter of coded information: analysis of the spatial and temporal pattern of stimulation may begin at the earliest stages.

Coding by Frequency

The *all-or-none* principle of nervous conduction, the principle that the action potentials of a particular neuron do not normally vary in size or duration, gained acceptance in the first decade of this century, but perhaps the most persuasive experiment was that reported in 1912 by Adrian: he showed that an impulse that has passed through a region of nerve, where its size is reduced by an anaesthetic or by cooling, will spontaneously regain its full strength when it re-enters normal nerve, provided only that it does succeed in getting through the region of decrement. The subsequent extension of the all-or-nothing principle to sensory nerves quickened the question of how the intensity of a stimulus is neurally represented. Previously it had been easy to postulate more or less of a *vis nervosa* or of an electrical potential. There now seemed two possibilities: as the stimulus increased in intensity either the number of active fibres might increase or the action potentials in a single fibre might become more frequent. It turned out that either or both of these principles might obtain in any particular sensory system. Experimental proof of coding by frequency came in Cambridge in 1925 when Adrian and Zotterman dissected a muscle of a frog until it probably contained only a single stretch receptor. Recording from the afferent[6] nerve and suspending various weights from a thread attached to the muscle, they found that nerve impulses became more frequent as the weight increased. Instances of frequency coding soon multiplied, especially when the introduction of the microelectrode made it much easier to record from single fibres. In Fig. 3.5 we show two examples,

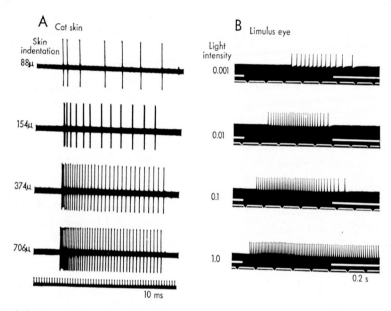

Fig. 3.5 The relation between stimulus intensity and the frequency of action potentials. The left-hand records (A) show the responses of a single afferent fibre in a cat's hairy skin as the indentation of the skin is increased. (From Mount-castle *In*: Eccles 1973.)

The right-hand panel shows the response of a single optic nerve fibre of *Limulus* to flashes of light of increasing intensity. The duration of the stimulus is shown by the gap in the white bar. (From Hartline, 1934.)

one drawn from the somatosensory system of the cat and one from the visual system of *Limulus*. Two additional features of these records are worthy of the reader's attention. Firstly, *adaptation* occurs: the frequency of action potentials wanes as a steady stimulus is maintained. Secondly, in the records for the *Limulus* eye an inverse relation can be seen between the intensity of the stimulus and the latency of the first action potential.

A vexed and notorious question is that of the mathematical relation

---

6. "Afferent" is used of fibres carrying signals to the brain; the antonym is "efferent".

between the intensity of the stimulus and the frequency of action potentials. Can we find in peripheral sensory nerves a basis for either the logarithmic or the power transforms discussed in chapter 2? It turns out that the psychophysiologist may secure almost any answer he wishes by choosing judiciously the modality he studies and the aspect of the response he measures. Thus, in a classic study of the *Limulus* eye, Hartline and Graham (1932) provided support for both logarithmic and power laws (Fig. 3.6).

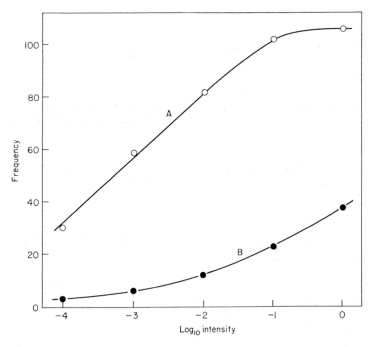

Fig. 3.6 The relation between the logarithm of the intensity of stimulating light and the frequency of action potentials (number per second) in a single optic nerve fibre of *Limulus*. Curve A shows the frequency of the initial maximal discharge. Curve B shows the frequency of discharge 3.5 s after the onset of illumination.

They teased out a single fibre from the optic nerve and recorded the frequency of action potentials produced by a wide range of light intensity. Curve *A* of Fig. 3.6 shows the frequency of impulses in the initial burst that follows the onset of light whereas curve *B* shows the frequency 3·5 seconds later: the former curve supports a logarithmic law, the latter a power law. A very similar choice of functions for the initial and steady states is available in the case of taste: during the first second of stimulation the frequency of impulses in a single taste fibre of the rat is related to the logarithm of the concentration of a salt solution, but five seconds after the onset of stimulation the relation is better described by a power function (Sato, 1971; Ogawa *et al.* 1974).

However, whether a power function or a logarithmic function proves the better description, we can separately ask how well neural frequency is related to perceived magnitude and here the most remarkable results are those of Zotterman (1971). By a quirk of nature one of the taste nerves, the *chorda tympani*, passes through the cavity of the middle ear (see chapter 5

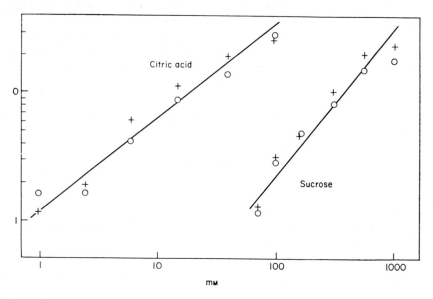

Fig. 3.7 Mean value of neural response (open circles) and of subjective response from two patients plotted against molarity of citric acid and sucrose solution.

p. 115) and during certain surgical operations it is exposed in a way that allows direct recording of the gross neural response to substances that are applied to the anterior part of the tongue. From a small number of patients, Zotterman and his collaborators have been able to obtain both neural recordings and psychophysical magnitude-estimations (see chapter 8) for the same stimulus solutions. Fig. 3.7 shows the intriguing agreement that has been obtained.

Before we leave the coding of intensity, we must be content to mention two complications. Firstly, we cannot predict *a priori* whether a particular physical dimension will or will not be represented by frequency within the nervous system: thus kinesthesis would not normally be classed among the intensive dimensions, the sensory continua that vary in intensity, and yet the position of a joint appears to be represented by the frequency of action potentials (Mountcastle et al 1963, see also chapter 5 p. 154). Secondly, an increase in temperature (Poulos and Lende, 1970) or in visual intensity (Kuffler, 1953; De Valois et al. 1965b) may lead to a fall in the activity of some sensory neurons, whereas a decrease in intensity leads to an increase in activity.

Coding by Place

In 1825 in Germany a prominent citizen was attacked and beaten one night by a political enemy. He sued for damages. The plaintiff told the court that the night was so dark he could not see his hand in front of his face and the judge was led to ask how then he had recognised his assailant. "It was very easy", replied the plaintiff, "in the lightning that occurred when he struck me in the eye I easily recognised the evil face of the accused."

It is said that it was this incident, much discussed in the contemporary newspapers, that led Johannes Müller to formulate in 1826 his doctrine of "specific nerve energies": sensations of different quality arise according to which nerve is excited and not according to the stimulus that excites the nerve.[7] Thus, if pressure on the eyeball stimulates the retina, we perceive light rather than pressure; and most of the senses can be excited by electricity, although the resulting sensation varies with the modality stimulated. It is the specialization of the sense-organs that ensures that particular nerves are normally excited only by their proper (or "adequate") stimulus. Müller supposed that the specificity of the sensation associated with each modality had its basis either in the central portion of the nerve or in the termination of the nerve in a sensorium where the soul enjoyed intercourse with the brain.

Müller tended to consider each sensory modality as a whole, postulating just five specific energies, one for each of the senses; but John Elliot (1780),

7. Müller's priority has often been debated, but he himself acknowledged the many scattered anticipations of his doctrine that stretch back to Aristotle (Müller, 1838). Perhaps the most systematic anticipation is to be found in the writings of the obscure, neglected and ill-fated Englishman, John Elliot, whose scientific career was abruptly ended in 1787 when he was committed to Newgate for "wilfully and maliciously discharging two pistols" at the person of the unfaithful Miss Boydell (Elliot, 1780, 1786, 1787). Through a study of the subjective sounds and colours produced by mechanical irritation of the ear and eye the unhappy Elliot became one of the first to appreciate the existence of specific transducers: he argued that physical vibrations were not, as many of his contemporaries supposed, directly conducted along the sensory nerves. This physiological insight in turn led him to the realization that the physical spectrum might extend into the infrared and the ultra-violet in the same way as there were acoustic stimuli of too high or too low a frequency for us to hear them. Much of the confusion that marked the physical theory of light and colour during the eighteenth century arose because few men were able to grasp that our eyes might be limited in their sensitivity and their discrimination.

Thomas Young (1801) and the mysterious G. Palmer (1786) had already suggested that different nerve fibres mediate the perception of different colours, and Müller himself was prepared to entertain a "place" theory for retinal position (Müller, 1838, Vol. 5, p. 351). It was, however, v. Helmholtz who most notably and most boldly extended the doctrine to individual fibres within a modality: he explicitly suggested that each of several thousand individual fibres in the auditory nerve was specific to a particular pitch. Yet the nature of the neural excitation was in every case the same (v. Helmholtz, 1863).

The representation of a stimulus attribute by which one of a set of neurons is active is now commonly known as *coding by place* (the reader may also come across references to the *labelled line hypothesis*). In Fig. 3.8A are shown modern *tuning curves* obtained by recording with microelectrodes from individual fibres in the cochlea nerve[8] (Evans, 1972): for each of several cells the intensity of a stimulating tone needed to give a detectable increase in activity is plotted against the frequency of the tone. Each fibre has its own *characteristic frequency* and the high-frequency side of the tuning curve is especially steep. How such fine tuning is achieved at so early a stage in the auditory system is an intriguing mystery (Evans, 1974a). In Fig. 3.8B are shown some analogous tuning curves for individual cells in the visual system. Here the abscissa is *spatial frequency*. It has been suggested in recent years, particularly by the Cambridge physiologists F. Campbell and J. Robson, that the visual system analyses the frequencies present in the spatial distribution of light on the retina just as the ear analyses the temporal frequencies present in a complex sound-wave. To the nature and function of this analysis of spatial frequency we shall return in the next chapter; and auditory analysis is further discussed in chapter 7.

In its simplest form the doctrine of specific nerve energies has never been acceptable; and it has seldom been held. As was fully appreciated by Müller himself (Müller, 1838, vol. 5, p. 272, *passim*) and, as has been especially emphasized by Gestaltist and phenomenological psychologists, our immediate perceptual experiences do not depend merely upon which sensory fibres are active, but are markedly influenced by our past experience, by our expectation and by interaction within and between sensory modalities. Many illustrations of this point will be found in later chapters of this book.

Although the doctrine of specific nerve energies needs to be qualified, it is the origin of most of the interesting problems in sensory psychology and we shall see in the next chapter that it is by no means dead: it has undergone a progressive encephalisation and reappears in the doctrine of the "trigger-feature detector" and that of the "grandmother cell". In thinking

8. The *cochlea* is the part of the inner ear that contains the auditory receptors.

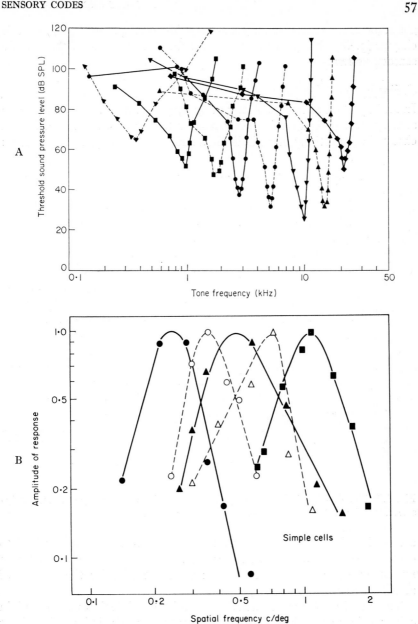

Fig. 3.8 Tuning curves for individual neurons in the cochlea nerve of the guinea pig (A) and in the visual cortex of the cat (B). Notice that in A it is the threshold that is plotted on the ordinate and sensitivity increases downwards, whereas in B the ordinate represents the relative size of the response to a stimulus of fixed contrast and varying frequency. (From Evans, 1972; Maffei and Fiorentini, 1973.)

c

about the doctrine it is well to recall the evidence, mentioned earlier in this
chapter (p. 48), that the neuron may not always be the functional unit of a
sensory system.

Coding by Spatial Pattern

In an important sense, absolute coding by place seldom occurs. Since no
sensory neuron has an infinitely narrow tuning curve (cf. Fig. 3.8), a
change in the activity of an individual neuron will always be ambiguous:

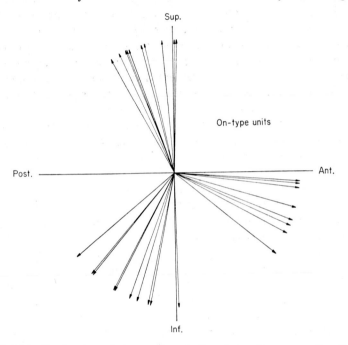

Fig. 3.9 The distribution of the preferred directions of on-type directionally-
selective units in the rabbit retina. (From Oyster, 1968.)

a drop in stimulus intensity or a slight qualitative change may lead to
exactly the same change in firing rate. A simple distinction between
frequency and place is not enough: we must consider the pattern of
activity in a population of neurons.[9]

The most celebrated illustration of this principle is to be found in
colour vision: at the initial stages of the visual system, information about

9. Helmholtz was quite clear about this; see his "Tonempfindungen," 1863 p. 219: Es
wird also schliesslich nur abhängen von der Feinheit, mit welcher die Erregungsstärke der
beiden entsprechenden Nervenfasern verglichen werden kann, wie kleine Abstufungen
der Tonhöne in dem Intervalle zweier Fasern wir noch werden unterscheiden können.'

wavelength is carried, almost certainly, by only three channels, each with broad sensitivities extending across most of the visible spectrum. Any individual visual receptor, any individual cone, is colour blind. It obeys the *Principle of Univariance* (Rushton, 1972): although its input may vary in wavelength and in intensity, its output varies only in one dimension—is *univariant*. Once a particular photon has been absorbed, all information about its wavelength (its energy-level) is lost. If stimulus intensity is suitably manipulated, different wavelengths can produce the same output from the cone. Thus information about colour is represented by the relative responses of different classes of cone (see chapter 6).

A nice analogy to the coding of colour can be found in the representation of the direction of movement in the rabbit's retina (Fig. 3.9). Some retinal ganglion cells in the rabbit respond maximally when an image moves across the retina in one particular direction, called the *preferred direction*. One class of such cells, those that respond best to relatively slow movement, have preferred directions that fall into just three groups (Oyster and Barlow, 1967). Such a population of units, each maximally sensitive to one of three preferred directions, would be able to represent unambiguously all possible directions of movement. Figure 3.9 is reminiscent of many geometrical representations of colour.

However, in the recent literature on vision only occasional lip-service has been paid to the ambiguity of the response of an individual neuron and the emphasis has been on *trigger features* (see chapter 4). It is in the case of the chemical senses that most has been made of coding by the pattern of activity in a set of neurons (Pfaffman, 1941; Ganchrow and Erickson, 1970; Sato, 1971). Most fibres of the *chorda tympani* seem to be concerned with more than one of the four classical qualities of taste—salt, sour, bitter and sweet. This can be seen in Fig. 3.10, which is taken from Ogawa *et al.* (1968) and which shows the mean responses of fifty fibres that have been ranked according to the strength of their response to salt (NaCl). The distribution among different fibres of sensitivity to each of the basic stimuli is not, however, entirely random; in both rat and hamster, for example, there are positive correlations among responses to hydrochloric acid (HCl), quinine ($C_{20}H_{24}N_2O_2$) and cooling and, in the hamster, sensitivity to sucrose ($C_{12}H_{22}O_{11}$) is negatively correlated with that to NaCl and positively correlated with that to warming. It is suggestive that in behavioural experiments those substances that prove least discriminable are those that produce similar patterns of neural activity in the *chorda tympani* (Marshall, 1968). It is also suggestive that the pattern of activity in a neural population may change as the concentration of a stimulus is increased, in a manner roughly similar to the way in which man the reported taste of some substances changes as intensity is increased. Thus the pattern of activity for potassium

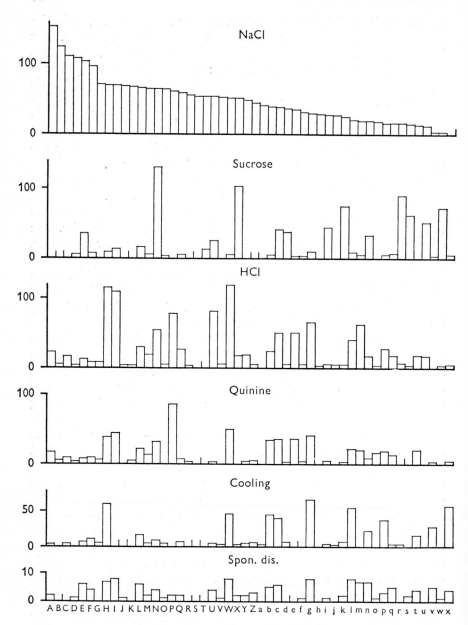

Fig. 3.10 Response profiles of fifty fibres in the chorda tympani of the rat (A, B, . . ., X). The fibres are arranged in order of their responsiveness to sodium chloride. The bottom row shows the spontaneous discharge. (From Ogawa *et al.* 1968.)

chloride (KCl) becomes more like that for salt as intensity increases and becomes less like that for weak sodium saccharine; and whereas at low concentrations the pattern for sodium saccharine (soluble saccharin $C_7H_4NNaO_3 S \cdot 2 H_2O$) has the characteristics associated with sweetness, it becomes more similar to those for NaCl and quinine as concentration increases (Ganchrow and Erickson, 1970).

Coding by temporal pattern

In principle, information could be carried by the pattern in time of action potentials within a single fibre or in a population of fibres. Such a hypothesis is most plausible where the stimulus information is itself intrinsically temporal: we could speak then of *temporal isomorphism*. There is indeed both psycho-acoustic and electrophysiological evidence for the *periodicity theory* of pitch perception, the theory that the period of a low-frequency sound-wave is represented directly in the cochlear nerve (see chapter 5 p. 119). Although any particular fibre may have a *best frequency*, a frequency to which it best responds, action potentials are found to be *phase locked*: they are most likely to occur in a fixed relation to the phase of a sinusoidal stimulus (see chapter 6) and thus they recur at integral multiples of the period of the stimulus. This is made clear in the histograms of Fig. 3.11 which are taken from Rose *et al.* (1967): the abscissae correspond to the intervals between successive action potentials and the ordinates to the number of impulses occurring at a particular interval. Notice that an individual fibre does not respond to every cycle of the stimulus even when the frequency is lower that 200 Hz; but we can imagine that in a population of fibres every cycle is represented. In the cat, phase-locking can be clearly seen up to 2500 Hz, but beyond 5000 Hz, if it is present, it cannot be detected in the records. That the human brain actually makes use of phase information is suggested by our capacity to localise low-frequency sounds purely on the basis of temporal differences between the two ears (see chapter 17 p. 463).

There has been a recurrent suggestion (but rather little evidence) that non-temporal qualities may be represented by temporal pattern (MacKay and McCulloch, 1952; Deutsch, 1955) and the hypothesis has most persistently been applied to the coding of wavelength (Troland, 1921; Fry, 1933; Myers, 1965). Thus Fry supposed that brightness was coded by the mean frequency of impulses but that this frequency could be modulated and that either the form or the period of the modulation-wave represented the wavelength of light. Saturation would correspond to the amplitude of the modulation. Most of the electrophysiological evidence now available to us suggests that colour is coded by place (De Valois *et al.* 1966; Zeki, 1973; Gouras 1974) and it is phenomenological evidence that is most often invoked

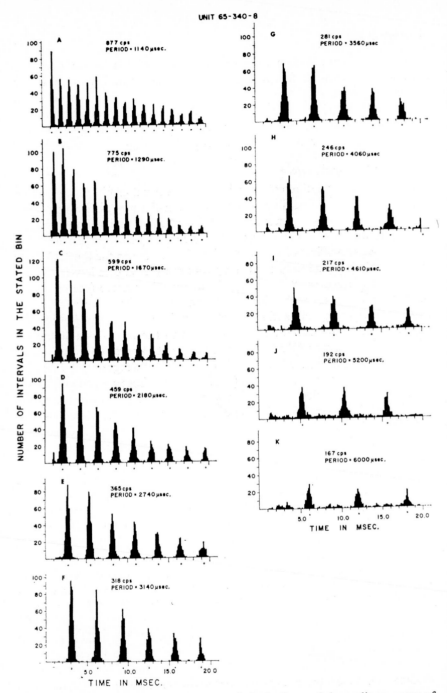

Fig. 3.11 Phase-locking in the responses of single fibres of the auditory nerve of squirrel monkeys. Each graph shows the distribution of interspike intervals for a particular frequency of the stimulating tone. The abscissa is the interval in milliseconds between successive action potentials and the ordinate shows the number of impulses occurring at each interval. Notice that the interspike intervals are clustered around integral multiples of the period of the stimulus. The best frequency for this particular neuron was 600 Hz.

in support of a temporal theory of colour vision. If a black and white disc such as that of Fig. 3.12 is rotated, one sees alternating bands of illusory

Fig. 3.12 A variant of Benham's top that has been designed to be rotated at 78 rpm. The reader is invited to photocopy it and try it out on his gramophone turntable (if you do not have access to a copying machine that reproduces solid tones, you will need to fill in the black areas; for, like the retina, most Xerox machines emphasize contours). If the disc is rotated clockwise, the innermost ring will be brownish-red and the outermost greenish-blue; if the sense of rotation is reversed the colours will be interchanged. Do not expect the illusory hues to be very rich; they are remarkable not for their saturation but because they occur at all. The best results are often achieved when the disc is lit by a tungsten reading lamp, but the effect can be obtained in daylight. It may be necessary to persevere a little, for the colours may become more salient after a little time. If you have difficulty, try different speeds, different viewing distances and different illuminations. You can also use this disc to examine the after-effect of seen movement. Fixate the centre of the disc as it rotates and then, after thirty seconds or so, switch your gaze to some stationary and textured object: it will appear to rotate in the opposite direction.

colours. These are the celebrated *Fechner-Benham colours* and it has been supposed that the sequence of black and white produces a neural sequence that mimics the code normally used to convey information about colour

(Fry, 1933; Festinger *et al.* 1971).[10] In judging this theory not too much weight should be placed on the dearth of electrophysiological evidence: the electrophysiologist tends not to see what he does not seek and it is only recently that the widespread introduction of small computers has allowed the detailed analysis of the temporal pattern of response.

In the case of stimulus properties that are usually held to be coded by the frequency of action potentials, subtler aspects of the temporal response may have been neglected. Werner and Mountcastle (1963), recording in monkeys from thalamic[11] neurons sensitive to the position of a joint (chapter 5 p. 152), have shown that the standard deviation of the intervals between successive action potentials is inversely and very highly correlated with frequency and thus carries the same information. This was true for both the spontaneous[12] and the driven activity of the cell, but the two types of activity could be distinguished by the slopes of the regression lines that related the frequency of impulses and the standard deviation of inter-spike intervals. Burkhardt and Whittle (1973) have gone further and have suggested that the degree of temporal jitter in the first of several spikes may carry information about stimulus intensity when the frequency of action potentials is unchanging: recording extracellularly from ganglion cells of the frog's retina and presenting brief flashes of different intensities, they showed that the variability of the latency of the first impulse could sometimes change markedly over a range of stimulus intensities where frequency was almost constant. Of course, a single ganglion cell does not have independent knowledge of when an individual flash occurred and thus cannot alone carry information about the latency of the response; but, if several such neurons respond in parallel, a later cell upon which they converge may respond the more strongly the more coincident the individual EPSP's. Burkhardt and Whittle's suggestion is important because it may explain a mysterious discrepancy between retinal physiology and human psychophysics: a dark-adapted man can discriminate the intensities of photopic[13] flashes over a ten-thousand-fold range (Whittle and

10. An alternative and even more venerable theory supposes that the different cone-mechanisms of the eye have different time constants. Mollon and Krauskopf (1973) provide some evidence that this is so. The latter paper and that by Festinger *et al.* provided further references.

11. The *thalamus*, a mass of cells in the centre of the brain (literally, and fancifully, the "couch" upon which each of the great cerebral hemispheres rests), is in part a relay station through which somatic and other sensory pathways reach the cortex and within which some sensory integration occurs.

12. Many sensory neurons are spontaneously active in the absence of an external stimulus. The reader can readily imagine that the synaptic influences upon the cell that produce spontaneous and driven activity are different and thus lend different statistical properties to its discharge.

13. *Photopic* vision is vision that depends on the cones of the retina; rod vision is referred to as scotopic. (See chapter 6, p. 110.)

Swanston, 1974), and yet such recordings as we have from the retinae of vertebrates suggest that single ganglion cells have, at any given level of adaptation, a dynamic range of only about one hundred to one (and the particular range does not vary much from cell to cell). A neural analysis of temporal jitter could perhaps extend this range.

Chung *et al.* (1970) have called attention to other ways in which the temporal pattern of discharge may be changed without a marked change in the average frequency of action potentials. They recorded from those fibres in the frog's optic nerve that discharge when a light is turned off, the "dimming fibres". In the dark the response of one class of dimming fibre is "bursty": groups of impulses are separated by silent intervals. The introduction of dim background illumination abolishes short inter-impulse intervals but leaves the longer intervals unchanged. In the case of another type of fibre a broad spectrum of inter-impulse intervals is recorded in the dark: dim illumination causes the distribution of intervals to become bimodal, so that only very long and very short intervals occur.

In assessing the plausibility of temporal coding the reader may wonder how a temporal pattern of action potentials could be recognized by later neural mechanisms. Two interesting possibilities arise from the fact that most axons end in hundreds or thousands of branches. If a second neuron, B, is to respond to one particular frequency of impulses in a presynaptic axon A, we might suppose that it receives direct excitation from one branch of A while a second branch excites an intermediate neuron that in turn itself excites B. If we further suppose that B responds only if it receives concurrent excitation over the direct and indirect pathways and that an impulse traversing the indirect pathway is subject to a fixed delay, then B will respond if the interval between successive impulses in A is equal to the delay introduced by the indirect pathway.[14] To prevent B responding to frequencies that are integral multiples of its preferred frequency we could add inhibitory circuits to our model or we could appeal to *refractoriness*, to the fact that a neuron remains inexcitable for a brief time after it has been depolarized. Neural refractoriness is indeed the crucial element in a theory of temporal pattern recognition proposed by Chung *et al.* The latter authors note that at each successive bifurcation the branches of an axon become finer, although the two new branches are seldom equal in diameter. It is known that refractory periods depend on axon diameter. Whether or not a particular branch of an axon will transmit a particular impulse will depend on the fibre's diameter and on the time since the last depolarization (as well as on the activity in adjacent fibres). Thus a temporal pattern will be converted into a spatial pattern of activity in the terminal branches of an axon.

14. Cf. the discussion of Exner's model of movement detection in chapter 4.

Thus it is clear that we cannot exclude temporal coding on the grounds that later neural mechanisms could not recognize a temporal pattern. However, we must end this section by mentioning two possible drawbacks of coding by temporal pattern. Firstly, since an impulse that immediately follows another is propagated with reduced velocity, a train of unequally spaced impulses will arrive more evenly spaced at the far end of a fibre (Brindley, 1970, p. 90). Secondly, in so far as a temporal pattern is used to represent non-temporal qualities of the stimulus it probably cannot also represent time itself: there must be a minimum sampling-interval and we must lose temporal resolution. However, our acuity in time is indeed very low and nature may compromise by providing us with specialized subsystems where accurate temporal information is required (Mollon, 1969): if a naive observer is to judge reliably the order of two events he needs an interval of as much as 100 ms*; and yet a difference of only 10μs* in arrival times at the two ears may change the apparent position of a click (Tobias and Zerlin, 1959) and an acuity of a similar order has been demonstrated electrophysiologically in single units of the inferior colliculus[15] (Rose et al. 1966). "Die Zeit erstarrt bei der Lokalisationsleistung zu Richtung im Raum" (Katz, 1944 p. 41).

Opponent Processes

Some sensory dimensions, such as brightness-darkness, direction of movement (cf. p. 73) and direction of curvature (cf. p. 74), have been described as *bipolar* or oppositional: the continuum has a central null-point at which neither of the complementary or antagonistic qualities are present.[16] Such dimensions are candidates for coding by *opponent process*. The presence of antagonistic physiological processes is suggested (though not proved) by the phenomenology of *simultaneous contrast* and of *complementary*, or *negative*, after-effects. A grey paper in a blue surround may look yellowish. If one fixates the centre of a disc such as that shown in Fig. 3.12 and allows the disc to rotate, stationary objects will afterwards appear to swirl around in the opposite direction. (On negative after-effects, see also chapters 4 and 6.)

The term *opponent process* has been used indiscriminately. Some who have used it have suggested that the same neuron may respond in two qualitatively distinct and antagonistic ways. In current neurophysiological usage, however, it usually refers to one of two less radical possibilities: (a) a special case of coding by frequency (or by graded potential) where opposite

---

* A millisecond (ms) is a thousandth of a second; a microsecond (μs) is a millionth. Thus we are faced here with a remarkable discrepancy of four orders of magnitude.

15. A mid-brain auditory centre ("colliculus" means "hillock").

16. Probably the best discussion of oppositional dimensions is still that by Gibson (1937).

sensory qualities cause the response to depart in opposite directions (increasing or decreasing) from an intermediate level of response that is defined as the null or resting level because it corresponds to either a physical or a phenomenological null-point; (b) a limiting case of coding by place, or by spatial pattern, where stimulus values on an oppositional dimension are represented by the relative activity in pairs (or in paired populations) of neurons, which may be linked by mutual inhibition.

To illustrate the first of these two possibilities we may take the suggestion of Flock (1965) that the hair cells in the lateral line organs[17] of fish may give opposite responses when the sensory hairs are bent in opposite directions, depolarization in one direction and hyperpolarization in the other (Fig. 3.13). Another, and much studied, example of a graded potential that may

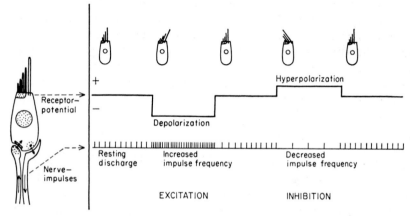

Fig. 3.13 Flock's theory of how hair cells operate, showing how the receptor potential and the frequency of nerve impulses depend on whether the sensory hairs are inclined toward or away from the Kinocilium.

decrease or increase according to the nature of the stimulus is the chromatic *S-potential* found in some vertebrate retinae. These potentials, first discovered by Svaetichin in the fish retina and originally thought to arise from cones, are now known to be the responses of one class of horizontal cells (Kaneko, 1970). The cell hyperpolarizes when the retina is stimulated with light from one part of the spectrum and depolarizes when it is stimulated with other wavelengths (see also chapter 5 and chapter 6, p. 169).

Of those sensory neurons that respond with discrete action potentials, many show a continuous discharge in the absence of any obvious stimulus.

17. The lateral-line canal organs in fishes are located in canals sunk below the skin and they detect movements of the surrounding water. The canals are filled with a viscous fluid that communicates with the outside water through narrow pores (See also chapter 5, p. 116.)

In principal, such a cell can signal by either an increase or a decrease in the frequency of action potentials. An interesting case is found in the afferent nerves from the *otolith organs*[18] of the thornback ray (Lowenstein and Roberts, 1950): tilting the organ in one direction from its normal position may increase the firing rate of a particular fibre and the opposite tilt may decrease it (Fig. 3.14A). Another and famous example is found in the response of some cells in the dorsal *lateral geniculate nucleus*[19] of the macaque monkey (De Valois *et al.* 1966): stimulation of the eye with light from one part of the spectrum will increase the frequency of action potentials; and stimulation with other wavelengths will reduce it (Fig. 3.14B).

However, in few such cases do we know for certain that both an increment and a decrement in firing-rate are treated as signals by later stages in the system. In the case of the so-called *opponent-colour* cells of the visual system, the inhibitory input, which causes the decrement in the spontaneous rate and which is assumed to arise from a distinct class of cones, may really serve to sharpen the spectral tuning of the cell rather than to generate a negative signal (Gouras, 1971). And usually, if neurons are found that respond with an increase to one attribute and with a decrease to its opposite, other cells are found that respond in the contrary fashion. Here we may have a situation akin to (B) above.

Three Final Remarks on Sensory Coding

We must end our discussion of sensory coding with three brief and general caveats.

Firstly, although we can correlate an aspect of the neural response with an attribute of the stimulus, we seldom know whether the aspect of the response that we examine is the one that is critical for later stages of the sensory system. We came across this difficulty in the case of the coding of intensity and again in the case of opponent processes.

Secondly, we may have neglected unduly the role of graded potentials: the transmission of information over long distances by means of discrete impulses may yet prove to be the dullest aspect of sensory analysis.

Thirdly, *coding* and *analysis*, usually confounded, may be worth distinguishing. Consider the two physiological theories of hearing that we briefly examined. When discussing coding by place we saw that auditory frequency could be represented by which neuron was active but we have also seen that low frequencies might be represented rather directly in the

18. The otolith organs are gravity-receptors and are concerned in the maintenance of an animal's equilibrium. (See chapter 5, p. 155.)

19. An extension of the thalamus, the lateral geniculate nucleus receives axons from the retina and projects in turn to the visual cortex of the brain.

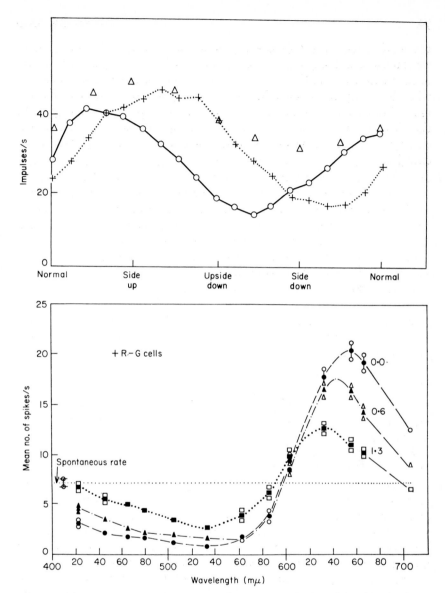

Fig. 3.14 Top. The responses of a single fibre of the utriculus of the thornback ray. The open triangles show the impulse frequencies recorded when the preparation was steady in a particular position. The circles and crosses show the frequencies obtained during continuous tilts in opposite directions. The solid curve is to be read from left to right and the dotted curve from right to left. (From Lowenstein and Roberts, 1950.)

Below. The responses of single cells in the lateral geniculate nucleus of the macaque monkey. All of these particular cells were excited by red light and inhibited by green. The dotted horizontal line in the figure shows the mean firing rate in the absence of stimulation. (From De Valois et al., 1966.)

temporal pattern of impulses. Many psychophysiologists, if pressed, would want to say that the two theories were not of the same kind and that in the former case some analysis, and even recognition, had already occurred, whereas a temporal or a spatial pattern was a mere code and would await recognition by a later neural mechanism. This, perhaps, is why place theories have proved so seductive to so many for so long. In the next chapter we shall return to this aspect of the doctrine of specific nerve energies.

4 | Neural Analysis

The Feature Detector

The last two decades have seen the doctrine of specific nerve energies elaborated in the concept of the "feature detector". The inquisitive micro-electrode has shown that vertebrate sensory systems contain neurons apparently designed to detect those features of the physical environment that either are of immediate biological significance to the animal, or else are especially informative for the identification of objects. Above all, we find neurons that are alert for a particular kind of change, the temporal change that may reveal prey or predator, the spatial change that may mark the contour of an object.[1]

The detection of movement, for example, is of universal and primitive importance and it has long been suspected from phenomenological evidence that in man's visual system there survive specialized mechanisms that detect movement. "It is experimentally certain", wrote William James, "that the feeling of motion is given to us as a direct and simple sensation." In the periphery of our visual field we can detect slight movements even when we cannot spatially resolve the starting and ending points of the movement. In unusual circumstances, movement may be phenomenally dissociated from change of position or of shape (Bowditch and Hall, 1880;

---

1. For further discussions of the matters covered in this chapter the reader may turn to Barlow (1972), Blakemore (1974), Dodwell (1970), Hubel (1963), Konorski (1967), Lettvin, Maturana, McCulloch and Pitts (1959), Virsu (1973) and Exner (1894). The neuro-physiology of auditory pattern recognition is reviewed by Evans (1974b). Much useful material is to be found in the successive volumes of the *Handbook of Sensory Physiology*, published by Springer-Verlag, and of the *Neurosciences Study Program*, published by the Rockefeller University Press (Vols I and II) and the MIT Press (Vol. III).

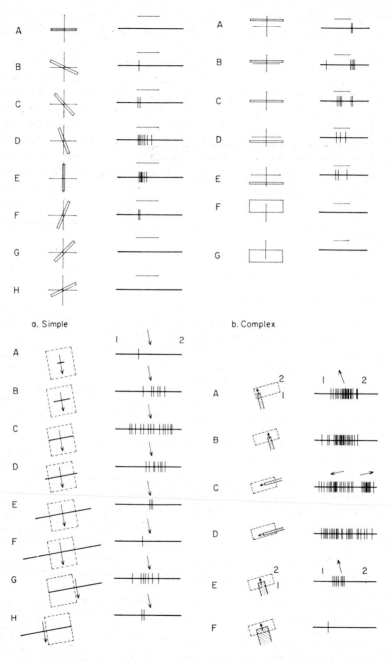

a. Simple

b. Complex

c. Lower-order hypercomplex

d. Higher-order hypercomplex

Wertheimer, 1912; Graybiel *et al.* 1946; see also chapter 16 p. 416); and movement, like other sensory qualities such as brightness and colour, can give rise to simultaneous and successive contrast. As early as 1894, considerations of this kind led the prescient psychophysiologist Exner to suggest that our visual system contains single cells sensitive to the direction of movement (see Fig. 4.5). Neurons of this kind, Exner argued, must occur at a stage before the signals from the two eyes are combined, for, if corresponding parts of the two retinae are simultaneously stimulated by movement in opposite directions, the direction of the illusory after-effect depends on which eye is tested. In 1953 Barlow published the first report of a class of ganglion cells in the retina of the frog that were particularly sensitive to a small object moving within their receptive field.[2] Such cells, he noted,

2. See also chapter 16 p. 415. The receptive-field of a cell is that area of the receptive surface, of the retina, say, or the skin, within which stimulation can affect the response of the cell concerned.

Fig. 4.1 Hubel and Wiesel's classification of the types of neuron found in the visual cortex of the cat.

In each case typical stimuli are shown to the left and the neural responses they characteristically evoke are shown to the right. In (*a*) and (*b*) the short lines above the neural records represent the period for which the stimulus was present and in (*c*) and (*d*) the arrows represent the direction of stimulus movement.

(a) *Simple cell.* The maximum response was elicited by a vertical slit of light that passed through the centre of the receptive field (*E*). The responses was reduced if the orientation or the position of the slit was changed. (From Hubel and Wiesel, 1959.)

(b) *Complex cell.* A horizontal slit evoked a response anywhere within a receptive field that had a diameter of three degrees of visual angle. When the slit was shone anywhere within the upper half of the receptive field the response was at the offset of the stimulus (*A, B*); in the lower part of the field the response was to the presence of a stimulus (*D, E*). When the slit was in an intermediate position (*C*), the cell responded at both onset and offset. However, and this is critical to the definition of a complex cell, a summation does not occur within the two parts of the field: large rectangles covering the entire lower or upper halves of the field (*F, G*) were completely ineffective. (From Hubel and Wiesel, 1962.)

(c) *Lower-order hypercomplex cell.* To evoke a strong response the stimulus had to be of a particular orientation and had not to extend beyond the boundaries shown by broken lines (*C*). The optimum length was about three degrees. In the case of this cell the left-hand antagonistic region seemed to be more powerful than the right hand one (compare *G* and *H*); and some lower-order hypercomplex units are stopped at only one end. (From Hubel and Wiesel, 1965.)

(d) *Higher-order hypercomplex cell.* The cell responded to a narrow tongue introduced into the receptive field in either of two orientations 90 degrees apart (compare *A* and *C*). The exact position of the tongue did not matter (compare *A* and *B*; and *C* and *D*) but if its width was increased the response was reduced (*E, F*). In *A, B, E, F* the duration of the samples was 5 s; in *C, D* it was 10 seconds. (From Hubel and Wiesel, 1965.)

could serve the frog well as "fly detectors". Cells with these properties, how-ever, have not proved exclusive to the insectivorous frog and have since been found in the retinae of many different vertebrates, including primates. Cells that are sensitive to the actual direction of movement have been discovered in the retinae of rabbits and pigeons; and, despite an earlier belief that the analysis of movement was *encephalized*[3] in higher mammals, such cells have now been reported in the retinae of cats (Hoffmann, 1973). A typical unit in the rabbit's retina responds with a burst of firing to movement in the preferred direction whether the stimulus is a white spot on a dark ground or a black spot on a light ground; it may be inhibited by movement in the opposite, or *null*, direction (Barlow *et al.* 1964).

The cells that are sensitive to the direction in which a delicate tactile stimulus is drawn across a particular area of skin have been found in the cortex (somatosensory Area 1) of the monkey (Whitsel *et al.* 1972). Similarly, cells specific to the direction of movement of a sound source have been reported in the auditory system of the cat (Al'tman and Markovich, 1969); but the truest auditory analogue to movement across the retina is perhaps move-ment along the basilar membrane (see chapter 7), that is, a change in the pitch of the stimulus. Whitfield and Evans (1965) have, in fact, described cells in the auditory cortex of the cat that respond to only one direction of change of acoustic frequency.

The catalogue of the feature detectors found in the major sensory systems is now a very long one. Figure 4.1 shows the classical types of unit described by Hubel and Wiesel in the visual cortex of the cat and the monkey (see also chapter 5). The *simple cell* has a bar-shaped receptive field that can be divided into discrete excitatory and inhibitory regions. The response to a stationary edge or bar can be predicted from a plot of the field made with flashing spots. Thus the simple cell responds optimally to a bar or edge in a particular orientation and a particular position. The *complex cell* typically has a larger receptive field and responds throughout its field to a bar or edge of a particular orientation; its receptive field, unlike that of a simple cell, cannot be divided into distinct excitatory and inhibitory regions and sustained firing is elicited by the movement of a bar across the field. The *lower-order hypercomplex cell* requires that the bar or edge be *stopped* at one or both ends: if the stimulus is too long, if it extends beyond the excitatory field, the response is inhibited. The *higher-order hypercomplex cell* responds to stimuli in either of two perpendicular orientations and could conceivably measure curvature. Hubel and Wiesel's classificatory scheme, introduced more than a decade ago, is still in general use, although it needs addition and modification and although, as we shall see, the model

3. Postponed until the cortex.

that it originally inspired is no longer tenable. The student should still read the classical papers (Hubel and Wiesel, 1962; 1965; 1968).

Often the specificity of a cell is to a conjunction or disjunction of stimulus qualities. Thus a particular unit may require that a bar is in a particular region of the visual field, is in a particular orientation, is of a particular colour and is moving in a particular direction (cf. Gouras, 1974, Fig. 10).

The Argument from After-effects

There is every reason to suppose that man's sensory systems are organized in a similar way to those of animals, but here we must rely primarily on psychological evidence. One of several indirect approaches has drawn upon *perceptual after-effects*. If a particular class of feature-detector is present in one of our sensory systems, then, it is argued, we may be able selectively to fatigue these feature-detectors and cause a change either in the detectability of the feature concerned or in its phenomenal appearance.[4]

By adapting to the grating of Fig. 4.2a and then looking at 4.2b the reader can experience one of the most celebrated of all after-effects, the *tilt after-effect*. Long before Hubel and Wiesel had made micro-electrode recordings from the visual cortex and thus before the existence of orientationally selective neurons was known, J. J. Gibson argued from the tilt after-effect that the orientation of a line should be regarded as a simple sensory quality, comparable, in fact, to brightness or to colour (Gibson, 1937).

A relatively recent addition to the catalogue of features extracted by the visual system is *spatial frequency*. The striking after-effect that can be obtained from Fig. 4.2c was first reported in 1969 by Blakemore and Sutton. Some years earlier visual scientists had begun to use stimuli that consisted of gratings in which luminance varied sinusoidally along one axis. Such a stimulus is a visual analogue of a pure tone (see chapter 7 and Fig. 7.1) and its frequency is usually expressed as the number of cycles per degree of visual angle. It initially recommended itself because it was the mathematically simplest of spatial stimuli, but there soon came the suspicion that the visual system contains channels tuned to particular spatial frequencies (Campbell and Robson, 1968) and single neurons with such selectivity have been discovered in the visual systems of cats and primates (see chapter 3 Fig. 3.8b). But what would be their role in perceptual analysis? Some suppose that these analysers of spatial frequency are directly responsible for pattern recognition, that, in fact, the visual system performs a spatial

4. An introductory account of perceptual after-effects is given by Mollon (1974). A comprehensive summary of visual after-effects will be found in Anstis (1975).

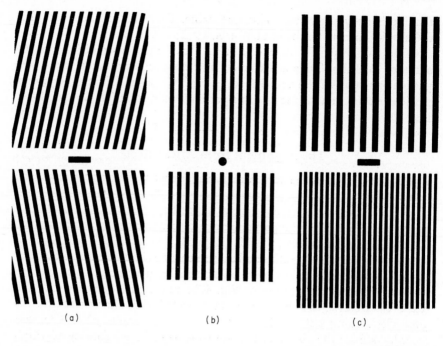

(a)   (b)   (c)

ıal ſtudies during the prir
:ds engaged in an Employı
l his intenſe application
ſible of any void ſpace in
:aſion for domeſtick ſociety
He left behind him about
Leibnitz, his rival, likewi
ıces, tho' not ſo rich : But
money which he had hoard
inary examples, and both

delt, began by taking hold of the
to climb to unknown principles;
them only in ſuch manner as they cot
chain of conſequences. The former ſe
clearly underſtands, to find out the
ſees; the latter ſets out from what h
find out the cauſe, whether it be c
ſelf-evident principles of the one
him to the cauſes of the phenomei
the phenomena do not always lea
ciples ſufficiently evident. The bout
two ſuch men in their purſuits thro
were not the boundaries of Their

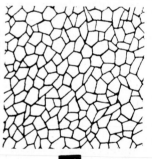

(d)

diſcovery of them, it is a ſight entirely new and
pected.
   What Sir Iſaac Newton aims at quite through
ticks, is the Anatomy of Light; this expreſſion is n
bold ſince it is no more than the thing it ſelf.
experiments, the ſmalleſt ray of Light that is co
into a dark room, and which cannot be ſo ſma
that it is yet compounded of an infinite number o
rays, is divided and diſſected in ſuch manner, tl
Elementary rays of which it is compoſed, are ſep
from each other, and diſcover themſelves ever
tinged with its particular colour, which after this
ration can no more be altered. The firſt total r
fore the diſſection, is white, and this whiteneſs
from all the particular colours of the Primitive
The ſeparating theſe rays is ſo difficult, that wher

delt, began by taking hold of the
to climb to unknown principles;
them only in ſuch manner as they cot
chain of conſequences. The former ſet
clearly underſtands, to find out the
ſees; the latter ſets out from what h
find out the cauſe, whether it be c
ſelf-evident principles of the one
him to the cauſes of the phenomei
the phenomena do not always lea
ciples ſufficiently evident. The bout
two ſuch men in their purſuits thro
were not the boundaries of Their

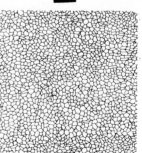

(e)   (f)

Fourier analysis[5] and that what is recognized is the resulting Fourier spectrum. However, the spatial frequency channels could have other functions. Firstly, they may serve to identify the density of texture of a surface and texture density may be on a par with colour: it allows the separation of figure from ground and of one object from another, a separation that is a preliminary to the recognition of form. In addition, *gradients* of texture density (see chapter 11 p. 310) are important in our judgments of distance (Gibson, 1950). Another function for the spatial-frequency channels might be seen in our ability to attend selectively to global or to local aspects of a visual stimulus: if we are looking at a page of text we can choose to attend to a single word or to a single letter of the word or to a serif on a particular letter.[6]

Classes of After-effect and Types of Code

The spatial-frequency after-effect belongs to a class of after-effects in which the test stimulus is phenomenally displaced away from the adapting stimulus along some perceptual dimension. Figure 4.3, which is based on a hypothesis introduced by von Békésy in 1929,[7] shows how such after-effects can be explained if the perceptual dimension is coded by place (see chapter 3 p. 55), if, for example, different spatial frequencies are represented by the activity of different members of a set of neurons. We must

5. Fourier analysis is the analysis of a complex waveform into a set of pure sine and cosine waves from which it could be reconstructed by simple addition. See chapter 7 p. 211 and Fig. 7.3.
6. The analysis of spatial frequency by the visual system is reviewed by Campbell (1974), by Campbell and Maffei (1974) and by Robson (1975).
7. An explanation of this kind was first extended to the tilt after-effect by Sutherland (1961) in a paper that has not received the acknowledgement it deserves.

Fig. 4.2 To obtain the tilt after-effect, gaze for about 30 seconds at the central horizontal bar of (a). Keep your eye moving to and fro along the length of the bar to avoid producing an ordinary after-image. Then switch your gaze rapidly to the central spot of (b). For a moment the vertical bars of (b) will appear tilted in directions opposite to those of the adapting grating in (a).

To obtain the spatial-frequency after-effect, move away from the page until the finest grating is still just clearly resolvable and look for about a minute at the central bar of Figure (c), again moving your eye to and fro along the bar. Then look quickly at the central spot of (b). For a moment the lower grating of (b) will look denser while the upper grating will appear coarser.

If you have difficulty securing either effect, try adapting for longer periods or try viewing from a different distance.

We do not have to use gratings. The two further adaptation figures, (d) and (f), and the test figure (e), allow the reader to judge the generality of the spatial frequency after-effect and its transfer from one kind of stimulus to another. (After Campbell and Maffei; Blakemore; Mayhew; Anstis.)

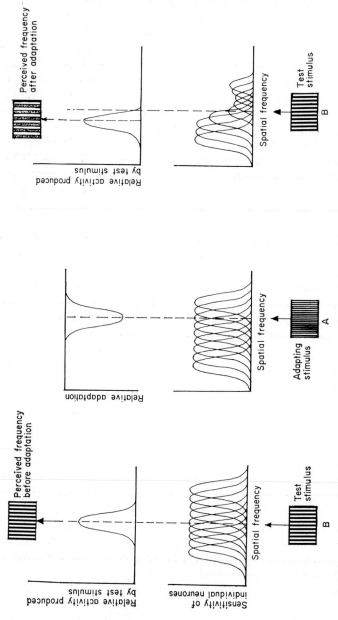

Fig. 4.3 A qualitative model of how after-effects occur when coding is by place. (After Békésy; Osgood; Sutherland; Blakemore.)

first make the assumption that neurons representing different values on the dimension have overlapping sensitivities and that decisions by later mechanisms are based on the position of peak activity in this population of neurons. Prolonged exposure of a particular value on the dimension (A in the figure, for example) will depress the corresponding neurons to an extent that is inversely related to their response to the adapting stimulus. If we now present a test stimulus (B) that lies to one side of A, the activity it produces must be weighted by the adaptation left by A. So the peak of activity produced by B, and thus perhaps its phenomenal appearance, will be displaced from A. If, however, the test stimulus is coincident with A, the peak activity will be reduced but will not be displaced (provided there are no asymmetries in the tuning curves of individual neurons in the series). Thus stimulus dimensions coded by place will show the *distance paradox*: the maximum after-effect will be for stimuli some distance along the dimension from the adapting stimulus. Appropriate measurements are available for the spatial-frequency after-effect and indeed distortion is greatest for test gratings lying one half to one octave[8] either side of the adapting frequency (Blakemore and Sutton, 1969).

The movement after-effect, which is one of the class of phenomena traditionally called *negative after-effects* (chapter 3 p. 66), seems to differ in a critical way from the Blakemore-Sutton effect that we have just been discussing. The relevant feature of the stimulus appears to change during the adaptation period: the movement comes to appear slower (Gibson, 1937) whereas spatial frequency does not appear to change during adaptation.[9] This observation may suggest that speed is not coded by place, but rather that all movement in a particular direction excites the same neuron, speed being represented by the frequency of impulses or the magnitude of a graded potential. Figure 4.4, which is based on a hypothesis introduced by Exner, shows schematically how the movement after-effect may arise. Two neurons are shown (L and R), one sensitive to movement to the left, the other sensitive to movement to the right. We have to assume that when their outputs are equal the later stages of visual analysis take the stimulus to be stationary and that we have here an example of an opponent process, a limiting case of coding by place such as discussed in chapter 3 (see p. 67). During prolonged stimulation by stimuli moving to the left, the response of neuron L slowly wanes. When stimulation ends the neuron will be depressed for several seconds and an inequality in the spontaneous activity of L and R may be treated as movement to the right. Alternatively, L and R may be

8. To say that a frequency is increased or decreased by an octave is to say that it is doubled or halved.
9. Since the adapting stimulus is here being regarded as a test stimulus the question is close to that of whether the distance paradox holds.

linked by mutual inhibition; and adaptation of L may transiently release R from inhibition.

Critical to this account of the movement after-effect is the question of what happens when we adapt to relatively slow movement and then look not at a stationary test stimulus but at one that is moving faster than the adapting stimulus. If speed is coded by frequency then the test stimulus should appear slower than normal; if speed is coded by place, the perceived speed should be displaced away from that of the adapting stimulus and the test stimulus should appear faster than it normally would. This crucial experiment has been neglected, but Carlson (1962a) did find one condition in which a test stimulus appeared to move faster after adaptation to slower movement.[10]

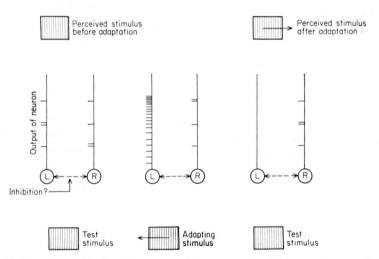

Fig. 4.4 Exner's explanation of the movement after-effect. Before adaptation both neurons are spontaneously active; after adaptation only R is active. Graded potentials could be substituted for action potentials.

A more clear-cut candidate for coding by frequency might be seen in apparent contrast. The apparent contrast of a grating, unlike apparent spatial frequency, does change during adaptation; and the maximum reduction in apparent contrast is at the adapting frequency (Blakemore and

10. There are other difficulties that face too simple an account of the movement after-effect. If the retina receives no patterned stimulation at the end of adaptation, the after-effect can be stored for several seconds at almost full strength (Wohlgemuth, 1911); adaptation for 15 minutes to a rotating spiral will produce a weak after-effect the next day (Maslin, 1969); and the after-effect of lateral movement can be abolished by the absence of a stationary framework (Day and Strelow, 1971). The present writer confirms these phenomena from his own observations.

Campbell, 1969). There is no distance paradox. We can draw conclusions only about the level of analysis at which adaptation occurs; but at this level, contrast would not seem to be coded by place.

Hierarchies

How do individual neurons gain their specificity to a complex feature of the stimulus? Although we have a good idea of the trigger features for neurons at different levels of different sensory systems, we know very little of how neurons are connected together to achieve these specificities. It is supposed,

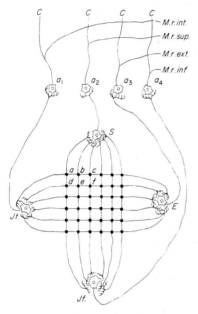

Fig. 4.5 Exner's model of directionally-selective movement detectors (Exner, 1894, p. 193). *a–f*, etc. are the projections of discrete retinal points. *S, E, Jt* and *Jf* are directionally-selective cells. Each retinal point is individually connected with each movement detector, but for simplicity the connections are shown in the diagram as passing through the projections of neighbouring retinal points. The time required for excitation from any particular retinal point to reach a particular movement detector is approximately proportional to the distance given in the diagram.

How does the model deal with dark objects moving on a bright ground? Exner supposes that considerable processing occurs between the retinal receptors and their central projections (*a–f*) and that by the stage shown in the diagram a dark object is represented by a positive signal.

The cells a_1–a_4 project to the external eye muscles (only four are shown in the diagram) and to the cortex.

however, that sensory neurons are organized into successive levels and that the specificity of a particular neuron is achieved by selective inputs, excitatory and inhibitory, from the previous level. The successive levels of analysis may reveal themselves in anatomically distinct layers, as in the retina, but elsewhere cells at different functional levels may be intermingled and we can only infer their connections from physiological and anatomical experiments.

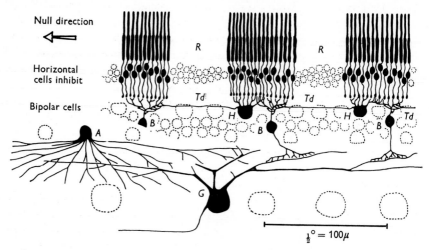

Fig. 4.6 Barlow and Levick's model for directional selectivity in the rabbit retina. Excitation passes from the light-sensitive receptors (R) via the bipolar cells (B) to the ganglion cell (G), but the bipolar cells can be inhibited by horizontal cells, which pick up from receptors in an adjacent region of the retina and conduct laterally in the null direction through a teledendron (Td) (but cf. Ch. 5 p. 106). Thus responses are inhibited when an image moves in the null direction but not when it moves in the preferred direction. A particular ganglion cell must receive inputs from a set of bipolars all selective for the same direction of movement; for although the receptive field may have a diameter of three degrees of visual angle, the directional selectivity may hold for movements of less than a quarter degree anywhere within a large region of the field. (From Barlow and Levick, 1965, *J. Physiol.*, **178**, 477–504.)

The principle of selective summation is explicitly embodied in Exner's model of movement detection (Fig. 4.5). The cell for leftward movement (Jt) receives input from horizontal rows in the retinal array and responds optimally only when it receives simultaneous input from several retinal elements. Exner called such a cell a "Summationszelle"; in modern jargon, it is an AND-gate. When a stimulus moves from c to a the excitation from later stimulated points travels over shorter paths and so the inputs are temporally coincident at Jt. The excitation reaching E on the other hand, is dispersed in time. We are to imagine that the set of movement-detectors, *Jt*, *Jf*, *S* and *E*, is reduplicated many times for different regions of the retina. When it did become possible to record from the movement-detectors that Exner had so remarkably foreseen, it turned out that his coincidence model was not enough and that inhibitory as well as excitatory processes were required. Figure 4.6 shows Barlow and Levick's model of directionally selective units in the rabbit retina (see: structure of retina, chapter 5 p. 101). When a stimulus moves in the *null*, or non-preferred, direction the delayed inhibition reaching the bipolar cell via the horizontal cells cancels the response to direct excitation, but when movement is in the preferred direction the inhibition arrives too late to prevent the excitatory response. The evidence for inhibition lies in the fact that a response to a spot moving in the null direction may be less than that to a stationary spot: a purely excitatory model could not account for this finding.

A model that is very similar in principle has been offered by Bishop *et al.* (1971) to account for the directional selectivity of simple cells in the cat's cortex; and the reader will readily see how an analogous scheme would explain the presence in the auditory system of neurons specific to a particular direction of change of frequency.[11]

The most celebrated of all hierarchical models is that offered by Hubel and Wiesel for the early stages of visual shape recognition in cat and monkey. Although it increasingly looks as if their account of the visual cortex may be wrong, the student should have some grasp of their model, because of the pervasive influence it has enjoyed for over a decade; and because of its beautiful simplicity.

We begin at the level of the bipolar cell of the retina (cf. Figs. 3.2, 4.6; see also chapter 5 p. 104). A typical unit may respond when light falls on the centre of its receptive field and be inhibited by light falling on a surrounding annulus (Fig. 4.7). Such a cell would be called an *on-centre* unit. It receives an excitatory input from those receptors that lie in the centre of its field and an inhibitory input from those in the surround; the latter input probably reaches it via horizontal cells. Other cells have *off-centres* and *on-surrounds* (see also chapter 6 pp. 168-170). Many retinal ganglion cells reflect the properties of the bipolar cells from which they receive their primary input. Thus already in the retina we have cells that have little interest in steady, diffuse light (which stimulates both *on* and *off* regions of the receptive field), but which respond strongly to local contrast, to edges and to spots. "Die Netzhaut . . . schematisiert und karikiert" (Mach, 1900).

11. Fernald (1971), however, has explained such specificity by a model that is formally similar to Exner's: the synaptic inputs on the dendrites of the summation cell lie at varying distances from the soma and so different sequences of input lead to either temporal coincidence or temporal dispersion of excitation.

The cells at the next level of the hierarchy, at the level of the lateral
geniculate nucleus (LGN), have receptive-field properties similar to those
of retinal ganglion cells, but are even less sensitive to diffuse light (chapter
6 pp. 111–113). It is now confirmed, by simultaneously recording from retina
and LGN, that most LGN units take their excitatory input from a very

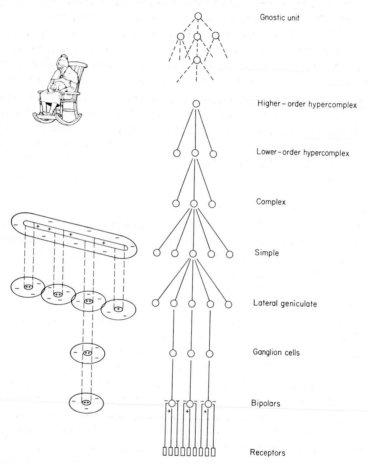

Fig. 4.7 The hierarchical model of the visual system. To the right are shown
schematically the classes of neuron and their connections. At the higher levels these
connections are strictly hypothetical.

To the left are represented typical receptive fields for cells at early stages of the
system. The plus and minus signs mark areas in which a stimulus produces
excitation and inhibition respectively. The diagram shows how the receptive field of
a simple cell might correspond to the receptive fields of a set of lateral geniculate
units.

The hypothetical "gnostic unit" is discussed later in the chapter.

small number of retinal ganglion cells of the same type (Cleland *et al.* 1971).

The next stage in Hubel and Wiesel's hierarchical model is the cortical simple cell. The orientational selectivity of the simple cell is achieved by taking a set of LGN units that have receptive fields lying in a row on the retina and feeding their outputs into the same simple cell (Fig. 4.7).

Simple cells in turn provide the input for complex cells. Each complex cell receives inputs from a set of simple cells that all have the same preferred orientation and so comes to have its characteristic property of responding to a bar of the correct orientation anywhere within the field.

Likewise, the complex cells furnish the input for lower-order hypercomplex cells. Thus a hypercomplex unit may come to be specific to length because it receives excitatory input from one complex cell and inhibitory input from other complex cells with fields lying at the end of its excitatory field. A higher-order hypercomplex cell may draw inputs from lower-order hypercomplex cells that have orthogonal preferred orientations (see chapter 12 pp. 337–340).

Difficulties for Hubel and Wiesel's model. X- Y- and W-cells
Unhappily this account of the sequential analysis of the visual cortex may no longer be tenable. It looks less and less likely that simple cells provide the exclusive input to complex cells. It seems certain that complex cells receive direct ("monosynaptic") input from the axons of LGN units: when the optic pathway is electrically stimulated and recordings are made from cortical units, complex cells respond with such a short latency and with so little variability that it is improbable that extra synapses are interposed (Stone, 1972; Toyama, *et al.* 1973; Singer, *et al.* 1975). Especially persuasive is the finding that some complex cells respond with a shorter latency than any simple cell in the same sample (Hoffman and Stone, 1971). Many complex cells do also receive inputs from other, as yet unidentified, cortical cells and it is an open question whether the direct or indirect inputs are most important in normal visual analysis. Indirect evidence against Hubel and Wiesel's hypothesis comes from a report that simple cells respond best to stimuli moving relatively slowly whereas complex cells often prefer higher velocities to which simple cells hardly respond (Movshon, 1974). Hammond and MacKay (1975) have recorded from the cat's visual cortex while stimulating the eye with the kind of "visual noise" that is obtained when a domestic television set is mistuned. If one area of such noise is moved relative to the rest, observers perceive contours at the boundaries of the moving area, even though a true contour is not present in the stimulus. Most simple cells proved to be indifferent to these "kinetic contours" but many complex cells responded vigorously to them. It is

unclear how this result would arise if complex cells took their main input from simple cells.

One possibility is that simple and complex cells are the respective projections of two different classes of retinal ganglion cell, *X-cells* and *Y-cells*. X- and Y-cells are primarily distinguished according to whether summation within their receptive field is linear: an X-cell does not respond when a sine-wave grating is so positioned that the changes in luminance over one half of the receptive field are the exact inverse of the changes over the other half and when, we may suppose, the inputs from the excitatory and inhibitory areas of the field directly cancel each other (Fig. 4.8); but null positions of this kind cannot be found for Y-cells, which respond to any variation of luminance within their field (Enroth-Cugell and Robson, 1966).

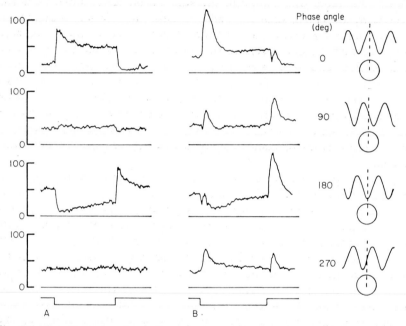

Fig. 4.8 The responses of an off-centre X-cell (A) and an off-centre Y-cell (B) to the introduction and withdrawal of a sinusoidal grating pattern. The ordinate of each graph shows the number of action potentials per second. The lowermost, rectangular trace shows when the sinusoidal pattern is turned off (downward deflexion) and when it is turned on (upward deflexion). To the right is shown the relation of the grating to the receptive field. (The "phase angle" is the angular position, in degrees, of the grating relative to the centre of the receptive field). Notice especially the difference in the responses of X and Y cells when the changes in luminance over half of the receptive field are the exact opposite of the changes over the other half, when, that is, the phase angle is 90 degrees or 270 degrees. (From Enroth-Cugell and Robson, 1966.)

There prove to be other differences between the two classes. Y-cells have large cell bodies and large axons and have high conduction velocities. Although their receptive fields can be divided into concentric ON and OFF areas, the centres are relatively large and the surrounds are notably so. X-cells have smaller somata, smaller axons, lower conduction speeds and smaller receptive fields. Y-cells respond only transiently to local illumination and prefer briskly moving stimuli; X-cells give a sustained response to local illumination. The axons of X-cells appear to project primarily to the lateral geniculate nucleus whereas those of Y-cells project both to the LGN and to the superior colliculus in the mid-brain. (Hoffman, 1973; Wright and Ikeda, 1974; Robson, 1975).[12] Are the Y-cells the sentinels that detect changes and events while leaving to the X-system the detailed analysis of form? The reader who knows the literature of the last hundred years will hear many an echo in such a speculation; and will hold his judgment.

LGN units can also be divided into X and Y classes and it has been supposed that the simple cells of the cortex receive excitatory input from X-cells while complex cells receive a parallel excitatory input from Y-cells (Stone, 1972; Stone and Dreher, 1973). Such a model accounts for many of the characteristic properties of simple and complex cells. A major difficulty for the hypothesis is the report of Singer *et al.* (1975) that both X and Y fibres project to both simple and complex cells, but in this study X and Y cells were distinguished only by the indirect criterion of conduction latency.

Hypercomplex cells have also fallen from their place in the hierarchy. Some hypercomplex cells receive input from X-cells of the LGN (Hoffman and Stone, 1971). Dreher (1972) has suggested that there are two types of hypercomplex unit, those with the properties of simple cells and those with the properties of complex cells: the former prefer slow movement and their receptive fields can be divided into distinct ON and OFF regions, whereas the latter respond best to faster movement and their fields cannot be divided into distinct regions. Rose (1974) has gone further and has argued that many of the cells that would conventionally be classified as simple or complex respond more strongly to short bars than to long and that there is no quantitative basis for regarding hypercomplex cells as a distinct class rather than as merely extreme cases of simple or complex cells.

12. A third type of ganglion cells, W-cells, have been described in the cat's retina. As a class, these cells are marked by very low conduction speeds, but they appear to be very heterogeneous in their properties, resembling many of the units that have been catalogued in the retinae of frogs and pigeons. Many have receptive fields that cannot be divided into centre and surround and some are directionally selective. Their cell bodies are thought to be very tiny and they are believed to project only to the superior colliculus. (Stone and Hoffman, 1973; Hoffman, 1973; Cleland and Levick, 1974).

The Gnostic Unit

It may be time to level Hubel and Wiesel's hierarchy, but whether the hierarchical model is wrong in principle or only in detail we do not know. Some have been ready to extrapolate beyond Hubel and Wiesel's experimental findings and to suppose that the hierarchical analysis was maintained through successively more abstract levels of feature extraction until was reached a single cell that detected a particular object or person or word. Konorski (1967a, b), who has given this view explicit expression, called such a cell a *gnostic unit*; another popular term has been *grandmother cell*. Barlow (1972) has spoken of *cardinal cells*. Although each gnostic unit can be regarded as lying at the top of a pyramidal structure, any particular receptor element lying at the base of the pyramid may contribute to very many such hierarchies and thus we may equally conceive of the pyramids as inverted. Konorski proposes that the only output from a particular perceptual hierarchy is from the gnostic unit at its apex: perceptual systems, he argues, are built to recognize objects and things, not the features or properties of objects. His conjecture is especially plausible in the case of hearing, for the untrained listener cannot identify the individual components that go to make up the sounds of speech. Man's sophisticated capacity to examine individual features of a visual stimulus depends, Konorski suggests, on the formation of special gnostic units.

The gnostic unit brings the doctrine of specific nerve energies to its ultimate development. The hypothesis has appealed because the means and the nature of recognition are made clear. It has been easy to imagine how linkages might be formed between a gnostic unit and an analogous cell that stood at the apex of an outflowing response hierarchy and controlled a spatial and temporal complex of individual muscle movements.

As we mentioned in chapter 3, earlier versions of the doctrine of specific nerve energies allowed that our immediate perceptual experiences depend not only on which sensory fibres are active but also upon our past experience, upon our expectations and upon interactions within and between sensory modalities. However, the hypothesis of the gnostic unit, as expressed in Barlow's Fourth Dogma (Barlow, 1972), supposes that there is a fixed relation between the activity of a cardinal cell and perceptual experience. When our perception of an object is changed by secondary influences, then what has changed is which gnostic unit is most active. We are to imagine that the input patterns that play upon a gnostic unit correspond not only to abstract descriptions of the sensory stimulus but also to the past and present states of other gnostic units.

The slender chances of finding a gnostic unit by electrophysiological recording in animals would be maximized by using stimuli that were of biological significance to the species. Funkenstein *et al.* (1971), recording from neurons in the primary auditory cortex of unanaesthetized squirrel monkeys, drew their stimuli from the monkey's elaborate repertoire of socially significant vocalizations and reported that some cells were specific to one particular class of call or to calls with very similar acoustic properties. Gross *et al.* (1972) have described a unit in the inferior temporal cortex of the macaque monkey that responded best to a cut-out silhouette of a monkey's hand that was held against an illuminated background in front of the animal.

What are we to make of such findings? It does seem that the very specificity of the response excludes an explanation in terms of general arousal; and Newman and Symmes (1974) have shown that the specificity to vocalizations of cortical units in the squirrel monkey does not change during changes of arousal that occur spontaneously or are produced by direct stimulation of the midbrain reticular formation. However, the electrophysiologist can never know that he has exhausted the set of stimuli that would lead to response in a particular unit: there may always be untried stimuli that would tease an equal, or stronger, response from the cell. Thus a more recent and thorough study of the responses of cortical units in the squirrel monkey shows that more than one class of vocalization will usually evoke a response from a given cell (Newman and Wollberg, 1973). The silhouette of a monkey's hand that was used by Gross *et al.* closely resembles the regular gratings that have more recently been found to evoke strong responses in primary visual areas.

The Association of Perceptual Qualities

As it stands, the doctrine of the gnostic unit presents an immediate difficulty. Within a particular hierarchy, information that is not relevant to the definition of the object is abandoned. In Hubel and Wiesel's model, for example, information about exact retinal position is lost between simple cell and complex cell. One kind of specificity is gained at the expense of others and the signals converging on the postulated gnostic unit cannot carry their ancestry with them. How then can accidental properties, such as position, be associated with the object? A man who looks at a busy expressway can report immediately that it is the Volkswagen that is yellow and is moving slowly towards Brooklyn whereas it is the Citroën that is silver and is moving swiftly towards Nassau County.

How is this perceptual synthesis achieved? Until now in this chapter we have been proposing that each of the major senses should be regarded as several sense-organs rather than as one and we have suggested, for example,

D

that the several properties of the retinal image (position, brightness, colour, direction and speed of movement, shape and so on) are analysed independently. We must now look more guardedly at the nature and extent of this independence.

The problem is one of the most acute, most central and least answered problems in perceptual theory. At the onset, however, we can exclude the two extreme possibilities. We cannot have a system in which the properties are not separated at all. It would be no good having single units, or cell assemblies, that were specific to yellow Volkswagens moving left at a distance of three metres or to Grandmother wearing her red shawl and bending to pick up a knitting needle. The primary difficulty here is not the numerical one of the number of cells required but the fact that we need to explain how we are able to recognize a Volkswagen for what it is independently of its accidental properties such as colour and position. Equally, however, the dissociation cannot be complete, for, as we have seen, accidental properties can be associated with their objects.

Let us consider briefly the types of psychological and physiological evidence that can be brought to bear on the question of the association of sensory qualities. We shall concentrate, in our illustrative examples, on the degree to which colour and form are dissociated in visual analysis.

Phenomenal Dissociation

In 1934 the British Post Office adopted a new design for its postage stamps. Plate I shows a halfpenny stamp of the old issue and a three-halfpenny stamp of the new issue. The changes from the typographic issue on the left to the photogravure issue on the right were slight ones: the fine etching of the typographic issue was absent on the newer issue; and the newer issue was the more saturated in colour. The reader is invited to try an experiment suggested by Creed (1935). Fuse the two stamps of Plate I by means of a stereoscope (see chapter 11 p. 293). Most observers see a brown stamp, differing only slightly in colour from the three-halfpenny stamp, but they also see the etching that is present on the cheek of King George V in the halfpenny stamp. Thus the hue of the fused image is drawn from one eye and the form is drawn from the other.

Here we have a dissociation of hue and form that is similar to the dissociation of movement from position or shape mentioned at the beginning of this chapter (p. 71). Another example is seen in the demonstration by Treisman (1962) that the colour of a stimulus may be suppressed in binocular rivalry[13] while the form of the stimulus still contributes to stereopsis.

13. When the two eyes are simultaneously stimulated by stimuli that are very different in form or in colour, the two stimuli often are not perceptually fused but are seen in rapid alternation. This alternation is known as *retinal* or *binocular rivalry*. (See chapter 11 p. 298).

Contingent After-effects

Evidence for the partial association of properties in analysis has been sought in the curious phenomena called *contingent after-effects*. Using Plate II the reader may observe for himself one of the most notable of these, the McCollough effect. This mysterious effect cannot be explained in terms of ordinary after-images (see chapter 6 p. 189), since any particular point on the retina has been stimulated equally by red and green light during the adaptation period. The illusory hues are contingent: they appear only when gratings of the appropriate orientation are present. It is argued that the McCollough effect reveals the existence of neurons that are specific to both colour and orientation. We have to assume that the apparent colour of a grating normally depends on the relative activity of orientation detectors tuned to different colours. During the adaptation period there occurs a selective depression of neurons specific to, say, green bars tilted 45 degrees to the right and of others specific to red bars tilted to the left. A black and white grating tilted right will then come to look pink.

Analogous after-effects of colour have been found that are contingent on direction of movement and on spatial frequency. Equally there is a tilt after-effect that is contingent on colour and there are movement after-effects that are contingent on colour or on spatial frequency. Table 4.1, which has been prepared by Dr. P. Thompson, conveniently summarizes most of the visual contingent after-effects that have so far been described. (For further references the reader may turn to the review by Skowbo *et al.* 1975.) In every case it is possible to argue that there are neurons selective for two, or more, properties of the stimulus.

In some ways, however, the contingent after-effects are more akin to the phenomena of conditioning. Firstly, for example, they persist much longer than sensory after-effects are normally thought to: ten or fifteen minutes of adaptation may produce a McCollough effect that lasts for days, weeks or months. Secondly, a McCollough effect is dissipated much more rapidly if the subject is repeatedly exposed (for example, in repeated testing) to black and white gratings after the end of the adaptation period (Jones and Holding, 1975; Skowbo *et al.* 1975) and this process resembles the extinction of a learned response. Thirdly, contingent movement after-effects have been reported to be stronger half-an-hour after the adaptation period than they were on immediate testing (Mayhew and Anstis, 1972); this is the phenomenon that in learning theory would be called *reminiscence*. But if the McCollough effect is a kind of conditioning why are the illusory colours roughly complementary to those associated with the gratings during adaptation? We have to suppose that the unconditioned response of the visual system to an excess of redness in the world is to turn down the gain

Table 4.1.

Dimension of Contingency

		Dimension of After-effect			
	Colour	Movement Direction	Spatial Frequency	Orientation (Tilt)	Brightness
Colour		Mayhew and Anstis 1972 Favreau, Emerson and Corballis 1972	Virsu and Haapasalo 1973	Held and Shattuck 1973	
Movement Direction	Hepler 1968 Stromeyer and Mansfield 1970				Mayhew and Anstis 1972
Movement Velocity	Hepler personal comm. to Stromeyer and Mansfield 1970				
Spatial Frequency	Harris 1970 Breitmeyer and Cooper 1972 Stromeyer 1972 Leppman 1973	Mayhew and Anstis 1972 Walker 1972		Wyatt 1974	
Orientation (Tilt)	McCollough 1965	Mayhew and Anstis 1972	Wyatt 1974		Mayhew and Anstis 1972
Curvature	Riggs 1973 Sigel and Nachmias 1974 Stromeyer and Riggs 1974				

of red-sensitive channels and that when later, in the testing situation, the appropriate grating (the conditioned stimulus) elicits this response the phenomenal result is that the black and white test-stimulus appears greenish. However, this learning process will have to be a rather special and local one: traditionally the McCollough effect has been produced by alternate presentation of red and green stimuli, but both red and green are concurrently present as we adapt to Plate II.

The problem of the association of properties during analysis has also been approached through the conventional, non-contingent after-effects:[14] it is asked whether an after-effect that has been established in the presence of some other sensory quality is still present when this second quality is changed. For example, Virsu and Haapasalo (1973) have shown that the Blakemore-Sutton effect (the spatial-frequency after-effect that we discussed earlier in this chapter) is as strong when adapting and test stimuli are heterochromatic as it is when they are of the same colour; and so they conclude that there are some channels at some stage of the visual system that are specific to spatial frequency and not specific to colour.

Electrophysiology

We have already mentioned electrophysiological evidence for units that are specific to more than one property of the stimulus, but the interesting question is whether this multiple specificity increases or decreases at successive levels of analysis, and here the answer, in the case of our example of colour and form, is contradictory. Hubel and Wiesel (1968) suggested that the analyses of form and colour were progressively dissociated in Area 17 of the monkey's cortex: the ON and OFF areas of the receptive fields of six out of twenty-six simple cells had different spectral sensitivities, whereas only 7 per cent of complex cells and a very few hypercomplex cells were colour-coded. Gouras (1974) has systematically examined the spatial and chromatic properties of cells in Area 17 and has reached a similar conclusion: most of the cells that had concentric receptive fields were opponent-colour cells whereas no hypercomplex cell in the sample was colour-selective. Yet Yates (1974) has reported the very contrary, that the more narrowly tuned is a cell to colour the more likely is it to have complex field properties. Zeki (1973), recording from an area he calls V4 in the prestriate cortex of the monkey, finds colour specificity associated with most of the types of receptive field described by Hubel and Wiesel.

However, Zeki's work addresses our question at a second level. He finds that almost every cell in V4 is specific for colour, whatever its other stimulus requirements. Elsewhere he finds an area of cortex in the rhesus

14. It could be argued that the majority of visual after-effects are contingent, if only upon retinal position.

monkey (the posterior bank of the superior temporal sulcus) where every cell is sensitive to movement and most are directionally specific; again the dominant feature was associated with varying degrees of specificity for form, but specificity for colour was apparently absent (Zeki, 1974).

With this suggestion that there are anatomically distinct centres for different stimulus properties we end our discussion of the evidence for independent analysis. Our purpose has been only to illustrate the types of finding that bear on this question. We have seen good evidence for partial independence; but the best argument against complete independence remains the *a priori* one with which we began. If we wish to retain a hierarchical model we must allow information to flow between hierarchies and in both directions within a hierarchy. There must be access to the Volkswagen's pedigree.

The Development of Neural Specificity

Lurking uncomfortably behind successive versions of the doctrine of specific nerve energies has always been the question of how neurons come to gain their specificity. Are animals equipped genetically with the rich and intricate pattern of feature-detectors that they need in order to face the environment into which they are born; or does the environment itself impress an organization upon an unschooled nervous system? Recent research begins to answer this ancient question. Few branches of sensory physiology are now so active and so intriguing.[15]

At first it seemed that much of the apparatus found in the visual cortex of the mature cat was present as soon as the kitten opened its eyes; for Hubel and Wiesel (1963) reported that both simple and complex cells could be found before the kitten had had any visual experience. These cells resembled those of the adult in every way except in their sluggishness and in the readiness with which they habituated to repeated stimulation. The question, however, has become controversial. Barlow and Pettigrew (1971) bluntly denied that there were any cortical neurons in the inexperienced kitten that were truly orientation-specific. A current view allows that some units are orientation-specific (Blakemore, 1974b; Barlow, 1975); but most units are not and it is clear that the inexperienced cortex is very different from that of the adult. Cells may have inputs from both eyes, they are almost always specific to the position of a stimulus, and they may be specific to the direction and velocity of movement, but most units are at once promiscuous and fickle in their response; and fine tuning for orientation and for binocular disparity waits upon visual experience (Pettigrew, 1971). That this is so is not remarkable in the light of anatomical evidence that less than 1 per cent

15. The reviews of this field by Blakemore (1974a, b) and by Barlow (1975) are recommended.

of synapses in the visual cortex develop before eye-opening in the kitten (Cragg, 1975).

The remarkable influence of early experience has been revealed by experiments in which animals have been reared in selective visual environ-

Fig. 4.9 An apparatus for exposing kittens to an environment containing stripes of only one orientation. The kitten wears a black ruff that prevents it seeing its own body. (From Blakemore and Cooper, 1970.)

ments. Hirsch and Spinelli (1970; 1971) brought up kittens in the dark for three weeks after birth and then fitted them with goggles that allowed one eye to see only an array of three vertical bars and the other eye to see only three horizontal bars. When, after several weeks of this restricted visual experience, recordings were made from the visual cortex of such a kitten, it was found that almost every cell was driven from only one eye and that if there was a stimulus orientation that excited the cell preferentially, then it corresponded to the orientation to which that eye had been exposed. Blakemore and Cooper (1970) reported a slightly different experiment with a similar result. They reared kittens in an environment containing only vertical lines or only horizontal ones. The kitten, fitted with a broad, black collar to prevent its seeing its own body, stood on a clear glass platform inside a tall cylinder covered with stripes in one of the two orientations (Fig. 4.9). When electrophysiological recordings were later made from such kittens it was found that the preferred orientations for cortical cells were clustered around the particular orientation to which the kitten had been exposed (Fig. 4.10). Similarly, when kittens are exposed to an environ-

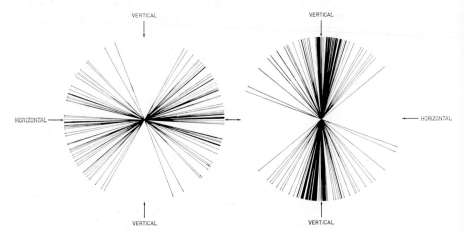

Fig. 4.10 The distribution of optimal orientations for 52 cortical neurons from a cat brought up in a visual world containing only horizontal stripes (left) and for 72 neurons from a cat exposed to vertical stripes (right). Each line represents the orientation to which one particular cell responded maximally. In the normal cat the optimal orientations are distributed randomly around the clock. (From Blakemore and Cooper, 1970.)

ment containing only coarsely-spaced white spots on a dark background, most cells come to respond as strongly to spots of a corresponding size as they do to the long lines that are normally so effective (Van Sluyters and Blakemore, 1973).

Is there a *critical period* during which the infant visual system can be modified especially readily? For the cat the effects of exposure to a particular orientation are greatest between the ages of 3 weeks and 14 weeks (Blakemore, 1974b). If one of a kitten's eyes is closed between the ages of 3 weeks and 8 weeks, there is a marked decline in the number of cortical cells driven by that eye, but this susceptibility to eye closures declines thereafter and disappears around the end of the third month (Hubel and

Wiesel, 1968). Monocular deprivation of this kind during the critical period has a permanent effect: even if the deprivation is followed by a long period of normal visual experience the properties of cortical cells remain abnormal (Wiesel and Hubel, 1965).

During the critical period an exposure to a biassed environment of only a few hours may change the responses of single units. However, the effects may take time to develop: Pettigrew and Garey (1974) exposed kittens to a vertical grating for 5–22 hours and found that if they immediately made electrophysiological recordings from the visual cortex then many cells responded to a broad range of stimuli and some responded to all orientations except the one that had been used during the initial exposure. After a number of hours had elapsed, many more cells responded to vertical stimuli with the fineness of tuning that is characteristic of the adult neuron.

How does selective experience exercise its dramatic effect on the visual cortex? If a kitten is exposed to vertical lines, do cells that might normally have been destined to respond to horizontal lines degenerate through desuetude, or do they instead come to respond to the prevailing stimulus?

The evidence suggests that the latter is the case. Firstly, the electro-physiologists do not find large areas of silent cortex that would correspond to the missing orientations and indeed the density of active cells is similar to that of the cortex of a normal animal (Pettigrew et al. 1974). Secondly, an unusual early environment may create units of a type not found in normal animals. Thus Hirsch and Spinelli (1971), in the study described above, found a few cells that had a receptive field consisting of three, parallel, bar-shaped regions and corresponding in configuration and size to the array of bars to which one eye had been exposed. Similarly, alternating exposure to vertical and horizontal bars may produce some units that are excited by both orientations and respond particularly well to a cross moving through the receptive field (Blakemore, 1974b).

The findings of the developmental electrophysiologists would appear to have important clinical implications for man. We should avoid subjecting the infant to a restricted or biassed visual environment. It is known, for example, that if an eye is astigmatic in the child no amount of optical correction can later restore normal acuity in the adult, and an explanation of this loss might be seen in the finding that kittens reared wearing cylindrical lenses lack cortical neurons sharply tuned to the orientation that has been blurred by the lenses (Freeman and Pettigrew, 1973).

We may end this chapter by concluding that higher mammals are equipped with a comprehensive armoury of feature-detectors and that, in phylogeny and in ontogeny, these feature-detectors are matched to the environment in which an animal finds itself. Whether the same principles are maintained in the analysis and recognition of objects, we do not know.

5 | The Different Senses and their Receptors

Vision

Detailed accounts of the visual receptors—the photosensitive cells of the eye, their inner structure, their interrelationship and their connection with the visual cortex—are available in most introductory textbooks (see e.g. Geldard 1972). For that reason this discussion is going to be restricted to relatively new aspects of the question, and to such points of view which must be considered especially significant. The general structure of the "camera-eye" of all vertebrates is the same, whereas the details may vary considerably from one species to another. As distinguished, for example, from the molluscs, the vertebrate *retina* which covers the entire posterior wall of the eyeball (see Fig. 5.1) is turned inside out. The tips of the

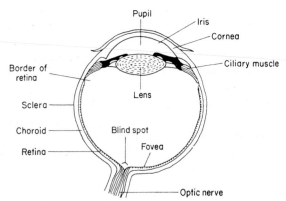

Fig. 5.1 Structure of the human eye. (From Geldard, 1972 p. 26.)

receptor cells point toward the rim of the eyeball, and the outer limiting membrane (*membrana limitans externa*) is pressed against the *choroid*, the great nutritive structure of the eyeball. On the other hand the optic nerve fibres, which branch out from the optic bundle and enter the eyeball through an opening at the optic disc, are spread out fanwise along the inner surface of the retina (*membrana limitans interna*). It might seem a little bit odd to non-specialist readers that the receptors are oriented away from the source of light which first has to penetrate the inner membrane and ¦the neural connective layers of the optic bundle. The diagram in Fig. 5.3) is probably helpful in illustrating this arrangement.

Most important is the fact that the optic bundle is a highly flexible conductor, which apparently permits the eyeball to move relatively freely within its oblong socket.

The choroid becomes modified in the front of the eye to form the *iris*. The retina extends nearly as far forward as the *ciliary body*, which is composed largely of muscular tissue and situated at the junction of iris and choroid. The *lens* is attached to the ciliary body by ligaments. The lens is completely encased within a membranous capsule which is under some tension in its normal state. This force tends to flatten the capsule, permitting accommodation for far vision. When focusing on a near stimulus the ciliary fibres relax, reducing the tension and permitting the lens to regain its more rounded shape. In early stages of vertebrate development the function of the lens was rather undeterminate (see e.g. Gibson 1966, p. 171). Its main purpose was to collect and focus incoming light rays into the photosensitive tissue of the eye. At higher stages of evolutionary development the lens became more flexible.

In colloquial usage the term "retinal image" is often heard. This image is thought of as originating when the light which enters the eyeball through the opening or *pupil* in the front of the eye hits the outer limiting layer (*membrana limitans externa*) of the retina. It is important to stress that in no way can we speak of an actual "image" or picture. The eyeball within its bone cavity is in constant slight vibratory motion (see chapter 16 p. 413), so that no clearly defined image can exist even for an instant. At the most, we can speak of a form with blurred edges.

During the last two decades interesting attempts have been made to point out the effects in visual performance caused by fixation: that is, staring with an immobile eye. Ditchburn and Ginsborg use the word *fixation* "when the subject is attempting to maintain his gaze on a stationary point" (1953, p. 1).

They were able to list three types of eye movements under those conditions:

1. *A quivering* at a frequency rate of 30 to 80 Hz showing an amplitude of 10 to 30 seconds of arc.
2. *Slow sliding movements* ("drifts") up to an amplitude of 6 minutes of arc.
3. *Rapid correcting movements* ("flicks") at intervals of 0·03 seconds to 5 seconds with amplitudes amounting 1 to 20 minutes of arc (see Ditchburn and Ginsborg 1953, p. 4).

Research based on better methods of registration is still going on but has in general granted verification of this data (see Pritchard, 1964, Moustgaard, 1969).

The ability of the organism to form clear sensory impressions on the basis of a vibrating blur generated by the beam of light depends on two factors: a highly developed lens, and a retina with specialized cell types. The zoologist Löwenstein has brought together for comparison examples of lens types from vertebrates at various levels of development (Fig. 5.2). In

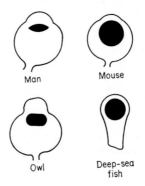

Fig. 5.2 The size of the lens in some animal species. (From v. Fieandt, 1972 p. 63.)

the mouse, the lens is almost spherical and astonishingly large, extending almost to the posterior wall of the eyeball. It admits a large amount of light, but this is not of much use in distinguishing outlines and shapes. For the mouse, a nocturnal animal, it is important to perceive rapidly the shadows cast in its field of vision by an approaching enemy. Similar large, spherical lenses also occur in deep sea fish. In the depths of the ocean there is very little light; thus it is important to catch even the weakest light rays, especially those emanating from other living organisms (bioluminiscence). The lens of the owl's eye is relatively flat and oblong, similar to that of man. But the eye of the owl shows the importance of the front part of the hard *sclera* which surrounds the eyeball. In the owl this transparent surface, the *cornea*, bulges considerably, thus permitting more effective gathering of light energy into the eye (Löwenstein, 1966, p. 54–55).

As the lens gains in size and importance, the necessity of its being able to focus or accommodate, becomes greater.

It would seem that the lens system and the retinal mosaic must have developed together. The primitive retina merely collects and combines the reactions occuring in its components; at higher stages of development it also integrates and structures these reactions. Structurally the retinal projection is not an "image" at all. According to Gibson, the so-called retinal image is only a sampling of the ambient light energy.

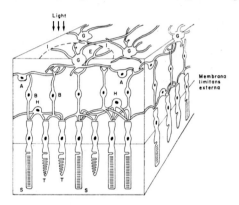

Fig. 5.3 Schematical picture of the structure of the retina. S = rods, T = cones, H = horizontal cells, E = surrounding area by means of stimulating light, I = broader enclosing area which in turn may inhibit the ganglion. The upper surface of the tissue represents the inmost border of the retina (*membrana limitans interna.*) (From Donner, 1973 p. 890.)

The retina as shown in Fig. 5.3 is seen to have a somewhat complicated structure. Altogether six main types of nerve cells can be distinguished on the human retina. Rods (S) and cones (T) at the bottom of the diagram point away from the front of the eye. In addition to these specialized light receptors the retina contains two kinds of elements: 1. conducting elements including bipolar cells (B) and two types of ganglion cells (G); 2. neural elements having a cross-connecting function: (H) horizontal cells; (A) amacrine cells. There are also sustentacular or supporting elements (see also chapter 3 p. 46 and Fig. 3.2).

The structure of the rods and the cones is schematically shown in Fig. 5.4. The tips of the outer segments of rods and cones are made up of hundreds, perhaps thousands of discs or *platelets*. In the cones they constitute a tremendously long double membrane and remain in continuous inter-action with the extra-cellular regions of the retina. In the rod each platelet is completely separate from its neighbours and remains isolated inside the surrounding membrane. According to Young (1971) new platelets are developed at the basic ends of the rods, whereas the lamina at the tip of the cells are continuously dissolved. Thus the outer segment of a rod is completely replaced within the period of a few weeks. In the cones on the other hand there is no corresponding locally-determined replacement of platelets. Apparently these tissues in the outer segments of the photoreceptors are the place at which the sensitive photopigments must reside (see Geldard, 1972 p. 32).

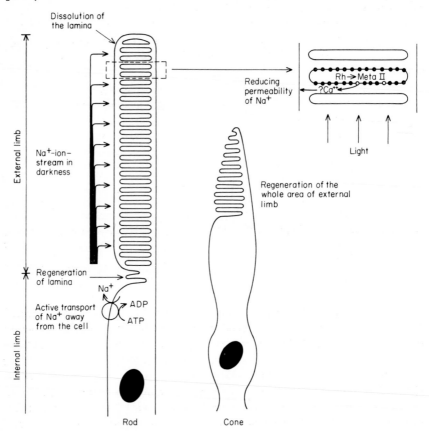

Fig. 5.4 The distal parts of the rods and cones of vertebrates. (From Donner, 1973 p. 886.)

The photosensitive material of the rods is known as *rhodopsin* or "visual purple". Around 80 per cent of the protein contained in the outer segments of rods consists of rhodopsin. The absorption of light in the rods is strongest when the light falls perpendicularly to the longitudinal axis of the cells (the light rays have to be parallel to the platelets on the tips) (Brown,

1972, Donner, 1973, p. 885). The rhodopsin is built of a specific protein, the cromophore component of which has an A-vitamin aldehyde configuration. After having been bleached, as a consequence of exposure to light radiation, the rhodopsin gets transformed to metarhodopsin II.

The changes in the membrane tensions of the visual cells have been registered recently (Tomita, 1970). It has been observed that the membrane of these cells becomes hyperpolarized as a consequence of light stimulation. Generally the opposite takes place in receptor tissues; as we know from chapter 3 p. 46 stimulation of a neuron usually brings about depolarization. Again, when a rod cell is stimulated by light the permeability of the membrane to natrium ions is restrained. This results in a hyperpolarization of the membrane (see Fig. 5.4).

Taken together these findings point to the conclusion that receptor cells display a maximum activity during darkness and that this activity decreases as a consequence of light.

Relatively less is known about the mechanisms mediating the effects of light found in the rhodopsin molecules to the cell membranes. It has been stated that the dissolution of the photosensitive material not only brings about stimulations in the neuronal tissues; it also changes the light sensitivity of the receptors. The sensitivity increases in a weak illumination. Rushton (1961a) made measurements in the part of the retina of a typical total (rod) monochromat (a colour deficiency to be described later, see p. 201). The patient had few, if any, functioning cones but a normal amount of functioning rods. Rushton studied this retina in two ways: (1) The dark adaptation curve in the usual psychophysical fashion was measured. (2) The regeneration of rhodopsin in the same region of the retina was measured by means of rhodopdin densitometry. The results are shown in Fig. 5.5. It is seen that a linear relation exists between the fraction of rhodopsin present and the logarithm of the threshold light intensity (Alpern et al. 1967).

Turning back to the picture of retinal anatomy (Fig. 5.3) we may notice that foveal cones connect more or less discretely through the bipolar cells while rods are said to be connected molecularly. That is, many rods impinge on a single bipolar cell. However, there is both convergence and divergence at work on the retina. A single end organ connects, for example, with several ganglion cells and a single ganglion receives collateral connections from several, sometimes many, receptor cells. The horizontal and the amacrine cells (Fig. 5.3) in particular provide collateral connections among various parts of the retina. Already this description of the structure implies the impossibility of visual signals directly mirroring light exposure variations on the retina, which could have been achieved only by means of simpler textures of inter-connections (Donner 1973, p. 890).

One of the basic processes was described by Kuffler (1953). Recording electrical activity in the retinal ganglia of the light-adapted cat's eye, he found that a whole series of retinal points would produce effects in a given ganglion cell when a tiny light spot was moved back and forth on the retina: "The discharge of a ganglion might be enhanced or depressed, depending on the spot stimulated. The whole retinal area from which changes could be evoked, known as the ganglion's *receptive field*, became

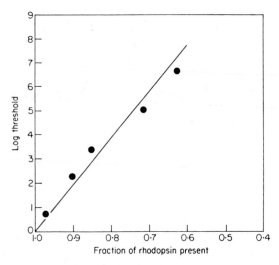

Fig. 5.5 Relation between log of the threshold of the rods and the fraction of rhodopsin remaining in the eye. (From Rushton, 1961.)

patterned in accordance with one of two plans. For some ganglia, there was a small area of the retina—that would discharge while the light was on and would subside promptly when it was extinguished. Surrounding this disc-like area, as a roughly circular annulus, there was another larger region that behaved in a quite different way" (Geldard 1972, pp. 70–71).

Briefly, in such a system, the centre of the receptive field is excitatory and the periphery is inhibitory (see chapter 4 pp. 83–85).

The second plan described by Kuffler is the reverse from the first one. There are ganglia with "off" centres and surrounding annular areas, which yield discharges only when the light falls on them. There thus always appears to be an antagonistic "centre-surround" mode of retinal organization (chapter 4 Fig. 4.7, pp. 84–85).

In 1932 Hartline and Granit—working separately—invented a method for registering impulses generated by light flashes in single neurons, and also from single fibres of the optic nerve (see chapter 3, Fig. 3.5 p. 52).

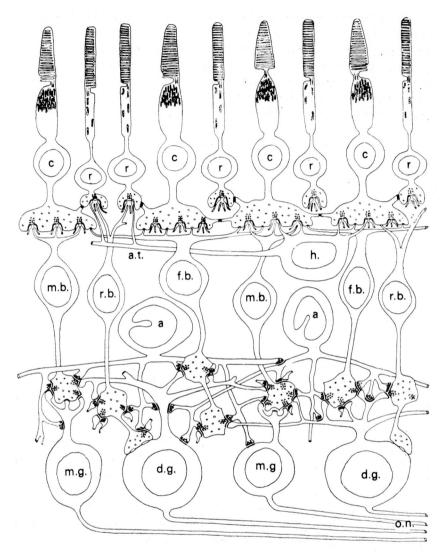

Fig. 5.6 Summary diagram of synaptic contacts between the principal types of retinal cells in the human retina. For details see the text. **r.**: rod; **c.**: cone; **m.b.**: midget bipolar; **f.b.**: flat bipolar; **r.b.**: rod bipolar; **h.**: horizontal cell; **a.t.**: horizontal cell axon terminals; **a.**: amacrine cell; **m.g.**: midget ganglion cell; **d.g.**: diffuse ganglion cell. (Reprinted from Boycott: Aspects of the comparative anatomy and physiology of the vertebrate retina.) (From Boycott, 1974.)

An up to date summary of synoptic contacts on the human retina has been given by Boycott, Fig. 5.6.

As mentioned above, hyperpolarization occurs in the receptor cells themselves. Stimulations from them to the ganglion cells are transmitted only by the bipolar cells of which two types have been distinguished. Figure 5.7 schematically represents the chain of events evoked by light falling directly on the receptors in an arbitrary receptor field (A). The impulses from the rod and cone cells are transmitted to the appropriate type of bipolar cell which becomes hyperpolarized as a consequence of the stimulation. Light falling on zones outside the receptor field (B) brings about depolarization of the above-mentioned type of bipolar cell. Instead, the opposite type of bipolars gets activated. When proceeding over the horizontal cells the hyperpolarization is spread out over a broad area, and thus light stimulations from zones *outside the receptor fields* are simultaneously transmitted. This implies a weakening of bigger amounts of graded potentials originating just in the receptive fields of the bipolars (Naka 1972). The first nerve impulses have been observed in the amacrine cells which, however, often respond by mere graded changes in their membrane potentials. Not until the level of amacrine cells have propagating neural impulses been observed. Although the changes in polarization spread over from receptors to bipolar cells, these changes don't appear as bursts of proceeding neural potentials. These chains of impulses actually can be recorded most effectively from the ganglion cells as shown in Fig. 5.7 (see Donner 1973, p. 892).

Contrary to the connective organization of the retinal cones, the rods are connected molecularly. Often several of them impinge upon a single bipolar. The innervation of the cones thus seems to favour specificity of response, while the lateral connections of the rods make for cooperation among them. Near the area with the greatest light sensitivity, the rods are only 1μ in thickness, while at the periphery diameters of $2 \cdot 5\mu$ have been measured. Foveal cones are similar in shape to the rods and measure about $1 \cdot 5\mu$ in diameter. It has sometimes been suggested that these cones are fundamentally different from those at the periphery, and that foveal cones are actually a kind of rod cell. However, both in structure and in type of synaptic connection they are clearly cones; the difference between foveal and extrafoveal cone cells is one only of degree, not of kind.

The only careful count of retinal cones and rods was carried out by Österberg (1935). He examined 164 different sample areas of the retina in a single human eye. The plot of his findings appears in Fig. 5.8. The shaded area of the inset shows where the counts were made. According to his measurement there are about six and a half million cones and 120 million rods on the human retina. Cone density is greatest at the centre of the fovea, while that of the rods increases from the fovea toward the periphery up to about 20°, after which it too gradually decreases.

At the point where the optic nerve fibres leave the eye, from the fovea toward the nose, is the so-called *blind spot*. It was first observed by Mariotte in 1666. In Fig. 5.8 the area corresponding to the blind spot is marked by

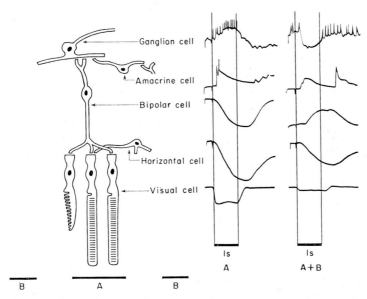

Fig. 5.7 Reaction of different cell-types to stimulation. A = exposure to light of the middle of the receptive field, B = exposure of parts outside the receptive field. The depolarization of a cell is indicated by upward deviations of curves concerned. (From Donner 1973 p.; 92. Courtesy of the author and the medical society Duodecim, Helsinki.)

two parallel vertical lines, indicating that there are neither rods nor cones in that area. In early sensory physiology it was assumed that the whole *macula lutea*, an area surrounding the fovea and including it, was free of rods. It is called the yellow spot, and measures about 2–3 mm in diameter, which is an angle of about 4°.

More than eighty years ago, two physiologists, Parinaud and von Kries, independently proposed the so called *duplicity theory* of the functioning of the human retina (see also chapter 6 p. 193). According to this theory the two kinds of cells, rods and cones, transmit different kinds of visual information. The rods register exclusively *degrees* of light energy (*intensity*). Thus the rods are useless in distinguishing colour hues; they are used only in the perception of small quantities of light in semi-darkness. As an instrument

of visual acuity (the ability to distinguish clear and definite outlines) they
are very weak. The cones come into play as the level of illumination rises,
and they make possible a considerable degree of visual acuity. According
to the extreme form of the duplicity theory the ability to distinguish colour
hues rests solely on the cones. The rods may be considered receptors for
night vision, the cones for daylight vision.

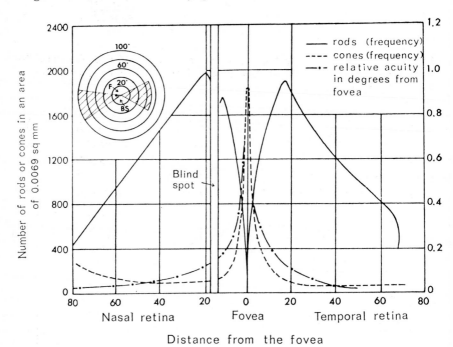

Fig. 5.8 Distribution of rods and cones throughout the retina. (From Geldard,
1972 p. 31.)

The two cell types further differ in their reaction to light stimuli of
different wavelength. Our normal visual world is "coloured" only when
observed in adequate illumination. When only the rod apparatus is in use,
we distinguish just degrees of grey, shades of white and black (chapter 3
p. 59).

Discrimination among wavelengths would presuppose at least two types
of cones, the absorption-curves of which are clearly separated. Thomas
Young (see chapter 6 p. 192) already proposed a trichromatic photosensitivity theory assuming specified visual receptors for reddish, greenish
and bluish radiation. For several decades investigators kept looking in vain
for photosensitive materials in the cones. Only ten years ago was the

existence of specific photopigments in the cones confirmed (see also chapters 3–4 and Chapter 6). Three corresponding types of cones have been found in the retina of rhesus-monkey and in man (Liebman 1972). In addition to the absorption-curve for rhodopsin Fig. 5.10 shows

Fig. 5.9 Demonstration of the blind spot. (From v. Fieandt, 1972 p. 67.) Close the left eye and keep fixating the cross with your right eye. At a viewing distance of 30 cm the disc disappears.

three approximate absorption curves for the cone-pigments in the human retina. The function of these differentially "tuned" cones is schematically shown in Fig. 5.11 (Donner 1973, 894). Everyone interested in more detailed description of the photochemistry of the retina may find a competent and substantial presentation in the paper by Wald (1968).

Spectral sensitivity curves are fundamental to colour specification. They

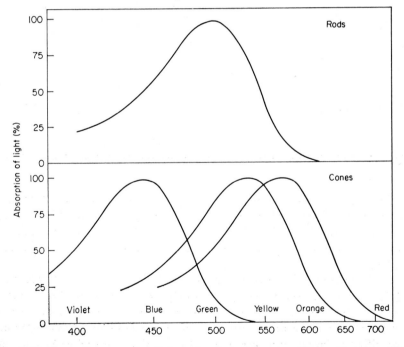

Fig. 5.10 Absorption curves of human photopigments. (From Donner, 1973 p. 885.)

show how the sensitivity of the eye changes with the wavelength of a monochromatic stimulus. As a quantititative indication of sensitivity we may
take the reciprocal of the relative amount of the light energy required to
evoke a constant visual response. If we make these measurements separately
in the periphery and at the fovea, two sensitivity curves are obtained (Fig.

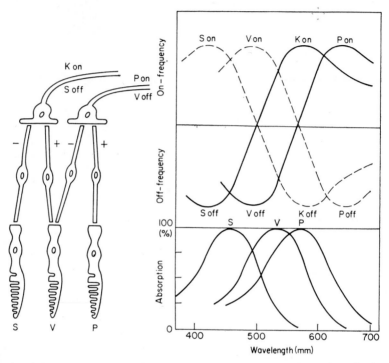

Fig. 5.11 The basic structure of the retinal system carrying information of colours.
There are three types of cones (*S*, *V*, *P*) which on the level of ganglion cells form
two pairs of colours, red–green and blue–yellow. The intermittent alterations are
mediated by the bipolar cells and the appearance of members of the colour pairs
depends upon antagonistic reactions in the visual nerve. The right part of the figure
shows approximated absorption spectra of different cone-pigments (below) and
on–off frequencies of the ganglion cells (above). The broken lines show frequency-
curves of the cells "*S* on–*K* off" and "*V* on–*P* off", respectively. (From Donner,
1973, p. 894. Courtesy of the author and the medical society Duodecim, Helsinki.)

5.12). A higher degree of sensitivity is displayed by the so called *scotopic*
curve which describes responses of rods. This higher curve shows the
results obtained in the periphery. The foveal curve indicates a lower degree
of sensitivity. Foveal responses are said to take place under the condition of
photopic or bright, visibility. At about 510 nm for the scotopic and around

555 nm for the photopic vision the sensitivity is at a maximum. This difference in sensitivity is called the *Purkinje shift* (see chapter 6 p. 189).

The fibres of each optic tract terminate in the *lateral-geniculate body*, a bulb-like protuberance on the *thalamus* of the midbrain, consisting of grey matter. There are two of these bodies, one on each side of the brainstem, and they function as an important way-station for messages travelling to

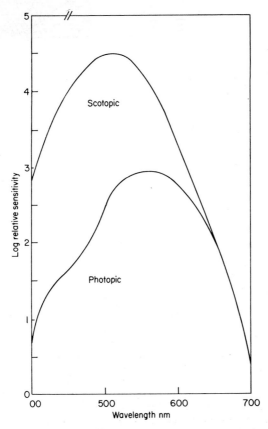

Fig. 5.12 Photopic and scotopic sensitivity curves. (From Wolman, 1973 p. 331.)

the ipsilateral visual cortex. What is known about these superimposed centra and their role in visual perception is mostly still based on the hierarchical model of Hubel and Wiesel (1962 and 1965). With a cross reference to what was discussed previously (chapter 4 pp. 83–85) the reader is asked to consult the schematic drawing in Fig. 5.14. It appears that receptive fields have been shown to exist also for the cells in the geniculate body. The

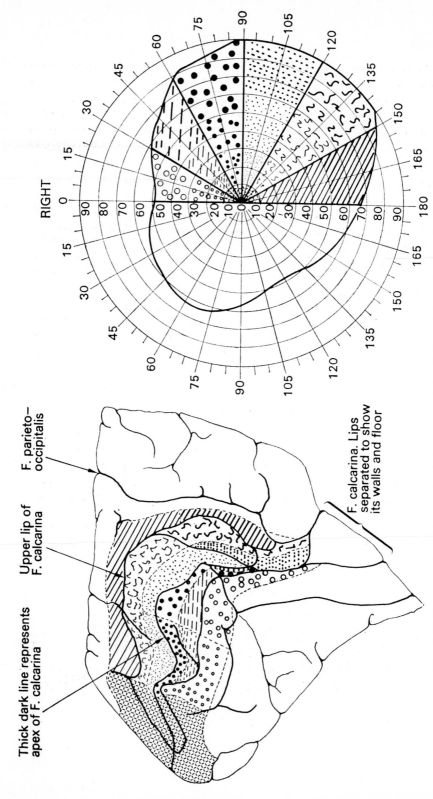

Thick dark line represents apex of F. calcarina

Upper lip of F. calcarina

F. parieto–occipitalis

F. calcarina. Lips separated to show its walls and floor

RIGHT

Fig. 5.13 Correspondence between visual centre and the field of vision. (From v. Fieandt, 1972 p. 70.)

findings are quite analogous to what was reported about the antagonistic functions of the retinal cells.

The geniculate body is connected by means of the geniculostriate axons to the striate area of the ipsilateral cortex (Brodmann's area 17). Figure 5.14 illustrates schematically the spatial correspondence between the left striate area and the right half of the field of vision, according to Holmes (1945).

The *simple* cortical cells can be stimulated by lines or contours showing a fixed consistent *orientation*. Obviously a far more specific stimulus situation is needed in order to activate cortical neurons than was required when stimulating retinal ganglion cells. In addition, superimposed *complex* and *hypercomplex* cells seem to be even more specialized; also the direction and speed of *movement* of lines or edges becomes important for activating the complex cells, whereas, for example, the length of a line in addition to its direction becomes decisive for the responses of hypercomplex structures. (See chapter 4 p. 84.)

An analysis of frequencies indicative of different properties of the visual image is apparently carried out in the centres of the pathway as a whole. This analysis is initiated already on the level of the retina, but at least in mammals it takes place mainly in the regions of thalamus and the cortex (Donner 1973, pp. 895–897; Geldard 1972, pp. 75–80).

Hearing

It is usually said that the receptor for the sense of hearing is the ear. However, the receiving and registering of individual stimuli is not sufficient. The complete auditory receptor system includes two ears, symmetrically located on either side of a movable head. When a sound stimulus occurs the head turns and orients itself in such a way that both ears function with the same receptor capacity.

Thus a single ear forms only half of the auditory receptor system. Figure 5.15 shows the four parts into which the ear is traditionally divided:

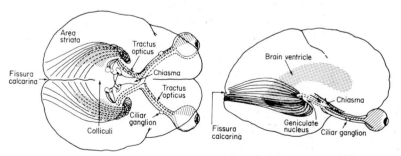

Fig. 5.14 The optical pathways. (From v. Fieandt, 1972 p. 69.)

the *external ear*, the *middle ear*, the *inner ear* and the *neural connections* which transmit impulses to the brain. We are all familiar with the outer ear or *pinna*, the most visible part of our auditory organ. As a device for collecting and focusing soundwaves it functions more effectively in many other mammals than in man. On the other hand the role of the human pinna in monaural localization has been experimentally shown by Batteau (1968). From the pinna, the air vibrations travel along the ear canal or *meatus*, which in man is about 2·5 cm long and 0·7 cm in diameter, to the eardrum or *tympanic membrane*, which can be considered the boundary between the outer and the middle ear. On the inner side of the tympanic membrane is a relatively spacious cavity or *tympanum*, about 1–2 cm³ in volume and irregular in shape. In the temporal bone near the middle of this cavity there are two openings which connect the middle and the inner ear; these are known, according to their shape, as the *oval* and the *round window*.

The oval window is located above the round one. Vibrations of the eardrum can be transmitted directly by air conduction through the middle ear cavity to the round window, but the oscillations are intensified by the lever system of the three *ossicles* which form a chain from the eardrum to the oval window. These tiny bones are the *hammer* (malleus), *anvil* (incus) and *stirrup* (stapes). The hammer is attached to the centre of the eardrum and thus vibrates with it. The vibrations are transferred to the anvil, which is connected to the hammer by an "elastic" ligament. The anvil in turn activates the stirrup through the lever system of another ligament, and the stirrup transmits vibrations to the oval window. (Fig. 5.16).

The *Eustachian tube*, which runs from the middle ear cavity to the throat, plays an important part in equalizing the pressure between the external and the middle ear. This is the third opening into the middle ear, and it connects the aural and the nasal-oral system of cavities. The lower end of the tube is normally closed, but it opens during swallowing.

Attached to the ossicles are two muscles, the *stapedius* and the *tensor tympani*. The former is attached to the stapes. When it contracts, it changes the articulation between the foot of the stapes and the oval window. Contraction of the tensor tympani, attached to the malleus, places the drum under greater tension and thus limits the extent of its movement. The muscles thus act as antagonists, the action of each being opposite to that of the other.

An essentially protective function of this muscle system has been demonstrated (v. Békésy 1939). The relation of the footplate of the stirrup to the oval window is such that, normally, the stirrup moves about a vertical axis. For exceptionally intense sounds however, the stapes rotates sidewise about an anteroposterior axis (at 90° to the former one). This reduces the amplitude of vibration from the tympanic membrane. Depending on frequency, the pressure per unit of area at the footplate may be more than 20 times that at the tympanic membrane.

A third way of transmitting the vibrations of the air outside the middle ear is by bone conduction. In this case, instead of passing through either of the windows of the middle ear, the vibrations are transmitted by the bone masses surrounding the inner ear. This is the normal manner of conduction in cases of partial deafness resulting from some structural defect or damage to the middle ear.

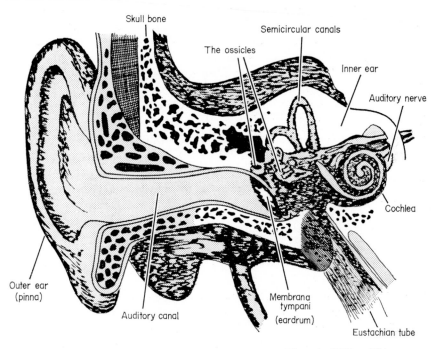

Fig. 5.15 Structure of the human ear. (From v. Fieandt, 1972 p. 72.)

The actual auditory receptor cells are located in the inner ear. Structually the inner ear corresponds to its name, the *labyrinth*. It is entirely embedded in the bony labyrinth, a system of cavities in the temporal bone (Fig. 5.17). It contains a transparent, watery fluid, the *perilymph*. Within the bony labyrinth and surrounded by fluid is the correspondingly shaped *membranous labyrinth* in which two parts can be distinguished: the so called *static labyrinth*, which regulates equilibrium (see p. 155) and the actual organ of hearing, the *cochlea*. Within the static labyrinth we can distinguish the *semicircular canals* and two sac formations, the *utricle* and the *saccule*. We will discuss more of their function in our discussion of proprioception (see subsequent paragraph, pp. 152–157). The membranous labyrinth is also filled with a clear fluid, the *endolymph*.

When the first terrestrial animals developed out of primitive aquatic organisms and became differentiated from them, it became essential to develop a receptor system for the perception of vibrations transmitted in

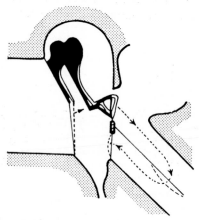

Fig. 5.16 Transmission of the oscillations in the middle ear. (From v. Fieandt, 1972 p. 73.)

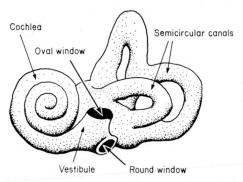

Cochlea

Oval window

Semicircular canals

Vestibule   Round window

Fig. 5.17 The bony labyrinth. (From v. Fieandt, 1966, p. 41).

air. It is this sytem which, by means of its canals and mechanical trans- mission components, transmits to the liquid-filled vessels of the inner ear those waves of vibration which in water organisms, for example fish, are mediated by the entire organism. In mammals this transmission of energy occurs specifically through the cochlea.

An important step in the development of the cochlea was the increase of its length, until it finally gained its present coiled-up form, resembling in man the shell of a snail. It consists of a cone-shaped central axis, the *modiolus*, and of a canal which is coiled around the central axis in a spiral form. In man this canal makes about 2¾ turns around the axis. In the fully developed inner ear the height of the cochlea from base to top is about 5 mm, while the width of the base is about 9 mm.

The entire length of the cochlea canal is divided into three parts or chambers. Figure 5.18 shows, uppermost (1) the *scala vestibuli*, below that

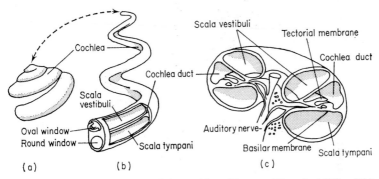

Fig. 5.18 Schematic pictures of the cochlea. (From v. Fieandt, 1972 p. 74.)

(2) the *cochlea duct* (*scala media*) and lowermost (3) the *scala tympani*. The first two chambers are divided from each other by *Ressner's membrane*, which spans the entire cochlea canal, while the cochlea duct is separated from the scala tympani by the *basilar membrane*. This membrane does not, however, divide the indicated cavities completely. At the extreme apex of the modiolus it leaves an opening between the two scalae, the *helicotrema*, which is scarcely larger than the eye of a needle (0·25 to 0·40 mm in diameter).

Extending from the modiolus, about half way to the outer wall of the cochlea, is a bony shelf which winds around the modiolus and forms a partial dividing wall between the scala tympani and the other chambers. At the base of this bony shelf and well protected by it is a large system of ganglia, the *spiral ganglion of Corti*, which also winds around the modiolus, and which is in direct contact with the auditory nerve bundle embedded within the modiolus. From this spiral ganglion the single afferent fibres branch out to the upper surface of the basilar membrane and into the *organ of Corti*, where they terminate in auditory cells. (Fig. 3.4A, chapter 3 p. 50.)

A schematic representation of the structure of the human cochlea is shown in Fig. 5.18 and Fig. 5.19. The sensory cells of the organ of Corti are called hair cells and are arranged in lengthwise rows on both sides of the pillars of Corti. One row lies inward from the pillars and contains the inner hair cells (see Fig. 5.19). On the opposite side are located the outer hair cells.

It is estimated that the cochlea of the human foetus contains about 3,500 inner hair cells and 13,500 outer hair cells. The density of the latter cells is maximal at the base of the cochlea, whereas the inner hair cells are uniformly distributed from the base to the apex.

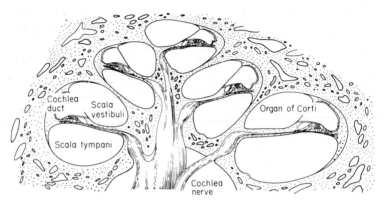

Fig. 5.19 The human cochlea. (From Békésy, 1957 p. 87.)

The hairs protrude from a fairly stiff plate (reticular lamina) which constitutes the free surface of both types of hair. When examined in cross section the hairs are found to be arranged in a W-pattern with the base of the W facing the so-called cells of Hensen. In the basal turn of the cochlea there are about 142 hairs in a single outer sensory cell (Kimura 1966).

As the apex is approached the bony cochlea necessarily becomes smaller and smaller in its cross-sectional area. Interestingly, the basilar membrane on the contrary becomes progressively wider. At the vestibular end it is about 0·08 mm wide. Near the helicotrema it has broadened to 0·52 mm. The length of the hair cells at the vestibular end of the cochlea averages 0·05 mm. At the apical end they are 0·085 to 0·1 mm in length.

To follow this structural description, however, it will be instructive in a study of hearing to follow the parts of the ear in terms of their function.

The most peripheral component of hearing is the mechanical transmission of vibration. This type of energy conduction also occurs, however, in the fluid-filled cavities of the inner ear and in the projections of the auditory cells in the organ of Corti.

The second component of the auditory event is the transformation of mechanical vibration into electrical impulses. The vibrations produce an electro-chemical process in the receptor cells. This in turn stimulates the nerve endings of the organ of Corti, and neural impulses are initiated. In our functional division this would constitute the third stage.

The auditory cells of the organ of Corti are located between the flexible tissues, the basilar membrane and the tectorial membrane. As the basilar membrane moves or contracts, the nerve endings of the auditory cells press against the tectorial membrane.

Numerous theories have been suggested as to the exact nature of the process by which mechanical energy, transmitted through a liquid medium, is transformed into an electro-chemical neural impulse, and as to the role played by the hair cells of the organ of Corti in this process. Any object whatsoever will share in the rhythmical vibration of its immediate environment, whether this be liquid or gas, if the specific frequency of the object corresponds to the frequency of the vibration in the environment. This is the phenomenon of resonance; for a more detailed description see pp. 120–122. In 1683 Du Verney, who did not know about the fluid contained within the inner ear, assumed that the auditory nerve endings resounded in response to movement of the central axis (modiolus) caused by air vibration. His theory included the assumption that the bony membrane of the modiolus possesses varying specific resonance at various points of the cochlea (see chapter 3 pp. 61–62).

About 200 years later v. Helmholtz put forth the so-called resonance theory of hearing. His assumption that the different nerve fibres react specifically to stimuli of differing frequencies has been shown to be incorrect. In order for discrete impulse series to be sufficiently sharply discriminated it would be essential for the resonators to be capable of abrupt damping; this does not occur in the inner ear.

In 1899 Ewald put forward his theory of the part played by static or standing waves in the origin of auditory sensations. He assumed a patterning of wave motion which, initiated by vibratory energy, would start at the base of the basilar membrane and travel across the surface of the membrane to the apex. This causes series of indentations or folds across the entire length of the basilar membrane, the number and size of which vary specifically with the frequency of the original vibration. This in turn causes different impulse patterns in the cells of the organ of Corti.

All the theories of hearing accepted today go back to the observations of v. Békésy (1928) in a publication based on a series of careful experiments with a model of the cochlea. Within a metal frame he placed a rubber membrane which in dimensions and structure corresponded exactly to the basilar membrane so that the membrane increased in thickness toward the wider end of the metal frame. He then scattered particles of coal dust across this artificial basilar membrane. When a tuning fork was struck he observed that the coal dust particles clearly shifted toward the "helicotrema" or apex of the membrane. These observations gave rise to a new theory of travelling wave movement. The wave begins in the stirrup in the middle ear and advances, depending on the frequency of the stimulus, to a particular point on the membrane, while the entire membrane participates in the vibratory movement. After reaching the critical points specific to that frequency in its movement toward the helicotrema the wave movement will be reversed in phase.

In subsequent experiments v. Békésy showed that the basilar membrane is not under tension. Even more, any tension which may exist is unimportant in the process of analysis. If tiny cuts are made in that membrane they do not pull apart. When stiff hairs are pressed endwise against it the membrane is seen to be flexible. The depressions assume a circular form near the apex of the cochlea and are slightly oval near the base, where the membrane is narrower and the tissue accordingly stiffer. The stiffness varies by a hundred-fold from one end to the other.

The movement of the travelling wave along the basilar membrane is shown in Fig. 5.21. The waves move from the narrower, stiffer end toward the broader, more flexible part of the apex. The maximum point, though broad, proves to be located in a characteristic place for a given frequency. The middlepoint is represented by a frequency of about 1600 Hz. For a low frequency tone, about 50 Hz (see chapter 7 p. 220), the basilar membrane vibrates as a whole. For other frequencies there is a difference in phase angle (see chapter 7 p. 210) between the movement of the stapes and a given point on the basilar membrane. The phase (see chapter 7 p. 212) of travelling wave changes progressively in its movement along the membrane (see Corso, *In* Wolman 1973, p. 357).

The concept of "travelling wave" must not be misunderstood. There is no simple progression along the length of the membrane like the shaking of a rope (Geldard 1972, pp. 175–176). The wave always travels from the stiffer to the broader, more yielding part. In cochlea models the wave might be made to proceed *toward* the driver, if placed at the broader part of the partition. "Travelling" is thus best thought of in terms of time relations. The principle that matters most is tissue elasticity, which varies more widely over the length of the membrane than any other. It thus has most to do with differentiation of response. According to v. Békésy (1957) the organ of Corti is built up in such a way that pressure on the basilar membrane is transformed into shearing forces many times larger on the side of the organ (Fig. 5.20). The altered shearing forces rub upon extremely sensitive cells attached to the nerve endings.

Several models of cochlea mechanics have been developed (see e.g. Flanagan 1962; Klatt and Peterson 1966). Some of them involve a set of differential equations that relate pressure and displacement in the inner ear. Equivalent computer networks have been built and tested. This extremely interesting research is still progressing, but its fruitfulness is dependent upon the construction of apparatus adequate to account for the various input parameters (chapter 3 pp. 61–64).

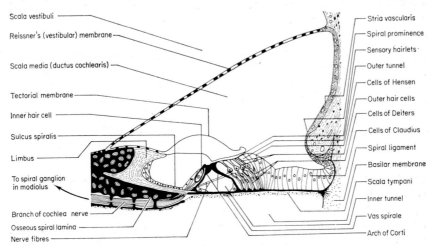

Fig. 5.20 The organ of Corti. (From Wolman, 1973 p. 357.)

There are several types of *electrical potentials* within the auditory system. The *endolymphatic potential* appears to be limited to the endolymphatic space bounded by Reissner's membrane and the reticular lamina. This excludes the basilar membrane of the organ of Corti (Tasaki, *et al.* 1954).

Cochlea microphonics was first systematically described and interpreted by Stevens and Davis in 1938 (1947). They pointed to the model provided by the piezoelectric effect. According to this hypothesis, which is now over-ridden by more recent research, when the hair cells of the organ of Corti are deformed by pressure they act as inorganic crystals and thus might be able to produce an electric current—much like a telephone-microphone. However, v. Békésy showed (1957) that there is no relation between the mechanical work done by a needle in displacing the basilar membrane and the resultant electrical output. He points to the tangential shearing action between the tectorial membrane and the organ of Corti mentioned above.

The *summating potentials* do not appear to arise simply as a result of nonlinearity of the cochlea microphonics-generators. According to Corso (1973) the summating potential is a product of an asymmetrical non-linearity. His model contains a nonlinear network with asymmetrical peak-clipping.

E

Nerve action potentials have been recorded from the fibres of the auditory nerve. There are about 30,000 individual fibres in this nerve. The fibres transmit neural impulses in the familiar all-or-none ways to the brain.

Coiled around the centre of the cochlea is Rosenthal's canal, which contains the most peripheral receptor ganglia. From here numerous neural fibres reach out to the hair cells. Each individual hair cell may be connected

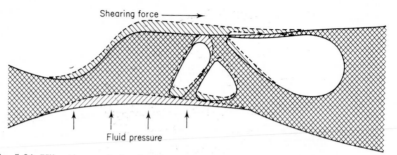

Fig. 5.21 Vibrations of the basilar membrane and the organ of Corti. (From v. Békésy, 1957 p. 87.)

with several nerve endings. The periodic pattern transmission along these fibres is even more exact and detailed than that possible by means of the basilar membrane, whose relatively large-scale and non-discrete impulse patterns become condensed in the ganglia. As we follow the sensory nerve connections up to the brain, the differentiation and specialization of neurons seem constantly to increase.

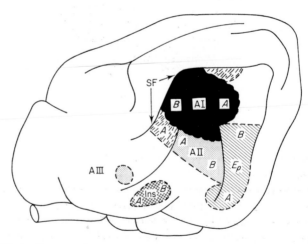

Fig. 5.22 Auditory projection areas of the cat. (From Geldard, 1972 p. 178.)

Upon leaving the base of the cochlea the auditory nerve enters the medulla of the brain. Here the majority of the fibres connect with others which cross to the contralateral side. By way of the lateral lemniscus they ascend to the *medialgeniculate body* of the thalamus. From this midway station radiating fibres spread to the cortex of the temporal lobe of the brain. Some regions of the cortex show a precise relation between locus

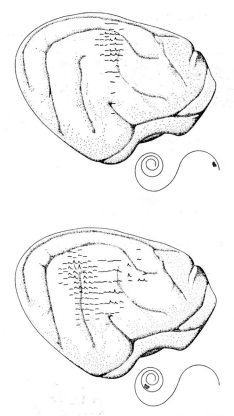

Fig. 5.23 Localization of nerve impulses on the brain of a cat. (From v. Békésy, 1957 p. 92.) The tiny drawing below shows stimulation spots in cochlea.

and tonal frequency. The ganglia involved are said to show *tonotopic localization* (Geldard 1972).

At present this much is certain: there are six more or less discrete areas on the cortex which involve auditory projections. Figure 5.22 shows their location in the cat. According to v. Békésy (1957) "the vibration of the basilar membrane produces in the auditory nerve volleys of electric spikes synchronous with the rhythm of the sound." The number of spikes packed into each period increases with increasing sound pressure. Two variables are transmitted to the cortex: (1) number of spikes, (2) their rhythm. These variables alone convey all information about the sound (see Fig. 5.23).

Above 60 Hz a new phenomenon comes in. The basilar membrane now begins to vibrate unequally over its area: each tone produces a maximal vibration in a different area of the membrane. Gradually this selectivity takes over the determination of pitch, for the rhythm of the spikes, which indicate the pitch at low frequencies, becomes irregular at the higher ones. Above 4000 Hz pitch is determined entirely by the location of the maximal vibration amplitude along the basilar membrane. (v. Békésy 1957, p. 92).

The recording *from single auditory neurons* has provided information on different levels of activity. In cats recordings have been made from the cochlea nerve, the cochlea nuclei, the geniculate bodies and the cerebral areas (see Fig. 3.8 chapter 3 p. 57).

All neurons at the periphery respond to both continuous and brief sounds. In upper brain structures many neurons respond only to brief sounds. An electrical potential origin which reflects both the intensity and the waveform of the stimulus has recently been found at the level of the inferior colliculi of the thalamus.

The tonotopic localization is more complete along the auditory tract than at the auditory cortex. There is evidence that the "projections" of the two ears become completely intermingled in the higher centres. Evidently each cochlea is represented bilaterally in the brain (Geldard 1972).

Smell and Taste

More primitive than vision and hearing in their level of phylogenetic development are those sensory modalities which react to *immediate* chemical stimuli coming in from the environment. The *chemical senses* are generally grouped into three modalities:

1. *The diffuse chemical sense.* The mucous membranes in the nasal and oral cavities are differentiated from the regions sensitive to general chemical influences. These regions are encountered everywhere around the openings of the body surface (eyes, mouth, intestinal region and sex organs). Animals at lower evolutionary levels, such as some types of fish, have chemical receptors all over the surface of their bodies and especially concentrated along their sides. These receptors are the undifferentiated nerve endings of fibres showing a general receptor sensitivity.

2. The sense of *smell*. This sense is traditionally defined in terms of the anatomical location of certain specific receptors, the olfactory cells. These cells are located within the nasal cavity, embedded in a small mucous

membrane in the upper part of the cavity. The terminal organs are elongated, spindle-shaped cells, the *olfactory rods*, from the ends of which fine hair-like formations extend through the mucous membrane into the nose.

3. The sense of *taste*, the receptors of which are located on the tongue and along the inner walls of the mouth. In aquatic organisms corresponding taste buds may occur all over the outer surface of the body. The terminal organs are selectively sensitive to various chemical stimuli.

More than anyone else Gibson (1966) has emphasized the fact that, from the psychological point of view, it does not make sense to classify modalities on the basis of the anatomical location of specific receptors. There is another way of classifying the chemical senses; they can be defined in terms of their function, smell being an accompaniment of breathing and taste of eating. In practice we do not consider as different tastes only those few sensory impressions which are transmitted exclusively by the specific gustatory receptors in the oral cavity, or as smells the nuances of a swallowed bit of food which follow from stimuli carried by the expired current of air. Thus ordinary language is not as misleading as might be assumed when it distinguishes smell and taste on grounds other than those of the specific olfactory and gustatory receptor fields (Gibson, 1966 p. 136). This fact has been observed before by numerous psychologists, e.g. Rubin (1936).

For practical reasons the specific olfactory and gustatory receptor functions will be described separately. In moving to a more psychological level of description, however, taste and smell will be discussed in large part as one undifferentiated modality.

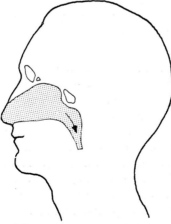

Fig. 5.24 The size of the nasal cavities. (From v. Fieandt, 1972 p. 81.)

The location and functioning of the *olfactory receptors* is based to a great extent on the dynamics of the air currents within the nasal cavities. The overall volume of these cavities in man is about 34·2 cm³ (for the two nostrils combined). Their location and relative size is shown in Fig. 5.24. Starting at the tip of the nose we first encounter the *nostrils (nares anteriores)* as the outermost part of the system. Correspondingly, there is a pair of outlets into the nasal chambers at the rear, the throat openings (*nares posteriores*). The inner surface of the nostrils is covered with a sensitive epithelial layer, an immediate continuation of the skin of the nose. This

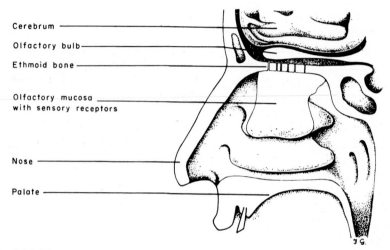

Fig. 5.25 The nasal cavity with the olfactory epithelium. (From Døving, 1967 p. 53, Fig. 19.)

epithelium is called *regio respiratoria*. The nostrils are separated by a partly bony and partly cartilaginous wall, the *septum nasale*. The bone forming the top and rear framework for the nasal structure is the *vomer*. Not all the air moving within the nose is able to mediate olfactory stimuli. Most of the inspired air passes in a high arc directly from the nostrils to the throat openings. In general the air current does not circulate around the three cartilaginous formations of the nose, but passes between and through them. (Fig. 5.25).

When we breathe quickly or deliberately "sniff" the air, part of the air current finds its way above and behind the highest cartilaginous wall, there encountering the well-protected *olfactory epithelium (regio olfactoria)*. In addition, some organs located in the septum are sensitive to smell. These *Jacobsonian organs (organon nasovomerale Jacobsoni)* are clearly rudimentary in the human adult. In the human embryo and during early infancy they are visible as openings in the inner walls of the two nostrils, one in each. In mammals other than man this organ is mainly composed of spongy tissue which can swell in order to affect the influx of air. During the process of smelling the swelling slackens, producing an air-sucking effect in the passages. It is not impossible that some of the peculiarities we ascribe to the perceptual world of dogs, and the differences in their sensory behaviour relative to that of man, might be due to their more developed vomeral organ. While sight and hearing are better in human beings, their olfactory organs seem to have degenerated.

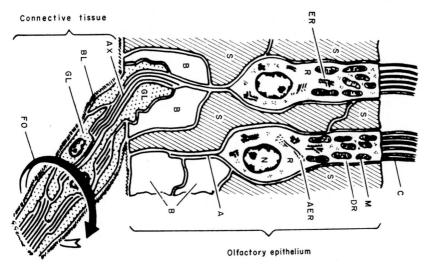

Fig. 5.26 Cell-types of the olfactory epithelium. (From Døving, 1972 p. 166.)
R = receptors, S = sustentacular cells, B = basal cells, C = cilia.

The olfactory epithelium is spread over an area of about 2·5 cm² in the upper part of each nostril cavity, as indicated in Fig. 5.25. Thus there are two separate tissues, one on each side of the septum. The tissue is yellowish-brown in colour. The surface of the olfactory epithelium consists of *columnar* or *sustentacular* cells which support and protect the oblong olfactory cells proper (Fig. 5.26). The columnar cells are pigmented, and are responsible for the yellowish colour of the tissue. The olfactory cells are actually free endings of the first cranial nerve, and there are about 50 millions of them in the epithelial tissue. At the extreme end of each cell are six to twelve brush-like formations which stand erect and penetrate through the mucous membrane which covers the tissue. The particles of matter which reach the nasal cavity first have to penetrate the mucous layer in order to reach the brush like projections. The density of receptors in the rabbit's mucosa is estimated to be 120,000 per mm², compared to at least 100,000 in man (Døving, 1973 p. 161). The basic layer of the mucous respiratory region is formed by the *basal cells* which have a pyramidal shape and a spherical nucleus.

The terminal organs formed by the junction of olfactory cells are called *olfactory rods*. In structure these organs showing a diametric measure of

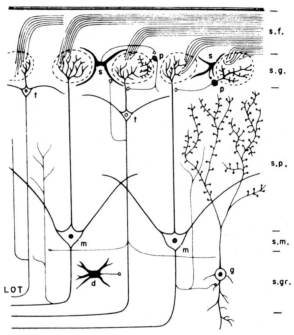

Fig. 5.27   Neural connections of the olfactory cells. (From Døving, 1972 p. 171.)
p = periglomerular cells, t = tufted cells, m = mitral cells, g = glomerular cell.

about 0·1μ are in many respects primitive, since they represent a combination of receptor and ganglion function in the same cell. There is no synapse at the level of the epithelial tissue; synaptic connections occur only when we reach the olfactory bulb. A similar duality of function is typical in the nervous system of the lower vertebrates, where the same receptor cell can serve both as generator and conductor of nerve impulses. This fact again indicates that the sense of smell represents the earliest stage in man's development.

Careful studies of the epithelial tissue of the rabbit show that there are no transverse connections between the olfactory nerve endings. After passing in bundles through the cribriform plate of ethmoid bone at the roof of the nasal cavity, they terminate in the olfactory bulb, the foremost extension of the brain tissue (for details, see Fig. 3.3B, chapter 3 and Fig. 8.3, chapter 8). The axons of the olfactory cells, about 0.2μ in diameter, are situated in close proximity to each other. Several hundred of them are encased in one common satellite cell (see Døving 1967, p. 54). In the olfactory bulb the receptor axons make synaptic contacts in the *glomeruli*, spherical structures near the bulbs surface (see Figs 5.27 and 5.28) about 0.2 mm in diameter.

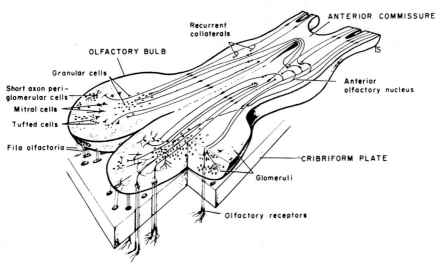

Fig. 5.28 The connecting pathways of the olfactory cells. (From Døving, 1964 p. 162.)

The second order neurons which take care of further nervous conduction are of three kinds: short axon *periglomeral cells*, small *tufted cells* situated in the external plexiform layer, and larger *mitral cells* making a distinct layer inside the former. Some of the axons of mitral cells pass directly backwards to form the olfactory tract. Others connect with nearby tufted cells which in turn send axons back to enter the glomeruli. By means of this "closed circuit" arrangement the olfactory system is provided with continuous *feedback*; this probably makes for "amplification" of the message thus accounting for the considerable sensitivity of the sense of smell. The structural conformity of the olfactory system throughout different animal phyla is shown in Fig. 5.29.

From the olfactory bulb, the *olfactory tract* or the first cranial nerve leads to the cortical olfactory areas. The best known way-stations are the cingulate gyrus, the amygdala and the pyriform area of the cortex.

The possibility of olfactory impulses being organized spatially, as those of other modalities seem to be, has given rise to a great deal of discussion. Some degree of regional projection has been found (see Adrian 1950, Le Gros Clark, 1951). Døving (1973, p. 163) points to the fact that some areas in the olfactory bulb of certain animals have been shown to specifically "pick up" information concerning strictly relevant groups of stimuli: in the

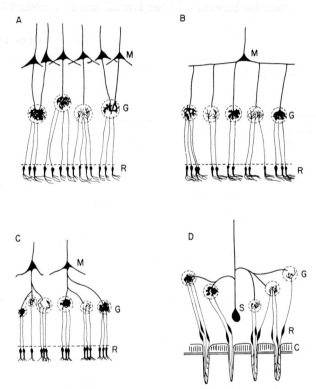

Fig. 5.29 Structural conformity of the olfactory connection system. (From Døving, 1967 p. 56, Fig. 22.) (A) Mammal; (B) Bird; (C) Fish; (D) Arthropod. (G) Glomeruli; (C) Cuticle.

rabbit the anterior part of that organ is most sensitive to substances soluble in water, whereas the posterior part takes care of materials soluble in fat.

The "smell brain" or rhinencephalon is often divided into three systems based on their connections to the olfactory bulb (Pribram and Kruger 1954). They are shown schematically in Fig. 5.30. The first system has direct connections with the olfactory bulb, the second system has connections with the first one but none with the bulb. There are also areas which lack direct connections with the bulb and with the first system, and instead are directly coupled with the second system alone. They are called the third system. It has to be pointed out that all these areas are not limited to olfactory function. It has been shown, for example, that lesions in the amygdala affect blood intake, temperature regulation and sleeping cycles, whereas lesions in the second system affect emotional behaviour.

The alternating activation and inhibition of the same sensory units, so characteristically demonstrated in the functions of vision and hearing, has its counterpart in the transmission system of olfactory messages. The admirably fine discrimination ability for different smell qualities is apparently based on selective activation of certain groups of receptive units simultaneously with the inhibition of others. Detailed results of *single cell recordings* on all levels of the olfactory system will be given later in chapter 8.

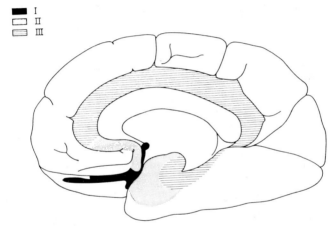

Fig. 5.30 Diagram of the olfactory brain centres in man. (From Døving, 1967 p. 58.)

The *gustatory receptors* of man are located on the tip, the sides and the back of the dorsal tongue surface. There are also regions responsive to taste stimuli on the soft palate, the front of the epiglottis and parts of the larynx. Adults are devoid of taste receptors on the underside of the tongue, on the middle of the tongue's upper surface, on the inner side of the lips and cheeks, the tonsils and the uvula. By contrast children, at least during their first decade, have taste receptors widely scattered about the whole surface of the tongue and even on the side walls of the mouth cavity. Since sensations of sweetness are based precisely on the receptor activity of the oral cavity, it is hardly surprising that children are particularly fond of sweets, while adults prefer spiced foods in which olfactory stimuli play a large part. From the point of view of comparative psychology, it is interesting to note that the gustatory cells are already clearly visible in the three-month old human fetus, and that they are actually spread over a wider area than in newborn infants. This pattern of organization is not unexpected; it has been shown that higher levels of ontogenetic development involve a gradual decrease in distinctiveness in olfactory and gustatory receptors, and their concentration over a more and more narrowly delimited area.

In contrast to the olfactory cells, the gustatory receptor cells act only as transductors. They make immediate synaptic connections to the actual afferent neurons. The taste receptors are located in small *taste buds*, spindle or onion shaped clusters of two to twelve receptor cells together with supporting and basal cells. The receptor cells themselves are generally spindle-shaped while the supporting (sustentacular) cells are columnar in shape. The taste buds are organized in papillae which, in the form of small nodelike swellings, cover the entire upper surface and edges of the tongue. One papilla may include hundreds of taste buds. In the buds, the sensory

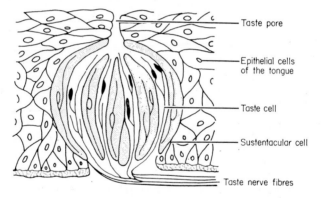

Fig. 5.31 Schematic structure of a taste bud. (From v. Fieandt, 1972 p. 86.)

cells are arranged as illustrated in Fig. 5.31 (De Lorenzo 1963). A noteworthy characteristic of these sensory cells is their brief average life span; in rats and rabbits they are "used up" and replaced within three to five days (see Beidler, 1963).

The different "cell types" traditionally distinguished within the taste bud actually represent, according to the most recent research, different stages of growth and decay of the receptor cell. New cells are constantly developing at the periphery of the taste bud, and as they mature they migrate to more central areas. It seems most likely (Wolsk 1967, p. 115 see also Davis, 1963) that the nerve endings do not "migrate" together with the receptor cell, but that the cell moves from one nerve conductor to another. Acceptance of this theory also involves recognizing that the stimulus sensitivity of a particular receptor cell changes according to the neuron to which it is connected at a given time. The neuron must be assumed to have a more constant structure over time than the varying sensory cell. The specificity of the neuron is in turn determined by its more central connection. Since specific sensitivity for various substances has been observed, this specialized sensitivity in the receptor cell must vary as it migrates within the taste bud.

Three different forms of papillae are traditionally distinguished: (1) *fungiform papillae*, mushroom-like in appearance, which are scattered irregularly over the upper tongue surface, (2) *circumvallate papillae*, much larger than the others, which are usually seven to ten in number and form a kind of ridge near the back of the tongue, and (3) *foliate papillae*, which are located in a series of folds along the outer edges of the back part of the tongue.

Contrary to what was hitherto rather mechanistically assumed concerning the functional basis of taste experiences, recent investigations have stressed the interactive complexity of taste phenomena. All naturally occurring tastes are a result of parallel stimulation of olfactory, temperature and touch receptors, as well as of the taste buds proper. By means of diffusion particles of matter moving with the air current escape from the mainstream and find their way to the uppermost reaches of the nasal chamber; this occurs during both inspiration and expiration. In all tasting of food the highly important, unanalysable overall quality, the taste experience, is based partly on food particles which come from the throat into the nasal cavity borne by the expired air stream. This olfactory stimulus is combined with the gustatory stimuli received by the receptors in the mouth. Thus taste perception is no longer conceived of as the mere additive result of some combined primaries or taste fundamentals. Admittedly, if we close our nostrils and taste only solutions at body temperature (about 37° C), we do experience a reduced world of tastes. In that situation we can distinguish four so-called primary tastes: sweet, bitter, salty and sour. It is obvious, however, that a bare series of qualities like this does not do justice to the richness of nuances encountered in natural free-tasting situations. All attempts to find and classify specific taste organs must be viewed against this background. Figure 5.33 shows the parts of the tongue which correspond specifically to the various primary tastes. This functional localization can, of course, be directly compared with the differences found in the structure of the papillae as shown in Fig. 5.32.

The determination of specific thresholds for the four types of receptors entered a new epoch when Pfaffmann (1959a) introduced his superb experimental techniques. By means of a series of electronic devices he was able to record the flow of discharges directly from the nerve fibres mediating gustatory stimulations. Thresholds for both sodium chloride (NaCl) and hydrochloric acid (HCl) were readily obtained by noting the minimal concentration which elicited a discharge of neural impulses. A modified

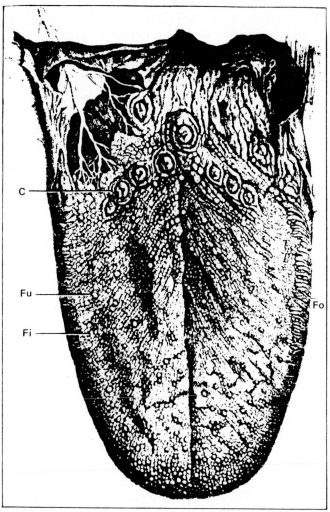

Fig. 5.32 The surface of the tongue. (From v. Fieandt, 1972 p. 87.)
C = circumvallate, Fu = fungiform, Fi = fibriform, Fo = foliate.

method of constant stimuli was used in which a series of stimuli, graded in composition and intensity, were dropped in random order onto the surface of the tongue. The presence of an impulse in the nerve fibre was observed by means of an oscilloscope and a loudspeaker attached to the recording

apparatus. The stimulus was then determined by the midpoint of the
frequency sum curve of nerve responses.

Interesting anatomical observations have come from the experiments by
v. Békésy (1964). The papillae which mediate stimulations from acids and
from salts appear to be structured differently from those responsive to

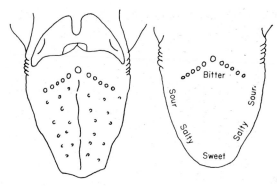

Fig. 5.33 Parts of the tongue which correspond to different primary tastes. (From
v. Fieandt, 1972 p. 88.)

bitter and also to sweet tastes. The sour-salt type is more rounded in shape
and contains capillaries producing distinguishable sub-surface loops.
Papillae of the bitter-sweet type have a more pointed shape and they
profit from a more deeply disposed vascular supply. There are also clear
differences in functions of the two kinds of papillae. Figure 5.34 presents
the differences in their responses to trains of electrical pulses. The salt-sour
type yields continuous sensations at 3 to 4 current pulses while a repetition
rate of 7 to 10 pulses is required to smooth out the bitter and sweet tastes
(Geldard 1972).

An observation made long ago, that gymnemic acid has the remarkable
property of acting on the tongue to suppress sweet and bitter tastes while leaving
sour and salty tastes unaffected, possibly fits in here also (Geldard 1972, p. 495).

Pfaffmann (1948, 1959a,b) was able to determine average specific
thresholds for five categories of chemical stimuli: sugar, salt, hydrochloric
acid, saccharin ($C_7H_5NO_3S$) and quinine sulfate ($2C_{20}H_{24}N_2O_2$. H_2SO_4 .
$2H_2O$). The differences in the order of magnitude of the thresholds were
considerable, varying from a 0·2–0·7 per cent concentration for sodium
chloride and sugar to 0·00003–0·00005 per cent for quinine sulfate and
saccharin ($C_7H_5NO_3S$).

Sugar produced practically no effect. Some activity following quinine
stimulation could be detected in the more optimal preparations. Pfaffmann

assumes that the nerve fibres conducting impulses for sweet may be of a relatively smaller diameter. They could, according to him, even be un-myelinated, so that action potentials in these fibres would prove quite difficult to record.

As Pfaffmann pointed out, the seventh and the ninth cranial nerves are of undoubted importance for taste while two others, the tenth and the fifth, are also involved. The tenth or *n. vagus* supplies fibres for the taste buds of

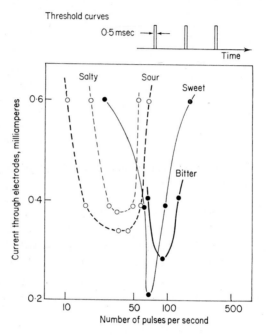

Fig. 5.34 Responses of papillae to trains of electrical pulses. (From Geldard, 1972 p. 495.)

the pharynx and larynx. According to Geldard (1972, p. 489) it is the fifth cranial nerve or the trigeminal which supplies the touch patterns that complicate both olfactory and gustatory perceptions. All these nerves run through different pathways to the medulla. The pathways carrying gusta-tory impulses seem to parallel those conveying cutaneous impulses from mouth and tongue all the way through the thalamus to the cerebral cortex.

A possibly separate gustatory projection area in man is presumably bilaterally represented and situated near the lower end of the postcentral gyrus, just above the fissure of Sylvius (Geldard 1972, p. 490). The central projection for taste is not to be found in rhinencephalon.

Self-regulation of the organism on the basis of the sense of taste could

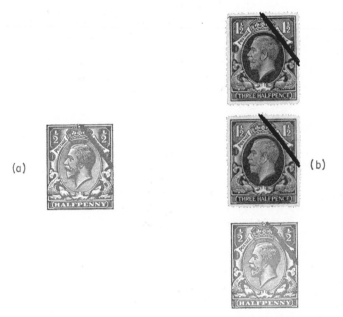

(a)

(b)

Plate I The halfpenny stamp on the left (a) is from the typographic issue of King George V; the three-halfpenny stamp (b) is from the photogravure series introduced in 1934. The stamps above and below b are to allow comparison between the fused image and the two monocular stimuli. If the brown stamp does not immediately dominate when you fuse the two, try attenuating the halfpenny stamp with a neutral filter (e.g., one lens of a pair of sunglasses). Colour reproduction is never perfect and the experiment is best attempted with the original stamps. (The 1934 photogravure issue can be identified from its dimensions, 22·25 mm × 18·3 mm; later issues were slightly smaller.) To comply with Post Office regulations it has been necessary to insert the oblique bar on the stamps.

Plate II To obtain the McCollough effect, gaze at the red and green pattern (A) for about three minutes. The viewing distance should be about two feet. Do not let your eye rest on any one point for very long and try to look as frequently at red as at green areas. Resist the temptation to tilt your head to one side.

Looking at the uncoloured pattern (B) you should see illusory colours that vary according to the orientation of the tilted lines: where the lines are tilted to the right you will see pinks and where they are tilted to the left you will see pale greens. Don't expect the illusory hues to be very strong: the effect is scientifically, rather than phenomenally, striking. Try tilting the book, or your head, 90 degrees to one side: the apparent colours should exchange positions.

One of the most remarkable aspects of the phenomenon is its persistence. Try testing yourself again after half an hour. If you gaze at the coloured figure for rather longer than three minutes—for, say, quarter of an hour—you may produce an effect that survives for days or weeks.

To obtain the basic effect some readers will need to look at the coloured pattern for a little longer than three minutes, some for a little less. Since the phenomenon, once established, is very stable, it does no harm to glance occasionally at the uncoloured patterns.

(a)

(b)

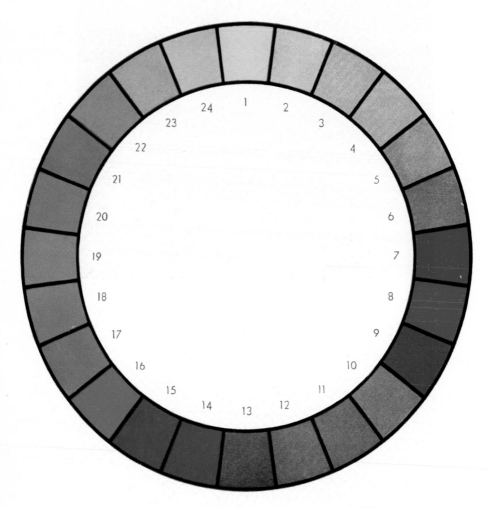

Plate III Ostwald's colour circle. See p. 172.

Plate IV The Munsell double cone and one of its vertical sections. See p. 174.
(Adapted from Kendler, H. H.: Basic Psychology, 1963.)

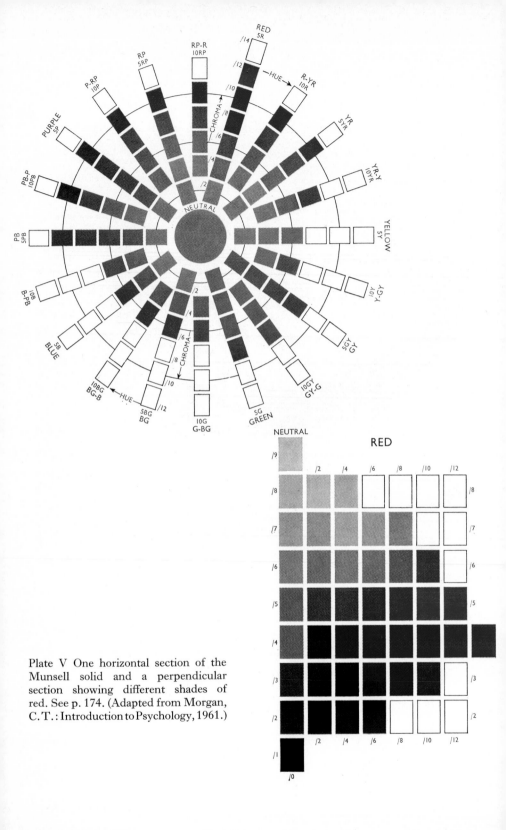

Plate V One horizontal section of the Munsell solid and a perpendicular section showing different shades of red. See p. 174. (Adapted from Morgan, C. T.: Introduction to Psychology, 1961.)

Plate VIa Additive colour mixture. See p. 183.

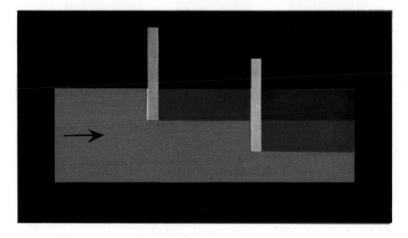

Plate VIb Subtractive colour mixture. See p. 184.

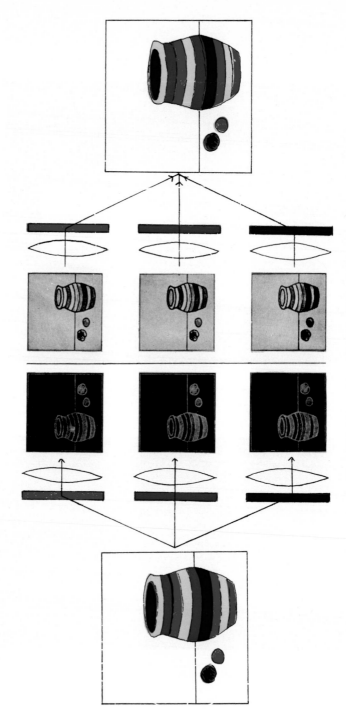

Plate VII Maxwell's experiment. See p. 192.

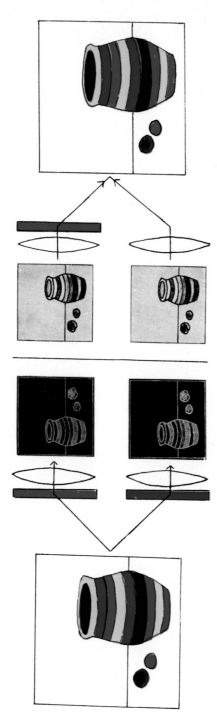

Plate VIII Land's experiment. See p. 205.

form a chapter of its own. Such self-regulation is seen both in taste preferences, to which a great deal of attention has been devoted, and in the ability of an animal to adapt its diet appropriately under conditions when the supply of some substance essential to life is seriously disturbed. These studies went back to the observations of Richter, published in 1943. When the adrenal gland was removed in experimental animals the sodium chloride level in the organism decreased so drastically that the animal was in serious danger. However, rats operated on in this way increased their intake of salt so greatly that the deficiency was compensated for.

Since Richter's investigations, careful and complex electro-physiological studies have shown that such metabolic disturbances do not entail changes in the specific sensitivity of the receptors themselves. The development of the gustatory cells and the differentiated cells of the taste buds also do not seem to offer explanation of these phenomena.

A possible explanation may stem from the findings of McBurney and Pfaffmann (1963) about the significance of saliva in gustatory adaptation. For instance, the sensitivity of the human tongue to a salt solution increases many hundred-fold when, instead of the normal saliva, the surface of the tongue is moistened with distilled water. The salt content, like other chemical components of saliva, is determined by the concentration of these substances in the blood. It is possible that metabolic changes are reflected in the composition of the blood and consequently also in that of the saliva, so that changes in the adaptation level of various gustatory sensations might occur without involving a corresponding change in the sensitivity of the receptor cells.

Taste has an interesting electrophysiology of its own. Changes in afferent nerve fibres carrying gustatory impulses have been demonstrated in different animal species. For example, the investigations by Pfaffmann have shown procedures in the gustatory fibres in the cat analogous to that found in afferents of other modalities.

Diamant et al. (1963) recorded impulses from the chorda tympani of 32 operated otosclerotic patients. Natriumchloride and sugars gave measurable electrophysiological responses. The relative magnitude of the electrical activity corresponded to the usual order of sweetness in various sugars. Interestingly in these human patients distilled water of tongue temperature had no effect whatsoever. It is known that chickens, dogs and monkeys all show clear potentials when stimulated by water. In general, large species differences have been detected: rats, guinea-pigs and hamsters give strong responses to NaCl and weak ones to KCl (see also chapter 3 pp. 59–61 and Fig. 3.10). On the other hand, cats, dogs and raccoons have large KCl responses and weaker NaCl responses (Geldard 1972).

Kimura and Beidler (1961) inserted tiny electrodes into individual taste cells in the rat's tongue. In response to various chemical stimuli they were able to record intracellular electrical changes. It turned out that no two taste cells are quite identical in sensitivity. Figure 5.35 shows a sample of functions for ten different taste cells. It is also apparent that each cell is normally responsible for two or more qualities. It is never "devoted" to only one single taste. There are cells which will respond to a wide "spectrum" of stimuli. The width of the spectrum also varies from one concentration to another. Specificity might occur on particular local sites; probably on the receptor cell's membrane.

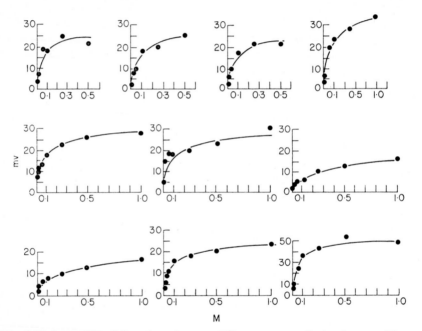

Fig. 5.35 A sample of functions for ten different taste cells in the rat. (From Geldard, 1972 p. 520.)

Single sensory fibres teased out of the corda tympani yield results that differ from those of the sense cell. They show trains of spaced impulses instead of potentials, (see analogous results with the olfactorial recordings p. 250). As with receptor cells, there are highly individual responses from fibre to fibre for a given stimulus (Geldard 1972, pp. 520–522).

Potentials may also be recorded at higher levels on the pathways to the cortex, though the technical difficulties appear to be even greater. Events seem not to be too different from what was recorded from the chorda tympani. The correspondence of recorded findings on the levels of the chorda tympani, the medulla and the thalamic centres is pictured in Fig. 5.36. So far it has proved rather frustrating to record gustatory potentials directly from the cortex.

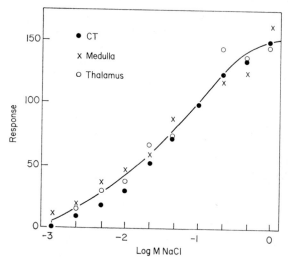

Fig. 5.36 Comparisons of responses in taste nerve (chorda tympani), medulla and the thalamic gustatory area of the rat. (From Geldard, 1972 p. 522.)

Of the receptors of the *general chemical sense*, those located in the nasal cavity are the most interesting ones. Stimuli are received by the free endings of the trigeminal nerve. Peculiar to the stimulation of these receptors is the "prickly" sensation, which occurs along with olfactory sensations, and which is accompanied by mucous secretion, weeping and sneezing. Many stimuli classified as smells activate this system as well as the olfactory network. In those areas of the oral cavity where taste receptors are absent, stimuli are transmitted by the receptors of the general chemical sense. These have the lowest sensitivity of all receptors of the olfactory and gustatory modality.

The Skin Senses

Of the five human senses distinguished by Aristotle, that of "touch" has since received the most critical treatment. Modern textbooks reject the old unitary sense of "touch". The Somaesthesis includes on the receptor level at least two different types, "mechanoreceptors" and "thermoreceptors", and possibly others also, (see Gibson 1966, Geldard 1972).

Up to now textbooks have generally classified sensory modalities in any of three ways: *qualitatively* (according to the sensation experienced), on the basis of the *stimulus*, or on *anatomical* grounds. The last is the most traditional; it is noteworthy that, even in psychologically-orientated discussions of perception, the sensory modalities are most persistently classified on the basis of structural characteristics. Since 150 years ago our sensory receptors have been divided into *external* and *internal* (exteroceptors and interoceptors). Since the turn of the century the category of *proprioceptors* has also been added: these receptors give information about the position of the body (Sherrington 1906).

The anatomical basis for classification seems to serve the needs of psychologists as long as their interest is attracted primarily to the tele-exteroceptors (vision and hearing). When we shift, however, to those modalities whose receptors are located in the skin or in internal organs, a classification based on anatomical criteria leads to considerable imprecision. The varying classifications and terminologies appearing in the textbooks of the field reflect, perhaps most drastically, the uncertainty which prevails on the subject. According to Geldard (1972, p. 260), the skin might best be considered as housing three sensory systems, one for *pressure*, one for *pain* and one for *temperature*.

A kind of mapping procedure has been applied to explore systematically the organs in the skin tissues. The common laboratory technique is to utilize a rubber stamp prepared in the form of a square grid, 20 mm on each side, with a total of 400 squares each 1 mm² in size. This then specifies a standardized sample area of the skin for exposure to experimental stimulation of different types. For investigation extended over longer periods of time a technique devised by Dallenbach has proved feasible: a small dot of Indian ink is hypodermically injected at the corners of the grid.

In order to explore warm and cold-sensitive spots, investigators applied temperature stimulators in which water at a controlled temperature circulated and kept the tip of the stimulator at a constant temperature. To produce pain stimuli, thin sharp metal objects (such as needles) are generally used.

At the turn of the century, Blix and Goldscheider observed that experiences of warmth or cold could not be obtained uniformly at all places on the skin surface. The specific temperature receptors are restricted to rather definite, circumscribed regions. Blix investigated the temperature-sensitive loci of the skin and was the first to define the different spots for warmth and cold. A little later, von Frey was able to extend the observation of punctate sensitivity to pain and pressure. That is why he gave a classification based on experienced qualities. As tools Frey used human and animal hairs attached at right angles to a small wooden holder. These hairs, varying from 0·05 to 0·2 mm in diameter, made it possible to carry out accurate point-by-point serial exploration of the skin surface.

With these methods Frey also tried to determine the specific end organs corresponding to the various categories of sensitivity. At first studies explicitly and rigidly followed the principle of specific nerve energies. Nowadays the interest in distinctions among specified transducers has lessened considerably. As Lewis puts it, nerve fibres are of interest at their endings rather than along their whole length. The way in which impulses travel is quite analogous from fibre to fibre.

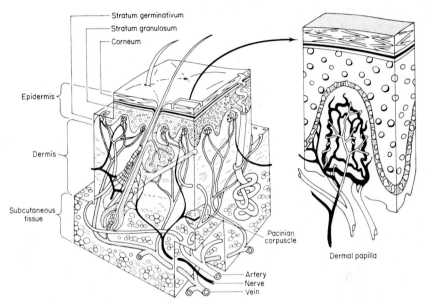

Fig. 5.37 Schematical drawing of human hairy skin. (From Kling and Riggs, 1971 p. 123.)

Although the question of the structural differences of the nerve endings located in various layers of the skin has lost most of its importance since the pattern theory suggested by Nafe (1934), Weddell (1955) and Sinclair (1967) set aside Frey's doctrine of specific receptors, a survey of the traditional approach to the problem of sensory qualities may be of interest.

Most of the known skin receptors are "free nerve endings" which reach up toward the surface of the skin. In some areas of the skin these nerve endings branch out into every cell of that skin layer. In their structure these endings show considerable variation. There are *bundles* (plexuses) which do not occur in the epidermis but which are quite numerous in the corium and in the subcutaneous layers. Phyletically they are sometimes regarded as the prototype of all other categories of skin receptors. However, no sharp boundary can be drawn between the more primitive and simple receptors and the large and complex *Pacinian corpuscles* (see Fig. 3.4, chapter 3 p. 50). But, while the free nerve endings terminate—mostly without any myelin sheath—in the epidermis, in recent decades more and more types of

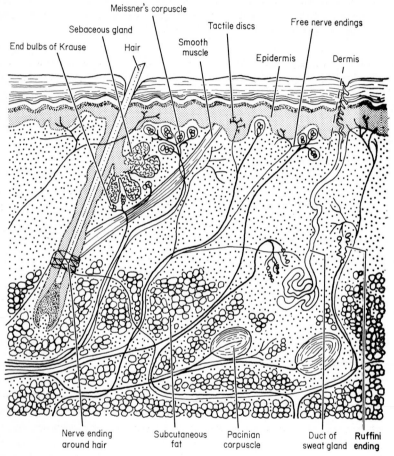

Fig. 5.38 The skin with some of its receptor-endings in cross section. (From Geldard, 1972 p. 273.)

encapsulated receptors have been identified in the deepest layers of the skin. Figure 5.38 illustrates, in addition to the free nerve endings, some of the most common basic types of encapsulated terminations. Among them are *Meissner's corpuscles*, found in hairless parts of the skin and particularly in the maze-like papilla ridges of the tips of the fingers. *Krause end bulbs* are distributed throughout the corium; they are most often found near the edge of the cornea in the eye, in the tissues of the external genitalia, and on the tongue. The *Ruffini cylinders*, also known as arboriform terminations, are located in the corium; sometimes they have also been found in the sub-cutaneous tissue proper. Not to be forgotten are the *skin hair follicles* with *basket-like free endings* coiled around them.

Similar to the encapsulated endings just mentioned are the *Golgi-Mazzoni corpuscles* and the Pacinian corpuscles; the latter are illustrated in Fig. 5.38. Both are rather large, onion-shaped formations which can be seen with the naked eye; they are quite widely distributed throughout various tissues. Golgi-Mazzoni endings are found especially in the junctions of tendons and muscles. Pacinian corpuscles occur in the deep subcutaneous layers, in the joints, the external genital organs, the connective tissue of the abdominal cavity, the covering of bones and near the walls of large blood vessels.

Opinions about Specificity of Receptors

As was observed in the preceding chapter (pp. 71–89), the modern view of perception holds that connections at a higher level than the receptor cells are more decisive in the transmission of various "sensory qualities" than the specific skin receptors themselves. As Melzack and Wall observe in their famous somaesthesis study (1962, p. 343):

> Receptors, then, are more specialized than von Frey could have envisaged more than sixty-five years ago. It is clear that there are not four kinds of special-ized receptors but a multitude of different kinds of specialization. To ram re-ceptors into one of a number of preconceived separate categories would be arbit-rary and artificial. It is much more reasonable to define the specialization of each skin receptor in terms of its position in a multi-dimensional space of physio-logical variables.

As these writers point out, the law of adequate stimuli and their con-duction can be maintained today even without assuming the one-to-one correspondence between receptor-cell structure and the created sensory impression which Frey insisted on.

Some words of caution have been uttered (e.g. by Geldard 1972, p. 277 and Kenshalo 1971, p. 125) against assumptions of precise specialization and selective powers of the mentioned receptor populations: "At different stages of development and in different body loci end organ shapes and sizes vary." (Geldard). The functions performed by the varieties of all listed encapsulations remain insufficiently known, according to Kenshalo: "Whatever their function, it appears certain that they do not provide nerve terminals with selective devices to permit differentiation of mechanical, thermal or painful stimuli."

For this reason the argument concerning the number and structure of the various skin receptor types has lost most of its significance.

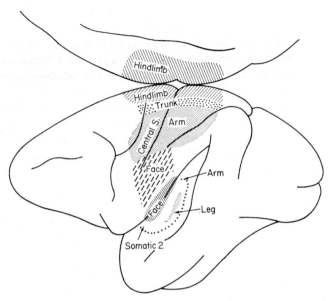

Fig. 5.39 Somatic sensory projections in the monkey. (From Geldard, 1972 p. 280.)

Neural Pathways and Cortical Projections

The entire surface of the body is represented along the post-central gyrus of the cerebral cortex. The fibres carrying impulses from the skin surfaces cross from one side of the spinal cord or brain stem to the other. The left half of the body thus becomes represented in the right cerebral hemisphere and the right side in the left hemisphere. The amount of cortex devoted to a particular site of the skin apparently also varies from one part of the body to another (Fig. 5.39).

As Kenshalo (1971, p. 128) points out, electrical activity observed in the postcentral gyrus is of a tactile quality, as are sensations produced by electrical stimulation: "Only rarely have thermal sensations been reported to result from electrical stimulation of the cortex; pain never has been."

The cortical projection areas are schematically outlined in Fig. 5.40. In tracing the progress of impulses from the receptor surface up to the cortex, two way-stations are of central interest: the thalamus and the cortex itself. There are two nuclear regions in the thalamus which show somewhat different properties. The one takes over impulses from fibres which are faster-conducting and which subserve touch, pressure and kinesthesis.

The other serves as a station for fibres which are predominantly slow and convey messages for temperature changes and some types of pain.

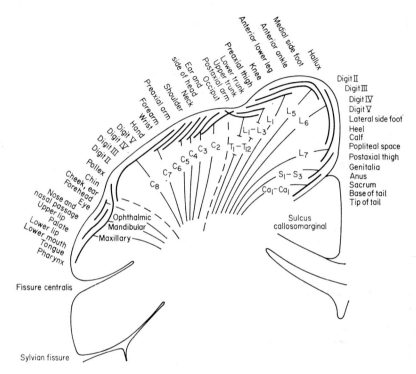

Fig. 5.40 Projection of the body surface on the central gyrus of the cortex. (From Geldard, 1972 p. 288.)

Receptive fields of individual cortical cells are more variable than are those anywhere else in the receptor system.

Temperature Sensitivity

Temperature sensitivity has proved especially troublesome for investigators. From the point of view of the physical stimulus conditions it may seem unnecessary to distinguish between two separate senses; the surface of the skin either loses heat to the surrounding environment or gains it. In the former case the organism should have a sensation of cold, in the latter, one of warmth. However, Katz has pointed out that the levelling of temperature differences during conduction occurs in several stages. Gradual levelling of temperature differences also occurs between the skin surface and the sub-cutaneous tissue layers. Using Gibson's modern terminology, we could say that *gradients of increasing or decreasing temperature* occur between the successive adjacent layers of the body surface.

The ability to perceive temperature changes seems to serve a two-fold function for the organism. First of all, if the body temperature, which normally remains within limited boundaries for some reason deviates sharply from these limits, a kind of neural control mechanism comes into play. There is an effort to return to the normal body temperature and, at the same time, the fluctuations are perceived qualitatively as sensations of warmth or of cold.

The skin of man is sensitive to temperatures below $+24°$ C and above $+35°$ C. The area between these two boundaries is called the physio-logical zero-area or indifference area. According to Nafe and Kenshalo (1966, p. 234), no exact values can be given for cold and warmth thresholds since such thresholds are highly dependent on the conditions under which they are measured. There are at least three factors which affect the thres-hold: the extent of the area under stimulation, the temperature of the skin and the extent of the change induced. Subjects are evidently less sensitive to cold than to warmth stimuli. The rapid cooling of the skin through perspiration may contribute to this difference. Weber's statement that the skin temperature as such acts as a stimulus, whereby the direction of change determines the sensation of cold or warmth, holds true within the limits of the so called zero area. When the skin is stimulated by a cold stimulator (below $+20°$ C) the sensation of cold may obstinately persist up to 30 seconds after the stimulus ceases. The sensation does not change to one of warmth, as Weber's theory would predict.

In the normal resting skin, maintaining as it does a thermal equilibrium with the external environment, the gradients for warmth and cold evidently cancel each other out. The cold receptors occupy a region in which the gradient is already quite steep to begin with. The conduction of heat away from the skin surface causes an abrupt sharpening of the gradient, and a sensation of cold is aroused. When the skin gains heat from the environ-ment, the opposite gradient, that of temperature increase, rises with similar sharpness; this increase is recorded by the warmth receptors, which are located at the greater depth under the skin surface. The reaction to a rise in temperature always occurs more slowly than that to a decline.

Nafe and Kenshalo (1966) question the validity of the gradient theory. In using heat-treatment or radar devices with ordinary radiation, sensations of warmth were aroused in the subject. Since these were infra-red or com-parable rays which *penetrate into the tissues* of the body, on the basis of the gradient theory, we would expect a very large change in the amount of stimulus energy necessary to reach the same warmth thresholds compared to ordinary, non-penetrating radiation. To the surprise of the investigators the changes in stimulus energy brought about by these techniques were hardly observable.

In experimenting with cats, Nafe and Kenshalo observed that when applying warmth-stimulators to the cat's back (which had been shaven bare), the temperature had to be raised to $+50°$ C before the animal would perform the task which it had been taught as the conditioned response to the stimulus of a heat sensation. With cold-stimulators, a temperature about $5-6°$ below the lower adaptation threshold of man evoked a corresponding reaction. This result is surprising, since the cat is generally known as an animal which is highly sensitive to warmth. When the stimuli were applied to the inside of the thighs the point of inflection remained equally high for warmth stimuli. The zero area was diminished to a narrower band than found in human subjects when the stimuli were applied to the face of the animal, close to the corners of the upper lip. The warmth threshold also decreased to $+33°$ C. Hensel and Kenshalo (in Thomae, 1966) conclude that, at least in the face of the cat, the same neural pathways transmit both warmth and cold impulses. A "cold" sensation would be due to activation of the conductors, one of "warmth" to inhibition of the same neural activity. They also stress the fact that there is no reason to assume a cortical projection of these impulses.

The boundaries of the physiological "indifference" area vary both from one individual to another, and from time to time in the same individual. This variation is greater in women than in men. Sensitivity to cold increases during the ovulation phase of the menstrual cycle. These results point to a close connection between the perception of temperature and the general metabolism of the body tissues.

Some of the studies on *single-unit* (e.g. Fig. 3.5A, chapter 3 p. 52), *preparations* and *single-cell* recordings which have been performed, e.g. with sensory nerves that supply hairy and hairless skin in response to identical stimulation, will be discussed later in chapter 9 together with a broader survey of electrophysiological investigations.

Pain Sensitivity

In the study of the perception of *pain* and *ache* the idea that certain specific receptors correspond to this experience must also be abandoned in the light of recent research. There are two reasons why the psychological study of pain perception is complex. First of all, a number of different receptors are able to receive and transmit pain stimuli; and secondly, the central nervous system clearly includes not one, but several pain centres.

It has turned out even more difficult to discover specialized pain receptors than to isolate those for warmth, cold and pressure. One of von Frey's favourite ideas was that pressure and pain formed two mutually independent perceptual systems, but this idea is no longer considered valid.

It was the widespread distribution of free nerve endings throughout the body which led von Frey to believe that these organs were the specific receptors for pain. For a long time there was disagreement over the role of the free nerve endings in the cornea of the eye. Since the cornea contains no other receptor organs, it was claimed that no sensations except pain could be elicited by corneal stimulation. As Geldard (1972) points out, however, experiments during the late 1930's showed that the cornea is also sensitive to pressure. Any tissue containing free nerve endings is capable of transmitting sensations of pressure as well as of pain.

All phenomenal mappings of pain impressions are of necessity rather subjective. The exact classification of different qualities or "shades" of pain is especially difficult. Dallenbach (1927, 1931) listed 44 different qualities. The most distinctive of these are such pains as "biting", "burning", "gnawing", "pressing", "tearing" and "twitching"; yet we can probably never achieve even such a degree of unanimity between different individuals as that achieved in naming colours. For instance, Lewis found that momentary stimulation of pain spots is called "pricking", while the same stimulus applied over a longer period of time is called "burning" pain. Furthermore, the more interior tissues of the body, such as muscles, form an "echo board" which differs from the sensations described above. A single, brief prick to the fingertip produces an experience consisting of *two successive pain sensations.* Immediately after the stimulus a mild and brief flash of pain occurs. After a short pause there follows a more persistent and generally more intense feeling of pain, as a kind of echo to the first. According to Lewis, the average lag of the second response is 1·9 s at the toe, 1·3 s at the knees and 0·9 s at the top of the thigh. On the basis of these observations a double system of pain transmission has been postulated. It is known that receptor nerve fibres transmit impulses at different rates: certain kinds of fibres, the α and β fibres, have a rapid transmission rate, while others, the γ fibres, transmit impulses more slowly. Thus it does not seem unreasonable to assume that the skin may be equipped with two parallel pain mediation systems: the first immediate pain sensation is transmitted by the fast β fibres, which are also thicker than γ fibres; the following "burning" pain is probably mediated by the thinner and slower γ fibres. Some supporting evidence comes from observation on pathological cases. Rapid reflexes, such as the withdrawal of the hand from a hot surface, are known to be mediated by the thick β fibres. The rate of transmission in the γ fibres is 0·5–1·0 m/s.; in the β fibres it is twenty times as fast. The quality of the sensation is the same regardless of the transmission system involved; furthermore, pain localization is equally good with both systems (Lewis, 1946).

Pain impressions originating in receptor systems of the deeper layers of the body are generally much more difficult to study. In particular, controversy has surrounded the issue of the origin and nature of so-called visceral pain. Lewis holds that no differences in connecting pathways or the resulting experiences can be shown to exist between pains in muscle tissue and in visceral organs; he feels that to avoid difficulties in the operational definitions it is wiser to confine our studies to muscle pains.

Part of the controversy is due to the insufficiency of our knowledge so far about afferent pathways from the visceral organs. Here we are concerned with types of pain which will come up later in connection with the proprioceptive receptors. The best assumption seems to be that free nerve endings typically act as the primary receptors in the deeper layers of the skin, and that they receive larger and more diffuse stimuli than the pain spots on the surface of the skin. There are varying opinions as to afferent visceral pathways. Ross, like his follower Wernøe, assumed that impulses are transmitted along two different paths. Direct visceral pain is presumably mediated by the vagus nerve; coordinated with this system is another, consisting of more peripheral subcutaneous tissues. Pain transduction is assumed to be a function of "vegetative reflexes" which contract the capillaries of the skin and bring about other changes affecting the dermal pain receptors. Referred pains are easily explained with this view, as are local hyperalgesia of the skin surface accompanying visceral pain, skin pallor and secretory disorders. According to Wernøe's modification of Ross's theory, two parallel spinal pathways are postulated: one for *splanchnic* (visceral) pain, the other for *somatic* (referred) pain.

Lewis considers that the concept of "vegetative receptor pathways" is apt to be misleading. The only thing we can say is that some afferent pathways associated with the spinal column, such as the vagus nerve, connect anatomically with some structures of the autonomic nervous system. Part of the confusion stems from the attempt to identify sympathetic ganglia as pain centres, despite the fact that these ganglia lack afferent fibres. The connections of both the vagus and the somatic nerves with the spinal cord are all in the dorsal roots. Lewis does not deny the possibility that there may be some direct neural pain mechanisms; although the visceral organs themselves lack pain receptors. In general all we can do is point to the general region from which the pain appears to be radiating, and to say that the pain is somewhere deep under the skin; sometimes we can decide whether it is located on the ventral or the dorsal side of the body.

When we come to projected pain, the picture is different. This is fully

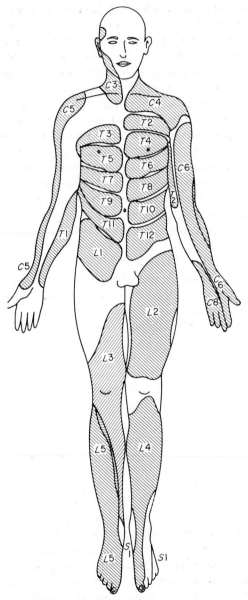

Fig. 5.41 Schematic picture of the dermatomes in man. (From Geldard, 1972 p. 279.)

analogous to the "deep pain" felt in muscle and connecting tissue. Nerves located in corresponding parts of the body produce identical pain sensations which are projected to some corresponding part of the skin surface. Schematic diagrams of the body surface have been developed to show the *skin segments* or dermatomes which are innervated by the known pain transmission systems, e.g. the cervical nerves. In a similar way those segments on the surface of the skin can be identified as those to which experimental subjects refer, deeper pains originating in muscle tissues (Fig. 5.41).

If blood circulation in a limb is artifically restricted and the muscles of the limb are then compelled to move, the subject suffers a diffuse indefinite pain which is hard to localize, and which has a quality different from any experience of pain sensations at the skin. There seems to be reason to distinguish between *superficial* or *epicritic* pain and *deep* or *protopathic* pain. These two are so different in quality that even the common term "pain" seems misleading, and perhaps the term "ache" should be substituted in describing the experience of deep pain.

On Midway Stations in the Brain Stem

Some light has been thrown upon the more central connections of pain sensations by recent investigations of the midway stations of the skin receptors in the brain stem. Comparative animal studies have been especially helpful in this regard. Attention has been drawn in particular to the so-called Gasserian ganglion, through which pass many of the pathways originating, for example, in the mucous membrane of the mouth.

Weitzman and his colleagues (1961) experimented with Rhesus monkeys; the animals were able by means of simple "right" or "wrong" reactions in a discrimination situation to regulate an electric current directed to the Gasserian ganglion. By means of these reactions the animal was actually regulating its own pain. When a dose of morphine was administered its effect was to raise the threshold. Without the morphine the animal did not strive toward a completely painless state. It seemed, on the contrary, that the monkey was reacting to a pain-inducing stimulus intensity. Sweet (1959) has commented, however, on the dangers involved in conclusions and generalizations drawn from animal experiments.

Werner and Mountcastle (1965 pp. 359–397) have studied the applicability of Weber's and Stevens' laws to pain sensation in cats and monkeys. A stimulus varying in duration from 1 to 1000 s was applied, and the frequency of the resultant nerve impulse firing was measured. The procedure, as is often the case in psychophysical research, was to formulate beforehand the exponential function expected for intensity variations. This was an equation similar to Stevens' power law, on the basis of which the variations in intensity indicated by Weber's law could be predicted. The empirical results of the experiments corresponded beautifully to the values predicted.

Intermodal connections and interactions have also recently been emphasized in the study of the pain modality. Thus Berman (1961) and Thompson *et al.* (1963) have shown that in the cortex of the cat there are close connections between the areas of general somatic sensation and those of auditory as well as visual perception.

Also worth noting is Scott's study of the receptors located in the dental bone uncovered by the enamel; these receptors are sensitive to many different stimuli (warmth, cold, pressure), but they produce only one message at a central level, that of pain (Grossman and Hattis 1967).

Kinesthetic and Labyrinthine Sensitivity

We have already mentioned the group of sensory receptors called proprioceptors, and the discussion of pain frequently touched upon phenomena which could with equal justice be considered either proprioceptive or interoceptive. It is often pointed out that the proprioceptors function almost exclusively as mechanical receptors, i.e. they are primarily fired by mechanical stimuli; pain receptors, including non-interoceptors, may also receive chemical stimuli.

The terminations of mechanoreceptors are found in practically all the tissues of the body. There hardly exists a piece of tissue which is not able to transmit impulses from the microscopically small mechanoreceptors contained in it. The following types of receptors have been distinguished (Gibson 1966 pp. 106–109):

1. Free nerve endings. These may occur for instance between and around muscle fibres, sometimes fan-shaped, sometimes as spirals (Fig. 5.42).

2. Encapsulated nerve endings, node-like, spindle-shaped or cylindrical.

3. Microscopically small hair cells (not to be confused with the hairs of the skin). These are especially sensitive to various phenomena of movement.

By distribution, these receptors can be grouped as follows: (a) those located in the hairy parts of the body, (b) those in the joints of movable limbs, (c) those in muscle and tendon tissue, (d) those surrounding blood vessels, and (e) receptor organs of the inner ear.

What is common to all these parts of the body is their mobility. But the tissues in which these receptors are located move in different ways. From the point of view of the information transmitted by these receptor systems, Müller's problem of specific pathways is completely meaningless. Even if subjective sensory qualities were mediated by anatomically differentiated nerve connections, the fact remains that messages about body movement and position rest on information from interlocking receptors of different types and on simultaneous overall stimulus patterns (Melzack and Wall 1962).

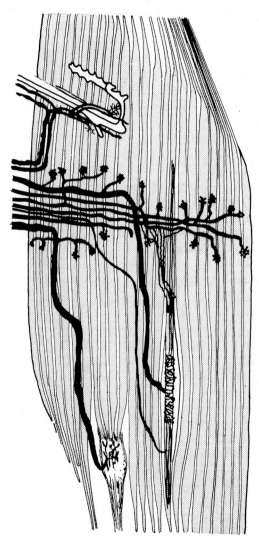

Fig. 5.42 Nerve endings in muscle. (From Geldard, 1972 p. 382.)

Muscles and joints differ in function, but complement each other. The muscle varies in length and in degree of contraction, while the joint varies in angle of movement. In Gibson's opinion, sensitivity to the position of the

F

joints is of decisive importance in the perception of space and movement. The perception of muscle tension, on the other hand, is less important. Rose and Mountcastle have shown that the organism is able to sense the angles of leverage and inclination prevailing between the bony parts of the mobile limbs. It is misleading to claim that variations in muscle-fibre length can be sensed (see Gibson 1966). It is true that *tension receptors* transmit information as to the degree of contraction. Recorded discharges from two tension receptors are shown in Fig. 5.43. But there are no impulses concerning the length of the fibres at any given moment (see also chapter 3 p. 49).

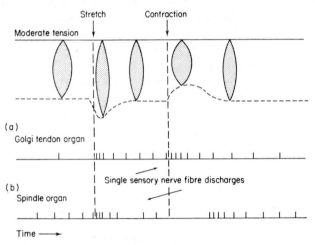

Fig. 5.43 Discharges of sensory fibers from a Golgi tendon organ and a spindle organ. (From Geldard, 1972 p. 384.)

Thus the perception of *movement* or *kinesthesis* is dependent on a complex system of receptors. This includes movement of the organism as a whole, of the body and of the individual limbs relative to the environment. The observation that not all supraliminal stimuli induce phenomenal sensory impressions concerns all the receptors, interoceptors and proprioceptors which transmit information as to movement and position. The information which the organism receives from these receptors is clear and unambiguous; the threshold must be determined indirectly from the behaviour of the organism.

There is no exclusive "muscle sense" or "sense of motion" (Gibson 1966 p. 111). The modalities of touch and of pressure, together with the perception of movement, interact in many different ways. No sharp modality boundaries can be postulated here either. "We sense the structure and shape of a chair when we sit in it" (Gibson 1966 p. 112). In using tools we simultaneously feel the touch and pressure of the object on the skin of the hand and the objects and surfaces in our environment which are touched by the tool. The receptors in our joints enable us to use scissors even in the dark: we experience kinesthetically the position of the blades and the way in which they cut (see chapter 3 p. 64).

The structure of the *labyrinthine receptor system* has already been partly described in connection with the sense of hearing. Of the organs located in the inner ear, the utriculus and the sacculus serve primarily in the preservation of balance, while the semicircular canals react delicately to changes in direction and rate of movement. The earlier conception of a sharp division between the functions of the semicircular canals and other labyrinthine organs has to be abandoned here also.

The sensory tissues along the inner walls of these organs are located in planes at right angle to each other. The nerve terminations consist of hair cells embedded in a gelatinous substance (the macula). Above the hairs are suspended thin crystals of calcium carbonate, the so-called otoliths (chapter 3 p. 68); when the rate of movement of the head either accelerates or decelerates, these otoliths press upon the hairs. Tilting of the head in any direction causes similar reactions.

Congenitally deaf individuals, or those in whom the entire inner ear has been destroyed by infection, are still able to maintain equilibrium and move about surprisingly well. Only when the patient is asked to stand on one leg with his eyes closed does the abnormal state of his utricle and saccule become apparent. The receptor system of the labyrinth should perhaps be named the *sense of spatial orientation*. Some evidence in favour of this opinion is provided by the orthogonal arrangement of the receptor surfaces, which holds not only of the vestibular sacs but also of the semicircular canals. As we know, the three canals are located at right angles to each other. Also in human depth perception the system of orthogonal coordinates, based on the vertical force of gravity and the axis at right angles to it, has played a dominant role (see below chapters 12 and 13).

The canals lead at either end into the utricle, and the entire system is filled with endolymph. At the juncture point each canal expands to form an *ampulla*, and it is this ampulla which contains the receptors sensitive to changes in velocity and direction of the organism's own movement. These receptors consist of hair-like cells, ten to twenty of which branch out from a common flexible stem, the *crista*. The upper part of the crista is submerged in a gelatinous substance, the *cupula* (Fig. 5.44).

The principle according to which these hair cells function is simple. Every new movement or every change of speed in a previously even movement brings about a change in the direction of flow of the endolymph. The small hairs bend in the direction of the current of the moving liquid, transmitting information as to the extent, direction and changes in velocity of the movement. Since the canals are located in planes which intersect at right angles to each other, all possible movements of the head in three-

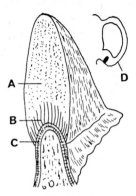

Fig. 5.44 The structure of a crista and the location of it in a semicircular canal. (From v. Fieandt, 1972 p. 107.)

dimensional space influence the stimulus pattern. The receptors of the semi-circular canals can be stimulated by sharp changes in temperature, by pressure or by electric shock, in addition to changes in movement (Fig. 5.45).

The function of the proprioceptors of the inner ear in human beings is

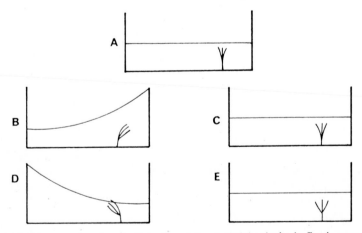

Fig. 5.45 Diagram showing the function of the static labyrinth. A. Stationary state; B. Left acceleration; C. Constant speed; D. Stopping of motion; E. Stationary state. (From v. Fieandt, 1972 p. 108.)

more interrelated with that of other modalities than is the case at lower levels of development. Unlike reptiles and birds, man is able to compensate by means of sight, touch and movement sensations for damaged labyrinthine receptors. These are connected by numerous pathways to the thalamus and the cerebellum, so that even changes in *muscle tonus* are determined to a high degree by labyrinthine stimulation. Since the labyrinthine receptors can be stimulated in a variety of ways, they make it possible to investigate cross-modal interaction in terms of observable and measurable *tonic reflexes* such as *eye movements* (nystagmus), which can be elicited by a variety of different parallel sense stimuli.

Part Two

The Hierarchical Organization
of Perception

6 | Light and Colour

Colour research has fascinated great philosophers, biologists and other scientists through the history of mankind, especially during the last few centuries. Men like Leonardo da Vinci, Newton, Goethe, Maxwell, v. Helmholtz and Hering have made interesting contributions. Colour vision, apparently, is a subject that is the concern of a host of sciences and arts. Among others physicists, anatomists, pathologists, physiologists, psychologists, light bulb and paint manufacturers, artists and architects have been interested in colour from different points of view. The layman usually equates colour with hue, but the specialist is more likely to speak of colours in terms of their hue, brightness and saturation. In this text the term "chromatic" will be preferred whenever no reference is made to brightness differences alone or to "neutral colours".

Because this is a book on *perception* it could be questioned whether *colour vision* belongs to its topic at all. Boynton (1971), for example, has made a distinction between "colour vision" and "colour perception", in the sense of assigning to the former the treatment of the functional, neurophysiological display of the visual apparatus, whereas "colour perception" contains a sphere of problems which can be approached only from a phenomenological point of view.

The neurophysiology of colour sensation has developed at an astonishing speed especially during the last two decades. It seems necessary, in order to give the right background to a psychological treatment proper, to outline some general sensorimotor trends in the function of the visual apparatus before proceeding to questions like colour appearances, colour-names and diagrams, memory colours, colour constancies, etc. The first two sub-headings, before dealing with descriptions of experiences, are presented in functional and behaviouristic terms. Toward the middle and the end of this chapter a mainly phenomenological approach will be applied.

"Colour vision" aspects will however be handled as briefly as possible before going over to problems in "colour perception".

Nature of the Light Energy

The basis of our visual stimulation consists of radiant energy, emanating from varoius sources and reflected in various ways from the surfaces of bodies around us. Stimulation leading to visual perception is caused in the human eye by only a small part of the range of electromagnetic radiation

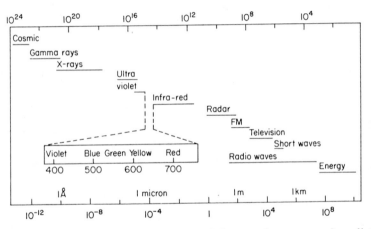

Fig. 6.1 The visible spectrum as related to all known electromagnetic radiation. (From v. Fieandt, 1972 p. 109.)

which has been physically studied. Light is usually defined as vibration with a *wavelength* of 380–760 nanometers (nm; 1 nm = 1 millionth of a millimeter). The shorter the wavelength, the higher the number of vibrations per unit of time, i.e. the frequency. Thus wavelength and frequency are inversely related.[1]

How narrow a range of all known electromagnetic radiation stimulates our eyes as *light*? A demonstration is given by the diagram in Fig. 6.1. Physically this radiation belongs to a series extending from cosmic rays, with an extremely short wavelength but great penetrating force, to radio

1. Concerning specific concepts of photometry see Riggs *In* Kling and Riggs (1971, pp. 276–278).

waves, with a wavelength of several kilometers. In the middle part of the figure (to the left) the portion representing the *spectrum* of visible light (wavelengths between 380 and 760) is shown considerably magnified. In sensory physiology light is defined as that range of electromagnetic radiation to which the organism reacts when the visual tissue of its eye is stimulated. The second part of the definition is crucial. It is important that both wavelength and amount of energy are high enough to transcend the absolute threshold of stimulation.

Fig. 6.2 Correspondence between radiation wavelength and various parts of the spectrum. (From v. Fieandt, 1972 p. 110.)

Figure 6.2 shows the correspondence between radiation wavelength and various parts of the spectrum, defined and measured according to relative specific intensities required for equal visibility. When pure white light passes through a prism it breaks up into a series of chromatic components, ranging from violet at 400 nm to red at 760 nm. In passing through the prism the shortest wavelengths are refracted to the greatest extent, long wavelengths the least. The spectrum thus appears as shown in Fig. 6.2. At one extreme are the *red* components with a radiation wavelength of about 760 nm. This is followed by orange, primary yellow (about 580 nm), olive, primary green (500 nm) and finally by primary blue (450 nm). At both boundaries of the spectrum of sunlight there are also rays which do not stimulate our sense of vision: beyond the visible violet rays are the so-called *ultra-violet* rays with strong powers of penetration, and at the other

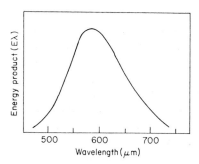

Fig. 6.3 Schematic drawing of luminance distribution of a type of red light. (From v. Fieandt, 1972 p. 111.)

extreme, beyond the red band of the spectrum, are the *infra-red* rays with longer wave-lengths. Since electromagnetic radiation also has heat characteristics the existence of these rays can be demonstrated by means of thermometers located at both extremes of the spectrum.

General Conditions for Chromatic Vision

In our time, when roads in big cities are lit by yellow-looking sodium-vapour lamps, most people have had strong experiences as to what happens with light-reflecting object surfaces in an almost monochromatic illumination. A food-store window close to the yellowish illuminated road looks achromatic, and shows its familiar *Kellogg's* corn flakes packages and other advertisements only in shades of black and white. The sodium vapour lamp emits almost all of its energy in a very narrow part of the visible spectrum, and this band, close to the primary yellow, has been chosen because the respective light yields the strongest visibility at a certain expense of energy. From these every-day experiences we might conclude that although mono-chromatic light is sufficient for brightness discrimination to take place, chromatic discrimination is not possible when reflecting surfaces are illuminated by such a light source. It does not matter that we are surrounded by objects which reflect radiations varying along a wide scale of wave-lengths. This rich multiple variation of chromatic surfaces is seen only under a favourable spectral distribution of light. Yet there are some other requirements too for chromatic vision of surfaces to occur. We shall try to analyse some of them beginning with the spectral reflectances of surfaces.

Spectral Distribution and the Reflectance of Surfaces

"Hues can best be discriminated when objects are illuminated by a source of light that emits a continuous and balanced sprectrum" (Boynton 1971). Sunlight represents a source of this type. The evolution of chromatic vision is partly understandable as a response to the availability of this kind of illumination throughout evolutionary history.

The property of a surface that is highly correlated with its perceived colour is its *diffuse reflectance*. Diffusely reflected light is scattered back from a surface in all possible directions. A *specularly reflecting* surface on the other hand reflects incident light in such a manner that the angle of reflection is the same as the angle of incidence. Coloured blotting paper is a rather good example of a diffuse surface, whereas a mirror is almost completely specular.

Specularly reflecting surfaces usually reflect light non-selectively as a function of wavelength. Diffuse reflection, in contrast, is often quite selective with wavelength. Figure 6.4 is an example of *spectral reflection*

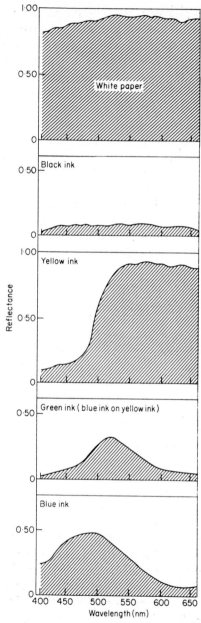

Fig. 6.4 Spectral reflection curves of white paper, untreated (top) and covered by inks of various hues as indicated. Each graph shows the percentage of diffusely reflected light measured at each of the wavelengths indicated by the vertical bars. (Adapted from Pirenne, 1948.)

curves which can be prepared for light radiation reflected from various object surfaces. A prerequisite for this kind of spectra is, in fact, that they are sampled from equal energy spectra, i.e. they show spectral reflectance of surfaces under white light producing equal energy at all wavelengths. In preparing spectral reflection curves we first mark the various wavelengths of which the light is composed on the *x*-axis, and then the amount of *reflected light energy* for each wavelength on the *y*-axis. In this way we can illustrate, for example, the physical differences between the light reflected from a tomato and an orange (Fig. 6.5). To a remarkable degree, the

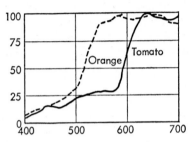

Fig. 6.5 Spectral reflection curves of the skins of orange and tomato. (From v. Fieandt, 1966 p. 77.)

colour of a surface is not much affected by wide variations in the nature of the illuminant.

The visual system is sometimes defined as primarily an organ of analysis. This is, however, only its secondary function: it is primarily a discriminating and integrating system. Almost without exception diffuse reflectance from a homogeneous surface is experienced, regardless of its composition, as a single colour. If, for example, we look at a piece of orange peel, we perceive a uniform red-yellow rather than a series of blue, bluish green, reddish-yellow and red hues. This integration forms the basis of colour mixture.

Several Types of Visual Receptors

Chromatic vision, though, would not be brought about unless the receiving organism were capable of selecting, transforming and processing the radiant energy. Throughout the history of colour vision research speculation has continuously persisted about the number of specific receptor systems required in order to render the variation of subjective chromatic experiences possible. The investigators have suggested two possibilities whereby the visual receptors could respond differentially to the spectral variation of colour stimuli.

Unquestionably, over the luminance range for which chromatic vision occurs, at least two differing spectral distributions must produce different reactions.

(1) The first possibility is that the cone receptors (see chapter 5 p. 102) are all alike but capable of responding positively to one part of the spectrum and negatively to another.
(2) The other possibility is that the eye contains at least two classes of receptors and that these receptors differ in their spectral sensitivities.

This second possibility seems to be more favoured by experimental evidence, and research workers almost unanimously agree upon a scheme of three types of cone receptors. Should the receptors all have the same spectral sensitivity, then the visual procedure would result in a kind of achromatic vision familiar to us from the functioning of the rod apparatus at low levels of illumination.

Differentiation of Signal Transmission
Granted the arrangement with specific types of photoreceptors at the retinal level for several spectral radiation zones, the question arises as to whether these chromatically separated signals can be forwarded as relatively independent messages to the higher order organization centra. Since the days of Young and v. Helmholtz it has been supposed that signals emanating from each type of receptor might be transmitted along separate pathways all the way up to the visual brain level. Modern thinking does not emphasize the painstaking separation of three signal-systems. On the contrary, what is important is a transmission of signals that reflects differences between the outputs of two systems. Single cell recordings carried out on the retinal level, as will be demonstrated further on in the text (p. 169), have sufficiently demonstrated how, even in this channel system, a higher degree of reliability can be achieved by the mixing of signals in certain seemingly complicated ways. The three presumed systems of signals must not necessarily be kept separate during the transmission procedure.

Qualitatively Different Sensations
Even neural messages which transmit the results of photo-receptor processes do not as such imply an occurrence of chromatic visual activity. The differences among the transmitted signals should manifest themselves as experiences, i.e. chromatic and achromatic sensations, including red, green, yellow, white, black and all combinations of these.
At the cortical level, if only one type of colour information were achieved, the brain would fail to produce colour vision no matter how well the chromatic differentiation was carried out on the receptor level, or how

efficiently the specific signals got transmitted to the higher order visual centra. This psychological requirement for colour vision is even more necessary than the three enumerated "more objective" conditions for adequate chromatic discrimination.

Chromatic Specificity of Sensory Processes

The Pigment Level

As mentioned above, scientists long ago agreed upon a neurophysiological scheme of three types of cone receptors. The very first non-optical event in the chromatic vision process is the absorption of light by different photo-pigments contained in these cone-cells (see chapter 5 pp. 108–110). Unfortunately it has proved very difficult to reveal the three photopigments of the cones.

The best known and carefully examined among the photo-receptor pigments has hitherto been the *rhodopsin*, also called visual purple, extracted from the rods.

Retinal densitometry is a method that enables us to determine and register the degree of concentration of visual photopigments in the receptors illuminated. A very narrow beam of light can be directed through the pupil onto the parts of retina to be investigated. The light reflected back through the pupil will vary slightly depending on the concentration level of the visual pigment in the respective photoreceptors. If the photopigment has been bleached as a consequence of a certain spectral composition of the light, the sensitive photomultiplier tube of the apparatus denotes the corresponding maximum of the spectral sensitivity in the different types of cones. Such measurements define the *action spectrum* of a pigment.

Around ten years ago another method was invented (Marks *et al.* 1964, Wald 1964); the *micro-spectrophotometry*. This surprisingly fine technique allows measurement of light passing through single cells. By means of two beams of light directed at a group of cone cells fastened on a microscope slide it has been possible to measure absorption of light in the outer segment of the cone, using the outside beam as a control.

These two methods together unquestionably confirm the existence of at least three types of photopigments in cones. There is some evidence too that a single cone contains only one type of these pigments considered.

The Level of Retinal Potentials

The painstaking investigation of the photoreceptor pigments has definitely shown how at the very initial level of vision there exists arrangements for specific chromatic discrimination. Until the Second World War it was generally supposed that the very laws of colour mixture and colour adaptation could be accounted for by "absorption" and "reconcentration" processes in the photosensitive pigment at the retinal level. Thus the well-known *bipolarity* of certain colour experiences (red-green, blue-yellow, white-black), which already interested Goethe and Mach, was explained by assumed functions of antagonistic processes at the level of single photo-receptors on the retina. This was the meaning of the so-called opponent-colours theory, first presented by Hering during the years from 1905 to 1911 (Hering 1920) and later elaborated by G. E. Müller (1930) and by Hurvich and Jameson (1966).

Recent investigation during the 1950's and 1960's has convincingly demonstrated that both assumptions—the idea of trichromatic photo-pigment and the opponent colours hypothesis—account for procedures on the retinal level without any actual controversy. All we need is a scheme

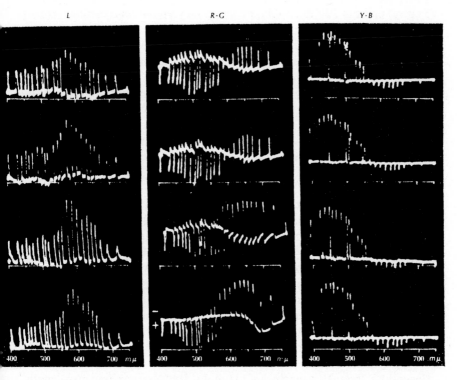

Fig. 6.6 *S*-potentials recorded near the cones of fish (Svaetichin 1956.) (From Kling and Riggs, 1971 p. 324.) Column (L): responses indicate signals of luminosity; Column (R–G): responses vary in sign depending upon wave-length; Column (Y–B): responses with long neutral wave-span.

allowing for a first trichromatic stage of photosensitivity and a second stage of recording the signals in terms of bipolarity-systems of specific neuronal transmission.

Svaetichin (1956) working with microelectrodes at the level of retinal receptors was able to record single cell potentials (see chapter 3 p. 52) showing specific properties as a function of wavelength. Within the fish retina investigated, some electrode placements gave responses to luminosity, others gave rise to responses that varied in sign (positive v. negative potentials) *depending upon wavelength* as shown in Fig. 6.6. When the *neural* wavelength was relatively long Svaetichin called these responses "R–G" (red-green) signals; when it was relatively short he called them signals from "Y–B" (yellow-blue) units. At each wavelength light of the same energy was used. Nevertheless, for the "R–G" unit the sign of the response was negative for wavelengths below about 550 nm and positive for longer wavelengths. The positive climax is around 650 nm. There is a neutral point at 550 to 580 nm at which no response is recorded.

Further work by Svaetichin and McNichol proved that these responses were not given by single cones in the fish retina, as was originally assumed by Svaetichin. The potentials actually showed up only when the eletrodes were placed very near but not in the receptor cells. Their result convinced the experimenters that the "bipolar response" does not originate in the receptor. This finding has been amply confirmed by Tomita (1966), among others. He also demonstrated that the bioelectric responses from individual cones are all of the same sign, varying only in size as a function of wavelength and intensity of the stimulus.

The Level of Midbrain Nuclei

In a long row of studies beginning in the early sixties, De Valois (1960, 1965a, b, 1966, 1972) has recorded from the lateral geniculate bodies (see chapter 3 p. 69) single cell activities which are clearly specific in response to chromatic stimulation. These cell units exhibit in the absence of stimulation a resting potential at a relatively low rate of spike firings. Depending on the composition of stimulating light, short wavelengths produce a vivid response. Long wavelengths bring about a decrease in the spontaneous spike frequency but exhibit an increasing rate when the light goes out. It thus appears that even these chromaticity-specific single units are functioning on a "on-off" basis of release (see chapter 3 p. 68). The wavelength is encoded "as either an increase or a decrease in firing rate, depending upon whether the light stimulus is of short or long wavelength" (Boynton 1971, p. 326).

Parallel with these chromaticity-specific reception encoding and transmission arrangements—beginning with differentially reacting pigments at the receptor level and ending with conversion of the specific signals into neural messages—there must be supposed to exist a system for mediating *achromatic information.* Already at the level of single receptor units it can be seen that quite a number of responses don't show any variations in sign, whatever the wavelength of the stimulating light. The same holds true for certain units in the lateral geniculate nucleus. "The substitution of one wavelength for another in this way has been called *silent substitution*" (Boynton 1971, p. 326).

Suitable intensity adjustment is the only prerequisite for a response within the frame of this achromatic system of transmission. In chapter 5 the conditions and the shape of scotopic and photopic luminosity curves has been discussed (p. 110). The spectral sensitivity curve has been determined for single substituting units at both the retinal and geniculate levels. As shown by De Valois (1965) the resulting curve of the geniculate body from primates is identical to the photopic luminosity curve of these animals. The luminosity level of any given colour clearly shows a variation independently of its specific hue. The phenomenal dimension corresponding to luminance is called *brightness* (see chapter 13).

Apparently the nonspecific brightness system coexists with the chromatic one. If the chromatic systems could be turned off, only achromatic vision would remain. It is a well-known fact that colour-defective individuals whose achromatic vision is missing altogether are in possession of a perfectly normal colour vision (see Weale 1953). As a consequence of the fact that brightness vision is mediated by a unitary system, luminances of lights of different colours should be additive. This statement, known as *Abney's Law,* has been shown actually to hold true within limits of experimental errors (Boynton 1971, p. 327). The colour mixture phenomena will be more closely taken up in a subsequent subheading (pp. 183–187).

As a conclusion, we have a picture to account equally well for the encoding and transmission of specific chromatic colour information at three levels (pigmental, retino-cellular and brain stem), as for the existence of a parallel system for mediating achromatic information.

Dimensional Descriptions of Colour Systems

The concept of a one-to-one correspondence between wavelengths at a particular spectral band and specific colour tone has nowadays been abandoned. It is nevertheless useful to examine various three-dimensional descriptive models based on the former doctrine of the specific correspondence between physical dimensions and phenomenal attributes (see chapter 10).

It is open to question whether a phenomenal descriptive system of perceived colours is reasonable or not, or even whether it is possible to construct an adequate and exhaustive system of phenomenal colours. The fact is, that there do exist a number of such systematic descriptions, and that they are not without significance; for example, in the commercial use of colours in printing or packaging, or in art workshops and other places concerned with the laws of colour mixture. We shall now compare three descriptive systems, those of Ostwald, Munsell and the CIE system.

Ostwald's Colour System

This model is based on the principle that all the colours in our natural environment can be represented, without remainder, by a three-dimensional body.

Phenomenal colours are traditionally classified into

1. *chromatic* or *spectral* colours, and
2. *achromatic* or *neutral* colours.

The achromatic colours are shades of grey ranging from deepest black to brightest white. Since they can be ordered on a single scale, they can be said to posses one dimension only, that of *brightness*.

All other colours are chromatic. In addition to differing in brightness, they also differ in *hue*. Even when white, achromatic light falls upon object surfaces these surfaces reflect the radiation selectively; they absorb certain wavelengths and reflect others. Surfaces of different qualities absorb and reflect the wavelengths represented in the spectrum in different ways. The greater the reflective selectivity of a surface, the more *saturated* is the perceived chromatic hue; and conversely, the more components of varying wavelength are contained in the reflected light, the more *unsaturated* the hue appears. The relations between different hues and saturations can be well represented by Ostwald's colour wheel. As his starting point he chose primary yellow (575 nm); it is located at the topmost point of the wheel, and has the number 1. Of all spectral colours, pure yellow has the highest degree of brightness in normal daylight. It is also the colour most easily recognized; we are quick to observe it when other radiation components are mixed with it. Clockwise from this primary yellow are located successively redder hues from orange to primary red. The wheel continues through purple and violet to primary blue (440 nm), and from there to dark blue, which is located at the bottom of the circle opposite primary yellow. This is followed by green-blue, blue-green, leaf green and primary green. After olive hues we return to number 1, primary yellow. This system makes a distinction among 24 hues along the colour wheel, proposing a system of numbers as norms for referring to chromatic hues. Complementary colours are always diametrically opposite each other on the wheel. The four primary colours are given the numbers 1, 7, 13 and 19 (yellow, red, blue and green). For practical purposes a hue scale with 24 steps has turned out to be adequate. Every hue on the wheel could be produced by mixing an equal amount of both neighbouring hues (i.e. their spectral components) in a single stimulus. Furthermore, if we assume that every hue has its complementary, and if only the hues of one half of the circle are known, we could produce all the rest, since the unknowns would then be complementaries of the knowns (see Plate III). A practical method for finding out what a complementary to a given colour looks like is to produce after images of that primary colour. The subject is asked to stare at a patch containing the primary and to keep looking at it for 20 to 25 seconds.

After this stimulation a negative after image usually appears in a complementary colour. (For a detailed discussion of after images see the subheading "Varieties of chromatic adaptation", p. 187).

The brightness of the colours varies from point to point along the wheel. As mentioned above, in daylight, yellow is the brightest; this is followed in both directions by ever darker hues, until at the bottom of the wheel we reach number 13, the darkest. The steps of the brightness scale from hue to hue are not, however, all equal. The brightness differences between adjacent hues are smaller in the blue and green zones of the wheel than among the reds and yellows.

The third of Ostwald's dimensions is *saturation*. The saturation or purity of a hue can be defined as the distance between it and the main axis, which is imagined as running through the centre of the colour wheel and perpendicular to it. Since the colours occurring in our natural environment are mostly relatively unsaturated, our eyes are able to discriminate between

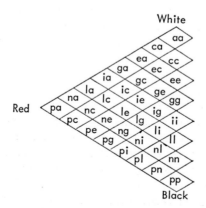

Fig. 6.7 One isotonic triangle from Ostwald's system. (From v. Fieandt 1966 p. 83.)

degrees of brightness combined with degrees of saturation. These varying shades are called the *valences* of a hue. In primary red 100 valences can be distinguished. In order to describe this system Ostwald uses isotonic triangles (Fig. 6.7): the vertical white-black axis serves as a common base for all these triangles; their apices are located along the colour wheel, representing the greatest degree of saturation. The resulting three-dimensional body is called Ostwald's double cone.

Munsell's Colour System

Since the Second World War Ostwald's system of colour classification has lost a great deal of its significance. It is still applied in Central Europe as a device for colour use and classification, but its standard norms have become difficult to obtain. In recent textbooks of psychology the Munsell system is becoming more and more prevalent.

Munsell's system is based on the same principles as that of Ostwald. Due to the great importance of colours in modern society, we are constantly faced with problems of colour terminology and classification. The fields of colour printing, textile manufacture and paint and pigment production must pay constant attention to the popularity of the colours of their standard products. Munsell developed a double cone of the same types as that of Ostwald described above. He worked out a number system to correspond to the three dimensions of each colour body. His system of colour norms is presented in the *Munsell Book of Color*, in which hues of varying brightness and saturation are arranged in stepwise series. The sections along the axis of the double cone are similar to the isotonic triangles of the Ostwald system; one difference is that the successive colour norms are presented in the form of small rectangles (see Plate IV).

Munsell's book contains numerical symbols for every conceivable colour selection. The classification can therefore be used to specify a desired hue in exact terms. Instead of ordering, for example, coloured paper of "light rose pink and medium saturation", one can, if one is acquainted with the Munsell classification system, request the colour 5.OR 6/6. The pigment manufacturer, after glancing at the reference work mentioned above, knows exactly what colour is desired.

The uppermost part of Plate V shows a series of colour scales of varying hue and saturation, all of which represent the same degree of brightness, that is, they all originate from the same horizontal section surface of the Munsell solid. In this case the brightness value is /5. The series of reds in the uppermost vertical scale of the figure is denoted by 10 RP 5/10. The Munsell colour circle includes 40 different hues. Different shades belonging to the same hue are located in the same perpendicular section of the double cone. The similarity to the Ostwald classification is also seen in the fact that the achromatic colours occur in a perpendicular dimension along the axis of the solid.

The *colour triangle* is an attempt at a graphic model of the laws of colour mixture, of which more will be said below. *It is independent of the three-dimensional phenomenal colour system*, (e.g. Munsell, Ostwald), and should be kept sharply distinct from it. The principle of the colour triangle is the following: if A has the weight *m*, B the weight *n*, the location of the mixed colour is always the centre of gravity of A and B. In this way the points along a straight line (e.g. AB) represent all the proportions of hue mixtures.

The CIE-System

The standardized description of colour mixture, the *Chart of Chromaticity*, was adopted in 1931 by the *Commission Internationale d'Eclairage* (CIE) (Fig. 6.8). If, in the same system of coordinates, we represent every wave-length of Fig. 6.8, i.e. every colour hue relative to the sensory thresholds of both rods and cones for that particular point of the spectrum, we obtain a model of a colour system which possesses many methodological advantages (Fig. 6.9). Among others, it touches upon the purely empirical colour triangle and upon the international colour classification system derived from it. Following Granit's train of thought, the values along the *x*-axis represent wavelengths which affect cone cells; values along the *y*-axis thus affect rod tissue (Willmer, 1946).

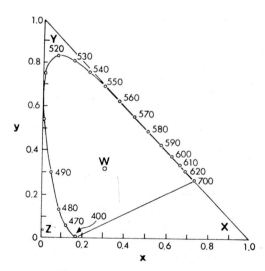

Fig. 6.8 The CIE Chart of Chromaticity (Kling and Riggs, p. 357). (From v. Fieandt, 1972 p. 119.)

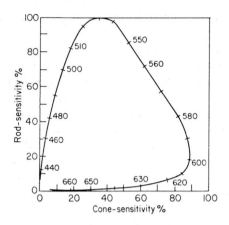

Fig. 6.9 Willmer's graph of chromaticity. (From v. Fieandt, 1972 p. 119.)

The CIE system is also useful in quantitatively representing differences in saturation of various hues. Saturation here means the inverse of the ease with which a given hue of the spectrum, under conditions of adaptation, loses its chromaticity and approaches the diagonal. Saturation can thus be calculated directly from the distance from the diagonal, and the result compared to the empirical graphs described above.

The Appearances of Colour

One purpose of the double cone, as of other psychological colour systems, was to arrange and classify the colours of our phenomenal experience. Neither Ostwald's nor Munsell's colour solid has, however, succeeded in this attempt. Nor can either of them be considered a classification of the colour stimuli themselves. One consequence of the physicalistic approach originated by Newton has been that the phenomenal appearances of colour have been studied exclusively on the basis of the spectrum, as though the only important factor in the colours were the specific wavelengths producing them. Other important components of the appearances of colours are left out, such as the preceding retinal stimulation and simultaneous stimulation outside the focal area (see for example Kanisza *In* Thomae, 1966). Hurvich and Jameson in their important studies have paid special attention to these factors (Heaton, 1968, p. 56). When consideration of their effects is omitted, a three-dimensional colour model is not adequate to describe colour experience exhaustively.

"Pure" spectral colours, the brightness of which appears to correspond to the intensity of the light reaching the retina, are seen only in highly artificial conditions, for example, in laboratory spectroscope experiments or in the work of highly realistic and analytic artists. Such colours are called, following Katz (1935), *film colours*. They appear to be immaterial, separate from objects, and they seem to be located perpendicular to our line of vision. They cannot be seen as following the surface or shape of an object. The distance of a film colour from the perceiver is also difficult to determine because of its transparency. If we look at a cloudless sky we get an idea of this difficulty. The experience of film colour occurs when some field of vision is perceived under *reduced* conditions, that is, when the number of objects or other cues in the field of vision is limited. This kind of isolation of part of the real visual environment can also be achieved by the use of a reduction screen. This is a screen which covers the entire field of vision, except for a hole in the middle, which is completely filled by the light reflected from some surface. This kind of "hole colour" is described by Feldman and Weld (1935) as follows:

When we ordinarily inspect an object—say, a polished piece of wood—the outcome of our perceiving is rich in scope. We perceive the *grain* and *polish* of the wood, its *hardness* and its *weight*. We can tell whether the wood retains its *natural colour* or whether it has been stained. We see it in a definite *place* and as having a definite *orientation*. We can perceive the *shadows* clinging to its surface and the lights reflected from its interior. When the same piece of wood is observed through the opening in the reduction screen, *all* the products of perceiving just listed *drop out*. Instead, one sees an objectless plane of colour with a soft, skylike texture. This colour plane has no resemblance to the surface of a solid object. (Cited in Boring *et al.*, 1935, p. 284.)

Film colours thus differ from *surface colours*, which seem to be a part of objects (Heaton 1968, p. 56). The colour seems to follow the surface of the object and to possess the structural properties characteristic of the object surface (polish, smoothness, granularity, transparency). The experience of surface colour is always linked with that of three-dimensionality; the colour may thus be located in a plane at any angle to the line of sight whatsoever.

Of the colour concepts distinguished by Katz, the most difficult to understand is perhaps *volume colour* or *illumination colour*. The stimulus source of such colour consists of various surfaces and the light reflected from them (together with a certain amount of light reaching the receptors directly from a light source). But in some cases the perceiver experiences a *transparent light, which fills the space and which lies in front of other coloured surfaces*. The visual apparatus thus seems to analyse the surfaces lying behind the illumination separately from the illumination itself. Another example of such volume colour is, for example, a mildly chromatic transparent solution in a glass bowl through which the surfaces lying behind the bowl are visible, or the somewhat dimly chromatic total illumination of a room at a fancy dancing party.

When the illumination of a room changes from daylight to candlelight, the perceiver rapidly sees a new red-yellow overtone which was not characteristic of the earlier illumination. After about five minutes this new chromaticity already seems much weaker. The object surfaces, with their surface colours, are perceived as much more invariably neutral than at the first instance. This is a case of so-called colour constancy, of which more will be said later (chapter 13).

The experience of volume colours (Katz 1935, p. 21) is said to be due to the articulation of the visual field. In some cases the subject may fail to construct his perceptual world: *he does not experience objects coloured "by themselves" in several ways—say in a red–yellow illumination*. If he does not perceive objects as independent coloured surfaces, he presumably cannot experience them as unaffected by the illumination. In an artificial "reddish" illumination they appear more chromatic than in normal daylight.

Gelb (1938), Teuber *et al.* (1960) and Critchley (1965) cite cases of brain-damaged patients in whom the normal perception of surface colours is impaired, often because of a wound in the occipital lobe. In patients suffering from hemianopia, where peripheral vision is reduced because of some occipital damage on one side of the brain (see chapter 5 p. 113) and where only half of each retina is able to transmit stimulus information, surface colours may lose their normal character, they become "indefinite" and "obscure". The ability to distinguish between surface colours probably does in fact presume analysis at the cortical level, since in Gelb's and Teuber's patients this type of deterioration in colour perception was most likely to occur. Colour hues no longer followed the outer surfaces of the objects perceived, but seemed to lie upon them in an indefinite mass. They had the properties of film colours. A patient pressing a pencil against paper was unable to write because the point of the pencil seemed to penetrate through a white film covering the paper. Such patients were also unable to see object surfaces of specific colour in an illumination of a different colour (Heaton 1968, p. 170; Goldstein and Gelb, 1920, p. 193; Teuber *et al.* 1960; Critchley, 1965).

Other spatial colour appearances are *transparent film and surface colours, reflections, lustre, shine* and *glow*. Katz also points out, in speaking of reduction techniques, that any surface colour can be transformed into a film colour by sufficiently reducing the field of vision. If, for example, we look at the opposite wall or a room through a hole 2 cm in diameter in a screen held at arm's length, the colour which fills the opening loses its surface colour characteristics. What is seen, in the plane of the reduction screen, is a film colour.

Effects of Different Illuminations

Earlier conclusions so far discussed concerning our ability to distinguish between *illumination* and the *object illuminated* (see chapter 13 p. 371) are in some respects no longer valid. The following statement would today be more appropriate: *within certain limits* the organism is capable of making such a discrimination, and this ability has reached a developmental level corresponding to biologically relevant natural life conditions, such as prevailed up to the last few decades. The human visual system enabled us to make adequate discriminations given the amount of variation prevailing out of doors, both in full daylight and under the more chromatic conditions of sunset and sunrise. It also functioned adequately with the relatively even and monotonic variations in radiation energy, represented by fires and other hot light sources.

The wealth of observations and experimental results of the well known colour psychologists, especially G. E. Müller, Bühler and Katz, were obtained mainly under daylight conditions or in illumination from *incandescent lamps*, which is not very different from sunlight in its spectral composition, viz. the spectrum being also continuous.

Light sources produce light mainly in three different ways: (1) heating a body to a high temperature, (2) effecting an electric discharge in a metal vapour or in a gas, (3) utilizing fluorescent materials. To the first type belong flame sources, where carbon particles heated to incandescence emit light, and incandescent lamps, where a filament is heated by means of electric current. Examples of the second type are mercury-vapour and sodium-vapour lamps, and xenon-lamps. The third type is represented by fluorescent lamps, where mercury vapour in an electrical discharge generates ultra-violet radiation, which is transformed into visible radiation by fluorescent powders. The main part of the artificial light in the world is nowadays produced by the last mentioned method.

The use of fluorescent illumination has brought about a revolution in the conditions of colour vision especially in two respects:

1. The higher illuminances now possible caused a considerable rise in the brightness of reflecting surfaces. For this reason alone hues measurable and definable under laboratory conditions have changed compared with comparable traditional colours under incandescent illumination.

2. Depending on the material composition of the substance used, fluorescent light shows a wide variation of intensity across the conventional band of the spectrum. We can assume that the human eye originally developed especially for the purpose of facilitating man's locomotion and orientation under conditions of variation in intensity and hue of natural sunlight. At different times of the day the brightness of the objects in the environment varies considerably. In order to recognize our environment as constant, "the same", we need a delicate sense of the *relative amount* of light reflected from

different objects. The *brightness constancy* or invariance of perceived brightness is in fact very high (see chapter 13 p. 374).

In natural daylight conditions, differences between successive hues throughout the chromatic continuum are more gradual than under fluorescent illumination. There is a shift in the appearance of some portions of the spectrum when cone vision changes to rod vision in dark adaptation, but from the point of view of the perception of colour in general these changes are minimal. Even when incandescent light was substituted for daylight in laboratory research, this merely meant an intensity shift toward the "redder" end of the spectrum.

As will be shown later, the experience of *hue constancy or invariance* is probably brought about as much by certain stimulus proportions of reflected surface intensities (i.e. degrees of brightness) as by their spectral chromaticity proper.

Memory Colours or Invariances?

Colour "invariance" or colour "constancy" is a concept which can be traced back to the terminology of Hering (1920) and what he wrote over 50 years ago about the *"memory colour"* (*Gedächtnisfarbe*) which he considered peculiar to each object we experience. Familiar objects appear to us to have relatively constant colours even in very different illuminations. We always experience grass as green, coal as black, chalk as white, etc. regardless of the conditions under which we see them.

Subsequently v. Helmholtz made a distinction in his theory of perception between the reflecting characteristics of the surface of an object and the prevailing conditions of illumination.

We learn by experience to distinguish between the illumination and the surface illuminated, "because we continuously have a tendency to distinguish between that aspect of the colour or the appearance of an object which is caused by the illumination and that which originates from the particular surface of the object itself" ("weil wir fortdauernd die Neigung haben zu trennen, was in der Farbe oder dem Aussehen eines Körpers von der Beleuchtung und was von der Eigentümlichkeit der Körperoberfläche selbst herrührt").

In terms of strictly physical stimuli, such a visual achievement would be hard to explain. The stimulus array impinging on our photoreceptors cannot be separated into an independently stimulating "illumination" and an independent colour surface "behind it". The direct radiation from the light sources and the reflected radiation are fused in the stimulus pattern, and what should be perceived is the mixed colour resulting from these components. Since our perception here does not conform to these traditionally

assumed conditions, v. Helmholtz had to postulate a higher-order perceptual regulating system. The psychological nature of this regulatory
component remained hypothetical throughout v. Helmholtz's presentation.
The most cited reference in this context is the first edition of the well
known *Handbuch* by v. Helmholtz (1867, p. 430). By that time he had coined
the expression "unconscious inferences". He wanted to point out that
combinations of mental images and identification processes of frequently-
memorized items constitute important prerequisites for veridical perceptions of object colours. These combinations, which are similar to
inferences, the "logical chains" of which remain unconscious, "allow for the
role of illumination" when perceiving light reflecting surfaces of objects.
Less familiar is his article 27 years later (Helmholtz 1894, pp. 81–96) in
which he specifies the regulating process as "induction-inferences". He
clearly points to the role of previous learning. Frequency and similarity in
the occurrence of experiences gives us *knowledge* about familiar objects, that
leads to *expectancies* and governs our perceptions. Knowledge ought to be
distinguished from information—a product of conscious logical inferences.
Yet v. Helmholtz still speaks of these "identifications of things" as "silent
inner inferences" (1894, p. 89).

Hering (1907, 1920) on the other hand, in his well-known criticism of
Helmholtz, could not accept explanations based on analogies with "intellectual judgments". He pointed to some logical difficulties within this chain of
thought which sound paradoxical: first we must know the object colour in
order to utilize the reflected light as an index of illumination, yet on the
contrary we must know the illumination in order to use the reflected light
as an index of object colour. (See Woodworth and Schlosberg 1955
p. 432).

The exact and careful experimental studies of Katz, even though they
explain colour appearances as phenomenal experiences, nevertheless reveal
the effect on his theory of the Helmholtzian way of thinking. The dualism
inherent in that influence is evident in all explanations presented by
Katz.

The distinction between the concepts of "normal illumination" and
"specific object colour" is a purely phenomenalistic one, yet these concepts
are applicable only to specific laboratory conditions. We thus end up with
the peculiar situation that the empirical descriptions of Katz provide us
with a clear enumeration of colour, but leave us without any point of
departure for an understanding of the correspondence between stimuli and
perception.

Gelb was the first to provide us with a key, and a surprisingly modern
one, to the question of colour constancy.

In 1929 he described a new constancy-contrast illusory situation, which since then has shown itself to be of great theoretical and empirical interest (cf. e.g., Koffka, Metzger, Stewart, Wallach). A black cardboard disc hangs from thin black threads in the open door of a dark room, behind it is a dark hallway. A projector in the room illuminates the black disc but not the door frame, so that a subject who stands in the dark room sees a strongly illuminated disc and nothing else with strong illumination; the shadow of the disc and the illuminated wall in the hall and ceiling of the hall are invisible to the subject behind the door frame. Under these conditions the disc looks white, even though it is "black" in the sense that it only reflects a small proportion of the light falling upon it. It is a well-known fact that the expression *reflectance* of a surface refers to the ratio of the light *reflected* by that surface to the amount of *incident* light. If the surface colour investigated is achromatic, i.e. it consists of a mixture of white and black components, its reflectance is called *albedo*. In other words, the albedo of a grey is measured by the ratio of the reflected to the incident light. Albedo-values are usually given in percentages. The albedos of some most familiar commercial stuffs show a variation between the upper limit of 90 per cent (chalk-powder) and the lower one of around 1 per cent (deep black velvet). In the first stage of the Gelb-experiment his disc suspended in the door frame looks white, even though it has a low albedo (see Bühler 1922, pp. 73–75, Woodworth-Schlosberg 1955, p. 430). If now a small piece of white paper is held in front of a part of the disc or at its edge, the disc immediately looks black. When the piece of white paper is removed again the disc regains its original appearance.

Let us begin with the problem of *brightness constancy*, since it is less complex.

We often wrongly assume that illumination is perceived independently of the brightness of the illuminated surfaces. In reality, whenever some perception of brightness invariance occurs, it depends on the simultaneously perceived *relations among the intensities of reflected radiations*. According to this theory, it is the organism's ability to perceive the *relative stimulus intensities of reflecting surfaces* which makes possible the existence of *brightness constancies*. The organism can thus adapt to its familiar environment, even at times of the day when the general illumination varies in intensity.

Gelb's observations on the relative nature of colour constancies also imply that the intensity gradient of light reflected from adjacent surfaces will be displaced if the illumination itself changes in spectral composition. This is, of course, exactly what happens when the illumination in a familiar room changes from incandescent to fluorescent.

Mixtures of Radiation

Colour Addition and Substraction

As already pointed out on p. 166 our visual apparatus functions primarily as an integrating system. This makes it possible for us to perceive the same colour as a result of a number of different wavelength combinations. The colour of an orange, for example, can be based on a mixture of different colour components in varying proportions.

It has been stated earlier (p. 171) that *brightness vision*—despite the three types of photopigments in the cones—is mediated by a unitary system. Therefore the luminances of lights of different colours are additive. As a matter of fact, if the light beams of two or more monochromatic light sources are superimposed, the resulting mixture of radiations is always stronger in luminance and looks brighter than each one of the mono-chromatic components. In an "ideal observer" the corresponding colour mixture experience is "brighter" than the hues of the components, coming close to what is represented by the *sum* of the respective luminances. Radiation mixture of the monochromatic components is additive in its luminosity.

When research workers speak of "colour mixture" they usually refer to this mixture of direct radiations from the light sources. It is called *colour addition* or *additive colour mixture*. It hardly has any significance at all for our practical manipulation of colour in everyday life, yet it is easily shown by means of a projector system in laboratory conditions.

In Newton's experiment, white light was broken up into its spectral components. Conversely, if the absorption quanta of these components could be added up and combined in a suitable manner—because of the addition principle mentioned above—an experience of *white* light should occur. That is what happens under "ideal" laboratory conditions, and is schematically shown on Plate VIa. A completely achromatic mixture can be achieved by means of combining two chromatic primaries, granted adequate difference in the wavelengths and suitably adjusted intensities. This is the well-known case of the *complementaries* (see pp. 172–173).

If the colour addition of radiations results in a *luminosity* equalling the sum of the luminances of the components, what about the *hue* in an additive mixture? Because we have three types of pigments in the cones, and all information about the wavelength is lost when absorption occurs in the respective pigment, any two wavelengths can, if suitably adjusted for intensity, produce identical effects upon any single type of pigment. The action of an additive mixture of wavelengths comes from the sum of the individual mixing components. "If two physically different stimuli produce the same absorption in all three types of photopigment, it follows that these stimuli should look exactly alike in all respects" (Boynton 1971, p. 350).

The laboratory device for making additive colour mixtures consists of colour discs, which can be placed in various overlapping positions. By varying the size of the visible sectors, the experimenter can regulate the proportions of the components in the mixture (Fig. 6.10). When the discs

Fig. 6.10 Colour discs as mounted concentrically on a colour mixer. (From v. Fieandt, 1966 p. 89.)

are rotated at a suitable speed the radiations reflected from them combine producing a colour mixture determined by the proportions of the rotating chromatic sectors. According to *Talbot's Law,* the brightness of the mixed colour is equal to that which would be produced if the *successive* stimuli hit the retina *simultaneously*. In other words, brightness is equal to that which would result if the sectors of the wheel were spread out, so that their radiations came from the entire area of the wheel, but with an intensity reduced in proportion to the increase in surface area.

Subtractive colour mixture results when a reflecting surface is covered with a different colour hue, as is done, for example, in mixing paints. Everyone is familiar with the techniques used by artists in mixing paints and pigments to produce new colours. Pigment mixtures are never additive because the *colour subtraction* principle implies that they attain their colour by absorbing light from some portions of the spectrum and reflecting other portions. When two pigments are mixed, a part of the light which is not absorbed by one may be absorbed by the other. Light of some wavelengths may not be absorbed at all. This light produces the resultant colour. A subtractive mixture results in a hue which is *less bright* than its components (Plate VIb).

A further characteristic of subtractive colour mixture is that, while it is determined by the absorbing properties of pigment colours, the illumination in which the colour mixture is seen will always have a considerable effect on the appearance of the resulting colour. Different pigments absorb spectral components of radiations in different proportions.

Colour Equations

In addition to three projectors producing monochromatic light beams as shown on Plate VIa, imagine a fourth projector S_U (Fig. 6.11) which casts light to one side of the patch produced by the others. The spot it produces is less saturated but also chromatic.

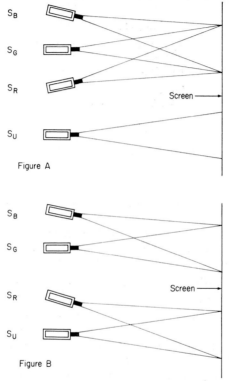

Fig. 6.11 Experimental set-up for producing additive colour mixture. (From Wolman, 1973 p. 334.)

It follows from the statements given above that if the luminances S_R, S_G, S_B (red, green, blue) are suitably adjusted, the spot of light they produce can be brought to match that of S_U. The equality produced can be expressed by an equation:

$$L_U(S_U) \equiv L_R(S_R) + L_G(S_G) + L_B(S_B)$$

In other words:

L_U units of light S_U match the sum of L_R units of
S_R, L_G units of S_G and L_B units of S_B.

G

A combination of three primaries R, G and B is seldom saturated enough to match the monochromatic U completely. Yet if the primary projectors are free to move, so that their light can be mixed with S_U, one really succeeds in producing two mixed patches of light which look completely equal in hue and saturation. This arrangement can be described as follows:

$$u(U) + r(R) \equiv g(G) + b(B)$$

For a test wavelength of 490 nm it reads

$$0 \cdot 082(U) + 0 \cdot 058(R) \equiv 0 \cdot 057(G) + 0 \cdot 083(B)$$

(see Boynton, 1971).

The statement is purely empirical. The plus signs are borrowed from mathematics in order to indicate chromatic addition. The symbol " $\equiv$ " does not imply mathematical equality, it only indicates a coincidence of the type familiar from psychophysical measurements.

However, analogous mathematical statements might be written down and handled according to elementary rules of algebra. It turns out that quite a series of interesting calculations can be made, which actually predict the results of new colour matching experiments.

As illustrative examples let us assume after having mixed together paper discs of complementary colours (e.g. red + green on one disc and blue + yellow on another) that a pair of colour equations obtain in the following way:

$$195^\circ\, R + 165^\circ\, G \equiv 205^\circ\, B + 155^\circ\, Y$$

(Both mixtures of complementaries have been matched against a mixture of black and white.)

As a result of algebraic calculations the following statements for additive colour mixture have been derived:

1. Every hue has its complementary which, when mixed with it in proper proportions, produces achromatic grey. If the proportions are not exactly right, the mixed colour resembles the more strongly represented component, but its saturation is reduced.

2. If hues other than complementary ones are mixed together, no proportion of the components will yield an achromatic grey. The mixed colour resembles the component which is more strongly represented in the mixture, and its saturation is weaker the greater the difference between the saturations of the component hues. If three hues are chosen in such a way that each of them has its complementary located between the other two on the colour circle, all other hues can be produced by mixing these three together in appropriate proportions.

3. If the mixtures resulting from two pairs of hues a and b appear identical,

and two other pairs c and d also yield an identical result, appropriate mixture of a and c or of b and d will also yield an identical result.

Rayleigh studied how subjects mixed red and green to match a certain yellow; he was astonished to find that some individuals could discriminate the hues correctly but did not combine them in the usual proportions or would not accept the usually approved mixture to match the yellow. In accordance with the prevailing *Young-Helmholtz three-colour theory*, Rayleigh assumed that these individuals represented some intermediate step between total colour blindness and normal sight. Pickford (1951) later demonstrated that *Rayleigh's equations* can be used as diagnostic aids in achieving a more precise classification of colour perception anomalies by way of his excellent apparatus known as an "anomaloscope". According to him red-green vision shows a normal frequency distribution, except for individuals suffering from certain colour vision anomalies and certain forms of colour blindness (see pp. 201–204). For these individuals, the values fall far beyond either end of the normal distribution.

Varieties of Chromatic Adaptation

In our everyday experience, objects are perceived as located in a certain place and arranged in a certain way. There is articulation and organization within the field of vision, and we are able to discriminate, for example, between the relative size, distance, colour and shape of given objects. Along the edges of every area seen as an "object" there is a sharp gradient of light reflectance, which we perceive as a *contour*. Colours can vary gradually, or they can appear as continuous surfaces which are experienced as *figures*. These contour phenomena thus form the basis of all object perception.

The articulation of our visual world is further reinforced by *contrast*. This emphasizes the location of contours and makes them sharper since the effect of contrast is to make adjacent parts of a surface more distinct from each other. Thus we can speak of both brightness and hue contrast. The area of a surface in which contrast is caused is called the *test area* or *centre area*, that which causes the contrast is called the *inducing* or *surrounding area*. In actual fact these areas have a reciprocal effect on each other. In experimental work a relatively small test area is usually surrounded by a large inducing area. In this way a maximal contrast effect is achieved.

Brightness contrast is best demonstrated by offering the subject two grey discs of the same degree of brightness side by side, one against a white and the other against a black background. Discs cut from the same grey paper appear to possess a different degree of brightness; that shown against a black background is clearly brighter. Only when the part played by the context is completely eliminated, for example, by covering the black and the white surfaces, do the two discs appear identical. In this way we can show that phenomenal brightness is determined both by the intensity of the light reflected from a surface and by the immediate environment of the stimulus area, the so-called perceptual context.

Chromatic contrast can be produced in many ways. For example, equal grey discs can be placed against a red and a blue background. The grey which is surrounded by red appears greenish, that which is surrounded by blue appears yellow. Again, if we place a pale, unsaturated yellow disc against a strongly saturated blue background, the light yellow becomes a deep and saturated colour.

In order to produce a strong contrast effect, the articulation into figure and ground (see chapter 12 pp. 323–327) should be clear, but the "object" character of the areas should be weak. The figure and the ground should be placed on the same plane, and the colours should be strong, preferably film colours. By using a colour-wheel or by covering pigment colours with transparent tissue paper, the effect of film colour can be achieved.

Two adjacent complementary colours increase each other's saturation by means of a reciprocal contrast effect, and the resulting saturations can considerably exceed those normally found in the spectrum. On the other hand, if the two areas differ in saturation but have the same hue, the apparent difference in saturation decreases because of the contrast.

If the spatial distance between contrast-inducing fields is increased the effect is weakened; even a relatively small displacement has this effect. A black border or contour also weakens contrast.

Contrast phenomena are considered to result from summation and inhibition processes in the retina. On the other hand, they are believed to reflect the functions of the single neurons which have been found in the lateral geniculate body (see chapter 3 p. 68) and of the inhibition which has been shown to occur in their impulse firing. The impulses coming from the test area may, for instance, be inhibited when the impulse frequency from the surrounding area, for one reason or another, is higher than the density of those from the former. This kind of effect of a higher impulse density is called *induction* in normal psychological usage (Osgood, 1953, p. 253).

According to Helson and Bevan (1968), phenomena of adaptation, contrast, assimilation and constancy (the last two of which will be discussed in a later chapter) should be seen as resulting from a single underlying mechanism. By assimilation they mean the inverse phenomenon of the classical contrast effect. White stripes against a chromatic background are known to make it brighter, while dark stripes make it appear darker.

In the opinion of Helson and Bevan, all these phenomena represent the activity of the same receptor connections. On the neural level, inhibition underlies phenomena of contrast while facilitation or summation produces phenomena of assimilation. They emphasize the close relationship between adaptation and contrast (Helson and Bevan 1968, p. 326).

According to the point of view adopted here, however, constancy should be considered a higher-level process connected with object perception, and an invariance at a more cognitive level of mental procedures, as will be shown later (see chapter 13).

The contrast phenomena described above are often called *simultaneous contrast*, as distinct from *successive contrast*; the latter term refers to changes in the brightness or hue of a visual object as an after-effect immediately following an intensive stimulation. These after-effects are usually known as *physiological after-images*.

If we stare at a red disc against a grey background, after some 10–20 seconds the disc may fade or even disappear. If the disc is removed while the subject continues to stare, its place will generally be taken by an after-image of *complementary colour*, in this case a green disc. If the distance between the subject and the background is increased, the area of the after-image increases in direct proportion to the square of the distance (*Emmert's Law*). The same phenomena of induction which are characteristic of simultaneous contrast are generally used to account for after-images. In the stimulated areas of the retina the photosensitive matter undergoes, as it were, a state of deprivation.

According to Helson's concept of *level of adaptation* (see chapter 2 p. 41), continued stimulation of some limited receptor area causes adaptation in the receptor tissue and local changes in the adaptation level take place; the effort at re-establishment of the original level is experienced phenomenally as a complementary colour (see Helson and Bevan 1968, pp. 327–328).

In everyday life, contrast phenomena play an essential role in the organization of the visual field and in the perception of objects as distinct from each other and from their backgrounds, since different objects normally reflect radiation differently.

The Purkinje Shift

When the prevailing general illumination becomes weaker, colours gradually appear dimmer. As can easily be observed during twilight on a summer evening, differences in brightness become more dominant than differences in colour, and scotopic vision dominates over photopic (the reader may read the meaning of these terms; see chapter 3 p. 64). The brightness maximum shifts from the yellow–red end of the spectrum toward the blue–green end. This is due to the fact that the central areas of the retina are more sensitive to longer wavelengths and the peripheral areas to shorter ones. In full daylight the maximum sensitivity lies at the light yellow band

(572 nm), at twilight it is at blue–green (511 nm). This phenomenon is known as the *Purkinje shift*. Together with the shift in the brightness maximum there is also a decrease in visual acuity, as vision shifts to the non-foveal zones. We may use both our dark-adapted eyes to improve visual acuity, since both retinas together undergo a physiological process of summation which does not occur in eyes adapted to daylight. Everyday experience yields examples as easily as does the laboratory: in daylight a blue canoe appears darker than the red boathouse behind it, but at twilight the canoe appears bright against the darker background of the boathouse. In the laboratory we can control the amount of light reflected from surfaces and make sure that it is everywhere identical, but the phenomenon persists with undiminished clarity.

The structural organization characteristic of surface colours is a result of cooperation between the fovea and the visual cortex (Gelb and Goldstein, Teuber and others). Peripheral areas of the retina are more primitive than that of the centre, and peripherally mediated colour experiences are, at best, only film colours (Katz 1935). When surface colours are reduced to film colours, the result is the same as in peripheral colour perception. On the other hand, the peripheral areas of the retina are more sensitive to *movement stimuli* in the visual field; this may have biological meaning, since movement within the visual field may be the sign of danger or of prey.

On Colour Theories

Colour theories up to now have generally followed the line of thought implicit in Newton's physical optics. Goethe is usually mentioned as the earliest and best known investigator to seek a different solution to the problem of colour perception from that of Newton, one specifically appropriate to the phenomenal point of view. Goethe's ideas, however, were mostly loose speculations which failed to meet strict scientific criteria. It is clear why anyone trying to oppose Newton at that time would have failed: methods and terminology were not yet developed to a stage where they could be applied to a phenomenal analysis from a psychophysical point of view.

Newton's discovery that white light can be split into its components by conduction through a prism was so revolutionary that it has dominated *all subsequent colour research*, including that of psychologists. But the theory which Newton constructed on the basis of his findings, with regard for instance to the nature of colour stimuli, was above all a product of its time. In many respects it reflected the age of invention, when the natural sciences were above all analytic, when the atomic theory was developed to describe chemical compounding, and when ultimate units or elements were posited to explain events in animate nature also. After the discovery of the spectrum there was a strong tendency to assume that in our natural environment there occurred "pure hues", representing a highly restricted wavelength band. Although such relatively monochromatic bands can be found in the spectrum, they can be obtained in the laboratory only by heating various chemical elements in their pure form. There is, however, no reason to assume that even the complete spectrum of sunlight, which is a compound of spectroscopically recorded radiations from glowing elements in the sun, should exhaustively represent the chromatic stimuli in our real natural environment.

In keeping with the Newtonian way of thinking, the *primary colours*, as visual stimuli, have also been described as particular and relatively narrow bands of the spectrum. The theory of specific nerve energies (see pp. 55–97) then led to the conclusion that each chromatic receptor functions as a recording device for a particular pure, narrow and precisely defined band of the spectrum. This view can briefly be stated as follows:

A given rate of refraction always corresponds to the same experienced hue, and a given hue always corresponds to the same rate of refraction.

As we survey the colour theories suggested since the beginning of the nineteenth century, we thus ought to remember that, according to the principles of Newton's optics:

1. the specific stimulus of a chromatic perception was assumed to be either the wavelength of a "pure radiation" represented in the spectrum and experienced as a primary colour, or a particular summation of these wavelengths experienced as a mixed colour;
2. the brightness gradient was never considered as part of the stimulus basis in the perception of hues, which were offered "strictly monochromatically".

Particular specialized cells were assumed to function as receptors for certain "pure" monochromatic hues, i.e. the primaries. This reasoning completely ignored the role played by the brightness gradient which is characteristic of each primary.

In speaking of cells and their role in the transmission of visual information, the "classical" point of departure has been the assumption that transduction specific to the intensity and the wavelength of the stimulus could occur only at the level of the retinal tissue (see e.g. p. 168). Actually, the colour theories set forth up to the present can be divided into three classes, according to the physiological function which they ascribe to the receptors. According to the classification of retinal receptors, we can speak of *three-colour theories* and of *opponent colour theories*. Both of these must be distinguished from the more modern *zone or stage theories*. The first two types are represented respectively by the Young–Helmholtz theory and by the theory of Hering.

The Young–Helmholtz Theory

The laws of colour mixture formulated by Newton implied that any perceived colour could be produced by combining three "pure colours" or primaries in the appropriate proportions. (Newton originally proposed altogether seven "pure radiations": violet, indigo, blue, green, yellow, orange and red.) In 1801, at an early age, Thomas Young read a paper before the Royal Society, setting forth his conviction that the perception of all conceivable hues could be explained on the basis of three specific processes in the retina. Each of these processes, according to Young, corresponded to a particular band of radiation (again using Newton's spectrum as the point of departure); any experienced colour would thus depend on the intensity relations of different radiation wavelengths.

This "three-colour theory" was soon forgotten, but it was revived by v. Helmholtz in 1860. His version of the theory was based primarily on the colour mixture experiments of J. C. Maxwell, then the first-ranking physicist in England. In 1855 this superb research worker had already devised a method for producing the world's first colour photograph. Maxwell took pictures of a given still life or landscape in the ordinary way, using achromatic negatives but taking each picture three times and masking the lens alternately with red, green and blue filters. The three negatives were developed into positive black and white transparencies. Using three projectors simultaneously, and placing the same chromatic filters in front of the respective transparencies, the three pictures were superimposed on the screen, resulting in a *projected colour photograph, which had not only the three filter colours, but all the colours of the originally photographed scene* (see Plate VII). It should be emphasized that it is not sufficient to project three

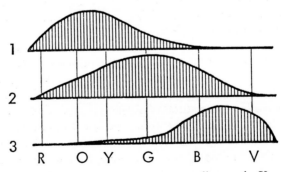

Fig. 6.12 The three-colour response systems according to the Young–Helmholtz theory. (From v. Fieandt, 1966 p. 97.)

identical black and white transparencies through three primary-colour filters; three different achromatic negatives must first be obtained by photographing through chromatic filters. This process retains differences in the brightness distribution of the surfaces photographed.

On the basis of Maxwell's experiments, v. Helmholtz developed Young's theory to state that, while all types of receptors respond to radiation of all wavelengths, they are especially sensitive to radiation of a particular wavelength area, according to the diagram in Fig. 6.12.

Maxwell was able empirically to derive three such sensitivity curves. By studying a case of colour blindness (dichromat), he was also able to confirm the occurrence of separate colour response systems. These sensitivity distribution curves for different sets of receptors were later specified mathematically by König and Dieterici.

At about the same time, Schultze presented the duplicity theory, already described above (see p. 107), which maintained that there are two types of receptor cells in the retina. This theory was further developed by v. Kries in 1894, and it required a revision of the Young–Helmholtz theory. It proved necessary to assume three types of cones to allow for specific sensitivity to particular wavelength bands. They were as follows:

1. *First type of receptor*
   Most sensitive to red, but responsive to radiation of other wavelengths also.
2. *Second type of receptor*
   Most sensitive to green, but responsive to all kinds of radiation.
3. *Third type of receptor*
   Most sensitive to blue and violet, but responsive to all kinds of radiation.

The emphasis of the Young–Helmholtz theory is on physiology. It explains the phenomena of colour mixture in a satisfactory way, taking the situation into account by the colour triangle. It has not been as successful in accounting for the large number of phenomenal regularities discovered by experimental psychology in the field of colour perception.

For example, what part of the spectrum should be postulated to correspond to the sensitivity peak of each receptor type? Young at first assumed the three maximum points to correspond to particular shades of red, yellow and blue. He later spoke of red, green and violet primary stimuli. Actually, the most suitable colours would be orange-red, yellowish-green and violet-blue; these would enable us most easily to produce the complementary of any of the three from a mixture of the two. Maxwell's colour photography filters, in fact, had spectral compositions very similar to these. Nowadays, however, all filters are more or less polychromatic, so that the Helmholtzian three-colour theory cannot be fully confirmed by means of this method. In 1881 Donders published a study of colour blindness which partly supported v. Helmholtz's theory but partly called for a revision into closer agreement with Hering's theory.

Any criticism of the Young–Helmholtz theory must consider its weakness in accounting for some of the phenomenal facts of colour. We know that white, black and yellow appear as independent primaries in our immediate experience. Thus psychologically speaking they cannot be considered colour mixtures, as the theory assumes. From the point of view of a correspondence between stimuli and sensations, the most important thing to remember about this theory is its assumption of functional integration between three types of cone cells.

The Hering Theory

Hering's explanatory model had its own predecessors. In several connections Mach expressed ideas which clearly affected Hering's conclusions. Thus, when writing on the parallel laws (Parallelgesetze) of function and experience, he pointed out that yellow can never be *experienced* as a mixed colour, although the three-colour theory would define it as such. In addition to the primary colours distinguished by Young, white, black and yellow play an equally fundamental role in experience, and we would therefore expect some equally basic physiological process to underlie all six.

In the same year as Mach (1865), Aubert also sharply criticized the Young–Helmholtz theory. He emphasized the lack of correspondence between the physiological stimulus elements, the primary colours, and the psychologically distinguished categories, as indicated, for example, by colour names. Actually it was Aubert who first introduced the term *Hauptfarbe* (main colour, fundamental colour) to signify the phenomenally elementary or "primary" colours. Hering's theory assumes the occurrence of one of three processes in the visual tissue, depending on its structure. Each of these three is an event of metabolic assimilation or dissimilation. The presumed physico-chemical basis for these processes is the alternating absorption and reconcentration of the photosensitive substance in the cells. The change occurs in three parallel, mutually independent systems:

	Substances		
	White–Black	Yellow–Blue	Red–Green
Dissimilation	White	Yellow	Red
Assimilation	Black	Blue	Green

The table should be read as follows: dissimilation of the white–black substance causes an experience of white; an assimilation of the same substance causes black vision. Dissimilation of the yellow–blue substance gives rise to an experience of yellow, etc. The shifts occur alternately in opposite directions, but they cannot maintain a balance except in the case of black and white, where such an equilibrium is assumed. The corresponding experience is then one of a neutral grey. When the stimulus radiation does not fall within the limits of any of these six fundamental stimuli, simultaneous processes of change occur within all three systems. There are types of radiation which cause dissimilation of one of the substances simultaneously with the assimilation of another. When white is produced by a mixture of complementaries, this is not due to a summation-type combination of chromatic sensations. According to Hering, visual white is the result of equilibration between opposing processes, of a neutralization between the chromatic complementary components of a complex radiation. The chromatic valences nullify each other so that only white valences remain, resulting in a perception of white.

The Hering theory also encounters difficulties: for example, although the primaries yellow and blue turn out to be complementary colours, this is not true of primary red and green, which do not cancel each other out. In order to bring about a grey mixture, we need a combination of purple-red and olive-green, or of an orange-tinted red and a bluish green.

The Opponent Colour Theory of Hurvich and Jameson

A more modern version of the opponent colour theory is that of Hurvich and Jameson, also based on the concept of substances functioning in bipolar opposition (e.g. Thomae, 1966, pp. 131–160). Hurvich and Jameson try to show that a definition of phenomenal colour which is based on processes brought about by stimulation of a particular point in the retina is not sufficient: those physiological induction effects which are due to stimuli elsewhere in the visual field or to earlier stimulation of the retina should also be taken into account.

The basic empirical findings of Hurvich and Jameson are the following:

The saturation of a focal stimulus is reduced by the surround of the stimulus; the reduction is in direct proportion to the luminosity ratio (the ratio between the intensities of the focal stimulus and the background see chapter 13 p. 376).

The perceived hue of a focal stimulus is either reduced or changed to its opposite by the surround of the stimulus; the reduction is directly proportional to the luminosity ratio between the background and the focal stimulus.

The perceived brightness of a focal stimulus is strongly reduced by the hue and luminance of the surround of the stimulus in cases where the luminance of the stimulus is less than that of the background. The reduction is stronger if the hue of the background is the same as that of the stimulus.

These findings indicate that the experienced colour depends (a) on the photo-chemical and neural processes activated by stimulation of a particular point in the retina, and (b) on neural activity opposite to that of (a), caused by psychological processes in the environment of the stimulated point.

The Granit Theory

Granit (1947, 1955) emphasizes the fundamental importance for colour perception of variations in impulse frequency along the afferent receptor fibres. These variations depend not only on the intensity of the light stimulus but *also on its wavelength*. The various hues of the spectrum cause different impulse frequencies. In addition to coding by intensity there is also coding by frequency (cf. chapter 3 pp. 51–55). Differences in stimulus sensitivity depending on the hue of the illumination used can also be empirically demonstrated. In this way we can determine which parts of the spectrum exhibit sensitivity peaks, and can draw conclusions about the corresponding nerve conductors.

Although the areas of greatest sensitivity coincide with the spectral zones of red, green and blue, it is obvious that the organization is more complex than that assumed by Young.

Granit believes that smaller zones can be shown to exist within each of the three bands mentioned above: red, green and blue (Fig. 6.13). Within the area of each primary colour he has found two zones. These occur at similar points in the spectrum for various animal species, but their number varies from one species to another. According to his theory, the perception of different colours is based on the activity of cone cells specifically sensitive to different wavelengths—the so-called *modulators*. There are at least six different kinds of these, in the human eye possibly even more. Most numerous are the *dominators*, which occur everywhere in the retina and which serve in the perception of thegeneralbrightness dimension, that is, of white light, which is represented as a component in radiation of all colours. According to this theory, then, the sense of brightness is more abundantly represented by receptors than the actual sense of colour. This appears from the general brightness distribution of the spectrum. The following detail from Granit's experimental methodology deserves attention.

Let us assume that a dominator consists of a group of inter-connected modulators. Thus, if a dominator corresponding to a broad area of sensitivity is based on the joint effect of red, green and blue modulators, can each of these in turn be eliminated from the dominator in an experiment? By exhausting the eye by means of chromatic light this can, in fact, be achieved.

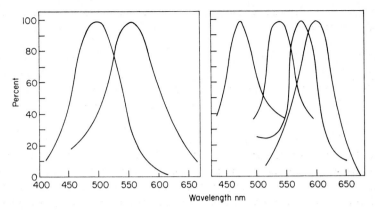

Fig. 6.13 Dominator and modulator curves from the frog (Granit and Svaetichin, 1939). (From Wolman, 1973 p. 343.)

In addition to the compound dominators there also exist various modulators, which modulate the perception of diffuse brightness to one of a particular hue.

Colour blindness, in Granit's opinion, can be explained by the elimination of particular single modulators. The dominators, however, preserve their ability to function to a sufficiently great extent so that the receptor sensitivity to light intensity remains normal.

Zone or Stage Theories

What all the described theories have in common is a greater emphasis on the part played by tissues at a higher or more central level than on that of the light-sensitive retinal receptor-cells, in the perception both of diffuse brightness and in the discrimination of specific colours. Interest in the study of these more central levels was aroused above all by the considerably improved techniques of light-stimulus focusing and of impulse recording from the neural pathways of individual cells. As mentioned above (p. 93), in this way it has been possible to record measurements from individual cone cells, from ganglia located in deeper layers of the retina with lateral connections between different receptor pathways, and most recently also from the large lateral geniculate bodies in the centres of the brain stem.

Svaetichin, *et al.* (1960) carried on the investigations originated by Svaetichin (see pp. 169–170) around the problem of light-sensitive single cones. They experimented with two species of fish, both shallow-water species, whose behaviour indicates that they discriminate colours fairly reliably. The retinae of the fish are fairly easy to isolate and prepare. The tissue was kept alive during the experiment. From the exceptionally large cone cells of these fish the experimenters were able to record reactions both to general luminosity (L) and (for certain cones) to chromatic, red–green stimuli (R–G). By varying the focusing of the point-like light-beam so that the light alternately hit the tip of a particular cone closer to the centre of the eyeball, they were able to demonstrate convincingly the light sensitivity of the cones. When the light beam hit the tissue lying between the cones the amplitude of the potentials recorded from the nerve fibres fell to about one-third of its previous height.

Svaetichin and McNichol (see pp. 169–170) have repeated and revised the experiments carried out by Svaetichin concerning the visual apparatus and performance of certain teleost fish. The amplitude variations of the photopic impulse curve from the light-adapted retina represent three different types. As mentioned above, the L-type is the name given to a wide-range decrease in amplitude corresponding to wavelengths covering the entire spectrum; in addition, recordings corresponding to certain cone-cells yield specific chromatic potentials, the R–G (red–green) and Y–B (yellow–blue) potentials. What is significant is that the peaks of opposite polarity are consistent with the Hering colour theory; shallow-water species living at depth of 1 to 2 metres show specific reaction curves for both colour pairs, R–G and Y–B, while deep-water species are sensitive only to one or the other of these. In general it was observed that the thresholds and amplitudes of the L-reactions remained unchanged regardless of whether specific chromatic responses occurred at the same time or not. The findings of Rushton (1963) seem to indicate that L-reactions can be recorded from ganglia cells in which synaptic connections from all different types of chromatically specialized cells terminate. The amplitude increase of the L-potentials is directly proportional to the logarithm of the stimulus intensity, as assumed by Weber's law.

If the chromatically sensitive cones are stimulated simultaneously by two equally intense complementary colours (e.g. red and green), or by perfectly white light, the result is an activation of the L-response. The ecological observations of these researchers also confirm the finding that deep-water fishes living at depths of 30–70 m demonstrate only L-reactions in this tissue as a consequence of their homogeneously "bluish" life environment. In rivers and lagoons which are only a few metres deep, the water is a yellowish orange, and the fish show both R–G and Y–B responses.

Hubel and Wiesel (1960) studied receptor areas in ganglial connections of the optic nerve in macaque and spider monkeys (see also chapter 4 pp. 93–94). Two types of neural units could be distinguished. In one the centre of the stimulus area gives a facilitating reaction, while the periphery acts to inhibit; in the other the division of labour is the opposite. There are ganglia which react specifically to chromatic radiation. For example, if white light was conducted through a blue filter, in certain fibres a strong "on" reaction was aroused. A red filter aroused the corresponding "off" reaction. In general, wavelengths over 500 nm have an inhibitory effect; shorter wavelengths a facilitating effect.

It would thus seem that, in keeping with the claim made by Svaetichin and McNichol (1958), the polarity evident in higher neural connections is consistent with the opponent system of Hering's theory, while everything that we know about the sensitivity areas of the receptor cells themselves indicates the accuracy of the three-colour theory. It must, however, be remembered that not all information regarding colour hues is transmitted by these polarized connections.

An evaluation and criticism of the hierarchical model presented by Hubel and Wiesel has been given above in chapter 4 (pp. 85–87).

A Stage Theory Closely Investigated

Instead of the traditional "colour vision" or "colour perception" theories which provided us with "all over" explanations and almost universal colour detection models—presumably valid at all levels of the receptive apparatus— works like those by Svaetichin (1956), Svaetichin and McNichol (1958), Wald (1964, 1967) and DeValois (1965, 1972) have resulted in *hierarchies* of subordinated explanation models (see chapter 3 pp. 81–85). Evidently appara- tuses that are responsible for one or another functional level or stage within the frame of the visual system obey their specific rules and "working principles". What goes on at the level of rods and cones must be described in different terms from what holds true at the stage of retinal interaction. Based on this consideration quite a number of plural explanation models, "zone" or "stage" theories have seen the sunlight. Most familiar among these, dealing occasionally with processes on only one of the "zones", are the theories of Judd (1951), Hurvich and Jameson (1955), Rushton (1963) and Boynton (1960). Recently there has appeared a new explanation model by Boynton (in Kling and Riggs, 1971), which could be labelled a "plural zone or stage theory". It deserves some consideration as a very typical example.

The schematic diagram in Fig. 6.14 gives a pretty good idea about his way of reasoning. The outputs of the red, green and blue cones are in- dicated by a, b and c in the foot of each receptor. Outputs of G and R cones summate $(a+b)$ at a luminosity unit (L). The L-signal is passed along by the bipolar cells and evidently modulates the resting level of activity in the ganglion cells. All different L units converging upon each ganglion cell transmit information about the amount of white light in the stimulus.

From the R-cone a second branch of output is delivered to a chromatic cell (C_1). From the G-cone a branch is also delivered to C_1. The output of C_1

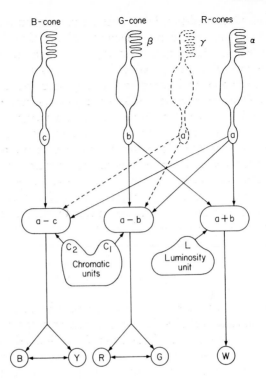

Fig. 6.14 The model derived by Boynton for chromatic information processing. (From Kling and Riggs, 1971 p. 331.)

in turn is just the difference of the two signals, *a–b*. An *imbalance* between the relative stimulation of R- and G-cones is thus assumed to exist.

At the level of ganglion cells, if output from C_1 is totally missing (*a* equals *b*) the resulting potential shows a "resting frequency". The meaning of this message may be coded as "neither red nor green". In case C_1 gives a positive output, the resting frequency just mentioned increases. That means "red". A negative output which decreases the frequency, means "green". The activity in the optic R–G fibres thus signals either red or green.

The model described so far represents a dichromatic system, and it accounts fairly well for the function of a corresponding class of colour defective people (see below, p. 202).

Analogous to the C_1-system is the C_2-system. If *a* exceeds *b* the optic fibres signal "yellow"; when *b* takes over the signal gives "blue". "For most spectral stimuli there will be nonzero contributions from both the C_1 and C_2 systems. When this happens, the result will be the simultaneous activity of brain units: either B or Y units on the one hand together with either R or G units on the other." (Boynton 1971, p. 333). Thus this dual activity might produce four types of "composite sensations".

The diagram in Fig. 6.14 also accounts for the possibility that a minority of the R-cones (dotted in the figure) contain γ-pigment normally prevalent in B-cones. These units are supposed to account for the existence of unique blue in the spectrum—sensitive as these units are, especially to short waves.

A zone- or stage-model, like the one examined above, naturally oversimplifies the actual chains of processes in several ways. Among others this scheme overlooks the area-problem. The outputs of cone cells actually don't summate linearly. The appearance of colour is also a function of the area stimulated. Even the shape of the receptor potentials speaks against the presumption of linearity in outputs. Nevertheless, illustrative schemes like this one have contributed remarkably to our understanding of the tricky underlying processes of our colour vision.

Abnormal Colour Vision

It is a generally accepted conviction among representatives of behavioural sciences, that biological variables show an almost normal distribution. The thesis has played a predominant role especially in the field of differential psychology, where it has provided the basis for nearly all construction of performance tests. A closer look at individual psychology, however, reveals a lot of variables which are largely physiologically determined, and hardly show any variability at all within 90 per cent of mankind. Deficiences in chromatic vision belong to this class of variables. Only a handful of people are chromatically *blind*—their discrimination ability is restricted only to differences inside the dimension of black and white. Among chromatically *defective* people 8 per cent of all males deviate markedly from the average in their visual performance. Among females the corresponding number comes up to 3 cases in every 10,000. This minority group of colour deficient individuals in both sexes can be divided into six subgroups, the performances of which are almost completely unrelated.

Several routine devices have been developed for the classification of colour defects. The most reliable method, however, consists of colour-matching experiments by means of an apparatus called an *anomaloscope* which has been particularly developed and improved by Pickford (1951). The subject is confronted with a split field, on one side of which a monochromatic hue, usually yellow, is projected. By turning a knob the subject is able to adjust the energy of this monochromatic source. On the other side of the split field a mixture of two monochromatic lights (red and green) is provided. Their ratio can be varied by turning another knob. For a subject without deficiences there will be only one setting of the second knob that will produce a yellow that matches the hue of the monochromatic yellow.

Among the chromatically deficient people about a quarter are *dichromatic colour mixers*. The dichromats need only two primaries to produce all their phenomenal chromatic tones instead of the three primaries needed by normals. The dichromat seemingly has only one longwave-sensitive receptor system. He finds that there are many combinations of settings of the red and green primaries that will produce the same visual result. The two general forms of dichromatism are protanopia (red blindness) and deuteranopia (green blindness).

"The protanope is distinguished by a large insensitivity to stimuli in the long-wave end of the spectrum, requiring five to ten times as much energy to perceive a level of brightness apparently equal to what the normal subject sees. The deuteranope's perception of luminosity, as measured by brightness matching methods, is essentially normal." (Boynton 1971, p. 363). The protanope lacks sensitivity in the red end of the spectrum, the deuter-anope, on the other hand, lacks sensitivity to the middle part of the spectrum. Deuteranopes are more sensitive than normals to the red end of the spectrum, whereas protanopes are more sensitive than normals to the middle of the spectrum. Deuteranopia according to Pickford (1951) reveals itself as difficulty in distinguishing orange and green, although red may be seen normally.

A third type of dichromatism is called tritanopia. This deficiency reveals itself in a difficulty to discriminate between blue and yellow. This type is very rare indeed, and even the term "tritanopia" is questioned by Pickford (1951, p. 90). He points to the danger in dividing blue–yellow deficiencies in subgroups (tritanopia and tetrartanopia) as has sometimes been done. It causes the whole classification to be linked up with an implicit conviction about a three-colour theory. As a matter of fact, all cases of blue–yellow deficiencies are "minor defects". They show no sex-linked hereditary influences.

The largest group of colour defective people consists of *anomalous trichromats*. Anomaly refers to minor peculiarity in perceiving red and green. The anomalous are generally unaware of their defect even though they are willing to accept quite exceptional colour mixtures. Paradoxically, being unaware of their deficiency, they are even more handicapped by their defect than the definitely chromatically defective (red or green blind) people.

Before closing this section let us have a look at the classification scheme of chromatic vision deficiencies presented by Pickford (1951, pp. 27–28 see also v. Fieandt, 1966, p. 109).

Classification scheme of chromatic vision deficiencies
(Pickford)

I. *Total colour blindness* occurs very rarely and is clearly inherited but not sex-linked. According to the old duplicity theory it is due to defective functioning of the cones.

II. *Acquired total colour blindness* may be caused by a variety of factors such as poisoning, accident, and even hysteric conditions.

III. *Night blindness* or *twilight blindness* (hemeralopia) is a deficiency in dark adaptation but does not involve impaired daylight vision.

IV. *Red–green deficiency* is inherited; it is sex-linked and recessive in females but dominant in males, occurring in about 8 per cent of them. There are three subcategories:
   1. *Red blindness* or *protanopia*
   2. *Green blindness* or *deuteranopia*
   3. *Green anomaly*

V. *Non-inherited red–green deficiencies* occur in two groups:
   1. *Red–green deviation*, with a colour spectrum in which either the red or the green region, or both, have a restricted range.
   2. *Red–green weakness*, in which the differential threshold for red and green radiations is double that of the normal eye.

VI. *Blue–yellow deficiency*, which is neither sex-linked nor inherited.

As a basis for these categories he has chosen the range of dispersion outside the distribution proper. He had already shown that red–green vision in an unselected sample yields a normal distribution. As for red–green blindness, cases scattered within the limits of one standard deviation from the modal score of the normal distribution Pickford called *normal*, those ranging within the limits of one to two standard deviations he called *deviant*, and those within the limits of two to three standard deviations he regarded as *colour weak*. The last two categories overlap considerably in the case of blue–yellow deficiency, because of the greater number of deviants within this aspect of capacity for colour vision. Cases of actual colour vision anomalies and of colour blindness clearly fall beyond the limits of these six standard deviations.

The frequency distributions published by Pickford on the basis of his experiments with more than 1,000 normal and deficient individuals clearly show that protanopes are distributed as an extremely small group, far beyond the limits of the normal distribution. Closest to them fall the deuteranopes, who are located far out in the tails of the normal distribution. The green anomalous are close to the deuteranopes but are scattered widely throughout the tails of the continuous distribution. The colour weaks and deviants fall clearly within the range of the normal distribution.

While Pickford's contribution may be criticized, there is no question about the usefulness of his treating colour differences dimensionally, of showing the continuity of their variation in consistently applied differential tests, and of pointing out typical characteristics of those cases which fall outside the scope of biologically normal variation.

Some Recent Advances in Colour Research

Investigating Higher Levels of the Visual System

According to the most fundamental assumptions in classical psychophysics there should exist "underlying" patterns of function in the brain corresponding to the contents of "red" and "green" experiences respectively. The research so far remains short of strict evidence in support of this hypothesis. Measurement of spectral sensitivity curves carried out "on the sensation level" does not answer the question as to whether these curves represent only outputs from single retinal units, or whether they result from complex interaction procedures. As will be shown more precisely during some subsequent chapters, investigators still argue about the ways chromatic information gets encoded. There is much evidence in favour of the *pattern theory* (see Melzack and Wall 1962), which points out the *mode of activation* of the units in the brain. As pointed out before (chapter 3 p. 55) the *place theory* too, according to which the location and number of units is decisive, has its strong advocates. The enormous advances in the technique of electrophysiology might allow us to explore the tuning characteristics of visual brain cells, applying the hitherto successful method of micro-electrode-registering directly from brain areas.

Single Unit Recording

The foremost achievement of the microelectrode procedure has been the recording of single-cell potentials. During his early studies Granit (1947) developed a technique for recording impulses from single ganglion cells in the retina. This led him to classify the functioning retinal units as either modulators or dominators, as mentioned earlier in connection with his theory.

As pointed out already, McNichol and together with him Wagner and Wolbarsht (1963), have further elaborated this supreme investigation technique. Their results led to the well-known descriptions of *receptive fields*. The "on" and "off" centres of respective ganglion cells have been explored and registered (see chapter 4 pp. 83–85). As we know, this antagonism of the centre and the margin areas becomes especially evident with coloured stimuli. The same microelectrode can be applied to pick up both electroretinograms of specific retinal areas and corresponding single spike potentials. It has been showed that these two responses have similar spectral sensitivities.

There are some species of primates which show almost human trichromatic sensitivity. DeValois in particular, together with his co-workers, (1965a, b, 1966, 1972) has collected an immense amount of data from single unit recordings in macaque monkeys, relevant to their psychophysically explored colour reactions. In the geniculate bodies of this animal both so-called *broad band cells* and *spectral opponent cells* were identified. The broad band cells are believed to mediate brightness vision. They show either an increase or a decrease in frequency as a consequence of stimulating light of all wavelengths. Opponent cells show excitation at some wavelengths and inhibition at others. In general they respond less to changes in luminance as to changes in wavelength (De Valois, *et al.* 1966).

When single units fire in the geniculate bodies, it is due to the combined action of several stimulus parameters. The same unit may react strongly to changes in wavelength, luminance and the dimensions of the stimulus field. Also in the receptive areas of these cells, the centre and the surround are often opposite in their response characteristics.

The results available so far evidently show that even at higher levels of the visual system the information—accountable as it is in terms of a trichromatic model when explored at the peripheral receptor stage—preserves its characteristic traits of opponent colour functional arrangements.

The Land-Phenomenon. Some Future Prospects

Let us now return to the starting point of all colour theory development, the Newtonian doctrine of "pure" chromatic stimuli, representing different points along the spectrum, and of the colour mixtures brought about by their additive combination. In Maxwell's colour photography experiment (see p. 192) the essential point was that he exposed three black–white negatives through *red*, *green* and *blue* filters and thus found the least number of cues sufficient to activate the retinal receptors which mediate chromatic messages. But Maxwell's explanation of the phenomena still involved the assumption of *specialized receptors stimulated by the chromaticity of the filters and the additive combination of their information.*

In 1955 Land, the inventor of the Polaroid Land self-developing camera, began to repeat Maxwell's experiments with the purpose of developing a camera capable of reproducing colour by means of black and white negatives combined with appropriate filters. Working with three parallel projectors, he once happened to turn off the blue-filtered projector and remove the green filter from one of the other two. He was astonished to find that, although the picture projected consisted only of red and of white radiation (the latter containing a maximum of different wavelengths), both projected through two different black- and-white negatives, the result was a coloured picture beautifully and realistically reproducing all the original hues.

Thus only one "primary chromatic stimulus", red, was needed in addition to white light in order to produce all the hues occurring in the environment (see Plate VIII). Land first thought that what he was seeing was an illusion due to eye fatigue, but repetitions of the experiment yielded the same result. Since then he has continued his experiments, varying them in several ways, and has presented quite convincing explanations of the data in a number of articles (Land, 1959a, b).

It seems that two negatives are sufficient, if they are taken through filters representing parts of the spectrum sufficiently far from each other. The filters do not have to represent the Young–Helmholtz primaries; wavelengths as close together as 579 nm and 599 nm are sufficient. *In projecting the resulting diapositives, the chromatic filter can be removed from one of the projectors.* Land himself almost always removes the filter with the shorter wavelength, greenish in colour. These experiments suggest that the colour theory based on Newtonian physics need not assume *specific receptors corresponding to particular wavelengths.* The stimulus cues which activate perception of a given hue are not the wavelength of the radiation, but rather the *gradients* existing among the light-reflecting surfaces. It is evident that the primary colours of Maxwell and Helmholtz just happened to represent sufficiently distant areas of the spectrum to divide the reflecting surfaces of the environment into two categories in the way described by Land. Instead of assuming that each colour of the spectrum occurs as a stimulus, either singly or combined into a mixed colour, a sufficient stimulus cue is the division of the environment into two kinds of surfaces, those reflecting "long waves" and those reflecting "short waves".

The basis of the system of information transmission, whereby two black and white pictures taken through different chromatic filters can convey a polychromatic picture, is formed by the *brightness gradients* associated with each hue. Gelb's pioneering work demonstrating the importance of the *intensity gradients* of visual object surfaces has already been mentioned (p. 181). Land's findings seem to show that the visual receptors need only enough chromaticity to make the maxima of intensity distribution of various surfaces stand out, and thus provide a *frame of reference.* The rich variety of colours we normally perceive is determined by the relative *amounts of light* reflected by different surfaces, information about which is abundantly conveyed by a black-and-white photograph.

Actually, it is astonishing that the stimulus pattern provided by intensity gradients has not earlier been taken into account in trying to explain our experiences of the hue of reflecting surfaces. This is all the more remarkable since it would seem, on the basis of what has been said above (p. 170), that our receptors are considerably more sensitive to variations in intensity than to shifts in the spectral composition of light.

It seems clear that the views set forth by Land have a bearing on the psychology of colour perception. If the brightness gradient were without significance, why should three *different* black-and-white diapositives be necessary in Maxwell's experiments? If wavelength were the only stimulus to hue, one would have expected three identical transparencies, super-imposed through different primary filters, to provide an equally good picture.

Land's theories have already aroused criticism in psychological literature. The scientific validity of his experimental setups has especially been faulted. Walls (1960) points out that there is insufficient information about the monochromaticity of the *filters* and of the spectral composition of the pro-jection lamp. The "white" light which is always one of the two used, might contain precisely the yellow components needed to produce dichromatic effects when combined with the red from the other projector. He also points out that Land has never been able to achieve a natural blue colour. Although Walls has not repeated the experiments which he is criticizing, he does not deny the perceptual phenomena in question; rather, he tries to explain them in terms of the *induced* or *contrast* colours produced by a strongly illuminated area on all adjacent areas. The review justifiably compares the phenomena described by Land with the *chromatic shadow* described by Goethe, which has never been sufficiently studied.

Already in 1940 Judd had pointed out that figures looked at in red and in normal "white" light varied in hue depending on the illumination of the background. There was considerable variation in the responses of the subjects, which Judd ascribed to adaptation level and possibly to memory colour.

Wheeler (1963) studied how the colour responses to complex and simple figures differ from each other when they are illuminated in the same way as in Land's experiments. A complex square was formed of 100 small squares, representing altogether ten shades of grey, each shade represented in turn by ten small squares. The small squares were arranged in such a way that the same shade of grey occurred in each row of the large square only once. There were two of the large squares, both exactly the same in composition; one was illuminated with "white" light, the other with red. The task of the subjects was to identify the hue of each small square in terms of the corresponding Munsell colour hue.

As simple figures, each of the small squares of the preceding experiment was used singly. All possible pairs were formed in such a way that one square was illuminated with white, the other with red light. In the stimuli was squares of each pair were superimposed in projection, and the background of the figures was illuminated at various stages of the experiment with red, pink, "black" and "white" light. Again the task of the subjects was to find the corresponding Munsell colour.

Using the complex figure, it was possible, according to Wheeler, to produce all the hues which Land was able to produce in his own experiments. With the simple figures, the hues varied much less, except when the background was illuminated with a pink light. An important point is that Wheeler's large figures, in which there was wide variation in hue, were synthetic "mosaics" rather than photographs of real objects like those of Land.

Wheeler's experiments do not offer sufficient ammunition for an attack on the theories advanced by Land, according to which intensity gradients play a crucial role in the perception of surface colours. Wheeler's colour figures are artifacts of the laboratory, and they do not provide a basis for drawing conclusions as to the way in which we experience radiation reflected from adjacent object surfaces. (See also Wheeler 1965, 1967.)

Tone (in Akishige 1967) studied Land's phenomenon in two experiments. The variables studied were (1) the effect of the projection background on experienced hues, and (2) the effect of the chromatic saturation of the projection light on chromatic shadow. It turned out that when projection background was divided into more than two components differing in intensity of reflection, the hues appeared most richly differentiated in chromatic illumination. The saturation of the chromatic shadow was the greater the less white light was contained in the chromatic (e.g. red) light source. According to Marriott (Davson 1962), the Land phenomenon is based on the simultaneous effect of the colour invariance tendency and simultaneous contrast. There is a tendency, when the entire visual field appears in chromatic illumination, to "disregard" that common hue and to "correct" the object colours so as to correspond to their normal constant hue.

Even if sound criticism should show that the significance of Land's observations has been exaggerated, the fact remains that he has been able to achieve a polychromaticity formerly assumed to require a mixture of three primaries, by means of *achromatic* diapositives representing almost any two parts of the spectrum, and using only one filtered projector. Thus the part played by intensity gradients in our colour perception and the way in which it is tied to the object world has been clearly demonstrated. The boundary between the filters representing different ends of the spectrum must be placed, on the basis of research up to the present, at 588 nm.

7 | Sound

The auditory modality involves the study of variables in three major disciplines: acoustics, auditory physiology and psychology. Since the structure and function of the auditory receptors were described in chapter 5, the physiological characteristics of the modality will not be touched upon here. On the other hand, a survey of the elements of acoustics is necessary for an understanding of auditory stimuli and their effects.

Sound Stimuli

The *adequate auditory stimulus* is an oscillation in the pressure, particle displacement or particle velocity of an "elastic" medium, such as air or water. A solid substance may also mediate sound stimuli: an example is the case of bone conduction directly to the inner ear. The instantaneous acoustic pressure alternates rhythmically, corresponding respectively to the portions of compression and rarefaction in the sound wave. The individual air molecules never move very far to and fro, yet the changes in air pressure produced by them are transmitted rapidly through the medium. In dry air at 0° C, the velocity of the wave is approximately 330 m/s (1100 ft/s).

A simple type of vibration, shown for example by a vibrating tuning fork, is called *simple sine wave motion*. By means of a moving-picture camera the motion of a tuning fork prong could be photographed: a graph as shown in Fig. 7.1 would be obtained. This graph portrays what can be described mathematically as a sine function. After having performed one oscillation to and fro on both sides of its starting position, the vibrating object returns to that original position. By this time it has finished one complete *cycle* of motion. The *frequency* of vibration is defined as the number of such cycles of vibration per second. (The abbreviation cps is often used for cycles per second; the German-oriented European scholarship uses the abbreviation Hz, which stands for Hertz's unit—a symbol recently adopted in the scientific language of the United States as well.)

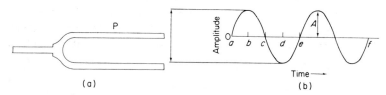

Fig. 7.1 Sinusoid graph produced by a pure tone. (From Kling and Riggs, 1971 p. 224.)

Regardless of the physical complexity of the sound, there are two basic ways of describing an acoustic wave and specifying its dimensions in quantitative terms: *waveform* and *spectrum*. The use of each is facilitated by laboratory techniques which make it possible to convert acoustic signals into electrical ones and vice versa.

The characteristics of the waveform are *frequency* and *amplitude*. A pure or sine wave tone (see Fig. 7.1) can be described in addition to these two

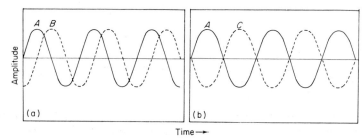

Fig. 7.2 Diagrams of two sine waves which are "out of phase." (From Kling and Riggs, 1971 p. 224.)

parameters, by determining the *phase* of the corresponding wave form. The two sine waves *A* and *B* in Fig. 7.2 are said to be out of phase. Sine wave *B* starts upward from the baseline a quarter of a cycle later than wave *A*. It is said to lag by one quarter cycle.

Simple sine-wave stimuli used in the laboratory are typically produced as electrical sine-wave stimuli by an instrument known as an oscillator. The maximum value that the instantaneous oscillation-amplitude attains (visible on the screen of the oscilloscope) is called the peak amplitude. The maximum amplitude of the wave is given by this maximum displacement of the function.

The variety of waveforms observed on the oscilloscope depends on the particular source of the sound and its duration. Clicks or pulses which have short duration do not attain a steady state; sounds of longer duration do attain a steady state. It may be repetitive or non-repetitive in waveform.

Most of the sound waves which reach our ears under normal circumstances are *aperiodic sounds* or *noises*. Their wave-structure is generally highly complex and involved, since it consists of a number of tones representing different wavelengths.

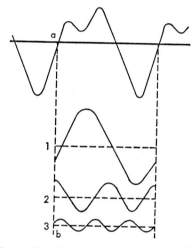

Fig. 7.3 A compound sound and its components isolated by means of Fourier analysis. (From v. Fieandt, 1966 p. 116.)

Periodic sounds are particularly common in music. Sounds which are composed of both periodic and aperiodic oscillations are called *soles*. These occur particularly in human speech. Certain combinations of tones are called *chords*.

In 1882 Fourier invented a method by means of which any soundwave whatsoever can be broken down into simpler, sine-shaped curves, which represent pure tone. This procedure, called Fourier analysis, thus makes it possible to describe the combined sound wave in terms of the amplitudes and phase-differences of the components.

Figure 7.3 gives an example of such an operation. Nowadays, if the waveform is repetitive as in the case of musical tones, the analysis may be performed mechanically, mathematically or electronically by means of harmonic wave analysers. With nonrepetitive continuous sounds application of electronic noise analysers is necessary (see also chapter 4 p. 77).

When a repetitive waveform has been analysed, the results will be represented in the form of a line spectrum. "The components are discretely located on the horizontal axis at appropriate frequencies and their relative amplitudes are shown on the ordinate, with phase angle as the

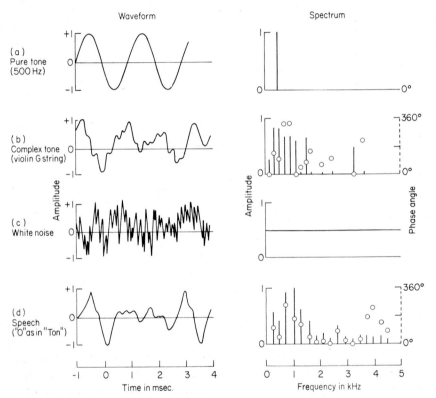

Fig. 7.4 Some acoustic stimuli represented by waveform and spectrum. (From Wolman, 1973 p. 350.)

parameter." (Corso in Wolman 1973, p. 349.) The spectrum with its three dimensions (frequency, amplitude and phase) completely describes a sound wave, as does the waveform with its two dimensions. In most cases, however, one or the other of these modes of description is more convenient and better suited to a given purpose. Figure 7.4 shows a series of representations of some typical acoustic stimuli by waveform and spectrum.

Composition of Musical and other Complex Sounds

Summation and Reciprocal Reinforcement of Oscillations

A typical spectrum of the first 10 frequency components in a violin tone is shown in Fig. 7.5. For this complex musical stimulus the *fundamental* or

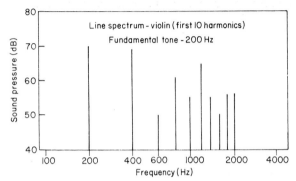

Fig. 7.5 The first 10 frequency components in a violin tone. (From Kling and Riggs, 1971 p. 226.)

lowest tone is 200 Hz, but there are additional frequencies called *harmonics*, which are multiples of the fundamental (400, 600, 800 and so on). The terminological complexity is increased by the use of the term *partial* tone; the fundamental is then called the first partial, the first harmonic is equivalent to the second partial, etc. as summarized in the following table:

> First partial = the fundamental
> Second partial = first harmonic
> Third partial = second harmonic
> Fourth partial = third harmonic

The sounds made by musical instruments, for example by a vibrating piano string, have simple integral ratios between the frequencies of the partials, such as 1 : 2 : 3 : 4, etc. Such sounds are called by their fundamental tone or first partial, which is the one most easily distinguished by the human ear.

Not all complex sounds have their frequency components arranged as simple multiples of a fundamental. As stated above, noises usually consist of quite a number of tones at different frequencies. In general two kinds of noise are often used in psychoacoustic experiments: random noise and white noise. *Random* (Gaussian) *noise* is a particular kind of noise in which the distribution of amplitudes of the wave-form as a function of time follows the normal (Gaussian) probability distribution. *White noise* (or "thermal noise") can be thought of as being composed of an infinite number of different frequencies of the same amplitude with no systematic relation between the phases of the components. White noise is often produced for laboratory purposes in restricted frequency regions. A noise with frequencies below 1 000 Hz only is called "low-pass" noise. A 1 000–2 000 bandpass noise, on the other hand, has frequencies in the band of 1 000–2 000 Hz only. White noises are often used in the laboratory as masking stimuli (see pp. 232–233). White noise sounds like a rush of steam released under pressure.

Units of Measurement

Of the various acoustical parameters we have already mentioned frequency (cps). The *intensity* of an auditory stimulus can be expressed in terms of either pressure, particle displacement or particle velocity. By convention, the measure of intensity mostly resorted to is pressure, the unit of which is dynes pr cm². Figure 7.6 shows the minimum audible pressure necessary

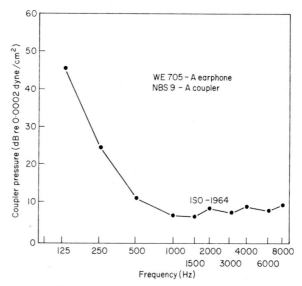

Fig. 7.6 Minimum audible pressure for absolute threshold of hearing as a function of stimulus frequency. (From Kling and Riggs, 1971 p. 233.)

for threshold at frequencies from 125 to 8 000 Hz. Our auditory system is extremely sensitive. In the most sensitive region, the displacement of the eardrum at threshold is less than the diameter of a hydrogen molecule. In terms of energy the weakest sound which can be distinguished by the human ear is about one billionth of the erg per second (1 erg = the work necessary to move 1 mg a distance of 1 cm). The energy needed to transmit vibration through a medium varies directly with the square of the pressure. Most units of pressure are in fact calculated as squares of the corresponding units of energy. Under given circumstances energy is proportional to the square of pressure.

Threshold values for sonic frequencies have been standardized by the International Organization for Standardization (ISO). As a matter of fact the graph shown in Fig. 7.6 represents the present zero reference level recommended by the ISO for audiometers: special devices for determining hearing acuity in different individuals.

Ultrasonic Frequencies

What about the frequency limits of hearing? Some young people can hear frequencies up to about 24 000 Hz (Wever 1949, Corso 1967). The hearing of low frequencies by humans has been recorded down to a few cycles per second (Corso 1958). Could these limits of hearing be extended by bone conduction? If the transducer is pressed firmly against the mastoid bone of the skull (Chapter 5 p. 115), the upper limit of hearing can be extended considerably. Corso (1963) found an upper threshold value of 100 000 Hz. Some animals like the bat and the common seal make use of ultrasones at high frequencies (up to 180 000 Hz). With deaf children sensitivity to tones around 62 000 Hz has been demonstrated (Corso in Wolman 1973, p. 361).

The Decibel Scales of Sound Pressure

A more convenient way to express variations in intensity is to give sound pressure as a ratio of two sounds. The unit of measurement on this scale is the *decibel* (db); the range of human hearing covers approximately 120 dB. The number of decibels N is calculated by the formula

$$N = 10 \log \frac{E_1}{E_2} = 20 \log \frac{P_1}{P_2}$$

in which E_1 and E_2 represent energies and P_1 and P_2 are corresponding pressures.

The decibel thus always expresses a *ratio between two intensities*. If a db value is used to express a single intensity, the denominator of the ratio must be explicitly stated. This pressure reference level is usually the absolute threshold at a given frequency. The perceptual threshold for a sound of 1 000 Hz, in units of energy, is about 0·0002 dynes/cm^2: this value is generally used as a standardized point of reference in comparing intensities.

Figure 7.7 shows the intensity in db of some familiar sounds compared to the standard reference intensity.

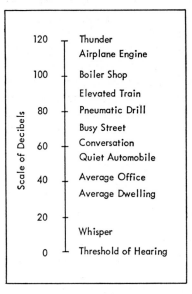

Fig. 7.7   Relative intensities of some sounds. (From v. Fieandt, 1966 p. 117.)

Some Units of Loudness

As an auditory dimension, *loudness* is measured on a psychological scale. Units used for the measurement are the *phon* and the *sone*, of which the latter derived by Stevens properly measures *phenomenal loudness* or *sonority*. The *phon* corresponds to the loudness threshold, and the point of reference is a sound of 1 000 Hz. Stevens defined one sone as the loudness of a 1 000 Hz tone of 40 phons. If we want to measure the phon-value of a sound, the procedure is to vary the intensity of a 1 000 Hz sound until it sounds equal in loudness to the sound we are interested in. The db-value of the sound obtained by this matching procedure is equivalent to the phon value of the unknown sound. One disadvantage of the phon-scale is that it does not accurately convey loudness relations between two phon-levels, except for just distinguishing between "stronger" and "weaker" loudness. How sones are measured, and what they signify, will be discussed later.

Signal Detection and Discrimination

In our discussion of threshold measurements so far, we have used the concepts and procedures of classical psychophysics. The development of signal detection theory has naturally meant a clear break with the earlier ways of thinking, and it has necessitated a relativistic interpretation of perceptual thresholds in the area of auditory perception also. The concept of a more or less fixed and precisely determinable threshold is replaced here, as in other applications of signal detection theory, by a probability of occurrence of the signal. This theory, in fact, is at present one of the most significant explanations of the basic phenomena of sound perception. Some kind of selective filtering of sounds apparently goes on in the auditory system. On the basis of physiological discoveries the occurrence of such a process seems highly probable. Signal detection within the frame of this system is, according to Licklider, based on a system of filters both at the purely sensory level and at higher levels of perception (Koch, 1959, I, p. 131).

What distinguishes signal detection theory experimentally is that the observer is usually required to detect the presence of a sinusoidal signal in a background of noise. Signal detection theories therefore typically involve noise. There are studies around this theory which have certainly advanced our understanding of auditory processes.

Detectability functions for signals of different *durations* and *intensities* have been determined from judgmental data of equal loudness. The form of the intensity duration function for constant loudness could be shown to agree with the intensity function for a constant level of detectability.

Corso (1973) has reported a number of studies which have uncovered a kind of "pedestal effect" in the detection of sinusoid tones in noise. When tone pulses are delivered as in-phase-additions to a continuous standard tone (pedestal) that is embedded in a steady background noise, these additions give a greater audibility than when the pulses are delivered in noise alone. Given a constant level of detectability of, for example, 75 per cent correct responses, a 1 000 Hz tone requires less intensity when presented with the pedestal than without, regardless of its duration.

Signal detectability theory has been continually revised to accomodate new experimental situations. It is now possible to predict the level of monaural detection of a pure tone in noise by solving a series of equations, to apply theory of signal detection to matching procedures and to develop rating scales (Corso in Wolman 1973, p. 363).

How does the subject's awareness of his previous results affect his level of performance? Studies by Carterette *et al.* (1966) clearly indicate that on easy discrimination tasks no knowledge of results is better than partial or complete feedback. On a difficult task, feedback after each trial secures a better performance.

Monetary motivation has very little effect on auditory detection tasks. Similarly, the effects of practice are limited to the first session.

H

Temporal Summation at Threshold

As is the case for other senses, the auditory system is capable of temporal summation. In other words, the effects of a stimulus are accumulated over short periods of time. As shown in Fig. 7.8 less energy is required for

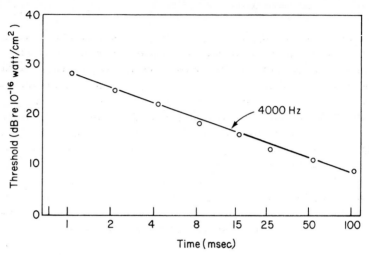

Fig. 7.8 Threshold intensity as a function of duration of the tone. (From Kling and Riggs, 1971 p. 234.)

threshold as the duration of a tonal stimulus is increased. Garner and Miller (1947) have given the equation

$$t(I - I_0) = k$$

where k is a constant, t is effective stimulus duration, I is the overall power of the signal in Watts/cm² and I_0 represents a constant minimal intensity. Any excess in intensity over I_0 will lead to proportionate neural effects. They in turn will be summed up over time by the auditory system. If the experimenter obtains detection with a stimulus intensity I_1 at duration t_1, and then doubles the stimulus duration (t_1) he needs to use only half as large a value of ($I_1 - I_0$) to obtain the same total neural effect required for threshold. This statement holds true up to a certain length of duration.

Zwislocki (1960) has derived a theory of temporal summation. The locus of this process of integration presupposed by temporal summation effects is placed by him above the level of first order neurons. The ear is considered as a power integrator showing a time constant of 200 ms.

Maximum summation effects occur only when the frequency components in the sound are not considerably separated from each other. They must be contained within a "critical band" of frequencies (see p. 233). If a tone spreads out beyond the critical band, then it is not integrated perfectly. There may thus be a *lower* limit of duration for perfect integration as well as an upper duration limit.

The "Dimensions" and "Attributes" of Sounds

As will be shown in chapter 10, the study of sound perception contributed significantly to the theory of *sensory attributes* which was so important at the end of the last century. Thus, after Titchener established the *volume* of a sound as an attribute in its own right independent of *pitch*, the way of thinking prevalent at the time made it of great importance to discover what aspects of the stimulus, if any, corresponded as specific and measurable correlates of the attributes experienced in perception. In its most extreme form this isomorphism postulated frequency as the correlate of the attribute of *pitch*, and amplitude as the correlate of *loudness*.

In chapter 10, the stand taken by the authors toward the theory of attributes and the value placed on this theory in modern psychology will be sufficiently clearly defined. For practical reasons psychologists have mostly accepted some distinctions among "attributes" for example:

1. location
2. duration (the dimension of time)
3. loudness
4. timbre
5. pitch, including
   a. brightness
   b. tonal quality
6. vocality (cf. Wellek 1934, 1935).

Following the viewpoints of Titchener and Stevens (see chapter 10) two more should be added to the list (see Fig. 10.2 p. 282):

7. volume
8. compactness or density.

Pitch The traditional concept of the specific correspondence between pitch and frequency was correct insofar as *phenomenal* pitch does depend *primarily* on frequency. Stevens and Davis (1947), however, pointed out that phenomenal pitch is a function of two physical variables: frequency and time pattern.

Each of these gives rise to a differentially conditioned experience of pitch. (1) *Place pitch* is controlled by the location of maximum excitation along the basilar membrane. It thus depends on the frequency spectrum.

(2) *Periodicity pitch* is associated with the time pattern or periodicity of the acoustic stimulus.

The existence of place pitch is more firmly established and it will be considered from several aspects in this representation. It is generally observed that low frequency tones are localized towards the apical end of the cochlea, whereas high frequency tones belong to the basal end. A simple tonotopic theory of pitch seems however to be insufficient. Because the patterning along the cochlear partition provides rather broad maxima of amplitude, it seems highly probable that sharpening occurs somewhere inside the auditory system, especially for frequencies below 500 Hz (see also chapter 3 p. 61).

There has been much argument among neurophysiologists as to the locus and nature of a postulated sharpening mechanism. According to v. Békésy (1960) the localization of response is sharpened neurologically through inhibitory processes from the neural system of the inner ear. Additionally, differences might occur among arrival times of stimulations in different sections of the basilar membrane. Carhart *et al.* (1967) developed a model of sharpening in the central nervous system, apparently at the level of the cochlea nucleus.

Place pitch clearly depends on the upper and lower limits of audible frequency. While of course vibration frequencies can in principle vary far outside these limits, the human ear generally does not react to vibration below 20 Hz or above 20 000 Hz. (For additional statements see p. 265.) The lowest frequency distinguished by human ear is said to be 16–24 Hz i.e. about C_1 (Révész 1946, v. Békésy 1960, p. 258).[1] In experiments with tuning forks an upper boundary of 22 500 Hz (around F_{13}) has been obtained, but this value varies with the nature of the source of vibration. Earlier (p. 215) we briefly touched upon the case of *ultrasonic stimuli* (e.g. 10 Hz); such vibration may sometimes activate other sensory modalities (v. Békésy 1960, pp. 257–267). These findings will be described in more detail in connection with our discussion of the skin senses.

The common association of pitch with frequency is in part due to the fact that the tonal scale of our musical system is basically a *frequency* scale. Only oscillations lying between 60 Hz and 4 000 Hz (i.e. approximately C_2 and C_8) are perceived as musical in quality. For the sake of simplicity, the symbols for tones used in this book follow the standard international usage, which was agreed upon in 1962, and which is meant to be adapted to both old European and newer American tonal scales. In Fig. 7.9, which is adapted from Marianne Mörner's excellent presentation (1963), the new

---

1. Of the many existing systems for denoting and abbreviating sounds, the one adapted here is the new international standard system: tones are denoted by capital letters, octaves by subscripts. See following paragraph and Fig. 7.9.

international symbols are shown in the bottom row, along the bottom edge of the figure. Along the upper edge are the keys of the piano with the corresponding octave divisions; below that the older European system of notation, followed by the corresponding frequency bands. The pitch levels of the human voice, including both chest tones and head tones, are shown in the middle.

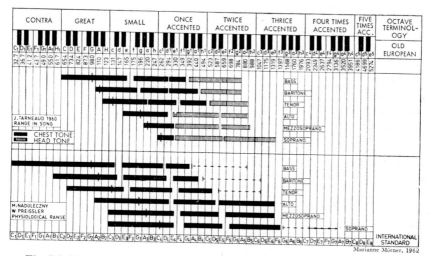

Fig. 7.9 Various registers of the singing voice. (From v. Fieandt, 1966 p. 121.)

The impetus for investigating the relationship between pitch and intensity (Stevens 1936) came from a familiar everyday experience: if a tuning fork producing an ordinary C_4 is brought closer to the ear of a listener who is trying to reproduce it accurately by singing, the resulting increase in intensity (i.e. loudness) causes him to sing lower. The closer the tuning fork is brought, the lower the pitch of the singer's voice. Thus *a louder tone is experienced as lower in pitch.* A systematic study of the phenomenon leads to the results illustrated in Fig. 7.10. The curves represent so-called *equal pitch contours*, and they indicate the effect of changes in intensity on the perceived pitch of tones of certain frequencies. *As intensity increases the pitch of tones at low frequencies (150–500 Hz) falls, while that of high tones (4 000–12 000 Hz) rises.* These studies of Stevens have been replicated by Cohen (1961). He observed only a very restricted magnitude of the shifts. The pitch of low tones is also shifted downward by masking wide band noise, and upward for high frequency tones.

Periodicity pitch is reflected, for example, in a phenomenon which appears inconsistent in terms of ordinary place theory. In several kinds of experiment a definite pitch is heard which does not correspond to any component present in Fourier analysis of the stimulus. If a sound is composed of two tones at least 100 Hz apart, the phenomenal pitch does not correspond to their averaged frequency. Instead, what is perceived, in addition to two fundamental components p and g, is a variety of new tones which can be derived fairly simply from the original frequencies (e.g. $p+g$, $p-g$, $2p-g$, $2g-p$, etc.). If, furthermore, the stimulus is a sound

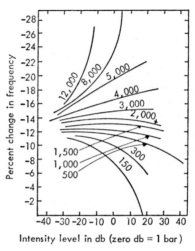

Fig. 7.10 Equal pitch contours. (From v. Fieandt, 1966 p. 122.)

composed of the three tones 400 Hz, 600 Hz, and 800 Hz, and tones at 500, 700 and 900 Hz are then added, *the pitch of the entire sound seems to fall by an octave*. This is due to the fact that the lowest difference tone was previously 200 Hz (600–400), but is now 100 Hz. A consequence of this phenomenon is that a phenomenal pitch can be maintained even when the fundamental frequency to which it corresponds is absent. If the frequency differences between the harmonics is equal to the frequency of the fundamental, the experienced pitch is not changed by eliminating the fundamental.

This type of low pitch occurs for clusters of high frequency harmonics up to about 5 000 Hz. This described "residue phenomenon" can be elicited at low signal intensities. Obviously it is not an artifact produced by possible distortions in the ear.

As for the relation between pitch and duration, let us here point out only that the accuracy with which pitch is perceived is up to some limit directly proportionate to the duration of the stimulus. For example, when a stimulus lies within a range of frequencies with a high pitch discrimination threshold, a longer duration is needed for accurate recognition of the pitch.

The revolutionary method of electronically founded single unit analysis has secured a row of quite remarkable results. Interrelations between pitch discrimination and individual reactions of neuronal units in the auditory system imply that (1) only a "time-locked" mechanism for pitch occurs below 300 Hz; (2) only a place-sensitive mechanism operates above 5 000 Hz; (3) between these limits there is an overlapping operation of the two mechanisms (Corso in Wolman 1973, p. 369).

As is the case with investigations of the visual system, the auditory connections have also been subjected to several neuropsychological models of explanation. Licklider (1959) proposed a triplex theory. The acoustic patterns are said first to undergo a mechanical frequency analysis in the cochlea (traditional place explanation). Then the first stage of correlational analysis in centres of the nervous system consist of sound localization, whereas the third stage is responsible for mediating periodicity pitch.

Other investigators, while accepting periodicity pitch, do not agree upon the explanation model of a special mechanism central to the cochlea. v. Békésy (1960) doubts that the periodicity principle alone is sufficient to determine the pitch of a sound: a band of low frequency noise gives rise to a pitch corresponding to upper and lower edges of that band, even if no specific periodicity accounts for these pitches.

In 1937 Stevens and his collaborators established a quantitative scale for place pitch. They related pitch to pure-tone frequency. The unit of this scale is the *mel*; by definition a pitch of 1 000 mels is equivalent to one of 1 000 Hz at 40 db above the threshold. For example, a tone of 2 000 mels sounds half as high as one of 4 000 mels, but twice as high as one of 1 000 mels. This scale was thus developed by a process of subdivision into fractions from a standardized pitch. Siegel (1965) was able to confirm this relation for frequencies below 5 000 Hz (see Stevens and Davis, 1947).

According to Shephard (1964) the pitch of complex tones can be said to possess two attributes: (1) *tone height*, a monotonic function of frequency and measured in mels; (2) *tonality*, which is cyclical with a period of little more than a physical octave.

Loudness With certain reservations, the traditional concept of loudness can also be said to be correct. Perceived loudness does depend to a great extent on the intensity of the stimulus, but a complex variety of other stimuli also contribute to it. As Stevens and Davis (1947, p. 25) also observe in this connection, loudness is not identical with perceived intensity, nor is the decibel a unit of phenomenal loudness.

Systematic investigation has in fact shown that loudness varies considerably with the frequency of the stimulus. For the purposes of measurement a psychological scale derived by Stevens is adopted. A unit called the *sone* has been developed, similar to the mel in measuring pitch. A tone has a loudness of 1 sone if its loudness is equal to that of a tone of 1 000 Hz heard binaurally at an intensity of 40 db above the absolute threshold. By means of this phenomenal unit, it has been possible to construct graphs of the function of loudness (Fig 7.11). The graphs give the loudness in sones

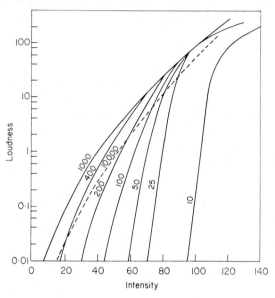

Fig. 7.11 The loudness of tones of various intensities and various frequencies. (From v. Fieandt, 1972 p. 168.)

of tones of various frequencies as a function of intensity (in db values above the absolute threshold). Tones of low frequency must be presented at intensities many times greater than high frequency tones in order to be heard as equally loud. For example, a tone of 25 Hz at 80 db is heard as equally loud as a tone of 1 000 Hz at 40 db. If we consider the shape of the auditory area (see Fig. 7.12), this relation is quite reasonable. Figure 7.11 also indicates that loudness rises more steeply with increasing intensity for low rather than for middle frequency tones. Within the optimal frequency zone of 1 000–4 000 Hz, even low intensities (0–15 db) yield maximal loudness.

In his studies concerned with Weber's law, Stevens (1956) became interested in the accuracy with which a subject can distinguish and label loudness differences on the basis of direct estimation of sensory loudness. It turned out, for example, that the subjects were surprisingly easily able to subdivide the loudness of a 1 000 Hz tone into the required "loudness fractions", using the halving method. According to Stevens' law the loudness of a 1 000 Hz tone increases as a power function of sound pressure. Loudness can thus be calculated by means of the formula

$$L = k(p - p_0)^{0.6},$$

where L is loudness, p is sound pressure, k is a constant that depends upon units, and p_0 is the threshold value.

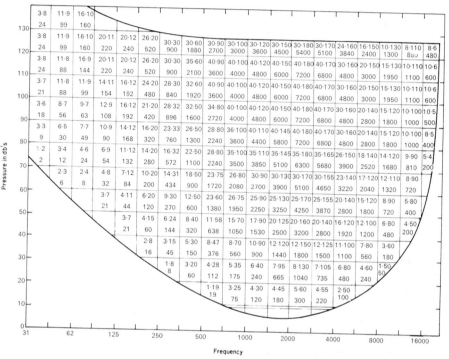

Fig. 7.12 Numbers of tones within the auditory area. (From v. Fieandt, 1972 p. 169.) Limits of the area determined by auditory thresholds (bottom) and thresholds for touch (top).

Cross-modality matches have also been made between loudness and ten other perceptual continua (Stevens 1966a). The data indicate that the loudness exponent in the power function considered lies around 0·64.

The human ear can distinguish among about 1 500 different *pitches*. The differential threshold for *loudness* allows for about 325 separately perceived levels within the region of greatest sensitivity (about 1 000–4 000 Hz). If we multiply the number of discriminable pitches by the corresponding number of discriminable loudness in different regions of the auditory area, we obtain a total of about 340 000; the number of discriminably different tones. It is interesting to note that, if we calculate all the discriminable *colour* shades by multiplying discriminable degree of brightness, saturation and hue, we come up with a figure of roughly the same order of magnitude. In Fig. 7.12 the auditory area is divided up into rectangles for the purposes of this calculation. The first number in each rectangle gives the differential threshold for intensity (in db's calculated from a standard intensity), the second figure gives the differential threshold for frequency (in Hz), the third is the result of multiplication between them.

The fact that loudness is a function of frequency in addition to intensity has rendered it possible to derive *equal loudness contours* or *isophonic contours*. A sample of such curves (Robinson and Dadson 1956) is shown in Fig. 7.13. These contours typically show sound pressure level plotted as a

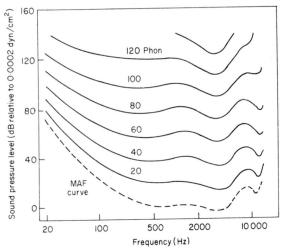

Fig. 7.13 Equal-loudness contours. (From Kling and Riggs, 1971 p. 246.)

function of frequency. The loudness level is indicated in phons. The contours are somewhat asymmetrical. For equal increments in intensity low frequency tones increase in loudness more than high frequency tones, in the region of 20 to 500 Hz.

According to Corso and Levine (1965) isophonic contours for bone-conducted sounds are similar in form to contours for air conduction, however, higher frequencies might be transmitted.

Loudness is also a function of stimulus duration. From 50 to 500 ms the loudness of a 1 000 Hz tone increases as a logarithmic function of duration.

Additionally, loudness reflects the contribution of two other attributes: volume and density. As for threshold functions and psychophysical determination of these variables see pp. 228-229.

Timbre is that auditory attribute in terms of which a listener can judge that two sounds are dissimilar even though they have the same pitch and loudness. Earlier investigators assumed that the specific timbre of an instrument reflects the combination of a fundamental in a sound with one or several of its harmonics (e.g. Révész 1946). Very few instruments are able to produce all the possible harmonics. The shape of the oscillation curve characteristic of each instrument was said to depend on the number and intensity of the partials; this was given as the basis of the characteristically different phenomenal tones or timbres.

v. Helmholtz summed up his account of the physical correlates of various timbres as follows:

Composition of stimulus	Timbre
Fundamental alone	Soft
Fundamental + first harmonic	Mellow
Fundamental + several harmonics	Broad
Fundamental + high harmonics	Sharp
Fundamental dominating	Full
Harmonics dominating	Hollow
Odd partials dominating	Nasal
Discordant partial dominating	Rough
High discordant partials dominating	Screeching

An alternative theory to the classical one is called *formant theory* of musical quality. According to this explanation the characteristic sound of an instrument is due to strengthening of deliberate partials, provided they lie within a relatively fixed region of the musical scale. The term for this region is a *formant* of the said tone. One tone may have a lot of formants. The partials nearest this region are strengthened in intensity. The frequencies in the formant region do not need to be harmonically related to the fundamental of the tone.

Timbre, however, is determined not only by the partials represented in the sound, but also by aperiodic noises and by periodic variations in intensity.

In some investigations from the early sixties (e.g. Jenkins 1961, v. Békésy 1960) attention is paid to the resonant characteristics of the cochlea structure. It is suggested that the total acoustic stimulus undergoes a kind of differential filtering along the cochlea partition.

When broad areas of the basilar membrane are stimulated, there may occur, according to v. Békésy, interactions between the neural connections mediating high and low frequencies. All of his subjects, for example, reported that if a 50 Hz tone was increased in intensity, its timbre also changed. This also happens with absolute pure tones. It is also assumed that the asymmetrical structure of the ear and its nonlinearity as a conducting system plays a certain part in the phenomenon (v. Békésy 1960, pp. 218–219).

In acoustic and musical theory we also encounter the concept of *harmonic undertones*, analogous to the overtones considered here. The frequency ratios of undertones are $\frac{1}{2}$, $\frac{1}{3}$, $\frac{1}{4}$, etc. They are, however, of theoretical interest only, and are not considered, for example, in musical practice.

Volume and density are the most controversial attributes of sound perception. Some psychologists have even tried to deny the independence

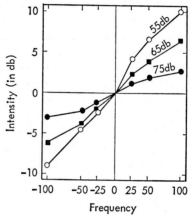

Fig. 7.14 Equal volume contours as functions of intensity and frequency. (From v. Fieandt, 1966 p. 127.) The parameters show intensities (in db) of comparison tones.

of volume as a separate attribute. The meaning of the concept of volume, the "space-filling" quality of a sound, becomes clear if we compare the tone of an organ and a flute, musically equivalent in other respects (pitch, loudness, etc.). The tone of the organ seems "larger", "broader", "richer" than that of the flute. As the dimension of the stimulus corresponding to phenomenal volume, research workers already in the 1930's postulated the *volume* or *size* of the resonating system (e.g. Heinitz 1931). Some researchers have concluded that the threshold values for volume are not independent of those for pitch and loudness. But the findings remain controversial. Stevens was able to determine "equal volume contours", using a method analogous to that for finding equal pitch and equal loudness contours. The subjects were presented alternately with two different tones, and they were to adjust the second of these until it matched the first in volume. *Two tones might have equal phenomenal volume even if they differed in both pitch and loudness.* The resulting curves were similar to those in Fig. 7.14, and they indicate that, when volume is held constant, frequency increases with an increase in intensity. In other words, frequency is inversely proportional to volume, intensity being constant.

We must, however, stress the uncertainty of our knowledge; the contours have been established only for a very restricted frequency and intensity area. Furthermore, no unit of phenomenal volume has been established after the manner of the units for pitch and loudness. The systematic errors involved in the experiments are also of a high order of magnitude.

The concept of *density* is subject to some of the same reservations. Some sounds are heard as "harder" or "more compact" than others. Stevens also extended his methods to this dimension of experience. In order to define the concept of density to the subjects, they were presented with tones of 200 and of 4 000 Hz respectively, for comparison. The higher tones sounded more compact. The results of Stevens' experiments showed that density can in a sense be considered a separate phenomenal dimension or attribute.

Beats When two tones differing slightly in frequency are heard simultaneously, the waves are summated. As a result, they sometimes strengthen and sometimes weaken each other, depending on their differences in phase (see Fig. 7.15). This phenomenon is called *beat*. For example, when we press down two adjacent keys of the piano and listen to the gradual fading off of the compound sound, we can usually hear a periodically alternating intensification and weakening of the sound.

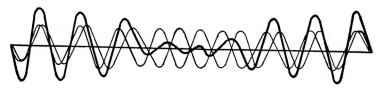

Fig. 7.15 The production of beats. (From v. Fieandt, 1966 p. 128.)

Our ear is not a perfect frequency analyser. Instead, our perception of beats is related to fluctuations in the amplitude of the waveform. These in turn are produced by two frequencies simultaneously stimulating the same physical system. If our ear were a perfect analyser, and if each frequency really—in accordance with the "place theory"—were isolated at a separate place in the ear, beats would not occur.

In investigating this phenomenon, stimuli are used in which two tones, originally identical in frequency, are made to differ more and more. Phenomenally the following stages can then be distinguished:

1. loudness increases and decreases periodically
2. the beat is perceived as a series of intermittent pulses
3. a continuous harsh sound is heard.

For the first stage, determination of the threshold actually depends on the patience of the subject. During this stage, the beats occur once every two minutes or more. The lower threshold for the second stage is 6 to 7 alternations per second.

Thus the rate of the beat has a crucial effect on the perceptual experience which results. A minor and slow beat does not disturb the listener noticeably, but faster beats are apt to cause an unpleasant and irritating wavering effect, comparable to the disturbing flickering of a movie when the projector is slowed down. If the rate of the beat is accelerated more, successive phases are no longer discriminated; instead, a continuous harsh noise is perceived.

Combination tones As stated above, the phenomenon of beat is thought to be due not to the fact that the receptors as single units independently act as originators of auditory impulses, but that the basilar membrane as a totality functions like a tuned "sound analyser". The distorting effect of single tones caused by the asymmetry of the entire outer ear may lead to *amplitude* and *frequency displacements* (see p. 210). Fusions of two such simultaneously displaced tones are called *combination tones*, and they may be either *difference* or *summation tones*. Combination tones are due to *displacement of amplitude or frequency*, whereas beat is a result of periodic *alternations in intensity*.

How can the loudness of a combination tone present be measured? (1) When measuring *audible* distortion an additional frequency is introduced, which equals that of the distortion frequency to be measured. The sound pressure and phase of the tone of this additional frequency are adjusted until the pitch corresponding to the distortion frequency vanishes (Goldstein 1967). (2) Another method is to increase the intensities of the two primary frequencies. A critical threshold appears at the intensity level which permits the distortion frequency (produced by the two primary frequencies) to be just detected by the observer.

Von Békésy (1960) showed by a series of experiments that difference tones could be produced by nonlinearity in the middle ear. Harmonics on the other hand were shown not to arise from middle-ear distortion. Tonndorf (1958) was able to show that audible harmonics occur at sound levels at which eddies appear in the fluid of an inner ear model constructed by him.

The number of combination tones formed in the inner ear is truly astonishing. When the cochlea of a cat was stimulated by tones of 700 and 1 200 Hz, at an intensity of 90 db above the absolute threshold, no fewer than 66 combination tones could be detected by microphone (Stevens and Davis 1947, p. 162). This gives some idea of the rich articulation undergone by the spectrum of any tonal stimulus on its way to the receptors of the inner ear. It is hardly possible to imagine the richness and articulation of the sound spectrum produced by the tonal configurations emitted by a symphony orchestra, already in themselves composed of a rich variety of frequency components.

Modulation and vibration The phenomenon of *vibrato*, which is a special case of modulation, has already been mentioned in connection with the discussion of beat. *Modulation* can be defined as the *intentional variation of the amplitude, frequency or phase of a sound*. Figure 7.16 illustrates how

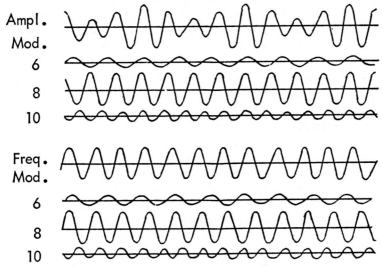

Fig. 7.16 The role of the same components in amplitude—and in frequency modulation. (From v. Fieandt, 1966 p. 130.)

either amplitude or frequency modulation can be achieved, depending on the phase relations of three superimposed tonal components. This method is of considerable importance in sound spectrum analysis, in which the tonal components of complex noises, tones and soles are studied. When we vary frequencies across the spectrum by means of an oscillator, the listener is unable to distinguish separate successive spectral components; instead, a kind of beat is experienced, in the form of *continuous pitch variation*. Correspondingly, when we modulate amplitude, what is heard is *a sound of constant pitch but of continuously varying loudness*. Beat may be considered a special case of *frequency modulation*, affecting a spectrum of only two components.

Vibrato is the fundamental type of frequency modulation. It is often heard in the playing of a virtuoso violinist, who by means of rapid rhythmical pressure of the finger brings about slight changes in the length of the vibrating string. The rate of musical vibrato is usually about seven alternations per second.

Masking In everyday life there is much listening in situations where noise is present. We try to detect a specific signal, yet the noise interferes. Masking is the process by which the absolute threshold of a test tone rises because of the presence of another tone heard either immediately before or simultaneously. This tone is then said to be *masking* the test tone. The *masking value* is defined as the difference, expressed in db, between the normal absolute threshold (in silence) and the higher threshold due to the presence of the masking tone. Already in the late 1800's Mayer observed that low tones have a different masking effect from high tones. He formulated this by saying that *the lower of two tones can mask the higher completely, but the reverse does not hold.*

The classic contribution stems from Wegel and Lane (1924). Their research produced the following statements: (1) Tones of adjacent frequencies produce greater masking than widely separated frequencies. (2) Low tones mask higher frequency tones considerably better than high tones mask lower frequencies. (3) When the intensity of the masking tone is increased, masking also increases but at a rate dependent upon the frequency of the masked tone (see Corso in Wolman, 1973, p. 363).

When two sounds occur simultaneously, the phenomenal experience depends greatly on the frequency and intensity relations of the two, according to the effects described above. The non-linearity of our auditory receptor system brings about harmonic partials in some cases; in others summation or difference tones.

Evidence is restricted and controversial concerning the locus of the masking effect—whether peripheral or central. At the peripheral level some investigators have pointed to the shortage of available neural elements in the hair cells activated by the masking sound. This lack of transmission capacity presumably heightens the threshold of the signal sound. An increase in the signal intensity is rendered unavoidable.

Masking by noise—Critical bandwidths Fletcher (1940) developed the concept of *critical bandwidth* to account for pure tone masking data when a masking noise was applied instead of masking by tones. He first assumed that the masking of a pure tone by noise was actually produced by a narrow band of frequencies around the frequency of the tone. All eventual masking effects contained in the noise outside this relatively narrow band could be ignored. His second assumption implied that the acoustic power of the noise components contained in the band equals the power of the tone to be masked if measurements are performed on the just audible level of the tone in the given noise.

These assumptions are based on laboratory experiments applying *white noise* as a masker. Such a sound raises the thresholds for all frequencies of a sound spectrum. However, only a small part of the noise, the frequency components of which lie in the immediate vicinity of the masking tone, are sufficient to bring about the masking. This contributing band is called the *critical band*. Figure 7.17 schematically shows how the threshold for a pure tone (vertical line) at the centre of the spectrum first remains unaffected as a white noise is narrowed. Subsequently, as the noise is very narrow, the tone becomes clearly audible. So the critical band is "marked out" by the

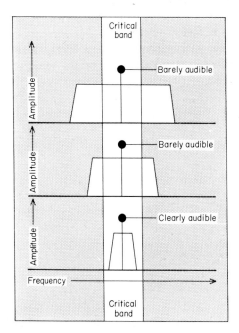

Fig. 7.17 The critical band. (From *Psychology Today. An Introduction.* CRM Books p. 266.)

two "frequency thresholds" between which the masked tone becomes clearly perceivable despite the masker. The width of this critical band is plotted as a function of the frequency of the masked tone in Fig. 7.18.

It has been pointed out that a critical band corresponds to a distance of 1 mm along the basilar membrane in the cochlea. On the other hand, "auditory signal detection" experiments (Green 1958) do not support the notion of a fixed bandwidth. Listeners might be able (even unconsciously) to vary the characteristics of their auditory systems to match signals which ought to be detected.

When we recall the significance of bands in signal detection theory in reformulating the old threshold laws, we realize the broad possibilities of application available with the concept of the critical band.

Musical scales The structure of tonal systems in European music has been directed by three different principles at various times: the *principle of consonance*, the *principle of fifths* and the *pragmatic principle*. Comparative musicology has shown that the interval called an *octave* has played a special role in the music of various peoples, both in ancient and in modern times, in civilized and in primitive cultures. The series of tones constituting a scale generally falls within an octave, which is the fundamental interval. When pairs of tones within this interval are compared, it is observed that certain pairs sound pleasant, others unpleasant. The former are called consonant tones or *consonances*, the latter *dissonances*. Even in ancient times it was known that consonant intervals are based on the simplest relations between tone frequencies.

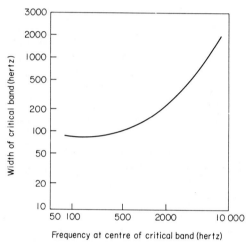

Fig. 7.18 The width of the critical band as a function of the frequency of masked tone. (From *Psychology Today, An Introduction*. CRM Books, Fig. 14.16 p. 267.)

The octave is defined as a tone pair whose frequencies are related by the ratio of 1 : 2 (see Fig. 7.9). The frequency ratios of other intervals are derived from this basic interval, as follows:

16 : 15	diatonic semitone	3 : 2	pure fifth
10 : 9	minor whole step	8 : 5	minor sixth
9 : 8	major whole step	5 : 3	major sixth
6 : 5	minor third	9 : 5	minor seventh
5 : 4	major third	15 : 8	major seventh
4 : 3	pure fourth	2 : 1	pure octave.

If the interval relations within the limits of an octave follow this scheme, the tuning is called *pure* or *mathematical*.

A more richly articulated scale within the octave is obtained by means of the 12-tone chromatic scale, in which intermediate tones are interpolated into all whole-tone intervals. This can be done either by multiplying the frequencies of c, d, f, g and a by 25/24, producing c sharp, d sharp, f sharp, g sharp and a sharp, or by multiplying the frequencies of d, e, g, a and b by 24/25, yielding d flat, e flat, g flat, a flat and b flat. Finally, we must mention the so-called *enharmonic scale*, which contains all the intermediate tones listed above:

c	c	d	d	d	e	e	e	f	f	f
1	25/24	27/25	9/8	75/64	6/5	5/4	32/25	125/96	4/3	25/18

g	g	g	a	a	a	b	b	c	c
36/25	3/2	25/16	8/5	5/3	125/72	9/5	15/8	48/25	2

Pure tuning has proved impossible in permanently tuned instruments, especially when played in harmony or in accompanying a human singer, since corresponding intervals cannot be made of equal size in different keys. This is due largely to the fact that 12 pure fifths and 7 pure octaves are not precisely equivalent, as would be necessary in order to fulfill the above condition. Thus permanently tuned keyboard instruments such as piano or the organ, with their constant intervals, do not fit perfectly with string instruments following pure tuning or with the human voice, which can easily shift the enharmonic intervals to a new scale. The solution has been to compromise on the purity of sound in order to achieve more constant tone step relations, by constructing the equidistant or tempered scale.

The principle of fifths means that the scale is constructed of basic intervals. After the octave, the most harmonious interval is the fifth. We then end up with the seven-step *Pythagorean scale*. However, this solution also has its draw-backs. When an instrument is tuned according to the principle of fifths, the *major* third becomes too large and sounds somewhat impure; this is due to the fact that the note e^1 in this scale obtains a frequency of 324 Hz, while in the diatonic scale it corresponds to 320 Hz. It is this deviation from the natural major third which limits the use of the Pythagorean scale in polyphonic music.

In the end, the most widely adapted solution has been that based on what Révész called the *pragmatic principle*. This led first to the *partially tempered scale*. Within the limits of the octave, the tonal steps were adjusted in such a way that fifths and fourths remained pure as in diatonic scale, while thirds and sixths, not to mention seconds and sevenths, were allowed a certain amount of impurity. The alternative was to tune the thirds to purity, compromising on the fifths, which thus become too small. However, even this scale caused some difficulty in choice of key. In the end, the octave was divided into *twelve equidistant intervals*, compromising on the purity of each. The scale thus obtained was called the *well-tempered scale*. By making the half-tone steps equivalent in size, the difference between *c* sharp and *d* flat, for example, is eliminated. For practical reasons they are considered equivalent, although a trained ear can under certain circumstances distinguish a difference in pitch between them.

Due to the great adaptability of our sense of hearing, we have become *used* to impure intervals in music since the days of Johann Sebastian Bach, so that they do not interfere with our enjoyment of music. On the other hand, pure intervals are still highly important wherever string instruments or the human voice are allowed free play, without interference from keyboard instruments. Pure chamber music allows us to realize the aesthetic values which we have lost by adapting tempered scales.

Speech Perception

It has been said that the highest achievement of the human auditory sense is the reception of the information contained in human speech and its transmission to the perceptual centres. This amazing performance includes the perception of a wide range of information, even to the frame of mind, socio-economic position and feelings of the speaker.

Production of the Speech Sounds

The human speech apparatus, which produces the verbal stimuli involved here, is more delicately articulated than any known musical instrument. Speech stimuli are based on the rhythmic thrusts of the breathing organs, often accompanied by resonance of the trachea. Superimposed on these muscular movements are complex movements of the larynx, the tongue, the soft palate and the lips. As a result of all these movements, a rhythmical articulation is imposed upon the continuous stream of air. The science of phonetics has been especially interested in the analysis of various vowels on the basis of their spectral composition. A spectrum of the vowel *a*, for instance, is shown in Fig. 7.19. The peaks F_1 and F_2 refer to first and second formants, respectively. (As mentioned on pp. 227–228 a "formant" signifies concentration of acoustic energy in a restricted frequency region.) The perceived sound of a recognized vowel depends on the frequency location of the formants F_1, F_2 and/or F_3 as shown in Fig. 7.20.

In addition to vowels, human speech contains various types of consonants. Characteristically consonant sounds are generated by narrowing or closing the "throughways" of the vocal tract.

The main method of registering speech sounds for laboratory use is the automatic *sound spectrography*.

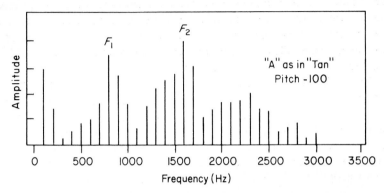

Fig. 7.19 Amplitude of the frequency components of the vowel a. (From Kling and Riggs, 1971 p. 250.)

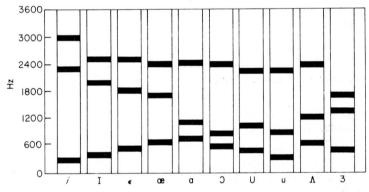

Fig. 7.20 Frequency regions for formants of different vowel sounds. (From Kling and Riggs, 1971 p. 251.)

An inverse procedure to that one represented by the spectrography is performed by the *"synthesis of speech"*. From visual analytic patterns similar to those shown in Fig. 7.21 a "play back" apparatus reproduces speech sounds. Such a technique provides an excellent opportunity to analyse carefully the role of various minimal cues for the articulation of speech. A minimal change in the darkness or the continuity of a spectrogram section, for example, strongly influences the perception of the speech sounds.

Much work is going on in order to demonstrate invariant cues for given sounds and the transitions between them. When we hear a particular consonant in cases where no specific structural cue can be shown on the spectrogram, there might exist, given articulatory movement, "a motor command to the tongue", as it were, which actually constitutes an invariant accompaniment of that consonant. Such an explanation is favoured by Libermann *et al.* (1962), among others. On the basis of pathological cases which involve inability to produce articulated sounds despite normal under-

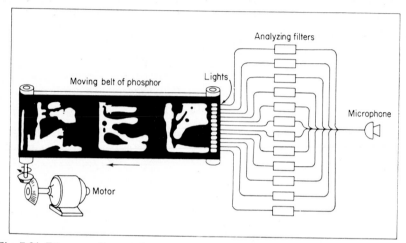

Fig. 7.21 Diagram of a sound-spectrograph. (From Kling and Riggs, 1971 p. 251.)

standing of speech, Libermann's theory has been questioned by other investigators. The newest speech synthesizing devices require the use of data machines.

Intelligibility Determinants in Speech

How can we measure the intelligibility of speech? The most common method is to list the number of words an observer hears correctly.

Speakers who perform their task as "stimulus generators" in the experiments are subjected to the wide inter-individual variation in speech articulation. The perception of speech is strongly influenced by the personality of the speaker. The content and the sampling of idioms, too, has enormous relevance. One standard procedure consists of providing the listener with one-syllable words. Again, the percentage of vowel and consonants in these words should be representative of the language investigated. Figure 7.22 shows how the percentage of correctly perceived syllables increases proportionally to the intensity of the voice of the speaker. Intelligibility is determined by the frequency of occurrence with which the test words have been used in everyday speech. The threshold for recognition of a word heard in noise is inversely related to the logarithm of the frequency of occurrence of the word (Thurlow in Kling and Riggs 1971, p. 255; Jauhiainen, 1974, p. 75). This observation brings us close to the problem of the "context" and of the phonetic word structure in auditory perception. If the subject knows the set of words that are to be used in the experiment, the above-mentioned effect of word frequency does not occur. If subjects know which words are to be used, less intensity is required for correct recognition. Words presented in the context of a sentence can be perceived more easily.

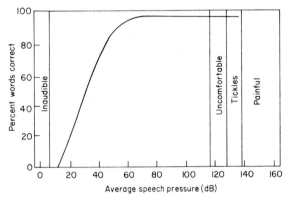

Fig. 7.22 Percentage of perceived syllables as a function of intensity. (From Kling and Riggs, 1971 p. 254.)

It is well known how much easier it is to understand a foreign language when the speaker is also seen and not only listened to.

In a "phone voice" there is not only a lot of masking, filtering and distortion on technical grounds—most important is the invisibility of the face and the dropping out of mimic reactions. "Nonverbal communication" plays a predominant role when we look at the face and the global movement of a speaker. The advantage of these visual cues is increased as the noise level increases relative to the speech. Visual cues gain in importance in cases where less auditory information was provided (O'Neill 1957).

Distortion in Perceived Speech

Distortions in speech-transmission systems have a remarkable influence on the intelligibility of speech. There are several investigations showing the effect of eliminating one or other frequency region from speech. Some classes of the formants can also be "clipped away". In most of the studies it has been shown that intelligibility considerably deteriorates as more and more of the high frequencies or more and more of the low frequencies are eliminated. According to Fletcher (1953) eliminating high frequencies affects consonant intelligibility more than vowel intelligibility. The opposite is true for elimination of low frequencies.

Interruptions in the speech flow affect the intelligibility to a higher extent if the interruption is "time spending" (say 50 per cent of the transmission time continuously on speech and 50 per cent on break). Yet intelligibility rises at higher rates of interruption. It has been shown that words can be made 2·5 times faster than normal by "chopping out" syllables without loss of intelligibility. Shifting the frequencies in speech will cause a decrease in its intelligibility.

In everyday situations the effect of noise varies considerably depending on several stimulus conditions. The threshold for detectability of speech increases proportionally to the level of masking noise, as shown in Fig. 7.23.

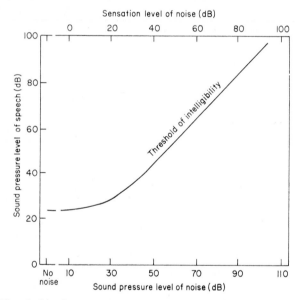

Fig. 7.23 Threshold of intelligibility as a function of pressure of noise. (From Kling and Riggs, 1971 p. 257.)

It has been found possible to predict interference with speech in many practical situations, where the noise spectrum is not uniform, by taking an average of noise levels in certain octave bands, e.g. in bands of 600 to 1 200, 1 200 to 2 400, 2 400 to 4 800 Hz. Thus it is possible to make recommendations about desirable and permissable noise levels in offices and ships, for example by knowing how these noises interfere with speech (Thurlow in Kling and Riggs, 1971, p. 258).

Voice Ranges

With a few exceptions, the human voice ranges over a pitch area from C_2 to E_6—that is, from about 65 Hz to 1 319 Hz. The pitch range of a single individual, however, rarely extends over more than two to three octaves. It is important to distinguish between singing register and speaking register. For example, the speech range of a baritone, whose *voice range* can be represented by F_3 (the upper boundary of the fully vibrating voice) might extend from C_2 to B_4, whereas the limits of his singing voice are likely to be near G_2 and F_4. These relations are illustrated below (adapted from Sovijärvi 1938, 1974).

The entire speaking and singing range of the individual is determined by the middle tone of his entire voice range, defined by the frequency of the medial tone of his voice range. The middle tone of a baritone voice is generally F_3. If we assume that his voice range extends over about three octaves, it can be represented by the schema in Fig. 7.24, which also shows

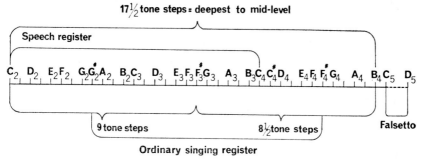

Fig. 7.24 Total voice register of a man whose middle tone is f. (From v. Fieandt, 1966 p. 134.)

the various *registers*. *The wider the speech range, the wider also the singing range*. The boundaries of voice registers cannot be defined in absolute terms, since there are individual differences even within each voice category. Sovijärvi (1938, 1976) lists the following typical characteristic tones for male and female voice category, the range of which can be assumed to extend individually about an octave to each side of the tone or more:

		International standard			International standard
Soprano	a^1	A_4	Tenor	a	A_3
Mezzosoprano	f^1	F_4	Baritone	f	F_3
Alto	d^1	D_4	Bass	d	D_3
Contralto	c^1	C_4			

The soprano, mezzosoprano, alto and contralto are female voices; the tenor, baritone and bass male voices. Human voices, in addition to pitch range, also differ in timbre. The untrained voice generally is capable of producing only 13 tonal steps at will. The registers (see Fig. 7.25) are the following: *deepest range* (3 steps), *deep level* (3½ steps), *mid-level* (3 steps), *high level* (2 steps) and *highest range* (1½ steps). The *chest voice* ranges through all these registers except the high B_4 level, and is followed at higher pitch levels by *head voice*, which includes the *highest range*. Chest voice is characterized by its greater *fullness*, head voice by its shrillness and sharpness.

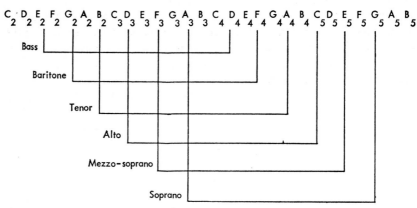

Fig. 7.25 Voice ranges. (From v. Fieandt, 1966 p. 135.)

Information Variables Available in Speech

According to Gibson, traditional acoustic research was too limited when it was content to analyse complex sounds into their Fourier components and concerned itself primarily with the frequencies and amplitudes of various sine-shaped waves. The deliberate and meaningful articulations of human speech vary far more complexly than can be described in terms of pitch, loudness and duration. The numerous variables contained in the configurations of human speech may be combined into "higher-order" variables, which are individual and unique in their phenomenal nature. These are difficult to generate or simulate so as to sound genuine, and precisely for this reason they contain a great deal of information. It is just these complex variables that the normal auditory system perceives and discriminates most sensitively (Gibson 1966, p. 87).

Study of the spectral composition of these stimuli has been more fruitful than the traditional analysis based on sine waves. It has been shown that the frequency relations between various parts of the spectrum are more essential to the discrimination of speech stimuli than, for example, absolute frequencies as such.

The perception of speech sounds and the comprehension of their symbolic content are two different complementary processes. The most interesting aspect of this event is the occurrence of certain invariances, which remain even with variations in pitch, loudness and duration. The vocal range of a woman lies about one octave higher than that of a man, but the vocalic or consonantal characteristics of speech sounds are retained. Vowels can be sung in different keys, speech sounds can be shouted or whispered at a hardly audible level, but they are still discriminated. In the same way the rapidity of speech may vary within very broad limits. As long as the sequential configurations are preserved, the speech will be understandable. All this demonstrates conclusively that the realizations of phonemes and the speech units can be transposed across the various dimensions of pitch, loudness and duration. Our "inner ear" is able to discriminate the invariance available in the complex stimulus field of human speech.

8 | Smell and Taste

Two Modes of Primordial Sensory Experience

When we come to smell and taste, we are dealing with senses which in many respects must be considered more primitive and more vital, in a way more personal, than the more specialized distal senses of sight and hearing. To use Schachtel's terminology, smell and taste are *autocentric*, subjective forms of perception, as opposed to *allocentric* or objective. Schachtel considers that traditional psychophysical concepts—thresholds, discrimination, etc.—have been given too prominent a place in the earlier approach to smell and taste modalities. Briefly stated, the scientific approach to these phenomena has been too rationalistic.

However, according to Schachtel, in the early stages of all sensory perception the autocentric form of experience is dominant. Probably the newborn infant draws no boundary between the ego and the external world (Schachtel 1959, pp. 81–84). Smells in particular are directly involved in the fundamental drives of our existence. Many studies have demonstrated the connection between the sense of smell and sexual attraction. In order to understand the role of unconscious sensations in arousing erotic stimulation, we should recall the difference between the stimulus threshold and the recognition threshold, as discussed in chapter 2 (see p. 25). The recognition threshold for smell, unlike other thresholds, is frequently not precisely empirically measurable. It varies considerably from moment to moment; in some cases these variations are hardly worth mentioning, while in others they may be extremely large. According to Henning, the perceptual threshold has been formed, at which point characteristically the *name* of the perceived object is also recalled.

Significance of Odours in Everyday Life

Stimuli falling below the threshold of recognition nevertheless affect our behaviour and our performance without our being aware of it. It is well known that the *timbre* of the human voice can play a part in arousing sexual stimulation. Similarly, unconsciously registered olfactory stimulus factors may play a decisive role in the indescribable total impression created by the "presence of the beloved". The characteristic odour of any person, his "personal aura", as it were, depends to a large extent on the secretions of his skin glands. "Oft ist der Geruch der Vorläufer der Liebe." ("Often smell is the harbinger of love.") This personal aura is often supplemented and enhanced by means of artificial odours. In all cultures known to history this has been an incentive for the production of perfumes. Indeed, in this sense, the use of cosmetics is as old as culture itself.

On the other hand, small impressions are known to produce equally strong feelings of disgust, even in cases when they are purely imaginary and due to a kind of perceptual analogy. Certain animals take advantage of this phenomenon and protect themselves biologically by means of ill-smelling secretions. Even the most pleasant odours, if enjoyed in excess, involve the danger of intoxication and in extreme cases of poisoning. It is not unusual for a branch of cherry or a bunch of lily-of-the-valley left overnight in a bedroom to produce a feeling of nausea, or at least of strong satiation and unpleasantness, in the sleeper.

Schachtel (1959, p. 299) points out that no other sense arouses such a strong feeling of disgust or leads so easily and violently to nausea and vomiting as does the sense of smell. The same can of course also be said of taste (as pointed out in chapter 5 p. 133): the olfactory components of our taste sensations are of great importance, while the olfactory pathways terminate close to the gustatory centres in the midbrain.

The violence of our reactions is due to the fact that both pleasure and disgust are much more closely tied to the proximal than to the distal senses. "Thus some particular smell or taste, or the proprioceptive feeling following from some accidentally assumed position, may with near-magical vividness bring to the mind some memory of far-away childhood. Sometimes the memory is only a vivid recall of the exact smell of Sunday evening at home, or the mother's dress, or the father's study. At other times some entire situation from childhood may be recalled in every detail." (Schachtel 1959, p. 160).

Skramlik tells the amusing story of the lady in whom roses aroused a strong feeling of disgust. Once, when another lady visited her wearing a hat with a rose in it, the result was a severe attack of nausea. The sight of the rose was enough to arouse the unpleasant feelings normally associated with the smell—and in this case, in fact, the rose was an artificial one.

Long before the child is aware of the mother's external appearance, he is familiar with her smell and taste. It is likely that an angry or insecure mother tastes and smells differently to the child from one who is calm or comfortable. As far as we know, under these circumstances the mother also looks different to the somewhat older child. The child experiences through taste, smell and touch before it becomes aware of visual or auditory sensation.

Olfactory Sensitivity Adaptation and Arousal

Investigators have been curious about individual differences in olfactory sensitivity. It has often been observed how good is the performance of women in discerning minimal amount of odours. The sensitivity of both sexes also shows considerable variation from one part of the day to another. Early in the morning people generally are most sensitive, yet inter-individual differences are considerable. The persons called *introverts* by Eysenck are supposed by him to be more sensitive than the so-called *extroverts*. A study by Koelega (1970) did not confirm this hypothesis. Four groups (introvert men, extrovert men, introvert women, extrovert women) were compared as to their olfactory thresholds. The introvert men were the weakest performers. The women in both groups were the best. There was no covariation between sensitivity and arousal, but most women were best in the morning.

Adaptation and recovery was measured by Steinmetz *et al.* (1970). The odourant applied was methyl-isobutyl ketone $= CH_3COCH_2CH(CH_3)_2$. The authors made use of two psychophysical methods: modified category scalings and determinations of thresholds. Both methods rendered similar results in what concerned lowering of the sensitivity and recovery of it as a function of stimulus time and stimulus intensity. More than 50 per cent of the adaptation and of the recovery occurred during the first two minutes of stimulation.

Sensorial Models and Terminology of Odours

Schachtel feels that western civilization in particular has neglected the cultivation, development and description of the olfactory and gustatory senses. They have been labelled as "animal senses" and invested with taboos, warning signs of untouchability and avoidance. As the development of the individual follows that of the species, the child's proximal senses, so delicate in the beginning, later degenerate; but Schachtel claims that this process is accelerated by the rejecting attitude on the part of the culture toward these senses (Schachtel 1959, p. 299).

Additional light is cast upon this cultural development by the fact that languages in general offer only a limited set of words for describing smell and taste experiences. There are no actual conceptual names for tastes and smells. Compared with the rich vocabulary we have to describe the shapes and colours of the visual world, the terms for odours and tastes are concrete and tied to the stimulus object itself. This is probably evidence of the small degree of articulation of the sensory impressions themselves. Colloquial language has no names, for example, for the phenomenal sensory experiences which would correspond to the direct colour names characteristic of our visual perception. Shades of smell experience can be expressed only by reference to the objects which are most often the source of the smell. We speak, for example, of the odour of a rose or of lavender, or we say that something smells like a rotten egg.

Some kinds of wine may be described as dry, others as sweet, in taste; the terms heavy, soft, fullbodied are also used. None of these, however, give the complete picture of the *aroma* of the wine (Broadbent 1975).

According to Henning, the linguistic objectification of olfactory impressions, their anchoring to names of objects, is due to the following reasons:

(1) Physically speaking, smells are more "substantial" than light, that is they are actually carried on by particles, whereas light radiation stimulates substrates on the retina.
(2) Smells are physiologically more closely tied to a particular source.
(3) A smell experience is conceptually linked up with a particular, concrete and substantial stimulus material. A colour experience is conceptually more abstract and "independent".
(4) The attempt to use the names of smells as symbols ("transposing" them) as we do with those of colours would be meaningless.
(5) Two "similar" smells cannot give rise to the same accurate impression of identity, as do colours with the same name.
(6) We can have colour concepts or images, but images based on un-objectified smells are difficult to evoke, though we may be justified in speaking of "after-sensations" of smell.
(7) Compared with visual perception, which represents a kind of luxurious complexity, smell is a biological reality, close to life. Its logic is that of a primitive *striving* (in Brentano's sense), rather than a higher-level logic of *representation* (in the sense of a symbolic language).
(8) The world of smell experiences has not yet undergone the division into two categories of names, one to denote the object sources of sensations, the other these sensations themselves.

Henning has proposed the following inventory of smell "primaries":

> *Flowery*, originating in flowers and plants.
> *Resinous*, originating in balsam and odorous resins.
> *Fruity*, from flowers, fruits, oils, wines.
> *Spicy*, from spices and roots.
> *Burnt*, the smell of burnt organic matter.
> *Foul*, originated in rotten and decaying matter.

These six primaries form the six points of his "smell solid" or prism. This representation was based partly on observations, partly on deduction, but it has not received empirical support. For example, the location of "mixed smells" along the continuum between two primaries has caused difficulty.

During the last decades of research it has become apparent that dimensional descriptions are needed in order to account for the stimulus continua corresponding to our smell experiences. Engen (1962) pointed out that the subjective smell response comes along several dimensions at once. He extracted three factors from the data of his subjects, who had been presented with homologous series of alcohols. One factor decreased with chain length, another, increasing with chain length, appeared to be a musty "smell". The third factor stood for a "pleasantness-unpleasantness" dimension. Beebe-Center (1931) had subjects rank odours on some sort of pleasantness-scale. However, the correlations between different subjects for the same odour were rather moderate, about $r = 0.42$ (after Mozell in Kling and Riggs 1971).

A more modern attempt to construct a classification of basic smells is that of Amoore and his colleagues (Amoore *et al.* 1964). Their seven-point classification consists of the smells of camphor ($C_{10}H_{16}O$), musk, flower, peppermint, ethyl ether ($C_2H_5OC_2H_5$), pungency and rot. A desirable aspect of such classificatory systems is their attempt at greater control of the stimulus correlates of olfactory impressions. The question arises whether the chemical structure and composition of a given stimulus substance is the correlate of the odour category aroused by the stimulus. In other words, do substances which smell the same also share related structural characteristics? Amoore claims, for example, that substances causing a camphor-like smell all share a similar molecular structure; their molecules are similar in size and shape. Furthermore, he assumes the existence of specialized locations and cavities within the olfactory tissue, which react to molecules of specific size and shape. This is an interesting assumption, which may offer a solution to the psychophysical riddles posed by the more important categories of taste sensation. This kind of psychophysical experiment, including the analysis of smell similarity analysis, has been carried out at the

Institute of Psychology of the University of Stockholm, under the direction of G. Ekman. We will return later to these problems.

The Evidence from Single Cell Recordings

The material presented in chapters 5 and 6 concerning the contributions of neurophysiology in the study of the visual modality, and especially of colour perception, has its counterparts in single-cell recordings on various levels of the olfactory tracts. Corresponding to *electroretinograms* (ERG) and to single cells on the retinal level (see p. 168) *electro-olfactograms* (EOG) have been obtained from the single receptor neurons of the olfactory mucosa (Ottoson 1956, Shibuya and Shibuya 1963, O'Connell and Mozell 1969). Technical difficulties in recording from these very small single units in the mucosa, led to working with potentials from specific neural tissue in the bulbus olfactorius, which might be considered as a counterpart to visual stimulation recordings from the brain stem nuclei (see chapter 3 p. 68, chapter 4 p. 84). There is a growing body of evidence supporting the idea that there may be some quality differentiation of incoming odours right at the periphery, within the olfactory epithelium (Geldard 1972, p. 468).

An experiment of Mozell (1966) on the function of the olfactory nerve of the frog points to the existence of different spatio-temporal patterns of discharge for different odours. Although there has been a lot of disappointment as to the possibility of grouping together odourants which specifically act on single types of neurons, the EOG has proved a useful indicator of the intensity of stimulation in various parts of the receptive tissue. Modern investigators make use of the amplitude of the EOG in order to determine the time limits of the most efficient phase in the local stimulation. There remains quite a lot of work to do in the efforts of quantification among the frequencies with which each odourant stimulates a given unit.

An excellent contribution to the mapping of the big ganglion cell system in the bulbus has been given by Døving (1965, 1966a, 1966b, 1967, 1970, 1972, 1973) primarily working with frogs. Every odourant he used was classified as to whether it excited, inhibited or had no effect upon a given bulbar neuron. Each odourant was then compared to every other odourant. In a homologous chemical series chosen by him it appeared that odourants representing the same molecular weights were more likely to be classified together than those with more variant molecular weights.

In his earliest studies (1964, 1965) Døving minutely and laboriously analysed the reciprocity and correspondence between the width of the EOG spike potentials and the rate of discharge in single bulbar units. Simultaneous recording (as represented e.g. in Fig. 8.1) offers a convenient

I

method for this kind of comparison. It can be clearly shown that the period of highest amplitude in EOG (lower trace) temporaly coincides with the highest rate of discharge of the bulbar unit. This correspondence however,

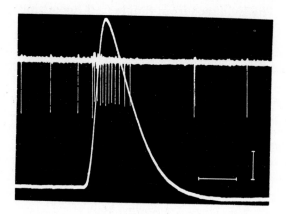

Fig. 8.1 Simultaneous recording of EOG (lower trace) and discharge of single bulbar unit (upper trace). (From Døving, 1964 p. 153.)

is only one part of the story. As shown in Fig. 8.2A and B stimulation on the receptor level might in some instances result in an activation (A) of the bulbar single neuron transmission (see Fig. 3.2b), in some other cases (B)

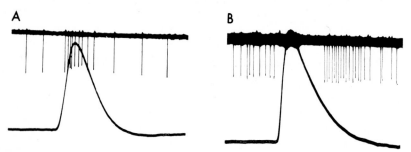

Fig. 8.2 Excitatory (A) and inhibitory (B) types of responses. (From Døving, 1967 p. 66.)

it might elicit a phase of inhibition in the bulbar activity recorded. Thus the bulbar single neuron units apparently show a considerable degree of selectivity toward the "stimulation pulses" on the receptor tissue. A certain class of odourants are secured "free entrance" by a type of bulbar units which might "close the doors" to other series of odourants.

A vast amount of conflicting data could be selected from Døving's papers on the responses of the bulbar neurons. The black dots in Fig. 8.3 show the main areas which were used by the investigator for implanting his electrodes. Founded on the differences in the conductance capacity illustrated by Fig. 8.4 (p. 252), the effect of odour stimulation on the bulb units was classified into excitatory and inhibitory types of response. Døving investigated each of 93 bulbar units for five odours. Between any two odours in the experimental series the degree of association in stimulative properties was measured. For each pair of odours, the number excited by both odours, the number of units inhibited by both, and the number of units giving opposite responses to the two stimuli, was counted.

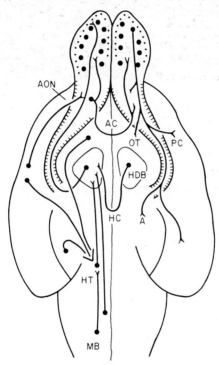

Fig. 8.3 Schematic drawing of the olfactory pathways in the frog. (From Døving, 1965.)

These values were placed in a 2 × 2 contingency table and the chi-square values for the pairs calculated.

In Døving's study 14 per cent elicited similar types of responses to the five odours used. For combinations of 4, 3 and 2 odours of the five in this experimental series, the corresponding percentages were 21, 33 and 52. The theoretical probability of response similarity was calculated on the assumption that the odours had been independent scores about 10 per cent lower than the obtained values.

A theoretical drawback in Døving's studies on the specificity in the bulbus was his taking Amoore's scheme of classification as a frame of reference. As pointed out before (see p. 248), Amoore's speculations about the significance of the molecular structure of the odorant substance for the

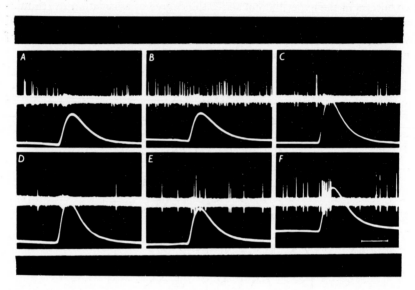

Fig. 8.4 Differences in the conductance capacity in a sample consisting of six neuronal units. (From Døving 1965.)

selective outcome of the receptor stimulation hardly holds true, and his psychological odour system requires updating and increased precision. Nevertheless, even another study (Døving 1966b) applying stimulating odours selected from homologous aliphatic series of alcohols, ketones and acetates reveals the same type of very complicated relationships between the molecular structure of the odourant and the degree of selectivity in the neural responses.

Mozell (Kling and Riggs 1971, p. 217) suspects that Døving's system is a rather coarse matrix upon which to measure the similarity of odorant effects. There is also some question about the precision with which the information from the secondary units recorded in these studies can be extrapolated back across a really complex synapse to account for the procedure of discrimination on the level of receptor cells.

In any case a promising method had been developed for improved continuous efforts.

Theories of Smell

It was formerly assumed that smell particles can affect the mucous membranes of the nasal cavity only *through the air*. It has been experimentally demonstrated, however, that water can also mediate stimuli of smell. As shown, for example, by Døving (1965, 1966a, 1973) fishes are excellent smellers. It does not seem to matter what medium functions as carrier of the chemical stimulating particles, as long as the medium itself does not stimulate or damage the sensorial apparatus.

In the case of man, odours are first sensed during inhalation, then during exhalation of the same air stream. From the point of view of taste sensation, the latter phase is more important. The human taste perceptions achieve their full proportions when olfactory stimuli also become involved. As for man and most species of terrestrial animals, the current of air coming from the lungs carries particles of swallowed food or drink through the nasal cavities, and their effect is added to those caused by taste.

What is still unknown is the chain of events in the receptor tissue during stimulation. There are *three main theories* about the physiological event involved. According to one explanation, the stimulus consists of particles emanating from the smell source. The second assumes that stimulation actually consists of direct chemical changes within reach of the receptor cells. The third proposes a mechanism involving non-visual electromagnetic radiation (ultraviolet or infrared) interacting with the inspired air after it has entered the nasal cavities.

The first assumption is easily shown to be evidently exclusive. Immediate olfactory stimuli differ in many ways from radiation-type energy. Smells travel with the streams of air or water; they do not penetrate thin transparent membranes, nor are they reflected from surfaces. Temperature variation has been shown to play a crucial role in the intensity of smells.

The second assumption has since been formulated more precisely by Kistiakowsky. According to him, the olfactory tissue contains enzymes which enable the sensory fibres to maintain a state of equilibrium. Each smell substance has an inhibitory effect on one specific enzyme or smell of them, of which there is exactly the same number as of the "smell primaries". In this revised form, the theory is fairly consistent with what we know of the physiology of the olfactory sense. Its most serious difficulty lies in its inability to account for the amazing rapidity with which smell sensations are initiated, and their flexible adaptation to temporal conditions. Geldard (1972) feels that this cannot be explained without recourse to "absorption gradients", whose steepness would depend on the velocity with which the odour-saturated air or water strikes the olfactory tissue. Should this interpretation be correct, it would give us a further indication that gradients of stimulation are fundamental correlates of our phenomenal experience, as postulated by modern psychophysics.

The third theory assumed a vibratory interaction between the air current and the receptor tissues (in terrestrial animals). The observations of a number of investigators have concentrated on possible vibration of the stimulus-substance molecules. Such vibration would follow the rates of light and heat absorption specific to each substance. A warm organism emits infrared radiation, which is absorbed by the vibrating odour substances in various proportions, depending on their own absorption spectra. Such a mechanism would produce local cooling gradients of specific zones of the receptor tissue. The actual stimuli, according to this theory, would consist of temperature changes within relatively circumscribed areas of the receptor tissue. But this theory, too, runs into difficulties; there are substances with precisely equivalent absorption properties which nevertheless have easily distinguishable smells.

The smell-producing capacity of a substance depends on its *vapour tension*. To maintain its power as an olfactory stimulus, the substance must be suspended in vapour on the surface of an object. The more the vapour tension rises, the faster the substance evaporates from the object surface. The intense smell of warm food, excreta, etc. is well known. A rise in temperature increases the vapour tension. On the other hand, particles can be made to adhere to previously indifferent surfaces by decreasing the vapour tension. Every hunter knows that the dog does the best job of following its prey if the wind is still and the weather is slightly humid. Under these conditions, the odours of the game animal adhere best to the shrubbery, the moss and the ground. Even astonishingly small drops of water may carry distilled "vapourized" odour particles familiar to everybody from the "aroma" of a forest in the hours of dawn. Dry, warm and windy weather hastens evaporation and thus interferes with a prolonged chase. On the other hand, of course, if the ground is very wet the odour particles are so completely bound that evaporation cannot occur at all.

Taste and Oral Perception in General

As has already been mentioned in chapter 5, Gibson particularly stresses the indistinguishability of smell and taste. "They can be defined by their functions in use, smell being an accompaniment of breathing and taste of eating." (Gibson 1966, p. 136). Considered in this way, taste is primarily part of the system of nourishment control. Such a control system occurs in all animals; its specific function is to exercise control in situations in which certain substances are accepted as food while others are rejected. The act of swallowing is preceded by a complex of eating (ingesting) behaviour, an essential part of which consists of searching and selection. In some cases, swallowing may lead to choking or coughing.

Recent study of the sensorimotor functioning of the oral cavity (see, e.g. Bosma 1967) has confirmed that its receptor activity belongs to a number of modalities. But all the stimulus messages—those of touch, pressure and vibration as well as of the chemical sense and of taste—go back to the same substance, the morsel of food which is manipulated by the various glands and muscular systems of the mouth and whose properties are recorded by various receptors. It would be misleading to assume that the activity in the oral cavity is directed only to preparing the food to be swallowed. The oral movements are simultaneously exploratory; they analyse the food and initiate stimulus connections. The act of chewing isolates and analyses liquids and taste substances, which are moved by the tongue so as to come in contact with the receptor surfaces. Thus tasting, as interpreted by Gibson, is a kind of attention (Gibson 1966, p. 139).

In the United States, research teams composed of neurologists, physiologists, odontologists and psychologists have studied the conditions under which the mucous membranes of the mouth are able to receive and conduct messages about object perception. The experiments concerning sensorimotor activity (McDonald and Aungst, 1967) and three-dimensional perception within the mouth (Shelton et al. 1967) are especially illuminating. They also included a replication and extension of the series of experiments planned by McDonald and Solomon in 1962. These experiments measured the ability of children five years of age and older to distinguish various surface structures, objects, weights and shapes in the mouth. The structure test consisted of a series of plastic buttons, smooth in surface and about an inch in diameter, the surface of which differed sufficiently from button to button to produce different feeling sensations. Weight was measured by means of plastic objects, which had the same volumes but whose weight differed on account of the varying number of lead pellets they contained. The test for object shape perception consisted of five different shapes: a ball, a cube, a pyramid, a cross and a cylinder. These objects were all about 1 cm in diameter. They were placed directly in the subject's mouth, so that he was unable to see them, and he was allowed to move them about with his tongue and mouth muscles as much as he liked. He then had to identify the shape of the "morsel" by saying which of the same series of objects placed on the table was the same shape as that in his mouth.

This test, however, turned out to be too easy. McDonald and Aungst therefore designed a more extensive test of 25 items (see Fig. 8.5). It was carefully weighted, and a factor analysis based on the point scores of each item produced six different factor groupings. Experiments carried out with about 250 subjects of various ages showed that the ability to recognize the shape of three-dimensional objects rises between the ages of six and fifteen or sixteen, after which it stabilizes. The average point score for older people (50–89 years) was only about half of that for 13 year olds. The ball-shaped object (item 25) was again the easiest one to recognize, the flat and oval shaped object (item 15) the most difficult.

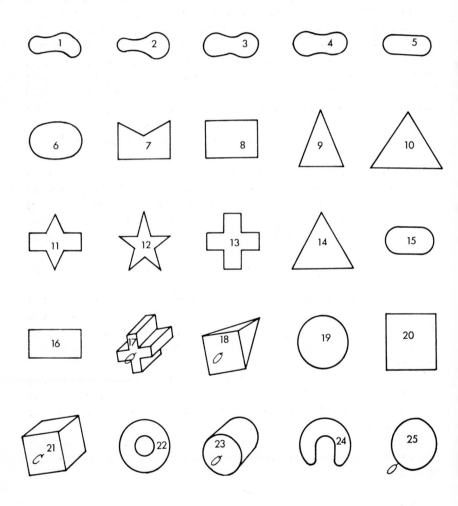

Fig. 8.5 Items of the McDonald and Aungst test for form discrimination in the mouth. (From v. Fieandt, 1972 p. 213.)

According to the classification of sensory modalities suggested by Schachtel, taste would represent the most basic type of the autocentric senses. It is the earliest of the senses to begin functioning after birth in the development of the individual, and its messages are inextricably bound up with feelings of pleasure or unpleasantness. The other receptors of the oral cavity, those mediating kinesthetic-tactile messages as well as those belonging to the sphere of warmth and hearing, further the possibilities of taste objectification. As Schachtel points out, recognition of the sensory object is considerably less important than it is in the visual modality (Schachtel 1959, p. 81). Tasting is in fact more a process of sensation than of perception. We really feel the gustatory stimulus on the receptor surface in the oral cavity.

According to experiments in 1940 by Stirnimann (see Schachtel 1959), differentiated taste reactions occur in newborn infants on the first day of life. When offered four different solutions in distilled water: lactose $(C_{12}H_{22}O_{11})$ 7 per cent, citric acid $(C_6H_8O_7 . H_2O)$ 0·5 per cent, sodium chloride (NaCl) 2 per cent and quinine sulphate $(2C_{20}H_{24}N_2O_2 . H_2SO_4 . 2H_2O)$ 0·01 per cent, alternately at different times, the child was able to distinguish the four "primary tastes" better than an adult.

Schachtel emphasizes the fact that, although the performance range of the mouth expands after the first year of life to include the recognition necessary in food intake, the pleasure–pain effect of touch stimuli in the oral cavity of adults still continues, *due to the autocentric nature of the taste modality*, to be stronger and more prominent than that stemming from contact with the hands.

It is a well known fact from daily experience that temperature conditions have a remarkable effect upon apparent sweetness. Puddings and jellies are often considered too sweet when served uncooled at an inappropriate temperature. When supra-liminal mixtures of glucose $(C_6H_{12}O_6)$ and fructose $(C_6H_{12}O_6)$ are offered,[1] the effect of temperature as well as that produced by the pH-concentration of the stimulant can be experimentally determined (see chapter 3 p. 59).

In the study by Stone et al. (1969) the test-stimuli consisted of glucose and fructose at different temperature-levels, and in the second part of the experiment at different pH-values. The control-stimulus consisted of a 0·25 M sucrose $(C_{12}H_{22}O_{11})$ solution.[2]

When presented with each of the stimuli the subject had to indicate what he experienced as a relative degree of sweetness when compared with the control stimulus.

1. grape sugar + fruit sugar.
2. The symbol "M" is an abbreviation for *mole*. A solution has a concentration of 1 mole if the molecular weight of the substance, in grams, is added to enough water to make exactly one litre of solution.

An increase in temperature from $+5°$ C to $+50°$ C did not change the apparent sweetness of glucose or fructose, nor of the compounds of these stimuli. On the other hand, when the pH-value was lowered from 5·8 to 2·7, the relative sweetness of all stimuli went down by about 5 per cent. The outcome of the temperature experiment, of course, was very surprising.

Moskowitz (1970) was interested in sweetness and in intensity of artificial sweeteners. The concentration level of the stimulus-solutions was indicated as percents per unit of weight. The taste substances consisted of cyclamate-salts (e.g. sodium cyclamate $C_6H_{11}NHSO_3Na$), sodium saccharin ($C_7H_5NO_3S$) and mixtures of cyclamate and saccharin. The subjects were selected among college students. Each of the subjects in turn was confronted simultaneously with the series of 40–50 solutions.

The subjects had to tell the degree of sweetness (in other words the intensity of the solutions) and had to rate this level by assigning respective comparison numbers to them. They were instructed to wash their mouth carefully after each act of judgment.

Within a middle range of the intensity scale of the stimulus solutions the apparent sweetness and "strongness" seem to vary as a function of stimulus intensity.

The four traditional qualities of taste have been closely investigated within the frame of several research programmes. Tarow (1969) started from the qualities "sweet", "bitter", "acid" and "salty". Within the frame of each quality-dimension he prepared 10 standard solutions, located with equidistant intervals on a T-scale. Additionally he made use of four solutions, one for each "main quality" and 96 compounds of two solutions at a time. Four professional tasters and four laymen were attracted as subjects. They were asked to match each one of the stimuli to a standard, with the aim of determining the amount of masking of the receptive stimuli by an adjacent one. A considerable reciprocal masking between sucrose and quinine sulphate could be observed.

In the study by Smith and McBurney (1969) the subject also had to judge the quality and intensity of the taste stimulants along the familiar dimensions of "sweet", "bitter", "acid" and "salty", and additionally to give their impression on the intensity of each of the stimuli. The experimenters first prepared 12 solutions of different salts and had their subjects adapt their tongues during one hour—in one part of the experiment using distilled water (HOH), in another part of the experiment 0·1 M solution of NaCl.

The authors found a weak effect of gustatory cross-adaptation. After having adapted to NaCl the subjects had no supra-liminal impressions of a salty quality. Instead the acid and bitter components of same solutions gained in conspicuity. It could be concluded that the cross-adaptation effects depended on qualitative similarity between the stimulus to be adapted and the test-stimulus. One single mechanism is supposed to be responsible for the registering of a taste of "salty".

Taste, Food and Nutritional behaviour

The objective of the tasting of food substances is generally to distinguish between edible and inedible substances. In this respect, our perception does not always provide a completely reliable picture of the environment. Most animals occasionally eat harmful or even fatal substances. There are poisons which do not in any way warn us by their taste. On the other hand, evil-tasting substances are not always harmful. Experiments have been performed serving small children with "cafeteria meals"; the purpose of these has been to discover the extent to which the children select a well-balanced diet on the basis of their taste sensations (Rosa Katz 1941, p. 177). The results have pointed to meaningful nutritional behaviour; but the experiment naturally did not include any poisons. The old theory of the organism as a self-regulating mechanism is evidently valid, in that clear deficiences of one nutritional element or another are reflected as specific "hungers" or "appetites" as for example in the "whims" of pregnancy.

Modern civilized man rarely encounters food in its natural state. It has generally been industrially processed and packaged. Diet is becoming more and more conventional, and there are ever fewer occasions on which unsuitable "raw materials" must be rejected on the basis of taste sensations. This situation has both its advantages and its drawbacks. On the other hand, the standardization of food products and effective supervision of their production and marketing may protect us from the dangers of infection, which we would no longer be able to avoid on the basis of the relatively poor senses of smell and taste as developed in human species. On the other hand, "factory production" may even lead to new dangers, connected with methods of preservation and packaging—for instance the destructive effects of deep freezing. In any case, this tendency will even further impoverish the ability of our "most primitive modality" to sense, analyse and experience the natural complexity of our life environment (see Gibson 1966, pp. 141–142).

9 | Somaesthesis: Touch, Vibration and Temperature

In chapter 5 we described the structure of the skin senses and the historical background of the research which led to the classification of specific pressure and touch receptors. Melzack's and Wall's study (1962, pp. 332–333), which has clearly forced a reformulation of von Frey's conception of the part played by separate and specific receptors in the transmission of the actual perceptual information (p. 141), has also been mentioned. According to Melzack and Wall, the crucial question to be asked concerns the way in which the cells of the central stations and the brain stem nuclei abstract information from the spatial and temporal patterns of the nerve impulses which results in our rich qualitative experiences.

Information Transmission from the Skin Surface

One alternative to von Frey's thinking is provided by the theory of impulse patterning in the nerves. According to that theory, similar skin receptors, for example, may be physiologically specialized to receive and transmit different types of stimuli (see chapter 5 p. 143). The receptors may for example vary in their threshold sensitivity to various pressure stimuli. The study of organisms at different stages of development has shown that in mammals, and in particular in man, the free nerve endings of the skin, the Pacinian corpuscles and the hair sheaths play a role as terminal organs of the sensory process. According to Melzack and Wall, the transmission capacity of any sensory receptor whatsoever depends upon the pressure-sensitive threshold of the skin, on the lower and upper thresholds of temperature-variation sensitivity, on the thresholds for sensitivity of chemical changes, and last but not least, on the adaptation period of the receptor. The arborized or branching endings of the terminal area "filter out" certain components of the message to be transmitted before the lowest synaptic level. Also affecting the nerve impulse are other neural phenomena, such as inhibition, facilitation and synchronization (chapter 3 and chapter 4).

The receptivity of cells at higher levels of the central nervous system is determined by their thresholds of stimulation, as well as by the spatial and temporal summations which occur as the impulses advance upward. According to Melzack and Wall, the centres of the skin senses in the brain are capable of selecting and analysing impulse patterns corresponding to sensory qualities from the incoming stream of information. Thus the specificity of touch and pressure sensations is due not to a fixed spatial, topographical organization prevailing throughout the entire system at all levels, but to the analysis performed by the central neurons on the basis of the information containing the messages transmitted from "below".

Stimulus Systems of Touch

The most common mechanical stimulus affecting the sense of touch is a *deformation* of the surface tissues of the skin; this may occur as a *compression* of superposited tissues or as a *displacement* along the surface.

The static aspect of a force applied to the skin as maintained pressure or tension was formerly thought of as a decisive factor in the tactual stimulation. Later experimental work (e.g. Kenshalo and Nafe, 1962) has convincingly shown that movement of the skin tissue rather than a steady pressure is the adequate stimulus for touch. Already Meissner (1859) pointed out that pressure itself was imperceptible. His famous experiment (dipping a finger in a glass of mercury) evidently proved that the pressure of the fluid itself remained outside the subject's experience. A "ring of pressure" was observable only at the area where the finger emerged from the fluid. Meissner therefore contended that tactile receptors responded to a *gradient of pressure* rather than to pressure *per se*. This gradient model was slightly elaborated by von Frey and Kiesow (1899).

Nafe and Wagoner (1941) and Nafe and Kenshalo (1958) have performed extensive experiments on rodents and men around the problem of *adaptation* to tactile stimuli. They made use of a series of weights which sank into the skin, and measured the amount of deformation along with recordings of nerve action potentials from single tactile fibres terminating in the skin beneath the stimulator (Figs. 9.1 and 9.2). The results evidently show that adaptation in the tactile sense is a stimulus phenomenon (Kenshalo in

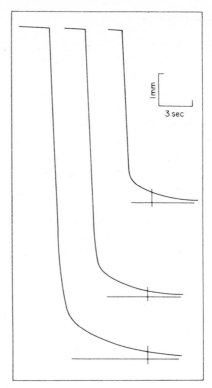

Fig. 9.1 Records of the tactile stimuli as they sank into the skin. (From Kling and Riggs, 1971 p. 130.) Weights applied: 35, 17·5 and 8·75 g.

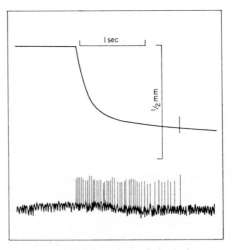

Fig. 9.2 Record of a tactile stimulus as it sank into the tongue of a rat. (From Kling and Riggs, 1971 p. 132.) Lower record: action potentials from a single tactile fibre.

Kling and Riggs 1971, pp. 131–133). Most of the receptors adapted almost instantly to *a completely steady* stimulus. The *movement* of the compressed tissues was decisive. A dip or an inward movement is not indispensable. Pinching the skin "upward" gives a sufficiently analogical displacement of the tissue. Thus adaptation resulted as a consequence of the failure of a static stimulus to stimulate the tactile receptors. The adaptation did not indicate a change in the state of sensitivity in the receptors. We do not observe the steady pressure of our clothes unless we move our bodies or limbs, and change the position of skin against the stimuli.

As pointed out by Gibson (1966, p. 117), compression or displacement of the skin surface is not by any means the only adequate stimulus for the sense of touch, nor can it even be considered the most primitive. If, for example, a rubber spiral is coiled around the skin and moved either clockwise or anti-clockwise, the direction of movement is perceived correctly. By means of rubber-pointed forceps we can bring about either stretching or contraction of the skin, by enlarging or reducing the distance between the two points. The experience is described as movement, although the points of the touch stimuli—the points of the compasses—do not move over the surface of the skin. Gibson also rightly refers to the question of how differently shaped object surfaces moving across the skin are correctly recognized, even by a blind person; this phenomenon may be based on the experience of *vibration* and would thus be related to acoustic sensation.

If we continue to employ a psychophysiological classification, the qualities of sensation mediated by the touch and pressure senses can be classified as *touch*, *pressure* and *tickle* in cases where the stimulation continues uninterrupted for some time. When the stimulus is intermittent but persistent, we can speak of experiences of *vibration*. In addition to *superficial* touch, physiologists also speak of *deep* touch. The differences said to exist between these sensations have caused some disagreement, similar to that involved in the concept of deep pain. Whatever the final answer to these questions, it does not have much bearing on a psychological approach to this sensory modality.

According to Head (1920), there are three layers of tissue involved in touch perception. These layers mediate different perceptual qualities:

(1) Deep sensitivity, which allows us to experience touch qualities even without our skin receptors being activated.

(2) Protopathic sensitivity, which provides us with sensations of smoothness and roughness, pain, cold and warmth.

(3) Epicritic sensitivity, which enables us to feel light strokes on the skin, slight temperature variations and minor superficial deformations or displacements.

Goldscheider and Hoefer (1923) distinguish among:

(1) The *sense of touch* proper, which functions on the receptors in the spots of the skin, and which mediates impressions of *granularity* and makes localization (orientation) possible.

(2) Other types of skin sensitivity, whose neural receptor basis has already been shown to be independent of the "touch spots".

(3) Deep sensitivity.

This classification reflects some of the difficulties involved when we try to explain touch impression on the basis of point-like receptors. If the modality of touch and pressure is interpreted more broadly from the point of view of the perceiving individual, as for example by Gibson (1966), the part played by the so-called *joint receptors* and body position receptors in the touch event indicates that this sensory modality is much more primary as a basis for object perception. It is not restricted to the three modal qualities listed above (p. 263).

The experience of tickle differs in many respects from those of touch, pressure and vibration. Here also, von Frey distinguished between *skin tickle*, mediated by the touch spots, and *deep tickle*, mediated by muscle receptor groups. The quality of *itch* is apparently related to simultaneously occurring components of pain.

Absolute thresholds for the perception of touch and of tickle are generally the same, but only stimuli just above the threshold can bring about experiences of tickle. Another necessary condition for tickle is the *movement* of the stimulus along the skin at an appropriate speed. Thus a sensation of tickle in the palm of the hand is brought about by a weight of 0·2 g, moving at a rate of 1·2 cm/s. Skramlik (1937) points out the importance of set; the same stimulus may cause an experience of touch on one occasion and tickle on another, depending on the perceptual set of the subject (see chapter 20).

The Stimulus Basis of Vibration Perception

In connection with our discussion of the normal human auditory area (see Fig. 7.12 p. 225), we may mention that this area covers the space which is left in our diagram between threshold curves of *touch sensations* and those of *hearing*. The human auditory threshold is quite high for sound stimuli under 12 Hz in frequency, but at a frequency of 800 Hz the intensity threshold is only a small fraction of that for low frequencies. On the other hand, stimuli under 10 Hz in frequency produce clear pressure and touch sensations in the auditory organs at lower intensities (measured in dynes/cm²) than those necessary for auditory perception. Such an impression of touch and pressure continues to occur when we increase the frequency of the stimulus, even when tones are heard in the normal way, as long as the intensity is raised to the level of the absolute "touch threshold", i.e. about 10^3 dynes above the reference level (see Fig. 9.3). This figure is presented by v. Békésy (1960, p. 258). The values of the auditory threshold curve are based on measurements with monaural hearing. The abscissa gives the frequencies of the stimuli in Hz; the ordinate the units of pressure

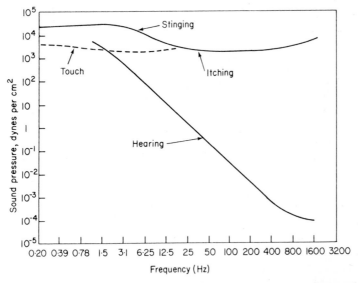

Fig. 9.3 Absolute sensation threshold rates for hearing and some other modalities (After v. Békésy 1960). (From v. Fieandt, 1972 p. 198.)

at the eardrum. When the frequency falls below 10 Hz, monaural listening results in a *touch-like sensation* of *pressure*. If the amplitude of the stimulus then remains constant, while at the same time a stimulus of gradually rising intensity is presented at the other ear, the subject frequently finds that the impression of touch is masked. When the loudness of the sound reaches the same level in both ears, the result is often the localization of a touch sensation as a nonuniform auditory impression inside the head.

It seems apparent that the reaction of the "senses" of hearing and of touch to vibrations at very low frequencies are to a great extent analogous. When the stimulus frequency falls below 10 Hz the threshold curve dips downward, due to the harmonics aroused in the middle ear by pressure over 10,000 dynes, which serve to lower the threshold. Stevens and Davis claim that these non-auditory sensations of pressure occur everywhere above the upper auditory boundary, whenever the intensity is sufficiently great. These threshold values are somewhat vaguely called the "thresholds of feeling" (Stevens and Davis, 1947).

While a constant pressure on the tip of the finger generally results in rapid adaptation, the cochlea adaptation is much slower. The tactual sensation remains constant over a period of several minutes.

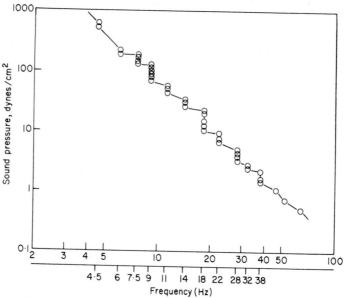

Fig. 9.4 The threshold-curve for slowly raising tone pressures. (From v. Fieandt, 1972 p. 199.)

Careful studies have shown that changes in the auditory threshold for low-frequency tones reflects gradual increases in the number of functioning neural transmissions (see chapter 3 p. 56). When the frequency of varying tone pressures was slowly raised without affecting their intensity over a range of 2–50 Hz, the sound impressions did not change continually but rather stepwise, as shown by the threshold curve (Fig. 9.4). This discontinuous shape is clearest for the 18 Hz stimulus. When the 18 Hz boundary was passed the number of simultaneously distinguished impulses was doubled; at the same time the sensation became more complex and a sound impression was combined with one of touch.

When a sound stimulus directed toward the ear rises in intensity, a level is reached above which a feeling of tickle is added to the auditory impression. At frequencies below 10 Hz, the tickle shifts clearly to a localized pricking sensation, which is most strongly felt at the point of the pressure maximum. This pricking is felt deeper in the ear than are impressions of touch.

When two tones of, say, 50 and 400 Hz are produced simultaneously by means of two sound generators, and these are then adjusted to intensities above the threshold for tickle, it is found that an impression of tickle occurs which is completely different from that produced when the subject places the tip of his finger on a moving vibrator. During this phase of the experiment, the vibrator replaced acoustical amplifiers. When the pressure was raised even more, the impressions of loudness and of tickle both rose independently of each other. The impression of tickle was determined primarily by the maximum intensity of pressure, while the way in which the pressure is produced does not affect the sensation (v. Békésy 1960, pp. 257–263).

These brief reports suffice to indicate the close relationship between the senses of vibration and of hearing, and the groundlessness of earlier attempts by physiologists to interpret the perception of vibration as a special case belonging to the modality of the skin senses, despite the evidence that resonance of the body cavities is often perceived as vibration similarly to the phenomena occurring at the boundaries of auditory perception. Human beings possess two senses for the perception of mechanical vibration in the environment: the sense of vibration and the sense of hearing. It is possible that the latter of the two developed out of the former at a later evolutionary stage (see Fig. 9.5).

Probably also some stimulus constituents of the chemical senses (smell and taste) do affect several types of our skin receptors, at least at greater concentrations.

The sense of vibration, like the sense of hearing, has its fusion point. When the frequency falls below 10 Hz the impression of continuous vibration is replaced by perception of individual beats. The boundary is, however, less rigid than it is in hearing. There is more controversy over the upper boundary of vibration perception than over the lower. Katz and his followers originally spoke of an upper boundary of 500–520 Hz, Brecher of 1 500 Hz and others of a boundary of 3 000 Hz, as long as the amplitude is great enough.

Some earlier classical experiments have also shown that the senses of vibration and of hearing operate in a reciprocal manner. For example, if a vibrating tuning fork held in the hand cannot be *heard* (because of earplugs in the ears), its vibration is *felt* in the hand. If the tuning fork is brought close enough to the ear to be heard, the feeling of vibration disappears at the same moment that the tone is heard (Rubin 1949, pp. 348–356).

Absolute vibratory thresholds, as measured by the displacement of the stimulator probe, reflect a duplex function of the vibration frequency. This duplex effect is interesting enough, because it shows two receptive elements, each with different sensitivities to mechanical vibration which combine to form the resulting threshold curve—rather like the visual dark-adaptation curve divided up in two parts due to the different effects of rod and cone transmission (see Fig. 9.7).

Are there specific nerve terminals responsible for such a duplex threshold-curve? Verrillo (1968), after having performed careful threshold-measurements on skin surfaces at various sites of the body, found the dermal nerve network and Pacinian corpuscles (see Fig. 3.3 and Fig. 5.38) together responsible for a duplex threshold-curve. When a tissue was used that lacked Pacinian corpuscles, the absolute threshold for vibration did not

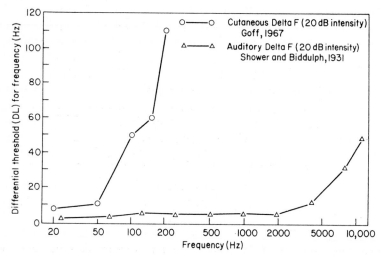

Fig. 9.5 Comparison of cutaneous and auditory differential thresholds (DLS). (From Kling and Riggs, 1971 p. 135.)

decrease at frequencies between 90–300 Hz (see Mountcastle *et al.* 1972, p. 122, Merzenich and Harrington 1969, pp. 236–260). Loewenstein (1959) removed the successive lamellar coats of the Pacinian corpuscle and observed that *two major electrical events* occurred in the stripped-down bare core of the onion-like structure. (The surrounding layers turned out to be irrelevant.)

(1) there is set up a graded response (generator potential) which reflects the intensity of the mechanical stimulus;
(2) the all-or-nothing discharge of the attached myelinated fibre comes about through a flow of current (Fig. 9.6).

This receptor-type was shown to provide a high threshold to vibration at frequencies below 60 Hz, a low threshold at 250 Hz and an elevated threshold at higher rates (Kenshalo in Kling and Riggs 1971, p. 138).

In his psychophysical studies Stevens (1959b) denoted phenomenal intensity of vibration—as expressed in arbitrary units—*vib*. In analogy with loudness the concept of *vibness* was coined by him. When equal-vibness contours have been mapped at different intensity-levels over the range of 50–250 Hz, an interesting increase of the exponent in the power function (see pp. 31–36) could be observed.

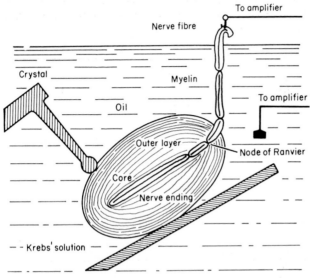

Fig. 9.6 The Loewenstein–Rathcamp experiment with the Pacinian corpuscle. (From Geldard, 1972 p. 296.)

Franzén (1969) determined detection thresholds for vibrations applied to the tip of the index finger as well as corresponding thresholds for vibrations applied to the second toe. He also found vibness at low frequencies (50 to 100 Hz) linearly related to the physical input. An abrupt shift to a power function with a steeper slope occurred at 250 Hz signals. The author found some evidence in favour of a duplex afferential system on the sensorial level as well as on the level of single cortical cells.

Differential sensitivity (see chapter 2 p. 15) to vibration is apparently relatively independent of frequency. Over the range of 16 to 600 Hz we can discriminate only about 25–30 different rates of vibration, while the sense of hearing can discriminate about 1 000 different pitches over the same range. The differential threshold (DL), when other frequencies were used as a standard, and the auditory DLs are shown in Fig. 9.5. Compared to the ear, the skin is a reasonably good frequency discriminator at low frequencies but deteriorates rapidly at high frequencies.

The effect of *masking* on vibrotactile thresholds was determined experimentally by Gilson (1969). He first obtained the absolute threshold with a Sherrick vibrator from the test locus on the left thigh (ventral side) of the subject. The stimulus was a 200 ms burst of 150 Hz vibration. He then measured the threshold elevation (TE) caused by a simultaneous equivalent masking stimulus applied alternately to quite a number of masker sites. These sites were located at various distances from the test site and they contained equal numbers (5) of contralateral and ipsilateral loci with respect to the test locus.

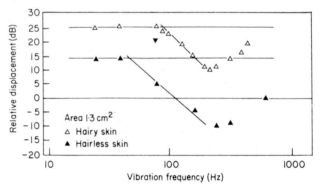

Fig. 9.7 Vibrotactile absolute thresholds measured on hairy and hairless skin. Hairy skin is less sensitive to all frequencies. (From Kling and Riggs, 1971 p. 135.)

The masking effect appeared to be systematically affected by the distance of the masker site from the test locus. As the longitudinal separation from the test locus or its contralateral homologous site increased on the body in either direction, the amount of TE decreased. Interestingly enough this weakening of the masking effect with the increase of the distance to the masker site was roughly equal on both lateral halves of the body. Contralateral maskers were no less effective in elevating the threshold at the test site than ipsilateral maskers. The interference between the stimulated points clearly does not occur at the peripheral level but at some central site or sites.

Subjective Intensities of Vibration

In his study (1959), Stevens suggested a unit for the measurement of subjective intensity of vibration. This unit is called the *vib*, and the phenomenal intensity which it measures is obtained by means of the following formula:

$$V = kA^{0.95},$$

in which A denotes amplitude. The value of the constant k depends on the constant amplitude assumed to correspond to an experienced intensity of one vib.

In his work, Stevens has been especially interested in the question of the analogy between the function of experienced vibration and the function of loudness. In fact, the power functions determined experimentally show great similarity for a stimulus of 60 Hz.

The phenomenal intensity of vibration can thus be described as a function of amplitude. When the tip of the finger is stimulated (either by holding a vibrating rod between the fingertips or by placing the fingertip on a generator), the psychological function follows Steven's well known law. Experienced intensity is measured in two ways, by means of magnitude estimation and by judgments of equal-appearing intervals. As it turned out, the two scales do not correspond linearly to each other.

Geldard (1972, pp. 308–310) distinguishes between "loudness" and "pitch" as vibratory dimensions.

Some discussion has sometimes occurred as to whether weak vibrotactile signals, presented singularly to different fingers of the subject, show any spatial summation effects. Franzén et al. (1970) demonstrated in a series of experiments that the detectability of the vibration stimulus is not actually greater when the tips of the index and the middle finger are stimulated simultaneously, than in situations where either of these fingers receive the same stimulation alone. That no spatial summation of vibrotactile stimuli for two fingers results is—according to the authors—consistent with a single-channel model of attention. When resting the tip of his index finger on a small disk which will be set into motion, and the tip of his middle finger on an adjacent disk, the subject can attend at any instant only to inputs to a single channel—and no spatial summation occurs.

Even in cases where the subject was left uncertain about which one of the disks was going to vibrate on a given trial and he apparently showed spatial summation, the authors got clear evidence that this appearance was misleading. Actually, the response even then reflected a decrement in the performance of the single fingers.

Interpretation of the Vibratory Experience

In his biological interpretation of vibratory perception, Katz employs a kind of duplicity principle. The receptors for touch and pressure are actually *proximal senses*, but in mediating vibration they are simultaneously *distal senses*; thus they fulfill a double function. In terms of evolution, the "sense of vibration" is an intermediate between touch and hearing proper. Probably this intermediate sense represents the first step of the differentiation of the touch organs into auditory receptors.

Half a century ago there persisted a considerable controversy between investigators who held that there existed a separate "vibratory sense" and those who viewed vibratory sensations as "pressure in movement". When referring to the opinions of Katz we rightly provide his term with quotation marks. As a phenomenologist he wanted to speak of vibration experiences as a sense in its own right regardless of the question whether this "sense" is in possession of special receptors and nerve supply. He claimed that different senses—in the psychological meaning of the word—without any difficulty can share common afferent neural connections. Thus what he actually had in mind as a neural correlate to perceived vibration was intermittent oscillatory pressure. Such an interpretation eliminates the controversy which—according to Geldard (1972, p. 302)—"may now be said to have been resolved in favour of the conclusion that the vibratory pattern is, in fact, 'pressure in movement' ".

Even man, at his phyletic level, lives in a world which is *vibratory* as well as *auditory*. A driver or a sailor, by means of his "vibratory sense", perceives the variations in pressure between the wheels and the road or between the boat and the water. The "vibratory sense" also serves us in many daily tasks, such as shaving or writing a letter.

The organization and articulation of our touch percepts proper will be discussed in later chapters.

The Perception of Temperature

The physiological basis of temperature perception was described in chapter 5. At that point the theory of Nafe and Kenshalo about the specific sensitivity of different areas of the skin surface and the biological basis of subjective "warmth" and "cold" thresholds was also discussed.

Since the classic instance of a temperature contrast experiment was pointed out by John Locke in 1690, it has been a commonplace in basic perceptual texts that two plates of equal temperature can be made to feel different, if the subject adapts his hands in advance to different temperatures. After having rested his right hand for about a minute on a 32° C plate and his left one on a 35° C plate, the subject feels a 40° C plate placed under the right hand warmer than the physically equal stimulus given to the left hand. Egeth *et al.* (1970) have shown—interestingly enough—that not only perceptual contrast occurs in situations like that mentioned above, *assimila-*

tion too can be demonstrated to exist under appropriate conditions. In cases of short adaptation duration (about 10 s) and a fairly high overall range of temperature spanned by the stimuli (e.g. 21° C and 35° C adaptation temperatures against 40° C test temperature) assimilation responses obtained. The plate touched by the hand, stimulated in advance at a *higher* temperature, actually felt *warmer*.

The hands of human beings are particularly sensitive to temperature changes under normal workday conditions. Experienced cooks and bakers are said to be able to estimate temperatures up to 250° C with an accuracy of 2° without a thermometer, merely by touching the surface of a hot loaf of bread lightly with the hand. The drawback of such "natural thermometers", however, is their *narrow stimulus range*, which considerably impairs perception of temperature variation over longer periods of time. As mentioned earlier (p. 146), "pure sensations of warmth" can be experienced only within a stimulus range of about +20° C to +45° C.

The stimuli of temperature perception are determined not only by the relative temperatures of objects in contact with the skin. *Specific heat* and *thermal conductivity* of the surface material also affect the skin temperature. Specific heat is the heat required to raise a unit volume of a substance by 1° C and thermal conductivity is the ability of a substance to transfer heat at a nearly constant temperature level through itself. The reduction of differences between temperatures occurs in at least two phases. First of all, heat is conducted from the surface of the skin into surrounding objects and substances, including the air, or alternatively from the environment into the skin. Secondly, a balance is established in an analogous manner between the temperatures of the skin surface and its underlying layers of tissue. At the same temperature, cotton feels warmer than wood, which in turn feels warmer than glass or metal. Water and air, each at 20° C, do not feel equally cold. In the experiments by Katz (1925), metal and glass felt hot, but wood and cotton only lukewarm when all these substances were applied at a temperature considerably higher than that of the body.

Radiant heat energy from electric lamps has been used to change skin temperature and to produce warm sensations. Dry ice has served to absorb heat and produce cool sensations. By means of these methods it is possible to stimulate either very large or very small areas of skin.

General "behavioural variables" affecting thermal absolute thresholds have been discussed. Women show lower thresholds for cold during the postovulatory phase of the menstrual cycle than for the period from the onset of menses to ovulation (see also chapter 5, p. 147). One requirement is, however, that the skin be adapted to temperatures above 36° C. Both males and females report lower cool thresholds in the afternoon than in the morning. Psychological stress, for example, the anticipation of a "hard" exam, increases the absolute cool threshold, but only when the skin has been adapted to temperatures higher than 36° C.

"Paradoxical cold" is a phenomenon in which some cold spots when touched with an hot stimulator (45° C) give sensations of cold. The opposite would be "paradoxical warmth", a warm sensation as a consequence of stimulation of some warm spots with a cold stimulator. Paradoxical cold cannot be aroused by applying a hot stimulus to a large area. Everybody knows about the momentary confusion of cold and hot that frequently occurs when a hand or a foot is dipped into hot water.

It is sometimes held that "heat" sensations are uniquely different in quality from that of warmth or pain. In addition to warmth, a slight stinging sensation seems to occur when "feeling heat".

Two theories have been advanced. Alrutz (1908) ascribed "heat" to a simultaneous stimulation of warm and cold receptors. Herget and Hardy (1942) assumed an "own special receptor type" for mediating heat. Evidence in favour of the Alrutz theory has later been brought up, especially by Burnett and Dallenbach (1927) and Ferral and Dallenbach (1930). Jenkins (1938) without any success tried to repeat these earlier investigations. Studies of the spatial summation of thresholds for warm or cool sensations pointed in the direction of the Herget and Hardy theory. There was less spatial summation for heat than for either threshold warm or cool sensations (Kenshalo 1971, pp. 147–149).

Since the recent advances in neurophysiological methods there has developed a number of investigations centred on registrations from the afferent temperature fibres. Temperature-sensitive fibres have been found both among the myelinated fibres and the very thinly myelinated or unmyelinated fibres. The cold fibres seem somewhat more thoroughly mapped and identified. A rewarding point of departure was found in the quite detailed correspondence between some of the thermal-receptive tissues in the face of the cat on the one hand and the human upper limb on the other (see e.g. Järvilehto 1973). Correlations of behavioural thresholds and neural activities have been made in order to show how behavioural and neurophysiological methods can be used to complement one another in this field of research.

Attached to the works of Hensel (1952, 1973) the neuropsychologist Järvilehto (1973) first determined cold thresholds of single cold spots by way of ordinary psychophysical methods from the human forearm and thereafter correlated his findings to recordings of potentials in the single afferent cold fibres of the cat using the same stimuli as in man. As shown in Fig. 9.8 the relation between the average reaction in man and average fibre activity in cats to a cold stimulus of 5·9° is rather unambiguous. The threshold sensation correlated with an impulse frequency of 46–75 imp/s, but a cumulative number of impulses evidently is of significance for the central nervous system to receive sufficient information about the duration of the effective stimulus. To quote the author: "The coding action of the CNS could be even more generally conceived as an integration of cumulative numbers of impulses rather than as an action of the frequency analysis" (Järvilehto 1973, p. 61). These considerations have been based on the assumption that a cold spot in man is served by a single cold fibre. Comparisons of the single fibre activity in the cat and reactions in man support this assumption.

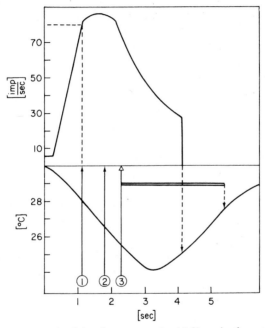

Fig. 9.8 Average changes in firing frequency of cold fibres in the cat (upper graph) and reaction in man (double line) to a temperature stimulus of 5·9° C (lower graph). Arrows: 1, Instant for exceeding the threshold frequency in periphery; 2, Instant of exceeding "central threshold"; 3, Instant of reaction in man. (From Järvilehto, 1973 p. 60.)

The modality of temperature perception also shows tendencies toward the *objectification or somatization* of impressions, particularly when simultaneous touch sensations are available. We say that we have "shivers running down our back". "Object-gestalten" could in fact hardly ever form on the basis of temperature sensations unless our perceptual experiences were actually referred or transferred to "outer objects", organized and built up on the basis of information from quite other modalities.

Part Three

Higher Achievements of Perception

The Concept of Sensory Attributes in Perceptual Psychology

10

Historical Background

The frame of thought dominant in the natural sciences throughout the latter half of the nineteenth century and in the beginning of the twentieth can suitably be called the Galileo-Newtonian world view. An example of this conception of the universe is offered by the idea, part of Newton's theory of colour, that in the spectrum of white light each successive pure chromatic band is the sole and unique stimulus correlate of the respective phenomenally experienced colour hue. The principle of an absolute isomorphism (to be explained later p. 282) between the stimulus world and that of experience, inherent from Wundt's early psychological laboratory and inspired by the spirit of unconditional mechanical law, was in evidence until the 1920's. This principle is often called *the constancy hypothesis* (see e.g. Gibson 1950, p. 62). It assumed simple and unvarying one-to-one relationships between the stimulus basis and certain variables or components of the corresponding sensation. When the leading associationist theorists after Wundt attempted to formulate their psychological research programme—which they considered to belong to the natural sciences—within the framework of this world view, the term "sensory attribute", which at that time had already become widespread, seemed to offer a natural foundation for their programme.

The names for various aspects and characteristics of sensations, which were at first used accidentally and randomly, now became a standard part of the conceptual system which even today, despite the considerable revaluation of the Galileo-Newtonian system, seems to play a fundamental role in the thinking of scientific psychologists. It is therefore appropriate to devote some consideration, even if only out of terminological interest, to the history of the concept of sensory attribtues, and to is semantic meaning in present-day psychology.

According to Edwin Boring (1942, p. 19), Wundt should also be considered one of the pioneers in this part of the conceptual inventory of psychology, although he does not seem to have used the term "attribute" explicitly and systematically. Wundt's train of thought in this context seems to have been more or less as follows: in every perceived object there are present certain characteristics, traits, properties (Merkmale, Eigenschaften), of which it is constituted. The perception of a ripe apple inseparably involves a particular rounded shape, perceived by sight and touch; a particular colour and smell; a particular surface structure felt against the skin; and a particular resistant and porous material. The components bearing these properties are "attributes".

Sensations in general always have two attributes: quality and intensity.

In Külpe (1893) we first encounter a formalized doctrine of attributes. Attributes, he said, are inseparable from sensations, by which they are determined. All five senses have three attributes: quality, intensity, duration. "A sensation without quality, intensity, duration cannot exist" (Külpe). In the case of sight and touch sensation, a fourth attribute was added: extension of spatiality.

Attributes conceived of as Independent Variables

The most essential point in Külpe's ideas is that *these four attributes are independently variable*. In this way the foundation was created for the doctrine of the *dimensionality* of attributes. In contrast to Wundt's theory of attributes, which in addition to quality and intensity also included *feeling* as a third dimension in the system, Külpe observed that feeling cannot be a sensory attribute since it has attributes of its own. Once the doctrine of attributes had become established as an officially accepted system, new and corresponding dimensions soon began to appear in the various sensory modalities. The confusion prevalent at this stage, due to the simple reason that no clear distinction was drawn between *descriptions on the level of experience* and those *on the level of stimulation*, was particularly characteristic of the situation.

In the field of visual perception research, *three attributes of colour* were found and named: brightness, hue and saturation. Here the description, of course, is on the level of experience. But in the middle of this description, the question may occur: What has happened to intensity? Why has it been forgotten? In discussing vision, intensity was customarily considered a stimulus variable, with brightness as its phenomenal counterpart. Similar confusion and shifting from level to level soon began to appear also in the modality of auditory perception, in speaking of the attributes of tones (see Fig. 10.1).

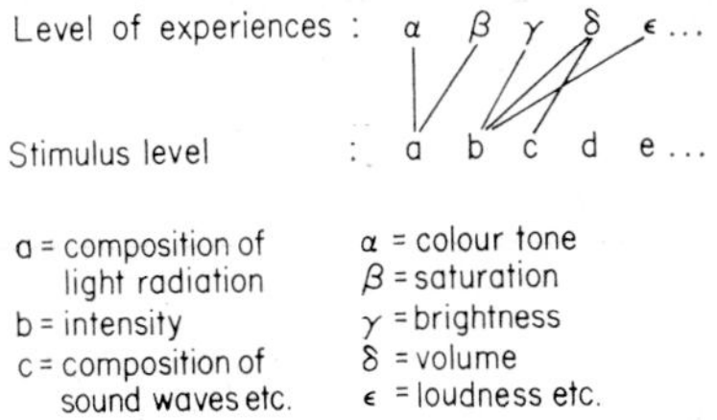

Level of experiences : α β γ δ ε ...

Stimulus level : a b c d e ...

a = composition of   α = colour tone
    light radiation   β = saturation
b = intensity   γ = brightness
c = composition of   δ = volume
    sound waves etc.   ε = loudness etc.

Fig. 10.1 The presupposed pairwise correspondence between the "experience" level and the "stimulus" level of sensory attributes. (From v. Fieandt, 1972 p. 189.)

Thus Titchener (1908) adopted the *volume* of a tone as a new attribute. It was observed that *stimuli of the same intensity sound fuller or louder when occurring at a lower pitch than when at a higher pitch.* This observation in turn aroused the question: if pitch and volume vary together, how can they be two different independently variable attributes? To this Titchener replied that a small change in pitch may occur without a corresponding change in volume.[1] Thus attributes as dimensional variables were at least formally preserved, although on the other hand more and more complex questions concerning the doctrine of correspondence arose (Fig. 10.2).

In the second decade of the twentieth century, in the years 1912–1913, the *phenomenological* trend of thought which was sweeping across Europe began to be reflected in the study of perception. Especially in describing the dimensions of sound experience, psychologists no longer wanted to be confined by the traditional classifications. In the Institute directed by Carl Stumpf in Hamburg, a large-scale study was undertaken to chart the various attributes or dimensions of sound on a purely phenomenological basis, regardless of whether or not some stimulus variables were involved as a basis of description.

An addition made later by Külpe to his original theory, came to play a fundamental role in the definition of units or elements typical of the associationist tradition. In the end, attributes were real units of sensation and image formation: "the attribute may be all that exists in the mind at the observational moment" (Boring 1942, p. 23). Corresponding elements or variables on the stimulus level were then called *dimensions*.

1. Heinitz (1934) already gave an explanation of the stimulus basis for volume (see also chapter 7, pp. 228–229).

K

Reenpää (1961) in his sensory-physiological theory of perception, when presenting his axiomatic system came back—as it were—to what has been described above as a doctrine of mutually independent sensory dimensions. According to his axiom of independence the dimensions of sense-elements are orthogonally oriented in relation to each other: a variation along one dimension does not affect—according to him—variations along other dimensions. Thus a "surface colour" could be described as a combination

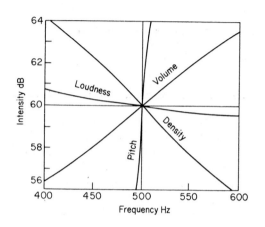

Fig. 10.2 The volume, pitch and density of a sound as functions of intensity and frequency. (From v. Fieandt, 1972 p. 163.)

of a certain colour *tone* and of its "*location* in space". This argumentation, however, does not fit conceptual frames of contemporary perceptual psychology. Reenpää's theory will be given a detailed evaluation in chapter 19.

The Doctrine of Isomorphism

Isomorphism is the name given by Boring to the characteristic way of thinking about sensation and perception by psychologists up to the 1920's. The assumption, mentioned earlier, that to every attribute of sensation, such as the pitch or loudness of a tone, there corresponds a unique and specific stimulus variable—in this case frequency or amplitude—must be taken above all as an example of the isomorphic way of thinking. This approach was especially popular in analysing acoustic dimensions. This, then, was the rigid doctrine of correspondence into which the study of sensory attributes had drifted during the first half of our century.

One of the steps along this road was the observation made by Rahn (1913) that everything indicated by a psychophysical experiment has to do with attributes. According to this opinion the task of any psychophysical experiment is to evaluate the part played by a particular attribute. Later, Titchener (1915) began to speak of the "dimensions of experience", thus leading directly to the postulates of the paired relationship of stimulus and sensation dimensions.

The doctrine of isomorphism treated such correspondences as rather self-evident events.

Out of such analysis grew, says Boring (1942), the false belief that every simple dimension of sensation is correlated to a simple dimension of the stimulus . . . (Boring 1942, p. 89).

The Case of Modern Colour Psychology

Modern colour psychology may be used as an illustrative example showing that a simple isomorphism, as described above, does not correspond to reality. Our eye, as an optical instrument, functions not only analytically, but also by integration; thus the radiation reflected in it which we call, for example, green, may contain a number of various spectral stimulus components. The reaction "green" can be obtained by means of an infinite number of different stimulus combinations. Furthermore, it seems certain that stimulus relations determine the perception of colour hue more crucially than do single radiation elements of the stimulus. The colour which is perceived in response to a particular spectral stimulus combination appearing in some part of visual space depends on the radiation available simultaneously in other parts of that same space.

Land's experiment (see chapter 6 pp. 205–208) has shown conclusively that, in the perception of chromatic object surfaces, other factors are significant besides immediate simple point stimuli. It is a question not only of the spectral frequency of the radiation reaching the eye at any given point, but also of the relative brightness distribution of the entire visual field achieved by means of each particular chromatic filter; this brightness distribution contains the stimulus relationships for the discriminative encoding of certain specific hues. The perception of a particular colour thus corresponds not only to some specific rate of frequency, but any chromatic tone is highly dependent on all stimulus relations prevaling in the total situation.

Whatever we may think of Gibson's description of the transmission of information and its processing at a central level (see p. 242), his theory of the *irrelevance of sensory dimensions* to the process of perception seems undeniable. It is unnecessary to assume particular distinct sensory dimensions, corresponding to stimulus variations, in order to understand and account for the process of perception.

The Problem of Tonal Attributes

To return to the attributes of sounds: we can imagine a researcher attempting to find two tones of different frequencies with the same loudness in a psychophysical experiment. Systematic variation of the attribute named loudness is not accomplished by variation of *intensity* as a stimulus variable. When two tones to be compared have different frequencies, the "stimulus factors" of the loudness reaction are not specifiable as single units. The same number of decibels which is said to serve as a specific or unique stimulus for loudness with a tone, for instance, of 600 Hz, does not produce an equally loud tone at 400 Hz; a correspondingly greater intensity must be used. In the case of acoustic attributes, the requirement of systematic variation of stimulus variables is extremely difficult to carry out, on account of the number of possible different stimulus combinations corresponding to similarly perceived tones. The phenomenal tone is complexly determined. This is one of the reasons why Reenpää's idea about an "orthogonal independence of dimensions" has not been approved of in this presentation.

The Place of Attributes in Modern Descriptions

From the point of view of present-day perceptual psychology, the traditionally distinguished attributes are not much more than highly arbitrary conventions. Their terminological history shows that they were artificially isolated on the basis of certain assumptions as to the one-to-one correspondence between particular stimuli and particular perceptual categories.

If we want to use the term sensory attribute in modern psychology at all, it would seem more justifiable in the light of the above discussion to reserve for it the same usage as that by the European phenomenologists during the 1910's. At that time, attributes were freely distinguished in the perceptual experience, without allowing the concept of isomorphism to restrict the complexity of the description.

When absolute systematic variation of stimulus variables is demanded in research, this represents a return to the old doctrine of the one-to-one correspondence between phenomenal attributes and stimulus variables. It would seem to be unwise to maintain such an attribute doctrine, since it may easily lead to arbitrarily selected and one-sided stimulus variation.

11 | Differentiation of Visual-Tactual Space

Introduction

"Space" is one of the keywords in everyday language as well as among the scientists of our time. The technical terminology developed by planning and programming centres of satellites and aerial navigation uses the expression almost synonymously with the "astronomic universe" even outside our solar system. Yet the word "space" has a wider and more "organismic" or more "behavioural" meaning. As the Texan university rector Ransom (1958) put it: "In an age preoccupied with outer space the area still most important to education is that which lies between the human ears" (1958, p. viii). The conception of space as an explanative tool within perceptual theory and philosophy of knowledge is much older than are the inventions of astronautic technology.

The earliest contributions to a theory of perceptual space date back to the medieval and Renaissance eras. Thinkers like Ibn al Haytham, Leonardo da Vinci and Kepler had been strongly interested in the way our visual organs convey information about our environmental-behavioural space. Descartes decisively improved the methods of description when he introduced the imaginary coordinate system as a kind of frame for our space impressions.

Since this time it has become customary to define space in terms of Euclidean geometry. (As to the fruitfulness of this proposition, see p. 300.) According to this explanatory model, the individual's own body can be considered a kind of point of origin for his three-dimensional frame of reference. The three *cardinal dimensions* of our visual perceptual space intersect at right angles at a point between our eyes. These phenomenal cardinal dimensions or planes, are the vertical, the horizontal and the sagittal. The sagittal plane can be conceived of as a partition between the two eyes, continuing vertically in front and in back of the individual and dividing phenomenal space into a right and a left side. When it cuts exactly halfway between the eyes, it is called the median plane. Perpendicular to the sagittal plane and parallel with the forehead is the frontal or vertical plane, which intersects at right angles with the line of vision. The third plane is the horizontal, which lies through the pupils of the eyes. These planes divide the space into corresponding sectors: something is seen "above" or "below" (the horizontal), or something appears "in front of" or "behind" (the vertical), or, finally, something can be seen "to the right" or "to the left" (from the sagittal plane).

It must be observed that the phenomenal space is *anisotropic*, that is, metrically and proportionally it does not follow Euclidean rules. For right-handers it nearly corresponds to the visual field of the right eye (see Takala 1951).

During the second half of the nineteenth and especially in the twentieth century the research in space perception developed rapidly. Some perceptual psychologists held the opinion that space perception must develop into a field of its own. According to them this specific branch of psychology has to deal exclusively with factors of *differentiation of space* (depth cues, the effects of motion, form, colour, etc.) and of a possible interaction of all of these. Alternatively, it presumably faces a lot of special problems, which were considered curious, for instance, *amodal perception* (how we are able to "perceive" a total, complete cube despite the fact that half the number of its sides are "hidden", i.e. "turned away" from the observer). Other "specific problems" are the preconditions of geometric illusions, the size, shape and colour of after-effects, the phenomenon of "object constancy", and so on.

During the last decades neuropsychological investigations, primarily among scientists in Soviet-Russia, as well as in America, have pointed to another reason why we should consider space perception research as a field of its own. Any kind of "normal" (non-deviant) behaviour is orienting in nature. Orientation behaviour is biologically significant among most animal species: their behaviour looks "purposive"; "goal directed". Such orientation implies that the information mediated by the sense organs is differentiated, at least in some respects. The messages have to be *veridical*; they have to represent the world around the organism with accuracy, in a reliable manner. If there were no veridical perception in the life of an organism it would not be able to look for food, nor could it escape from its enemies or interact with other members of its species. Yet achievements like these do not require only veridical perception. They are built on several types of so called "perceptual constancies" and invariances. In order to behave in an adequate way, the organism should also perceive environmental objects as generally similar in spite of variations in time, perceptual conditions and local positions of sources of stimuli.

Determinants of Perceptual Space

Primary Gravitational Effects

In addition to veridical perception there exist several perceptual events which must be regarded as *nonveridical*. All that is seen, heard, smelled, tasted or tactually and kinemathically perceived does not correspond to physically described reality. The discrepancies are moreover quite systematic in some way or other. The *cardinal dimensions* (the vertical, the horizontal and the sagittal) have been abundantly shown to dominate the way we locate visual objects in our closest neighbourhood.

In the literature dealing with human spatial orientation there is some confusion concerning the use of the concepts of *orientation* and *localization*. In this text we use "orientation" when in a broad sense we speak about the complex of perceptual functioning securing an adequate behaviour in space. The perception of the various specific spatial relations, (1) between the perceiver and objects in space and (2) among objects reciprocally, we call "localization".

A widely accepted distinction of long standing (Hering 1861) is that between the above mentioned type of localization called *egocentric* and what is known as the *exocentric* one (Glick 1968).

It has been argued (e.g. Gibson 1966) that gravitational force has played a decisive role for our adequate body-orientation, and that this "pressure toward the vertical" is observable among the most primordial species of organisms. One remarkable characteristic of that *nonveridical* way of perceiving is that it generally organizes and simplifies the features of the behavioural space. The environment of the perceiving organism is by no means rendered chaotic or unorganized. In this context we have been reminded by v. Békésy (1967) of the important role of all kinds of sensory inhibition. Should we really perceive as veridical all information carried by the stimuli available, the situation would probably be rendered too difficult to be worked out. Perception is therefore often nonveridical in the sense of *omissions*—a substantial part of the stimuli are not processed at all. And there is a high degree of *selectivity* in our perceptual performance. The perceptual acts seem to be governed by the *goal directedness* of the organism. All things that point in the direction of orientation behaviour play a predominant role in the way the organism picks up information from the numerous surrounding stimuli.

Visual Correlates, Inversion of the Retinal Image

The man in the street most likely believes that the way in which we perceive space is based exclusively on our sense of sight: that our space is a visual one. The fact of the matter, however, is that visual space is supplemented psychologically by auditory, kinesthetic, olfactory and gustatory space. In addition, numerous other spatial cues, such as vestibular stimuli and body image cues (see chapter 15), must also be taken into account. These various spaces, naturally, are not mutually independent, but form an interlocking system.

In the following pages it must be kept in mind that, especially in human spatial perception, the various variables ("cues") very seldom have clear phenomenal correlates in spite of the fact that they, in an unmistakable way, influence our perceived spatial world.

In any case, the human organism receives information concerning the perceptual environment by means of the visual sense. It has been proved that human space orientation in complete visual deprivation—in a state of darkness—can function mainly through the impulses from the vestibular apparatus. The predominant role played by vision in spatial perception is easily understood when we recall that vision is a "distance sense"; of all our senses, it is able to detect stimuli from the broadest area. Hearing is usually considered another distance sense, but the space it encompasses is much narrower than that reached by our eyes.

The human eye has sometimes been compared to a camera. The analogy itself is inaccurate and misleading—yet, in the sense of an explanatory model, the retina could be thought of as a counterpart to the light sensitive film, and the lens of the eye as a counterpart to the lens of the camera. As Leonardo da Vinci pointed out, if we do not assume some kind of double lens system in the eye, the refracted light rays must be expected to cross. In any case it would result in an *inverted retinal image*. No wonder that research workers throughout centuries were preoccupied by the question: how do we nevertheless see things right side up. Actually—as modern investigations have verified at different instances—in the process of spatial perception, peripheral receptors, afferent neural events and central mechanisms all act together, forming a quite wonderful system of organized interaction. A great deal of the details in this communication and transformation procedure remain hidden to the scientific observers so far. Evidently, as has already been pointed out (see p. 99), the matter is much more complicated than would be a simultaneous transmission of a locally determined mosaic-pattern. What counts is a *system of relationships*—as for relational explanation systems, see p. 513—therefore, whatever the orientation of a retinal projection, it does not prevent a flexible development of the significant flow of messages.

Thus, during our perceptual process—as far as vision is concerned—two subsequent inversions take place. First, there is an optical inversion on the level of the retina, and second there is a neural inversion in the visual area of the cortex. Numerous fascinating experiments have been performed around this phenomenon.

Kohler (1951) used spectacles, mirrors and other kind of optical devices to produce gross distortions in the space and colour aspects of the habitual visual world. After wearing the distorting glasses for weeks, subjects gradually became able to compensate for these distortions. These like other analogous experiments convincingly show *that the organism habituates*—as it were—when carrying out its space-perception procedure, to previously unknown and distorted systems of stimuli. Analogical reactions occur when—after completed adaptation—the distorting glasses and prisms have been removed again. At first the positions and orientations of familiar things appear reversed. Yet in the long run *rehabituation* takes over. In reaction experiments the subject behaves "correctly" in everything concerning orientation and he also has verdical experiences about what happens in the environment. The degree and efficiency of such a stabilization process can be seen in the fact that one of Kohler's subjects was finally able to ski in the Alps with his distorting lenses on, having had sufficient opportunity to become accustomed to them (see this chapter p. 320 and chapter 23 p. 617).

Perception of Depth and Distance

How depth and distance are perceived depends on the information mediated by various sense organs. It has been customary to analyse and enlist quite a number of *depth cues* for three-dimensional vision. Several sense-modalities generally participate in mediating cues of depth and distance. As a rule each one of these modalities might act independently, which implies that each one is capable of mediating an incontroversial presentation about the locational distances of all visible environmental objects. Yet a complete picture of the environment of a given person requires some degree of *modal interaction*. The term *"intermodal perception"* has been coined (see, e.g. Gibson 1966, v. Fieandt 1958, 1965) to account for the extensive, global administration of all sensorial information available. This point of view is in accordance with that of Rubin who considered the perception of space as illustrative of a biological generality called *the multiviatic principle*, i.e. all fundamental procedures are secured in a certain multitude of ways (personal communication).

The most important depth cues have been grouped as follows:

Gross tactual-kinesthetic cues in near depth The sense of touch gains in importance if we consider the conditions for most effective cues in the immediate near space. The movements of muscles and the motion of the receptive body surfaces play a predominant role in all that is known as sensations of touch. Therefore one should preferably speak of *tactual-kinematic cues*, instead of mere tactual cues.

In this context the role played by the *perception of the subject's body* becomes indisputable. As a matter of fact the perceiver's body forms a *frame of reference*; a basic *measurement coordination system* as it were. The relative distances of the perceived environmental objects are referred back to this basic measure unit. On the other hand we are unable to preserve this system of measures as completely consistent and invariant. This fact in turn depends upon the influences from perceived environmental conditions upon what is perceived as belonging to the "body image" of the observer. When stretching out his arm the subject actually perceives it as longer than when it is held in a completely relaxed position (see also Fig. 15.4 p. 408).

Visual Organismic Cues

Ocular musculature Within the frame of this presentation the visual cues could be classified, first as *organismic cues*—immediately dependent upon the structure and the functions of the perceiving organism—and further as *perceptual cues*, which presuppose not only motor aspects, but also an actively creative process on the part of the perceiving organism. Among these visual perceptual cues the *binocular ones* are distinguished from merely *monocular* cues.

Most of the visual organismic cues depend on the function of ocular musculature. Two of them have been systematically treated since the days of Berkeley (1709): *convergence* and *accommodation*. In addition *retinal size*, which depends among other factors upon *visual angle*, is often referred to this main category.

Accommodation In order to obtain a clear picture of an object the eye focuses on it by changing the convexity of the lens. The adjustment is accomplished by the *ciliary muscle*.

As mentioned above (p. 99) the lens is held in position by the *suspensory ligaments* which are attached to these ciliary muscles. It is worth noticing that the lens, left to itself, assumes a convex shape by virtue of its own elasticity. When focussed on near objects the pull of the suspensory ligaments is therefore reduced in order to render the lens its shape of maximum convexity. When, on the other hand, the eye is focussed on distant objects, the lens is flattened by the radial pull of the suspensory ligaments and the ciliary processes. The lens is said to be in a state of *relaxed accommodation*. In constrained accommodation on near objects, the relaxation of the

suspensory ligaments is accomplished by the contraction of certain muscles
attached to the ciliary ones.

In Berkeley's time it was supposed that the observer judged the distance
of the seen object on the basis of the muscular strain he could feel in his
eyes. Nowadays one speaks of information to the brain signalled by kinesthetic impulses in order to avoid a phenomenalistic way of expression.
Could the degree of contraction in the ciliary muscle provide us with a
depth cue? This mechanism has been subjected to relatively abundant
investigation. To estimate its value as a cue has proved extremely difficult
because all visual perceptual cues ought to be controlled by the experiment.
From around 1890 to 1975 investigators have attacked the problem by
means of ever-refined experimental design. This research has convincingly
shown that accommodation plays a very subordinate role as a cue, even at
short distances (Fig. 11.1).

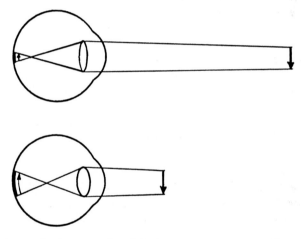

Fig. 11.1 Changes in the convexity of the lens as a consequence of accommodation
to objects at varying distances. (From v. Fieandt, 1966 p. 244.)

Convergence When focusing on an object the observer keeps innervating
another system of muscles too, the eye muscles for horizontal movements
of the eyeballs, the *internal* and *external recti*. The inward rotation of the
eyeballs, the convergence, gets stronger and stronger the closer the object
perceived. If we imagine the lines of sight crossing somewhere behind the
visual object we get a triangle. The base line is formed by the interocular
distance of the perceiver. To this quantity of his body system he must be
thoroughly habituated. "This distance taken together with the record in his
nervous system of what degree of convergence his eyes have been ordered

to assume, furnishes a possible distance cue." (Hochberg 1971b, p. 479). Several experiments during the 1930's and 50's (Frank 1930, Adams 1955) have evidently shown that apparent size decreases as a function of increased convergence (Fig. 11.2). The perceived object apparently gets closer too.

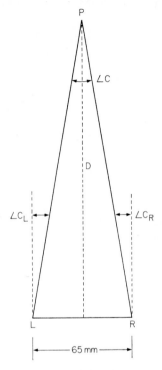

Fig. 11.2 The angle of convergence and the distance of the fixated object. (From Kling and Riggs, 1971 p. 478.)

Most of the experiments have been performed by means of the *mirror stereoscope* (Fig. 11.3), which makes it easy to vary the degree of convergence. As for its importance as a distance cue, convergence can only give some secondary information of the distances of objects, and for distances greater than 6 to 7 m the lines of sight are practically parallel. Obviously the correct adjustment of the eyes must first be achieved in response to some other cues.

Retinal size The size of the retinal image is proportional to the ratio of object size to distance,

$$s = n(S/D)$$

if s is the size of the retinal image and n is the distance from the focal point of the lens to the retina, S the size of the stimulus object and D its distance from the eye (Fig. 11.4). This ratio S/D for all small angles like that one shown in the figure, is the tangent of the visual angle subtended by the object. For example, on a railroad track seen in linear perspective, each railroad tie subtends successively smaller visual angles.

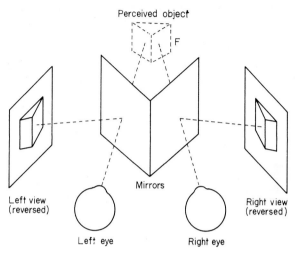

Fig. 11.3 Diagram of the mirror stereoscope. (From Kling and Riggs, 1971 p. 482.)

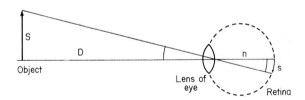

Fig. 11.4 Schematic presentation of the relationship between visual size and depth. (From Kling and Riggs, 1971 p. 477.)

Retinal size gains some importance as a depth cue only together with other cues, and its role, for example, in combined size-distance judgments will be discussed later. It is one of the determinants of size-constancy phenomena in familiar objects. Although the retinal size changes with changes in distance, the apparent or judged size tends to remain constant. In Helmholtzian terms it is as though distance were "allowed for" in judging size (see p. 181).

Visual Perceptual Cues

Binocular Vision and Non-correspondent points on the Retinas

If a person looks at the edge *C* in the prism *ABC* (Fig. 11.5) he accommodates and converges his eyes until the image of *C* is brought to the foveal centre of each retina. These foveal centres are corresponding points in the anatomical sense that they are linked by fibres of the optic tract to a

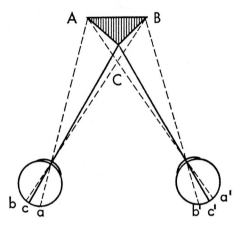

Fig. 11.5 Demonstration of binocular disparity. (From v. Fieandt, 1966 p. 242.)

common locus in the visual projection areas of the cortex. The degree of correspondence of both retinal images makes it possible to localize parts of the stimulus objects which do not fall on corresponding loci as either closer to us or further away than the *horopter* surface, on which the fixated edge is located. The horopter is defined as the locus of all points seen as single in binocular vision, that is the locus of all points whose images fall on corresponding points of the two retinas. In the horizontal plane the theoretical horopter is a circle which passes through the fixation point and the centres of the two eyes. If the edge *C* in the prism *ABC* is foveally and correspondingly projected, the other edges are noncorrespondingly projected on the retinas, resulting in the impression of three-dimensionality.

Double images are produced by projections to noncorresponding points on the retina. Their significance as possible depth cues had been noted early, but has often been overlooked (see Fig. 11.6). They must have a certain functional importance, yet it is very difficult to demonstrate anything of their contribution. There are no ways of isolating them experimentally from other types of binocular cues.

Binocular disparity is a measurable quantity, which increases with the difference in depth as shown in Fig. 11.7. "Disparity is equal to the convergence angle of the nearer point minus the convergence angle of the farther point." (Hochberg 1971b, p. 482). Regardless of the way it is measured, retinal disparity is a possible depth cue. It gives information

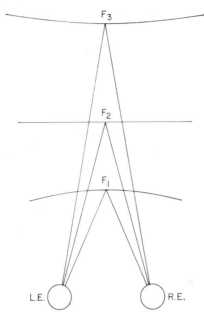

Fig. 11.6 Explanation of double images through the conception of an empirical horopter. (From Kling and Riggs, 1971 p. 480.)

about the distance of visual point stimuli, whether they are nearer than the horopter or not. However its effect is greatest at short distances, where it acts as a considerable aid when we are reaching out our hands or aiming at near objects.

That perception can be artificially misled by retinal disparity is demonstrated by the stereoscope. There have been manufactured several types of these devices, explicitly designed to produce disparate projections of lines or pictures on the two retinas, and thus to yield illusions of three-dimensionality while using two-dimensional stimuli.

Traditional *stereograms* have mostly been photographically prepared by taking two photographs from different positions, separated at least by the interocular distance. During the early sixties Julész (1960, 1963, 1964) elaborated a very practical form of stereograms (Fig. 11.8). A computer prints out two identical patterns of dots in a random display. In one of the patterns an entire region is displaced horizontally. Because the original pattern is random, the displacement of this region cannot be observed when directly looking at the monocular pattern. When the original is presented to one eye and the altered pattern to the other, the displaced region is clearly visible. It appears floating in space as it were, at a different distance than the rest of the pattern (see Hochberg 1971b, p. 483).

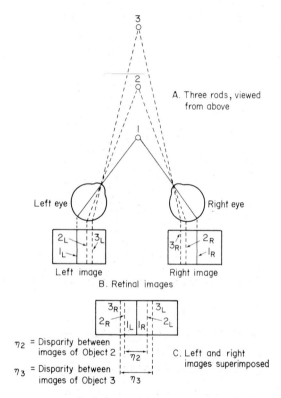

Fig. 11.7 Depth and binocular disparity. (From Kling and Riggs, 1971 p. 481.)

There has been quite extensive research done around this visual depth cue. By means of the stereoscope it has been easy to discover first the limits for the accuracy of stereoscopically discriminated depth differences, secondly something about the fusion rules for stereopsis, and third the way stereopsis has contributed to the perception of objects in space.

Fig. 11.8 Dot pattern stereo-effects as developed by Julész.

Disparity and Stereopsis

In the early 1850's Lotze formulated his theory of "local signs" (Lokal-zeichen). According to this theory each point stimulated on the retina gives information of the direction of the fixated object and its distance from the observer. Hering (1861) elaborated this explanation and expressed it as follows: each retinal point furnishes sensations of light, colour and direction (i.e. two-dimensionally determined position) in addition to a sensation of *depth*. By this theory, these depth sensations are positive (meaning

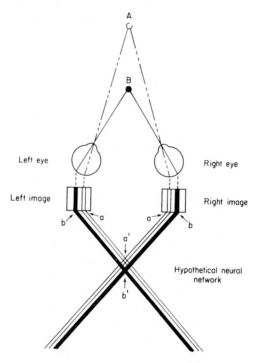

Fig. 11.9 A diagram of a fusion network theory of stereopsis. (From Kling and Riggs, 1971 p. 490.)

"farther") in the nasal halves of the retinas, negative ("nearer") in the temporal halves. Furthermore, they are identical but opposite in sign at corresponding points, identical and of the same sign at symmetrically placed retinal points (Hochberg 1971b, p. 490). This formal doctrine of retinal signs had been opposed already by v. Helmholtz. Recently Hochberg has presented us with an alternative model (after Boring 1933, Charnwood 1951, Dodwell and Engel 1963), shown in Fig. 11.9. Images falling on the two eyes can be made to fuse by means of a network hypothesized in the brain. Lines from *a, a* can fuse only on the point *a'*; similarly lines from *b, b* can fuse only at *b'*. The geometry of the spatial relations that give rise to the disparity has here been reconstructed inside the head. Against this explanation the following arguments can be raised (according to Hochberg 1971b):

(1) Fusion is not necessary for depth perception. Even when disparities are so large that double images are seen, the appropriate depth is perceived.

(2) The images may not really be fused in stereoscopic "fusion". If stereograms have been prepared with their half-views printed in complementary colours, a marked rivalry results in the combined view. This competition between two complementary colours, for example, red and green, does not prevent depth from being seen in the combined view.

Kaufman (1965) replaced the dots in the matrix stereograms of Julész with letters. He presented his subjects with two matrices of letters, identical except that the area outlined by a dotted line had been shifted over one column. As with Julész' patterns, a square of letters is seen at some different depth from the surround.

Observations like these seem to support a model of stereopsis based on suppression at least as well as on fusion.

(3) The nature of binocular disparity. As Koffka (1935), Woodworth (1938), Werner (1937) and Linschoten (1956) have shown, a definition of disparity in terms of points alone is clearly insufficient. The disparity effective for stereopsis seems to be a disparity between *patterns* that are similar in some fashion. Look at the two half-views in Fig. 11.10. If the stereogram is produced by means of modulating the luminance of letters in the inner region, a pattern might arise. In addition the pattern in the left half-view has been shifted one letter to the right. Subjects first reported the inner region as standing *in front* of the surroundings. After a while, this impression shifted into a kind of reversible figure, the depth articulation in figure and ground shifting from time to time.

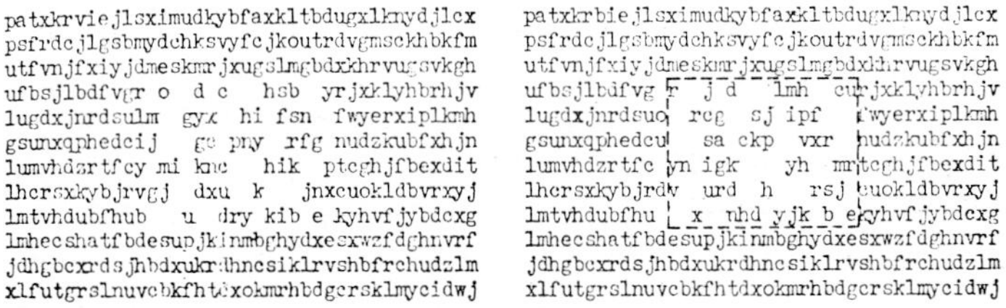

(a)   (b)

Fig. 11.10 Stereogram produced by means of modulating luminance of typescript. (From Kling and Riggs, 1971 p. 491.)

The physical space in which we move our eyes and body can be adequately described in terms of Euclidean geometry. It would be expected that the same geometry would be reflected in our judgments about objects and their locations, see p. 285. However, as a matter of fact, judgments about apparent space are not consistent with Euclidean space. If a subject is asked to arrange a set of lights in an otherwise dark room so that they appear to line up in two parallel rows symmetrically placed around the median plane, and he is also asked to arrange two rows of lights so that the distances between points of each pair that lie in the same frontal plane are equal, the two tasks do not produce equivalent results. There might be some lawfulness, however, in the sphere of these inconsistencies. Among others Luneburg (1950) proposed that the visual space may be non-Euclidean. There has been a lot of argument around this Luneburg theory of space; sufficient evidence is however lacking in favour of the form given to it so far (see Koch I 1959, pp. 395–426).

Some Prevalent Monocular Cues of Depth

In addition to retinal size, already discussed above (pp. 292–293) there are a number of primary monocular cues often referred to as *pictorial cues* of depth. Contrary to the binocular cues this group in terms of Brunswik represents either *ambiguous, irrelevant* or *erroneous* cues. Most of them are at least ambiguous, yet they must frequently be regarded as good indicators of depth and distance. The following cues have been subjected to most intensive research.

Familiar or assumed size This cue is particularly important to the study of space perception. By its very definition it requires past experience with a particular object rather than previous learning of a general rule. Hochberg and Hochberg (1952) argued that this cue of familiar size should be distinguished from that of relative size.

In the well-known Ittelson (1951) experiment each of 3 playing cards was presented singly to the subject under completely *reduced conditions* (monocular vision without any support from other ordinary binocular or monocular cues). One of the cards was normal in size, one twice the normal and one half the normal in size. The distance judgment was made by setting a target to the apparent distance of the playing card. This variable was perceived under *unreduced conditions* (binocularly with all usual distant cues available). Hochberg (1971b) reprints the results for five subjects:

Card	Predicted D	Obtained D
Normal	7·5	7·5
Half-size	15·0	15·0
Double-size	3·8	4·6

Although there has been much controversy around the question of the reliability of these results, one might conclude with the words of Hochberg, "that realistic representations of familiar objects do indeed affect the distance judgments" (Hochberg, 1971b, p. 496). One prerequisite is that the subjects have been instructed to judge distance relationships in the absence of the usual depth cues.

Interposed Objects in Space A perceived distance refers to some model or spatial arrangement which guides the subjects' spatial behaviour. Such behaviour quite typically is determined by a map or schema of the world that the subject has experienced to exist in the external surroundings of his empirical body. The more this world is articulated, that is the more it is "filled up" with objects, the more reliable and precise is the opinion of the subject regarding the depth and distance conditions. It is a commonplace that distances viewed over a water landscape are underestimated, probably as a consequence of the sparse representation of interposed, spacefilling objects on the water surface.

This observation reminds us of the familiar *Oppel-illusion*. Of a bisected line, that half looks longer which in turn has been divided up by tightly interspersed querlines. A bigger number of articulating objects builds out the phenomenal space.

Natural and Linear Perspective

The angles subtended by objects when viewed by means of one eye yield a wide range of variation depending on the distance and direction of the object considered. The straight lines defining this array of visual angles constitute the "visual pyramid" or "pyramid of sight". The effect of these visual angles may be called *natural perspective*.

Linear perspective as used by artists and architects, on the other hand refers to the pattern of lines given by the central projection of the objects on a surface . . . the centre of projection being the relevant point in the eye. The perspective projection thus consists of the intersection of the pyramid of sight by the picture surface. Natural perspective therefore is more general in scope than linear perspective . . . (Pirenne 1970, pp. 56–57).

What is generally referred to by these considerations of Pirenne is the *polar projection*, with one or more vanishing points at the horizon (Fig. 11.11A). The eye however definitely also accepts *parallel projections* of various kinds (Fig. 11.11B–E). Because of the lacking convergence in the lines of the last mentioned projections, those drawings are rendered ambiguous. They easily provide us with a type of *reversible patterns*. Perspective ambiguity probably is no characteristic of nature. Stavrianos (1945) and Freeman (1966) found that subjects, when comparing slants of plane rectangles of different sizes, constantly judged larger rectangles to have greater slant. Linear perspective would normally produce fore-shorting and convergence in perspective views of objects.

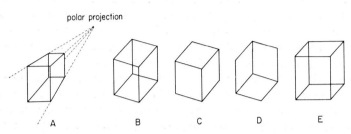

Fig. 11.11 The same object in different perspectives. A polar projection, B–E parallel projection. (From Kling and Riggs, 1971 p. 499.)

Since the time of the physicist and philosopher Ernst Mach (1900) a governing perceptual principle, often labelled the *minimum principle* of pattern perception, has been demonstrated. As Attneave and Frost (1969) were able to show by means of a series of experiments, subjects presented with drawings of cubes showing inconsistent perspective always preferred that apparent slant of the edges, which rendered a maximum amount of homogeneity among all angles and all line lengths and slopes in the per-ceived object. This *minimum principle* ought to be kept in mind when considering superficial interpretations of the function of linear perspective. It is sometimes declared simply an outcome of previous learning. Actually the depth organization of a drawing gives even trapezoid shaped surfaces and often makes oblique angles look more rectangular than does the frontal-parallel alternative of these shapes on a linear pattern without perspective impressions.

Since the time of great Renaissance artists the linear perspective has proved a supreme tool in rendering depth to pictorial art, especially in efforts to portray a scene or a landscape as faithfully and as compellingly as possible. Later, when photography took over the task of realistic repro-ductions regarding our surroundings and objects, artists have applied the rules of perspective in order to reduce apparent depth or to provide incongruities and capturing controversies on their canvas. Modern art not infrequently resorts to inconsistent or partly inverted perspectives.

Hochberg (1971b, p. 500) has pointed out that the spatial information communicated by even sketchy perspective does not work within the frame of other cultures. For instance African natives might be unable to perceive the spatial layout in pictures of people and animals (see also chapter 22 p. 588).

The role of perspective transformations will be discussed in the chapter on perception of movement and time.

Colour perspective In Baroque art the spatial articulation effect of various hues was clearly a well known rule and a technical device. Rembrandt especially preferred to colour the central or most prominent parts of the painting in "warm", reddish, orange or yellow hues. The apparent difference in location of various spectral hues becomes later quite obvious in works of great artists like Goya and van Gogh. Yet Cezanne in particular was a master in placing his human figures at different distances from the observer simply by means of colouring them in different shades. It is an empirically proven fact that surfaces reflecting short wave radiations (bluish and violet objects) are located further away than surfaces reflecting long wave radiation.

In the Psychological Institute of the University of Helsinki, Järvinen (1964) carried out a series of experiments in a "vision tunnel" carefully designed for this purpose and excluding all usual depth cues except for the two flat chromatic objects, the depth difference of which the subject had to judge applying the method of paired comparison.

In incandescent light the most significant differences in the localizations appeared between red and dark green, and orange and light green. The blue however did not differ significantly from red, nor from the orange. In fluorescent light the experienced difference between red and blue is extremely significant due to the apparent displacement of blue toward the dark green regions of the spectrum. (v. Fieandt *et al.* 1964b.)

Aerial perspective When it is often claimed that distant mountains are blue "in the clear country air", this is not only a matter of colour perspective. There are such spacious and wide layers of clear air between the spectator and the mountains that light gets absorbed, and some portions of radiation disappear during travel through the air masses. This accentuating of depth through the light absorption can be more strikingly shown in vistas of great cities, where interposed layers of smoggy air and dust render the buildings just a few blocks ahead an unclear and dim appearance (Fig. 11.12). This effect is known as "aerial perspective" and it may play some role as an ambiguous cue, which is however relevant only over relatively long distances. There has not been any systematic research on its effectiveness so far.

Distribution of lights and shadows In addition to colour and aerial perspective one might consider a *brightness perspective* too. The depth accentuating role played by the distribution of light has clearly been familiar to great artists like Rembrandt and Cezanne, who created numerous masterpieces showing *gradients* of light. If we employ a more modern expression, coined by Gibson (1950), instead of "colour perspective" we could have spoken of "gradients of location of hues".

Leonardo da Vinci distinguished three kinds of subjective shadow phenomena: object shadow, spatial shadow and cast shadow. Object shadow occurs when some opaque object, for example a sphere, stands in the path of light coming from a source. Space shadow means that some part of space appears darker than the immediate environment; a good example is the corner of a room in shadow. Cast shadows, with their strong effect on the articulation on space, are exemplified by the work discussed in the chapter on visual art (e.g. Rembrandt's *Night Watch*).

Fig. 11.12 The effect of aerial perspective. (From v. Fieandt, 1966 p. 246.)

If a light coming from one side and sharply delimited in direction falls upon a surface with relief-like elevations and depressions, the object shadows in the depressions occur on the side opposite to those on the elevations (Fig. 11.13). One phenomenological consequence of this is that when the surface (e.g. a board) is turned upside down, what was formerly a depression now appears an elevation and vice versa. There is a tendency to perceive the direction of the illumination as constant; thus the strongest invariant in perception is that of the direction of illumination, and the perceptual whole is structured so as to correspond to it. This *illumination continuity*, to which the surface relief corresponds, may be veridical, but it may also deviate from the real stimulus basis. In many cases, however, the observer forms an integrated illuminational whole, in terms of which he perceives the locations of shadows and the relief of the surface.

There has been a great deal of discussion about whether some one direction of illumination is more favoured than others in forming this illuminational whole. This problem has been empirically studied by von Fieandt (1938b). The results indicated that an illuminational whole which assumes a source of light located above is more favoured than others. This assumption of overhead lighting seems to be as strong in 4–7 year-old children as in adults. At the same time, the research revealed another

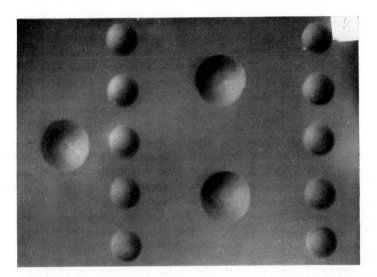

Fig. 11.13 The role of light and shadow in the depth articulation of a surface. (From v. Fieandt, 1972 p. 277.)

perceptual coherency, in competition with the former; this can be called the *coherence of depth shapes*. Especially strong is the tendency for all shapes to be perceived as *elevations*; for some subjects, this was so strong that it prevailed at the expense of the coherence of illumination (v. Fieandt, 1938b, 1949).

The above mentioned conformity in the reactions of children and adults does not mean that the preference for configurations illuminated from above should be innate as to character. Hess (1961) later showed by means of animal experiments that previous experience may in some cases determine how the object surface is articulated on the basis of shadow. If young chicks, seven weeks of age, had been reared in cages lit from below, they

showed a marked tendency to pick at photographs of wheat grains corresponding to an illumination from below. However, a second experiment was
less successful. This time adjustment to lighting from below was quite
difficult. Overhead lighting was probably after all more in accordance with
spontaneous ways of behaviour (Fig. 11.14).

The controversy between nativistic and empiristic explanations is old
and strong and can be raised in connection with almost every one of the

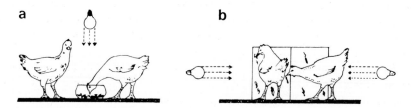

Fig. 11.14 *a* and *b*. Schematic drawing of the Hess experiment with chicks reared in
variously oriented illuminations. (From v. Fieandt, 1972 p. 279.)

Fig. 11.15 The "Falling Arch of Fort Knox" illusion. (From Antonitis, *Am. J.
Psychol.* **82**, 1969.)

depth cues (see chapter 13 p. 380). So far as humans are concerned experimental evidence is hard to obtain; so much spatial learning might occur during the first months of life.

Like the reversible brightness-distribution pattern shown in Fig. 11.13, there can be produced quite striking ambiguous figures in cases where brightness gradients on rounded surfaces, on the one hand, and linear perspective factors, on the other, have been brought to combine. A beautiful case is the "falling arch of Fort Knox illusion" (Fig. 11.15). If the picture is turned over, the "falling arch" transforms into a peculiar and impressive protrusion in the shape of a broken cone. The transformation could hardly occur without the effects produced by the deep shadows around the edges of the "falling arch" considered.

Partly overlapping or covering This cue was originally listed by Brunswik as an ambiguous one, and sometimes it can prove even quite erroneous. Generally speaking, further objects often appear partly or totally covered by nearer ones, so the common contour of two objects may give a rather good indication of which one is in front. Yet overlapping contours can be provided in plane figures without any differences as to their location in the third dimension. And, referring to the well known experiment by Osgood (1953, p. 263), it is a familiar fact that we are easily deceived by this cue if the "overlapping" is replaced by inverted size-conditions for the object and appropriate sections in the otherwise unbroken and continuous contour of the physically nearer object (Fig. 11.16).

Helmholtz gave the rule that the contour line of the covering object usually does not change its direction where it joins the covered object. Experimental evidence is not in favour of this criterion, which apparently does not hold true under all circumstances (see the examples in Fig. 11.17).

Gradients Gibson (1950) has emphasized the fact that a number of depth cues have been completely omitted in the traditional investigations of perception, which have usually been based on some kind of abstract concept of "empty three-dimensional space". The third dimension, "depth", has been conceived of as the shortest distance between the object and the retina. Thus research has been concentrated on the effort to discover how objects are localized in the third dimension. Actually, however, *differentiated or structured depth* is almost always perceived in such a way that *objects are seen as rising from surfaces or lying on them.* Perceptual distance is represented not by straight lines running horizontally at eye level, but by a plane reaching from the observer to the object, somewhat below eye level. It is this plane which is projected in its entirety, as an organized whole, onto the retina. Thus distances are quite concretely represented on the retina.

As a matter of fact Gibson did not approve of the expression "depth cue". The organism does not gather information by way of reacting to cues.

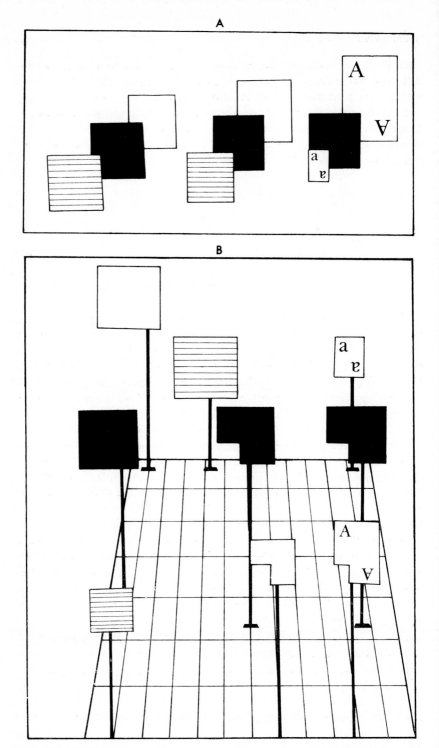

Fig. 11.16 Illusion of size differences created by partial masking (A) and how this illusion was created (B). Courtesy of *Life* No. 28, 1950. (From Osgood, 1953 p. 264.)

Thus it would not be appropriate to list,—as it has been done in this book—his findings as a category among the "depth cues". It was the Berkeley-Helmholtzian way of reasoning which needed "cues" as explanation for how we form a visual space despite "two-dimensional retinal images". Hochberg points out that Gibson prefers explanations in terms of invariances, that is, invariant features, within the total organization of the perceptual world (Hochberg 1971b, p. 503).

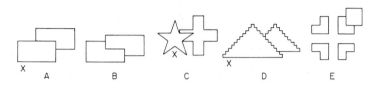

Fig. 11.17 Effect of overlapping contours. (From Kling and Riggs, 1971 p. 498.)

This proposition of predominant invariances governing the overall perceptual organization would thus seem to be irreconcilable with the "cue hypothesis". In the opinion of the authors of this volume such an inference however could not be legitimate. It has been found on several occasions that various kinds of *stimulus enrichment* support more articulated, well organized and veridical perceptual structure. If the "cue" concept is deprived of its mere mechanistic, "point-by-point" significance, we can handle the traditional depth cues as instances of well-controlled and partly isolated enriching stimulation, which contributes to stronger organization invariances. In this sense, depth cues certainly lose a lot of their individual, isolated explanatory value. They are no ultimate entities fixed in number, capable of being listed, or additive as to their cumulative effects. They just contribute as stimulus variables to the information needed for three-dimensional perception.

Additionally, it deserves mentioning that *"cues"* in the traditional sense of the word (e.g. Tolman, Brunswik, etc.) refers to stimulus variables the effects of which presumably might be "hidden" and unconscious rather than conscious to the perceiving organism.

The more recent concept of *"stimulus information"* has the advantage of covering both types of situation:

(1) those situations which involve conscious observations and consideration during the perceptual act,
(2) those situations in which our actions are spontaneous and lack deliberation.

What are the perceptual invariances according to Gibson? They could be called *relational invariances* in the sense that stimulus relationships have proved more powerful determinants of perceptual space than single stimuli by themselves. The relational variables most stressed by Gibson are the *gradients*. If there is any regular marking or visible texture on the ground, this texture undergoes perspective transformation such that in the retinal

Fig. 11.18 The gradient of texture density in a surface. (From v. Fieandt, 1972 p. 276.)

image there is a gradient of texture density. If the pattern projected on the retina consists of components of evenly increasing or decreasing density, what is perceived is a surface receding from the viewer, with the texture density greater at greater distances (Fig. 11.18).

According to Gibson it is the gradient which is the appropriate stimulus variable to consider, not the lines in a drawn stimulus, nor the points of retinal stimulation (cf. the "local signs" of Lotze). "These gradients in the retinal image are directly correlated with objective arrangements on the one hand and . . . with the subjective perceptions of those arrangements on the other." (Hochberg 1971b, p. 501.)

The concept of gradient has a much wider relevance in the theory of perception than that originally ascribed to it by Gibson when discussing determinants of visual depth. It is applicable in most instances in which relational invariances have been resorted to as explanations of perceptual organization. We shall turn back to it later (see Johansson 1975).

Motion parallax and motion perspective Before discussing some relational theories of object perception we still have to consider one systematic determinant of visual space or "cue", if we use the older terminology.

The relative motion of parts of the field of view gives rise to motion parallaxes and motor perspective. "Relative" motion implies that these depth determinants not only start functioning when objects move in the world but also when we ourselves move about in the world in relation to the objects. For the process of developing a perceptual space this primordial *sensory exploration* has certainly been of tremendous importance. It is by way of this active moving about that we gather the basic information concerning the surrounding physical world.

Parallax in general is the change in the visual field resulting from a change in the spectator's position. The projections of the objects in the "picture plan" (e.g. a train window) all move about if you keep moving yourself. This "cue" has relevance both for monocular and for binocular vision. Yet it gets especially important in cases where, for example, as a consequence of partial blindness, binocular sight has been impaired. We often see a one-eyed person moving the head to and fro in a horizontal plane. The farther objects seem to move slower than the closer ones, each velocity being a smoothly graded function of the objects' real distance.

Gibson has suggested that the significance of this kind of mediator of information should be considered in a wider context. According to him the visual system might respond directly to some features of the continuous transformations which are due to motion confronting the eye (see also the contributions of Johansson, chapter 19).

The space-determining role of those types of transformations, as well as that of the perspective reversals, will be evaluated in subsequent chapters of this book.

Relational Variables in Object Perception

The conception of relational stimulus variables (see p. 364) has led to propositions concerning the role of some relatively simple ratios governing our experience of objects in space.

Size-distance invariance The apparent size of an object is interrelated with its apparent distance. It has been argued that we must take an object's distance into account in order to judge its size. In other words, it is the perceived distance, not the physical distance, that affects the size that will be perceived as a response to a given retinal image. Thus the perceived distance is one of the determinants of perceived size.

Physically the relationship is simple enough. Let s be the size of the retinal image of an object having the physical size of S, and D be the distance of the object from the eye. The retinal size s is proportional to S/D, which means that the ratio of size to distance is constant. There has been a lot of discussion as to whether the same thing holds true for apparent size S' and apparent distance D'. Can we write:

$$S'/D' = k?$$

The experimental evidence in favour of this hypothesis remains controversial so far. A closer examination of it will be postponed until the chapter on perceptual invariances.

Slant-shape invariance is closely related to the above-mentioned relationship. It presumes that the shape of a slanted object (e.g. a rectangle) would be correctly perceived if slant and shape were coupled perceptually as they are physically. "In the usual experiments to study the judgments of the shape of an object, a subject tries to match the shape of an object (the standard) that is presented to him at one slant, by choosing from among a set of objects having different configurations (the variables) which are viewed at another slant." (Hochberg 1971b, p. 515.) The subject usually chooses a shape which is intermediate between one which presupposes the two objects as having the same physical configuration, and one which would presuppose equality of shape in the retinal image. As Hochberg points out, there is little support for the proposition that the information about slant and shape should first manifest itself as perceived. On the contrary, some information of the degree of slant can be achieved and it might effect the perceptual behaviour without necessarily having been directly perceived (Hochberg 1971b, p. 517). To Gibson again, information about the object's shape can be potentially available in features which remain invariant during the transformations that its projection directly undergoes in the optic array.

Auditory Cues

Our perceptual space is partly also auditory determined, in various ways. With the same degree of adequacy—and with the reservations expressed on p. 309—we could speak of "auditory cues". They are analogous in many respects to the visual ones. Information about distance in space is mediated by sound intensity, frequency and the time differences among various signals located at different directions and distances in space. Among the last-mentioned, time differences between auditory and visual sensations of the same object must also be taken into account.

The importance of frequency was shown by v. Békésy (see chapter 7 on frequency). In the sound spectra emitted or reflected by sounding objects lower tones are characteristic for relatively closely located, higher tones characteristic of further located, sounding components of the object.

Interrelations between Appearances, Spatial Orientation and Distance

Developmental Factors—Innate v. Acquired Determinants of Perceptual Space

The spatial coordinate system develops as a product of visual-tactual inter-action in the sensitive organism. By the end of its first year of age a baby is normally tactually very alert and motivated. It moves its limbs continuously, especially its hands and fingers, grasping around eagerly. Compared to the sense of vision which develops later and at a slower rate, the sense of touch is well matured and highly elaborated in early childhood. During these important months the still rather ambiguous visual percepts of the baby have improved through these frequent controls mediated by receptors of non-visual modalities.

The role played by the sense of hearing cannot be regarded as equally primordial. Sounds always provide efficient aids in our efforts at localizing objects. However, a strictly organized space built on auditory sensations proper is extremely rare. It is a well known fact that in experiments with hidden loudspeakers or when listening to other sounds in twilight, subjects tend to *objectify* the hidden sources: the stimulus is ascribed to some of the simultaneous visual or tactual objects in the room (cf. the experiment by Somerkivi 1947, and chapter 17 p. 469).

The intermodal anchoring of the human perceptual space has been convincingly demonstrated through the *cross modal transfer*-experiments. In Brynn Mawr College at Pennsylvania young Rhesus-monkeys had been conditioned to discriminate between tactually provided small three-dimensional objects in geometrically elementary shapes (balls, cubes, cones, cylinders, etc.). The sight of the animal was screened during the experiment. The paired comparison method was employed.

The well trained animals then had to compare two-dimensional pictures of the same geometrical figures. A cross modal transfer-effect was significantly achieved. After the conditioning period with tactual stimuli the learning product was transferred to yield right answers when working with visual stimuli of the objects. (Verbal communication by Mrs. Wilson in 1963.)

L

Orientation refers to the way of moving around in our daily environment. This control is better performed the richer the stimulus context encountered. Stimulus enrichment means increasing the amount of criteria for veridical perception. The more this stimulus context is *reduced* during the experiment the less veridical and enduring are the object-experiences. In order to investigate laws of perception under poor articulation conditions this method of experimental *reduction* is often employed. Most of the perceptual depth cues can be controlled by various methods of reduction. If that method is carried far enough, there is nothing left of the usual depth-context of the frame of reference. What is perceived is a diffuse, unorganized, dim, white-looking space, a "Ganzfeld".

Gradual Differentiation of a Homogeneous Space

Metzger (1929b) studied monotonous, uniform visual stimulation by producing a *homogeneous visual field*. His procedure was as follows: the subject sat opposite a wall painted a homogeneous flat white, at a distance somewhat over a metre, and fixed his sight on a point in its centre. All edges and corners were eliminated by means of rounded cardboard sheets which inclined imperceptibly toward the subject. The illumination was homogeneous and could gradually be increased. In the dimmest illumination the subjects reported a diffuse "light fog", which was phenomenally "*space-filling*", similar to the *space colours* described in chapter 6. It could not be localized as lying on any plane or at any particular distance. When the illumination was raised above a given threshold, the visual field was experienced as a concave surface, oriented at right angles to the line of vision and perceived as a *film colour* at a distance more or less equivalent to the real distance of the wall, but devoid of the depth structure and articulation of a surface colour. As the illumination continued to rise, another threshold was encountered above which the normal surface articulation and *surface colour* of the wall was perceived.

Thus, in the first stage of the experiment, the only thing perceived was an undifferentiated, unarticulated light fog, the so-called *homogeneous visual field* or *Ganzfeld*. The German term is commonly used in English-speaking countries also. Gibson (1966) suggests the term "white-out", in analogy to black-out, to describe a phenomenon experienced in the Arctic wilderness. When this occurs, the unarticulated white light leads to a confusing impression in which the details of the landscape and even the horizon itself disappears entirely from the observer's field of vision.

This homogeneous light fog can be produced experimentally in a number of ways. Cohen's procedure (1957) is based on a large sphere whitewashed inside and out. When the subject looks into this sphere from further away through a round hole, he does not perceive the inside at all, since the visual space is completely unarticulated. Another ingenious method is to place split pingpong balls in front of each eye in the manner of eyeglasses (Gibson 1966, pp. 212–213).

An object surface can be seen as a surface, with a particular shape and colour, *only* when the illumination is strong enough to allow the eye to accommodate to the irregularities of the surface. The illumination must thus exceed the threshold determined by the distance and other factors affecting accommodation. If accommodation is successful, the diffuse visual field is differentiated into object surfaces. Gibson also suggests that borders of intensity are necessary in the homogeneous light surrounding the eye in order for the location and organization of surfaces to be distinguished at all (Gibson 1966, p. 212). As soon as structural variation appears in the visual field, a framework or system of reference can be formed which in turn serves as the basis for further perceptual articulation.

Koffka (1935 pp. 115–119) sums up Metzger's results with the following four statements:

1. An undefined unarticulated visual field appears space-filling. Even the lowest degree of articulation requires some degree of irregularity in the object surface.
2. The perception of a surface is already evidence of a considerable degree of articulation; objectless space and the coloured surface have been distinguished from each other.
3. Perception of the surface as a film colour is the first stage in the process of gradually increasing articulation.
4. Phenomenal space occupies the least possible volume given the circumstances.

These statements also imply that, even in cases as simple as the perception of two-dimensional plane figures, no figures or gestalten will be perceived unless there is some degree of *irregularity* or non-uniformity in the stimulus pattern. As soon as some possibilities of perceiving non-uniformity are present many interesting figural articulations arise. As a simple illustration, let us imagine an inkblot on a sheet of white paper. Given some discontinuity, those parts of the whole configuration which are sufficiently internally consistent and unitary are *differentiated from the rest of the stimulus field*. The emergence of a gestalt presupposes, in addition to mere segregation from the environment, also the formation of a figural pattern. Generally speaking *homogeneous* stimulation initiates cohesive, unifying field tensions, while non-homogeneous stimulation leads to isolating, segregating tensions in the pre-supposed bioelectrical field of the visual cortex (see Köhler 1920).

According to the gestalt psychologists visual gestalten emerge from the fine-grained interaction between internal and external conditions. As soon as the homogeneity of the ganzfeld is disturbed in some way, different potential articulations arise, which follow the familiar gestalt laws of perceptual organization in bringing about the fundamental differentiation between plane figures and their background

Pattern Discrimination on Plane Surfaces

The prerequisites for figure formations and pattern recognition as based upon changes in the array of light, has been analysed, so far, in terms characteristic for the gestalt theory of perception (Metzger's laws of the segregation of stimuli, Koffka's statements on figural articulation, Köhler's presumptions of isomorphic correlates of stimulus patterns within cortical bioelectric fields). This survey might have been purposive and interesting as a historical background to modern attempts at satisfactory explanations. The gestalt theory mostly reports interesting analogies and suggestions on the very level of pure descriptions. That kind of approach evidently deserves some credit for having pointed out the important fact of "stimulus equivalence", that is, the fact that all "squares" and all "circles" seem to contain certain unique shape characteristics. A square is recognized as a square despite its size, its colour, the number and retinal orientation of its stimulus elements. The stimulus-equivalence of all squares, despite the completely different elements they are "built upon", is something peculiar.

Even the traditional supposition of "isomorphy" between "neural brain fields" and stimulus configurations gives no explanation for the very processes of pattern recognitions. Nowadays the vast amount of neurophysiological findings (see p. 74), especially the impact from single cell recordings since the time of Hubel and Wiesel, has provided us with previously unexpected ingredients for neuropsychological model constructions.

The next step in the attempt to explain the "stimulus equivalence", was, according to Dodwell, represented by Lashley's ideas of interference patterns as circles of resonance which get globaly propagated throughout the cortical cell-tissue. It was also envisaged in Hebb's neural cell models for perceptual learning, especially the primary cortical detector systems of his presupposed "cell assemblies".

The third step was taken by Deutsch (1955), Sutherland (1957) and Dodwell (1957, 1964) who developed their explanation models for pattern recognition on the background of relatively fresh evidence from single cell recordings on various levels of the visual system. The basic model designed by Dodwell looks, as far as sensory functions are concerned, somewhat like the combinations in the following schematic figure (Fig. 11.19).

It has to be observed that the contour-information contained in retinal stimulation is propagated to C as a first stage of communication. At this stage the representation is merely spatial in nature. Mediation of spatial information requires a *topological* correspondence between the input at the R-level and the input in C. Yet such a correspondence does not necessarily imply a *topographic* identity. It is only on the third stage that a temporal organization of the message is prevailed during the transmission procedure from C to D.

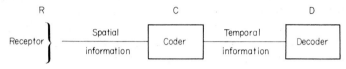

Fig. 11.19 Schematical drawing of the pattern-coding model. (From Dodwell, 1970 p. 22.)

This is not the right place for discussing the above-mentioned explanation model in all its details, in the way they have been presented by Dodwell. The essential aspect is stressed by pointing out that he further elaborated the structures of the coder as well as the decoder in terms of either singular or joint activation of respective neural elements. These elements act as receivers and mediators of messages and they presumably are linked together in systems of rows and columns, the orientation of which represents the horizontal and the vertical main dimensions respectively in the anatomical structure of the retina. That means faster and more effective central visual coding of stimulus patterns, for instance a square, the main extension of which coincides with either the vertical or the horizontal axis of the retina.

Neurophysiological Evidence for the Structure of Explanation Schemata

Criticism has rightly arisen against this kind of descriptive model construction, of which Dodwell's scheme has only provided an illustrative example. There could be listed several of them, of course, all of that type. They are highly abstract, logically founded and even mathematically derived constructions for what has been inferred mainly from findings in animal experiments. Yet certain features, especially in Dodwell's explanatory model, fit some of the results of the Hubel and Wiesel research line so nicely, that something very striking must be hiding behind his ideas.

When Hubel and Wiesel (1962) mapped the receptive fields for single neurons in the cortex of cats, they found some correspondence to the arrangements with the receptive fields on the level of single cells in the geniculate bodies and even on the level of the retina. Yet the cortical fields turned out to be much more complicated. What is surprising on the other hand is the "economy" and "simplicity" in the functional solutions of the system.

First, there are "simple receptive fields", the elements of which might be grouped, for example, as indicated in Fig. 11.20. The "on" responses occur along an axis of the field, whereas the rest of the field elicits "off" responses only (for explanation see chapter 4 pp. 83–85). Very interesting are the changes in responses elicited by contours which are moving across the field in a direction perpendicular to the field's axis (Dodwell 1970, p. 57).

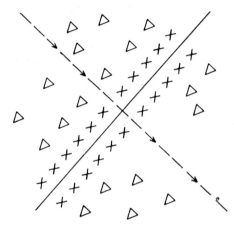

Fig. 11.20 Patterns of response in geniculate and cortical receptive fields. (From Dodwell, 1970 p. 57.)

Yet there are also "complex fields" at a higher level of organization. Some of the cortical cells give combined "on–off" responses. Within these fields strict localization required for optimal stimulation no longer holds. "On" and "off" summations occur only in rather specific ways.

In experiments with cats it turned out that a horizontally oriented rectangle (▨▨▨▨▨▨▨) elicited cortical potentials varying in frequency according to the location of the stimulated area of the retina. Tilted rectangles equal in size and proportions did not affect the cortical cells at all.

In addition to these cell assemblies in area 17, Hubel and Wiesel identified hypercomplex field-units in area 18. Most of these field units are responsive to highly specific moving contours. If a narrow rectangle with its longer sides deviating from the vertical orientation by an amount of 30–45° keeps moving over the field, the receptive system is evidently extremely sensitive to variations in the *width* of the rectangle. In other words, a rectangle showing the same *proportions* between its edges would not activate these receptor fields unless the edge oriented along the direction of the movement remains unchanged. *On the contrary, it does not matter across what parts of the retina it keeps moving.*

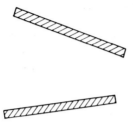

Fig. 11.21 Cell activated only by left (contra-lateral) eye over a field approximately 5 × 5°, situated 10° to the left and above, area centralis. (From Dodwell, 1970 p. 60.)

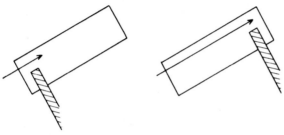

Fig. 11.22 Responses to a dark tongue 1/2° wide introduced from below in four different positions. (From Dodwell, 1970 p. 70.)

Dodwell is inclined to assume that stimulus-equivalence is at least partly achieved by means of perceptual learning.

In Dodwell's experiments with rats, the animals performed well when required to distinguish between stripe patterns where the stimuli followed the main orientation of the cardinal dimensions (+).

However, when confronted with rotated patterns, even if they were perpendicular to each other (×) the animals showed great difficulties in their behaviour (Dodwell 1970, pp. 73–74).

According to Sutherland, the octopus has a very consistent preference for certain shapes in its discrimination-learning behaviour. This animal easily learns to discriminate between horizontal and vertical contours, and it has a coding system fitted to detect the inner relationships of the structure.

Interestingly enough the model elaborated by Dodwell renders itself appropriately for computer simulations of the activated visual system. What is more, it seems to account for the impressive readaptation procedures to optically distorted patterned inputs.

Evidence from Readaptation to Optically Distorted Patterns

Since the contributions by Stratton (1897), Erismann (1946) and Kohler (1951), it has been a well known fact that the visual system, after having undergone conditions of long lasting regular distortions is able to adapt remarkably fast and in a very efficient way to these distortions (see further Pick *et al.* 1963). The word "regular" is extremely important. In other words: "rearrangements" occur in response to regular distortions. These rearrangements are highly predictive. The visual system seems to apply a kind of calculating transformation.

The point with all the interesting distortion effects presented by Kohler, and later on summarized by, for example, Smith and Smith (1962) and Harris (1965), is that these lenses, mirrors and wedge prisms did not—as a rule—produce *arbitrary distortions*. What happens in the visual world is predictable if we know the optical structure of the distorting devices. In case of "irregular" distortions no "rearrangement" occurs. There will arise "disarrangement" in the system.

One of the advantages with Dodwell's explanation model is that it allows for mathematical calculations of the conformal transformations by means of which the visual reactions of the subject are easily understandable. There are strong relational invariants hidden in all translations, reflections and inversions, etc. effected by the distorting optical instruments. What the visual system performs is a kind of transformation analysis. By way of conformal transformations the visual system adapts to what remains essential during all kind of regular distortions: the relational invariances.

There are impressive experiments on *some influences of stabilized retinal images* as a consequence of continuous fixation. In staying constant and relatively stable, in spite of continuous movements of the eyeballs (see chapter 5 p. 99), particular portions of the perceived figure-pattern stand out as compared with the other parts of the configuration. When fading off, as a consequence of enduring stimulation of some areas on the retina, these preferred elements remain visible for a longer period. These persisting portions are not arbitrary: a human face-shaped figure is more persistent than an occasional line-pattern on the same level of complexity (Pritchard *et al.* 1960). The following "unstructured regenerations" of a fading pattern are interesting (Fig. 11.23):

In the after-effect regenerations (*b, c, d*) of the original pattern the orthogonal crossing part of the vertical-horizontal axes never dropped out.

Campbell and Kulikowski (1966) investigated interference-effects of simultaneously presented *sinusoidal gratings*. The grating with a lighter background was applied with the purpose of acting as a masking pattern to a darker grating of equal dimensions. The masking effect was strongest in cases where the stripes in both gratings had the same orientation (vertical). With an increasing angle between the main dimensions of the stripes in the patterns compared, the interference decreases.

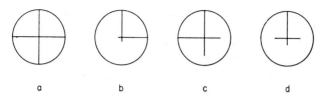

a   b   c   d

Fig. 11.23 Image, shown as a target (a) and regenerations of it in "structured" and "unstructured" forms (b, c, d). (From Dodwell, 1970 p. 195.)

The authors call for centrally-organized detectors of edges in specific orientation. Dodwell points out (1970, p. 198) that orientation-specific "field organizations must be presumed to exist within the visual system of man". On the other hand some caution must be called for when considering the explanation model of Dodwell. Conclusive neurophysiological evidence has not yet been obtained.

The Olson and Attneave Experiments

The explanation models presented so far are closely connected with the research marked out by Hubel and Wiesel. In view of the fact that their assumption of specific edge detectors has been questioned, a somewhat different approach toward the pattern recognition problem deserves mentioning. In their clear study on "similarity grouping" (1970, pp. 1–21) Olson and Attneave pointed out that at least the "slant analysers" suggested by Hubel and Wiesel are—presumably—insufficient when looking for explanations for some of their main results: the discriminative superiority of the subjects when confronted with the line patterns—the crossing symmetric axes of which coincided with the cardinal dimensions. The symmetric axis, e.g. of a right angle, is the straight bisection line of it. If the elements in a sub-area of an elsewhere homogeneous pattern had their symmetric or main axes differing by a 90° rotation (see Fig. 11.24), this sub-area was definitely segregated more quickly from the perceptual whole than were elements that differed from each other by 180°. Patterns like those in Fig. 11.24a were easier to recognize than the patterns pictured in Fig. 11.24b.

Olson and Attneave presented their subjects with circular fields—the area of which was filled up with tightly dispersed pattern elements (line segments varying in slope, in curvature and linearity, straight angles in

varying orientations, etc.). A 90° sector of the circular field contained somewhat different elements (see Fig. 11.25, a and b). The patterns were
tachistoscopically projected, and reaction times for right answers were precisely registered. The enclosing contour was left out of these circular areas.

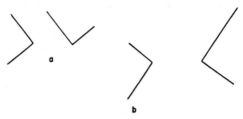

Fig. 11.24 Rectangle-pattern elements as used by Olson and Attneave. (From Olson
and Attneave, *Am. J. Psychol.* **83**, 1970 pp. 1–21.)

It turned out that the subject performed better if the sector to be
segregated was oriented with its imagined "border lines" along the horizontal-vertical main axes of the figure, than if these borders coincided with the
45° rotated axes (Fig. 11.25 b).

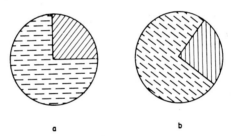

Fig. 11.25 Segregation patterns with differentially structured sector-elements and
positions. (From Olson and Attneave, 1970.)

On the transmission levels so far investigated by Hubel and Wiesel there
have not—at least in anthropoids—been found such a prevalence of H–V-
oriented receptive fields that would be required in order to explain the
results of Olson and Attneave. According to these authors the relative
amounts of variously oriented receptive fields in man are still unexplored.
They give arguments in favour of "descriptors" on a higher level of the
visual system than was proposed by Hubel and Wiesel. Some of these
descriptors might be directly sensitive to organizational factors effected by
the cardinal dimensions.

Most interesting were the experiments during which the head of the
subject had to be tilted by 45° when reacting to the pattern. By means of

these trials the authors wanted to assess whether *gravitational* factors were more influential than the *retinal* ones. It turned out that the subject performed best when the orientation of the sectors had changed. Yet the reactions remained consistent when judged from the point of view of retinal orientation. The problem of the significance of a broader, intermodal frame for what is called *visual* pattern recognition will be touched upon in the next chapter.

Pattern Ambiguity—Figure and Ground

Already during the era of the first decades of laboratory psychology the attention of the investigators was drawn to several types of reversible patterns; varying situations bring about different cases of reversibility.

A pattern might appear reversible because the stimulus configuration provides alternatives for what is standing out as a "figure" against a "background". The classical treatment is given by Rubin (1921). In other cases

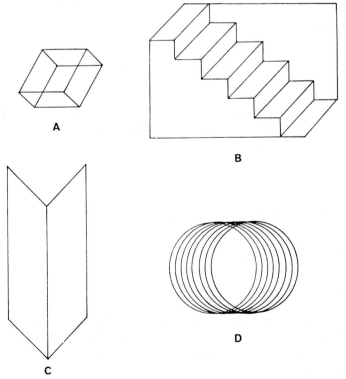

Fig. 11.26 A sample of reversible patterns displaying ambiquity as a consequence of lacking projective perspective. (From v. Fieandt, 1972 p. 259.)

there are line patterns which can be conceived of as plane projections of three-dimensional figures: cubes, open books, staircases etc. If the perspective cue in these drawings is left out, that is, if parallel lines do not converge in the depth, the flat projection may become ambiguous and results in a reversible pattern (e.g. the Necker cube). Figure 11.26 illustrates some of the best-known types of reversible figures, represented by plane figures drawn without perspective.

Various experimental approaches have been utilized in the attempt to discover some neurophysiological events corresponding to the phenomenal distinction between figure and ground articulation. Rubin examined a variety of visual plane figures. In figures 11.27 and 11.28, if one part

Fig. 11.27 Effect of the degree of articulation on the segregation of figures. (From v. Fieandt, 1972 p. 260.)

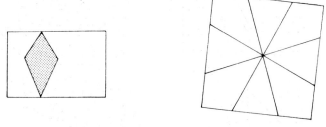

Fig. 11.28 Brightness differences and factor of proximity as contributing to figure-ground articulation. (From v. Fieandt, 1966 p. 231.)

is perceived as a figure the rest of the pattern becomes a ground, which seems to continue behind the part seen as figure. The ambiguous parts reverse, with what was previously seen as ground becoming figure, while the field previously seen as figure becomes ground. In these patterns the contours of the seen figures do not look like sharp "breaks" in the plane on which the figure is seen, yet the figure seems somehow closer to the observer than the rest of the pattern, as though it were lying on top of the ground.

It is a well known fact that in a pattern with two cross-shaped fields (Fig. 11.29) in complementary colours, the chromatic simultaneous contrast, which either one of the crosses undergoes, gets stronger when the cross phenomenally is *the figure* and the rest of the pattern is seen as background.

Fig. 11.29 Ambiguous figure-ground articulation. (From v. Fieandt, 1966 p. 231.)

Coren (1969) in one of his three experiments confirmed these results through brightness contrasts by applying the women–rabbit figure (Fig. 11.30). In the second experiment he was interested in the brightness con-

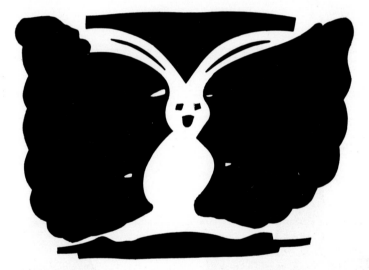

Fig. 11.30 Woman or rabbit? (From Coren, 1969.)

trast of the enclosed circle in stereo-views (Fig. 11.31) without figure and ground reversals. If depth cues are added as in Fig. 11.31B, the contrast is strengthened. Coren's point is that some cognitive factor—the figure experience of an area—influences the phenomenal amount of contrast. The third experiment dealt with Benary's cross. The little triangle in Fig. 11.32A appears lighter than the physically equal triangle in Fig. 11.32B. Coren manipulated the small triangles with additional stereoscopic cues, until the triangles in the *B*-type pattern became more easily discernable than the corresponding triangle in the *A*-patterns.

These cognitive factors, according to him, give evidence in favour of the Helmholtzian theory of the role of unconscious inferences in perceptual situations.

Lindauer and Lindauer (1970) systematically determined the role of brightness differences in figure-ground articulations. The rate of reversals was one of the things to be investigated; so too the duration of the immediate response.

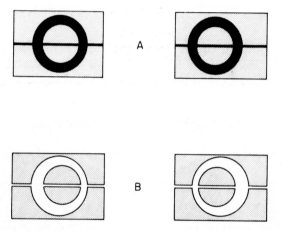

Fig. 11.31 The enclosed circles applied in Coren's stereo-experiments. (From Coren, 1969.)

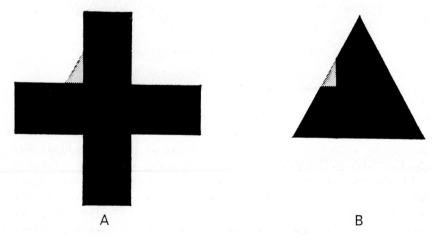

Fig. 11.32 Coren's experiment with Benary's cross. (From Coren, 1969.)

A series of Rubin's well known "vase and faces" patterns was elaborated The brightness-level varies in ten steps of clearly distinguishable pictures (three examples are shown in Fig. 11.33). There was also a "white" picture showing just the contours with 0 per cent fill. The filled area was more likely to be perceived as figure, the more strongly perceived, the higher the percentage of fill. In the "white" picture the face-response quite dominated. The rate of reversals was negatively correlated to the duration of the exposition.

Fig. 11.33 Three brightness-levels of the well-known "vase and face" pattern of Rubin. (From Lindauer and Lindauer, 1970.)

The following principles can be drawn about two dimensional figure-ground organization (after Koffka 1935, pp. 190–197):

1. Other things being equal, those subparts aligned with the vertical and horizontal cardinal dimensions are preferred as figures.
2. A part which is *smaller* than the entire patterned field or is *completely surrounded by it* is more likely to be seen as a figure.
3. More *richly detailed* and *better articulated* parts tend to become figures.
4. *Symmetrically* organized parts of the field are more likely to be seen as figures (see also Rubin 1921).

Developmental Factors in Figure Discrimination
Orientation of the main dimensions in a figural pattern has proved a source of ambiguity even if no reversal is suggested by the arrangements of the elements. Mach (1865) had observed difficulties in children if confronted with patterns which included "rotated duplicates" or "mirror images" of original simple patterns. Huttenlocher (1967) concluded that discrimination along the "left–right dimension" is more difficult for children than discriminations along the "up–down" dimension.

In Huttenlocher's situations (Fig. 11.34) right–left discriminations turned out to be more difficult than up–down discriminations, if right–left patterns were exposed as mirror images to each other. The orientation of the "open side" in the frame was extremely decisive. Enterline (1970) confirmed experimental results with the same patterns.

In addition she was interested in the relative difficulty evoked by "showed relative positions".

According to Piaget (1954) discrimination of the figures should be easier when they are placed "at different levels"; while next in easiness should be the situation with "frames opening in opposite directions", and most difficult should be the vertically symmetrical arrangement.

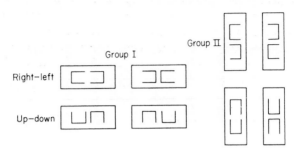

Fig. 11.34 The Huttenlocher patterns in the figural orientation experiments. (From Enterline, 1970.)

According to the results of the author "the showed relative position did indeed make it easier for the young child to learn to discriminate between two figures". The left–right orientational differences even now proved more difficult to discriminate than differences in up–down orientations.

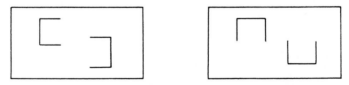

Fig. 11.35 The complementary patterns as devised by Enterline. (From Enterline, 1970.)

The accuracy of the recognition by children of short slanted lines was investigated by Over and Over (1967). They pointed out, that children got mixed up in situations with mirror images of figures, probably because of their inability to keep the various categories conceptually apart. Small children apparently do *see* correctly, there is nothing wrong with the sensory coding, yet cognitive factors are strongly involved. In tasks of detecting mirror-image obliques the subjects did better than in tasks of recognition. Another problem in connection with pattern perception has been the effect of "visual noise" (Munsinger and Gummerman 1967). The concept of noise is important for the signal detection theory. The evolutional point of view was observed in the structure of the sample. There were high school students from the second and the fifth level as well as some college-students (34 subjects in all).

The authors rendered the figures dimmer and more confused by masking them with networks of lines or stripes. The visual noise was either "systematic", consisting of equidistant parallel lines, or "occasional", with randomized location and distance of the masking lines.

Pattern recognition in visual noise turns out to be a fairly complicated achievement, depending on the density and quality of the noise, the age of the subject, and his experience with visual distortions. Children manage to distinguish the stimulus pattern better in the systematic than in the occasional noise-situation.

12 | Behaviour and Orientation in Tactual-gravitational Space

When considering Dodwell's ideas and models on the one hand and, for example, those represented by Olson and Attneave on the other (see pp. 316–322), some attention was given to the question of the meanings of the word "visual" in connection with pattern recognition. Traditional perceptual research was wrong according to Gibson in stressing the role of other sense modalities in the construction of a "visual world". Dodwell in turn is of the opposite opinion that visual cues are continuously controlled and interpreted in conjunction with information from other sense modalities (see Dodwell 1970, pp. 206–207).

In this respect we are in accordance with the opinion of Dodwell and we are inclined to stress the empirical evidence pointing to a very intimate interplay among our different sense modalities in spatial orientation and localization. Some trends of this evidence have been reviewed and discussed by Moustgaard (1975a).

In the following sections we are going to re-examine some of the impressive findings concerning the interaction of gravitational, positional and visual factors governing the visual orientation in three-dimensional space.

Visual-gravitational Orientation in Three-dimensional Space

Mach (1875) was supposedly the first investigator to work experimentally with a modification of the conditions of muscular tonus during investigations of the role of tonus for localization and orientation. His method consisted in affecting the subject's head with a rotative force by means of a sort of helmet. The subject had the helmet fastened on his head. The helmet and the head, and—via muscles of the neck—the body, could be subjected to a rotative force generated by the pull of strings passing over two pulleys and carrying two containers full of water. The subject was asked to keep his head still in spite of the force acting on it, thus resisting by strength of muscle the rotative force.

By varying the amount of water in the containers and thereby the rotating force too, Mach was able to provoke various forms of altered head and/or body localization, for example, as described in the following words:

Lässt man nun das Wasser aus den Gefässen abfliessen, so fühlt man eine Drehung des Kopfes entgegen demjenigen Sinne, in welchem er durch die Gewichte gedreht würde. Bemerkenswerth ist, dass alle diese Drehungen sehr stark empfunden, aber nur unmerklich ausgeführt werden (Mach 1875, p. 71). (If the water is tapped out of the containers the subject feels his head turned in a direction opposite to the previous turn caused by the weights. It deserves mentioning that these turns are strongly experienced but actually just slightly carried out. Translated by the authors.)

This method was taken over by Kleint in some of his experiments during the late 1930's. Regrettably, Kleint's very interesting work *Versuche über die Wahrnehmung* which was published in a series of articles in the years 1936–1940 is not well known. A study of this work clearly indicates, however, that Kleint anticipated the Sensory-tonic-field Theory of Perception (STF-theory, see pp. 331–334), both with regard to a series of experiments concerning perceptual localization and to important theoretical constructions (Kleint 1940).

Kleint's work is much too extensive and rich in detail to be referred to here and we shall confine ourselves to describing a couple of experiments conducted in line with Mach's method. These experiments have since become the prototype of a vast number of investigations concerning influence of muscle tonus conditions on perceived localization (see also Kleint's experiment described p. 332).

The first experiment to be mentioned concerned the perception of the vertical dimension in darkness. The subject was sitting in front of an illuminated perpendicular line located at his actual median. When the rotative force was added (by pouring water into the containers) he perceived the line as definitely slanting, its upper end appearing to tilt to the right if the force pulled to the left, and vice versa (Kleint 1940, p. 58).

Later on Kleint carried out experiments on visual autokinesis, using the same equipment. The illuminated line had now been replaced by a small spot of light which was fixated by the subject. The reports of the subjects stated that when the rotative force began to act, the spot of light was perceived as moving in the opposite direction to that in which the force acted. During relaxation—when the containers were emptied—the spot moved mainly in the same direction as that in which the force acted. The results of the two series of experiments have been independently confirmed in all essentials by other investigators since then (see also pp. 333–337).

Kleint points out that localization must depend on an inter-play of sensory and tonic processes. This is expressed, for instance, in the following passage on the cause of the autokinetic effect:

Nach dieser Annahme gilt . . . folgendes: die sensorischen Bedingungen wirken regulierend auf den gesamten Tonus . . . , bei zunehmender Verarmung des gesamten Wahrnehmungsfeldes nimmt diese Regulation und Eindeutigkeit des Tonus entsprechend ab und das gesamte Tonussystem gerät in einen natürlichen phasischen Verlauf (1940a, p. 127).

(According to this assumption the following things occur: the sensorial conditions act in a regulatory way on the whole tonus, . . . with increasing reduction of the present perceptual field this regulation and together with it the unambiguity of the tonus get diminished. A natural phasic trend is taken by the whole tonic system. Translation by the authors.)

As mentioned above this experimental paradigm has been one of the most important tools in the hands of STF-investigators. The Sensory-tonic-field Theory of Perception was brought forward by Werner and his collaborator Wapner a quarter of a century ago (Werner and Wapner 1949, 1952) and has been elaborated in co-operation with their colleagues and students since then. The authors stress that ". . . the theory cannot be fully understood unless we relinquish the traditional notion of perception as a self-contained unit and replace it by a field concept which defines the relationship between organism and object." (1949, p. 92).

Among the other key concepts of the theory "tonus" is the most important. It is used in a very wide connotation: "It includes the state of organismic tension as evidenced by the visceral as well as by the somatic (muscular-skeletal) reactivity. It refers to the dynamic (motion) and the static (posture) status of the organism." (Werner and Wapner 1949, p. 91).

The main structure of the part of STF theory concerning spatial orientation and localization may be reviewed by the following postulates:

1. Stimuli, whether mediated by exteroceptors or interoceptors, and regardless of their origin in the external, proximal or internal environment, have always sensory as well as tonic effects on the organism, and both specifically sensory (visual, auditory stimuli, etc.) and motor (position, motion) events are based on a simultaneous sensory-tonic state.

2. "Principally, the stimuli may or may not interfere with the present

organismic state. If the stimuli interfere . . . there emerges a tendency in the organism to change its state in the direction toward establishment of equilibrium between body and object. We believe that the perceived properties of the object are a mirror of these dynamic relations between object stimuli and ensuing body activity." (Werner and Wapner 1952, p. 325).

3. In relation to a certain percept, for instance a luminous line in an experienced position, a variation of the visual stimulation may have the same effect as a direct manipulation of muscular tonus. In other words, "there is functional equivalence between sensory and muscular factors with respect to a perceptual end-product." (Krus, Werner and Wapner 1953, p. 603).

Within the frame of this text it is possible only to consider a few of the experimental investigations the results of which support these basic assumptions and generalizations of the theory.

As in the case of Kleint's investigations mentioned above, the main idea in the most common experimental set up applied by the members of the STF-school has been to induce an asymmetry of muscular tonus in the perceiver in order to investigate the influence on his spatial orientation and on various processes of his localization-tendencies.

In accordance with Kleint's results in similar experiments (Kleint 1940, p. 58) Wapner, Werner and Chandler (1951) showed that the upper end of a vertical luminous line seen in the dark is experienced as if it were tilted toward the side of the body which displayed a heightened tonus. In the basic experimental situation the subject instructed the experimenter how to turn the luminous line until it *appeared* vertical.

When no other stimuli were present the upper end of the light band was usually tilted slightly leftwards from the vertical position in order to appear vertical to the subject—which actually fits the fact that the subject was righthanded (mean degree of tilt was 1·4°). The question of whether the subjects were also *righteyed* was not discussed here.

If other stimuli were presented as approaching from one side only, for example, a sound or an electric shock via the sternocleido-mastoid muscle on the right side of the neck, the light band had to be tilted in the opposite direction of the stimulated side (*in casu* to the left) to appear vertical to the subject.

Tilting of the subject himself likewise necessitated compensatory tilting of the line. This situation is very complicated with regard to the whole field of stimuli, however, and it has not been possible to find any generality concerning the direction of the compensatory tilt (see Howard and Templeton 1966 and Day and Wade 1969).

In various experiments, conducted chiefly by STF-investigators, the median and the eye level of the subject have been manipulated by means of induced tonus asymmetry. The amount of details is too vast to be discussed here. We shall, however, give the following brief summary of the literature concerning the phenomenal median plane: the factual median is generally perceived as being displaced in the direction to the side of the body which has a higher degree of tonus.

As far as the eye level is concerned there has been found to exist a general, and for each individual, rather constant difference between experienced and factual eye level, so that a line situated at the factual eye level in darkness will be perceived as being placed *above* the experienced eye level (Glick, Wapner and Werner 1965, Howard and Templeton 1966). This corresponds to the fact that the tonus of that very group of eye-muscles which move the eye vertically and diagonally upwards is higher than in other muscle groups (Adler 1965, p. 493).

The natural tonus asymmetry which reflects itself in lateral dominance (handedness and eyedness) has been shown by Wapner, Werner and Chandler (1951) and Wishner and Shipley (1954) to have an effect on spatial localization analogous with that of induced tonus asymmetry.

Investigations by Blane (1962), using persons suffering from residual paralysis caused by poliomyelitis as subjects, confirmed earlier results concerning the systematic influence of muscular tonus on the experience of a vertical luminous line in dark. The phenomenal tilt was always in the direction of greater tonus.

Based upon the STF-theory Meisel and Wapner (1969) investigated the conditions of sensorial and muscular interactions in some orientational situations.

The experiment builds on earlier findings, related above, that dark room perception of the median plane or the "straight ahead" is influenced by sensorial as well as tonic conditions. The following two conditions of stimulation were investigated: the asymmetrical, "one sided" extent of the stimulus object and increased uniocular-muscular involvement.

A luminous square with vertical and horizontal contours was placed symmetrically with reference to the median plane of the observer. With fixation of the left edge of the square the apparent median plane shifts relatively to the right. Again, with fixation of the right edge of the luminous square, the apparent median plane shifts relatively to the left. Asymmetry of convergence was introduced by having the subject wear a prism with the base placed temporally in front of the right eye. Relatively greater ocular-muscular strain to the left was introduced in the right eye; that is, there is greater convergence in the right eye. The effects of asymmetrical convergence could be assessed by comparing under symmetrical extent the conditions of left asymmetrical convergence, right asymmetrical convergence and normal symmetrical convergence (no prism).

The authors applied a factorial design in order to assess their summative hypothesis with focus on the fit between predictor values derived from adding single effects and observed values of simultaneously operating factors.

Although the results indicate that some interaction between sensorial and muscular factors exists, the most important criterion (agreement of predictive values and perception values) was not sufficiently supported. Probably a summation hypothesis is too oversimplified and schematic.

Individual differences in responsiveness probably deserves closer investigation.

Experimental studies concerning the effects of lateral head, body and trunk tilt on kinesthetic orientation have been carried on continuously during recent years. Hazlewood and Singer (1969) seated their subjects in a movable chair, the teeth gripping a biteboard. The subjects were blindfolded during the experiment and they had to grip a kinesthetic bar with their hand and adjust it to what they felt was a vertical position.

The degree of head, body and trunk tilt was always 30° with left–right counterbalancing. The arm opposite the side of the tilt was used in making the judgments (see Fig. 12.1).

The authors distinguish among *head tilt* (HT), *body tilt* (BT) and *trunk tilt* (TT). They found that HT and BT resulted in equal and significant opposite tilting-effects. On the contrary, TT did not provoke any significant effect. The results are fairly consistent with those reported by Wade (1968). According to him all three categories of tilt (30°) produced significant results. There was no difference between the tilt toward the right and that toward the left. Wade concluded that the otholit system was an important source of information in visual orientation constancy.

Churchill (1969) restricted his study to the effect of head movement in visual kinesthetic localization. This experiment is not concerned with the problem of apparent verticality. He simply wanted to control the degree of accuracy which we can expect from a subject who has to judge kinesthetically the location of visually perceived objects. The apparatus consists of a big bent bar and a segment of circle (0–100°) at the eye level of the subject and at a stretched-arm distance from his shoulder (Fig. 12.2).

In the first part of the experiment the subject had to adjust a pointer on an invisible arc-shaped dial so as to coincide with the position of a visible pointer on the arc in front of him. The invisible arc and the hands of the subject were masked by a piece of black canvas. Ten locations of the visible pointer were provided successively in a randomized order.

In the second part of the experiment the subject first touched the hidden

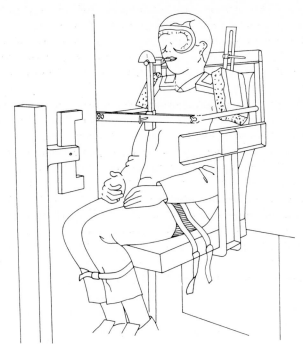

Fig. 12.1 Experimental set-up in the Hazlewood and Singer experiment. (From Hazlewood and Singer, 1969 p. 141.)

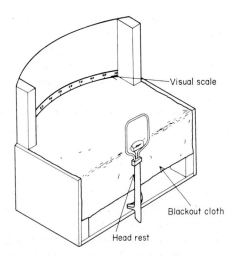

Fig. 12.2 Effect of head movements in visual kinesthetic localization (apparatus, front view). (From Churchill, 1969 p. 785.)

pointer on the invisible scale and then adjusted the visible pointer to fit the sensed position. There were again 10 random order trials.

Both parts of the experiment were run under two conditions, the free-head and the fixed-head conditions. It turned out that the subjects performed equally well under the free-head and fixed-head conditions of visual-kinesthetic localization.

Hay and Sawyer (1969) investigated the interrelationships between the motions of the perceiver's head and visually perceived movement. The subject had to nod and raise his head several times in a vertical direction. He was seated in a darkened room staring at a single light spot moving up and down in the medial plane in front of him.

The light spot actually was produced by letting the subject converge his eyes, thus bringing two identical spots to fusion. The spot was "programmed", either to follow the nods of the head or to move in an opposite direction. Sometimes it remained stationary all the time. The subject manipulated a potentiometer device by means of which he had to stop the movement of the light spot and keep it stationary.

Three situations of convergence were applied:

(a) The spot to the left was visible to the left eye, the spot to the right to the right eye. Angle of convergency 2°.

(b) The same single spot was visible to both eyes, "normal convergency" at an 11° angle

(c) The spot to the left visible to the right eye, the spot to the right to the left eye. Angle of convergency 18°.

The constancy of the location of a light spot in the dark depends, according to the experimental results, on the situation of convergency.

In situation (b) the spot was perceived as stationary when its location remained constant within the frame of the room and the observer. In situation (a) it had to move up and down following the nods of the head in order to remain apparently stationary.

In situation (c) it had to move up and down opposite the direction of the head movements in order to remain apparently stationary.

Determinants of Spatial Orientation

When discussing pattern perception in the previous chapter the very interesting role played by the cardinal dimensions (the vertical and the horizontal) was touched upon (see pp. 287–289). The discrimination among main dimensions of patterns is strongest when they are vertically or horizontally oriented. As mentioned above, several explanations have been put forward, and in recent times neurophysiological models (e.g. Dodwell

1970) have gained in importance. We also found that, together with this orthogonal co-ordinate system, the right angle is sometimes preferred as an "optimal solution" among "organizing tendencies" of ambiguous patterns.

Maffei and Campbell (1970) looked for orientation effects in electro-retinograms. A simple grating was shown in an oscilloscope, oscillating through a radius of 180° during periods of eight seconds. This moving pattern easily generates potentials which can be recorded equally well from the occipital lobe as from the eye ball.

If the grating was vertically or horizontally oriented the resulting wave-patterns were fairly similar in their amplitude and frequency. When obliquely oriented the pattern produced a lower rate of frequency.

The authors conclude that there must exist electrophysical correlates to our psychophysical observations. The visual discrimination power is more restricted in obliquely-oriented stimulus patterns than it is in cases of vertical or horizontal orientation. The effect of this mechanism must originate somewhere between the level of the EEG and the level of the cortical potentials. As mentioned earlier (p. 73) it has been observed in cats that cortical visual cell assemblies devoted to central visual perform-ances have more orientationally-selective units for the vertical and the horizontal co-ordinates. The authors refer to histological findings confirming this assumption.

The perception of directions in phenomenal space is based on an inter-esting set of relations. When aboard ship in a rough sea, visual directions are predominant. Although we are aware of the rolling of the ship, the walls of the cabin still appear phenomenally vertical and the floor and ceiling as horizontal, while other observations are made to conform to these cardinal dimensions. The clothes on their hangers swing out into space, away from the vertical direction of the walls in a rather ghost-like manner, approaching a phenomenal horizontal. *The immediate part of our visual space,* delimited by the walls of the cabin, *takes over the role of a visual system of reference, and the cardinal-spatial dimensions are likely to be identified with the dominant directions of the subordinate system.* Another situation in which it is very difficult to recognize the true basic dimensions is in an airplane coming in to land and inclined to one side; at such a time the surface of the earth or of the water seems to be tilted upward toward the plane.

In 1911 Jaensch demonstrated the *tendency toward orthogonal localization* (die orthogone Lokalisationstendenz). There seems to exist a perceptual tendency to localize objects in such a way that their main dimension lies at right angles to the line of vision. This appears especially clear with mono-cular vision. The law was restated by Rausch (1952), who generalized it to a tendency for straight lines to intersect phenomenally at right angles. Many so-called optical illusions can be reduced to this principle. A related principle observed by Rausch is the tendency of observers to straighten or "flatten out" zigzag lines. Yet another tendency noted by Rausch is that of the "phenogram", that is, the way in which a parallelogram is perceived by subjects. This phenogram can be observed by means of psychophysical measurements or by recall tests, and is found to be "squarer", closer to a system of right angles, than the original stimulus, the "ontogram".

In his extensive and many-sided monograph the Finnish researcher Järvinen (1969) has been able to demonstrate the existence of this orthogonal localization tendency in a series of experiments. At the same time he developed and refined the concept of orthogonality itself. The first experiment was designed to measure the phenomenal declination from the horizontal line of vision of a homogeneous black surface covered with a large number of dim light spots. The localization of this surface in the subject's visual space turned out to be non-veridical; in each of the eight positions offered it was perceived as more upright, less tilted than the physical stimulus warranted. Predictably, this tendency was even more pronounced in the case of monocular vision. In the reduced conditions of monocular vision, subjective factors play an even greater part in perception.

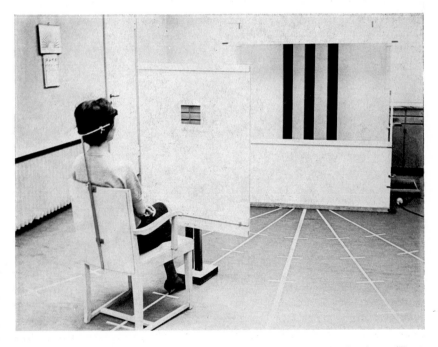

Fig. 12.3 Experimental design in the localization tasks devised by Järvinen. (From v. Fieandt, 1972 p. 269.)

Similar results were obtained when Jaensch's well-known rod experiment was reproduced under modern conditions. The basic stimulus consisted of three rods arranged so as to form a plane; one of the end rods was then moved either closer or further away from the subject, whose task was to place the other end rod in such a way that all three rods again formed a plane perpendicular to the line of vision. Planes accepted by the subjects as satisfying these conditions were in fact tilted away from the perpendicular. Monocular vision again induced a greater "tolerance"; the deviations from veridical perception were greater than in the case of binocular vision (Fig. 12.3).

According to Järvinen, the orthogonal tendency is weakest in the case of right angles in a plane figure. It was possible by means of the tachistoscope to repeat Rausch's parallellogram phenomena, but the orthogonal tendency in zigzag lines was not replicable; it is apparently determined by perceptual factors other than the tendency toward orthogonality.

Kleint Effects and the Illusion of the Tilted Room

Kleint (1940) has studied the frame of reference effects in a number of ways. Some of his experiments have been based on phenomenal experiences in various amusement park devices, such as the "witch's hut", a small cabin which can be rotated round its horizontal axis while the subject sits in a stationary chair (Fig. 12.4). When a small weight is suspended from the ceiling by a string, and the cabin is slowly and silently tilted, the subject

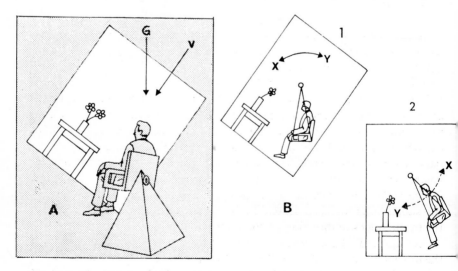

Fig. 12.4 The "swing and rotating cabin experiments" by Kleint. (From v. Fieandt, 1972 p. 270.) A: gravitational axis (G), perceived vertical axis (V). B: In position (1) the subject "feels" hanging like in (2).

perceives the string as diverging from the vertical direction while everything else remains normal; the walls, ceiling and floor retain their ordinary position. In another of Kleint's experiments, slides of landscapes, 2 × 2 metres in size, were projected on the white walls of a darkened room. The subject, standing about 1 metre from the picture, was asked to report the apparent position of the picture: that is, whether it was upright or tilted, and if the latter, how many degrees. Although the projected pictures were physically tilted, subjects judged them to be normally oriented up to a considerable angle; the subjects changed their position to correspond to that of the pictures, to such an extent that some of them were actually in danger of falling down. After subjects looked at the pictures for some time, however, they perceived them more and more veridically as corresponding to the real cardinal dimensions.

In addition to the everyday experiences in moving ships and planes mentioned above, a number of further examples could be mentioned. These are sometimes combined with apparent movement, as when we look at a landscape through the window of a moving vehicle. The internal dimensions of the vehicle are phenomenally identified with the gravitationally determined physical dimensions of space, so that if the train, for example, tilts on a curve, the buildings and trees framed by the window appear to tilt, while the internal space of the vehicle remains stable. This impression vanishes as soon as you put your head out the window; then the factual dimensions of the outside world take over and the internal space of train is "sensed" as tilted.

Thus it has been demonstrated that the horizontal, vertical and sagittal planes dominate the way in which we localize visual objects in proximal space. The orientations of objects are perceived as closer to these basic planes than is physically the case.

Consider the case of a vertical fluorescent line on a clearly differentiated background. At first, in strong illumination, the line is perceived veridically as upright. As the main illumination of the room is decreased and the cues to the surface structure of the wall are no longer available, the location of the line becomes difficult to determine. This uncertainty is greatest in the dark, when visual cues to the basic dimensions of space are completely absent and the subject is dependent on his proprioceptive sensations. Under such conditions, the so-called Aubert phenomenon might occur: if the subject tilts his head against his shoulder, the vertical line appears to tilt in the opposite direction (Aubert 1861).

As Nagel (1898) pointed out clearly in his careful and detailed analysis of the phenomenon, the effect of tilting in the opposite direction occurs even in normal illumination conditions, yet the illusion increases with an angle of 30–40° after a "longer stay in a darkened room" (Nagel 1898, p. 375).

This very significance of reduced perception conditions on the experienced verticality was systematically investigated in a series of experiments (Singer *et al.* 1970). In the first experiment the subject was confronted with a miniature interior of a room with its front side opened and showing a luminescent vertical bar on the wall opposite to the observer. The "room" could be tilted at various angles around its horizontal axis. As a rule the bar was perceived as tilted in opposite directions. The level of articulation in the room-space varied during the experiment: an empty room, a room with a striped back wall, and—in the highly differentiated situations—some furniture was added to the interior (Fig. 12.5b). There were 117 subjects in all and the room was tilted at angles of 22·5°, 45° and 67·5°. The effect of the articulation could be clearly shown. Yet this illusion of a tilted bar increased only to an upper limit of 45°.

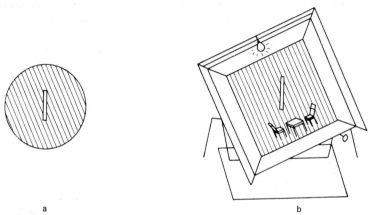

a   b

Fig. 12.5 a and b Effect of stimulus-framework reductions in different situations upon the amount of the tilted room illusion. (From Singer, Purcell and Austin, 1970 p. 250.)

In the second experiment the subject inspected the room by means of a tube which efficiently reduced all articulating stimuli except a circular field including the vertical bar (Fig. 12.5a). The same degree of tilt was employed as in the first experiment. Consistent with the Kleint experiments, the illusion was considerably weaker in all the "reduced situations" at all angles of tilt, and the illusion also appeared functionally different from that perceived under the "tilted room" conditions.

The Problem of Perceptual Learning

From a modest beginning, when it was interpreted specifically as the problem of the effect of earlier experience on perception, *perceptual learning* has developed into an autonomous and intricate complex of questions (see E. J. Gibson 1969). The primary object of this research is to define the extent to which forms of perception are already determined at birth, or on the other hand, the conditions under which factors of learning and experience can bring about structural changes in the way we perceive.

According to E. J. Gibson (1969), perceptual learning is represented by an increased ability to gather relevant information from the environment as a result of experience with the environment. When a human being has lived in continous interaction with his environment, it is natural to expect changes in perceptual functioning to occur in the form of more efficient ways of obtaining information.

The question of the part played by experience in certain fundamental perceptual activities has been approached by means of the so-called *deprivation* technique: young individuals are raised in a relatively impoverished, stimulus-poor environment, without the experiences normally available in the environment. These individuals are then tested for their motor behaviour, their ability to orientate themselves in the environment and to discriminate colours and shapes under normal conditions. Understandably, such experiments are usually performed with animals, since it is impossible for both legal and moral reasons to deprive human babies for extended periods of time of the conditions for normal development.

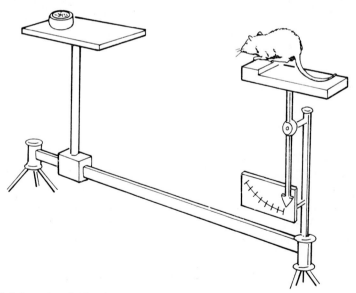

Fig. 12.6 Jumping device for rats in the Lashley and Russell experiment. (From v. Fieandt, 1972 p. 263.)

As early as 1934, Lashley and Russel raised 13 rats in complete darkness for one hundred days (except for a few seconds each day when some dim light came into the cages during feeding time). After this period of deprivation, the rats were placed in pairs on a jumping board, from which they had to jump to another "shelf", the feeding rack, 20–40 cm away. It took only three days for the dark-reared rats to regulate their jumping impetus (i.e. estimate the distance) as effectively as those which had been raised in the light (Day 1969 pp. 162–163 and Fig. 12.6).

Walk et al. (1957) studied the behaviour of dark-raised rats on the visual cliff. An experiment of depth perception with children (Fig. 12.7) produced similar results. Rats which had been raised in the dark for 30–90 days chose the shallow side of the structure without any practice. Animals which had been kept for almost ten months in the dark, however, apparently lost the ability to perceive the depth differences of the cliff. A month of experience in normal light was necessary for them to show appropriate behaviour (Nealy and Riley 1963).

In 1959, Gibson et al. were able to show that rats raised in the dark had no difficulty in learning to discriminate visual shapes. When kittens were raised in the dark for four weeks after birth, they were at first unable to perceive depth relations, but the avoidance behaviour patterns at the edge of the visual cliff appeared soon after they were exposed to normal light. The "fear" of the cliff was thus stronger than the "rewarding" experiences gained by walking over the glass shelf without falling (cf. Fig. 12.7) (Walk and Gibson 1961).

The experiments described so far concern situations of light or object stimulus deprivation with binocular vision. The same researchers extended their experiment to monocular deprivation. In the end, the animals had no other cues to depth relations except the monocular motion parallax. Nevertheless, kittens raised under such "half-blind" conditions avoided the edge of the cliff just as consistently, once they had become adapted to the light.

More recently Somervill and Sharratt (1970) made a series of experiments on the significance of the retinal size for visual discrimination in the above mentioned "cliff-situation". A group of one-day old chicks were confronted in the first experiment with, either (1) "empty" mirrors on the "deep" and the "shallow" side of the cliff, or (2) with texture patterns the elements of which, on both sides of the cliff, corresponded to an equal size in the retinal projections of the pattern-figures. No behaviour preferences could be observed.

In the second experiment the effect of the motion parallax was maximized by means of using three-dimensional patternings on both sides of the cliff. Sometimes the patterns corresponded to equal retinal projection sizes

Fig. 12.7 The striking experiment of the visual cliff. (From v. Fieandt, 1972 p. 263.)

on both sides of the cliff; sometimes veridical stimulus proportions were applied.

The experiments proved that depth discrimination in young animals can be radically modified by extreme changes in the retinal-projective "steepness proportions" of the cliff. Threshold determinations of the limits in depth-discrimination do not appear meaningful unless the total pattern is taken into consideration.

Riesen and his associates have been studying the effect of visual stimulus deprivation on spatial perception in chimpanzees and certain tailed monkeys since 1947. In the earliest experiment, chimpanzees spent the first sixteen months of their life in complete darkness. As pointed out by critics among Riesen's collegues, such extended deprivation may cause deterioration of the retina itself, thus eliminating possibilities even of effective perceptual learning (W. Köhler, personal communication 1957). Subsequently Riesen et al. (1964) repeated these experiments, using a translucent plastic helmet which completely encased the animal's head and allowed diffuse light to pass through. The animals thus grew up in a *Ganzfeld*, a homogeneous light fog (see p. 314). According to Wilson and Riesen (1966) these animals were able to discriminate black and white surfaces, triangles and squares or horizontal and vertical directions as easily as the comparison groups raised in normal illumination.

Chow and Nissen (1955) gave newborn chimpanzees light figure stimuli to one eye, while the other eye received only homogeneous light fog. The learned figure discrimination was not immediately transferred to the other eye, but the partial stimulation did mean a considerable saving in binocular learning.

Similar results have been obtained in deprivation experiments concerning the other senses also, e.g. by depriving chimpanzees of stimulation during the period when their tactual perception is developing (Nissen et al. 1951; Fig. 12.8.)

Comparative research has also helped to give a positive answer to the question of whether certain organizational tendencies in perception are already functionally present at birth (see E. J. Gibson 1969, pp. 263–368). In addition to the avoidance reaction on the visual cliff already described, there is evidence of the existence of *imprinting*—behaviour patterns which are released independently of any learning effect. For example, the remarkably accurate and perfect imitation of pantomimic expression patterns by young chimpanzees, which made possible the experiment by the Gardners in which the chimpanzee baby Washoe was taught the human deaf-and-dumb sign language code (Fig. 12.9). Another example is the tendency of baby ducklings, immediately after hatching, to follow any larger object which moves like the mother duck and emits her characteristic sounds

(Fig. 12.10; Hess 1959, pp. 133–141). Finally, concerning problems of human ontogenetic development, certain "instinctive" perceptual reactions can be beautifully demonstrated. Such a reaction is the innate ability of the newborn infant to look at "targets" containing simple circles and line figures, for the most part in black and white, but also including red and yellow circles (Fantz 1963).

Ahrens has continued the experiments carried out by Eino Kaila and Charlotte Bühler, investigating the minimal conditions necessary to arouse

Fig. 12.8 Sensory deprivation is used in order to study the role of early experience in perception. (From v. Fieandt, 1972 p. 265.)

Fig. 12.9 The chimpanzee Washoe is taught how to get something to drink. (From v. Fieandt, 1972 p. 266.)

the "social smile" in children which normally occurs in response to a human face (1954).

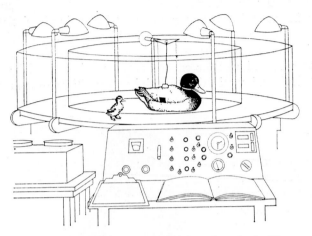

Fig. 12.10 Baby duckling following an artificial mother duck. (From v. Fieandt, 1972 p. 266.)

The Independence of Tactual Space

Perceptual psychologists have often been accused of describing the perception of space in purely visual terms. This is not very surprising if we remember how dominant a sense vision is in man. Visual stimuli give us the clearest idea of our position in the three-dimensional world. This visual dominance is so great that if a person with normal sight, in the dark, is asked to form an image of his position, his location and his immediate environment, he immediately turns to his visual memory images in formulating the answer. When a person with normal sight receives diffuse and inarticulated perceptual stimuli (e.g. smells or sounds), he starts *looking for* the source of the stimuli. Individuals who have lost their sight continue for some time, some even permanently, to maintain a visual attitude toward their spatial experiences. We have already mentioned that visual space is functionally closely related to tactual space; the latter is actually more reliable as a basis for describing the environment metrically.

The interdependency of visual and tactual improvements in perceptual learning was clarified in an investigation by Bower *et al.* (1970). They observed the grasping function in babies one week to five months in age. The method and strength of grasping was determined in two experimental situations. In situation one, a toy invisible to the baby was handed over by the experimenter. In situation 2, a three-dimensional object was presented by means of a stereoscopic shadow-caster. The projected stereoscopic images looked hard, solid and very "realistic", but no touch impression could be obtained from them.

The behaviour was analysed by means of a film. The authors observed a distinctive development in the method of grasping. Until they were five months old the babies grasped stereotypically closing all their fingers simultaneously several times. The visual orientation behaviour seemed rather dominant: aiming at the mere shadow-projection without touching the object caused strong frustrated behaviour, crying and anxiety. Artificially produced distortions in the visual world can be corrected by means of touch impressions: this has been shown empirically in some instances of *amodal perception* (Michotte *et al.* 1967). In many respects, spatial touch perception functions autonomously. Although the basic principles, according to which the surrounding world is perceived, remain more or less constant from one sensory modality to another, the haptic space also exhibits some regularities of its own. These appear most clearly in the congenitally blind; thus it is easiest to study tactual perception on such subjects. In the behaviour of persons born blind, it is the sense of touch which takes over most of the *space-determining functions*; they try, for example, to *objectify smells* by means of their sense of touch. The tactual sense has been shown to be highly adaptable; like sight and hearing, this modality can be developed to mediate symbolization, as shown by the invention and widespread use of the Braille alphabet.

Warren and Pick (1970) studied intermodality relations in blind and sighted people. The proportional contributions of visual, auditory and proprioceptive impressions in judging spatial directions was experimentally determined. The subjects were blind children of various ages, a suitable method for determining age trends during a period of expected differentiation. Neither a follow up study nor the observation of age trends confirmed a modality differentiation hypothesis. The interdependency of these modalities was retained through the age-range to a considerable degree.

A strongly integrative function was ascribed to sight, yet it does not seem to compensate for what is achieved with other senses.

The way in which an articulated tactual space is gradually built up is reminiscent in many ways of the corresponding phenomena in the visual modality. The visual space is most indefinite when the illumination is at its lowest. The normal haptic analogue to illumination is *movement* or *kinemathics*. If a congenitally blind person stands or lies absolutely still, an egocentric organism space is developed, a *body-space*, which phenomenally is extremely restricted in all its dimensions. This can be experienced only by those born blind; closing the eyes does not lead to a loss of visual images.

This body space is functionally essentially a near space. Spatial images are restricted to the proprioceptive images of one's own body. The only tactual impressions are those due to the *weight* of those parts of the body supported upon a surface. In all other respects there is nothing but an *empty space without dimensions*. The primary position of the vertical and horizontal is reduced to a bare minimum.

This body space of an immobile person is an extreme case. As soon as he makes even the smallest movement he experiences a *movement space*. This is more extended than the body space and more articulated into distances and directions, but the experienced position of the individual is still rather vague and uncertain.

The body space and the movement space are early, primitive stages of the object space. In order to understand how the tactual object space is gradually built up, we must recall what was said earlier about the sense of touch as a sense for short distances. Unlike hearing and sight, tactual experience presupposes some direct contact between the perceiving individual and the objects serving as stimuli. Our sense of touch is characterized by a kind of bipolarity: there is the subjective aspect, the sensation of what is happening at the receptor surface, and the objective aspect, the experience of the object as a participant in the perceptual event. Let us imagine a person born blind, who is moving about in his movement space and comes into contact with the back of a chair. Immediately, the closed somatic space opens up and the objective aspect becomes dominant: what he actually experiences is something in the "outside world".

The basic conditions for spatial perception are thus the same for both visual and tactual space. In each case a sufficiently articulated total situation is a prerequisite to the perception of three-dimensional objects. For both, a moving receptor surface is necessary; in the haptic modality this is an essential factor, since movement plays the part analogous to illumination in visual articulation.

The tactual perception phenomena dealt with so far can be included under *object haptics* and *space haptics*. *Form haptics* then include those special characteristics which distinguish the products of tactual perception from those of visual perception.

In classifying various types of tactile performances of the hand, Heller has distinguished between (1) the non-moving hand, (2) the moving hand and (3) the grasping hand. Touching by a non-moving hand is *synthetic*, since we aim at an immediate image of the object touched; *analytic* touching occurs when the hand is gradually moved. In the latter case we try to form an image which gradually expands to larger and larger wholes. Révész (1950) has made a corresponding distinction between *simultaneous* and *successive* tactile perception; the criterion in this case is not that of movement of the hand, but of whether the aim is to form an overall immediate image or an extended and articulated one bit by bit. The latter occurs by means of successive touch, since *haptic forms* or *gestalten* are generally *temporal configurations*, in contrast to simultaneous visual gestalten. The criterion of hand movement is used by Révész to distinguish between *static* and *dynamic* touch; the latter is much more important, since it is by means of this that a reliable judgment of the structure of an object is made.

Structural Principles of Tactual Forms

The study of congenitally blind individuals and of their modelling and sculpting performances has led to the formulation by Révész of the following principles of tactual perception:

1. *The stereoplastic principle*, according to which there is a strong tendency to grasp the object or parts of it in succession; this enables the observer to form a simultaneous three-dimensional articulation in a way peculiar to tactual perception, as in exploring a strange object in the dark or with the eyes closed.

2. The principle of *successive perception*. No real haptic gestalten are possible without constructions based on successive sensations. This generally occurs in forming the first overall inarticulated impression.

3. The *kinematic* principle appears as a compulsive need to move the hands and fingertips, even when the object surface itself is already moving. An example of this is the way in which we examine the thickness of a piece of paper or cloth.

4. The *metric* principle. The necessity in all measurement of direct contact between the object and some measuring device or scale appears most clearly in the tactual manipulation of objects.

5. The principle of *alternation between receptive and conative attitudes*. This is the contrast between passive reception and active seeking out. It has sometimes been claimed that visual perception is purely receptive, tactile perception purely conative. This would mean that in the sphere of the tactile modality only *haptomorphic gestalten* could be achieved by means or a receptive position, while a conative attitude would lead to synthetic forms, and in persons other than congenitally blind also to visualized, *optomorphic* forms.

6. The *schematic* principle appears as a tendency to perceive "preferred" forms, disregarding individual details in favour of a formulaic overall concept.

7. The principle of *transposition*; persons with normal sight and those who have become blind tend to visualize their haptic sensations.

8. The principle of *structural analysis* means that the first overall impression is gradually articulated by a method of analysis.

9. The principle of *constructive synthesis*: in contrast to immediately perceived visual forms, we have here a successive construction. The parts gradually added to a total form do not retain their mutual harmony.

10. The principle of *autonomous formative activity*. In spite of these restrictions, there is a tendency in tactual perception to form configurations and gestalten according to autonomous laws, which differ from those valid for visual perception.

These principles are most clearly observable if we compare object perception in persons born blind to that of normally seeing people. It has already been pointed out that detailed articulation in all modalities generally occur by means of *successive structural analysis*. Although our visual gestalten are usually simultaneous, a process of successive analysis may occur even in this modality. An example of Révész's will illustrate this: if we stand too close to a complex building such as a Gothic cathedral, our overall general view must be built up from a successive explanation of details.

In this example, the observer builds up his overall concept by a process of successive structural analysis. A global, *simultaneous* view could be achieved by standing further off, in which case the entire cathedral would be visible at once. The congenitally blind have no other possibility except a step-by-step structural analysis, and for this reason it is said that true tactile configurations are generally successive in nature. When a simultaneous concept is obtained by means of touch, this is usually either an act of recognition or (as in normally sighted people with their eyes closed, or those blinded in later life) a process involving visual images.

For these reasons, when a congenitally blind person models a three-dimensional object, certain peculiarities are observable. Through a successive kinematic structural form analysis, they develop a topographical map of isolated details of the object. These details in themselves may be accurate, but they do not fit together. The different parts of the human body, for example, may be modelled on a different scale, since the blind person has no overall concept of the subject. The Finnish psychologist E. Ketonen makes the comment that the congenitally blind person works like a child who in his preoccupation with an elaborate detail forgets the whole.

As pointed out at the beginning of this chapter, the separation between visual and tactual functions can be justified only on the grounds of clarity of presentation: it is necessary to emphasize the autonomy and self-determination of tactual gestalten in trying to understand a congenitally blind person's picture of the world, or in trying to isolate the part played by visual components in the articulation of space by normal persons. Let us not forget, however, that in all normally sensing persons the perceptual functions are global and intermodal, forming a synthesized view of the world on the basis of information from all the senses. We have already seen that the localization of perceptual objects is intermodally determined. Each animal species has its dominant sensory modality. The diffuse impressions from various senses lacking a clear-cut objective nature (in man the primitive "short-distance" modalities) are referred to the frame of reference offered by the better-developed telereceptors.

Analogies between Tactual and other Modal Space Determinants

The dominant frame of reference in dogs and closely related animals is based on *olfactory impressions*; this functions in a manner analogous to the visual-tactile system in man. Eino Kaila describes the behaviour of his dog, who preferred to follow the olfactory track of a moving ball rather than its visual track (Kaila 1962). The role of olfaction in man cannot, for a number of reasons, be compared to that of the other long-distance modalities. Already the longer *reaction times* reduce its importance. On the other hand, the sense of touch is superior to either sight or hearing in enabling us to determine precisely where and when a stimulus is in contact with our body, while as a receptor of more distant stimuli, with the exception of the sense of vibration, the tactual modality is poor.

The conditions for tactual-kinesthetic perception of length were investigated by Cheng (1968). How dependent are visual and tactual-kinesthetic spatial perceptions of length? Is one of these modalities based on the functions of the other ones? The experimental results did not give any support to the assumption of a priority of visual space determinants in the procedure of tactual-kinesthetic discrimination. On the other hand, our visual space is not based on a tactual-kinesthetic frame of reference.

A radial extent is always overestimated compared to a tangential one. A tangential extent which is more remote is tactual-kinesthetically underestimated in relation to a closer tangential one.

When comparing two visual stimuli, a more remote radial extent is underestimated although both stimuli are equal in length. Tactual-kinesthetic comparison of two equal radial extents gives a veridical result.

Relatively accurate after-images have been shown to occur on the surface of the skin following simultaneous pressure stimuli patterns. Figure completion phenomena, in the sense in which this term is used in connection with visual after-images, does not seem to occur. The hole in a ring remains a hole, in contrast to the visual after-image in which it is filled. On the other hand, the tendency toward "good gestalt", the so-called prägnanz tendency, has been clearly demonstrated in successive tactual patterns. Thus Benussi, for example, was able to produce an apparent circular motion on the skin surface by means of a stimulus of three sharp pointers arranged in the shape of an equilateral triangle and touching the skin in a regular rhythmical pattern (ABCABC, etc.).

What findings there are concerning tactual *eidetic phenomena* are of a controversial nature; in particular, Révész's comments on the perception of haptic forms lead us to doubt that such phenomena occur.

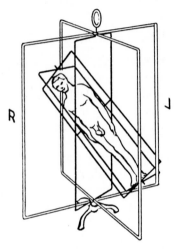

Fig. 12.11 Rotation apparatus used in the experiment on the recognition of body orientation. (From v. Fieandt, 1966 p. 256.)

Articulation into figure and ground in haptic perception occurs in a manner analogous to that in visual perception. The corresponding *framework* in tactual impressions is the *haptic peristasis*, in terms of which all tactual objects are localized by the observer. In persons with normal vision, however, this perceptual framework cannot be demonstrated, since it coincides with the visual frame of reference.

Haptic factors play at least some part in the localization of one's own body. In order to isolate the various factors and assess their relative importance, various rotational devices have been constructed (see Fig. 12.11). These can be used, for example, to isolate pressure sensations coming from the internal organs and those coming from the surface of the skin, and by this means to assess the relative part played by gravity acting between the earth and the subject in different cases. In these devices the subject is usually attached to a rotating frame, in such a way that he cannot fall off in any position, and his task is simply to report the position in which he feels himself to be located. Révész has frequently made the claim that, once the visual frame of reference is reduced and the subject has to rely exclusively on his haptic sensations, the dominance of the vertical and horizontal dimensions is eliminated in perceptual experience. The empirical results, however, indicate that position is determined most accurately when it lies

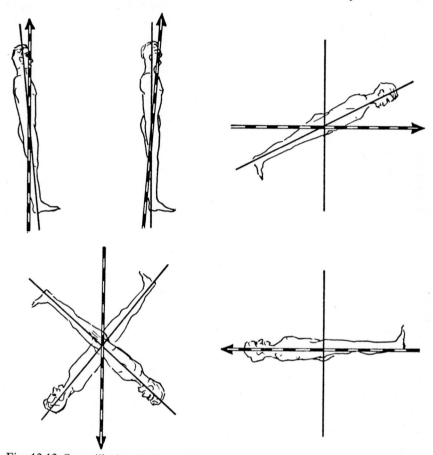

Fig. 12.12 Some illusions in the experience of body orientation. (From v. Fieandt, 1966 p. 257.) Thick arrows: positions as perceived by the subject.

within these directions, while in all other directions deviations from the veridical of some 10, 20 or or more degrees occur (see Fig. 12.12).

It would in fact be surprising if this were not the case. The centres of equilibrium in the cerebellum are connected with the thalamic way-stations of most sensory pathways, and kinesthetic sensations, tactual and visual orientation thus all cooperate with the sense of equilibrium.

Path Recognition: Animal Space Perception and Human Navigation in Space

With the recent developments in space flight there has been a reinforced concentration of interest in the Pavlovian tradition inside sensory physiology. Research workers inspired by this tradition (Vygotsky, Leontiev, Sokolev and to some extent Lindsley in the USA) have stressed the primordial role of motor activity in what is generally called perceptual functions. Perception would never arise unless a certain activity—and especially a motor activity—occurs prior to them in the behaviour of the perceiving organism. *Orientation reflexes* and *exploration behaviour* mean a manipulation of the objects to be perceived is needed to tune the receiving apparatus for picking up information from stimuli within the organism and within its environment. Before exploring the stimulus object by moving around and grasping, or looking, the child is said to be unable to carry out perceptual tasks. In this respect the ideas of v. Uexküll (1934), Buytendijk (1936), Brunswik (1936) and Saugstad (1958, 1965) could celebrate their enthusiastic "come-back" in the theory of perception. On the other hand E. J. Gibson (1969) has consistently pointed to the development of perception as an act of differentiation which cannot be exhaustively treated as mere cumulative orientation reflexes. What was referred to earlier in this chapter regarding the visual and tactual-kinesthetic components of spatial orientation (see pp. 330–337) thus gains increasing relevance in this context.

The attention of the scientists was first captured by the astonishing, almost unbelievable achievement of some ambulatory animal species. It has been known for years that migrating animals have sensitive equipment for recognizing their habitual path. Earthbound animals resort to their sense of smell in order to keep track of paths at a variety of distances. Smell signals guide the orientation at least of social insects and of the shrew. There are also caterpillar larvae which find their way "home" along thin webs woven by themselves as they move forwards to fresh growths in the topmost branches of a pine tree (Fabre in Breland and Breland 1966). Ants and bees learn to rely on *menotaxis*; keeping their direction of movement constant by means of the angle between the direction of the prevailing sun rays and their linear locomotion.

Migrating birds make use of a host of orientation signals. Moon and stars on bright nights, the colour of sunrises and sunsets, wind and landmarks all contribute to their incoming information.

The training of pilots has, during several decades, been based on some experiments in space perception. The information mediated by the gravitational sense and the otholite system of proprioceptors plays a predominant role when the pilot has to rely on the cardinal dimensions of his behavioural field. The visually perceived horizontal plane is extremely important for the pilot, more important than all pointers on several dials and optic instruments. Extraordinary gravitational fields are produced when the aeroplane swings and circles, rolling up or down in the sky. These new gravitational fields interfere with the normal pressure on the vestibular apparatus. In the optical control systems for pilots a TV-simulator reflects a sensitive visual image of a horizon. The deviations from this apparent horizon are thus signalled to the pilot—far more efficiently than by all other devices.

The Pensacola Naval Base provides a good example of the significance of the vestibular system when preparing astronauts for a space flight. To quote Wolsk (1967 p. 132):

... there is a large room placed at the end of a huge rotating beam. The room is furnished for sleeping, eating and so on. A constant rotation speed of 5–10 revolutions a minute creates a new constant line of force on the otolithic membrane—this force is a combination of the usual vertical gravity vector plus the new horizontal centrifugal-force vector. The results are at first rather devastating on volunteers who live in the room and try to perform manual tasks. Trying to walk in a straight line produces a curved path; throwing a dart at a dart-board results in a large miss to one side; any sudden head movements produce immediate dizziness. – – – After a few days of this life, the brain seems to make some adjustments in its circuitry, as all aspects of behaviour slowly return to normal.

Social Interpersonal Aspects of Space Perception

The German psychologist Paul (1970) has pointed to an interesting possibility in the development of spatial abilities in preschool children. At an early stage of differentiation the child's conception of spatial relationships and his concept of his own position within a social "near-space" seem to be closely interrelated. There is some empirical evidence in favour of the explanation that spatially confused, disoriented children also have difficulties in perceiving their relation to friends and age-mates in their social environment. What originally is geographically close or distant to a person —even to an adult—probably becomes socially close or distant. There are some analogies between the territorial behaviour of herd animals (birds, deer, wolves and dogs) and the housing of human families in residential areas of modern cities. According to Morris this demand for private territory is a trait very well known to all investigators of the big apes.

But there are of course exceptions to these topographical analogies: a son in the family who is socially very remote to his parents and whose sweetheart—the socially closest person—might at present live at a distance of several thousand miles.

13 | Phenomena of Constancy and Perceptual Invariance

The Concept of Constancy

The most significant regularities of our perceptual world are those which are called the *invariants or constancies of perceptual objects*. What is common to these phenomena is that the perceptual impression which arises is not determined solely by the stimulus basis available at a certain time and in a certain place; the information we have about the objects we perceive depends on the stimuli available from a wider stimulus environment or context. All constancy phenomena thus depend on the context occurring outside the perceptual object, and independently of it. The part played by these associated and contributory stimulus systems can most fruitfully be approached by means of experiments in which the stimuli which normally supplement the restricted stimulus basis are gradually eliminated to a greater or lesser extent. Such an experimental technique is termed *gradual reduction* of the stimulus context.

Technically, reduction can be achieved in a number of ways, all of which involve reducing or impoverishing the number of simultaneously available stimulus "cues". For example, the field of vision may be drastically reduced in size, the exposure time may be shortened to a fraction of a second, the illumination level may be made exceptionally low, or the visual objects may be presented greatly reduced in scale. The common effect of all these measures, when applied to perceptual objects, is a reduction in constancy.

Object constancy thus means that shape, size, colour, weight, intensity of sounds, etc. are perceived as constant within certain limits, regardless of the variations of proximal stimuli; in fact, these phenomenal properties more or less coincide with the "real", i.e. physical shape, size, colour, weight, intensity, etc.

Shapes at Different Angles of Inclination

Let us first examine the concept of *constancy of shape*. This means that, whatever the angle from which we observe an object, it preserves its solid and permanent shape. The classic example is that of the round dinner plates on the table. From wherever we look at them, the plates preserve their characteristic round shape, although their retinal projections consist of various elliptical forms depending on their position relative to the observer. Again, when a car comes toward us in the dark and then turns off on a side-road, its headlights do not appear first as round, then as ever narrower ovals and finally as lines; they tend, as familiar objects, to preserve their round shape even as they turn away from us (see. Fig. 13.1).

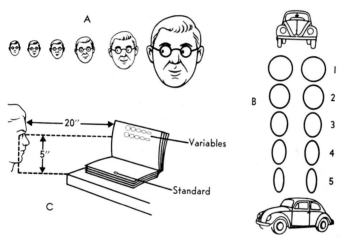

Fig. 13.1 Some examples of visual constancies. (From Hochberg, 1964 p. 49.) C: Place a standard disc on the opposite page. You might check shape constancy in series B.

If a round disc with a shining white surface is slowly turned around its axis to an ablique position in a sufficiently dark environment in which other surfaces are not visible, and far enough so that the lens of the eye cannot accommodate to parts of the disc located at different distances, constancy of shape is no longer preserved. The subject soon announces that he sees an oval shape. The measure of shape constancy or *invariance* is generally defined as the size of the angle formed by the original and the new position of the disc at which the disc still preserves its phenomenal roundness. A large number of shape constancy studies have been carried out using this definition.

Careful research has led to the claim that the phenomenon called shape constancy actually means that the object is experienced as *unchanged in shape but as tilted to an oblique plane*. If the subject reports that he saw the disc as round, he also reports it as lying at an oblique angle. If the possibility of perceiving the angle of tilt of the disc was completely eliminated constancy would also disappear, and instead of a round disc, an oval was perceived.

Investigations concerning Degree of Tilt and Shape Constancy

The problem of perceived tilt and its connection with shape constancy has been closely studied by Flock *et al.* (1967). He used an experimental setup in which 12 paper rectangles were each pasted onto a separate sheet of Plexiglass ("safety glass"). These transparent plates were then placed in frames in such a way that by changing the frame the angle of inclination of the plate could be varied. Each rectangle could be offered at an angle of either 30° or 15° for one group of subjects, and at angles 30°, 20° or 10° for the other group, inclined both toward the subject and away from him. The task of the subjects was to estimate the shape of the rectangle in front of him on the basis of its position, and to place a moveable "comparison plane" at the same angle of inclination. The sizes of the rectangles were 36·8, 5·7, 1·3, 0·9, 0·4 and 0·06 square inches in one series, and 26·4, 3, 0·8, 0·2, 0·05 and 0·01 square inches in the other.

The series of tilt-estimations for each subject was represented by means of a linear regression-coefficient: b. For each subject three regression-coefficients thus had to be computed, in that each one of the coefficients stood for one of the rectangle-situations. The median b-value was then computed for each one of the presented paper-rectangles.

The results quite clearly indicated that with a decreasing angle of inclination the median b-value also dropped reaching a zero-probability level at an angle of 1·2°. In other words, with a decreasing angle of inclination within a rectangle the impression of tilt—evoked by the figure—also diminishes approaching the level of zero-probability.

Our ability to perceive the angle of inclination of a surface veridically depends on the structural articulation of the surface, consisting of texture and illumination gradients which vary with the degree of inclination (see the remarks made by Gibson in chapter 11). In his own theoretical explanation Flock rejects Gibson's ideas of surface structure analysis, and bases his theory above all on an optical description of the stimulus variables and their relation to the eye.

Freeman has in turn criticized Flock's approach as placing too much stress on optical variables (1966). He refers to a number of studies indicating that contour shape is an important factor in estimating a plane and its inclination.

Epstein and Mountford (1963) questioned whether the plane can be judged at all in reduced conditions on the basis of only one "cue", that of contour. Among the other stimulus cues, they were most interested in the degree of differentiation of the surface of the plane. They asked whether surface articulation, in itself, is a sufficient "cue" for perception of plane inclination. The experiments were carried out with great care, and the answer to the above question was negative. Articulated and unarticulated planes were perceived at different angles of inclination, and the plane perceived was found to be determined by the retinal projection, rather than by the actual inclination. The greater the surface area of the plane, the more reliable its perception.

These results make it understandable that shape judged on the basis of inclination remains more or less constant. Slant is experienced as tied more closely to stimulus variation in a given stimulus situation, while the shape of an object or a figure is preserved in various inclinations, regardless of stimulus variation.

Relational Invariances in Object Perception

Such a conclusion in a way extends the original problem of perceptual constancy to encompass the meaning of a *constant relationship* between one group of stimulus factors (e.g. the shape of the retinal projection) and another (e.g. tilt). The stimulus basis of object constancy should not be defined as a single variable, such as the retinal shape, but rather as the *shape in relation to the tilt of the stimulus surface perceived.*

This general statement has, when further elaborated and systematized by a group of investigators, given rise to the well known *shape-slant invariance* hypothesis (cf. Hochberg, 1971b). Analogously with the *size-distance invariance* hypothesis, this assumption looks for a more precise operational-ization of the relationship between apparent shape P' and apparent slant V'. Actually the implication of this hypothesis is that apparent shape is directly proportional to apparent slant: in order to achieve the above mentioned shape constancy, the perceptual system has to work as if it were solving the equation

$$k = P'/V' \quad \text{for} \quad P'.$$

In the words of a fairly well-established perceptual-psychological slogan: the degree of slant has to be taken into account by the perceptual act in achieving shape constancy.

Beck and Gibson (1955) hypothesized that a given retinal projection determines a family of "apparent-shapes-at-apparent-slants". According to Hochberg (in Kling and Riggs 1971, p. 516) this shape–slant invariance hypothesis "does not imply that slant is taken into account to arrive at a shape judgement": it implies only a correlation.

In connection with the problem of size constancy and the size–distance invariance hypothesis this line of .thought will be further discussed. Here it might be sufficient to stress the following two points: (1) The assumption of a linear relation between physical shape and physical slant might prove valid only as long as small magnitudes, for instance, small inclination angles and simple line dimensions in the pattern are concerned. (2) Evidently a linear relationship can not be expected to exist between the psychophysical data involved, because of the rather complicated form of elementary psychophysical functions (cf. the power law of Stevens).

Here we are confronted with the question of the actual stimulus prerequisites which serve as the basis of phenomenal constancy. Is it perhaps more accurate in a functional description to speak of certain relational invariances of the stimulus basis which are realized as the experienced constancy of perceptual objects? One of the corner-stones of Gibson's theory of perception is the assumption that the really decisive stimulus may consist of two or more physical variables related to each other on the basis of a system of gradients. The underlying idea is that our object perception is not a mirror-like one-to-one registration of single elements (coded in the form of sensory energy), but a reaction to a system of relations among elements. From this point of view, one of the real problems of psychophysics is to find and describe the systems of relationships which act as crucial stimuli. Eino Kaila (1944) came close to this way of reasoning. Our eye is surprisingly well able to detect and follow the increasing curvature of a spiral, so that we are able to continue the spiral freehand without error. Kaila says that this is due to the fact that the real stimulus in this case is a relational variable, the gradient of curvature. Only the entire context presented by the environment can produce an articulated and relatively veridical perceptual space, and all registered messages are interpreted in terms of this context.

In Epstein's and Mountford's (1963) experiments, when a larger portion of the plane was offered to the subjects, the approximate constancy of inclination improved, i.e. perception became more veridical. On the basis of this single concrete case, however, the figural relations of the structure of the surface cannot yet be assigned a decisive role; the degree of surface differentiation did not provide sufficient stimulus background for constancy of inclination. Constancy was not improved in these experiments by surface differentiation, even when this was offered together with relational systems which in themselves brought about a certain degree of constancy.

The Problem of Size Constancy

It is well known that within certain limits there is a considerable degree of *size constancy* in the perception of objects. A person who is walking away from us does not appear to become smaller in proportion to the reduction in size of the retinal projection, i.e. in proportion to the square of the distance. This constancy has been well established.

Size constancy also is actually a case of *relational constancy* or invariance. This means that the size we perceive is determined by the *relation* between the *real size* of an object (the distal stimulus) and its *perceived distance* (the proximal stimulus). Research by Gibson and by the husband-and-wife team of the Smiths (1954) has indicated that *size constancy* disappears if all "cues" to distance are eliminated. The frame of reference here consists of the gradients of the surfaces which recede from the observer. In the following, the term *perceptual constancy* will generally be used to mean the constancy or invariability of objects, in the old sense. We shall let the term *perceptual invariance* stand for the relational invariants which are assumed to form the true stimulus basis for such object constancy.

If two squares are reflected into the subject's eyes, in the manner indicated in Fig. 13.2, the perceived difference in size between them may be due to one of two reasons. *Either* A and B are actually (as stimulus objects) at an equal distance from the observer, but B is in reality smaller than A (case I), *or* the squares are actually equal in size, but B is further away than A bringing about a smaller retinal image (case II).

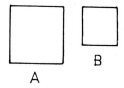

Fig. 13.2 Two squares A and B which might look equal in size if located at different distances from the observer. (From v. Fieandt, 1972 p. 233.)

Each setup could, of course, be used alternately to bring about an exactly identical retinal projection, if the squares used were chosen with sufficient care. Let us assume that we have two such situations, one based on case I, the other on case II. The question arises whether the naive subject is able to discriminate the two situations. It turns out that when *distance* "cues" are offered together with "cues" concerning the *surface structure* of the squares, the subject is amazingly well able to carry out the task. This after all is generally the case with different sized objects appearing in our normal environment. Along with the size of the image reflected on our retina, information concerning the distance of the perceived object is simultaneously available.

On the other hand, there have been numerous studies of the way in which distance "cues" may be obscured and their function rendered indefinite or even misleading, when certain stimulus constellations are brought into mutual conflict. Here the cue-concept is employed merely as a "technical" description of some depth perception conditions. The reader is asked to repeat our theoretical evaluation of the "cue concept", see p. 309. Thus the distances between various objects can be made to appear the reverse of what they really are, so that those which are closer are perceived as more distant and vice versa. In other cases objects of *various sizes* located at *different distances* are made to appear as lying at an equal distance from the observer.

The former effect has been conclusively demonstrated by Ames in his well known series of experiments. He used cards, placed in a vertical and overlapping position and with a small rectangular piece cut out of the lower left-hand corner of each card. In this way he was able to make the card which was further away seem closer, as though it were lying in front of the others and covering them. In addition to this "interposition cue of depth", which was artificially produced, objects familiar from everyday experience (playing cards) were used to bring about an impression of distance. Over (1963) has carried out experiments showing how, in a non-reduced situation, objects located at different distances can be made to appear equally far away.

The most effective stimulus system giving "cues" to distance consists of the consecutive gradients of the underlying surface extending directly in front of the observer. The significance of such gradients as "cues" to distance is illustrated by Fig. 11.18, p. 310. Under normal conditions, objects at different distances are always seen as rising above some surface. If in the experimental situation the normally observable *depth gradients* are eliminated, and, if by allowing the subject to use only one eye, other "distance cues" are also reduced, it becomes very difficult to distinguish between cases I and II (Fig. 13.2). But in the normal living environment there is a tendency for the object to maintain a constant size with variations in distance. *The invariance in question here is that of the relation between perceived size and perceived distance.*

At this point it seems appropriate to link up some of the leading perspectives in the present analysis with that which was pointed out in a previous chapter regarding the problem of apparent size and apparent distance (chapter 11 pp. 311–312). The assumption that apparent size S' is directly proportional to apparent distance D' has been termed the *size–*

distance invariance hypothesis. Hochberg (1971b p. 513) claims that the stimulus variables on which judgements of size are based, and those on which judgements of distance are based, are normally closely coupled to each other in the physical world. Nevertheless, judgements of size and judgements of distance need not in other respects be related to each other.

Stated more precisely in the terms some investigators have given to it the size–distance invariance hypothesis means that apparent size S' and apparent distance D' are linearly related. In order to secure the so-called size constancy to an apparent object, the perceptual system should—as it were—be able to solve the equation

$$k = S'/D'$$

for the value of S' in a given situation.

At this point it ought to be clearly pointed out that insufficient evidence has been brought about in favour of this particular statement. Although all our knowledge about the sensory and neurophysiological basis of object constancies leads us to assume that strong relational stimulus invariances exist which govern our experiences of constant objects, these invariances can by no means be assumed to follow simple rules of linearity. Elementary psychophysical invariances—as we know—reveal a much higher degree of complexity. That stated earlier when discussing the shape–slant invariance hypothesis thus evidently holds true for size and distance relationships.

The relational theories of size constancy do not presuppose any necessary psychological relationship between perceived size and perceived distance. Correct size judgements and correct distance judgements will (e.g. according to Gibson) both be made on the basis of the information in the texture gradient. Any reduction in the stimulus display that destroys the texture density gradient will remove both the information about distance and the information about size. For that reason, "the fact that size constancy and shape constancy both are lost when the depth cues are removed offers no proof that those constancies rest on taking distance into account." (Hochberg 1971b). Rock and Ebenholtz (1959) suggested that the stimulus correlate for an object's apparent size is the ratio of its retinal image size to the retinal size of some neighbouring object which serves as a *frame of reference.* Here again we meet the significance of the relationship between a single stimulus and a totality of contemporal adjacent stimuli.

On the contrary, the so called size–distance theory takes the size of the object's retinal image as the starting point for size perception. As has been shown in several series of experiments, subjects can judge when their retinal images are equal. When all stimuli of depth are reduced, the subjects might make use of the size–distance invariance hypothesis. They might assume that the standard and variable are at the same distance and make their match in terms of equal object sizes (a perceptual coupling between size and distance). On the other hand, Brunswik and his associates found the size matching of the subjects in his experiments highly dependent on the form of instructions. The subjects could be instructed to make retinal size matches, to make objective size matches and to match the apparent size. That kind of performance evidently presupposes a fully developed degree of object constancy, such as we know from the school of Brunswik, that size constancy as well as shape or colour constancy has undergone a process of development with the climax of constancy-performances somewhere between 10–15 years of age.

Winters and Baldwin (1971) investigated the development of size constancy under restricted cue-conditions. Five groups of subjects (one of the groups consisting of adults, the other four of children) had to match the sizes of pairs of circles. The location of the circles varied within a two-dimensional stimulus arrangement as well as three-dimensionally in some parts of the experiments. With the three-dimensional set-up, size constancy could be shown to exist in the age of 4 years. It further developed in the 6 to 10 year-groups. No variation in constancy and in the ratings concerning the location of the circles was found when applying the two-dimensional conditions of the experiments.

McDermott (1969) was interested in the joint effect of two "distance cues" together on the perception of size. Each one of the "distance cues" was paired in turn with the effect of the linear perspective (see pp. 301–302). The task of the subject was to match the size of the standard stimulus to that of the variable with one pair of the above mentioned depth "cues" alternately present.

Four different viewing conditions were applied

(1) through a monocular artificial pupil
(2) through a 5 mm monocular pupil
(3) binocular through two 1, 7 mm ϕ artificial pupils
(4) monocular in motion parallax-conditions.

The artificial 9 mm ϕ pupil was fastened to the moving eye of the subject, allowing for the motion parallax.

The subject always had to match a variable triangle to a standard. The author concluded from his results that a relative or familiar size is more important for size perception than the often discussed "cues of distance".

Measurement of the Degree of Constancy

Brunswik once postulated that the shape and size invariances described, were a kind of compromise between the constantly changing retinal images, i.e. the proximal stimuli and absolute object constancy. Constancy of visual size, for example, generally is not perfect. Visual size is preserved with growing distance, but not in proportion to the actual size of the distal stimulus object. Brunswik derived a mathematical formula, according to which the degree of constancy can be calculated if we know the experienced size of the object investigated, further the dimensions of the proximal stimulus (retinal image) and the real dimensions of the distal stimulus object.

In its general form, Brunswik's formula is the following:

$$R = 100 \, \frac{s-p}{r-p},$$

in which R is the degree of constancy in per cent, r is the dimension of the distal object functioning as the stimulus (e.g. in cases of size constancy the real height and width of the object), p denotes the corresponding dimension of the proximal stimulus, i.e. in our example the dimensions of the retinal projection, and s the phenomenal dimension of the object as experienced (phenomenal size, shape, tilt, etc.). This formula is most easily calculated for cases of size constancy, but it is widely applicable to all types of object constancy.

The constancy of size, shape or brightness, for example, is always obtained in terms of percentages, which are the higher the more veridical the perception, i.e. the closer the phenomenally perceived object proportions are to those of the "distal stimulus object".

McDonald (1962), however, has shown that Brunswik's formula is suffering an algebraic defect, which considerably reduces its applicability. McDonald himself, on the basis of his observations, questions the usefulness of the formula at all.

Poulsen (1972) also gives a critical analysis of the applicability of Brunswik's formula (pp. 105–108) in his experiments concerning individual differences in perceptual constancy. According to him the formula would work in momentaneous measurement situations only. However, it gives a misleading impression when comparing individual trends in series of successive measurements.

The specific aim of the experiments was to find out whether subjects react in a consistent way with regard to their degree of constancy in size and brightness perception. No such consistency was found however.

The point of view presented by Carlson (1962b) differs from that of Brunswik in that it sets up a direct relation between the veridical and the phenomenal size of the object as the basis of size constancy, rather than the traditionally postulated compromise between the object and its projection. Carlson has carried out experiments in support of this hypothesis, using different types of instructions. The subjects were instructed to estimate the objects alternately by means of "perspectival", "objective", "projective" and "direct" perception. Like the Japanese Akishige and his school, Carlson has also studied the effect on size constancy of sleep and rest deprivation. He found that extended lack of sleep increases perceptual constancy.

Over (1963) was able to demonstrate that an important factor in size and distance judgements is the wavelengths of the light reflected by the perceived object. The longer the wavelength, the larger and closer the object is perceived to be.

The relative constancy of the retinal projection has also begun to draw the attention of researchers. Thus Heinemann (1961), working with photographs of the stimulus area of the eye, found that the distance of an object from the eye may vary from 25 to 100 cm without affecting the size of the retinal image. He attributes this constancy at small distances to accommodation.

Size and Distance

The prerequisites for apparent *distance perception* have also been investigated on several occasions. Coltheart (1969) has reported on the influence of haptic size information upon visual judgements of distance. He has shown convincingly that an intermodal transposition of information readily takes place. He brought each subject blindfolded into a completely dark room. The blindfold was removed and the subject directed to look across towards the diagonally opposite corner of the room, using his preferred eye and viewing through a monocular viewing tube. Fourteen feet from the subject at his eye level was the visual stimulus, an illuminated equilateral triangle. While the subject was viewing this visual stimulus, the author handed him the haptic stimulus, an equilateral triangle made of masonite. The subject was instructed to judge the distance of the visible triangle from the size of the "haptic triangle" in his hands; the stimuli were said to be equal in size and shape. It appeared that the subject could make use of this intermodally transposed information.

During 1964–65, large-scale research into the constancy of size was carried out by Kirmse (1964) in order to determine the parts played by accommodation of the lens and by eyeball convergence in the object size constancy, which occurs when the visual object recedes from the viewer and the retinal projection simultaneously decreases in size. Twenty subjects were presented with two triangles of the same shape located at different distances; their task was to adjust the size of the nearer triangle until it agreed with the one further away.

At a distance of 12·5–100 cm, the nearer triangle was adjusted almost exactly to the size of the one further away (in binocular viewing). Constancy of size was then almost perfect.

In corresponding monocular viewing situations, according to Kirmse, the reduction of the retinal projection is also compensated for, although the constancy indices deviated by a relatively fixed amount from those prevailing in binocular viewing.

When the conditions for accommodation were reduced by means of screening spectacles with small apertures for focussing binocular sight, constancy was completely lost in both monocular and binocular vision. The triangles were perceived as equally large only when equal projections were produced. When the constancy values obtained in such a reduced situation were expressed as percentages of the values obtained for unrestricted viewing, it was found that size constancy rose in direct proportion to the nearness of the object located further away, i.e. to the degree of *accommodation*. On the other hand, expression of the results of monocular measurements in terms of those obtained with binocular vision did not reveal any such relation to the degree of *convergence*.

Freeman (1968) was interested in the role played by the natural visual perspective as a determinant of size constancy.

Before the crucial part of the experiments two groups of cats were trained for discriminatory behaviour in a corridor with natural perspective walls. In the first part of the main experiment a set of lines producing clearly distorted perspective were painted on the walls of the runway. When the cats were allowed, using both their eyes (binocular set-up), to approach the "discriminanda" objects in the distorted alley, a considerable decline in their object size constancy could be observed, despite the fact that the distorting lines were planned to generate over-, rather than under-, constancy.

In the second part of the experiment the cats had to view the objects in the alley monocularly. When, as a consequence of this arrangement, the effects of the binocular parallax as well as the motion parallax had been eliminated, the animals regained some of the normal size constancy which had been lost in the previous part of the experiment. Cats apparently are capable of accurate monocular size-judgements, even without the contribution normally provided by the motion parallax, if they are provided with a natural undistorted perspective as a main "reference-cue" in their visual field.

The idea of the fundamental importance of the invariant relation between size and distance has also been frequently criticized. According to Gogel, the invariance of this relation is important only when a stimulus comparison field is used (1963). In such a case, there is a large number of "comparison cues" serving as the basis of perception. In reality, constancy of size cannot be determined solely on the basis of complementary visual stimulus systems; thus a reliable picture of the conditions of constancy is obtained only by using tactual or kinesthetic comparisons in our measurements. Gogel distinguishes between the concepts of *distance*, by which he means the space between the observer and the object of perception, and *depth*, denoting the spatial relations between objects of perception. The most important factor in estimating distance is not the egocentric point of reference, i.e. the distance between the perceiver and the object, but rather the *relations prevailing within the stimulus field*. According to Gogel, the basic factors in psychological object size constancy are perceived relative size and distance. The distance perceived as "absolute" is derived from the "relative depth" by a process of perceptual summation.

In the post-Brunswikian research which has been described here, new empirical evidence has been brought to bear upon the discussion concerning the relation between phenomenal size and distance. These studies have also had some bearing on theory formation. In particular Gogel's ideas, although they add in a crucial way to our earlier conceptions of the meaning of stimulus relation information, seem to go too far in certain respects. It has after all been conclusively demonstrated that our visual apparatus includes various physiological "distance receptors" (e.g. accommodation, convergence, binocular parallax), which function independently of background frame of reference.

Constancy of size, like the other constancies pertaining to perceptual objects, is directly proportional to the overall articulation of the visual field. Only the importance of binocular parallax (see Fig. 11.5, chapter 11, pp. 294–296) is less considerable here than in the case of shape constancy. As an additional condition connected specifically with constancy of size, let us mention the significance of the cardinal dimensions, in particular the horizontal. We experience those objects most veridically (corresponding to their "distal" physical dimensions), when they are located in the horizontal dimension, i.e. rising from the surface of the ground in front of us. Size constancy decreases when an object recedes from us in a vertical direction. A metal plate located 15 m in front of the observer on the surface of the ground seems bigger than if it is placed at a distance of 15 m above the viewer's head.

Colour Constancy

Colour constancy has been the subject of systematic study for over a century. The invariances considered are directly related to the phenomenal appearances of colours, touched upon in chapter 6, in that only external *surface colours* (as defined by Katz) are sufficiently invariant to allow us to speak of constancy. It should also be remembered that a substantial degree of constancy of surface colours hold only for objects seen in natural daylight, with its relatively minor variations in brightness and chromaticity.

The classic experiments on colour constancy were made using artificial light sources which varied only slightly in their intensity and their energy distribution. When the traditional light sources, gas, carbon-arc and incandescent lights were replaced by fluorescent lighting, the intensity gradients of the reflected radiation became steeper and more variable. The following examples are not valid for all spectral wavelengths when fluorescent lighting is used. The yellowish and reddish portions of the spectrum are especially liable to change with a change in the type of lighting.

The traditional problems are most understandable if we recall some of the phenomenal changes which we experience in ordinary daylight conditions. Looking at the galvanized iron roof of a neighbouring house at dawn, we may see a bright, shiny white, which, particularly in late autumn, yields a compelling impression of snow. The brilliant reflected light is seen as something substantially connected with the surface itself, as a white colour belonging to it. We may have been misled by capricious climatic conditions, however; the impression of whiteness is caused by the wetness of the roof reflecting large amounts of light. As soon as the error is realized, the phenomenal colour of the roof changes; instead of a white surface colour, we perceive one which is nearly black, but which is far more lustrous and glowing than when it was perceived as snow. Or we may notice a small grey spot of dust on our jacket sleeve. The smallest movement, however, may reveal it as a spot of sunlight coming through a hole in the curtain. As soon as it is displaced by movement, we are no longer capable of seeing it as dust. These examples concern *brightness constancy* with variations in light intensity. Corresponding examples could be adduced for hue constancy when the chromaticity of the illumination is varied.

Interest in these problems was aroused by Hering with his interesting remarks on the subject in his book on the "sense of illumination". He introduced the concept of "memory colour", by which he meant the "specific" constant colour which we tend to ascribe to objects (see chapter 6 p. 180). In primitive thought, colour is regarded as an inherent property of the object. Memory colour plays a central role in Hering's attempt to understand and account for colour constancy phenomena. He also resorted to various physiological mechanisms (pupillary reaction, successive adaptation and simultaneous contrast), which are frequently, though not necessarily, omitted in later explanations. The concept of memory colour served as the point of departure for Katz in constructing his theory of colour psychology. In his work *The World of Colour* (1935) he claimed that every object has its own "specific colour", which depends on the spectral energy distribution of the light reflected by the object surface, and which can be determined in "normal illumination", by which he meant that in the cloudy northern sky at 12 o'clock noon. Under "abnormal" illumination conditions, our colour sensations are *transformed* in the direction of the specific colour. Katz interpreted his experimental data to indicate that there are two processes involved in human vision, one at a lower and one at a higher developmental level. The more primitive process is that which allows us to perceive film colour; it takes place in the periphery of the retina.

"Retinal vision" is governed by the ordinary optical laws of refraction and reflection, and can thus be artificially produced in situations of "reduced observation". Immediate, natural vision, however, is also governed by a "higher", more "central" component. This was the assumption which led Katz to his concept of "transformation".

As has been pointed out earlier in chapter 6 on colour perception (p. 181), and again rightly by Hochberg (1971a, p. 402), the explanations given by Katz are not at all too different from the Helmholtzian point of view. All the theories of this general type, which presuppose some functions or organizations at a "higher level", i.e. the participation of cerebral factors "in carrying out brightness constancy", reveal the explanatory role ascribed to some kind of "cognitive factor". To that type belong, e.g. the theories of Gelb (1929), Koffka (1935), Judd (1940) and Helson (1964), although they mostly avoid the specific connotations given by v. Helmholtz (cf. above, chapter 6, pp. 180–181) and put it more elegantly. The main point in all these explanations is, that for the equation

$$R=L/E$$

(in which R stands for reflectance of a grey paper disc, L for luminance and E for incident illumination on the disc surface) the subject must be able to receive information about E that he cannot perceive immediately. This information is mediated by some process that involves more than mere sensory coding as to its nature (e.g. learning products, inferences, transformation, new adaptation).

Opposite to this group of explanations are all direct sensory theories of brightness constancy, which can be traced back to the simple mechanisms postulated by Hering (cf. above chapter 6, pp. 180–181). To believe that these more immediate physiological adjustments could not involve learning products is certainly a biased point of view. Another schematic way of thinking is that of presuming more peripheral, sensory level arrangments to account for brightness and colour *constancy* phenomena if they have been accepted to hold for brightness and colour *contrast* phenomena. As will be shown in the last section of this chapter such a confrontation between constancy and contrast does not fit at all.

Let us illustrate the conditions of brightness constancy by means of one of Katz's experiments (Fig. 13.3). In front of the subject on a table, visible to him simultaneously, are two round colour mixers. They stand parallel against a neutral grey background, which also screens the motors of the mixers from the subject. All light falling on the circular discs of the mixers comes from a side window, and a sagittal screen located between the two

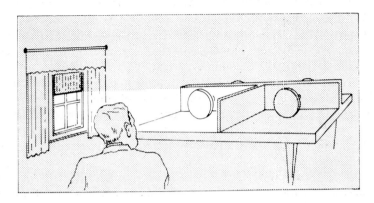

Fig. 13.3 The fundamental brightness constancy experiment. (From v. Fieandt, 1972 p. 242.)

mixers prevents light from falling on the one further away from the window. Before starting the experiment the same proportions of white and black are mounted on both mixers. The resulting grey colour mixtures look different *in two different ways*. First of all, the shadowed disc naturally looks darker. In order to achieve a colour equation—a situation in which the subject perceives the two discs as identical in brightness—the white sector on the shadowed disc must be enlarged. The existence of brightness constancy is convincingly demonstrated in this experiment, since *the white sector of the shadowed disc does not need to be enlarged to the extent which would optically compensate for the reduction in the amount of reflected light.* On the contrary: the shadowed disc appears *almost invariant in surface colour behind the darkness of the shadow.* Only a slight amount of white needs to be added to the grey of the shadowed colour mixture. The colour equation thus produced under conditions of free observation differs considerably from that obtained when the subject views the two discs through a reduction screen, and is then required to match the two discs. In the latter case, what is being compared are two *film colours*; the articulation into a coloured surface and the shadow cast upon it cannot occur.

There is, however, another way in which the two discs appear different. Even when the colour equation has been achieved which satisfies the subject under conditions of free observation, the two grey hues are not experienced as equivalent. This difference has been conclusively demonstrated by Katz. When the phenomenal brightness of the two greys is identical, the shadowed disc appears clearer; to use Katz's term, it has greater "*salience*" (Eindringlichkeit).

Degree of Colour Constancy

In his extensive work, Katz presented a method of measuring brightness constancy. (a) He defined his B-quotient as the ratio of the albedo of the unshadowed disc to that of the shadowed one, when the two appear equal in brightness in the free observation situation $(B = s/r)$. (b) The Q-quotient is defined as the ratio of albedo of the unshadowed disc freely observed to that of the same disc viewed through a reduction screen $(Q = s/p)$. Thus for example

$$B = \frac{200}{300} \quad \text{and} \quad Q = \frac{200}{20}.$$

These values could of course be equally well calculated by means of Brunswik's constancy formula (see above, p. 367). In that case, the albedo of the *shadowed* disc under free observation $= r$, that of the unshadowed disc $= s$, and that of the unshadowed disc seen through a reduction screen $= p$. Our example would then yield

$$R = 100 \, \frac{200 - 20}{300 - 20} = 64.$$

The significance of the concept "albedo" has been clarified earlier, see chapter 6 p. 182.

Theoretical Explanations

It was Gelb's influence which provided the impetus for relational theories of colour constancy. With this approach the old problem of reconciling psychological and physiological points of view becomes a pseudoproblem. The relational principles have implications specifically for the interpretation of brightness constancy phenomena. On the other hand, the brightness gradients present in the light falling upon a chromatically perceived surface can also provide the key to problems of hue constancy.

The conventional distinction between the "illumination" and the "illuminated surface" is actually not a very fruitful one. Whenever a perceptual event involves colour constancy we can always discover a constant ratio, a relational invariance in the prevailing stimulus basis, between the light intensities reflected from the surfaces in the visual field.

Brightness constancy cannot occur unless the observer has information available to him concerning the *relation* between the amount of light reflected from surface *A* and that from surface *B*. Thus the stimulus basis has to contain a system of relations between reflectance intensities. In his textbook of perceptual psychology Lian (1969, p. 70) calls these relational stimuli the *reference white*.

Additional Contributions Given by Lie

The starting point in a series of investigations by Lie (1969) was the dimensionality problem in connection with achromatic colour perception touched upon already by Katz (see p. 373) in his above mentioned experiments.

In Koffka's terminology (1935) the two dimensions distinguished by Katz would be called "whiteness" and "brightness" of the reflecting achromatic surface.

Brightness refers directly to physical reflectance of the surface, whiteness, on the other hand, or albedo (see chapter 6 p. 182), is given by the ratio of reflected light intensity to the illumination originally received by the surface.

In his experiments Lie had the subjects match the phenomenal brightness of two squares (6 × 6 cm) cut from grey paper in comparison with whiteness, in a series of situations in which the illumination of the background was also systematically varied.

All the participants were able—after a short training period—to distinguish "whiteness" from what they called "brightness". As Hochberg pointed out (Kling and Riggs 1971, p. 423), the evaluation of whiteness is decisively dependent upon the distance between the stimuli to be compared as well as on the relationships among the illumination levels of different parts of the visual field.

The results reported by Lie render some more evidence in favour of the conclusion that brightness is determined by the absolute level of the illumination, whereas whiteness must be regarded a function of the ratios between the luminances.

The role played by the sagittal screen in the classical experiment by Katz (see p. 373) was investigated by Lie in another series of experiments. How the subjects perceive the whiteness of the two rotating discs depends strongly upon some features of the dividing screen. The length of the screen affects the "separation-experience" of the discs. If the screen stretches out closer to the observer, the two discs are most frequently experienced as being located in separately "illuminated rooms". In all the other situations (with shorter or lower screens) the subject experiences the discs as located *in front of* two differentially illuminated rooms. According to predictions made by the author the effect of the screen should have decreased with the decrease of difference between the reflectancies of the standard and the variable respectively. This prediction did not hold true. The whiteness-judgements are invariably dependent on the illumination-level-ratio between the standard and the background stimuli. The whiteness-rating graphs computed from the results of different observers are essentially the same regardless of whether or not a shadow casting screen had been placed between the two rotating achromatic discs in the experiment. This calls for a unitary applicable explanation model, according to Lie, in all constancy experiments of the general type presented by Katz in his discussed experiments.

The author assumes that ordinary brightness contrast could provide us with the necessary basic explanatory model. To that end he goes on with experimenting on the contrast producing conditions in shadow-casting situations, or with measuring the distance from the background of either of the discs, therewith contributing to the sagittal location difference between the discs to be compared.

As will be shown in the last section of this chapter, we nevertheless lack evidence for simply bringing the complex phenomenon of brightness constancy back to mere effects of some *brightness contrast* differences (see p. 379).

A related issue concerns the effect on colour perception of the structure of the total visual field. Gelb not only pointed to intensity gradients as the basis of colour constancy, but also stressed the way in which these gradients depend on spatial conditions. In his brilliant "paradoxical experiment", he demolished Katz's concept of "normal illumination". Using Katz's experimental paradigm described earlier (see p. 373), Gelb placed the subject in the same illumination as that which fell upon the shadowed disc. Under these conditions the phenomenal change occurred in the colour of the other disc: the unshadowed one which Katz considered the standard disc in "normal illumination".

The role played by the context was convincingly demonstrated by Wallach's experiment. A round black disc was surrounded by a white ring: these could be illuminated independently. It then turned out that the experienced greyness of the disc was determined by the phenomenal brightness of the surrounding ring. Finally, Wallach doubled the entire arrangement. Using four projectors, four areas of grey were produced, yielding two circular discs each surrounded by a ring (Fig. 13.4). Let us call the reflection intensity of the left-hand disc i_1 and that of the corresponding ring I_1. Wallach then chose i_1 and I_1 such that the relative intensity i_1/I_1 was, for example, 1/2. If the right-hand ring was then made to reflect light with an intensity I_2, which represented a given fraction of I_1, the task of the subject was to adjust the intensity of the right-hand disc so that *its appearance corresponded as closely as possible to that of the left-hand disc.* Repeating

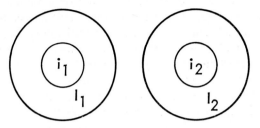

Fig. 13.4 Wallach's experiment. (From v. Fieandt, 1966 p. 223.)

the experiment with a number of different values, the same equation was always obtained:

$$i_2 : I_2 = i_1 : I_2.$$

Wallach's experiment clearly demonstrates that the constant grey of a perceived object depends on a system of relations, i.e. on gradients of reflected radiation. It is important to remember, however, that all four colour fields in the experiment were located on a *common plane surface*, so that the result could also be due to contrast.

In considering the results of Wallach's work, it is well to bear in mind that they may have been determined by the specific conditions of the experiment. If the room had not been darkened, and if the areas under comparison had been located differently with respect to each other, quite different results might have been obtained.

On the Relationship between Constancy and Contrast

In traditional textbooks on the subject Gelb's findings would have been interpreted as due to brightness contrast. In a particularly extensive study, Moed has paid special attention to the connection between brightness constancy and brightness contrast (1964, 1965). In his experiments comparing various grey surfaces he used a specially constructed series of rectangular cards of grey paper, graduated from the whitest white to the blackest black, over a scale of 37 different degrees of grey. In measuring the constancy of the grey stimulus object, the card was compared to a revolving black and white colour mixture disc. When the grey resulting from the black and white mixture corresponded to the grey of the card, this shade of grey was matched against the grey shade of the darker card next in the series. This card was placed *in front* of the colour wheel, and thus closer to the light source.

N

If brightness constancy is expressed, in Brunswik's terms, as "stimulus equivalence" at pole p, and "object equivalence" at pole s (see the presentation of Brunswik's bipolar formula $s-p$ for determining the degree of constancy, p. 367), then Moed's results mean that measurement values in his constancy experiments assume an intermediate position between complete constancy and complete stimulus-determined perception, although much closer to the latter than to the former.

In Japan, the research group led by Akishige has carried out a number of experiments in recent years on the measurement of constancy (1961, 1967). Akishige (1969) has derived a law concerning the conservation of perceptual information in visual space, which has certain points of similarity with Brunswik's formula.

The relationship between illumination constancy and illumination contrast has been studied by Akishige's colleague Ohmura (1961). He carried out five different experiments. In experiment 1, a standard area was used together with a comparison area. The reflectances of the two were identical, but the standard area was covered by a dim transparent screen while the comparison area was not. The results confirmed earlier observations by Ohmura and Hsia (1961; 1943), according to which the rise of phenomenal whiteness of an area is inversely proportional to the fall of intensity of the prevailing illumination. This occurs even if "retinal intensities" are made equivalent. If the *experienced* light intensity of the background falls, the phenomenal brightness of a neutral area seen against the background rises proportionately.

In experiment 2 the setup was the same as in the first, except that the illumination of the standard area was no longer covered by a background varying in intensity. Instead, it was surrounded by a light beam. In comparing these experiments, Ohmura claims that the first exemplifies a contrast phenomenon, which in Jaensch's and Müller's terms can be called a "tissue-contrast" (Florkontrast), and the second a marginal contrast (Randkontrast). The differences between the experimental conditions led to considerable differences in the way in which the subjects judged the illumination. Illumination can thus be used to bring about "masking" effects in object colour. There were, however, differences between the results obtained by Ohmura and those of Jaensch and Müller, which may be due to the fact that in the latter experiments the reflectances of the focal stimulus and of the background surfaces were different, while in the former they were identical.

In experiments 3 and 4, both the standard and the comparison areas were covered by the background; they differed in that the reflectances of the areas were different in experiment 3, but identical in experiment 4.

The results of experiment 3 indicate a certain amount of illumination contrast. On the other hand, the constancy increased with a decrease in the illumination difference between the backgrounds of the two areas. In experiment 4, illumination constancy did not occur.

In experiment 5, the intensities of the illumination backgrounds of the two areas were made to vary continually in such a way that the intensities of the two backgrounds were constantly alternating. No clear boundary line could be observed between the two backgrounds. According to the results of this experiment, illumination constancy rose when the illumination level of the background was relatively high. At the same time, differences between individual subjects decreased.

In the light of modern object constancy theory, the data can be explained without any recourse to contrast. Basically we are dealing with what is known in the psychology of learning as stimulus generalization.

The grey object colours represented by the discs can be perceived as similar only when the rings surrounding them function as "references" for whiteness. As pointed out in the discussion of Gelb's experiment, the primary whiteness references are the internal reflectance relations prevailing in the stimulus field, rather than the absolute localized values of light energy.

Freeman's Contribution

If we follow the scientific terminology of the 1960's, the explanation of brightness constancy offered by Gelb (and also by Wallach) should be called the *"luminance-ratio theory"*. Other approaches which have received considerable support more recently are, as mentioned above, the *contrast theory*, the *adaptation level theory*, and certain theories based on the effect of the surrounding surfaces, such as the *induced opponent response theory* suggested by Jameson and Hurvich.

An exhaustive comparative survey of the field has been carried out by Freeman (1967). Summing up, he finds that "there is little experimental confirmation for the brightness-contrast approach to brightness constancy" (op. cit., p. 185). In the few cases which have provided results consistent with the theory, the experiments can be equally convincingly interpreted in terms of alternative theories (those of the luminance ratios and of adaptation level).

Instead of contrast, Freeman feels that we should speak in terms of simultaneous or consecutive *brightness induction*. He thus defines contrast very broadly as the relation between the phenomenal brightness of an object and its luminance in relation to that of the surrounding surfaces.[1] It is clear that on this basis Wallach's results can easily be offered in

1. Measured *luminance*, according to Freeman, must be sharply distinguished from *reflectance* or albedo and from *brightness*, which is a ϕ-concept.

support of a contrast approach to constancy. Freeman in fact criticizes Wallach for not offering any data concerning the possible inducing effect of the surrounding rings.

Freeman's excellent survey follows, point by point, all the rigorous research into the conditions under which brightness contrast occurs. If all the conditions necessary for the occurrence of simultaneous or successive induction can be shown to be conditions for constancy also, then the contrast theory can be substituted for that suggested by Wallach.

Although the similarity and correspondence between these two phenomena is surprisingly extensive, certain results achieved by Kozaki (1963, 1965) nevertheless indicate that variations in the degree of contrast do not necessarily affect brightness constancy, and that, for example, a factor as essential to brightness contrast as the size of the inducing area has no effect on the constancy of the surface subject to induction.

Helson's theory of adaptation level (see p. 41) significantly seems to enable us to account for brightness constancy, in terms of the part played by the reflecting surfaces around the perceptual object in bringing about the brightness impression. According to Helson, constancy is based on the adaptation level pertaining to the perceived surface at the moment of perception. In fact it seems likely that, compared to the perceptual object, any white surface functioning in Kozaki's terms as a kind of "white anchor" produces the strongest brightness constancy in that object. Here the analogy with Gelb's paradoxical experiment (see p. 376) would be striking.

Thus, while Freeman seems inclined to favour a return to Hering-like optical and retinal explanations of brightness constancy, from the point of view of the integrated approach of this work we should instead stress the *simultaneous reflectancies of the surrounding surfaces* as the common starting point of most theories.

Attempts at General Constancy Explanations

With regard to the rather uniform type of relational invariances postulated and, to some extent confirmed to exist, as a basis for several object constancies,

(1) $k = P'/V'$ for shape
(2) $k = S'/D'$ for size
(3) $R = L/E$ for brightness,

it should not be surprising to find general theoretical principles applicable to all of them. As a matter of fact such general constancy explanations have been presented. One could group them in several ways. Sometimes a difference is made between *nativistic* and *empiricist* approaches—the former usually includes presumptions of inborn regulatory mechanisms that correct for random variations in the stimuli. The empiricist approaches have relied more on occasional regulatory processes on the receptor level and look for learning products and final achievements that govern the way we get along with external objects. Not completely overlapping this classification, is the beforementioned alternative: either higher organized central regulations (cognitive factors) are supposed to be involved, or the reactions of the organism are considered explicable on a sensory level of functioning.

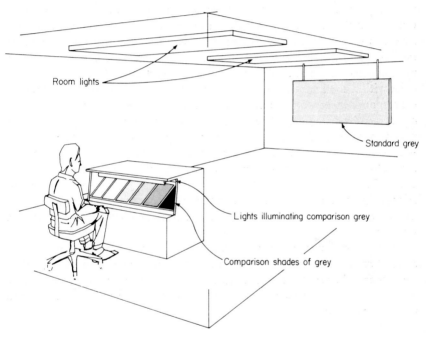

Fig. 13.5 Another classical setup for measuring brightness constancy. (From Cornsweet, 1971 p. 367.)

Let us begin with theories on *brightness constancy* because the discussion has there proceeded further than in most other instances, and the alternatives can be followed up in detail. Hochberg (1971a, pp. 395–426) has given a good survey of the early background and the development of all the main ideas, so for the most part it might suffice to quote him on the essential points of view.

Considering all Helmholtzian types of explanations (resorting to the contribution of cognitive factors) Hochberg points out the lack of evidence in favour of cerebral regulation mechanisms. He also keeps stressing the fact that these cognitive theories very strongly imply the necessity of *having learned illumination cues* and thus of the constancy as an unlearned reaction. This implication in turn is weakened by Burzlaff's (1931) and Brunswik's (1929) experiments on brightness constancy in children and Burkamp's (1923) results with goldfish. All these developmental studies indicated a well established brightness and hue constancy to exist at an early stage of development.

Turning to the other alternative we have seen (see pp. 370–371) that Hering was apt to explain brightness constancy from a series of rather peripheral sensory and senso-motoric mechanisms (adaptation, regulative opening of the pupil, contrast effects among different parts of the retinal field). In the opinion of the present authors, Hochberg at this point goes too far in elaborating the sensory type of explanation in only one direction. He takes all the peripheral interaction phenomena observed and confirmed to exist within the realm of *brightness contrast* as a starting point for applying corresponding sensory explanations to what happens in the *brightness constancy* experiments. Obviously, one dominating trend in the contemporary perceptual theory is to move away from "psychological" (experience —and learning oriented) explanation models toward more strict and accurate neurophysiological ways of reasoning (see for example, Cornsweet 1971, pp. 365–370). As Cornsweet has shown (Fig. 13.5 and 13.6) such a sensory explanation can at present be given for the case of brightness constancy, but *he does not make a mistaken analogy between contrast and constancy.* Cornsweet points out that in research on object constancies *the subjects in the classical experiments* (Katz, Gelb, Koffka, Kardos) responded not to the *amount of light* a surface reflected, but to the stimulus as an *object surface* (cardboard) (Cornsweet 1971, p. 366). Hochberg has not sufficiently pointed out that in order for brigthness constancy or colour constancy to occur, the subject has to perceive one or several *objects*, i.e. *surface colours* in his environment. As the experiments of Gelb (1938) and Goldstein and Gelb (1920) have evidently shown, *the achievement of perceiving surface colours is a cortical function.* In cases where brightness and hue contrast are —in the sense of Hering—regarded as adaptation and regulation mechanisms on the retinal level, *brightness and hue constancy of object surfaces cannot be regarded merely a parallel case to contrast interactions among different parts of the retinal field.* That we, on the other hand, should also include contrast-effects in what might be considered a cortical achievement looks quite superfluous and anachronistic.

It is in fact amazing that this amount of effort has been taken in order to bring brightness (and hue) *constancy* together with *contrast* on common denominators (see pp. 377–380 and Hochberg 1971a, pp. 407–412) when we consider how well colour and brightness constancies seem to obey common principles with other object constancies, especially the constancies of shape and size of familiar objects. Consider once more the *relational stimulus variables* as expressed in the equations (1) to (3) on p. 380.

Quite regardless of the exaggerated accuracy in these formulations, would it not be more simple to suppose that *all prevailing stimuli together influence the perception of the relative dimensions of objects and relative light*

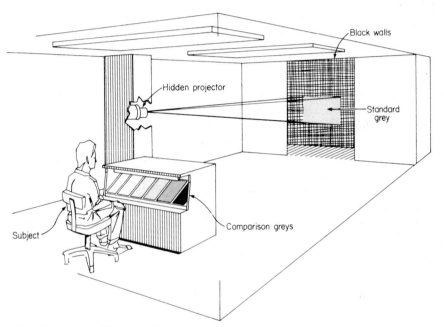

Fig. 13.6 A modification of the traditional setup in brightness-constancy experiment. (From Cornsweet, 1971 p. 368.)

intensities thus contributing to what we have called "object constancy" (see Cornsweet 1971, pp. 379–380)? How this achievement is carried out physiologically, is a matter for neuropsychology.

When Gibson introduced his concept of "higher order stimuli" he was thinking about relational stimulus variables. What really determines the way we perceive objects seems not to be a direct correspondence between isolated stimulus-elements and resulting information about the object. Most relevant for perception, apparently, are the relationships between single elementary stimuli. What happens or what is available in adjacent parts of the entire stimulus situation clearly determines the way we perceive shapes, sizes and colours of object surfaces. Stated in this way, the object constancies actually provide *instances of enrichments of the stimulus field* or of *stimulus generalization* in the terms of learning theory. The concept of *stimulus context* or of the *frame of reference* thus becomes extremely important for the "constancies" we ascribe to the objects.

There is nothing mysterious about an organism's preferred reactions to relational stimulus variables. We do not need to regard this as something "cognitive" in the sense of a Helmholtzian explanation. The essential condition for an object surface to retain its outlook in changing stimulus conditions is the presence of the *relational gradients among the stimuli*. Remember the crucial Gelb-experiment (see p. 181). When the small piece of white paper had been removed, the subject perceived the rotating black *once more as white* (just as before the experience with the white sticker). Cognitive factors thus do not seem to be essential—the relational gradient of visual stimulation has to be present in the situation.

It is symptomatic that Hochberg, in his otherwise excellent presentation, refers to Wallach's experiment as confirming the analogy of brightness contrast and brightness constancy (Hochberg 1971a, p. 413), whereas Cornsweet has rightly understood it as referring to the role of the ratios within the field of stimulation: "changing all the reflectances in a fixed ratio is identical, visually, with changing the incident illumination" (Cornsweet 1971, p. 374). His general conclusion after having applied his neurophysiological model also coincides with the formulation in this book: "When ratios do remain constant, brightness constancy holds, that is, the brightnesses of the objects remain approximately constant" (Cornsweet 1971, p. 372).

Evidence from other Modalities in Favour of the given Constancy Theory

It is interesting that a lot of investigations on the degree of constancy in other modality dimensions strongly support the evidence so far gathered from what is known about visual objects. Mohrmann (1939) carried out a series on experiments on *loudness constancy* when varying the distance of the sound source from the observer. The degree of constancy was astonishingly high when expressed in terms of Brunswik's ratio (see p. 367). The subjects evidently tend to react according to the *emission-intensity* of the sound, not according to its *reception-intensity*. More importantly, however, the stimulus most articulated among all of them, the *human voice*, resulted in the highest degree of loudness constancy. The hum of an electromotor or even better, a single organ pipe had a very poor constancy. The more articulated the field, the richer the context of present parallel stimuli and the higher the degree of constancy.

Some interesting cases of *gustatory constancy* have been reported by

Gregson and Paris (1967). They refer to Brunswik's interpretation of the object constancy phenomena. According to him, perception of one sensory dimension should be regarded in part as the consequence of "collateral sensory input from other dimensions". This latter information is supposed to be used by the organism and results in "an invariant response to what is physically an invariant distal stimulus magnitude experienced under very varied circumstances" (Gregson and Paris 1967, p. 483).

Their taste experiences were built upon collateral stimulation from volume, weight, temperature, viscosity, etc. They were thus faced with the possibility that the organism tries to preserve some perceptual invariances which might affect the veridicality of other aspects of the simultaneous information. Gregson and Paris were able to show in a series of careful experiments that *perceived taste quantity* preferably constitutes one of these fundamental gustatory constancies.

If citric acid at three concentration levels is given as a taste stimulus in paired comparison experiments, there is shown to exist an interaction between taste quantity and volume on the one hand, and between taste quantity and concentration on the other. Applying pairs of samples which (1) had the same concentration but differing volume, and (2) were equal in volume but unequal in concentration, the authors found that intensity and volume constancies break down. They assume that this result is due to the organism's striving to preserve a taste quantity constancy.

The latter constancy breaks down in favour of volume or intensity constancies as soon as the magnitudes of these two sensory dimensions are large, because the amount of stimulation then involved is sufficient to swamp the perceptual noise in the task which permits the quantity constancy to operate to yield nonveridical perception. (Gregson and Paris, op. cit., p. 486.)

Whether or not these gustatory constancies are analogies of visual constancies—for instance the size-distance constancies—remains an open question.

The Role of the Frame of Reference

It is evident in any case that the frame of reference is a condition of crucial importance in all phenomena of object constancy and its preservation. Measurements of constancy, whether of shape, size, colour, sound or taste, have indicated the overwhelming importance of the stimulus environment which is simultaneously available with the "constant" perceptual object. The broader this simultaneously available stimulus context is, the higher the degree of constancy. Whenever impoverishment or reduction of the broader stimulus field occurs, the result is also a reduction in constancy. Research seems to show that the extent to which stimulus relations can be perceived depends upon the broadness of the context. The narrower the perceptual field, the poorer the articulation and the more limited the stimulus relations available.

Gelb is sometimes said to be the first to adapt simultaneous intensity gradients as an explanation of colour constancy, though he was himself unaware of this. What he was actually looking for in his study of colour perception were the relational invariants which we mentioned above in connection with the constancy of shape. Just as constancy of shape depends on the *relation* between the projectional shape of the surface and its angle of inclination, and constancy of size depends on the *relation* between perspectival size and distance, so our perception of brightness and hue as constant is based on the *relation* between prevailing local reflectances and the radiation reflected from surrounding surfaces.

In finding and defining the relational invariances underlying phenomena of constancy, the concept of gradients has been of great importance. This was originally adopted to account for the relations between elements of receding surfaces in depth, but has since been extended to include more and more types of relational invariants.

When, for example, Kohler (1951) in his famous experiments with distorting eyeglasses, altered and deformed the visual space of the subject, certain relational invariances caused by the optical properties of the lenses were preserved under deformation (see Dodwell's arguments in chapter 11, pp. 320–321). We can assume that these invariances helped the subject to compensate for the distortions in his visual world. In principle it is just as natural that the reflectance relations which remained in the black and white picture in Land's phenomenon (see p. 205) formed the relational invariances on the basis of which the lost chromatic scale could be restored. It is thus that our perception of objects as "real" is governed by the invariant relations between stimulus elements referred to already by Kaila (see p. 362) in speaking of the goals of modern natural science.

14 | Constituents of Object Perception

Species-Determined Perceptual Worlds

In studying the way in which organisms perceive their environment, a common error is to regard the stimulus basis too physically, too objectively, as a set of quantities which exists independently of other regularities. With this approach, an important aspect of the stimulus world is disregarded. Gibson calls this aspect *ecology* (Gibson, 1966). From the point of view of the organism as it reacts to stimuli, there is no such thing as a universe of neutral, objective, and mutually equivalent stimuli. The existence of such a universe has been postulated as the object of physical description, and it corresponds in particular to the outermost circle of Fig. 1.1. Even in a functional description of the organism and its environment, using phenomenalistic language, we must keep in mind that a stimulus exists for the organism only insofar as it belongs to the perceptual world which is relevant for that species.

Every species thus has its own characteristic perceptual universe, its ecological environment. Even the world of stimuli experienced by human beings is determined by our perceptual equipment. It is impossible for us to know whether there is some more objective, more stable world "outside" or "beyond" what we perceive.

One investigator who has given us incomparable analyses and descriptions of the perceptual and functional world of animals is the biologist J. von Uexküll. In his article "Streifzüge durch die Umwelten von Tieren und Menschen" (1934), later published in English in Schiller (1957), he gives captivating descriptions of the perceptual world characteristic of certain animal species. Such an attempt must naturally remain somewhat speculative; we cannot know what is perceived by an insect, a lamprey, or a lemur. A great deal, however, can be concluded on the basis of the animal's behaviour, at least as far as its *discriminative* ability is concerned; and that is all we need to know in empirical psychology.

Uexküll distinguishes between the biological environment of the animal (*Umgebung*) and the functional world which it experiences (*Umwelt*). Only the first can be described in physical, objective terms.

Functional "Goal-Objects" of Animals

The world that surrounds moving, eating, preying, mating, attacking and fleeing animals is meaningful insofar as it is a *world of objects*. Uexküll's phrase has become famous: "The world of the dragonfly contains only dragonfly objects". Generalizing, we can say that the environment is perceived on account of the objects it contains, as a world of objects.

The perception of these objects is of crucial importance to the behaviour of animals. Perception and action are always tied together. There is nothing which is "exclusively perceived", "exclusively seen", "heard", or "smelled". Objects are discriminated from one another only to the extent that they are independent objects of manipulation or activity.

We speak of the objects perceived by *animals*, but these objects are not comparable to the constant and clearly articulated objects that *we* perceive; they are primarily *signal bearers*. They form the basis for the signals which vary from situation to situation. They may be, for instance, enemy-signal objects, food-signal objects, mating-signal objects, and the like. They exist for the animal only when a signal meaning is linked to them, as objects which release activity of one kind or another.

When a dog comes into a beautifully furnished room containing various colours, his perceptual activity may be aroused only by the *food objects* on the table, the *chewing objects* on the floor or chairs, the *dragging-around objects* lying around loose, and perhaps the objects which offer a warm, soft place to *sit down*, which offer a strong activity stimulus.

We have a tendency to take an anthropomorphic view of what happens in the animal world. When bees attack us at swarming time, for example, we imagine that they perceive us as a large and sharply delimited object shape. In actual fact, as careful experiments have shown, these insects sting in reaction to various signals emanating from human beings: a person's movement, a dark article of clothing, a characteristic odour, and the like. The objects perceived by animals, in fact, can only rarely appear clearly delimited in a simultaneous perceptual field, since they are usually primarily visual objects.

In studying the perception of shapes in his dog, Buytendijk (1924) observed that when the dog was on the leash it was often unable to obtain a good visual picture of an object. Part of the form perception process in the dog must include motor activity: running-around and sniffing exploration. Motor adaptation to optically sensed conditions is a high-level achievement, which is by no means automatic in an animal at the level of the dog. Only long practice can make it possible.

Compared to the perceptual objects of human beings, then, the perceptual objects of most animal species may be very primitive. They usually have the characteristics of mere functional activity signals. The "sameness" of an object through time, its *identity*, as well as its *permanence*, its object *constancy* (of size, shape and colour) and its *transgredience*[1] (the permanence of its "actual contents") independent of all variation in perceptual aspect, in short that which we consider characteristic of perception in human beings, appear only as isolated and incidental tendencies in animals. Animals may react to or disregard one and the same perceptual signal depending on the overall situation. Both Uexküll and Buytendijk thus have placed strong emphasis on the *selective* nature of perception. According to this view, a hungry frog behaves quite differently with regard to inanimate objects after it has obtained a worm or a spider to eat. After such a gastronomic experience, even matchsticks and bits of moss in the environment acquire temporary value as stimuli.

Close contact between the organism and the objects of its environment makes the inanimate nature dynamic. For example, some characteristic of prey may acquire absolute dominance in the perceptual world of the hungry animal. For the frog, such a characteristic, in natural feeding, is *movement of the prey*; when this feature is absent, the prey is not perceived as prey.

For the fish, the bait or fly of the fisherman may exist specifically as a signal object, insofar as it possesses some of the characteristics of the usual prey. The fish also reacts to the shadow of the boat moving over the water, to the net, or to voices as to "enemy objects". For the child, the "qualities of expression" of the objects surrounding it have been preserved to a much greater extent than for the adult.

Volkelt's Experiments

From this point of view, the experiments carried out by Volkelt with spiders are especially illuminating. For the spider waiting beside its web, only a living fly shaking the web acts as a prey object. Only this highly specific stimulus system is registered as "prey", and serves as the bio-

1. This term was coined by Kaila (1962). In a sense it stands for what Piaget (1930) had called *transitivity*: something that is perceived as "essential" and "substantial" in an object despite the endless variations of aspects under which it is observed (see p. 395).

logically appropriate object of attack. When confronted with a living fly away from the web, the spider may take to flight, since such a fly does not have the characteristics of the spider's prey. Furthermore, a dead fly placed in the web also fails to arouse the spider's interest, although it may avoid or even explore it. But if the web is touched by the end of a wire, so as to make it tremble, this may serve as the releasing signal to make the spider attack the dead fly.

When the spider does attack as a consequence of the vibration of the web, the progress of the reaction may be bound to the situation down to the last detail. The signal qualities denoting the object may vary from one situation to another. For the wrapping of the prey, perceived vibration is crucial (Baltzer, 1923). To release the eating reaction, smell and taste stimuli are also necessary, and these may in turn become the dominant characteristics of the "prey object".

Attraction and Repulsion Values of Human Perceptual Things

In the development of perception in man and his biological ancestors, certain objects and their functionally dominant characteristics have played a crucial role. Primitive objects of perception generally are either of a desirable or of a threatening nature. The textbooks have probably erred in describing the structure of the perceptual world merely in terms of afferent receptivity, emphasizing the receptive aspect of perception. This way of thinking leads us to overemphasize the importance of visual information, since as adults, having learned to move around among objects, we recognize them primarily by means of visual perception. But the formation of perceptual objects, the original experience of a particular perceptual content as an object, is probably possible only by means of *polymodal anchoring*. A grey piece of stone, suitable in shape to be used as a tool, probably does not stand out very much from the rock around it. But when prehistoric man seized the stone and used it as a weapon or as a working tool, it became articulated as a quite distinct object in his perceptual world.

According to Brunswik's famous article entitled "Psychology in Terms of Objects" (1936), such research should take into account not only the "stimulus cues" of a perceptual object, but also its "functional cues", as defined by Uexküll. Experiments about problem solving by Duncker (1945), Saugstad (1958), Raaheim (1961) and others indicate that certain objects in the physical environment are perceived under quite different conditions and, as it were, more effectively, when their functional or instrumental character becomes evident to the problem solver.

What the knowledge about the purpose of an unfamiliar instrument or apparatus means for the comprehension of the structure of such an object and for the right way of manipulating it was stressed already by Rubin (1920, pp. 210–225). The decisive factors in this acquaintance with the object (in his case actually a camera occluder) are—according to the author: (1) *the "task-character"* ascribed to the act of assembly by its performer, (2) *the merging of fertile ideas* which seem relevant to the purpose of the object as conceived of by the assembler. The task-mindedness of the subject thus becomes highly motivating for his behaviour and keeps activating his readiness to efficient means-ends combinations.

In discussing the selective nature of perception, Lewin (1936) has also stressed the functional aspect of perceptual objects for man. From the point of view of the activity, goals, or intentions of the perceiver, objects of perception may be either positive or negative. Those units which have such a valence (to use Lewin's terminology) most easily become objects of perception. A ripe and juicy apple transmits the direct message "eat me", a fresh newspaper, "read me", a tempting sexual partner, "take me", and so on.

The Constituents of "Object Reality"

In one of his earlier publications (1958) the senior author held the opinion that the "material thing-quality of objects" actually reflects the degree of interaction of several modal perceptual systems. Should the organism actually undergo a deprivation of *all* modal stimulations, there scarcely would remain any "substance" or "material" whatsoever as a kind of carrier of "thing-qualities". Evidently the multi-dimensionality and the interaction of modalities strengthens the reality impressions of objects. Their material and substantial character is probably founded on the repeated modal anchoring of perceptions. These "moorings" arise from the coordination of the perceptions with basic optic and haptic elements, that is, from the process of "objectivizing" our rather specific sensations.

However, having become acquainted with the above-mentioned contributions of Brunswik and those of Michotte to be discussed below one feels inclined to revise and to complete that point of view. "Object reality" does not exclusively depend on interaction of different modal perceptual systems. There remains something constituently determined in experienced "objects" even devoid of all sensorial data. A real object is conceived not only as a carrier of numerous simultaneous modal aspects but also as a temporally continuous, enduring, imperishable unit in the world of experience. It shows *identity* approached from several directions; furthermore it has *permanence* over periods of time. And, quite decisively, it has "tool" character.

The "handleability" of objects, so nicely expressed by Brunswik, immediately deserves our attention when searching for criteria for spontaneous "reality impressions" within our system of perception. This "handleability" forms an interesting counterpart and complement to the concept of "availability of functions" which was developed by Saugstad (1958) and Raaheim (1961). These landmarks outline quite new directions for our considerations when trying to find out decisive constituents for what we perceive as objects in our phenomenal and behavioural world.

The "Reality Function" Cortically Determinated

In order to understand the perception of objects in human beings, however, cognition must also be taken into account; distinct and articulated object perception is evidently possible only on the basis of a certain level of cerebral activity. At the turn of the last century, the leading French psychopathologist Pierre Janet, in his work "Les Obsessions et la Psychoasthenié" (1903), suggested a scale of psychological activation levels. His basic ideas are still valid. In this connection we should point out that Janet's "reality function" operates at a very high level and assumes cerebral activity of a cognitive nature. Lowest in the hierarchy of activation levels are reflexes and other involuntary muscular movements; above these are emotional reactions, and above these, at the third level, is activity connected with the imagination. The fifth and highest level is occupied by the "reality function", which in terms of the objectivity of the experiential world means the greatest possible reality in the perceiver. As a late evolutionary step, this reality function is easily disturbed. In a healthy individual, it means the freshness and enticement of the world of objects, its tangible "handleability". A patient in whom the reality function has been disturbed continues to perceive the world, but the character of objects is not felt to be "material" or "real". In this connection, the significance of Gelb's well known study is apparent; he found that *external surface colours*, the strongest and most "real" colour experiences, are the ones which disappear most directly following damage to the brain. It is these colours which are most important from the point of view of object colour constancy (Gelb, 1938; Heaton 1968, p. 170).

Identity, Permanence, Transgredience

Three phenomena were mentioned above as important to object perception in man: *identity*, *permanence*, and *transgredience*. Identity means the fact that an object is perceived as a continuous and identical perceptual whole, regardless of its various appearances on different occasions. How is it possible that an object which is temporarily removed from our field of vision is perceived upon its return as the same, although it may have changed in shape, size, colour, or position? The usual explanation has recourse to memory and to the phenomenon of memory traces. According to John Stuart Mill, our belief in the existence and permanence of the body is nothing but the belief in the permanence and contingence of our sensations (Mill, 1863).

Piaget's careful studies of how the concept of probability develops in children have indicated that the notion of the identity and continuity of objects is related to experienced solidity, substance, and material resistance. Our sensory-motor experiences (the roles played by objects in our functional world) define objects as material and as, in a certain sense, solid and continuous. Only at about ten months of age does a child begin to understand that the same object reappears after being hidden under a blanket or behind a screen.

Experiments carried out by the German psychologist Ternus (1926) have presented convincing evidence that the experienced identity of objects plays a fundamental role in the perceptual world of adults as well. He used a mobile stimulus-projection system. Stroboscopic situations were created, first by means of two alternating projectors and later by drawing a strip of cardboard, with a hole in it, back and forth across a group of figures. Phenomenal identity occurred in two cases: (1) when the stimulus was projected several times onto the same spot on the retina; (2) when the stimulus was projected at time (a) onto a certain spot, and an exact copy of the stimulus at time (b) onto another spot. There was a strong tendency for the subjects to recognize and identify the new figures which were exactly similar to those shown previously, but even when qualitative differences occurred, such as when the brightness level changed, there was a strong tendency to identify the new stimuli as identical to the previous ones.

A good example of the phenomenon of *permanence* is offered by the research of Michotte and his school on *perception of movement*. The best and most complete picture of this research is given by the collection of articles published in 1962 as "Causalité, permanence et réalité phénoménales". This collection includes most of Michotte's articles on various subjects, certain of his previously unpublished writings and the most recent student projects carried out under his direction, both in French and English. Of the experiments, the most impressive is that on the so-called screen-and-tunnel effect. The experiment is set up in such a way that two rectangles A and B (25×5 mm) are visible simultaneously, as A moves toward B. If, as A comes alongside B, the shorter side of A, which has been in front, stops moving while the other short side continues to move (with the effect of shortening the rectangle), 100 per cent of the subjects see rectangle A as slipping behind B. At certain velocities the impression is quite inescapable.

In these experiments the rectangle A represents a highly consistent structural whole. It is experienced as moving and behaving as an unchanging whole, displaying a tendency toward continuity of movement.

If rectangle B is now replaced by a smaller one, measuring 3×5 mm, while A preserves its original dimensions, A can no longer be experienced as disappearing behind B. In spite of this, 95 per cent of the subjects continued to maintain that they saw A disappearing behind B.

In the next experiment, rectangle B is eliminated altogether, while A continues to move from left to right. At a certain point the right-hand upright side stops moving, while the other side parallel to it continues to move, shortening the rectangle, until the two shorter sides merge. In this experiment, 70 per cent of the subjects say that they perceive A as moving behind some other object, such as a dark screen.

This is accounted for in the following way: the front side of rectangle A is not experienced as having stopped moving. The static background becomes the figure and the vertical boundary of rectangle A becomes the boundary of a figure emerging from the background, behind which A is perceived as moving. Under these conditions the object is perceived as moving but unchanged in form, while objectively the opposite is true. In order for this phenomenon to occur, it is essential that the colouring of the rectangle be homogeneous. If the boundary is made discontinuous, the effect is weakened.

Perception of the same object as reappearing from behind a screen or "out of a tunnel" seems to be based on two essential factors: velocity of movement and the qualitative identity of the two objects separated by the screen phase. The part played by velocity is reflected both by the requirement that the object retain a constant speed and by certain conditions concerning the duration of the interval during which it is invisible. The interval must be of such phenomenal duration that an object of the size in question would have been able, at a constant velocity, to pass through the tunnel.

In a very illuminating paper Gibson *et al.* (1969) put forward the question: "What is actually meant by *the permanence of an object*? Is that a problem of discriminating between persisting and non-persisting things?"

The authors want to make a distinction between "objects going out of sight" and "objects going out of existence". Visually reacting organisms must be able to master situations with those alternatives. (One basic requirement is of course that the general level of illumination does not sink remarkably.) If an object disappears in normal daylight, how does the organism receive appropriate stimulus information in order to recognize the significant alternative?

"Going out of sight" occurs (a) because of occlusion (it is hidden behind another object or behind a phenomenal edge), (b) as a consequence of an ever increasing distance from the observer.

"Going out of existence" implies changes in the "material consistence" of the physcial stimulus object—a pond of water evaporates, a piece of biscuit gets consumed, an airplane explodes and disappears.

The opinion of the authors is that perceptual psychologists so far have been too exclusively interested in static occlusion (e.g. overlapping contours). Reynolds (1968) repeated the Michotte experiments. He was able to restate the role of movement in occluding situations. There must not actually exist a "real edge" in the stimulus configuration. Nevertheless, if within a random texture one topologically distinct part of the elements keeps consistently moving in relation to another static partition of the pattern, *an occluding edge instantly shows up*, and the "tunnel effect" of the moving elements arises.

By means of an interesting movie-material the authors convincingly demonstrate how their observers immediately discriminate between "going out of sight" and "going out of existence". There are some differences inherent in the functional basis of the stimulation. The first mentioned alternative is based on optically reversible transitions, the second one on optically irreversible transformations.

The tunnel effect described above is a special case of the so-called "amodal complementation phenomena". A new study of these phenomena by Michotte and his students has later appeared (Michotte *et al.* 1967).

Invariance or constancy of perception means that the characteristic properties of objects (their experienced colour, size, and shape) do not seem to change to any noticeable extent, even though considerable variations and changes may occur in the objective stimulus basis. From the point of view of permanence, that is, recognition of the object as the same, this invariance is of course of the greatest importance.

"But," Michotte points out, "the impression by which objects are experienced as continuous goes even further". Permanence means that an object is recognized as the same and invariable in itself, even though changes may occur in some of its properties. A piece of iron is experienced as the same, regardless of the red glow it acquires at the forge. A balloon that increases in size as it is inflated is still the same balloon. *The experience of identity gives an object its unchangingness, its permanence, in spite of its partial or complete absence from the field of vision.*

A good description of *transgredience* is given by Eino Kaila in his posthumously published work (1962):

Jeder perzeptuelle Gegenstand, zum Beispiel etwa ein abgespiegeltes Gesicht, ist in bezug auf seine einzelnen momentanen Erscheinungen transgredient.— Also fällt nicht einmal ein perzeptueller Gegenstand mit irgendeiner momentanen Erscheinung zusammen; ein solcher Gegenstand ist nicht in seinen momentanen Erscheinungen anwesend oder präsent. Aber diesen logischen Umstand können wir in der Praxis unbeachtet lassen, weil wir ja im Normalfall eine empirische Sicherheit darüber besitzen, dass gewisse implizite Antizipationen das Richtige stressen (Kaila, 1962, 26–27).

(Every perceivable object, for example, a mirrored face, is transgredient in its relationship to its instantaneous appearance.—Thus a perceivable object is never identical with any instantaneous appearance; such an object is not existent or present in its instantaneous appearance. But in practice we can ignore this logical condition because in normal cases we possess an empirical certainty about it, that particular implicit anticipations are confirmed.) (Translated by the authors.)

A good description of amodal perception is offered by Kaila's example of the matchbox which is placed on the table in front of the subject. The box is placed in such a way that only the upper striking surface, the blue bottom of the box and one narrow blue side are visible to the subject simultaneously with one eye. Thus the "object" from whose surfaces light is reflected into the focusing eye is only a kind of "semienclosed space", a spatial angle with its apex toward the viewer. *But this is not how it is experienced.* In our immediate description of the situation, we say that we perceive the entire box. What is amodal in this perceptual situation, to use Michotte's terminology, is that the missing gaps in the proximal stimulus figure are compensated for in the continuous perceptual whole which is formed by the perceiver. This *integral, complete,* immediate visual experience of the object, which is independent of our knowledge (since the box is seen as complete and integral even though only three sides of the spatial angle are actually offered), seems to be based on the anticipations which are connected with perceptual objects once they have been distinctly conceived. These contribute to the transgredience that characterizes an object with respect to its individual manifestations (cf. Kaila 1962, pp. 44–45).

Some experimental investigations made by the Danish psychologists Koseleff (1957) and Johansen (1957, 1959) have provided interesting cases of anticipations in what could be labelled "amodal perception situations" in the sense of Michotte. Koseleff was curious about the real nature of the so-called size–weight effect from a phenomenal point of view. It is a well-known fact that we judge the smaller of two objects with the same physical weight to be heavier and more dense than the bigger one (Koseleff 1957, p. 184). According to Koseleff the subjects in weight-lifting experiments often reported that "they expected" the bigger object to be the heavier one and the smaller object to be the lighter one; "therefore" they were deceived in their expectation when lifting; and it was only "therefore" that the smaller object appeared to be heavier than the bigger.

After having carried out a phenomenological analysis of the experiences and attitudes of his subjects Koseleff concluded that no anticipation whatsoever precedes the intention of lifting the weight Nr. 1. "The order is

Fig. 14.1 Two illustrative cases of Johansen's "amodal perception" figures. (From Johansen, 1959 p. 108.)

reversed, as it is the astonishment or disappointment, occurring when lifting Nr. 2, which *creates* the disappointed anticipation. And the teasing point is that this expectation is phenomenally localized at a moment prior to its creation." (Koseleff 1957, p. 186).

Johansen, on the basis of his experiments on volume-figural phenomena (1957) critically analysed the concept of "amodal perception" as coined by Michotte. Johansen presented his subjects with three dimensional objects, e.g. polyhedrons turning their stereogeometrically well-defined frontsides toward the subjects. They had to describe the outlook and the dimensions of the invisible backside of the object.

This investigator came to the conclusion that the nature and structure of our perceptual space is strongly determined by the objects available—as it also is the space that constitutes the voluminal aspects of the objects.

According to Johansen the term "amodal" must not be given the meaning of something that is sensorially nonexistent or unrealistic. The reverse side is "present" to the perceiver as a vivid sensorial reality. In the case where we are confronted with an unfamiliar object, some kinds of expectations might arise as to the potential forms of the hidden objects. Yet in spite of Bruner's point of view, in our everyday life we get along with objects without any detailed or specific expectations as to the surfaces of familiar objects in our environment.

The phenomena of object identity, permanence, and transgredience in general include perceptual anticipation. The absence of such anticipations causes even such mentally highly developed animals as chimpanzees and dogs to lack "objects" in the human sense. A dog following a moving ball does not understand the concept of a continuous path of motion; such a path does not take shape for the animal, who seems to be completely bound to the smell trace occurring in the path of the ball. Perception that involves the experience of some kind of elementary "reality", and to which anticipations are linked is already at a very primitive level. The dog, even if it lacks the concept of paths in the sense mentioned above, does react to a *throwing movement* without actually perceiving a flying ball, that is, it shows anticipations. Already at an early stage perception is directed to those things which have at least some stability and permanence.

On other hand, this means that in the perception of objects we utilize certain *invariants* which occur in the stimulus basis. The part played by these invariances leads us to the problem of phenomenal *constancy* dealt with in the previous chapter.

15 | Perception of Self

Origins of the Body Image

The phenomenal body image, i.e., one's own body as a perceptual object, is a complex sensory pattern, depending to a great extent upon impressions from skin, muscle, and visceral receptors. Again, the dominant role of visual experiences and the tendency to visualize sensory material transmitted by other modalities is clearly noticeable. The body image of blind persons, by contrast, reveals a corresponding hegemony of the touch modality as well as a tendency to objectify other sensory experiences tactually.

Although attention was called to body image phenomena by some observations on *amputees*, the concept has typically been discussed in the literature together with the somatic delusions of mentally ill and brain-injured patients. The perceptual syndromes of amputees were handled separately, without consideration of their interesting relationship to the body image of normal people. It was not until some research on the problem in recent decades that a coherent, systematic description of these perceptual phenomena was achieved.

This kind of investigation, too, reflected prevailing conceptual tendencies characteristic of a long period of psychological research. Head (1920) referred body image phenomena to impulses from skin, muscle and joint stimulation, the same ones which determine our awareness of body posture. These sensations, however, do not produce any percepts until they have been referred to earlier experiences within the frame of the entire organism. Jalavisto holds that tactual-kinesthetic sensations contribute only in part to the process of creating a body image.

Jalavisto (1942, 1948) seems to present a correct interpretation when she considers the body image a special case of object constancy. She appears to be the first investigator to express the psychological nature of this phenomenon so clearly. She wrote:

The fact that we perceive our mobile and sensing body as something unified and persistent despite the host of impressions overwhelming us at each moment must in my opinion be taken as an indication of some *object constancy* process in our appreciation of this sensory material—I refer to this very invariance when speaking of body image.

Jalavisto then examines the possibilities for the empirical determination of the body image in healthy people and for the stimuli upon which it could be based. The role played by skin sensations becomes quite apparent in cases of local anæsthesia. A person whose straight index finger had been anæsthetized later reported having felt his finger as clearly bent. This impression was so strong that only intense visual examination of the position of the finger could abolish it. A limb devoid of its natural sensitivity feels bent, as though the muscles concerned were in a resting state. This fact has some implications for what will be considered later about phantom limb phenomena.

The senior author undertook some observations at the Psychological Institute of the University of Helsinki on the formation and the appearance of the body image. The subjects were adults, normal as well as amputees. Patients' descriptions of their body image clearly indicate that their sensations predominantly correspond to stimuli which would come from the peripheral *surface* of the body. Touch and pain are both localized on the body surface. Their sensations are rarely if ever referred to deeper, more central parts of the organism. When the experimental subject is given the task of imagining his own body while closing his eyes, the *somatic periphery*, that is, the peripheral body surface, clearly directs the formation of this mental image.

Of more recent research in this area, that of Shontz (1967) deserves special mention. He was interested in particular in perceptual illusions concerning the dimensions of our own body or limbs. The prevailing claim is that overestimates are greatest with regard to the forearm and the width of the head. The hands and feet, on the other hand, are often underestimated. Shontz had his subjects make these estimates in two different ways: the somatic distances were marked on a horizontal line, and the body with its limbs was drawn on a 1:4 scale. He was also interested in the extent to which error estimates of these somatic relations correspond to personality differences as reflected in "draw-a-man" tests.

On the horizontal estimate scale, the subjects were required to indicate

13 somatic distances; these were controlled by means of estimates of 13 distances in the nearby environment, carried out in the same way. The free-hand drawings of the subjects were evaluated independently by two persons, according to the criteria of the Machover "draw-a-man" scale. There were 48 subjects altogether.

The distance-estimate test showed statistically significant differences between certain body-distance estimates and similar distances in the environment. The somatic dimensions were consistently overestimated, with the exception of the length of the hands. Certain details deserve mention: the width of the head and the length of the forearm were over-estimated the most, followed by the waist. The hands and the lower part of the trunk were most underestimated.

Shontz was also interested in the effect of estimates of wider wholes on those of partial distances. It turned out that all the parts of the body and the limbs were most exaggeratedly overestimated when they were estimated as parts of a single whole, rather than as individual distances.

Evidence from the Phantom-Limb Phenomena

As soon as the significance of the phantom limbs of amputees was properly understood, the interpretation of the body image was greatly clarified.

The term "phantom limb" refers to vivid sensory impressions of the lost limb in an amputee, persisting even for years after the amputation, and giving the illusion that the limb is intact and in its original shape and position. Since the turn of the century the phenomenon has been systematically investigated. First, it was observed that peripheral stimuli from the stump at least contributed to the development of the phenomenal limb. On the other hand, some investigators (e.g., Katz and Pitress) emphasized the influence of some central factors. It was found, for example, that phantom limbs could be influenced and transformed by means of hypnosis.

Some of Katz's experiments were technically outstanding, although nowadays his theoretical considerations sound fairly out of date. Let us consider some of his results and then give them a more modern interpretation.

The *structure* of a phantom limb does not correspond accurately with the anatomy of the amputated part of the body. Some details develop a predominant role in the perceptual pattern. In a phantom hand the surface of the palm, especially the inside of the thumb and the fingers, are well represented. Among the fingers, the thumb, index finger and little finger stand out as best perceived. Tendons, wrist and elbow are rather noticeable, but the forearm usually appears diffuse, while the upper arm is hardly felt at all. Katz (1921, pp. 23–30) presented data on 22 forearm

amputees, with the following number of cases reporting each given part as
very clearly perceived in the phantom limb:

Perceived forearm	1 case
Perceived wrist	2 cases
Perceived palm	5 cases
Perceived fingers	22 cases

The phantom fingers appeared straight in only one case, while in the 21
others the fingers were felt as bent against the palm. There is a striking
correspondence with the findings in the experiments on local anæsthesia.
In the long run, phantom fingers bend more and more and may in the most

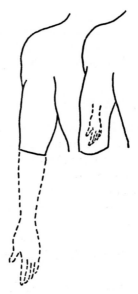

Fig. 15.1 Two kinds of phantom-limbs. (From v. Fieandt, 1966 p. 329.)

extreme cases even result in a permanent phenomenal fist. After a foot
amputation, the patient has his strongest phantom impressions of the sole,
toes, ankle, and especially the ankle bones. The legs are rarely perceived,
nor are the knees. Occasionally, the clearly discerned parts can appear as
separated from the rest of the limb; for example, the foot may appear to be
located at a distance corresponding to the missing part of the leg.

The spatial orientation of phantom limbs differs from that characteristic
of ordinary extremities. Not infrequently the bent phantom forms a 90°
angle, the forearm appearing phenomenally to be turned forwards or backwards; the leg being felt as lifted to a horizontal position straight back

from the knee. The phantom limb behaves in either of two intriguing ways when it overlaps in space with a physical object: the phantom hand may shorten and withdraw into its stump ("inner hand") or it may just appear to penetrate visible physical objects without avoiding them ("outer hand"). Katz described these alternatives and clarified them with illustrations (Fig. 15.1).

If the phantom limb belongs to the type which avoids obstructing p-objects, the body image really gives way, but only to the extent necessary— the phenomenal contours of the pattern are otherwise maintained with as much constancy as possible. The fingers, for example, are phenomenally preserved, yet they may be felt as withdrawn into the stump in certain situations.

Vividness and Mobility of Phantom Limbs

Occasionally, spontaneous *involuntary movements* are felt in a phantom limb, but this only happens rather rarely. Much more common instead are various degrees of *voluntary movement*. The phantom limb may feel readily movable or, at the other extreme, almost motionless. Usually the amputee feels capable of performing voluntary ϕ-movements, although he experiences them as stiff and as encountering much friction; the phantom limb seems to resist them. Not infrequently a condition for feeling voluntary movements is intentional motion of the healthy, preserved opposite limb (in which case the phantom limb is felt as swinging opposite the real one), in a way which corresponds to reciprocal motor innervation. That these parallel p-movements cannot be regarded as absolutely necessary conditions for perceived voluntary movements is shown by the fact that even bilateral amputees occasionally feel intentional movements in both their phantom hands.

Least difficult is the induced phenomenal innervation of *predominant, outstanding, salient* components of the body image. Such parts are the thumb and index finger of the hand and the big toe of the foot. It is not unusual for the amputee clearly to perceive a "localized effort to innervate" some of his phantom limbs; he may, for instance, experience trying to move one of his toes, although the effort does not result in any changes: the toe seems to have gone numb. Katz (1921, pp. 31–32) mentioned that 22 of his forearm amputees reported being able to move their phantom fingers. Most of them felt all their fingers movable, and some at least felt capable of straighteneing their bent phantom fingers from their relaxed curved position. Of the 27 upper arm amputees among Katz's subjects, 20 reported they felt they could move their phantom fingers. Sufficient observations of leg amputees have not yet been made.

The *vividness* of phantom limbs varies considerably. Generally they appear most vivid immediately after the operation, as soon as the pain has somewhat subsided. It is not rare for the phantom limb to shrink and disappear entirely after some 20 to 25 years. An impressive exception is the case of a patient who underwent amputation as an eight-year-old child and who vividly experienced the phantom limb even some 60 years later. In several instances the phantom limb maintains a *sensory vividness* for years. Patients often tell of their efforts to catch sliding objects with their phantom hand or to kick the door with their phantom foot when laboriously walking through it. Usually some bitter frustrations soon lead them to avoid reliance on such unrealistic impressions.

Especially curious was a case reported by Katz (1921, p. 23). A soldier, shortly before he was badly wounded in the arm, got a painful local wound just under the nail of his thumb. This painful thumb troubled him even after his arm was amputated, the pain appearing again in the phantom thumb as soon as there was some recovery from the pain of the amputation.

The phantom limb seldom shows up in patients' dreams. This fact has been considered to constitute strong evidence against Schilder's psycho-analytic explanation of the phantom-limb phenomenon. Inferiority feelings caused by the loss of a limb could be expected to show up in dreams rather than in conscious daytime imagination. According to Schilder, the phantom limb should be considered a protest against the violation of one's personal integrity (Schilder, 1950).

Later Research on the Phantom Limb

Of later researchers, Comalli (1966) investigated the question of whether the perception of verticality is affected by an amputation of one leg above the knee. Half of the patients had had their left leg amputated, half the right. All of them used artificial limbs. Estimates as to apparent verticality were made in three different situations: (1) the patient's own position was vertical, (2) he was tilted 30° to the left, (3) he was tilted 30° to the right. Comalli found that in (1) the experienced vertical was tilted to the side opposite to that of the amputated limb. If right-leg amputees were tilted away from the original vertical, they experienced verticality as even further tilted in the direction opposite to the laterality of the amputation (chapter 12 pp. 334–337).

After a subject with all his limbs normal and safe has been exposed to a tilted visual field his judgments of *apparent vertical* and of *apparent body position* vary considerably, depending on whether the body has been viewed in a mirror during exposure to visual tilt. Adaptation of the subject to tilted vision can be determined by means of letting him adjust a luminous bar until an apparent vertical position has been obtained. The amount of tilting in angle degrees directly gives a measure of adaptation. Several theories have been put forward in order to explain the role played by the perceptual-motor-coordination. According to *the reafference explanation* adaptation involves the gradual remapping of visual and kinæsthetic spatial senses. In this connection self-produced movement is said to give some "afference", which is compared with resulting changes in vision ("re-afference"). According to the positions-sense interpretation, adaptation is attributed to a shift in proprioception proper, and the sight of the body is considered particularly important to the eye-hand coordinations required by the experiment. The proprioception is supposed to get overridden by conflicting visual cues (see Harris, 1965). Quinlan (1970) in his experiments provided his subjects with five conditions (active walking, passive loco-motion and 3 gradations of body viewing). Body viewing in the "All" conditions was provided by a full-length mirror in which the subject viewed his body for about 8 min. of the total 20 min. exposure to tilted vision. In the "Hand viewing" conditions the subject kept one hand only in the field of view. In the "None" conditions the field of view became strongly restricted and thus prohibited the subject from viewing of any part of the body. In the "Active" conditions the subject had to walk a certain distance in the apartment and in the "Passive" conditions he rode on a trolley tub propelled by the investigator.

The "apparent vertical" and "apparent body position" judgments were approximately equivalent when tested with a repeated analysis of variance-design. Active subjects showed more adaptation than the passive ones in the combined "apparent vertical" and "apparent body position" experiments. Subjects with sight of their own bodies showed more adaptation than subjects viewing only objects in the environment. The findings are thus consistent with the reafference hypothesis. There are two additive components of adaptation, and they could be described as head-trunk orientation and eye-head orientation.

There are also several interesting symptoms of body image disturbances in mental patients.

What is the body image of patients suffering from hypochondria? Ueno (1967) has developed two hypotheses in answer to this question. (1) Patients with symptoms in the peripheral areas of the body will experience an "outer shell", surrounding the body and protecting it. (2) This experience will be absent in patients suffering from diseases of the internal organs. In head-ache cases, the presence or absence of such a phenomenal "shell" will also depend on whether the disease is of psychosomatic or organic origin. The results supported the first hypothesis. In headache patients, however, there was no difference in this respect between the two groups.

Body Image Explained as a Thing-Constancy Phenomenon

Jalavisto systematically considers each of the points we have raised as indications of how our consistent body image is developed and perceived. The constancy of this phenomenal image is the reason for perceiving the former somatic limits even in places where something is right now physically missing. In the long run, though, the body image is a function of many parallel determinants.

Jalavisto's interpretation is supported by the observation that phantom limbs do not develop in infant amputees, and yet peripheral irritations in the stump are hardly likely to be different at different age levels. If peripheral factors played a decisive role, age differences in stump stimulation patterns should be readily observed. Especially impressive is the case of Meyer, as reported by Jalavisto. The patient had to undergo two successive amputations on the same leg. The first cut was just below the knee. A usual phantom limb developed, including an apparent foot. After the second amputation, which was at the thigh, the patient continued to "feel" a phantom limb which this time, however, did only correspond to the shape and state of his leg after the first operation. This phantom leg had already "taken into account" the missing foot and ankle (see Jalavisto 1942, pp. 191–192).

Even if the body image is regarded as a case of the much discussed object constancies, this need not imply a perfect correspondence. This object constancy is apparently strongly affected by previous experience and learning. Following Jalavisto:

The way an infant reacts to visual experiences of hands and feet does not initially differ from his reactions to other visual patterns. Gradually the infant then starts to watch his limbs and tentatively performs some active movements. Even at this stage he may be unaware of the role of the skin surface in mediating touch impressions from alien bodies. After some time the infant clearly concentrates on his tactual experiences too. We can observe the child grasping his other hand or his fingers, even occasionally pinching or pressing parts of them. He looks surprised at the difference between these touch experiences and those he felt when handling surrounding objects. Characteristic of this stage of development is the reaction of the child who keeps striking the table and then suddenly, as if led by some haphazard impulse, turns the blows to his own arm or head and expresses the difference in what he experiences—sometimes even being hurt by his own activity!

Our Body as an Object of Our Perception

Most valuable are Jalavisto's conclusions concerning the cortical representation of the various parts of the phantom limb. Her observations concerning the salience of various phantom components, as well as concerning the loci of perceived phantom movements, are compared with Penfield and Boldrey's scheme of the proportional representation of body sensations in the cortex (Fig. 15.2 and 15.3). Thus, for example, the distinct experience of thumb and index finger in the phantom hand could be explained by their greater cortical representation.

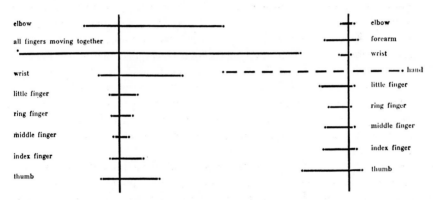

Fig. 15.2 Proportional motor and sensory cortical representation of the human hand. (From v. Fieandt, 1966 p. 333.)

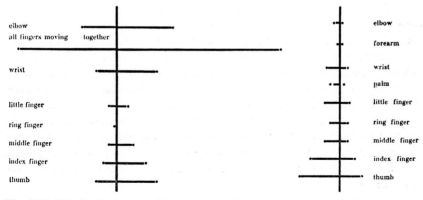

Fig. 15.3 Relative frequency of ϕ-movements in a phantom hand, and accuracy of its various parts. (From v. Fieandt, 1966 p. 333.)

Another factor, however, competes with this factor of structural pre-dominance. The *"borderline"* or *"extreme" parts* of a pattern stand out figurally. The index finger and the little finger constitute special, salient units in this respect. The names of these fingers are often learned first by young children. Distal extreme regions are in other ways also more strongly represented in the body image, as clearly shown by one of Révész' observations: if one stretches one's arms out straight ahead with eyes closed, the

Fig. 15.4 "Rejected"—clay sculpture of a congenitally blind (From ᵥ. Fieandt, 1972 p. 395.)

hands are kinesthetically perceived as the most salient and largest parts of both limbs. The parts of the arms connecting the hands with the trunk may sometimes even phenomenally disappear. This fact probably offers an explanation for the superficially disproportionate and clumsy, yet extremely expressive, clay sculptures of the blind, who are incapable of visually con-trolling their kinesthetic experiences (Fig. 15.4).

If we compare a work like that shown in the picture with Fulton's homunculus (Fig. 15.5) and Jalavisto's diagrams, the far-reaching similarity of the proportions can be readily observed.

Solonen (1962, pp. 11–14) sent a detailed 91-item questionnaire to 4000 Finnish disabled veterans, all of whom were amputees. He undertook statistical analyses on the 1000 best described cases, supplemented by 300 individual medical case histories. The time since amputation varied from

12 to 38 years. Of all the cases investigated, 945 (94·5 per cent) remembered having experienced phantom limbs, while 847 (84·7 per cent) reported them "right now" at the moment of the investigation.

The composition of Solonen's material is shown in Table 15.1. The additional individual explorations revealed that in only 5 per cent of the cases was the limb perceived in its original size and shape. Generally only the hand or the foot was present, usually not more than the fingers or the toes or even the most prominent among them (thumb, index finger, big

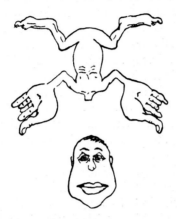

Fig. 15.5 Relative proportions of various motor centres in the cortex. (From v. Fieandt, 1966 p. 334.)

toe). Occasionally the palm or the heel could be discerned, sometimes the ankle, but rarely the elbow or knee. The closer to the trunk the amputation had been performed the more distinct was the phantom limb. It coincided with the prothesis in 22 per cent of the cases and seemed too large or too short in 9 per cent. In exceptional cases the phantom limb was larger than a normal one, but as a rule it appeared shorter.

Table 15.1. Solonen's cases according to locus of amputation

Type of Amputation	N
Upper arm	163
Forearm	97
Thigh	267
Leg	433
Ankle	9
Bilateral amputees	31

o

Ranta-Knuuttila (1962) studied 340 Finnish amputees (also disabled veterans), most of whom had phantom limbs and could feel intentional phantom movements. Continuous pain in the phantom limb was reported by 104, and occasional pain (with changes in the weather, etc.) occurred in 113. There were 123 without any distracting sensations. No significant differences could be shown to exist in this general distribution between arm and leg amputees, nor did the level of adaptation to the lesion make any substantial difference (Ranta-Knuuttila 1962, p. 111).

The interpretation of the phantom limb as an indication of the permanently perceived constant body image gains additional support from cases in which the patients's limbs are fully preserved but he is *unable to perceive one or more of them* due to some cortical damage. In patients who are able to feel phantom limbs, obviously their *intact cortex* plays a predominant role. Brain injuries can evidently in some way or another disturb the constancy of the body image. Such a patient may be bothered by the strange, unfamiliar, or weird appearance of one of his hands or feet. One case is known of an arm amputee who later suffered a cortical lesion. The phantom limb which had developed in the usual way disappeared immediately as a result of the brain damage.

Cases of *mescaline* ($C_{11}H_{17}NO_3$) *intoxication* give us further indications of the role played by the cortex in the articulation of the body image. The central symptom in this kind of disordered behaviour is the extreme variability of all perceptual objects. Jalavisto writes: "The experimentally intoxicated subject has the feeling of his limbs being isolated from the rest of his body; he feels, e.g. as though he could pick up his foot and hand it to somebody" (Jalavisto 1942, pp. 205–207).

Spatial Orientation of the Perceived Self

In connection with their investigations on the "oculogyral illusion" Clark and Graybiel (1949) noticed the "audiogyral illusion", the main features of which had already been discovered and described by Pierce (1901) and Bourdon (1902). If the subject is seated in a rotating chair and turned around several times (approximatively 10 rounds) at a moderately accelerating rate (from 0 to 20 rpm) he shows a tendency to misplace auditory stimuli (given during the acceleration) in the direction opposite to the rotation. This tendency is in agreement with the results of Gemelli (1935), who did not rotate the subject around his vertical axis but had the subject look from inside at a vertical rotating cylinder with vertical alternating black and white stripes, equal in width. Under these conditions the subject experienced himself as rotating in a direction opposite to the movement of the cylinder (see chapter 17). He also misplaced auditory stimuli *in a direction opposite to his apparent* (perceived) *rotation* and thus in a direction conforming to the rotation of the cylinder.

Two major classes of theories of auditory displacements can be distinguished:

(1) frame-of-reference theories in which information coming from the world is interpreted within different contexts,
(2) differential hearing change theories, which suggest that one ear becomes more sensitive than the other—and that sounds therefore are displaced toward the more sensitive ear.

Lester and Morant (1969) took up the question of whether the apparent displacement of the sound could be based on *a vestibularly-induced change in felt head position.*

In order to localize a sound with respect to the midline of his body, a subject must take into account the position of his head with respect to the rest of the body. Sound cues may allow the subject to localize a sound as directly in front of his face, but in order to report the sound's position accurately, he must consider the position of his head. (Lester and Morant 1969, 377.)

These investigators formed the idea of presenting the sound *behind the subject rather than in front of him.* This is the only condition during which opposite predictions can be derived from a "differential hearing change" theory and a "changed felt head" position theory. When reacting to sounds in front the subject may behave in the same way regardless of which one of the theories really holds true. Sounds from behind really render these explanations contradictory.

Two series of experiments were carried out with four well-trained subjects, one series performed in the absence of vestibular stimulation and the other one on localization during vestibular stimulation.

It turned out that the results confirmed the changed felt-head position explanation of sound displacement during vestibular stimulation. Due to the vestibular stimulation arising from the acceleration, the head is felt as having changed its position with respect to the body, and the displacement effect of sounds results from this change in felt-head posture during angular acceleration.

16 | Movement and Time

In recent years, psychologists have tended to emphasize the autonomy and spontaneity of the perception of movement. Among others, Vernon (1970a) has claimed that seen movement is phenomenally an independent event, since it cannot be derived merely from displacements occuring within the visual field. Confronted with a complex moving pattern the organism tends promptly to perform a perceptual motion analysis reminiscent of the Fourier analysis which occurs in the hearing of complex sounds (see chapter 7 p. 211).

Consider, for example, a lecturer pacing back and forth in front of his audience. If he nods his head several times up and down, we perceive his face moving in the vertical dimension at the same time as his body as a whole is perceived as moving horizontally. *We do not see* various points on his face moving along a sinusoidal curve, although that might be the path of the particular stimulus points involved.

Similarly, when we look at a railway passenger waving his hand on the platform of a moving train, we see his hand moving up and down simultaneously with the horizontal movement of the passenger together with the train.

Retinal Conditions and Displacement Explanations

The conditions for visually-determined perceived movement have traditionally been listed as follows:

(1) stationary eye, the object's image moves across the retina
(2) eye pursues the object, the image remains stationary on the retina
(3) stationary eye, entire field in motion
(4) observer in motion without fixation point.

As for cases (1) and (2) the experimental physiologists and psychologists in the early 1800's (Aubert, Roget, Faraday, Vierordt, Dvorak, Wundt) spoke of seen object motion. On the other hand points (3) and (4) indicate the prerequisites for the subject perceiving himself as moving, relative to the environment.

Before the interest of the investigators was focused on conditions (1) and (2) no psychological problem seemed to exist about visually perceived movement. Perception was thought of as simply recording *displacements of the retinal projections* caused by really moving objects. A certain confusion was evoked by the fact that objects can be seen moving *without any displacements of their projections* (see, e.g., case 2 above). For that reason it was assumed that the observer somehow takes his bodily positions and *intentional movements* into account, which all become "translated into stimulation of real movement". A special problem seemed to arise through the fact that a lateral pressure on the eyeball causes apparent movement of the entire visual field, whereas a corresponding volitional turn of the eyeball leaves the field stationary and immobile (Mayer-Hillebrand 1934).

Granted the "sensation of motion" would arise specifically from successive static stimulation of different points on the retina, that would not be a replication of a "true motion" in the external stimulus world. The stimulation is "jumping" from one receptor cell to another. In order to be perceived with a stationary eye the displacement has to exceed the value of 1—2' visual angle (i.e. the width occupied by 7 adjacent focal cone cells). In fact this explanation for seen movement, called the *retinal displacement theory*, runs into several difficulties when confronted with known empirical facts. Murch (1973) asks how the organism could obtain proper perception when several conditions bring about identical patterns of retinal stimulation. It has also been pointed out, several times, that a living eye is constantly in motion. How can the observer perceive motion when the movements of his eye are continuously creating new patterns of retinal stimulation?

The main criticism of this explanation model is given by the fact that a retinal displacement concept presupposes a passive observer. Actually, perception of motion, like all perceptual functions, requires *an active observer* who is continuously involved in extracting information from the environment.

The Ambient Array Hypothesis

It was Gibson (1966) who first pointed out the erroneous way of reasoning in the displacement theory. Instead of speaking of an image that gets displaced across the retina one should think of a moving retina, which continuously keeps scanning and picking up information from the light falling in through the lens system. This active retina is displaced across the image of the object. The source of motion perception is the actual displacement of the external object.

According to Gibson this perceptual achievement is the result of changes in the ambient array of light reflected by objects in the external environment. The changes occurring in that environment include all the four points listed above (p. 413). In particular he presupposes four types of transformations in the ambient light array, which all produce ambiguous retinal displacements. The visual system easily differentiates between each of the below-listed conditions because of the information contained in the ambient light array that is reflected and projected from the external environment:

Occlusion and disocclusion of environment by an object—Object motion

Transformation of the total ambient array—Observer movement

Eye sweeps over entire array—Eye movement

Occlusion and disocclusion at the borders of the visual field—Head or body turning

The ambient array hypothesis of motion perception thus explains perception in terms of movement in the environment rather than by an analysis of retinal stimulation. As it is in line with the main scope of this book and copes rather well with the instances of apparent movement and the kinetic depth effect it will be generally accepted throughout this presentation.

The Sensory Contributions of the Visual System

With outdating of the retinal displacement theory most discussions about the detailed physiological arrangements at different levels of the visual system have lost their importance for a psychologically-oriented presentation. Interest has centred on the active role played by the personality of the perceiver. Since, however, the involvement of the afferent receptive system in motion perception cannot be denied, we must not forget the recent findings concerning some "movement responsive units" within the cortical cell fields discovered by Barlow and Hill and Hoffmann (1973) as described in chapter 4 (p. 74). As stated above (see also chapter 11 p. 318) visual movement after effects (cf. chapter 4 p. 79) seem to be explicable in terms of neural units that are sensitive to the direction of displacement in the retinal image. Let us not forget that according to Sutherland (1961), based on his experiments with rats, a narrow rectangle or an edge moving at right angles to its axis of orientation was found to be particularly effective. "There is also some specialization, from cell to cell, in the most effective rate and direction of this transverse movement" (Riggs 1971, p. 295). There is some evidence in favour of specific movement detectors based on a series of animal experiments (Barlow *et al.* 1964, Barlow and Levick, 1965). In the octopus, according to Tomita (1966, 1970), "both orientation and direction of movement are preferentially established for single optic nerve fibres" (cited by Riggs 1971a, p. 295). Apparently research is going on in this field of sensory physiology. Yet we have to wait before a consistent description of the movement perception can be built upon the rewarding results of these investigations.

Apparent Motion

At the time when "real movement perception" did not seem to afford any problem of interest to experimental psychologists, their attention was evoked by "kinemathic illusions" (Roget's wagon wheel illusion, Faraday's wheels, the waterfall illusion by Addams, etc., see Boring 1942). The most characteristic trait in all of them is that the perceived movement did not seem to correspond with the "stimulus pattern". There was no simultaneous displacement across the retina of the perceiver's eye, yet a movement "illusion" was clearly experienced. In 1830 Plateau invented the first stroboscope, a device further developed by Sampfer and Horner. It provides a sensation of motion from successive static stimulation of different points on the retina, so long as the time interval of the stimulation of adjacent points is sufficiently small. Various mechanical devices have been developed to generate *stroboscopic movement*. The time interval in general must not exceed 800 milliseconds. What is essential in stroboscopic movement is the perception of successive static projections as uniform movement of an *object*.

What must have been regarded a rare peculiarity produced under laboratory conditions is today commonplace for people looking at their TV-sets or spending their evenings in cinemas. In the cinema the sensation of motion is produced by means of a series of successive images, each of which is physically motionless, but which succeed each other rapidly while the opening of the projector is obscured during the interval between pictures. The individual static images are not perceived.

Fifty years ago, a great deal of attention was drawn to the problem of defining the "blank interval", that is, the time interval between successive stimuli necessary and sufficient to generate an impression of continuous motion. Numerous experiments indicated that 30–200 ms. was the most significant range. If the interval is less than 30 ms., the two stimuli, A and B, are perceived as simultaneous. At the other extreme, if the interval is longer than 200 ms., the two stimuli are perceived as static images, flashing independently. No sensation of movement then occurs. Several kinds of apparent movement have been named. *Optimal movement* is produced with a blank interval of about 60 ms. in an arrangement developed by Wertheimer around 1910 when working with Schumann's tachistoscope. His stimulus situation was highly simplified, compared to those necessary for stroboscopic vision. Instead of a large number of static phases he used only two successive phases as visual stimuli. If these phases consist of two vertical lines presented successfully to the subject, *optimal movement* means an apparent motion of the line from one place to another. If the intervals are made somewhat longer *partial movement* seems to occur. Of major interest is what Wertheimer called *ϕ-movement* or *pure movement*. In his best known study, carried out in 1912, Wertheimer presented successive views to the subject, at a reading distance of two short vertical lines, A and B, of an equal length. The distance between them was 1 cm. A new type of movement phenomenon was then observed: even when A and B were simultaneously visible, something was perceived as "moving from A to B". This phenomenal movement differed from stroboscopic motion in that line A was not seen as moving from its place toward line B. Since this could not be considered a "sensation" in the traditional sense of the word, Wertheimer called it a "phenomenon", using a word adapted from the phenomenologists. The abbreviation of this term is ϕ-motion. It is apparent movement between two places even though no object appears to move. In his attempt to explain the phenomenon, Wertheimer (1912) inclined toward a theory of electro-chemical connections between stimulus projection points in the cerebral cortex.

Investigating the Wertheimer Phenomenon

Later on "phi phenomena" has become a collective term for four basic types of apparent movement: beta, gamma, delta and alfa movement.

In another experiment, Wertheimer used a slide projector in which pieces of cardboard could be placed in the frames; these could easily be superimposed. The lower stationary frame had figures cut into it, as shown for example in Fig. 16.1, and the other frame could be slid into place so as to cover only one of them. Thus the light pattern cast by the projector could be made to move suddenly from place *a* to place *b*. This is a case of ordinary stroboscopic movement, not of the ϕ-phenomenon. The latter was brought about by reducing the time interval, so that *a* and *b* were visible

Fig. 16.1 Successively presented phases *a* and *b* in the Wertheimer experiment. (From v. Fieandt, 1972 p. 311.)

almost simultaneously. Wertheimer varied the stimulus events in many ways, but the results were always the same. The events shown in Figs 16.2 and 16.3 are especially interesting. The side of the sharp angle always appears to move by the shortest possible path.

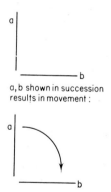

Fig. 16.2 Apparent movement over a right angle as studied by Wertheimer. (From v. Fieandt, 1972 p. 312.)

Wertheimer (1912) concentrated primarily on the type of apparent movement known as *beta movement* (the term is mostly used as equivalent to Wertheimer's optimal movement). Korte (1915) studied the inter-relationships between the optimal interval, optimal spatial distance and optimal illumination of the stimuli on the beta movement. He derived several basic principles known as Korte's laws. They represent an attempt to define the most obvious stimulus factors in order to produce beta-movement.

Gamma movement is a change in the apparent depth or apparent size of a stimulus produced by increasing and decreasing the illumination level of the stimulus. In *delta movement* the direction of movement is reversed when the second stimulus is more luminous than the first one.

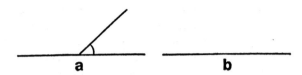

Fig. 16.3 Movement over the sharp angle. (From v. Fieandt, 1972 p. 313.)

Alpha movement is a special case of apparent movement designed by Benussi (1912). He presented the two portions of the Müller-Lyer illusion alternately and thus evoked apparent expansion and contraction of the straight line, middle part in the figure.

The results of later experiments are difficult to explain on the basis of gestalt theory. Smith (1948) stimulated the nasal areas of the left and right eye alternately. This produced clear instances of movement, although a cortical "short-circuit" effect could not be assumed, since the nasal parts of the eyes are projected onto different cerebral hemispheres. Gengerelli's experiments (1948) showed that the occurrence of ϕ-motion depends on particular anatomical relations between the stimulus field, the point of focus and the head, and cannot be interpreted simply as a phenomenon occurring in the brain. When the light points A, B, C and D are located at the corners of a square and are lit up in succession, the phenomenon of apparent movement is easier to produce in a vertical than in a horizontal direction. Vertical and horizontal ϕ movement occurred with equal probability only when the point of focus was located sufficiently far from the square.

Today no more is known than in Wetheimer's time about the neural basis of his ϕ-phenomenon. It seems unlikely, however, that there are any physiological connections between projected points corresponding to the perceived movement.

The German writer Linke (1907) believes that ϕ-motion can occur only under conditions in which the subject identifies both phases, experiencing them as the same object. The similarity and uniformity must be so great that the successive stimulus phases, as it were, duplicate the same visual object. In that case we may ask what part has been played by perceptual learning in generating the phenomenon.

Autokinetic Phenomena of Movement

Among the multitude of various apparent movements studied for more than one and a half centuries (Boring 1942), *autokinesis* is one of the best investigated phenomena.

A practical way to have a vivid impression of autokinetic movements is to fixate for a moment a lonely star in a starry night. At the same time you may compare your own description with the very first one given by v. Humboldt: "wonderful waving movements" (v. Humboldt 1799, p. 71) or with the more poetic expression by Exner ". . . wie die behaarte Frucht von Leontodon bei leiser Luftbewegung über die Wiese hinschwebt, oftmals die Richtung wechselnd, zeitweise aber auch lange nahezu geradlinige Strecken zurücklegend" (Exner 1896, p. 313).

Interest in this apparent movement among psychologists has been divided between one of investigating the phenomenon as such and one of using it as an "instrument" for experiments in social psychology, where Sherif (1935) was the pioneer, and finally one of testing, in the field of differential psychology, where Voth (1941) made the first steps.

Overviews of autokinesis as an instrument in the psychology of social perception is given by Moustgaard (1966), and of the use of it in differential psychology and experimental psychiatry by the same author in 1967.

Here we shall concentrate on autokinesis as a *phenomenon* of movement. As mentioned above, the first descriptions of autokinesis of stars was given by the famous astronomer v. Humboldt, and for half a century the phenomenon remained a problem for astronomers. Prompted by the descriptions given by v. Humboldt, Schweizer (1857 and 1858) started a systematic investigation of autokinesis of stars at his observatory at Moscow. It was this scientist, too, who started in his laboratory the long series of investigations of "artificial stars", that is, small spots of light fixated in a room, otherwise dark.

Concerning the development of the psychological research in the field of autokinesis we here must restrict ourselves to referring to relevant literature (Royce *et al.* 1966; Moustgaard 1969) and to stating the following results from this field of research.

Autokinesis has turned out to be a very complex field of phenomena—not a single phenomenon. In addition to the classical situation, where a pinpoint of faint light is fixated in an otherwise dark room, autokinetic movements also occur under more "natural" conditions, for instance when luminous configurations of spots "so large they fill half the visual field" are observed (Edwards 1954) in the dark, or when dark figures and other objects are fixated on a light background (Honisett and Oldfield, 1961).

Just as in the case of stroboscopic movement, analogous experiences of movement have been experimentally investigated in other modalities. Bernardin and Gruber (1957) and Andersen and Moss (1964) have, for instance, made interesting investigations of auditory autokinesis. Stimuli were simple sine-wave sounds from a loudspeaker in a dark room, and after a while the subjects experienced a movement of the sound very much like visual autokinesis. "The movement was often in three-dimensional space. It had the same rather ethereal, floating quality which is often reported in the visual case" (Bernardin and Gruber 1957, p. 134).

The perceiving person may either experience the autokinetic movement in a plane perpendicular to the line of sight, or as a three-dimensional movement (*ad–ab* movement) (Edwards 1954, Luchins 1954, Moustgaard 1969). Sometimes he may even experience his own body as moving in relation to the fixated object and/or to the whole external world (Moustgaard, 1969).

Ever since autokinesis was discovered, an intensive theoretical debate has taken place in the literature. Nevertheless no adequate theory covering the whole field of autokinetic phenomena has been set forth, because the phenomenal structure of this field is still insufficiently known.

An important distinction from a theoretical point of view between two types of autokinesis, namely *free* and *restricted* autokinetic movement, was made by Moustgaard (1963). *Free* autokinesis is characterized as a smooth, continuous movement along a rectilinear or slightly curved path. It often preserves its main direction for minutes. *Ad–ab* movements must be classified as free autokinesis, and the same thing holds good for all the phenomena of movement analogous to visual autokinesis.

The most important difference between the two types of autokinesis is that only the free type can have "paradoxical" aspects. Like a number of other movements free autokinesis has two main aspects, namely the aspect of *displacement* and the aspect of *"movingness"* (DeSilva, 1928). Both p_1-*movement* (experienced "movingness" without a corresponding displacement) and p_2-*movement* (experienced displacement without a corresponding "movingness") occur (Moustgaard, 1969).

Restricted autokinesis is a pure visual phenomenon and seems to be determined by a normal function of the mechanism of fixation control (see Fender, 1964). In its phenomenal aspect it is a jerky movement with frequent shifts of direction centred around a certain point in the visual field. While free autokinesis may have amplitudes of 60° or more, the amplitude of the restricted movement is very small (max. ca. 6') (Moustgaard, 1969).

Induced Motion Phenomena

In general the visual environment, in relation to which our perceptual objects are in motion, is stationary. The terrain with its hills and valleys, the floors and walls of rooms, and other objects such as buildings and trees are "standing still". It is in this static environment that objects are perceived as moving about. The information underlying constancy of movement thus originates in the immobility of the "visual frame". It follows that if the "pattern background", the "frame of reference", itself is made to move, non-moving visual objects will be perceived as in motion with respect to the visual frame. Such induced movement does in fact occur. The phenomenon is related to Kleint's "tilted cabin", described on p. 340.

Examples of induced movement can be found in everyday life, for instance, when the moon is seen as apparently moving through a large, slowly moving cloudbank, or when the train next to ours at the station is in steady and soundless motion, in which case our own train is felt to move in the opposite direction (see Duncker 1938).

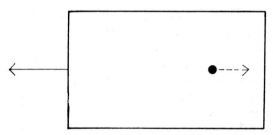

Fig. 16.4 An example of induced motion. (From v. Fieandt, 1972 p. 314.)

Of the newer studies concerning the phenomenon, that of Brosgole (1966) must be mentioned. The subject was placed in a dark room and shown a small round spot of light, surrounded by a fairly large (60 × 40 cm) luminescent rectangular contour. When the frame was shifted 20 cm to the left, the light spot was perceived as moving *within an immobile rectangle* about 8 cm to the right (Fig. 16.4). If the rectangle used was smaller, the distance travelled by the light spot under the same conditions was reduced. Since, however, the distance reported by the subject when using the large rectangle was only 8 cm, though the actual distance traversed by the frame was 20 cm, a kind of constancy phenomenon dominated the perception of the situation. Possibly the subject's proprioceptive sensations of his own immobility played a part in the constancy phenomenon, given an immobile light spot in the stimulus situation.

Kinetic Depth Effects in Sequential Patterns

Metzger (1934), in his study on depth effects based on two-dimensional moving patterns, mounted vertical rods on a turntable located in front of a light source casting shadows of the rods upon a translucent screen (see Fig. 16.5). A subject seated on the other side of the screen immediately perceived a set of vertical thin shadows moving horizontally toward and away from each other in a two-dimensional window. At rest, these

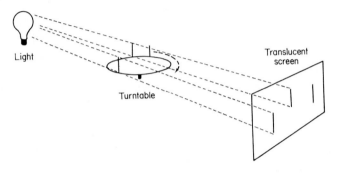

Fig. 16.5 Diagram of Metzger's kinetic depth experiment. (From Murch, 1973 p. 267.)

"distal stimuli" were clearly two-dimensional and described as such by all observers. When movement was introduced, most subjects reported a stereo-effect: the rods were experienced as moving in three dimensions and as belonging together. When performing this stereo-movement the three-dimensional "body" was clearer: it contained much less redundancy and the distance relations among the single dots rendered higher degrees of invariance.

Wallach and O'Connel (1953) who continued along this line of research proposed the term *kinetic depth-effect* to account for the transformations observed. They originally used wire forms (Fig. 16.6), the shadows of which were projected on a translucent screen. The forms were again seen as two-dimensional until they began to move. Initially the moving shadows brought about more variability and apparent redundancy, as long as the pattern continued to look flat and two-dimensional. After a while the shadow pattern was clearly seen as a turning three-dimensional consistent figure.

White and Mueser (1960) were able to produce noticeable depth effects with only two moving rods. Yet the impression of three-dimensionality increased with the number of elements shown in motion. Similarily Ross (1967) found that the stereo-movement became more and more stable as the number of moving rods in the shadow-window increased. Again, some new evidence in favour of the efficiency of richer articulation of the stimulus field!

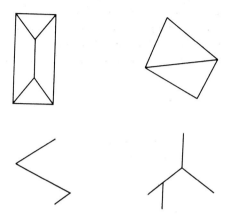

Fig. 16.6 Stimulus objects in Wallach & O'Connel's experiment. (From Murch, 1973 p. 268.)

A perceptual factor of interest is when the subject is able *to identify the direction of the rotation* veridically. Hershberger and Urban (1970) have carried out a study in which the role of three potentially effective "cues" was experimentally determined. By means of a diagram they carefully analyzed the polar projection conditions of a row of dots rotating in depth. They hypothesized three "cues":

(1) *Direction*: During clockwise rotation the leftmost and the rightmost dot both move to the subject's right; during counter-clockwise rotation both move to the subject's left.

(2) *Velocity*: If a dot moves more rapidly from left to right than right to left, the rotation is counter-clockwise and vice versa.

(3) *Order*: No two dots reach their respective limits simultaneously. The order in which they do might provide a "cue" to direction.

When the subjects in the actual experiment repeatedly viewed each of three polar projections of a dotted line rotated in depth, one incorporating only the *velocity cue*, another both *distance and velocity cues* and a third the *order and velocity* cues, it turned out that all three cues are used together. An increasing amount of accuracy resulted from a combination of several cues.

Not all investigators approve of Mach's "economy principle" (see p. 425)

—maximal degree of invariance, minimal redundancy—as an explanation of kinetic depth effects. Braunstein (1976) sought to explain the phenomena by identifying retinal cues for depth. Convincing experimental evidence is lacking concerning the differential thresholds of the shadows. According to Gibson's theory of motion (see p. 414), as the size of the shadow increases, so does the occlusion of the surrounding visual field.

Murch (1973, p. 269) conceives of the kinetic depth effect as an example of the manner in which the visual system interprets the changes or transformations in the ambient light array.

Consider the effects that occur when "flat" figure patterns are displayed on a frontally oriented rotating turntable, the so-called stereo-kinetic phenomenon.

The classic study of stereo-kinesis is Musatti's (1924) "Sui Fenomeni Stereokinetici", (Archivo Italiano di Psicologia). The experimental apparatus devised by Benussi, who discovered the phenomenon, is based on large, plate-sized vertical cardboard discs, presented monocularly in slow revolving motion (5–6 revolutions per minute). On the discs some figures are drawn near the edge: two intersecting circles, ellipses, points, etc. As the discs move, these two-dimensional figures are constantly changing place in relation to each other. At first the movement of the figures appears random and haphazard, but gradually a certain order is perceived. Whereas in the beginning each figure is perceived as a separate and independent stimulus, in the end they form a three-dimensional, stereo-kinetic motion pattern. These apparent three-dimensional motion patterns arise when the viewer seeks out in the two-dimensional plane the *motion configurations corresponding to the projections of the figures.*

One perceptual tendency which is always found as a prerequisite to stereo-kinetic perception is that toward greater constancy of localization. When two intersecting circles are presented, at a certain stage the subject no longer perceives the motion of each circle around its own centre, but rather the circles are seen as an integral whole which is fixed in space. Each point along the circumference of the circle seems to retain its own place.

Musatti stresses the view that stereo-kinetic effect represents quite a different level of reality from the solid body effect obtained by deduction from a drawing in perspective. Stereo-kinetic solidity is different in quality from the perspectival effect. In the stereo-kinetic effect we must assume the same kind of *unification* as that which occurs in stroboscopic motion. Physically separate static phases are perceptually transformed into a coherent moving "object". Similarly, in the stereo-kinetic situation different manifestations of the same object are transformed into a solid body of constant shape, seen in a series of different positions. In addition to this process of unification, according to Musatti, an event of *assimilation* is also considered central to the phenomenon.

It is surprising that Mach's "principle of economy" is never once brought to bear in Musatti's attempts to account for his observations, and even more surprising that it is never mentioned by Flock who approached the phenomenon later. This is perhaps a case of throwing the baby out with the bath water in the researcher's attempt to disassociate himself from Gestalt theory.

Studies carried out in Finland by Renvall upon the stereo-kinetic phenomenon indicate the basic importance of Mach's explanation (Flock 1962, Renvall 1929).

In Renvall's experiments there was a kind of "critical situation", in that a peripheral circle on the slowly rotating disc appears stationary whereas the radius in the frame of this circle is experienced as moving along the rim of the circle edge (Fig. 16.7). If familiar numbers from 1 to 12 are drawn along

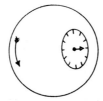

Fig. 16.7 Renvall's critical application of the stereo-kinetic experiment. (From v. Fieandt, 1972 p. 319.)

the periphery of the circle, the movement of the "hand" from number to number is certainly supported by strong empirical evidence. Yet the "hand" soon leaves this position and is seen as erect and pointing out from the disc surface toward the spectator. This is a case which should be explained in terms of "stronger economy" (Mach) or by means of the role played by maximal invariance of the relationship among parts of a perceived whole (see Metzger 1954, p. 219).

According to Mach (1900), under prevailing ambiguous stimulus conditions, and among the alternatives of resulting perceptual patterns, that one will be actualized which secures the highest degree of economy (or, to use a modern expression, a minimum of redundancy) of the transmitted information. The perception always follows the principle of strongest economy within the sphere of interpreting sensory messages. This is the famous "economy principle" of Mach. Hochberg (1971b, p. 524) points out how the "coupling" of perceptual attributes is also marked in cases like these. If slant in the rotating stereo-figure is perceived, at least some degrees of slant-shape invariance is displayed. If slant is not perceived the figures accordingly look non-rigid.

Recently, Knudsen (1974) systematically investigated a series of variables influencing the origin and appearance of kinethic depth effects: contours, position of light source, fixation conditions, eye movements, etc.

Perception of Rotary Movement

A number of experiments have been performed using "flat" (practically speaking) two-dimensional objects, slowly rotating around a vertical axis. The retinal projection corresponding to this motion consists of rhythmical expansions and contractions, which are the same regardless of the direction of the motion (clockwise or anti-clockwise). If we use physically three-dimensional objects, two of whose planes form an edge along the axis of revolution, the revolving motion of such a body can also be made to appear as back and forth oscillation.

Well known among those objects is the *trapezoidal window* (Fig. 16.8)

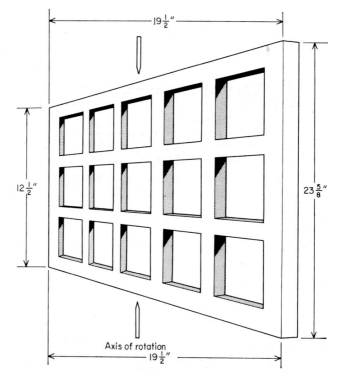

Fig. 16.8 The trapezoidal window as developed by Ames. (From Murch, 1973 p. 269.)

developed by Ames (see Ittelson and Kilpatrick, 1951). It appears to be a normal rectangular window, yet it is in fact trapezoidal. The painted shadows enhance the illusion: it appears to be a normal window seen from an angle. When rotated slowly about its vertical axis this window appears to stop and reverse its direction every 180°.

The explanation given by Ames was "Helmholtzian". He reasoned that the presumption the subject has formed about the shape of the moving object made him experience the reversals, because the seen rotation had been inconsistent with this previous assumption. One could also present Ames' explanation in terms of Mach's economy principle. The alternative of an illusion of motion secures a higher degree of invariance inside the system of dimensions of the figure. One vertical edge of the trapezoid is always longer, and perceiving it as located nearest to the observer maintains this constancy of the structure, and makes it pendulate back and forth to the observer.

Later, McGree (1963) and Cappone (1966) demonstrated that reinforcing the subject's assumption concerning the rectangularity of the window increased the magnitude of the illusion. That of course does not necessarily mean that some kind of inference governs the perceptual process of the observer. The preference in perceiving rectangular forms (see pp. 338–339)

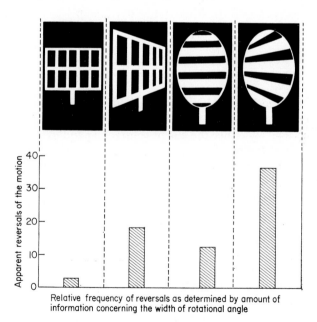

Relative frequency of reversals as determined by amount of information concerning the width of rotational angle

Fig. 16.9 Stimulus objects in the experiment by Day and Power. (From v. Fieandt, 1972 p. 315.)

is probably a strongly mediating factor. Haber (1965) was also able to show that the magnitude of the illusion decreased when subjects were provided with information about the true nature of the figure.

The empirical features of a real window need not be added to the trapezoidal object in order to produce the illusion. Zegers (1965) did not find a difference in the number of reversals reported for trapezoids designed to look like windows and for plain trapezoids. Freeman and Pasnak (1968) observed that the apparent reversals were affected by the visual angle subtended by the trapezoid, and by the amount of linear perspective given by the sloping horizontal lines. Day and Power (1963) among others found an apparent oscillation of circular, elliptical and quite irregular shapes (Fig. 16.9).

Pastore (1952) also reported apparent reversals of rotary motion with rectangular shapes, provided that the shapes subtended small visual angles (below 10°).

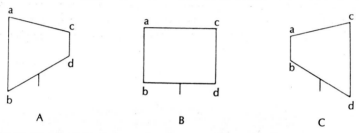

Fig. 16.10 The "cues" of contracting vs. expanding vertical edges and converging horizontals as examined together. (From Murch, 1973 p. 273.)

Power (1967) and Murch (1970) have carried out extensive investigations in order to analyze the "cues" of directional motion. Power sought to eliminate successively either the cue of contracting and extending vertical edges (*a, b* and *c, d*; Fig. 16.10) or the cue of converging horizontal lines (*a, c* and *b, d*) or both cues together. He was able to ascertain the relative importance of each cue in the detection of true motion. Power made use of the shapes shown in Fig. 16.11. The table below gives the mean number of apparent reversals for each shape:

Table 16.1 Reversals reported in Power's experiment

Shape	1	2	3	4
Mean reversals	4·7	8·1	19	18

The results clearly show that the lowest number of illusory reversals occurred for the full square. An equal number of reversals was exhibited by

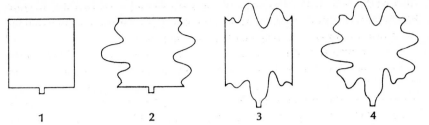

Fig. 16.11 Power's experiment with apparent reversals. (From Murch, 1973 p. 273.)

the shapes 3 and 4. The shape 3 provides only cue 1 (extension and contraction of the vertical edges). Power interpreted his results by suggesting that the most important cue is the change in the horizontal lines—the perspective effect.

Murch tested Power's conclusions with a modified design. Seven targets were made of fine wire, and some portions of them were painted with luminous paint (Fig. 16.12). Because the forms were shown in darkness only

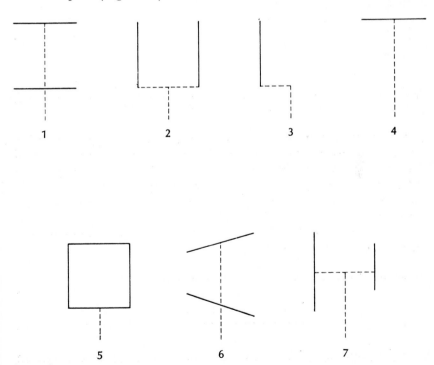

Fig. 16.12 The seven targets in Power's experiment. (From Murch, 1973 p. 275.)

the luminous parts remained visible. Objects 1 to 5 provided alternately or together both cues mentioned by Power. The objects 6 and 7 were based on the Ames trapezoidal figure. The experimental procedure was the same as in Power's investigation.

The mean frequencies of reversals are shown in Table 16.2.

Table 16.2 Reversals reported in Murch's experiment

Object	1	2	3	4	5	6	7
Mean reversals	8·93	11·32	17·21	15·04	6·61	21·82	17·18

No significant differences could be found among objects 1, 2 and 5. The number of apparent reversals was on the other hand significantly greater for both objects 3 and 4.

Murch concluded from his experiments that "the perception of true directional movement is obtained from information extracted by the interplay of vertical and horizontal elements of the square" (Murch 1973, p. 274). The results obtained with object 6 confirmed Power's suggestion: changes in the horizontal lines provide the most important cue. This seems to be the true outcome of Ames' contribution.

Evidently it can be concluded from all these experiments *that the perception of true rotary motion is a result of successive transformations in the ambient array of the rotating objects.* This transformation always proceeds in the direction of a higher degree of invariance among the spatial relations of the elements inside the configuration (see the next section concerning transformation analysis-investigations).

One series of experiments finally deserves mention. Cross and Cross (1969) have explored the contributions of inter-position and shadow during the illusory oscillations in the Ames figure. The conventional shadows on the "window bars" clearly provide a false interposition cue. It would not be true for a rotating figure that shadows retain their constant brightness values throughout the motion.

The objects designed by Cross and Cross are shown in Fig. 16.13. The values below the figures indicate the number of apparent reversals for all subjects out of 1000 observations reported. The perspective cue is strongly influential in the production of the illusion (objects 3 and 4). If the shadow interposition cue is in conflict with perspective (square object 5) it might reduce the number of reversals even if shadow cues usually increase the amount of the illusion. Even for the simple square 14·7 per cent of the trials evoked illusory oscillating movements.

In Johansson and Jansson's experiments (1968), apparent movement was brought about in three-dimensional space by offering the subject a line which varied in length at the same time that it turned around its mid-point in the frontal parallel plane. The experimental apparatus was constructed in such a way that, as the line moved in a plane, its projections at every moment corresponded to those which would be generated by a line of constant length in rotary motion. In this situation of ambiguous variation, the human perceptual apparatus seems to seek out the most essential

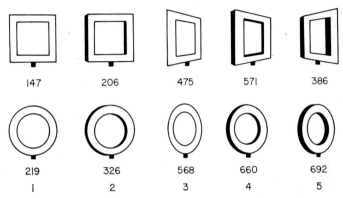

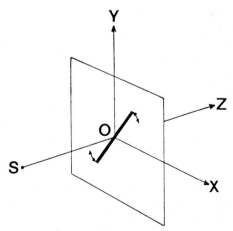

Fig. 16.13 Modification by Cross and Cross of the trapezoidal window experiment. (From Murch, 1973 p. 278.)

invariances, those of size and shape. When a three-dimensional space is available to the individual instead of a mere flat background, the ambiguity which is so difficult to resolve is eliminated and the invariances are maintained (Fig. 16.14). In this particular study the subjects were five psycho-

Fig. 16.14 The projection system of a rotating bar experiment. (From v. Fieandt, 1972 p. 317.)

logy students, and the perceived position of the line was investigated in detail, both by means of verbal descriptions and by means of paired comparison measurements.

The results reflect a tendency toward a kind of orthogonal localization: when the line is exposed in its maximum length, it is always perceived in frontal parallel position.

Jansson and Runeson (1969) carried out a series of experiments based on the above-mentioned study on perceived oscillation. The measurement conditions were highly improved by developing a comparison stimulus that could be presented under "full-cue" conditions. In their opinion the indicator of the perceived positions must not be presented under the same reduced conditions as the standard to be investigated. Indeed Jansson and Runeson preferred to show the standard stimulus under the "full-cue" condition. Therefore *an oscillating bar was this time presented under good lighting conditions.*

The first experiment was designed to find out the possible effect of difference in *distance* between subject and the standard stimulus. The subjects gave their responses by manipulating an apparatus consisting of two turnable discs located perpendicular to each other, and permitting the subject to indicate the tilt of the rod in one plane (the ϕ-angle) as well as the angle of rotation in the sagittal plane (the θ-angle). The authors concluded that the difference in distance to standard and comparison stimulus did not have any important effect on the responses. Nor had the use of one or two eyes any effect whatsoever. In the Johansson and Jansson (1968) experiments the θ-angle had been under-estimated (see p. 430). This underestimation of the θ-angle was not obtained in this experiment. The ϕ-angles were however overestimated.

In the second experiment three different locations of the comparison stimulus were employed, as shown in Fig. 16.15. The purpose was to determine whether the difference in *direction* to the standard and comparison stimulus had any effect on the subjects responses. Monocular vision was used.

The results indicated a rather good correspondence between standard and comparison stimulus. The overestimation of the ϕ-angle obtained in Exp. 1 was not repeated. Probably that overestimation was due to the somewhat asymmetrical position of the comparison stimulus in the first experiment.

The third experiment confirmed the effect of the spatial arrangements on the results of the measurement. It provided two response conditions: (1) the comparison stimulus being placed vertically before each response and the subject being instructed to reproduce the "more vertical" turning position first; (2) the comparison stimulus being placed horizontally in the

vertical plane through the line of sight and the subject being instructed to
reproduce the "less vertical" first. The effect of the response condition was
in the direction of starting position.

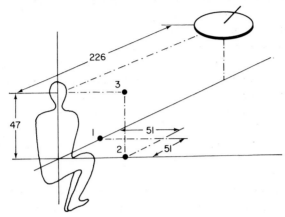

Fig. 16.15 Location of the comparison stimulus in the setup of Jansson and
Runeson. (From Jansson and Runeson, 1969 p. 30.)

The authors concluded from their experiments that the deviation of the
comparison from the standard was smaller than the deviation from the
predicted θ-angles in Johansson's and Jansson's experiment. They find it
probable that the result of that earlier study depended on the kind of
stimulation, and not on the response arrangement.

Transformation Analysis of Stereo-Patterns

Gibson has been interested in the part played by *perspectival transformation*
in the veridical perception of the motion of three-dimensional bodies. His
train of thought is the following: if we ignore the binocular disparity, and
both eyes are practically at rest, neither one has any other stimulus "cues"
available for the veridical perception of movement except the series of
projections cast by the consecutive positions of the moving body in a two-
dimensional plane (the plane of the retina). Each two-dimensional projection of the body is affected by continuous perspectival transformations,
brought about by the new "visual angles" which come up as the body
revolves. The perspectival changes caused in a two-dimensional plane by
the projections of a revolving body can be calculated by means of a kind of
"stimulus geometry".

In Gibson's opinion, a plane falling transversely across the radiation
entering the eye can be satisfactorily represented for experimental purposes

by means of a translucent glass wall. Upon this wall the shadows cast by three-dimensional objects (e.g. constructed of wire) can be projected onto a two-dimensional plane. His experiments are generally based upon this idea: the subject views, under various conditions, a translucent wall upon which shadow patterns are cast by means of an illuminated three-dimensional body concealed behind the wall (Gibson, 1969).

The mathematician Poincaré once asked whether the human eye was able, on the basis of shifting projections, to distinguish between the perspectival transformations due to *rotation* of a solid inanimate body and the corresponding transformations arising from the *two-dimensional expansion and contraction* of an elastic body. This problem was approached by v. Fieandt and Gibson (1959), using a network of rubber bands stretched upon a revolving frame. The perspective transformations cast by this device upon the translucent wall misleadingly resembled those caused by the *stretching* of a network located in the frontal parallel plane. The results showed that the subjects were able with amazing certainty to distinguish the two events. Somewhat later, Johansson repeated these experiments using much more precise apparatus (Johansson, 1964, 1975).

According to Johansson, experimental setups based on shadow patterns are not sufficiently reduced. What the experimenter has actually been observing is the veridicality with which distal stimuli, the shadow-casting objects, are perceived. Such a technique for producing figures may also be a source of errors. Johansson himself did not use distal objects; his experiments were concerned directly with the correspondence between "proximal" stimuli and the resulting perceptual formations.

He was able to satisfy these strict conditions by means of an oscilloscope linked to both low and high-phase generators. On the picture-tube of the oscilloscope the subject was alternately shown a square and a semi-parallellogram of varying size and other variables. These light figures had no reference plane or frame. We can say paradoxically that Johansson studied object perception without any real objects (Fig. 16.16 A and B).

For the purposes of describing phenomenal changes, Johansson presents the following system of dimensions:

x—the horizontal dimension
y—the vertical dimension
z—the sagittal dimension

His findings in general corroborate those of the Cornell school: any single change in size, shape or location in the two-dimensional plane may correspond to any one of several combinations of changes in movement and in shape in three-dimensional projection space. The transformation of a single proximal stimulus does not contain enough information to eliminate all except a particular type of motion configuration.

When shown a square varying only along the y-dimension, a great majority of the subjects perceived expansion and contraction in the *projection plane*; while a minority (one third) perceived the square as a rotating figure of constant size or shape.

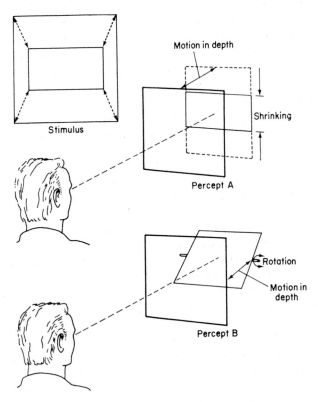

Fig. 16.16 The types of transformation in the projection experiment designed by Johansson. (From Johansson, 1975 p. 85.)

If the base of the square is allowed to expand and contract in such a way that the height of the figure is reduced in proportion, variation in the depth dimension is not eliminated, but other changes occur in addition. As the object varies in shape, it appears phenomenally to recede or approach. In addition, rotation may be perceived, in which case the shape of the object remains phenomenally invariant.

Perceptual Motion Analysis—Johansson's Experiments

At the beginning of this chapter the analytic character of movement perception was strongly accentuated. Illustrative examples of visual motion analysis can be found in Johansson's studies concerning sequential patterns of movement (Johansson, 1950). In his experimental situations the way a sequential pattern was perceived was clearly affected by the overall configuration faced by the subject. The entire human sensory apparatus is especially sensitive to stimuli which serve as signals relating to the total stimulus situation. *These systematic stimuli contained in the stimulus field are generally gradients which correspond to functional invariances* (brightness invariances, surface texture invariances, etc.).

Stated in terms of classical Gestalt psychology, Johansson found the configurations in event perception to obey what is called the *law of common motion state*. Consider the experimental situation shown in Fig. 16.17. Two

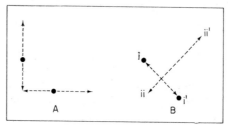

Fig. 16.17 A configuration in event perception (Johansson 1950). (From Kling and Riggs, 1971 p. 523.)

dots which move towards and away from each other are seen to do so on the diagonal $i - i'$. Less noticeably, the entire path of movement itself appears to move up and down on the diagonal shown at $ii - ii'$. The visual system has extracted a motion that is common to all parts ($ii = ii'$ in this case) and this motion itself has become the framework against which the residual movement is seen (Hochberg in Kling and Riggs 1971b, p. 523).

In one of Johansson's experiments he used four light spots (the small rings, Fig. 16.18) which were made to move along the paths indicated by the dotted lines, in a darkened room against a vertical background. If the components of the motion pattern are in phase, that is if all the points are simultaneously (1) at the highest point, (2) in the middle, and (3) at the lowest point of their paths, *the subject is unable to see two circular and two vertical paths separately*. Instead of that he perceives all four points as moving synchronously along a vertical path, while the two end-points, in addition, oscillate *back and forth horizontally*.

The law of the common state means that, as far as possible, changes in particular stimulus components are perceived as unitary changes in the state of the system as a whole. In our example above, vertical motion is perceived as a kind of coherent, self-contained system, to which the horizontal movements are appended as a deviant secondary system.

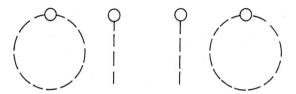

Fig. 16.18 An experiment in motion analysis. (From v. Fieandt, 1972 p. 322.)

Thus the perception of movement involves an analysis comparable to the mathematical analysis of physical motion. Of all the mathematically possible combinations, only a few are considered *phenomenally* real. The predominance of these alternatives, which are generally regarded as "natural" and self-evident, only becomes fully apparent in exceptional situations, such as in the dark, when the frame of reference with its familiar cues is no longer available. It is said that Galileo discovered the epicycloid equation late one night during the Tuscan peasant carnival, watching them roll wagon-wheels to which burning torches had been attached. In daylight the entire revolving wheel is visible; all its elements except for the centre appear to participate in the rotation, and the wheel is seen simultaneously as revolving and as advancing in its straight downhill path. In the dark, only the epicycloid path of one particular point is visible.

Johansson's w-phenomenon is an especially interesting perceptual event. If, for example, two adjacent round discs are illuminated from behind in such a way that the brightness of the left-hand disc decreases gradually as that of the right-hand disc increases, *something appears to be moving from the darkening disc to the brightening one*. If the brightness relations are reversed, the direction of motion is also reversed. *This perceived motion does not involve any moving object or pattern.* Analogous phenomena have been observed in sound perception if the intensities of the two sound sources increase and decrease alternately in reciprocal proportion. This "wandering phenomenon" is also found in the perception of vibration, for example, when the intensity of vibration is decreased in one hand as it is increased in the other.

In the wandering phenomenon, perception again seems to conform to an optimal meaningful invariant relation among the components of the situation. The sum of the intensities remains constant. Ekman compares this invariance to a physical analysis, theoretically performed.

Perception of Velocity

It took a great deal of independence from physical science for psychologists to realize that the perception of velocity is a problem in its own right. At first it was assumed that phenomenal speed was simply a function of time and distance, comparable to physical velocity, but it soon became apparent that this was not the case. Brown (1928, 1931c) found that phenomenal velocity depends on the shape of the moving object, on its position relative to the visual field, and on the direction of motion. Everyday experience again yields numerous examples. When a small motor-boat and a transatlantic steamer are moving physically at the same speed, it seems as though the smaller vessel were moving more rapidly. The scurrying of small insects on a warm rock has a phenomenal velocity out of all proportion to the actual physical speed of motion.

In perceived velocity, again, the constancy or invariance principle is observable. This is illustrated by Fig. 16.19. Just as the retinal projection

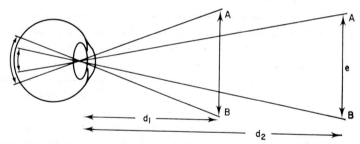

Fig. 16.19 Retinal velocity depends on distance of object. (From Day, 1969 p. 97.)

of an object is reduced in size as its distance from the observer increases, so a longer time is needed for the physical distance traversed by the object to be covered on the retina. The small object in the figure covers the distance e between points A and B in time t. In one case this motion occurs at a distance d_1 from the viewer, in another case at a distance d_2. The retinal projection of e is greater at the shorter distance d_1 than at d_2. Thus if two different motion paths, occupying the same time, occur at different distances from the eye, the retinal velocity of the motion closer to the observer must be greater.

Does phenomenal velocity display invariance in natural viewing situations? If the distance varies while physical velocity is unchanged, the question arises whether perceived velocity is determined by the angular velocity or by the physical velocity of the distal stimulus.

The most thorough investigation of this phenomenon was carried out by Brown in the 1930's. His experiments used two movable configurations, of which one, the *standard*, was placed alternately at a distance of 3·3, 6·6 and 10·0 metres from the viewer, while the other, the *variable*, was always at a distance of 1 metre. The experiments were performed in normal indoor illumination, and the task of the subject was to report when the variable appeared to be moving at the same speed as the standard at each of the three distances. The average velocities of the three subjects were 8·7, 8·7 and 8·3 cm/s, implying the existence of considerable invariance. By substituting, for example, a velocity of 8·3 cm/s at a distance of 10 metres in Brunswik's constancy formula (see p. 367), the degree of constancy obtained is 0·81.

The observer also obtains information about the distance of a moving object from the structure and size relationships of the environment. Thus an object moving at a given speed within a large fixed frame should seem to be moving more slowly than one moving at the same physical speed within a smaller frame, given that the two frames are located at an equal distance from the observer.

Brown used two frames, each with a rectangular opening within which moving objects were offered to the subjects. The two frames were exactly analogous, except that the proportions of one were half of those of the other. The standard figures used were, for example, round discs (1·6 cm in diameter and at a distance of 4 cm from each other), and corresponding figures one half the size (0·8 cm and 2 cm). The openings in the frames were 5 × 15 cm and 2·5 × 7·5 cm. The results of the experiments indicated that *the velocity of the comparison figures had to be set at one half the speed of the standard figures before the two appeared to be moving at the same speed.*

The most important result of Brown's research was the following: if both motions are presented in identical frames, but with different-sized circles, the velocity of the one with smaller figures is overestimated.

It has already been mentioned that the speed of peripherally perceived motion is generally overestimated. Brown was able to show that reduced illumination also leads to overestimation of velocity. According to the duplicity theory, the peripheral parts of the retina take over at low intensities of illumination.

His findings also concern the direction of motion: if the major dimension of the moving figure lies in the direction of motion, it appears to be moving faster than one whose main dimension is crosswise to the direction of motion. Takala (1951) continued Brown's work, designing analogous experiments and using technically improved apparatus. His results could not be accounted for by a single underlying principle, but the part played by the frame of reference was again beautifully demonstrated. As perceptual cues were reduced, the variability of estimated velocity and the systematic error (generally underestimation) increased. Different ways of reducing the situation were tried; at maximum reduction the stimulus was a single light spot moving in a darkened room, with all cues completely eliminated. A single cue was available when one other, immobile light point was shown together with the moving one. Under these conditions the variability and systematic deviation were clearly reduced. The effect of cue reduction similarly appears when a black figure is shown moving against a black background. Under these conditions the fovea is less sensitive and the role of the retinal periphery increases. As a result phenomenal velocity increases, consistently with the findings reported by Brown.

The Japanese researcher Toshima, a member of Akishige's research group, has specialized in the measurement of radial velocity along a circular path of motion (Toshima 1967). This phenomenal velocity again has its own perceptual constancy. Toshima undertook a mathematical analysis of the optical movement which was projected on the retina, and developed a model to describe the radial velocity constancy. After this he carried out empirical work to discover the factors affecting this constancy. (1) Regarding varying viewing distance and physical velocity, he found that the latter affects phenomenal velocity, while the former does not. (2) Distance also has no effect on the way in which radial velocity is perceived when the direction of motion is reversed. Thus the radial velocity constancy is maintained regardless of direction of revolution. (3) As in other types of perceptual constancy, the degree of constancy is reduced as the visual field becomes more homogeneous. (4) The length of the circular path plays a considerable role in apparent radial velocity.

If we consider only the perception of actual physical motion, disregarding apparent (e.g. stroboscopic) or induced motion, modern neurophysiology offers strong grounds for accepting the theory that the organism possesses sensory neurons which are specialized for the reception of motion stimuli (see the presentation at the beginning of this chapter p. 414). Today investigators cautiously state only that psychophysical correlates to the perception of motion continue to be found, but it is clear that such correlates on the neurophysiological level do exist. The ultimate explanation will probably be found in the connections of the central nervous system (see Day 1969, pp. 101–102).

Sensitivity to apparent movement toward the observer

Appropriate laboratory conditions have made it possible to create apparent visual movements toward or away from the observer. These rather artificial human situations are rendered interesting against the background of studies concerning conditions for heightened oriented responses in animals

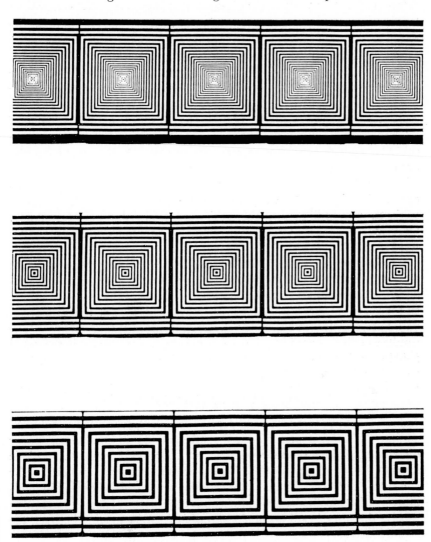

Fig. 16.20 Apparently approaching and receding patterns. (From Bernstein *et. al.*, 1971 p. 39.)

P

and man (Sokolov 1960, Maltzman and Raskin 1965, Bernstein 1970). Both galvanic skin responses (GSR) and pulse volume (PV) measurements have been applied, in order to demonstrate the activation level of the subject in a perceptual situation. This line of research is clearly relevant to the problem of "set" and other actual motivational states (see chapter 20) of the perceiver.

Bernstein (1970) put forward the thesis that greater response to increased loudness or brightness might be part of a generally heightened orienting response-sensitivity to stimuli, indicating the "approaching of something toward the organism".

In order to test this hypothesis, Bernstein *et al.* (1971) showed their subjects a set of movies which consisted of expanding and contracting black and white square patterns of the type shown in Fig. 16.20. Both the male and the female subjects were divided in four groups. By means of different running directions of the animate drawings, the square patterns could be made to expand or contract successively. On the other hand, the expanding or, alternately, the contracting, could be made to proceed stepwise (simple changes in the thickness and density of the lines) or continuously. The four alternatives, presented separately one to a group of subjects, were Still-Toward, Move-Toward, Still-Away and Move-Away. Only individual experiments were applied. Eyeblinks, GSRs and PVs were recorded.

Carefully performed statistical analysis of the orienting response-values clearly indicated that both movement-toward and movement-away produced stronger responses than those elicited by mere changes in thickness and density of the lines. However, movement toward the subject, in particular, triggered strong and relatively enduring orienting responses. The results were interpreted to suggest that the onset of movement in the visual field is associated with a momentary increase in perceptual receptivity.

Auditory and Tactual Event Perception

In his well known thesis on event perception (1950), Johansson also studied auditory *W*-motion under both dichotic and diotic conditions. Under dichotic conditions the tone was fed to a couple of earphones. In diotic hearing the sound sources were located at some distance from each other and from the subject. In the latter case the two signals, changing in loudness, reached both ears simultaneously. Subjects generally agreed in reports that they heard a sound *constant in intensity* moving between the sound sources.

Hearing might be called an "exclusive event sense". We must remember that auditory information rests upon successive temporal changes. The very model applied when interpreting visual motion analysis is borrowed from acoustical research (Fourier-analysis). Stroboscopic auditory motion had been produced and investigated since the early 1920's (Scholz 1925, Mathiesen 1931, Galli 1932). Certain parallels of Korte's laws, for example, have been shown to exist.

It is also interesting that changes in loudness when one of the ears is stimulated are preferably perceived as radial motion, in the same way that we perceive visual brightness changes as a constant stimulus fading away along a radial track from the observer (radial motion). (See also p. 420 on auditory autokinesis.)

Several investigators agree that there exists a *tactual counterpart to visual stroboscopic motions*. When two skin spots not far from each other are touched in rapid succession, a motion over the skin surface is perceived.

Based on his studies (see p. 272) Katz reported vibrations wandering between the two hands of the subject. He used an amplitude-modulated vibration in two vibrators. The result was perception of a vibration unit, "a vibration phantom" wandering between the two vibrators. There appear to be the same characteristics as in visual w-motion: constant ϕ-intensity + motion (personal communications given by G. Johansson).

Research concerning the Perception of Time

There seems to exist a tendency for organisms to be aware of time lapse. The question has sometimes been asked whether a specific "time sense" should be postulated, and how such a sense might function. Observation of the behaviour of animals and other organisms has shown that it is accurately adjusted both to many regularly periodic astronomic cycles and to their own metabolic phases. Man with his clocks (mechanical time-measuring scales) is not the only being conditioned to periodic changes (Fraisse 1964, pp. 17–63). Furthermore, human beings do not experience time as regularly and uniformly as might be expected judging by our mechanical timing devices. It is, however, important to discriminate between periodically repeated cyclical behaviour and a "sense of time". Psychological events exist along a dimension of time: they have a duration, as do motion events. This does not mean, however, that the duration of any particular event or movement is necessarily perceived. The concept of time perception should be reserved for cases in which a living organism is aware of the flow of time and divides it up in some way.

The fact that some kind of temporal awareness existed long before the invention of any mechanical devices for the measurement of time is not perhaps as surprising as it seems at first glance. All life processes have a certain rhythm; there is an individual timing process operating in our heartbeat, our breathing, the alternation of sleep and wakefulness and in many phases of motor activity (see M. Frankenhaeuser 1959, pp. 11–13).

According to Heidegger (1961) the origin of what we experience as the flow of time (which means phenomenal time) is anchored much deeper in the mental constitution of man. Firstly, "physical", chronological time as applied by the sciences and secondly, "inborn" psychological time are from this point of view considered "vulgar", construed and artificial. That is, in both of them we meet an inferred conceptual system, something that belongs to the *matters of being*, the dry rationalized entities exempted from all the strivings and intentions of the perceiving subject. The actual phenomenal world of man—so Heidegger argues—is filled up by *matters in hand*, by surrounding, available, potentially practicable entities. Therefore the essential root of the time sense and of all attempts at *timing* in human being is fixed in his insight into the limits or of the finiteness of his existence. This determination of all matters at hand make him put some final goals for his strivings, to estimate the remoteness of his aims, to *time* his steps and behaviour. However, Heidegger's refined epistemological perspectives exceed the frame of this presentation. An excellent survey is given by Reenpää (1966).

Precisely because it became impossible to point out any specific receptors for the perception of "vulgar" time, scientists belonging to the traditional psychophysical school have postulated some correlation between occasional time experiences and "veridically observable" organic processes. According to Fraisse, the part played by internal cues in the perception of time is of great importance. The biological clock, he claims, is part of the rhythmical cycle which can be found in the activities of all organisms, including man (Fraisse, 1964, pp. 40–48). The feeding periods of the great tit and of other birds have been carefully observed, and it has been found that they regularly search for food at the same hours, particularly during the nesting season. The intensity of the sunlight and its angle of incidence apparently serve as signals for initiating and terminating such activity. The "sense of time" of such insects as ants and bees has been especially thoroughly investigated; the role of the sunlight has been experimentally controlled, but the insects have nevertheless arrived punctually at their accustomed feeding places (Renner 1955). It is well known that dogs are able to go to meet a train at a particular time, expecting either to be fed or to meet a familiar and liked person. Human beings also have an awareness of time in this sense; we know, without looking at the clock, more or less what time it is. The investigation of "time sense" in animals was initiated as early as 1896 by Groos. How deeply rooted this sense of time can be is illustrated by the ability of some people to decide before falling asleep what time they want to get up; such an intention rarely fails if the motivation is great enough.

Ornstein (1969) feels that the concept of the biological clock may be relevant in explaining periodic physiological rhythms, but that these do not account for our experience of the flow of time. We have, according to him, made a serious error in all traditional research around the phenomenon of time perception. The search for "adequate stimuli" and eventual receptors of a "time sense" implies the presupposition that time could be considered as being something like a sensory process. This reasoning is characteristic of the psychophysical approach to the world of our experiences. This scientific approach takes physiological correlates of our experiences for granted, and the psychologists should be able to point out the correspondence. Among the explanatory models for time perception, which have been presented so far, this is called the *"sensory process metaphor"*.

This sensory process metaphor presupposes a "real" time to exist independent of us, in the same sense that there exists an outer object space of distal stimulus objects. We must not forget however, Ornstein insists, that no real physical time or no independent clock-time does exist. Something like a "real time" exists for us only as a result of our conventions and our pacemarker-instruments. Therefore all "time-sense" assumptions and "inner clock" explanations do not rely upon durable physical frames of reference in the same sense as does a psychological model for perception of space.

As a substitute or completion to the "sensory process methaphor" Ornstein provides us with his *"storage size metaphor"*. In his opinion the experience of time should be conceived of as a *cognitive process*. Duration is an experience which involves memory and a storage of "registered" events. There is no need for postulating a "time base" or an "inner clock", because duration ought to be amenable to a cognitive information processing analysis. Ornstein starts from the fact that the amount of information registered in consciousness determines the duration experience of a given interval. Anything which increases the "mental content" of a given interval relative to another interval, will also increase the amount in storage of that first interval. Ornstein goes on to demonstrate in general, information processing terms, how the same amount of information can, stored differently, subtend different storage sizes depending upon the way in which it is laid down. Instead of asking how "accurate" the subjects might be relative to the clock of hours and minutes and seconds, the representatives of this new approach are interested in experiences only of *relative* duration of different intervals. Subjects asked to judge duration should be asked *directly* to judge the experience of one interval relative to another. Ornstein declares that he is—for this purpose—going to use magnitude estimation scales only in his experiments on time.

In this respect he obviously approaches the time conception represented by Reenpää (1966) and referred to on p. 444 of this text when briefly discussing the existential time philosophy of Heidegger. Chronological time, founded in the movement of the heavenly bodies was an achievement of Aristotle; the concept of inborn "organic" time goes back to St. Augustine. Reenpää in accordance with Ornstein points out (1966, p. 63) that the time order, the way we immediately experience it, is unsuitable for all kinds of metrics. Therefore any autonomous physiological theory must be originally based on ordinal scales only. Reenpää presents several experimental investigations as evidence in favour of this alternative.

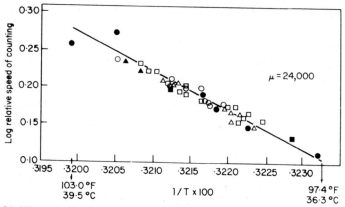

Fig. 16.21 The relationship between speed of counting and body temperature. (From Hoagland, 1935 p. 111.)

Since Francois (1927) and Hoagland (1933, 1935) published their studies, the body temperature has been considered an important factor regulating our subjective estimation of time. Hoagland (1935, pp. 108–112) relates some experiments of his own carried out on two patients (his wife and one of his colleagues, both suffering from influenza). The patients reported that during a state of heightened fever (from 36·3° C up to 39·5° C) time seemed to pass slowly. This was shown by the way in which certain tasks (e.g. the reading of number lists) were performed faster than normal. In that the life processes, especially the reactions of the patient, are running faster, time as measured by objective clocks must appear to go slower. Hoagland (1935, p. 110) reports the experiments of Francois which pointed in the same direction. A combined graph of the results from both investigations presented by Hoagland (1935, p. 111) clearly demonstrates the linear relationship between speed of counting and body temperature (Fig. 16.21).

Ornstein, on the other hand, points to some traits of aggravating weakness in Hoagland's experiments: for example that they were "run with extraordinary casualness", with few subjects (Ornstein 1969, p. 32). The investigation by Hoagland was repeated more carefully and with modern equipment by Pfaff (1968). It turned out that the subjects' time judgments decreased as the body temperature increased (method of production). If the method of estimation was applied, estimated duration increased with increasing body temperature. Katz finds that mental events can be interesting either for their content or their duration. If we are more interested in their content, our sense of time may be almost completely eliminated. At a dull lecture, when the content is not interesting, time may go by almost unbearably slowly. But when the listener is involved in the lecture, he may become completely unaware of the flow of time. Phenomenal (i.e. perceptual) time moves within fairly flexible boundaries. Attitudes and expectations may play a crucial role; when we are waiting for something, time appears to go by very slowly.

De Wolfe and Duncan (1959) had their subjects judge a 26-second interval using the reproduction method.

The "active condition" subjects worked on anagrams; in the "passive condition" subjects sat back in their chairs without doing anything. During both of these conditions the subjects had to judge the length of intervals: some subjects just got the interval presented by the experimenter, other had to reproduce the heard interval. The passive work condition was judged longer when the subjects actively reproduced the interval. The active-active and the passive-passive subjects did equally well.

Murch (1973) finds these results very natural. The influence of activity can only be assessed by comparing passively judged active periods with actively judged passive periods.

There has been some work done on comparing perceived duration in different senses. Goldstone et al. (1959) asked their subjects to indicate whether a sound or a light had been presented for a longer duration. They found that the visual second was consistently estimated to be longer than the auditory second.

Several studies (e.g. Zelkind and Ulehla 1968) have revealed some relationship between experienced duration and stimulus intensity. Ekman et al. (1969) varied the intensity of a vibrotactile stimulus and were able to show a regular and beautiful relationship to exist between the apparent duration and the intensity of the stimulation. Apparent duration can be described as a logarithmic function of the intensity.

The Phenomenal Present

The difference between phenomenal and "physical time" can most easily be seen when we consider the way in which "the present moment" is defined in each of them. The physical "now", as a mathematical abstraction, is without duration; it is a "point of time" (see Fraisse 1964, p. 100) lying on the single dimension of time and dividing it into the past and the future. The phenomenal "now", on the other hand, has been shown to vary within the boundaries of 0·2–3·0 seconds. It is "the minimum duration of the physiological process corresponding to a simple action" (Fraisse 1964, p. 102). Stimuli separated by more than three seconds are no longer perceived as simultaneous, while in some cases stimuli separated by as little as 0·2 seconds can be distinguished as successive in time. In most cases, stimuli occurring within these limits are experienced as falling within the same "present moment".

Here again Heidegger (1961) in accordance with his much broader epistemological time-theory would reject both concepts of the "present" in the sense they have been treated either by "physical" or by "psychological" explanations. He would, for instance, argue against the metaphor of time as an infinite straight line. Yet, as pointed out before, we must here desist from these extremely interesting philosophical considerations (see Reenpää 1966).

There is a clear difference between this succession within the present and a temporally unitary configuration. When two glasses are lightly struck in succession, there are two possible cases: *either* "now *A* is heard but *B* isn't yet" and "now *B* is heard but *A* isn't any more", *or* "now *AB* is heard", i.e. the sounds of *A* and *B* are heard as occurring simultaneously. This does not necessarily mean that *A* and *B* cannot be discriminated as two successive stages of one event (Fraisse, 1964, p. 84).

Phenomenal time differs from physical time in another way, and is reminiscent of spatial organization. The phenomenal present has a centre and a periphery, or to quote Fraisse once more, there is a *temporal horizon* (Fraisse 1964, p. 151). An event which has just occurred within the present moment is more recent than the events in the immediate past, and generally belongs to the present together with events occurring in the immediate future. The difference between phenomenal time and the physical concept of time, however, is not as great as the comparison with time as a mathematical abstraction might lead us to expect. The physics both of the macrocosm and of the microcosm (astronomy and nuclear physics) has encountered, with regard to appropriate measuring devices, somewhat the same limitations as human beings in their everyday perceptual experience. Like the mechanical concept of causality, the mathematical concept of time is as Ornstein points out, just "a convenience, used as an arbitrary standard". "Real time" doesn't exist in the universe (Ornstein 1969, pp. 34–37).

Studies by the Fraisse Group on the Psychology of Time

The investigation of time perception achieved a new and more scientific level with Fraisse's widescale survey of the subject (*Psychologie du temps*, 2nd ed. 1967, English translation 1964). In this fundamental monograph, Fraisse reviewed and summarized the many investigations on time experience and related this achievement to the "number of changes" which occur in a given interval. According to his theory of the experience of duration, with more "changes" or more "mental content" what is perceived as duration gets lengthened. His work thus paved the way for explanations which do conceive of duration experiences as *cognitive processes* (see Ornstein 1969, pp. 37–38).

The rest of this chapter will be devoted to an examination of the research into these questions which has been carried out in recent years under his direction. We will conclude with a brief look at contemporary investigations into the effect of certain drugs on the perception of time.

"Cues" as to the flow of time were effectively eliminated in experiments in which the subjects lived for weeks in underground caves or in shelter chambers. In a study by Fraisse et al. (1968), the subjects themselves kept records as to their periods of wakefulness and sleeping, their activities in-between meals, etc. The experimenters themselves took part in the experiment, one at a time; in general the estimates corresponded amazingly well to real time (errors of 10–20 per cent). One of the subjects however, was in the cave 174 days altogether, but thought that it was only 86 days. His daily rhythm was quite normal, except that the length of his day was 48 hours. He took a siesta each day after lunch, which in reality lasted as long as a normal night's sleep. The research by Thor and Crawford (1964) is concerned with similar problems.

Fraisse has been interested specifically in the problem of psychological rhythms. He stresses the rhythmical wholes formed by our motor activities. Fraisse and Voillaume (1969) have investigated conditioning linked to time. They measured (a) the latency period involved in the blockage of α-waves, and (b) the latency of a motor response aimed at simultaneity with a light stimulus. The former was somewhat shorter than the latter, and they were correlated with the individual performance level as a whole.

Of more general interest is Fraisse's study of the correlation between the duration of individual words and the speed of reading (1968). The experiment was based on lists of monosyllabic words beginning and ending with a consonant. Altogether six different lists were formed, consisting of 4, 8 and 16 words. The exposure times were 8, 12, 18, 27, 40, 60, 90 and 135 milliseconds. For each duration, the investigators calculated (a) the number of correct responses, and (b) the mean reaction time for the correct responses. The results appear in the following table (Table 16.3). The differences are highly significant. The reaction time of the verbal response decreases as the exposure time is increased. The upper boundary producing scatter is an exposure time of about 90 milliseconds.

Table 16.3 Times of verbal reactions and per cents of correct responses at different exposition conditions in the Fraisse-experiment

	Exposition time in ms	8	12	18	27	40	60	90	135
4 possibilities	per cent of correct responses	46	74	97	100	100	100	100	100
	time of the verbal reaction for the correct response	880	680	571	519	498	478	470	475
8 possibilities	per cent of correct responses	30	70	99	100	100	100	100	100
	time of the verbal reaction for the correct response	778	637	656	599	531	511	499	490
16 possibilities	per cent of correct responses	15	61	95	100	100	100	100	100
	time of the verbal reaction for the correct response	1152	851	696	621	563	539	521	526

In order to explore the part played by perceptual cues in the sense of time of six to twelve-year olds, Zuili and Fraisse compared two different experimental situations. In one, the child was asked to compare two durations and to give a rationale for his estimation. In the other, his attention is drawn to other factors in the situation before he makes his comparison.

The seven-year olds were confused by this additional information and the number of incorrect estimates increased, while the eleven-year olds were able to use the extra data in a deliberate manner in making their estimates. The stimuli consisted of series of slides, either 8 or 16 in number.

In another study by the same authors (Zuili and Fraisse, 1966), children of different ages moved small objects (rings and dice), estimating the time needed for the task. The objects were moved by means of small tongs; the rings were quick and easy to move, while the dice were slow and difficult. A majority of the children of five and nine paid attention primarily to the number of objects involved, and their responses showed that a larger number of moves corresponded to a longer time. The thirteen-year olds, on other hand, were able to recognize other factors also (the number of objects and the duration of each move, i.e. the rapidity of the moves). Even at this age, however, few of the subjects were able to take into account both these criteria.

The Estimation of Time Intervals and Durations

A few words must be said about the most typical methods in the research work on experienced time intervals. Most usual are the following three as listed by Underwood (1966):

(1) *Verbal estimation*: the experimenter presents a standard time interval and the subject has to give an estimation verbally (in seconds, minutes or even hours).

(2) *Production*: the subject has to produce a time interval—indicated verbally by the experimenter—by means of manipulating a signal device (e.g. pressing a telegraph key).

(3) *Reproduction*: experimenter presents a standard time interval and the subject has to reproduce the same interval by means of manipulating the reaction equipment (motor performance as above under point 2).

According to a number of studies applying these three methods, the results in time estimation experiments depend on which of these methods has been followed. It is a generally accepted observation, made consistently by several investigators, that in situations of time interval estimation which require some *motor performance* (methods 2 and 3), the subjects systematically tend to *underestimate* the given intervals (Murch 1973, pp. 292–294). Hornstein and Rotter (1969) found in their experiments applying the three above mentioned methods, that, in addition, working with method (1) caused significant *overestimation* (see p. 447).

What is the part played by continuous and discontinuous changes in our estimation of duration? This question is illuminated by the investigation of Bonnet (1967). In a dark room, figures (e.g. Oppel's illusion) were projected on a white screen by means of a tachistoscope, so that the projections fell upon different points of the screen using different frequencies. The results seem to indicate that the perception of duration is affected by velocity and by the projection frequency of a moving object. On the basis of Bounet's study it is possible to claim that the more articulated and eventful an interval is, the longer it is felt to last. This interpretation at least on the surface seems to contradict certain earlier observations (see p. 445).

Michon has tried to resolve this conflict in experiments which consider the relation between a phenomenal two-second duration and certain aspects of tasks performed during the duration by means of simple time estimates (1964, 1965). In the classic experiments of Wundt and of Katz the subjects were strongly motivated, and the tasks demanded close attention because of their strict sequential constraints. Under such conditions, the estimated duration of a second really is apparently shortened. On the other hand, when the information content consists of numerous unrelated elements which the subject must strain to follow, the phenomenal interval has a tendency to lengthen.

In Michon's experiments on the estimation of a two-second period the subjects regularly reacted too quickly, that is, the phenomenal interval was shortened. He investigated the effect on the estimate of relatively formal characteristics of the task, such as the uncertainty per stimulus or per response in multiple choice tasks. The subject had to respond by one of a number of reactions to one of a number of stimuli, while at the same time he performed a given constant response task at regular two-second intervals.

The results of these experiments indicate that stimulus uncertainty does not shorten phenomenal time, while response uncertainty and a complicated transmission situation do have a shortening effect (see the results of Hornstein and Rotter's study reported below).

In Hornstein and Rotter's study the same subjects were required to make time estimate ranging from two to 29 seconds under all three of the above-mentioned experimental conditions (p. 451). Table 16.4 presents their data: ratios of subjective time to real time as a function of the size of the estimated interval.

Table 16.4 Ratio of subjective time judgments to presented time

| Interval (s) | Method of judgment | | |
	Estimation	Production	Reproduction
2	1·18	0·78	0·78
5	1·13	0·93	0·88
8	1·10	0·96	0·95
11	1·13	0·98	0·96
14	1·07	0·98	0·96
17	1·06	0·98	0·96
20	1·07	0·99	0·96
23	1·03	0·97	0·95
26	1·05	0·99	0·93
29	1·03	0·99	0·98

A comparison of the performances of male and female subjects was additionally carried out by Hornstein and Rotter. Table 16.5 brings the mean ratios of subjective time and real time in all procedure-situations:

Table 16.5 Time judgments as a function of judging procedure and sex of the subjects

Method: Sex:	Verbal estimation	Production	Reproduction
Male	0·974	1·033	0·920
Female	1·191	0·881	0·947

Although the authors resist making conclusions from these weak differences, they allow for some considerations. The underestimation in the production was greater for women. They seemed to do their best job with the procedure of production. Males were generally a little more accurate; the overestimation in the verbal situation was stronger for the females.

The authors generally concluded that accuracy improves with increasing time interval.

All the above reported findings are consistent with those recently published by v. Fieandt and Näätänen (1970). In these experiments, estimates of a two-second interval were again studied. The subjects were not given any tasks to perform during the actual interval to be estimated, but the period was immediately preceded by a multiple choice reaction experiment. In all subject groups this resulted in a phenomenal period shorter than the physical one.

The consistent differences in the time-estimation data depending on whether the subjects had to behave *passively* (listening to or following time-interval presentations and verbalizing their judgments) or *actively* (motor performance) are in agreement with one of the main conclusions made by Vroon (1970a, b). He studied precisely the effects of presented and processed information on duration experience. "When the subject has to behave actively", he states, "i.e. by translating the stimuli into binary choices, it is found that experienced duration decreases with the number of processed bits."

In Bovet's experiment (1968), the subjects were asked to divide time periods in half. The periods offered ranged from 0·33 to 2·0 seconds, and were presented in terms of sound durations (Fig. 16.22). The subject pressed a buzzer when he considered that the stimulus was at its midpoint. The stimuli used were sounds of 1000 cps. The resulting scales are linear (Fig. 16.23), but an interesting observation may be mentioned: when the stimuli were presented in order of increasing duration, the mid-way point

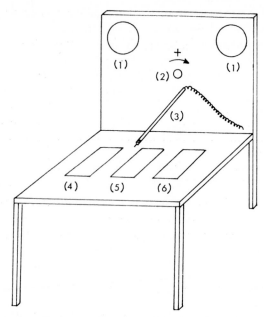

Fig. 16.22 Apparatus for measuring apparent duration of stimuli. (From v. Fieandt, 1972 p. 335.)

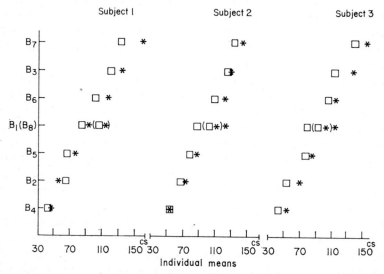

Fig. 16.23 The results of three subjects in Bovet's time-estimation experiment. Bisections were carried out both in ascending and descending series of presentations. Increases in durations as well as the linearity of scales is clearly reflected in the trends. (From v. Fieandt, 1972 p. 335.)

was systematically overestimated, while when the stimuli were reversed the opposite was true.

In his studies concerning phenomenal durations, Michon (1964) has examined differential sensitivity in the perception of repeated temporal intervals. It has already been shown that when subjects are offered time intervals as single presentations (defined by means of sound signals and very short in length, varying from 70 to 2700 ms) the area of greatest differential sensitivity is around 700 milliseconds. On the other hand, when the intervals are offered as rates of intermittent stimulation, the area of greatest differential sensitivity goes down to 110 milliseconds. On the basis of his careful experiments, Michon has been able to resolve this seeming contradiction. By introducing sufficient variation into both interval length and frequency, he has been able to derive a differential threshold curve which includes both these maximum sensitivity areas. His own opinion is that these reflect two relatively separate mechanisms, both part of our "inner clock".

Marianne Frankenhaeuser's Contributions

In her work "Estimation of Time", Marianne Frankenhaeuser considers those problems which she considers to be central in investigating the perception and experience of time. These are, in her opinion, (a) the relation between time perception and its retention in memory, (b) the conditions which affect time perception and (c) the conditions which affect retention.

Frankenhaeuser introduces the following three hypotheses: (1) Since the amount remembered is generally less than the amount perceived, the estimate of some past interval is less than the sum of the estimates of consecutive present moments on which the remembered amount is based. (2) The relation between the objective and the subjective second varies according to the mental content of the interval. If the mental content is enriched, the subjective second appears longer, and vice versa: if the mental content is impoverished, the objective second appears subjectively longer. (3) Under conditions which favour memory retention, the number of time units preserved in the memory for a given interval is greater than that retained under conditions which weaken retention (1959).

The first hypothesis has received clear empirical verification, indicating that the amount remembered is less than the amount perceived. The difference between them increases with an increasing time interval up to a period of 20 s, after which a relative balance is achieved (Frankenhaeuser 1959, pp. 50–55).

In order to demonstrate the validity of her following two hypotheses, she studied the effect of stimulating and depressing substances on the perception of time. If the subject is given a stimulant and is thus more alert, the amount of mental content is increased and memory retention is improved. Since according to the assumption, the perception of the present moment varies according to the mental content while retention depends on memory processes, both should be correlated with the degree of alertness.

In the experiments, 25 subjects were given three different drugs and were then given various tasks to perform. The substances were (1) 200 mg of nembutal or pentobarbiturate (a depressant $C_{11}H_{17}N_2O_3Na$), (2) 10 mg of pervitin or metamphetamine (a stimulant $C_{10}H_{15}N$. HCl) and (3) 700 mg of lactose ($C_{12}H_{22}O_{11}$) (for control purposes). The estimates both of the present and of the past were lower with the barbiturate and higher with the amphetamine than for the control group. Inter-individual variation was smaller in the group given the amphetamine than in the other groups. The individual rhythm was slowest in the barbiturate group and most rapid in the amphetamine group.

Frankenhaeuser has also investigated the effect of these substances on objective and subjective reaction time. Twelve subjects were given 15 mg of d-amphetamine ($C_9H_{13}N$), 200 mg of pentobarbiturate and milk sugar (lactose). Under the influence of the depressant, both subjective and objective reaction time increased, while subjects given the stimulant reacted more rapidly. It is worth mentioning, however, that the barbiturate led to more accurate subjective reaction times than the amphetamine.

Caffeine is generally considered to cause changes in neural activity and to increase alertness. In Frankenhaeuser's experiments with this substance, estimates of *past intervals* were lower than those of the *present*; the latter, in keeping with the hypothesis, were higher for subjects under the influence of caffeine than in the control group. The estimates of past time under the influence of caffeine were only slightly higher than corresponding estimates in the control group. The individual rhythm was again slightly faster in the experimental group (1958).

As far as other substances are concerned, the investigation of the effects of laughing gas, nitrous oxide (N_2O) led to highly varying results. In general the effect of the gas can be compared to that caused by a moderate consumption of alcohol, but the symptoms varied considerably from one individual to another from sleepiness to a state of excitement. A comparison of the effects of laughing gas and of oxygen (O_2) showed that (a) estimates of past time were considerably smaller than estimates of the present under all conditions, (b) estimates of the present were smaller under laughing gas and greater under oxygen, (c) estimates of the past were also smaller under laughing gas, and (d) laughing gas also led to lesser memory retention (Frankenhaeuser and Post 1966).

Hashish, marijuana, mescaline ($C_{11}H_{17}NO_3$) and LSD ($C_{20}H_{25}N_3O$)

caused extensive changes in consciousness and thus also in time estimates. In general, the present moment seems to be phenomenally extended in duration under the influence of these drugs, while the past appears shortened.

Summing up, we can say that those substances which in general act as stimulants (amphetamine, caffeine) tend to enrich mental content and cause changes favouring memory retention. Under their influence, estimations both of present and of past time intervals are greater than in the control situation or under the influence of depressant substances. Adrenaline ($C_9H_{13}NO_3$), hashish, marijuana, mescaline and LSD act as stimulants, laughing gas primarily as a depressant. Quinine does not appear to have any particular effect on the perception of time. General performance level improves with amphetamine and weakens with barbiturates. The results concerning reaction time, however, are not entirely consistent.

17 | Audition

The experience of time leads naturally to evaluations of the role of rhythm and of the time dimension in *auditory perception*. The time dimension is quite central to our auditory impressions, although *temporal units* can be found wherever changes and movements are perceived, such as in successive visual or tactual stimulations. Auditory gestalten always involve time. Auditory totalities such as rhythmic patterns or melodies would not be possible without temporal articulation.

The old controversy concerning the independence and the genesis of auditory space is usually handled nowadays by the conjecture that three-dimensional visual-tactual space provides the frame of reference for auditory experiences as well. It can hardly be denied that we do have spatially localized auditory impressions. In such cases the time dimension often enriches the otherwise static three-dimensional visual-tactual articulation. On the other hand, although our immediate auditory experiences are in some way or another spatially determined, and especially music is typically and richly spatially differentiated, the localization of our auditory impressions is nevertheless spatially imprecise and diffuse. Aside from the two-component theory of tone perception with its spiral model, which provides a kind of spatial organization for musical experiences, it appears reasonable to assume that all discernible sounds are referred to the visual-tactual system of coordinates. Auditory impressions are perceived within the framework of visual-tactual space, and if in addition they have their own particular spatial character, this is due at least in part to the time dimension.

Analogies between Visual and Auditory Space

Visual and auditory functioning are analogous in many respects; for example, there are temporal figure-ground phenomena: "behind" a brief sound we may hear another longer lasting, persistent one. In a really strict sense of the word this analogy does not hold completely true, however. Rubin especially was of the opinion that in order to be considered analogous the segregation phenomena in other modalities than the visual one should also include reversals of figure and ground. In general, the gestalt laws seem to hold for auditory as well as for visual perception.

Such analogies have led some investigators to draw far-reaching parallels between these two modalities, sometimes giving rise to loose and speculative thinking which is not properly tied to empirical facts. The previously mentioned "octave law of vowel" might be considered one such attempt. One must take more seriously the theoretical consequences of the fact that man is able to discriminate among as many sounds as colours, if one considers all the nuances of hue, brightness, and saturation. Whether or not there is a common organic basis for this correspondence, or how else one could explain it, remain unresolved questions.

Temporal Units: The Role Played by Rhythm

The significance of the time dimension for auditory gestalten can be seen in the role of *rhythm* in certain auditory articulations. Some musicians speak of "the sense of rhythm". This term refers primarily to body movements, but applies equally well to auditory events, in which rhythm is conceived to develop in parallel with the development of motor patterns of rhythm. Preschool children display nicely the coordination of both kinds of rhythm (Roiha 1966, p. 151). The auditory rhythmic pattern of our own gait is more easily recognized than is the visual one. At early stages of human development, rhythm is strongly and inextricably intermodal. Roiha (1966, p. 152) declares:

> Rhythm is temporal. That is, it is a whole which is differentiated and integrated in a certain way, with the differentiation arising from the listener's appreciation of the relation between the stressed and the unstressed phases of a sequence, and even just a dim awareness of the relations can suffice. Integration means that the stressed elements occupy a central position within the rhythmic whole, and that the unstressed elements are referred to these central components. In music stresses are beats, accents or cadences, but unstressed elements lack emphasis. Such words make us think about loudness, and undoubtedly loudness is of great importance for rhythmic accents, but they do not reflect loudness exclusively.

Accents can be produced by other components as well. Loudness, duration, pitch, timbre and harmonic as well as tonal factors all interact, influencing each other to a different extent and in different ways in different conditions. Attempts to force rhythmic articulations solely on the basis of varying intensity have not been very successful. (Roiha 1966, pp. 151–152.)

The duration of tones is an important factor in rhythmic articulation. In ancient music the lines of tempi were not indicated and accents were produced by relationships of durations, with the rhythm based upon the "width" of the elements. The phenomenal connections between the "weight" and the duration of a tone seem to be rather close, as shown by many psychological investigators. The stressed tone is often prolonged—a so-called irrational prolongation, not written in the note manuscripts. On the other hand, unstressed elements are sometimes really produced by tones of long duration inserted among shorter ones (Roiha 1966, p. 153).

Lehtovaara *et al.* (1966) have been interested in hereditary determinants of rhythm. They reported on a series of experiments carried out separately with 13 monozygotic and 14 dizygotic pairs of twins. There were three tests in all, two pencil tapping tests (preferred v. maximal speed) and a metronome test. Dizygotic intrapair differences turned out to be decisively stronger, yet the differences between mono- and dizygotic pairs were especially convincing when comparing results of males only. The reason for this result remains to be explained.

All kinds of rhythm imply regularity; this must, however, not be taken too literally. Instead of the "regular metre" of the old classicists, modern composers use a number of fixed intervals in the continuous tone series. These intervals are linked together in larger combinations.

Direction and Distance Localization

The localization of sounds is in many respects analogous to the localization of visual objects, whether we consider it merely a process of *fitting auditory percepts into a visual-tactual frame* or whether we consider such localization as perception of an auditory space in its own right. The physiological conditions for an auditory space are in any case harder to determine than are the conditions for visual localization. Even the factors which contribute to perceived direction in auditory space have proved complex.

The perception of auditory distance is determined by intensity and by the components of the sound spectrum in the field extending from the sound source, with lower frequencies in the sound spectrum relatively stronger near the sound source. This is due to differences in ease of absorption among sounds of different frequencies. Engelmann (1928) showed in a series of experiments that cats have a very well-developed capacity for auditory distance localization. The cat is a nocturnal animal, and the proper timing and coordination of its pounce upon moving prey in twilight or darkness is highly dependent on its ability to "scan" the right distances. The human auditory apparatus is, by comparison, quite underdeveloped.

The auditory localization of directions depends upon three different primary factors, all of which are *binaural: intensity, phase,* and *time* differences at the two ears. They are all based upon physical differences in proximal stimuli, i.e. at the very moment the sound waves arrive at the ears.

Binaural Intensity Differences

If the sound source is located on the sagittal plane, straight ahead of the listener, directly above him, or behind his back, the sound waves stimulate both ears with equal intensity. If the source is moved to one side of the sagittal plane, the ear nearer the sound source receives a higher intensity of stimulation than the other ear. This binaural intensity difference permits the sound source to be localized; one hears the sound as coming from the side receiving the higher intensity (see Fig. 17.1). The difference in

Fig. 17.1 The effect of head-position on the arrival of sound waves to the ears. (From v. Fieandt, 1972 p. 343.)

intensity is caused not only by the different distances of the two ears from the sound source; the further ear is also partly screened by the head. An object can function in this way only if the wavelength of the tone in question is small compared to the diameter of the head. Since the speed of sound in the atmosphere is about 34 500 cm/s, and since the linear dimension of the head is about 17 cm, only frequencies greater than 2000 Hz can lead to significant intensity differences. Classic experiments on this problem were carried out by Firestone (1930), using an artificial head in an open sound space. He observed an intensity difference between the two ears of about 10 db, with a stimulus tone of 4000 Hz.

High frequency components are somewhat damped before they reach the far ear, and some investigators (e.g., Wilska 1938) have suggested a tone

quality factor in addition to the customary intensity difference. In laboratory experiments the role of intensity has been studied by presenting
separate stimuli, differing in intensity, to the two ears. Subjects can readily
point to the apparent location of the sound source on the basis of the
intensity difference as soon as the differential threshold for intensities at the
two ears is passed. This threshold is easily measured, but varies with the
stimulus conditions, as thresholds generally do. Stewart claimed to have
found a simple relationship: phenomenal deviation (in degrees from the
sagittal plane) is directly proportional to the intensity difference (in db). It
is, however, hazardous to generalize this simple equation to all audible
frequencies and intensities (Stevens and Davis 1947, p. 171).

Binaural intensity differences unquestionably play a major role in the
localization of the direction of sounds, but this role becomes somewhat
complicated when complex sounds and noises are considered. The screening head, the structure of the outer ear, and the ear canal affect the intensity
differences in complex ways.

The classical method for investigating the role of intensity differences is
by means of using earphones. They allow for a complete control of the two
different signals reaching each ear separately. Because sinusoidal pure tones
very seldom occur as acoustical stimuli, the *phase differences* between
sounds reaching the two ears do not play nearly the same role as do the
intensity and *time* differences. By means of earphones, intensity and time
factors can be manipulated independently. In their study of shifts in
binaural images Elfner and Delaune (1970) have stressed the importance of
decreasing the intensity of the signal at the other ear simultaneously with
increasing it at one ear. As a consequence of this procedure the overall
intensity level remains approximately the same, and a simultaneous
variation in the signal intensity at both ears is achieved. Increasing the
intensity at just one ear is unfortunately quite frequently practiced, but
must be regarded as inappropriate and deviating from natural auditory
situations.

The authors applied a rating method to auditory lateralization, that is to
the shift in position of the tone image toward the ear receiving the more
intense signal. This rating method should tell us whether or not sensitivity
of the auditory system is different for low and high frequencies in a lateralization task.

By means of audio-oscillators signal trials and signal plus noise trials
were produced and mediated to the earphones. Interaural imbalances were
presented with right or left direction of shift an equal number of times.
Three frequencies, 500, 1000 and 2000 Hz were alternately employed. Two
practiced listeners and nine naive subjects were selected for the experiments.

In all cases the subjects responded by using a rating method in which a number was selected from a 4-point scale. A *one* response indicated certainty of shift, a *two* response uncertainty of shift, a *three* response indicated uncertainty of no-shift and a *four* response certainty of no-shift.

The most notable result was a high discriminability shown for the 500 Hz signal. Two listeners showed random responses to the 2000 Hz signal and one listener showed random responses for the 1000 Hz signal. In terms of left versus right shift, no clear indication of change in discriminability was apparent.

The experimental results demonstrated that the rating method is applicable to the study of auditory lateralization.

First-half and second-half comparisons were determined to check reliability of the technique and also to evaluate the effect of the number of trials. The results indicate that with practiced listeners it is possible to obtain reliable performance on the task with relatively few trials. Apparently shifts in the low-frequency signal are more easily discriminated than shifts in the higher-frequency signals. It is worth mentioning that the signals were calibrated to insure that no significant phase differences were produced by the apparatus. *Thus, even in the presence of contradictory phase information* (i.e. intensity increase without phase shift) the listeners were able to discriminate *shifts in the low frequencies* at a high level of performance.

Binaural Time Differences

If two identical sound stimuli reach the ears *at different times*, the sound is localized toward the side of the first stimulated ear. One of the early studies on the role of time differences in auditory localization was that of v. Hornbostel and Wertheimer (1920). They found that the optimum difference in time of arrival of a sound at the two ears has two thresholds: if the difference is too small, the auditory apparatus is unable to discriminate which ear was stimulated first; the upper limit consists of a difference so large that *two different sounds are heard*, one in each ear. The lower limit is of the order of magnitude of 0·1 ms, the upper limit around 2 milliseconds. The apparent direction of the sound is determined by where the time difference falls between these thresholds.

In their experiment v. Hornbostel and Wertheimer found that if the difference in the distance from which the two ears receive the sound is 1 cm, the phenomenal direction barely diverges from the sagittal plane. Such a distance difference equals a time difference of the magnitude of 30 $\sigma\sigma$ or 0·03 milliseconds. The phenomenal angle ϕ (between sound direction and sagittal plane) of perceived sounds is determined by the values of s and of the time difference. If s (the difference in length of path from sound source to the two ears) is 21 cm, ϕ is increased to 90° and the time difference to 630 $\sigma\sigma$. In actual hearing, the angle ϕ can be assumed to coincide with the actual physical angle α from which the sound is coming. Then s can be computed from the equation $s = k\sin\phi$, in which k stands for the distance between the ears. We know from elementary physics that the speed of sound can be computed from the equation $t = s/34\,000$ ($34\,000$ cm/s is the speed of sound travelling through air). If we insert this value for s, we then have a method for calculating the time difference. Actually, however, this simple trigonometric technique ignores the shadowing effect of the head on the more remote ear. This can to some extent be taken care of by including a correction for D, the diameter of the head, so that we end up with the new s:

$$s = D\left(1 \pm \frac{\sin\phi}{4}\right)\sin\phi.$$

Binaural Phase Differences

If we disregard sudden clicking noises or abrupt sound onsets, the only cues to time differences are phase differences in the sine curve. If the sound arrives at the farther ear more than one full cycle delayed, the stimulus becomes ambiguous. If the wavelength of a pure tone falls below 1 m, phase differences evidently lose their importance as cues to direction. This assumption has been verified in experiments conducted with pure tones offered in an open echo-free space. Stevens and Newman (1936) used three different stimuli: slowly and gradually beginning sine-shaped curves, clicks and noise stimuli spanning a wide frequency band. If the results are displayed graphically in the form of the localization phase curve, it becomes evident that localization is most accurate for the lowest and the highest frequencies (an average error of 10°) and least accurate in the middle range of frequencies (2000–5000 Hz, an average error of 20°). Both click and noise stimuli were localized very rapidly in these experiments, with an error margin of only 5°.

Stevens and Newman's results show conclusively that the localization of this kind of sound source requires an explanation on two different levels. The event is based on two parallel series of sound "cues": the binaural differentiation of low frequencies is based on time and phase differences, the differentiation of high frequencies depends on differences in intensity. In the frequency zone lying between these two extremes, errors in localization increase sharply. Complex sound stimuli are easier to localize than pure tones.

Stevens and Newman's research was later continued by Zwislocki and Feldman (1956) and by Mills (1958); the latter's work is especially notable for the determination of the lowest threshold value for the angle of orientation in relation to the median plane of the observer.

Localization of Sounds in a Closed Space

It might seem natural at first glance to extend the findings described above to the localization of sound stimuli under more realistic conditions. If the experiments are carried out, not in an echo-free chamber, but with sound-reflecting walls surrounding the subject on every side, it becomes well-nigh impossible to find a simple rule. Intensity cues become ambiguous, since the most varied differences may be present, depending on the geometrical shape of the room. Differences of phase as cues to the location of pure tones become similarly confusing, since the paths traversed by the soundwaves increase in complexity.

Wallach (1940) showed, in a series of brilliant experiments, the importance of sideways movement of the head in localization under natural conditions. This research has since been continued by Thurlow and Runge (1967) and by Thurlow et al. (1967). If it is impossible for the subject to turn his head, he may deduce the location of the sound source on the basis of several individually unreliable but complementary cues, offering the possibility of mutual control. Phase differences of tones of differing frequencies may then add to the reliability of the estimate; but such comparisons rapidly become overcomplex, and only the onset of the soundwave is reliable. As echo effects arise, these orientation cues also rapidly become confused.

In the case of sudden sound stimuli, the auditory organs function in exactly the same way. Localization occurs on the basis of the onset of the wave. This is the so-called *precedence effect* or Haas effect, discussed by Gardner in his "Historical Background of the Haas or Precedence Effect" (1968).

As mentioned earlier (p. 462, see Wallach et al. 1949) the various components of the stimulus can be best controlled by means of earphones. The sound effect produced in this way, however, is not the same as when the sound source is located further away from the ear. The subjects describe the sound as coming from somewhere inside their own skull. This *laterali-zation* phenomenon has been studied, together with the localization of a sound from within the head, in numerous ways. The subjects have been instructed to "show" the location of the sound by means of a manipulable air current (v. Békésy 1960), or by drawing a line within a picture of the head (Teas 1962). Another method used is to regulate the tones in each earphone until the sound is experienced as "in the middle of the head" (Kikuchi 1957; Jeffress and Blodgett 1962).

Deprivation of the above-mentioned binaural cues should be expected to have the same effect as temporal or intensity changes at one ear. As stated above, a change in intensity at one ear would cause the sound image to shift in position toward the ear receiving the more intense stimulus. If hearing with the other ear is inhibited in distorted auditory intensity—or sequential hearing conditions—is there any recovery in the spatial orientation ability due to previous training?

In their experimental study Perrot *et al.* (1969) first determined absolute monaural threshold-values for 350 Hz, 1000 Hz and 4000 Hz sounds. Thereafter a series of orientation tests were given. Three loudspeakers were hidden by a curtain in front of the subject, one of them located sagittally to the subject, the two others at 45° angles to the right and to the left of the one in the middle. The sound stimulus was audible at periods of 15 seconds.

After the plugging of one ear the subjects during the same repeated test-situations localized the sound in the direction of the free ear. Maximum shifts of the apparent source are observed for the 4000 Hz signal. Location of the 350- and 1000 Hz signals seems to be affected similarly, but less extensive shift is noted. For the 4000 Hz signal on the plugged ear side the apparent locus of the source is shifted to such an extent that it is initially located on the opposite side of the midline. This consistent lateral reversal is rarely observed under normal listening conditions. The results show the following effects to be significant: (1) stimulus frequency, (2) hours of exposure to distortion, (3) frequency by hours of exposure interaction, (4) place of speaker, (5) frequency by place, and (6) frequency by hours of exposure by place. The post-exposure data show that a considerable shift, toward the previously plugged ear side, occurs immediately after removal of the plug.

The result of this investigation clearly demonstrates that listeners can adapt to distortion of binaural input. The gradual return of localization toward baseline performance and more strikingly the post-exposure shift, demonstrate this effect.

The emphasis in recent research has been on neuro-physiological and dynamic points of view (Deatherage 1966).

Other Cues for Scanning and Localization

Some auditory localization is even possible monaurally. Several investigators have, indeed, considered auditory direction finding primarily monaural.

In 1971 Butler carried out a systematic study on subjects deprived of their binaural "cues" for sound localization. In the pilot experiments 5 subjects with one ear occluded were asked to locate tone bursts, 0·25, 0·4, 0·6, 0·9, 1·4, 2·0, 3·2, 4·8 and 7·2 kHz generated by concealed loudspeakers. The response required from the subjects was to call out that number from a series of numbers arranged horizontally, behind which they thought the signals originated. The five subjects were confronted with nine loudspeakers in all, but only loudspeakers at 10°, 30°, 50° and 70° from the subjects median sagittal plane were used. Each subject was oriented so that the array of loudspeakers extended from straight ahead to 80° toward the side of his occluded ear.

According to the obtained data, there was no indication that the subjects, when deprived of binaural cues, were locating sound sources with an accuracy exceeding chance. Interesting, however, from the point of view of the cardinal dimensions in auditory space, is the fact that tone bursts of 3·2 and 4·8 kHz were perceived as nearer the subject's median sagittal plane than were 0·9 and 2·0 kHz.

Within the three-dimensional visual space the sagittal and horizontal dimensions, intersecting on straight angles, are said to correspond to the vertical and horizontal dimensions of two-dimensional planes. Corresponding to assimilation effects in the direction of cardinal dimensions, familiar from experiments with visual two-dimensional fields and visual space, we encounter here too a kind of assimilation effect within the auditory space. Butler (1971) points to the possibility that subliminal stimuli impinging on the occluded ear might have brought about these apparent "assimilations". Therefore a patient totally deaf in one ear was given the same test, but was unable to locate most of the sound sources. More important, his placement of the tonal frequencies 0·9 kHz and above followed a pattern similar to that exhibited by the other five subjects.

In the main study only one loudspeaker was used, but the subjects were not told that just one loudspeaker was generating all the stimuli, which they had to locate in the same way as during the pilot study. This time 17 subjects, not tested before, participated. They were confronted with the same horizontal series of numbers as the subjects in the pilot study.

Almost without exception the subjects perceived all tonal frequencies to emanate from the side of the unoccluded ear. If the concept of intensity difference can be extended to a monaural listening situation, intensity at the ear or loudness was the single cue available for localization. The judgments of the subjects bore no consistent relation to the actual location of the sound source. Rather, the listeners showed a strong tendency to locate a tone burst, within the range of 0·9 to 7·2 kHz, in a fixed spatial relation to the next higher—or lower—pitched tone burst.

Distorting the pinna of the unoccluded ear—by pulling it tightly forward by means of a fastened tape—did not modify the observed perceptual pattern.

Still, in one respect the author regarded his findings as methodologically important: in these experiments a positive outcome of localization trials could not be explained in terms of word associations. In some earlier studies (Pratt 1930) with sound sources in the *vertical plane*, directly ahead of the subject, higher-pitched sounds were located above lower-pitched ones. It was argued that some interrelationship had been formed between the verbal description of tonal pitch and the frequency of the stimulus. Tullio and Kraus (Tullio 1929) suggested that the impression of an auditory direction may depend upon displacements in the labyrinthine endolymph (see chapter 5 p. 116), caused by pressure variations on the eardrum. There are known to be cases in which vestibular damage has produced anomalies in auditory localization, but such cases have been insufficiently investigated.

Monaural scanning and localization are also facilitated by differences in timbre and intensity. In familiar settings we may, on the basis of previous experience, accurately locate a well-known sound by recognition of its timbre.

Recent physical and psychological research in hearing has used a new approach to these problems, an approach which is more global and more dynamically oriented than earlier work. Especially interesting are the new attacks by Gemelli on auditory scanning and localization. No single cue alone can fully account for auditory discrimination of sound direction. In some studies of binaural stimulus differences the experimental procedure did not involve localization proper, but rather only the *lateralization* of a perceived sound. The subject estimates the approximate angle of the sound source rather than performing a genuine localization. The binaural cues can be conceived as operating on the horizontal plane running through the imaginary binaural axis connecting the ears. Wilska argues that the traditional approach, which has generally explored only the horizontal plane, reveals of a kind of "astigmatism" for localization on other planes. According to Wallach, equivalent binaural differences can be produced by all the loci on the surface of a cone whose central axis coincides with the binaural axis, and whose apex is centred directly between the two ears. Wallach (1939) has shown experimentally that the *change* in binaural differences with head movement relative to the sound source, resulting in changes in the cones of possible locations, is also a major cue in auditory localization.

Gemelli suspects that the problem of discrimination among auditory directions cannot be solved on the basis of physical stimulus differences alone. If that were the case, auditory scanning and localization would be primitive sensory functions. He feels that the fundamental fact of discrimination among directions must be thought due to some kind of frequency analysis by the ears. However, binaural theorists are also right in pointing out that auditory stimuli display a variety of binaural *physical* differences in accordance with the prevailing conditions.

On the other hand, it is clear that a given aspect of the auditory stimulus itself constitutes only a part of the total structure governing our impressions of directions and loci. Successful sound localization is apparently based upon complex, multi-dimensional processes in which separate features of the physical auditory stimulus constitute the chief factors and are complemented by one another as well as by further integrative and developmental factors. Scanning and localization of sounds cannot be considered "qualities" of auditory perception; rather, they constitute a differentiated perceptual process striving to achieve a clearer specification of the stimulus.

In actual life we not only localize sounds in our stationary system of coordinates, but, as pointed out by Wallach among others, we also move about and complement the usually considered localization processes with kinetic trials. This fact, too, conforms with our frequent emphasis upon the interaction among modalities. The perception of a sound is influenced not only by the auditory stimuli proper but also by proprioceptive messages from muscles controlling the head position, as well as by visual and vestibular stimuli. Furthermore, in most cases we also use our past experience of the probable location of particular sound sources to assist us in our attempts to localize familiar sounds.

Some experiments performed at the Psychological Institute of the University of Helsinki may serve to illustrate these problems. In 1944 the Institute cooperated with the Finnish Broadcasting Company in a study of the localization of simple mobile and stationary auditory stimuli in the horizontal plane. The results were intended to assist anti-aircraft batteries in the nocturnal localization of enemy planes. The experimental procedure, designed and carried out by Somerkivi, consisted in confronting the subject with loudspeakers in a large, darkened anechoic chamber. Monotonous recorded aircraft engine noise was transmitted from different positions on the front wall of the room. The subject pointed at the estimated direction with a 2 1/2 m-long stick which was attached at one end on a support at his eye level. The far end of the stick held a reference sound source, a buzzer which could be electrically operated by the subject.

Most important in the present connection were the following results: the scanning and the location of a moving sound source is actually no more difficult than pointing to stationary sources. The best results were obtained when the subject succeeded in keeping the observed sound continuously in his median plane (which results in the lowest threshold for directional sound localization). The improvement produced by a reference sound source in auditory localization tasks had already been pointed out by Wilska. In Somerkivi's experiment the "acoustic-optical condition", in which the tip of the pointer could be illuminated by the subject in addition to permitting the subject to sound the buzzer, was the most effective. Less accurate, but still comparable results were obtained with the "optical condition" (illuminated pointer without the sounding buzzer) or the "acoustic condition" (the tip of the pointer could be heard, but not seen because of the darkness).

The Role of Differentiation

From these results we might conclude that the additional information yielded by visual space articulation decisively supports sheer *auditory* scanning and localization of directions. The additional spatially differentiating perceptual cues seem to be equally effective whether they are visual or auditory. The best result is obtained with a combination of cues from both modalities in reciprocal interaction. *The more detailed and richer the differentiation of a stimulus situation, the greater the degree of constancy or invariance in the perceptual relationships investigated.* The experiments also revealed that subjects confronted with the task of discriminating between two identical sounds presented simultaneously from different directions did surprisingly well. If one of the stimuli kept moving, especially clearly differentiated percepts were achieved. The subjects reported an auditory figure-ground articulation: the stationary sound formed a background to which the moving sound source was referred, as something more temporary and incidental than the ground. Kock later demonstrated that our capacity to detect weak sounds in a complex of disturbing noise is directly proportional to the size of the angle between the directions of the sound and the noise sources.

In a subsequent chapter, when considering the role of attention and memory (see pp. 541–545), the short-term and long-term-storage models of Broadbent, Norman and Neisser will be discussed. In his experimental study Massaro (1970) tried to find some evidence in favour of the existence of an acoustical storage system. The subjects were presented with a high or low frequency sound of short duration, and its pitch had to be estimated as either high or low. The task was not difficult, granted a sufficient difference in rate between the two stimuli. The identification of the test sound as high or low is rendered more difficult, however, if a retroactive "masking" sound is given immediately after the test sound.

The author wanted to demonstrate that it is the perturbance effect of the masking sound which impedes the performance of the identification task. The task of the subjects was to identify the pitch of sound lasting for 20 milliseconds. After a silent inter-tone interval the masking tone was given. The results proved that the distortion caused by the masking tone was relatively independent of the similarity between the test and the masking tone. The authors are convinced of the existence of a store of short term auditory images.

Shifts in masking with time had been studied by Bilger and Melnick (1968). The signal to be masked was a 500 Hz pure sound. Both *remote masking* (a noise of 2000 to 4000 Hz) and *direct* masking (a noise from 200 to 4000 Hz) were applied.

The authors wanted to know (1) whether the threshold for the test tone changes in the direct masking situation (low frequency masking) during a period following the identification task; (2) if changes affected by direct masking do occur, are they different from changes evoked by remote masking or contralateral masking situations; (3) could some mechanisms be pointed out as standing for the effective duration of the masking procedure.

Each one of the seven subjects was first presented with a 500 Hz signal tone at his absolute threshold level of intensity. The height of the threshold was followed and indicated by the subject during the following masking situations: (1) remote v. direct masking, (2) constant noise v. constant signal, (3) a simultaneous v. a delayed identification task of the constant test parameter.

The results of the remote masking experiments clearly indicate that the lapse of time *after* the performance of the identification task has only some statistical relevance.

There could be consistently noted a tendency of decreasing intensity for direct as well as for remote masking stimuli. In case of direct masking the change was affected by the identification and the control procedures in the experiment, whereas changes occurring in remote masking situations appeared to be independent of these parameters.

Interaction of Visual and Auditory Cues

In the Psychological Institute of the University of Helsinki, Pentti (1955) undertook an investigation of auditory localization in an effort to develop a critical evaluation of some of Gemelli's (1935) theoretical proposals. The experimental subject was seated inside a vertical rotating cylinder. The inside wall of the cylinder consisted of narrow vertical stripes, about 10 cm in width, alternating black and white. The subject was given the task of indicating the apparent direction of a sound coming from outside, and presented successively from randomized points on the same horizontal plane. The nystagmic movements of the subject's eyes, and the visual stimulation from the rotating cylinder, soon produced the illusion that the subject and his chair were turning in an opposite direction, while the physically moving cylinder appeared stationary. This illusion produced a systematic displacement in judged localization, relative to performance inside the stationary cylinder. The subject's pointer had a strong flashlight which enabled the experimenter to record the readings precisely. The displacement averaged 17° and systematically followed the direction of rotation of the cylinder.

Satisfactorily in line with these results are the findings of some recent investigators. Thurlow and Kerr (1970) had their subjects localize both the source of sound and the phenomenal "straight ahead". In their experiments too, rotation of the vertically striped visual environment about the subject caused a "displacement" in both localization tasks in the direction of the rotation. The authors expected a correlation between the perceived direction of the head and the localization of sound, "since cues to head position must be taken into account in locating sounds" (Thurlow and Kerr, 1970, pp. 112–113). It was of interest to see whether displacement effects could be explained completely by shifts in the direction of "straight ahead".

Six experiments were performed, the setup of which is shown schematically in Fig. 17.2.

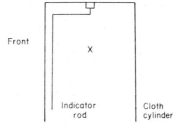

Fig. 17.2 Schematic of experimental setup used by Thurlow and Kerr. (From Thurlow and Kerr, 1970 p. 114.)

The subject was seated inside a vertically striped rotating cloth cylinder. Outside the cylinder, hidden from the subject, was a loudspeaker which could be placed at different angles clockwise or counterclockwise from the "straight ahead". The sound was a high frequency thermal (white) noise.

In the first experiment the subject had—by means of movable indicator rod—to point out the "straight ahead" and the direction of the sound when the loudspeaker was placed 32° to the right of the "straight ahead" of the subject. Measurements were performed equally well during the rotation of the cylinder as when the environment was stationary. The following two experiments repeated the procedure of the first, with the exception that the experimenter moved the indicator rod according to the ratings of the subject. This time the loudspeaker was moved 5° to the left of the "straight ahead" of the subject.

Of the three last experiments the two first were a kind of control. The subjects were not told to try to imagine themselves as moving. (Gemelli had found that the displacement effect was dependent upon the subject perceiving himself as moving.) The indicator rod was not used, and the subject pointed out the directions with his index finger. His pointing hand was not in his field of view. The source of sound was put 5° to the right of the "straight ahead". The fifth experiment only made use of a wider band of noise. In the sixth experiment the indicator response was again employed, and the subjects were asked to imagine themselves as moving.

The essential results are given in a condensed form in Table 17.1. The moving environment brought about a consistent displacement effect both on localization of sound and on location of "straight ahead." Compared with the 17° mean displacement of the s sound source in the experiments of Pentti (see p. 471), the corresponding effect was much weaker in the situations created by Thurlow and Kerr, varying from 10·2° to 12·9°. Even weaker was the displacement for location of "straight ahead". The authors are cautious in drawing conclusions, from the fact that the displacement seems to be greater in cases where the subjects perceived themselves as moving. There might be other factors involved when comparing experiments IV and V with the other four experiments.

The authors feel inclined to ascribe the displacement effects to the influence of nystagmic movements of the eyes occurring as a reaction to the moving environment.

Table 17.1 Mean shift in degrees for localization of sound and for "straight ahead" as a result of movement of striped environment

	Experiments					
	I	II	III	IV	V	VI
Number of subjects	13	10	10	9	20	10
Perception of self-movement	Yes	Yes	Yes	No	No	Yes
Shift in localization of sound (a)	11·7++	10·2++	12·9++	5·1+	4·2++	12·4++
Shift in "straight ahead" (b)	8·5++	5·3++	9·2++	0·5	2·7+	7·1++
Difference (a − b)	3·2	4·9++	3·7	4·6+	1·5+	5·3+

+ Significant at 0·10 level.
++ Significant at 0·01 level.

Roelofs and Van der Waals (1935), and Gemelli (1935) stressed that the body image serves as a frame of reference for auditory localization. When localizing auditory stimuli, at least, the human being relates them to the position of his own body. Pentti's experiment confirms this explanation and the above-mentioned results of Wertheimer demonstrate that this phenomenon may involve a primordial, inborn human capacity.

Q

How We Perceive Auditory Patterns

Research work which has been carried out so far on auditory pattern perception interestingly reveals features of regularity and lawfulness in central nervous organization, undeniably corresponding to some basic trends in visual organization. We have to stress especially the role played by orthogonally intersecting cardinal dimensions in the localization of spatial directions and the grouping principles of temporal patterns. The central processing time of acoustical signals does not seem to be a fixed value—as is often assumed, for example, in terms of a "one channel hypothesis", but depends among others on the amount of information input per unit of time. Certain "perceptual preferences" and "organization tendencies" are demonstrable (Tolkmitt 1970, pp. 174, 177, 179). To borrow an expression from Royer and Garner (1970): "the pattern organizations are wholistic" "...the organism selects a pattern or organization from a set of alternatives". This organizational selection is made on the basis of the whole pattern, not on parts of it built up sequentially (Royer and Garner 1970, p. 115).

If the task of the subject consists in localizing white noise rotating among eight sound sources (Tolkmitt 1970) his perception changes systematically at very reduced stimulus duration (down to 25 ms of burst duration of white noise). The auditory patterns are based equally well on spatial as on temporal features of the sound.

Spatial features are given by the abundantly discussed "binaural cues" and by the head movements of the subject. Temporal features refer to the fact that hearing is basically a temporal sense. Auditory organization implies discrimination of signal patterns in time. The minimum interstimulus interval for sequential processing in hearing lies in the vicinity of 250 milliseconds. Tolkmitt, in looking for internal organizational tendencies in audition, therefore started to manipulate both the spatial and temporal features: binaural cues and burst duration.

Eight hidden loudspeakers were arranged octogonally around the subject as shown in Fig. 17.3 A. The lateral angles of the speakers counting clockwise from the left lateral pole of the aural axis were 0, 45, 90, 135, 180, 225, 270 and 315°. These locations were referred to as left, front-left, front, front-right, right, back-right, back, back-left.

Three experiments were performed. The first one, employing twenty subjects, served as an exploratory study. The series of sound bursts produced by a white noise generator rotated clockwise among the loudspeakers. Seven burst durations (25, 40, 63, 100, 160, 250 and 400 ms) were used. Because of two head conditions (fixed v. moving head) there were 42 stimulus combinations in all. Each experimental session lasted one hour.

The subject had to give his reports on a set of cards, one card for each trial. He indicated the distance and the direction of the pattern (clockwise or counterclockwise) and finally described the spatial pattern of the sound. The alternatives were given on the card in form of 3-point scales or by choice among circle, broad ellipse, tight ellipse and oscillation.

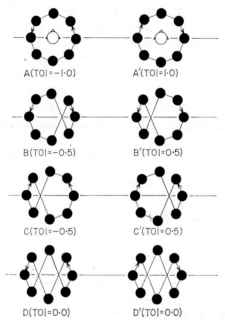

Fig. 17.3 The pattern population of the situations in Tolkmitt's experiments. (From Tolkmitt, 1970 p. 174.)

The pilot results are interesting. As for the *distance* of the sound pattern (actually 1·5 m) the subject had the impression of approaching sounds while the noise increased. With decreasing burst duration (below 100 ms) the subject lost the impression of *direction*. While burst duration decreased the subject perceived fewer speakers which led to the perception of tighter and tighter ellipses. *Moving* v. *fixed head* condition led only to an impairment of the overall impression without any other notable effects.

Most interesting was the second experiment, in that it introduced three distinctive noise patterns (*A, C, D*, Fig. 17.3) as a variable, and additionally included a variation of the starting point of the rotating pattern. Figure 17.3 shows the pattern population from which the various studies were sampled.

Three burst durations (250, 100 and 40 ms) and four starting points (front, right, back and left) were used.

The only difference in the third experiment was that it used both clockwise and counterclockwise patterns, all eight starting points, and that the burst duration was constant (160 ms). Ten subjects participated in the second and the third experiment.

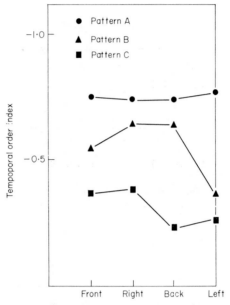

Fig. 17.4 Temporal order index as a function of starting point within the patterns *A* to *D* in Fig. 17.3 (From Tolkmitt, 1970 p. 175.)

Analysis of variance of the results produced significant effects for burst duration and pattern. With decreasing burst duration the number of located speakers decreased. The pattern also had an obvious influence. For pattern *D* it was harder to locate the loudspeaker. The effect of the temporal order (Fig. 17.4) was interesting. *Starting a trial at the right facilitated, while starting at the left inhibited, perception of a counterclockwise rotation.*

As for the role of the spatial cardinal dimensions, it turned out that localization difficulty is smallest for the loudspeakers in the aural axis (left v. right) followed by the two speakers in the median plane. From the answer cards of the subjects it was possible to compute the percentage of times each loudspeaker was located at each burst duration. The data are shown in Fig. 17.5. Apparently with decreasing burst duration the subject processed only speakers with the lowest information content.

Despite some obvious methodological restrictions (e.g. indirect measurement of the responses by means of rating procedures, previously fixed response alternatives on the cards, etc.) the study of Tolkmitt has convincingly demonstrated some basic organizational tendencies in auditory pattern perception. The author is inclined to ascribe the above-mentioned perceptual changes to a reduction of time allowance for locating single loudspeakers. A binary decision sequence was assumed to test speaker

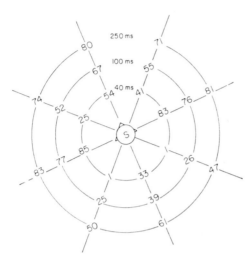

Fig. 17.5 Percentage of time each speaker was located at each duration. (From Tolkmitt, 1970 p. 176.)

locations in the following order of complexity: binaural frontal plane, median plane, intermediate planes. According to Tolkmitt (1970, p. 179): "By gradually shortening the time allowance, S eventually arrives at a decision rate which decreases the information loss enough to enable him to structure the processed stimuli".

The aim of Royer and Garner (1970) was to explore further the principles underlying preferred organizations of temporal auditory patterns.

Their experimental approach did not involve any localization tasks. They simply worked with repeated sequences of nine dichotomous elements of the following general type:

$$X \ X \ X \ X \ X \ O \ X \ O \ O \quad or$$
$$O \ X \ X \ O \ X \ X \ O \ X \ X$$

the X standing for a higher and the O for a lower tone (actually 180·9 Hz and 176·4 Hz in this investigation). The tones were emitted from two loudspeakers in front of the subject and 8 in. apart. The duration of each stimulus element was always one-half of the period. The subjects were required to describe the sequence after it became heard as an organized pattern. The presentation began at an extremely rapid rate that was gradually reduced. The deceleration was decreased as the rate approached 4·0 seconds.

The following patterning principles were observed:

(1) *Tonal frequency effects*: The majority of the descriptions began with the higher tone (66·8 per cent). This result might be due to a figure-ground phenomenon: the higher pitched tone is more easily followed and the subject tends to maintain organizations built on this higher tone.

(2) *Oranizing tendencies of temporal gestalten*: The subjects perceived the runs, *XXX, XXX, XXX* or e.g. *OO, OO*, as the psychologically meaningful units. These units are also established by the anticipated events that confirm a possible organization.

Preferences are shown for patterns that are balanced in time with long runs at the ends (e.g. *OOXOXXXXX*) and for patterns that have a directional simplicity with run lengths either increasing or decreasing in a regular order (e.g. *OXXOXXOXX* or *OOXOOXOOX*). Whenever a particular pattern is a preferred organization, so also is its temporal reversal. The point is that two patterns that are reversals are similar to each other only if it is assumed *that the pattern is perceived as a totality*. One cannot imagine a reversal unless one has perceived a totality.

The authors conclude with some remarks about the role of organization as inherent in the stimulation. Balance and directional simplicity are organizing principles. "Neither of these principles can be stated except in terms of the entire pattern. Thus, it is proper to speak of the structure of a stimulus and to ascribe to the stimulus a role in pattern organization" (Royer and Garner 1970, p. 120).

Conditions of structures are given in the environment. Instead of insisting upon organizing functions in the receptor-systems, we should probably speak of the sense organs as means of discerning existing structures in our stimulus-environment.

18 | Haptics and Vibratory Information

The place of tactual and haptic perceptual phenomena in human perception as a whole has received less attention from psychologists than has the part played by vision and hearing. In investigating these questions, the emphasis has been more purposefully on real-life, natural perceptual situations. Thus oriented, analysis has indeed revealed a number of striking correspondences with the way in which our visual world is articulated.

Dimensions of Touch and Modes of Appearance

Just as, in the chapter on colour perception, we could distinguish between "dimensions of colour" and "modes of appearance of colour", it seems reasonable to characterize *modes of appearance* of touch. On the other hand, the dimensions of colour, like brightness, saturation and hue, lack definite counterparts in the world of touch. It would not seem appropriate to construct "touch solids" to depict the various dimensions of touch. Superficially, even illumination seems to have no parallel in the tactual world. Should we, because of these limitations, give up any attempt to enumerate appearances?

According to Katz (1925), the poverty in the kinds of tactual dimensions which could be arranged in some sort of "solid" diagram is amply compensated for by a wonderful richness in the modes of appearance of touch. Although we must abandon a strict analogy to colour dimensions, we can readily distinguish between two modes of appearance, which Katz called *modifications* and *specifications*.

Titchener, who was interested in the dimensions of touch experiences, described only one continuum which could probably best be compared with the brightness dimension in colour vision. This continuum contains the various steps from the lightest, gentlest, "airiest" contact, to the "heaviest" pressure. This bare, qualitatively restricted variable would represent the only dimension comparable to that included in the three-dimensional colour diagram. Richer and more varied are the following tactual modifications:

Surface touch (*Oberflächentastung*) corresponds to surface colour. It can be observed when touching rigid objects (metal, wood, wool, or, for example, paper surfaces). The surface phenomenally forms a spatial boundary around the three-dimensional object, separating it from the rest of perceptual space. It is experienced as corresponding closely to the shape of the object. Even a thin sheet of cotton, smoothly spread out over the table, has a surface quality when touched during an experiment. Surface touch can be localized at any distance from the subject. "Space" is here referred to as the tactual space experienced by a normal blindfolded person.

Space-filling touch (*Raumfüllendes Tastquale*) is the touch experience of a medium. When walking against a rather strong wind, we experience a pressure which is diffuse, homogeneous, and without any reference to familiar surrounding objects. When the body surface is stimulated by a strong wind, no definite three-dimensional form can be experienced. Because this touch quality lacks articulation in form and location in space, Katz compares it to film colour. It is the most reduced touch experience. This same touch quality also occurs when we move our limbs around in a liquid of a certain viscosity (e.g. splash in a pool with our feet). This phenomenon provides an opportunity to discuss the old question of the two poles, the subjective and the objective, of certain sensations. When sensing a space-filling touch, we do not feel the distal stimulus as "something out there" or as an object in the way the distal stimulus in vision usually is represented, according to Gibson, in the light flux of the proximal stimulation. The objective pole fades in an impression of space-filling touch, yet it remains as an extremely weak component connected with the dominant subjective pole in tactual perception.

Touch transparency (*Raumhafte, Durchtastete Fläche*). This phenomenon occurs when a rather small, well-bounded object is perceived *behind a layer of softer material*. We can, for example, perceive a wristwatch through a sheet of cotton which completely covers the watch. The cotton is felt as *tactually transparent*—a medium, as it were—behind which the object is perceived. In the psychology of vision, *space colour* refers to something seen in chromatic illumination. Touching through a contact surface is in some sense of the word equivalent to perceiving a space colour. The same general rule holds, according to Katz, for both modalities: *The depth impressio, improves with increasing articulation of the object behind the medium* (Katz, 1925).

Activity Versus Passivity in Tactual Perception

Gibson, in his investigations, (1962, 1966), has emphasized the distinction between *active* and *passive* tactile perception. Passive touching actually means "being touched", the experience described by the subject whose eyes are closed or blindfolded and whose skin is stroked or pressed, either by himself or by others. The traditional way of exploring variations in sensitivity along the tactual surface had obviously taken into account only this alternative, called passive perception. Closely following the classical procedure—begun by v. Frey—are some modern studies on errors in tactile localization (see Culver, 1970). Applying the method of "point stimulators" the experimenter explores the palm of the hands of the subjects. In Culver's experiments, when the subjects were asked to point out the stimulated points on a map of their hand, it turned out that all subjects located these spots too close to their thumbs. In addition, left-handed subjects localized the "touch-spots" concerned closer to the wrist than did the right-handed.

When performing the task the subjects could not see the stimulated hand, as it remained hidden during the experiment.

The author sees in these localization-errors an outcome of some inhibitory processes (see v. Békésy, 1967). Another possible explanation could be found in the predominant representation of the thumb-area on the sensory cortex (see chapter 15 on body-scheme).

Active touch means the use of the movable limbs and especially of their surface *to explore the environment*. "It is only half the truth to realize that animals feel the layout of the earth and its furniture. They also *seek* contact with things." "The Metaphors of the search for contact hold true not only for the terrestrial, the sexual and the social realm, but also for the cognitive and the intellectual" (Gibson 1966, p. 123). Below we shall discuss tactile perception by means of the moving hand. Motion in this case is not a mere response to a stimulus, but, as Gibson appropriately points out, it actually *produces* the stimulation. The traditional assumption of a fusing between two components, a passive "tactile" sensation and a "kinesthetic" one, is artificial; the "kinesthetic sense" is interpreted too narrowly as muscle activity and spatial sensation, while sensory-motor limb activity and, for example, attitude sensations are ignored.

The psychology of the blind has thrown considerable light upon the achievements in active tactile perception. If congenitally blind subjects are asked to measure the length of variable rods by means of a standard rod available one might expect to find out how tactile-kinesthetic procedures are evaluated and adapted in a perceptual act. The congenitally blind are usually chosen as subjects in order to control all influences from previous experience.

Duran and Tufenkjian (1969) found, when providing their subjects—congenitally blind pupils aged from 5 to 14 years—with a set of steel rods varying from 1 in. to 12 1/2 in. in length, five distinct classes of methods for measuring length: spontaneous methods, body part as measuring instrument, kinesthesis, time duration and physical principles.

The method of constant stimuli (see p. 27) was used to determine the upper difference threshold for each standard, and the pairs were presented randomly in order to avoid learning by the subject.

In the *spontaneous methods* the subject resorted to two alternative ways of stating the coincidence or noncoincidence of the end points of the rods. He either juxtaposed them or used his palm span across the top of the two rods.

When using *a body part as instrument* the subject often placed the end of a rod at some point on the body surface and rested the rod against the adjacent skin. He could also use the width of his forefinger as a unit of measure in that he progressed over the total length of the rod grasping it between thumb and forefinger of both hands alternately.

Kinesthesis implies dynamic touching (Gibson 1966, p. 109), that is, stimulation of the skin and joints in combination with muscular exertion.

Most interesting was the *time duration estimation* of differences in length. The subject slid the tip of a finger along the rod from one end to the other, probably using the time needed to traverse the rod as a basis for the length measurements. This explanation interferes with the problem of the sensitivity of the subject to differences in surface properties, a problem not investigated by the authors.

When applying *physical principles* the subjects interestingly make use of vibration differences in rods of different lengths, either tapping them in order to listen to their pitch or waving the rod between the finger tips.

What is the actual effect of texture on tactually perceived length? Corsini and Pick (1969) offered their subjects five sets of stimuli. One set of stimuli consisted of objects made of oaktag paper pasted on cardboard. Objects of five different lengths were available. The material in the four other stimulus sets was sandpaper, varying from set to set in its degree of roughness. Also in these sets five levels of length were available.

When presenting the blindfolded subject with the stimuli the method of paired comparison was applied. He had to indicate which one of the two stimuli appeared longer to him.

Clear and quite convincing results were obtained: the finer the texture of the stimulus the longer it appears to the subject. With increasing roughness the length is finally underestimated.

Apparently the subjects did not make use of time duration in their estimates, since sliding the object between two fingers would have lasted longer for the relatively rough objects. They were, indeed, most underestimated.

When we touch an object with our hands, the various simultaneous sensations are intertwined into a highly complex whole, but even in this stimulus "stream" certain structured invariances can be found. It would be a mistake, however, to speak here of one single, delimited sensory modality.

Intermodal Correspondence

When considering the differentiation of visual space, we introduced the concept of *frame of reference*. Correspondingly, differentiation of the tactual world involves *a tactual framework* with certain *figures* standing out from it. This can be demonstrated by stroking the stiff hairs of a short-bristled brush with the palm of one's hand. The tips of the bristles are perceived together, forming a kind of coherent, consistent figure on an indeterminate background. The spaces among the hairs provide a kind of tactual frame, articulating the distinct configuration. What is amazing in a case like this is the impossibility of reversing this figure-ground configuration. There are few, if any, reversible tactual patterns. True, if we press a coarse-pronged fork against the skin we may sometimes perceive the "background" as more pronounced than the widely scattered "figure". These simple tactual figures convincingly demonstrate some features parallel to those observed in the articulation of visual stimulus configurations. For example, the *discrete patterning* of the discontinuous receptor surface does not prevent the perceiver from tactually experiencing a cohesive continuous plane. The five fingers of our hand together represent an "unbroken" consistent receptor field. Physically speaking, there are gaps in this phenomenally continuous sensorial field, for the fingertips are distinctly separated when scanning a tactual object. The spaces between the individual fingers correspond to the blind spot in the receptor field of the eye. Yet, in the same way as a moving retina can compensate for the lack of continuity and complete the discontinuities of the visual receptor area, so our five fingers can report continuous unitary surfaces without any breaks or "openings" between the tracks of the fingertips moving together across the object.

Gibson carried out some simple demonstration experiments, in which the subject "explored" an unfamiliar object which was concealed behind a cloth curtain. He found that even a touch limited to two fingers led to a unified object experience; simultaneous contacts with the fingertips from two different directions are sensed as belonging together, and the object is experienced as a single unitary one (Gibson 1962, p. 481).

The problem has even more relevance when, say, we *move* our hand along the edge of a table. There occurs a certain *invariance phenomenon* not too different from the one we encountered when we considered visual examination of physically stationary objects by moving our eyes along their contours. Although various groups of single receptor cells on the retina are successively stimulated, there is no phenomenal motion. On the contrary, there is a phenomenal constancy in the perceived stationary objects. According to Katz, the *moving sensory surface* is also of major significance in tactual invariances. As mentioned before, he is inclined to assign to the motion of the receptors a role in maintaining tactual constancy, comparable to that assigned to the prevailing illumination in accounting for colour constancy (Katz 1925, p. 58). Only by a stroking movement or through increasing pressure on the skin are we able to develop our surface touch experiences, which are actually the most ubiquitous impressions of touched objects. These conditions enable us, among other things, to experience constancy of surface touch at varying velocities of tactual movement.

To avoid misunderstanding we must emphasize that the immediate experience of surface touch is always completed by a *specification* of the tactual object. Such specification represents a tactual analogy to various colour hues. Human beings are so much less differentiated in tactual perception than in vision, that there are simply no specific "touch names". Terminology for touch contains no expressions comparable to "red", "blue", "green", etc.; the specific names for various colour impressions. This fact has many implications for the psychology of language. When speaking about touch qualities we must resort to expressions like "wooden", "leatherlike", "silky", etc. (Katz 1925, p. 33).

As for the intermodal perception conditions, some of the most convincing investigations have been carried out with vibrotactual stimulation coupled with auditory clicks or visual flashes. Because of the special features in the perception of vibration some of these intermodal correspondencies will be discussed at the end of this chapter together with the problem of haptically judged space.

A series of investigations, using ordinary tactual point stimuli, have centred around the problem of testing short-term storage models (see chapter 20 p. 536) for tactual perception. Hirsh and Sherrick (1961) in a paper on temporal resolution by the visual, tactile and auditory modalities, showed that temporal resolution for two sequentially presented stimuli was the same for all three modalities. This finding amounts to the often dis-

cussed problem: is there a common, central, temporal decision mecl
for these sensory systems?

Hill (1971) in completing an earlier study by Hill and Bliss (1968) became
interested in differences between tactile and visual localization ability and
temporal ordering ability. He made use of a sequential presentation of
4- and 6-point stimuli in a 3 × 8 matrix of stimulators. A computer system
was used to store stimulus patterns and the sequence of presentation. The
computer was connected either with an array of 24 tactual stimulators or
with a display box with 24 neon lamps.

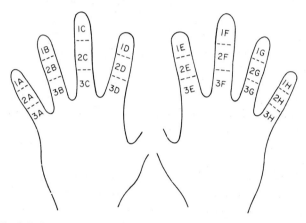

Fig. 18.1 The labelling systems of the fingers in the localization experiment. (From
Hill, 1968 p. 341.)

For the purpose of the experiment the fingers of the subject (thumbs
excluded) were divided into 24 phalanges and labelled for reporting as
indicated in Fig. 18.1. The front view of the light box is shown in Fig. 18.2.
Only the two 3 × 4 fields on black background were used during the
experiment. The centre lamp of the centre field (never on, but always
visible) served as fixation point. Either 4 or 6 of the phalanges of the hands
were sequentially stimulated by the tactile stimulator. Either 4 or 6 of the
lamps were sequentially turned on.

Two subjects participated. In both experiments they were asked to
report the position stimulated using the reporting alphabet shown in
Figs 18.1 and 18.2. A copy of Fig. 18.1 was before the subject during the
tactual experiment. There was no time limit set for the response of the
subject.

The experimental results indicated (a) that ordering a large number of
points required considerable larger onset intervals than ordering a smaller
number; (b) that ordering tactually presented points was more difficult

than ordering the same number of visually presented points; and (c) that the ability to localize the points reached a minimum with a 50 ms onset interval. This dip in performance with onset interval was not due to spatially dependent masking.

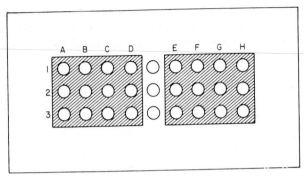

Fig. 18.2 The front view of the display box in the Hill experiment. (From Hill, 1968 p. 342.)

Preferred Forms

Révész (1950) was especially interested in the form perception of the congenitally blind and carried out some experiments connected with these questions on them. It is generally known that there are certain *preferred forms (ausgezeichnete Formen)* in *our visual world*. Their importance can be shown, for example, by referring to the tendency to maintain and reproduce shapes having a simple structure (circles, squares, symmetrical forms, etc.) that are so conspicious in visual perception. These preferred forms also emerge in the salience of certain proportions for the main dimensions in familiar plane figures. Occasionally it has even been claimed that some kind of aesthetic judgment tends to influence visual perception in a choice situation in which rectangles of varying proportions are to be compared. These influences have been referred to as the principle of the "golden section", which appears to govern our preferences for proportions. If a subject with normal sight is presented with a series of rectangles differing in the proportions of their main dimensions, and if he is asked to point to the "most agreeable", he usually chooses a rectangle the proportions of whose sides are 21 to 34. Despite the exaggerated emphasis some investigators since Fechner's time have given this principle as an "aesthetic achievement", it has some general implications from, for example, the point of view of gestalt psychology. Révész began his experimental study of this statement by presenting rectangular pieces of cardboard to subjects with normal vision. A clear majority preferred a rectangle with proportions of 1 : 1·6, or even more extreme ones, going far from the other extreme, the cardboard square (the maximum discrepancy in the length of the sides was 1 : 2) (Révész 1950, pp. 197–199).

When the same series was presented to blind subjects, a completely different result was obtained. The rectangle whose proportions were closest to the golden section was no longer most preferred, but instead the square (proportions 1 : 1) was. There apparently is a tendency to choose proportions explicitly avoided by the normally sighted (see Fig. 18.3).

Fig. 18.3 The left rectangle is preferred by visual perceivers, the square by tactual ones. (From v. Fieandt, 1966 p. 303.)

When the blind were asked to choose the "most agreeable", the task hardly made any sense to them. The majority choice of the square was regarded by them as rather arbitrary. Révész is of the opinion that no genuine aesthetic judgment is chosen on the basis of the metric principle; it is a form which is easy to handle kinesthetically and rhythmically, that is, it submits readily to a successive scanning process. Révész holds that form perception, even of normally sighted individuals up to an age of 10 to 16 years, follows the principles of construction and of simple symmetrical structure. This method of structural analysis in touch perception is a more primitive form of perception in general, and only later do the normally sighted become able to go further and appreciate relatively more complex structures (Révész 1950, pp. 199–200).

The *absence* of *gestalt completion phenomena* in tactual forms is conspicuous in comparison with visual ones. A visually presented open, slightly unclosed ring, is phenomenally completed in tachistoscopic or after-image experiments. Nothing of this kind happens in tactual experiments. *Missing parts in the concrete physical stimulus pattern cannot, contrary to what occurs in visual perception, appear in the complete final phenomenal configuration.* An opening remains an opening, a torso of a human figure remains a torso, without being *completed* as a total impression. Furthermore, as we have seen, predominantly tactual structural analysis proceeds *slowly* and *gradually, bit by bit.* Since no gestalt completion is possible in, for example, the sculpture or clay modelling of certain blind people, their productions mostly remain an *incidental collection of successive partial impressions of an unintegrated totality* (see pp. 352–353).

Expressive Value of Works Made by Congenitally Blind

Révész goes so far as to deny any expressive value to works created by congenitally blind subjects (1950, pp. 227–231). According to his observations visually normal people are incapable of entering into the "spirit" of a product of these patients, to say nothing about their inability to grasp its meaning. In one of his experiments Révész showed a series of 14 clay sculptures produced by the patients of the Institute for the Blind in Vienna (Wiener Blindeninstitut) to about 80 university students. The task was simply to write down for each of the sculptures what the students thought they might represent. Some of his results are shown as percentages in Table 18.1. Révész himself pointed out that interpretations which can be considered "adequate to" or "in agreement with" (*übereinstimmend*) the original meanings were rare. In some cases there were more "opposite" or inconsistent (*widersprechend*) interpretations than ones within the "same general motive" (*dasselbe Gebeit*) as that intended by the blind sculptor.

In the Psychological Institute of the University of Helskinki a group experiment was carried out in 1950 in an attempt to check further Révész's statements. Some of the same products of the blind were photographically reproduced and shown to 285 university students, namely "Horror", "Fury", and "The Rejected", but added to them was a series of modern artistic products all of which seemed to possess a considerable expressive value (Herzog's "Enjoyment", Minné's "Mother with Dying Child", Munch's "Cry", Picasso's "Face", and Schäffner's "Decency"). The pictures were projected on a screen and the classroom was sufficiently illuminated to allow the subjects to write their responses. In the instructions the subjects were asked "to judge whether, from any one of the pictures, they could obtain an impression of a certain sentiment, a certain emotional reaction or some kind of mood and, if so, to name their impression." The results, as well as Révész' comparable ones, appear in Table 18.1. The percentages vary considerably from picture to picture. Although "adequate" interpretations of the artists' products attained an average of 30·9 per cent compared to 14·3 per cent for the works of the blind, the difference is not overwhelming, and some of the latter products seem—according to these results—to be even more expressive than certain works of art.

Table 18.1. Distribution of answers in the first experiment compared with some of Révész' results

	No. 2 Horror		No. 6 Fury		No. 7 The Rejected		No. 8 Grief
	Révész	Exp. 1	Révész	Exp. 1	Révész	Exp. 1	Exp. 1
Adequate	8.2%	37.7%	4.9%	5.3%	1.3%	2.5%	14.7%
Same motif	34.9	36.8	34.1	17.5	28.0	24.2	30.5
Opposite content	10.8	3.5	—	42.8	—	14.7	1.4
Indeterminate	1.2	—	1.2	0.4	—	0.7	—
Other answers	42.2	23.2	56.1	30.9	69.3	55.4	52.6
No answer	2.4	1.8	3.7	3.2	1.3	3.2	1.1

Blind sculptors

	No. 1 Minné Exp. 1	No. 9 Picasso Exp. 1	No. 3 Munch Exp. 1	No. 7 Herzog Exp. 1	No. 5 Schäffner Exp. 1
Adequate	56.5%	48.4%	26.0%	14.7%	9.5%
Same motif	17.5	—	28.4	8.4	26.0
Opposite content	1.7	6.7	—	11.2	4.9
Indeterminate	—	4.6	—	5.6	5.3
Other answers	20.4	30.0	41.4	47.4	51.9
No answer	3.5	10.5	4.2	12.6	2.5

Expressionist artists

Pointing in the same direction are the results of a large contest on estimating the aesthetic value of works of some well-known modern artists and of some blind artists, which was arranged by the Finnish weekly magazine *Viikkosanomat* in 1958 without the contestants' knowing anything about the origin of the works to be judged. Three pictures of works by blind artists, "Loving Couple", "Old Man" and "Rejected", taken from Révész' book and called *A*, *C* and *E* respectively, had to be ranked according to their estimated artistic value with three others, *B* (Gwen Lux's "Eve"), *D* (Picasso's "Face"), and *F* (Herzog's "Enjoyment") without the title and artists being mentioned to the contestants. The results for the 1409 responding readers are presented in Table 18.2. The first place votes already showed unambiguously that *F* (Herzog), scored highest (47·4 per

Fig. 18.4 "Horror." (From v. Fieandt, 1972 p. 362.)

Fig. 18.5 "Fury." (From v. Fieandt, 1972 p. 362.)

Fig. 18.6 Minné: "Mother and Dying Child." (From v. Fieandt, 1972 p. 362.)

Fig. 18.7 Picasso: "Face." (From v. Fieandt, 1972 p. 362.)

cent); next was B (Gwen Lux, 30·7 per cent). The remaining 22 per cent were shared among Picasso and the blind sculptors. E and C, works of the blind, ranged third and fourth, after them came D, Picasso, and the smallest number of first place votes was given to A ("Loving Couple"), a product of a blind person.

Table 18·2. Distribution of responses in the second experiment

Picture

Order of Preference	A	B	C	D	E	F
1	65 = 4.9%	432 = 30.7% (430)	76 = 5.4%	68 = 4.8% (66)	99 = 7.0%	669 = 47.4% (665)
2	215 = 15.3	542 = 38.4 (539)	155 = 11.0	102 = 7.2 (101)	151 = 10.7 (144)	244 = 17.3 (242)
3	370 = 26.3 (368)	180 = 12.8 (177)	211 = 14.9	166 = 11.8	303 = 21.5 (301)	179 = 12.7 (178)
4	300 = 21.3 (297)	129 = 19.1	307 = 21.8 (303)	150 = 10.6	398 = 28.1 (397)	125 = 8.2
5	306 = 21.7 (304)	80 = 5.7	435 = 30.9 (431)	280 = 19.9	252 = 17.9 (251)	56 = 3.9 (55)
6	152 = 10.8 (151)	50 = 3.5	226 = 16.0	642 = 46.9 (637)	207 = 14.7 (205)	132 = 9.3

Thus it appears fairly safe to conclude that although the works of the blind do not seem to be particularly appreciated artistically, they cannot clearly be distinguished from certain products of modern art.

Fig. 18.8 Munch: "Cry." (From v. Fieandt, 1966 p. 307.)

Fig. 18.9 Schäffner: "Decency." (From v. Fieandt, 1966 p. 307.)

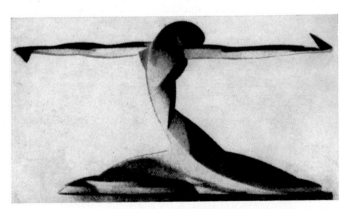

Fig. 18.10 Herzog: "Enjoyment." (From v. Fieandt, 1972 p. 363.)

The Gestalt Completion in Tactual Experiments

Turning back to the question of completion phenomena with tactual gestalten, we should distinguish between simultaneous tactual percepts produced by a deforming object placed on the skin surface and the cases reported on p. 483. In a deformed simultaneous depression, gestalt completions may indeed occur—a ring with an opening on the skin surface of the trunk, can be felt as a complete, continuous circle. Let us not forget, however, that touch receptors are sparsely scattered over the human chest and back. Maybe a physically missing bit of the ring did not actually stand out in the stimulus pattern because of the scarcity of receptors. We cannot quite compare these cases to visual completion of stimulus patterns, which really do skip considerable portions of the receptor tissue—counterparts of visually perceived motions are "tactual apparent movements". It is possible to produce motion illusion in tactual perception by alternately stimulating two spots on the skin in a sufficiently rapid tempo. Under favourable conditions a "back-and-forth" movement appears. Some investigators report having been able to *create apparent circular movements in which the effect of a prägnanz tendency can be discerned.*

The alternation—or fusion—of after-images is rapid in visual and slow in tactual perception. If we want to draw letters in the air with a moving flashlight, we must be quick about it. If comparable symbols are drawn on the skin surface, the movements must be sufficiently slow.

Really interesting is the "Frontal Plane Hypothesis" which accounts for the way finger drawings on the forehead and back of the head are oriented in the perceptual space of the observer.

This hypothesis was formulated by Duke (1966) as follows: "Symbols drawn upon anterior or posterior surfaces of the body are perceived as if they were drawn and viewed by *S* upon one common, transparent two-dimensional surface projected out in front of *S*."

Allen and Rudy (1970) experimented with four symbols ($\ulcorner$, $\urcorner$, $\subset$, $\supset$), which were traced on the foreheads and back of heads of 103 subjects. They were asked to reproduce the figures on a surface indicated by the experimenter. The hypothesis was confirmed. There was a tendency toward greater congruence in the posterior loci. Any sex differences, as postulated by Duke, could not be observed.

It is true that in tactual perception we *notice* and *take into account certain proportions,* but the *awareness of proportions is not generally a part of the immediate synthetic apprehension of the pattern.* When limited solely to tactual stimulation, we are often still able to distinguish a Latin cross (Fig. 18.11, *b* and *c*) from a Greek one (*a*) and sometimes even two Latin crosses from each other, but typical forms "such as owe their existence to the impression of proportions" do not become clear (Révész 1950, p. 133).

In a row of careful experiments Day and Avery (1970) were able to show that the horizontal-vertical illusion also occurs haptically (i.e. a haptic over-estimation of the vertical length) if tested with the $\perp$-pattern. On the other hand, an L-figure did not produce the said illusion. It has been generally claimed that some geometrical illusions also occur in haptic space if a raised line-pattern is presented to a blindfolded or blind subject (Révész

1934, Over 1963). The visual illusion effected by a L-pattern has been shown to depend on the correspondence of the two lines with retinal meridians. With the subject recumbent, the *horizontal* line is judged the longer (Künnapas, 1957). Because of this role played by retinal meridians the L-figure should have no preconditions for its haptical occurence.

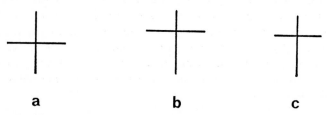

a   **b**   **c**

Fig. 18.11 Two Latin crosses (*b*, *c*) and a Greek one (*a*). (From v. Fieandt, 1972 p. 365.)

Révész' experiments show that *experienced relations of tactual percepts can even be transposed to a different scale.*

Our knowledge of the ability of congenitally blind persons to recognize contours of familiar objects on the basis of sequential vibrotactual patterns stimulated on their skin surface has improved considerably after the invention of tactual transmission of TV-images. How veridically do these vibrotactile percepts correspond to a visual line pattern of the same object? The structure of the apparatus has been described by White *et al.* (1970). The central device in this system consists of a TV-camera focused on a screen on which the "video-images" occur. The subject, seated on a chair behind the TV-camera (see Fig. 18.12), manipulates and directs the

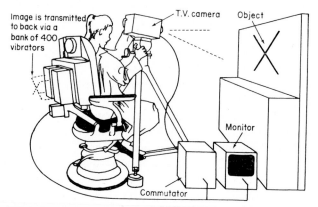

Fig. 18.12 Experimental design for "seeing with the skin." (From White, Saunders, Scadden, Bach-Y-Rita and Collins, 1970 pp. 23–27.)

camera toward the line-pattern, invisible to himself. The video-image gets electronically transformed in the apparatus and immediately transmitted to the back of the subject by means of 400 vibrators.

The subjects, 25 congenitally blind, were able to recognize simple structured patterns almost immediately. Their form discrimination ability improved rapidly if they were allowed to scan the visual pattern by means of the camera and if their errors were promptly corrected.

When the subjects were instructed to recognize a circle, a square and a triangle the performance did not exceed chance probability when they were not allowed to move the camera and were not corrected for wrong answers. However, they reached 100 per cent accuracy when these restrictions had been resolved.

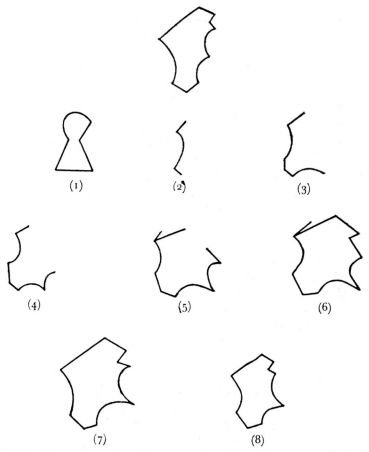

Fig. 18.13 A piece of cardboard (top centre) and how it was successively figured out. (From v. Fieandt, 1966 p. 311.)

They performed equally well as a control group of normally sighted persons.

When perceiving by touch alone, we *strive for symmetry in our gestalten*, a process which is in some ways parallel to the visual prägnanz tendency. At an early stage of their *structural analysis* blind persons aim at symmetrical wholes, a tendency which is, according to Révész, an outcome of the schematic principle. The result of this procedure can be seen in experiments with blindfolded normal subjects who are presented with a piece of cardboard, the shape of which they have to figure out (Fig. 18.13). *Photograms* taken of the movements of the middle finger during this scanning procedure show how difficult such tactual form perception is (Fig. 18.14) (Révész 1950, pp. 110–116).

 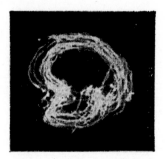

Fig. 18.14 A piece of cardboard (left) and outlining movements when trying to reproduce it. (From v. Fieandt, 1966 p. 312.)

The Role of Orientation in Tactual Pattern Recognition

Related to the above mentioned discussion around perceptual equivalence between visual and tactual patterns (Gestalten, geometrical illusions, etc.) is the problem of equivalences in spatial orientation of figures. Pick *et al.* (1966) have reported that consistent judgments of phenomenal orientation could be secured for non-representational visual forms but not for their tactual analogies.

In addition to the effect of the absolute orientation of the shapes to be recognized, Hake (1966) and Warm *et al.* (1970) have paid attention to the role of the relative orientation of the shapes compared to each other. Already when visual forms are concerned, differential orientation apparently impedes the recognition of the figures. Is there some evidence for intermodal correspondence in this respect in the central processing of pattern perception?

In the study of Warm *et al.* (1970) metric figures at two levels of complexity, 4×4 and 6×6 were used. The subjects were required to determine which of two choice figures was identical to a previously presented target (identity indicator response) or, if neither of the two choice figures was identical to the target (non-identity indicator response). Two orientation conditions were employed: (1) all figures were oriented in the same direction, and (2) choice figures were oriented in different directions relative to the target and to each other.

The impeding effects of differential orientation occur systematically in visual forms only when the subject is asked to make identity—as compared to nonidentity—responses.

The 24 figures employed in these tactual experiments resembled histograms and were generated by random selection of column heights, using 4×4 and 6×6 column matrices. A 4×4 matrix defines a population of 4^4 or 256 random four column metric figures, whereas a 6×6 matrix defines a population of 6^6 or 46·656 random six column metric figures. The stimuli were presented in a partially closed box which precluded visual inspection by the subject. He had to use his index finger for tactual inspection and to determine which, if either, of the choice stimuli was identical to the target stimulus.

Response accuracy and response time were recorded by the experimenter.

Two measures of performance were computed: (1) percentage of correct recognitions, (2) the median RT to correct recognitions. Mean percentages of correct recognitions are shown in Fig. 18.15. As can be seen, performance levels on the average exceed change expectations.

Means of median RTs for correct recognition are given for each of the

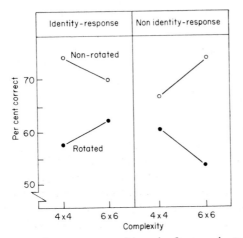

Fig. 18.15 Percentages of correct recognitions in figure orientation experiments. (From Warm, Clark and Foulke, 1970 p. 88.)

eight experimental conditions in Table 18.3. Analysis of variance has been carried out on these test data.

According to the results, differential orientation of the shapes degraded both the accuracy and speed of recognition. The negative effects of differential orientation were dependent upon figure complexity and the type of indicator response when perceptual performance was measured in terms of accuracy but not when a speed index was used. Patterns at the low level of complexity were recognized more rapidly than high complexity patterns only when a nonidentity indicator response was required. No differences between complexity levels were noted with identity indicator responses.

Table 18.3. Means of median response times (in seconds) to correct recognitions in the experiment of Warm *et al.*

Orientation	Indicator Response				M
	Identity		Nonidentity		
	4 × 4	6 × 6	4 × 4	6 × 6	
Rotated	9.93	10.98	9.27	11.17	10.34
Nonrotated	7.22	7.40	6.39	7.63	7.16
M	*8.85*	*9.19*	*7.83*	*9.40*	

Consistent with the information storage diagram given at the end of chapter 21 (see p. 544) is a theoretical model given by Howard and Templeton (1966). They maintain that a central processing mechanism scans all the information regarding both the features and the orientation of the stimulus, and that this information is stored in memory. Differential orientation, according to this model, should have a negative effect upon both tactual and visual form perception.

Discrimination Learning of Tactual Forms

Several types of hypotheses have been presented to account for the procedures and dynamics involved in discrimination learning of tactual forms.

According to the *scheme-hypothesis* all discrimination and identification involves matching of the sensory material or the cues to certain prototypes or models of stimulus-objects. The prototypes are formed as a result of persistent previous experience of the objects. Experience with the objects thus actualizes the formation and moulding of appropriate schemes.

The *discernible trait hypothesis* on the other hand presupposes that a discrimination learning of the differential specific traits of the objects takes place. According to this hypothesis the training process prepares the individual for his reactions to an ever-increasing amount of stimuli.

In order to test these hypotheses Pick (1965) in her experiments made use of black symbols, consisting of letters of the alphabet. The letters were cut out from a stiff wooden material and pasted on cardboard-rectangles. The subjects were 50 children on the pre-school level. There were two tactual and one visual discrimination task.

The evidence drawn from the experiments is decisively in favour of the *discernible trait hypothesis*. Subjects with practice in discrimination of traits were superior to the others in a transfer of training situation.

Gibson (1962) reports a series of experiments designed to investigate differences in the accuracy of shape perception in situations of passive and active touch. The subject sat in front of a table and placed his hands, palms up, behind a vertical curtain. Passive touch was induced by placing "plane figures" formed of metal wire against the subject's palm. In situations of active touch, the subject was allowed to bend his fingers and to curve them around the edges of the wire figures. The six shapes shown in Fig. 18.16 were offered in turn. Each stimulus object was offered five times altogether in each situation. There were 20 subjects, and they were required to recognize the felt shape from a series of drawings simultaneously visible.

Fig. 18.16 The six shapes in Gibson's tactual discrimination experiment. (From v. Fieandt, 1972 p. 367.)

The expected number of correct responses generated randomly would be 16·7 per cent. The level reached by passive touch was 49 per cent, and by active touch 95 per cent correct recognitions. This, of course, is due to the fact that fingertips are more sensitive than the palm of the hand. The real meaning of the experiment, however, lies in the observation that the unity, the "continuity" of the object is experienced so accurately with the discontinuous surfaces of the fingertips.

In later experiments Gibson (1966, pp. 124–126) used ambiguous sculptured three-dimensional objects (Fig. 18.17), all of which differed in some respect from each other. They did not resemble any familiar, easily recognizable object or simple geometrical shape. Each, however, had a regular convex reverse side, and each had six protuberances. The touching again occurred behind a curtain, invisible to the subject. An exact duplicate of the entire series of ten objects was, however, visible the whole time.

When the object was placed in the subject's hand, he (1) curved his hand around it, pressing his fingers into the cavities; (2) moved his fingers about in exploration; (3) pressed his thumb and other fingers alternately in opposition against different sides of the object. The principle aim seemed to be to obtain a series of different position sensations of the hand and fingers, while the movement served only as a means to this end. Not a single subject ever moved his hand along the entire outline in a systematic, exhaustive exploration.

Fig. 18.17 Sculptured three-dimensional tactual targets. (From v. Fieandt, 1972 p. 368.)

After an hour or so, the average adult is able to distinguish all the shapes from each other. This practice period also enables the subject to give an accurate verbal description of the features distinguishing the objects. Distances and dimensions mediated by the positions of the fingers seem to be more crucial than the extensive deformations of the skin surface.

In order to discover whether the law of simplicity familiar from visual perceptual structure (Mach, Köhler, Hochberg) also operates in haptic perception, Roeckelein (1968) continued Gibson's work with a series of experiments in which shapes of varying complexity were offered to the subject in the same manner as in Gibson's experiments. The objects used were Gibson's series of six three-dimensional objects (series A) and three of Hochberg's flat wooden figures, pasted onto a wooden block (series B). Each series was arranged in order of increasing difficulty, corresponding to increasing complexity. The subjects were twenty psychology students, divided into two groups of equal size. Each group was offered both series of stimuli, but one group used the method of paired comparisons to a them in order of simplicity, while the other was given all the s simultaneously for comparison.

Gibson paid no attention in his experiments to the effect of set on successful active tactual perception (see chapter 20 p. 524). Roeckelein continued his research with this problem in mind (1968). His approach involved a preliminary training phase to the experimental group, which according to the hypothesis should be in a more favourable position with regard to the perception of length proportions that the control groups. Each group was composed of six students. The RT (rod-training) group was given training in estimating the length of wooden rods, the LT (letter-training) group had practice in the recognition of flat wooden letters (similiar to Hochberg's figures), while the NT group received no training at all. The stimuli in the actual experiments were six letters of the alphabet formed of wooden rods, with a gap in the longest continuous straight part which divided the entire letter in half. The task was to estimate the relation between the length of the shape above and below the gap. The set created by preliminary training was clearly significant: the RT group produced by far the best performance of the three.

Spatial-intermodal Organization of some Tactual-perceptual Contents

As mentioned earlier (p. 484), some of the most productive investigations concerning interaction of modalities in the differentiation of visual-tactual space have been carried out with vibrotactual stimulation.

In the experiment by Attneave and Benson (1969) all the subject's fingertips were stimulated by 2 vibrators, each enclosed in its tube of aluminium. The tubes were fixed perpendicular to each other in a T-shaped structure (Fig. 18.18). Brushes of 60 Hz-frequency were applied as stimuli.

During the training period the tips of the six fingers involved in the experiment had to be associated with six letters: b, f, j, m, q, s (simple paired-association task).

Half the number of subjects started with their right hand on the upper bar, the other half the other way round. After 12 trials the hands were changed.

The results of the experiment indicated that the subjects had learned both ways of association, and cleared the transfer of training fairly well.

Strong evidence was found in favour of the statement *that spatial orientation is primarily transmitted visually*—even if the input is given by way of another modality. With eyes uncovered the subjects had stronger associations with the location of the bars than with the signs of the finger-tips.

The interaction-relationships between vibrotactual and auditory stimulation has been touched upon by many investigators. It is a well known fact that intense auditory stimulation may reduce the detectability of tactual stimuli (see e.g. Gescheider and Niblette 1967). After they had questioned the reliability of classical psychophysical methods concerning measurement of masking effects in this field, Gescheider *et al.* (1969) took the aspects of signal detection theory (see p. 41) as a new point of departure. They tried to find a method for independently evaluating possible changes in

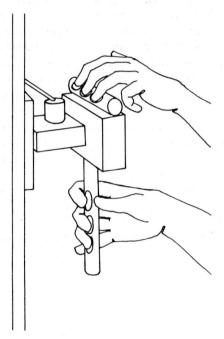

Fig. 18.18   Visual and nonvisual organization of tactual contents. (From Attneave and Benson, 1969 pp. 216–222.)

the judgment criterion of the subject and changes in stimulus detectability during the measurement-period. In their first experimental setup they had one pulse generator applied to a vibrator contactor. The duration of the major activity was approximately 10 ms and a single pulse was felt as a brief tap. Pulses from a second pulse generator were applied to a pair of earphones. The subject had to make judgments of the presence or absence of the vibrotactual stimuli on his right index fingertip. His task was to report whether his index fingertip had been stimulated in the first or second of two successive observation intervals separated by 1 second. He was told to ignore the auditory stimulus as much as possible and to concentrate on the tactual stimulus. The importance of his paying attention to the voltmeter, which would indicate the observation intervals was stressed.

The experimental design was a 4 × 4 factorial manipulation of tactual stimulus intensity and auditory masker intensity. The intensity levels of the tactual stimulus and the auditory masker were relative to each subject's tactual and auditory thresholds, measured by the method of limits prior to the experiment. Thus the intensity levels of the tactual stimulus, specified in terms of decibels above threshold, were − 4, − 2, 0 and 2 db. The intensity level of the auditory masker was likewise specified in decibels above threshold, and the values were 20, 50 and 80 db. The order in which the vibrotactual stimuli were administered was random, as was the order in which the auditory masker conditions were given. A total of 160 judgments were obtained from each subject under each of 16 conditions of the experiment over 16 sessions.

In the second experiment the authors tried to measure both the detectability of a tactual stimulus and the location of the subject's judgment criterion under various conditions of auditory masking. The subject was required to report the presence or absence of the tactual stimulus in a series of trials wherein the probability of stimulus occurrence was 0·50.

If the index of detectability, d', is defined as the difference between the means of the noise (expressed in terms of their standard deviation)—and signal plus noise distributions—then it was shown by the experiments that

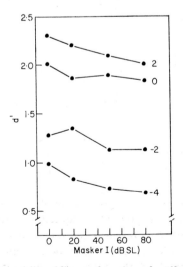

Fig. 18.19 Index of detectability (d') as a function of auditory masker intensity for tactual intensities. (From Gescheider *et al.*, 1969 p. 122.)

d' for detection of brief tactual stimuli decreased with increased intensity of a simultaneous auditory click. The main conclusion by the authors was that simultaneous auditory stimulation affected performance of reporting tactual stimuli by slightly decreasing stimulus detectability, while increasing likelihood ratio of the criterion. The auditory tactual masking thus seems to be a joint function of the operation of these two factors (Gescheider *et al.* 1969, p. 124).

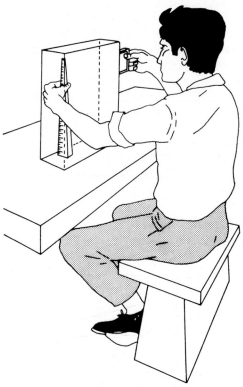

Fig. 18.20 Matching "thickness" of sheets—using left hand fingers and looking simultaneously into visual stereo-devices. Apparatus used for matching with the left hand the apparent depth of the object held with the right hand. (From Singer and Day 1969 p. 315.)

In Fig. 18.19 d' is plotted as a function of auditory masker intensity for each of the tactual stimulus intensities (i.e. −4 to 2 db.) It is apparent that for tactual stimuli at all four intensities, detectability decreased slightly as the intensity of the auditory masker was increased.

The authors lean toward the conclusion that the amount of inter-modality masking obtained by classical methods might be a function of both criterion shifts and decreased stimulus detectability. These two effects of an auditory masker might correspond to different neurological processes.

To what extent do visual stereo-experiences affect tactual perceptions of sheets with varying apparent visual "thickness"? Singer and Day (1969) presented their normally sighted subjects with three tactual stimuli successively, the thickness of which they had to match. The stimulus object was held with the right hand between the thumb and index finger in an apparatus shown in Fig. 18.20. Matching was performed with the left hand.

The first object A was a stereo pair. In front of two specially prepared "cartoon" pictures was a lenticular grid whose linear elements were actually long and very narrow cylindrical lenses. Refraction by these elongated elements caused each eye to view one of the two slightly disparate pictures. The picture was a "cartoon-scene" of animals in a wood and, although 0·135 in. deep, it conveyed a compelling impression of depth. The second object B was a coloured photograph of A, and it caused no apparent stereo-effect as did A, although colours and forms were faithfully reproduced. The third object C consisted of a plain buff-coloured card. The tactual stimulus was the same throughout.

It turned out that the object A was haptically judged much thicker than both B and C. Visual depth experiences evidently influence our haptical perceptions of objects.

The Difficulties in Perceiving Relief Pictures

A counterpart to the visually captured haptical judgments of normally sighted persons is offered by the difficulties blind people show in catching the meaning of relief productions in art. Again, some of the best contributions have been found among observations on blind artists.

One of the most interesting peculiarities of congenitally blind artists is their inability to understand relief pictures. This may sound somewhat paradoxical, since relief is not actually a *plane figure*, and therefore we could expect that it would be easily perceived by persons without sight. But we must remember that the whole idea of representations in relief is based upon a visually determined type of articulation: the figure-ground articulation. Relief provides no opportunity for the observer to apply the stereo-plastic principle. The most natural way of perceiving forms without visual aids would be by grasping. This cannot be done with reliefs, because they are accentuated forms of plane figures on a ground. Furthermore, the ground does not present tactually plane and distinct figures. For those born blind they represent only isolated, disconnected pieces of heads, arms, etc. mixed up in a chaotic way with the rest of a larger, diffuse object surface (Révész 1950, pp. 183–187).

R

Searching for Relational
19 | Invariances in Perceptual
Events

The Sensory-Physiological Theory of Y. Reenpää

It has been said that until the middle of this century sensory physiology had no perception theory of its own. Before the Second World War, however, such a theory was presented by the Finnish scholar, Yrjö Reenpää, from a more philosophical standpoint. It is not surprising that his view of sensory physiology seemed, even then, totally incomprehensible to traditionally-trained doctors. The conventional teachings concerning stimuli, sensations and perceptions were turned completely upside down by this "new direction" in physiology. One normally speaks of "stimuli" as the source of all sensation and perception, as if they were causal factors, so that the sensations corresponding to these "primary causes" are produced as a chain of cause and effect relations. When working as a university assistant on his thesis on threshold phenomena in the functioning of the gustatory sense, the young Yrjö Reenpää had already become convinced that the "stimulus-sensation" model, which had been generally accepted up to that time in classical sensory physiology, was not adequate as a basis for scientific explanation, since all we can directly experience are these sensations themselves. The stimuli, corresponding to some kind of classical minimal sensations, can only be established experimentally by inference. In his thesis, for example, Reenpää had to define the *intensity of gustatory experience* rather indirectly, so that it could be dealt with by methods based on physico-chemical constants.

Lack of Causality in Stimulus-sensation Relationships

In his later work, too, Reenpää (see for example, 1959, 1961) never tired of emphasizing that the ultimate phenomena that could be recognized in his science are precisely sensations. The concept of "stimulus" presupposes not directly experienced knowledge, but inferred or constructed knowledge, of the kind that knowledge in physics usually is, in fact. It is true that the latter is most accurately represented mathematically, in the form of axioms. However, Reenpää's pioneering claim is that the mathematical precision of physics is in part only apparent, since it is not based on elements of primary knowledge but on constructed concepts. The dependence relationship which holds between the primary "sensation" and the secondary "stimulus" Reenpää calls phenomenal-conceptual dependence.

The new direction which gradually developed in physiology, inspired by Reenpää's work, is thus based essentially on phenomenalist philosophy, and in particular on the works of Husserl and Heidegger and others, with whom Reenpää became acquainted later, during his professorship. In creating a conceptual system for sensory physiology the phenomenologist does not start from the magnitudes of physics, which describe relations between objects in the external world, because these magnitudes are secondary, based not upon sensations but upon the stimuli corresponding to them. They are quantities which, according to Fechner's psychophysical doctrine, have been used in attempts to describe our sensory experience *indirectly*, i.e. in terms of "equations" and "registering meters", for example. In place of these, Reenpää (1961) maintains, sensory physiology must create for its own a taxonomy which should be based on the sensory content of our primary experience.

The dependence relation between "stimulus" and "sensation" should thus be described not in terms of causality, but as a relation of "reflection" or correspondence. Stimuli, like the neurophysiological operations of the sense-receptors, are "parallel images", "reflections" of what the sensation phenomenologically contains. This duplicate, formed from the stimuli and the neural impulses and presented to the observer, corresponds to a certain degree of probability to the manifold sense data. Thus in this new theory, causal dependence becomes only an equivalence-relationship given in terms of a certain probability.

The Autonomous Axiomatic System

A system of quantities for sensory physiology may be created by developing for it an autonomous axiomatic system. Reenpää (1959) had begun by investigating the advantages of formulating mathematically the quantities of physics, i.e. the quantities corresponding to the stimulus level. These may be expressed by means of an easily graspable mathematical system.

After examining the theory of knowledge and symbolic logic he concluded that the equivalent level of description for mathematical formalization could most naturally be reached via an axiomatic system of the dependence relations in sensory physiology. By means of the so-called analytical reduction method, in which the intentionally goal-directed observer classifies or divides perceived objects into their "qualitative features", the following axioms are arrived at:

(1) the axiom of simultaneity
(2) the axiom of quantity
(3) the axiom of independence
(4) the axiom of inner discontinuity
(5) the axiom of maximal threshold
(6) the axiom of absolute threshold.

The first axiom states that all the different elements of the sensation content (e.g. time z, space r, quality q and intensity i) are linked by a simultaneity element g. They always occur at a given moment "now", which may actually mean simply the occurrence of several elements simultaneously.

The axiom of quantity means that every experience, e.g. of intensity or space, is a multiple of a certain minimal experience λ_e. According to the third axiom, the so-called basic elements of sensory experience, such as the surface area and colour of a seen object, vary independently of each other. In Reenpää's analysis of sensation they thus represent various dimensions: one element may vary without affecting the others. For this reason these dimensions of the basic elements may also be described as orthogonal system of axes (movement along one axis does not necessarily mean movement along the other). This independence axiom proposed by Reenpää is of great significance in perception psychology today, and will be discussed below.

The axiom of inner discontinuity expresses the "jerky" nature of the dimensions of the multiplicity perceived, and illustrates the fact that they are not perceived as continua. Here the claim is the same as the well known affirmation of classical sensory physiology: sensory dimensions do not occur as continua, but are "terraced" according to experience-discrimination thresholds. Each level of the "terrace", each step which can just be distinguished, is a discrimination threshold apart from the next.

The last two axioms also deal with a subject long familiar to sensory physiology: top sensation and sensation threshold. Several of the dimensions, for example, that of intensity, have highest and lowest possible values.

The former of these definable values is called the maximal, and the latter the minimal or absolute threshold experience.

A further point should be made here concerning the basic elements of the multiplicity of sensation already mentioned in connection with the third axiom. Like the dimensions listed above, these are the "end products of phenomenological reduction", the "pure sensations," which are revealed when *constituting sensory experience according to the theory of knowledge*. By means of this "analytical reduction", to which Reenpää refers repeatedly, the sensation may be released from being bound by time. Every sensation is, as an experience, merely a phenomenon: it occurs here and now. Only when it is released from being temporally bound does it become possible to achieve the necessary "generality" in a scientific description. A purely phenomenal experience may thus be represented in the language of concepts as a result of this analytical reduction. Using terms borrowed from symbolic logic, Reenpää distinguishes both one-place and many-place phenomenal elements. Many-place elements include, for example, simultaneity, which has already been discussed. However, colour, surface area and form, in the visual experience of an object are one-place phenomenal elements. Using Husserl's terminology, Reenpää speaks of the purposeful nature of all perception, its intentionality, which classifies and divides the objects of perception into their elements. Thus in the perception of an object one distinguishes e.g. its surface colour and its spatial location. By analytical reduction one also arrives at the basic elements: time, space, quality and intensity.

Correspondence of Experiences and Concepts

Reenpää says that he drew up his axiomatic system in such a way that sensory physiology might thus acquire an autonomous system of metrics, i.e. a system of measurable quantities independent of the quantities of other sciences and in particular of the physics of stimuli. In spite of this laudable reliance on autonomous units of measurement (especially the sensation thresholds), it is evident that the axiomatic system has been conceived in advance in such a way as to offer an adequately precise equivalent to the syntax of formal logic. Each and every axiom is formulated so that at the conceptual level, corresponding to perception, there is a specific corresponding expression (an axiom at the level of conception) for the assertion there of a pure sensory experience. Reenpää openly acknowledges this intention. He maintains that up to now the formal statements of the theory of knowledge have suffered from a lack of inner content, whereas sensory physiology, which is rich in detailed data, has been without a formalized syntax. The major aim of his life's work has been to achieve this synthesis;

and as regards his own field of science he may be said to have succeeded in this to a considerable degree. It is this which constitutes the strength of his achievement, but in some ways also its weakness.

The fundamental principle underlying Reenpää's theory of knowledge is the mutual complementation of the phenomenal level and the level of conception. It is as if between the laws of perception and the laws of thought there was an inner identity. Only at a high level of conception, where thinking occurs is it possible to become consciously aware of perceptions, with the aid of knowledge; to make them "a part of reality". The concepts of logic possess absolute invariance with respect to that which is perceived. And *seeking for these invariances* is the only way to discover the stimulus correspondence, the "Reizentsprechung", on which physiologists have long wished to base their theory of sensation. Not being sufficiently acquainted with the psychology of perception and its recent developments, Reenpää in making sensation his starting-point, in a way disregarded the levels of perception, insight and mental image, and jumped straight from the axiomatic description of sensation to the corresponding axioms of conceptual thought. He concludes that the axioms of these different levels occur in pairs, parallel to each other. According to this theory the thought process is thus analogous to the act of perceiving. The sign language of symbolic logic can be used to describe the structural relations between a phenomenon and the corresponding concept. In this way it has become possible to find the invariances, and to offer sensory physiologists an autonomous mathematical descriptive system comparable to that of the exact natural sciences.

Psychological Application of the Descriptive Model

How does Reenpää's contribution appear in the light of present-day perceptual psychology, and how should it be evaluated from the point of view of the general theory of perception? With the present compartmentalization of the sciences, it is significant, but also deeply regrettable, that the approach of this new sensory physiology receives so little attention in general surveys of perceptual psychology. On the points discussed above—the re-evaluation of the relation between stimulus and sensation, and the directing of actual empirical interest towards content, towards directly experienced quantities; and on the emphasis given to the perceiver's influence on everything he perceives,—there is general and fairly unanimous agreement among perceptual psychologists nowadays. The primariness of the quantities of perception as compared to those of physics is stressed at least by European perceptual psychologists, and presumably also by most Americans today. There can scarcely remain many of the so-called pure behaviourists, who refuse to consider experiences at all.

It cannot be denied that an axiomatic system which adequately describes dependence relations, and which can also be transposed so easily into the language of pure logic has meant a distinct gain to a science restricted to the phenomena of sensory physiology. Hensel, in his essay on general sensory physiology (1966), speaks of "practical alternatives in scientific explanation". This descriptive model has already proved its explanatory value in several experimental studies done by Reenpää and his followers.

From the point of view of perceptual psychology itself, however, something that is central and significant to its field of study is lost, if, following Reenpää, perception is simply considered as no more than an intermediate stage when setting up axioms for sensation parallel to the laws of thought. In the empirical descriptive systems of psychology—and indeed especially in these systems—the starting-point must be primary experiences and not secondary concepts.

The illustration of the axiom of simultaneity,

$$g = q : l = l : q,$$

which Reenpää gives as the formalized description of an object's surface colour, would not be considered viable today as a statement in perceptual psychology: according to it the *simultaneous* (g) experience of the colour quality (q) and the object's location (l) produce the surface colour.

In the psychological description of surface colour, however, it is not possible to represent it as the simultaneity of two dimensions. What we experience directly are undiscriminated wholes, such as objects in our environment. In the scientific description the "dimensions" attributed to them, such as a certain colour and its location, or the object's shape, are already the result of discrimination. In the psychological description of perceptions, the objects we perceive do not appear broken up into their elements, as argued in Husserl's study mentioned above. We do not experience for example, "simultaneously red and a location", but the total impression of a particular red object.

In axiomatic sensory physiology the expression given above is evidently acceptable, since on the conceptual side of the description there is the axiom of addition,

$$d = a + b = b + a,$$

corresponding to it so elegantly. Such conceptual correspondences would do violence to the psychological description of phenomena, and would go against the principles which also underlie the whole of the new sensory physiology itself.

rther evidence of this non-adaptability to the processes studied by ıology may be found in the case of the other axioms. Hytönen and Jauhiainen, according to Reenpää (1961, p. 23) have investigated the third axiom, that of the orthogonal independence of dimensions, with respect to the sense of hearing; they took the intensity and frequency of a sound as basic elements, and varied them independently of each other. In this way the axiom can indeed be verified in the laboratory by separating out the natural components of perception (and the axiom can be made to correspond to the conceptual axiom of the scalar product). But on the other hand, psychological research into aural perception has shown that the experience of the pitch of a sound and its loudness are closely dependent on each other. Here too, from the point of view of direct *psychological* description the sensory-physiological axiomatic description (in itself a successful analysis) appears arbitrary.

It must of course be granted that, by confining itself to phenomenology even more strictly than in Reenpää's description, psychology loses some degree of axiomaticization. Although psychology should also aim at the correspondence of conceptual level and direct description, in this science the "practical alternative" perhaps needs to be sought in a somewhat different way. Without searching for the direct stimulus-correspondences in the manner of classical, naive sensory physiology, psychology has made considerable progress in the analysis of the constant relations between stimulus variables. These relational invariances (Gibson, Johansson, Jansson) may perhaps offer an alternative base for quantifying perceptual psychology.

Concluding Remarks

In his general survey of sensory physiology Hensel says he doubts whether there is in the phenomena of experience the complete determination of concepts which is characteristic of logic. Perhaps, then, the presupposed identity of structure, (isomorphia) between phenomenal and logical similarity relations will only prove a fruitful mental construct in an approximate descriptive method. Hensel is perhaps right when he argues that the conceptual correspondences of sensations hold good most convincingly when the investigation concerns one sense modality at a time (sight, hearing, touch, etc.). Yet our natural perceptions are "general sensations". The mathematical study of their complex interrelations is only just beginning.

Considered as one alternative in the description of perception, Reenpää's theory is not isolated or detached. It has already inspired a good deal of research (Jalavisto, Bergström, Lindfors, Hytönen, Jauhiainen) in the

Helsinki Institute of Physiology, where it still holds a powerful position. Abroad, too, the theory has received considerable support from eminent sensory-physiologists (v. Weizäcker, Hensel, Armstrong, Keidel). The psychology of perception and modern sensory physiology have been offered a significant new point of contact by information theory in its various forms; and on both sides there have already been encouraging signs of the application of this connecting link.

Some Higher-order Stimulus Relationships (Kaila, Gibson, Johansson)

The examples given of visual perception of movement demonstrate most elegantly and convincingly the way in which our perception is actually a reaction to certain *invariances* in the stimulus conditions (i.e. to the stimulation available in the perceptual situation). These are usually specifically *relational invariances*. Even when the stimulus elements are continually changing, the essential relations or interactions among them remain constant. In Johansson's experiments on the analysis of movement (see chapter 16 p. 437, Fig. 16.18), given a fairly complex motion series of the light spots, the subject experienced only two straight motion paths, one horizontal and one vertical. He was actually based on the two most essential invariances in the stimulus constellation. Vertical motion can really be ascribed commonly to all the moving lights spots, granted that at the same time the other component of the configuration is also perceptually represented: the horizontal motion of two spots moving "in phase".

In a later experimental work by Johansson (1975), small flashlight bulbs were attached to the shoulders, elbows, wrists, hips, knees and ankles of the subject and a motion picture was taken of his movements in darkness. When the film was projected an impression of a moving man immediately appeared.

Again, Johansson claims that the necessary condition for the occurrence of the w-phenomenon of wandering brightness (see chapter 16 p. 438) from disc A to disc B is that the brightness *total* of the two discs remains constant. This is another demonstration of the way in which a particular motion perception is based on certain invariances.

Consider the case of perceiving a wagon wheel (chapter 16 p. 437) moving horizontally down the street. In this moving stimulus pattern two components are again represented:

1. the rotatory motion of the periphery of the wheel around its centre;
2. the proceeding movement of the whole wheel, the centre and periphery included.

Each one of the single points along the periphery of the wheel follows a path commonly known as *epicycloid*. It was exactly this curve the equation of which Galileo invented, when he was able to observe the path of *single isolated points* without having seen the motion of the wheel as a whole. When the Tuscan peasants (as pointed out in chapter 16 p. 437) had fastened burning torches to the rolling wagon wheels, the path of these single elements was rendered visible in the dark Mediterranean night. These epicycloids are actually the "real" stimuli of the seen movement: during daytime in ordinary visual conditions our visual system has sought out these two invariances of the motion of a wagon wheel: the translatory horizontal and the rotatory circular movements. This is an entirely unconscious motion analysis. The mathematical analysis carried out by a Galileo might on the contrary be called conscious.

In discussing his newer work, Johansson (private communication, 1970) has also tended to interpret the central processing of the retinal projections as a corresponding invariance phenomenon. The optical system of the eye does not produce static "retinal images", but rather a constantly varying distribution of light energy on the receptor tissue (see chapter 5 p. 101). Apparently the human eye is able to pick up and further process these invariant *relations*, prevalent in all stimulus configurations.

In his posthumous work, Eino Kaila says the following:

These perceptual invariances are biologically essential. What would be the consequence if they did not exist, if perceptual objects were experienced in keeping with the stimulus? Perceptual "errors" would constantly occur, false anticipations would be continuous. For the most part the stimuli as such and the imagined "sensations" which correspond to them are indifferent or secondary to the organism. What is important, on the other hand, are certain objectives, which the organism wants to achieve, and others which it wants to avoid. But this objective is something which the organism must anticipate; if the anticipation is incorrect, the goal will not be reached. To the hen searching for grain, what is important is to distinguish between edible and inedible particles; it is not interested in the amount of light reflected by the particle into its eye, or in the size or shape of its retinal projection depending on the perspective. The only thing of real importance is that edible particles are experienced, regardless of variations in stimulation, as sufficiently constant to be distinct from inedible ones (Kaila 1962, pp. 46–47).

Our perceptual world is basically and primarily a "world of perceived objects" (see chapter 14). "The environment is perceived on account of the objects it contains, as a world of objects" (p. 388). For this reason our object perceptions are to a very great extent based on far-reaching and powerful relational invariances in the stimulus configurations. In the preceding chapters, we have tried to show that the *identity*, the *permanence*, the *transgredience* and the *constancy* of perceptual objects are based on the high-level and manifold invariances contained in the stimulation which falls upon the sensory receptors.

Invariance of object perception, understood in this way, is a more general concept than, for instance, *constancy*. In examining the traditional forms of object constancy (constancy of size, of shape, of brightness and of hue) in chapter 13, we observed that in its most commonly accepted meaning the term refers to the relative constancy of the *sensory impression*—the visual, auditory, or tactual experience—in the prevailing, relatively variable stimulus conditions. From this meaning, the concept of constancy has been extended to denote a kind of stable relationship among the elements of the stimulus material as perceived in a given situation. The constancy of shape of an object is a common function of the projected shape, and of the angle of tilt from the frontal parallel plane. The constancy of size of an object is a function of the size of the projection and of the perceived distance of the object. Constancy of colour hue makes sense only in terms of the light reflected from object surfaces *relative* to the reflectance of the surrounding surfaces. This last condition was convincingly demonstrated by Gelb and Wallach in their experiments on brightness constancy (see chapter 13 pp. 377 and 384).

Thus when instead of constancy we speak of object invariance, the latter term, in its deeper theoretical meaning, refers to more than *experienced "constancy"* or unchangingness (in which sense it is also used). It should be reserved above all to refer to the *constant relations of stimuli* (e.g. the variable of projective shape relative to the variable of projective tilt), which we do not experience directly, but which are realized in our object perception. This aspect of invariance was referred to in chapter 13 p. 362: "Is it perhaps more accurate in a functional description to speak of certain relational invariances of the stimulus basis, which are realized as the experienced constancy of perceptual objects?"

In comparing object constancies to more primary or more peripheral perceptual functions, the connection with higher-level invariances is often forgotten. Brightness constancy is often simplistically compared to brightness contrast (see e.g. chapter 13 pp. 377–384). This disregards the fact that object invariances are almost always related to "anticipations", as observed among others by Kaila (1962, p. 50). Through these anticipations, the perceptual aspect of object constancy merges with the conceptual. We are dealing here with phenomena in which perception and cognition are closely interrelated.

Johansson, in his studies on the perception of movement, likes to emphasize the view that the visual system, "in utilizing the proximal stimuli available", always tries to include in the resulting perception the maximum amount possible under the circumstances of invariance in two or three dimensional stimulus patterns. For instance, when a moving object is perceived, those hierarchies of invariance which make possible the perception of motion also "guarantee' the preservation of the traditional "object constancies" (shape, size, etc.) to as great an extent as possible (see e.g. Johansson and Jansson's experiment chapter 16 pp. 430–433). In his interpretation of the way in which a two-dimensional monocular field undergoes perspective transformation (see above, p. 434), Johansson is actually performing a kind of vector analysis of the stimulus context. He claims that the visual system in a way similar to mathematical analysis, utilizes all those "cues" available in the proximal stimulus which are needed in order to experience three-dimensional perspective motion of outline figures (such as a rectangle). *The residual non-perspective components of the stimulus configuration are perceived as changes in the shape of the figure itself.*

Thus, for example, when the parallel sides of a two-dimensional parallelogram (see Fig. 16.16) are made to contract, in the resulting perception of motion *the figure is seen to recede.* The size and shape of the figure, *in relation to* the contraction, lead to the impression of approaching and receding movements in three-dimensional space. Again, if of the two opposite sides of the parallelogram one contracts more than the other, but symmetry is preserved in keeping with the laws of perspective, the resulting impression is one of receding motion simultaneously with rotation from the frontal parallel plane.

Again, if the proximal stimulus contains a figure which deviates from the projective image of a rectangle or trapezoid, these changes in shape are perceived as located within a rotating and receding rectangle, whose shape and size are otherwise preserved. The resulting experience of motion is dictated, as it were, by the hierarchical system of invariances.

The impression of three-dimensional motion with two-dimensional stimulus figures in the experiments of Johansson as well as those of Benussi, Musatti and Renvall with their stereokinetic discs (see p. 425), those of Wallach, Jansson *et al.*, Knudsen and of Ames (Kilpatrick), is based on certain fundamental relational invariances contained in the complex stimulus, which are "detected" by the visual system. The realization of these invariances and visual perceptions follows at the same time Mach's economy principle, or Kaila's (1962, p. 83) principle of the conceptual optimum (see chapter 13 p. 362). Thus some theory based on the relational invariances of stimuli, for example, a more precisely defined gradient theory, might well replace the vague phrases of Gestalt theory. It is worth noting that these invariances "dictate" perception not only in the visual modality. Kaila gives the amusing example of the lecturer walking back and forth in front of the audience, whose voice intensity is experienced almost as constant. We also know (see chapter 15) that man's perception of his own physical body is successfully accounted for on the basis of object invariances in this sphere of experience.

In this context it is especially relevant to recall those ideas of Kaila's as to the reality observed by modern science. According to Kaila (1939), the crucial contribution of Galileo was his conception of science as the *relations* which remain constant and unchanging in the midst of change. In Plato's time natural science had been defined as the search for *invariants*. But in classical thought, invariance or permanence could be characteristic only of *things* or *beings* (entities), never of *change*. For this reason, natural science based on Plato's thought remained static. It was incapable, for example, of discovering the laws governing the heavenly bodies and the universe, or of developing a technology to control space. It was Galileo's insight that constant, unchanging relationships are more important to science than unchanging entities. He spoke about *relational invariances* which turned the attention of science from the static approach of the time of Plato to the dynamic one of modern thought. This Galilean point of view has been adapted for centuries by the natural sciences in their study of reality. The invariances in relationships are the objects of modern natural sciences.

In chapter 13 (pp. 362 and 364), in connection with the discussion of object constancies, we referred to the usefulness of Gibson's concept of *gradients* in concrete cases, when we want to explain our perceptions as responses to complex but also clearly organized systems of stimulus relations.

In his classic work Gibson (1950) defined his new key concept of the *higher-order variable* (see chapter 7 p. 242 and this chapter, p. 518). Speaking of visual perception, he emphasized the way in which, in our search for veridical information about three-dimensional space, we utilize certain mathematical relations characteristic of the light energy reaching the eye. These relational variables, distinguishable in the stimulus array, he called "gradients". In most of the chapters of this book, the concept of gradient has been formulated and adapted to various purposes. It served as a useful concept in the analysis of touch and temperature sensations (chapter 5 p. 146), of chromatic vision and of the Land phenomenon (chapter 6 pp. 205–207), but above all in accounting for our perception of the spatial shape and size of three-dimensional objects (chapter 13 pp. 362–365) and in searching for the foundations of three-dimensional vision (chapter 11 p. 307). The concept of gradient is also highly useful in analyzing the perception of acoustical sequences, such as music or human speech (e.g. chapter 7 p. 238), and we encounter it in the depth articulation of pictorial art (chapter 22 p. 583).

Gibson has never suggested a mathematical definition for his concept of gradient. It would thus seem that he does not mean it to be taken as a strictly mathematical concept, although a rigorously defined concept by the same name is also known. (The gradient can be defined, for example, as a function whose value in a vector space, following a particular vector, continually increases or decreases in a given proportion.)

Gibson has continually emphasized the empirical and concrete nature of his concept of gradient. Its origin, in 1950, was primarily to explain gradients in the retinal projection—or, more precisely, to describe stimulus structure of the light energy arriving at the eye as a kind of "frozen array". Let us call this concept of the gradient that of *momenteanous structure*. Understood in this way, the concept can well be taken to represent Galilean relative invariances; the stimulus array, arrested at a particular moment into a frozen structure, always conceals manifold relational invariances. From the point of view of the general usefulness of the concept in perceptual psychology, however, it would be desirable to discard the original specialized meaning of the term and extend it to include a broader field of meaning. Although Gibson does not seem to have extended his concept of gradient from its successful application to size and shape constancy to corresponding phenomena in the perception of colour, in principle, it is just as applicable to the latter. Actually it is a consequence of relational invariances occurring in the array of light stimuli that we perceive a wavelength portion of the spectrum differently at different times (see chapter 6 pp. 205–208). As mentioned above, what is seen depends on the relation, among others, between the intensity of this radiation and that of other visible reflecting surfaces. Similarly, when I. Kohler with his distorting eyeglasses changed the whole visual space of the subject, so that, for example, everything seemed to be "elastically stretched", this transformation of visual space and of visual objects was naturally not arbitrary or random. Depending on the mathematical-optical properties of the prism attached to the glasses (i.e. on the so called coefficient of deflection), even when the stimulus system was distorted, certain relational invariances were preserved between the stimulus elements. The rapid correction of the false perceptions may be taken as a demonstration of this "gradient theory".

In Gibson's more recent work (Gibson 1966), he applies the concept of gradient more sparingly. It would seem, however, that instead of "the frozen structure of stimulus arrays", he is more interested nowadays in the invariances forming part of the information about moving objects detected by large moving receptor groups (head position-eye-hand). From these conditions for the perception of motion in moving organisms, we can expect above all that they will contain something "unchanging amidst change" in the Galilean sense. According to what has been said above (see p. 516), these invariances in the perception of motion—as compared to "frozen structure" determinants—should be considered "higher-order" invariances in Johansson's sense of the word.

In his discussion of the invariances of perception, Kaila listed some of the conditions for conceptualization in the perceptual world (Kaila 1962, p. 38). The first of these is the continual articulation of experience. Already, in discussing the relevance of the "context" or frame of reference in object constancy (chapter 13 pp. 384–386), we mentioned the importance of the level of articulation of the stimulus situation. The higher the level of articulation, the stronger the constancy. The part played by articulation is related to the possibility of *objectification* of the contents of various sensory modalities. Throughout the preceding chapters we noted, starting from the physiological level of the receptor channels and concluding at the level of higher achievements, above all at the level of integration of perception, that perceptual objects are rendered more "real" and undisputable in appearance the greater the number of modalities involved (v. Fieandt 1958, 1965). When the contents of a particular modality are easily connected with those of another (e.g. colours bound to tangible objects, sounds perceived as originating in moving objects, etc.), the result is a *polymodal interaction*, which apparently amounts to a higher degree of object invariance.

As one of the most crucial principles during this presentation, it has also been pointed out that the apparent specific continua of sensory modalities are actually strongly involved (see chapter 14 p. 390). Dimensions such as "bright" to "dark", "high" to "low", "light" to "heavy" are reflected in analogous statements whatever the modality concerned. Even more: a corresponding emotional dimension is mostly involved. There scarcely exist "matter-of-fact" perceptual qualities.

Crucial to an understanding of perceptual objects and the perceptual world, however, is the second condition mentioned by Kaila: the symbolic function. It is only the "corrections" of stimulus information on the level of cognition which make possible the continuous advance of intellectual development, towards an ever stronger conceptualization.

The theoretical aspect applied throughout the previous chapters, and in this recapitulation, toward the questions of "invariances", "higher-order-variables", "gradients", "context", etc. might well be labelled "phenomenalistic". However, this mode of examination is not a "naive" phenomenology as was the case in some Gestalt psychology. Instead of concentrating solely on the experiences of the individual the emphasis is on a form —as it were—of higher psychophysics. It is a matter of describing those very cases in which a phenomenal percept can be explained by some regularities obtaining in the stimulus relationships. The decreasing redundancy accomplished by stimulus invariances has been chosen as a goal of perceptual research. In this approach an attempt was made to follow the path marked out by Kaila, Gibson and Johansson.

Part Four

Personal Determinants and Appearances
of the Perceptual World

20 The Effect of some Transient Phases of the Organism on Perception: Set, Deprivation and Attention

In a previous chapter the perceptual sensitivity of the observer to apparent movement toward or away from himself was discussed (see chapter 16 pp. 441–442). It was found that there exists a close reciprocity between the alertness of the receptive organism and certain perceptual processes. Again, this is a good instance of the effect of the "dynamic state" of the organism on what is likely to "enter the perceptual channels". Something perceived as approaching the organism is accompanied by increased arousal, measured by means of several indicators: SC (skin conductance), PV, EEG, etc.

The organism seems to be especially "tuned" to cope with certain groups of stimuli, which are relevant in some way or other to its welfare and persistence.

The important problem of "perceptual context" has been touched upon on several occasions in this book. It is one of the key concepts in the realm of modern psychophysics but in this context its major relevance became apparent in connection with the object constancy phenomena, and especially when discussing conditions of perceived movement (pp. 438–440).

In its widest sense, the word "context" includes preceding and ongoing stimuli which might influence the perception of a new or novel stimulus introduced in the field. It has been claimed that the test perception is affected by the *previous experience* given by the preceding or ongoing events. In this case "experience" is a word used in its broadest sense. It includes events like preliminary staring at stimuli in visual after-image experiments, instructions given to the subject concerning his manner of observing spatial relationships, shapes and colours of objects in traditional laboratory experiments, illumination and noises in the room, etc.

Perceptual Set

This term refers to the tendency of an organism to pay attention to certain features of a stimulus pattern. In addition to predispositions or biases brought about by previous experience and learning effects in general, sets may also be taken to mean some influences of more "deeply anchored" motivational states: personality involved perceptual tendencies. Despite the abundant variety of meanings connected with the concept of *set*, it can generally be taken to describe:

> *either*   relatively short-term, temporary and personality-unintegrated states, due to preceding events in general
> *or*   relatively long lasting and personality-integrated, inborn or deeply anchored directive tendencies.

This distinction apparently has many advantages from the point of view of an instructive presentation, and it will therefore be adopted throughout the present work.

This chapter will be devoted to the discussion of nonlasting "transient states" brought about by conditions such as short-term subliminal perception, deprivation and attention conditions. The question of personality-determined perceptual tendencies will be taken up in chapter 21.

The objects of our perceptual world possess certain "attraction" or "repulsion" valences (see chapter 14). Thus our expectations concerning perceptual objects, especially our wishes or fears, give them an emotional colouring. We continuously *ignore, complete* and *change* the contents of objects, not to mention several other clear-cut or compound perceptual tendencies. We thus achieve products of our cognitive styles as they affect our perceptual functions. Perceptual events are always going on under the contributions of sensory processes on the one side and motivational processes on the other. In the course of time a great deal of discussion concerning the definition of perceptual processes as such has taken place. Some investigators (e.g. Johansson, Hochberg) have argued for a narrow concept of perception, pointing out that if this concept is broadened to include individual motivational factors the phenomena have more to do with cognition than with perception. Other psychologists have argued for a broader concept of perception, stressing that perceptive processes are fully dependent on a variety of motivational states (e.g. Hartshorne 1934, Bruner 1951, 1957).

To give a comprehensive and readily understandable presentation of the role played by perceptual sets seems rather difficult and confusing, because of the ambiguity prevalent among all definitions of the "set"-concept. Despite its long history, reaching back to what German psychologists meant by their term *Einstellung* around the turn of the century (see, for example, v. Kries 1894), it was never given a sufficiently precise and appropriate definition. According to v. Kries, a *connective attitude (konnektive Einstellung)* is a "cerebral change as a result of which one certain visual percept may evoke sometimes one, sometimes another mental image or idea" (v. Kries 1894, p. 4). He was convinced of the role of varying procedures in the brain as the reason for this kind of directive effect on the association of ideas. "The unknown change that evokes the alternations of the mental associations . . . I would call a changing attitude (Einstellung). Undoubtedly these changes are cerebral, we want to speak of cerebral attitudes."

A *dispositive attitude* on the other hand, in the terminology of v. Kries, indicates a state of readiness corresponding to the broad contents of general ideas; a disposition, for example, to visualize a certain shade of red out of the general idea of that colour (v. Kries 1894, p. 17). From (1959), in his study on apperception has pointed to this forgotten chain of concepts. According to From we are dealing here with the influence of set—or a whole system of sets—upon the processing of physical stimuli, and thereby on one's expectations. This point of view has been further developed and applied in his study of person perception (From 1971).

On the other hand, a survey of this research history evidently demonstrates the significance of this type of concept when describing often remarkable modifications in perceptual contents without being able to point out—so far at least—corresponding changes in the stimulus-context. (Take for example the shifts of figure and ground, pp. 323–327, the reversible patterns of ambiguous figures, p. 325, etc.)

After the *Einstellung*-concept of the early physiological psychologists and the Wundtian structuralists, there was the input from Gestalt psychologists. They questioned the conceptual line of classic psychophysics and looked for a number of variables to be simultaneously investigated. Since the Second World War new trends of research have developed, emphasizing the importance of experiments in order to account for the relevance of those multiple variables. This approach is often called "directive state theory", since it claims that the state of the perceiving individual has a crucial influence on perceptual processes. In the 1940's the group of psychologists representing this point of view received the name "new-look psychologists".

Fechner was already aware that there exist considerable differences between the relative thresholds of various individuals. Each threshold curve contains an unknown factor of variance, which we may call, for example, S_s. Similarly, the complexity of the background stimulation also affects the height of the threshold curve; this variance factor depends on the degree of reduction. Let us call this component S_r. The question now arises, whether some general formula can be devised which would be independent of inter-individual variations of differences in adaptation levels and of different experimental conditions, and which would account for the relationship between stimulus intensity and the threshold; in other words, whether S_i is independent of S_s and S_r.

In order to approach this problem, we shall first examine the traditional concept of set in the realm of this chapter. It will be followed by a survey on recent theory formation and research concerning effects of needs and current motivational states on perceptual events.

Set Produced By Specific Experience

Stimuli which act as affecting and provoking the set of a perceiver may be *specific*, such as certain visual or auditory events. They can also be *nonspecific*, such as the result of the general experiences derived from life in a certain culture. So far the influence of specific experience has been studied more abundantly in experimental laboratories.

How does specific perceptual experience direct the perceptual organization built upon ambiguous visual or auditory stimuli? Bugelski and Alampay (1961) presented two groups of subjects with the ambiguous drawing shown in Fig. 20.1. One group had been confronted only with "human" pictures prior to presentation of this test figure, the other group had seen as many "animal" pictures before they made their judgment of the figure. Without this influence of "set" the alternative of a bespectacled "human face" is reported in 81 per cent of the cases, whereas a "rat" is seen in the minority. The influence of the subject's specific experience is clearly shown in Table 20.1.

The results show clearly that the same ambiguous figure was perceived quite differently, depending on the pre-established set. For the "animal alternative" the frequency with which the rat was reported increased as a function of the number of animal pictures presented.

Toch and Schulte (1961) concentrated their attention on the influence of certain long-range experiences. The tendency known as *binocular rivalry* (see chapter 11 p. 299) results in either an alternation between the two pictures presented to the left and the right eye respectively, or in their fusion. Toch and Schulte had chosen distinctly different pictures which were impossible to combine in a meaningful fusion. They argued that the observer's past experience might bring about a preference for either one of the pictures. One group of their subjects had undergone extensive training

Fig. 20.1 "Human face" or "rat"? An ambiguous picture. (From Murch, 1973 Fig. 8.1 p. 301.)

Table 20.1 Response-percentages to the rat/man drawing

	Animal pictures				Human pictures			
	1	2	3	4	1	2	3	4
per cent rat	74	82	91	100	27	25	27	20
per cent man	26	18	9	0	73	75	73	80

in police work; the members of the other group were beginners. All subjects were shown the same pair of drawings in a stereoscope. There was always a violent and a non-violent scene presented simultaneously, as shown in Fig. 20.2.

Out of 18 pairs of drawings, subjects with police training saw an average of 9·37 of the violent scenes, the beginners in training saw only 4·69. A control group of college students reported an average of 4·03 violent scenes. Obviously the training provided a set for the perception of violence.

The ambiguous drawing in Fig. 20.3 (after Hill) can be perceived either

Fig. 20.2 The two scenes applied in a binocular rivalry experiment. (From Murch, 1973 Fig. 8.2 p. 303.)

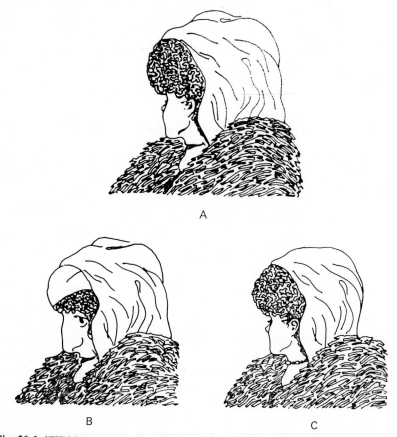

Fig. 20.3 "Wife" and "Mother-in-Law" in three versions. A, the ambiguous drawing. B, unambiguous old woman. C, unambiguous young woman. (From Murch, 1973 Fig. 8.4, Fig. 8.5 pp. 304–305.)

as an old woman ("mother-in-law") or as a young woman ("wife"). Leeper (1935) prepared two *unambiguous pictures* (Fig. 20.3 A and B) based on Hill's drawing. His first experimental group was confronted only with Fig. 20.3. The second group was given a *verbal* description of an old woman prior to the exposure of Fig. 20.3, and the third group a previous *verbal* description of a young woman. The fourth group got to see Fig. 20.3 A and the fifth group Fig. 20.3 B prior to the exposure of the ambiguous figure. The results are shown in Table 20.2.

Table 20.2 Subjects describing Fig. 20.3 as young or old

Groups	% reporting young figure	% reporting old figure
1 Control	65	35
2 Verbal old	67	33
3 Verbal young	63	37
4 Visual old	6	94
5 Visual young	100	0

Apparently, the verbal descriptions were unable to produce the expected perceptual set, whereas the previously exposed figures had a remarkably strong effect. However, Murch (1973, p. 305) could not confirm this result. Despite his experiments with several hundred students in psychology classes, he could not create a tendency to see the old woman by way of previously showing Fig. 20.3 A. Probably the figure was too well-known to the students.

In Steinfeld's experiments (1967), the ocean-liner drawing by Street was employed (Fig. 20.4). Before seeing this picture, subjects in a first group were told a story about the sinking of an ocean-going liner and a second group listened to a story about a scrubwoman who lost her purse in a large building. Additionally there was a control group looking at the figure without hearing any preceding stories. Table 20.3 gives the time required by each group to perceive the ambiguous figure as a ship.

Table 20.3 Recognition times for the ocean-liner drawing

Set	Mean time	SD
Group A (Sinking ship story)	4,5 s	3,15
Group B (Scrubwoman story)	38,1 ,,	39,69
Group C (Control)	24,1 ,,	30,48

The ship story had a strong set-producing effect. Group *A* organized the test figure more efficiently than did the other groups. The weak tendency in the direction away from a ship-interpretation in the *B*-group does not provide a basis for speculations in favour of a "negative set" (see Steinfeld 1967), because of the high scatter values for both groups *B* and *C*.

In the three above mentioned experiments one tendency towards error must be kept in mind. The previous training or experiences, the effects of which are interpreted as "sets", might have created "response sets" as well as actual perceptual sets. It is hard to insist upon real modifications or alterations in the way different groups of subjects *perceive* the presented stimuli. What they have seen or heard before the test figure might have directed their response tendencies without any changes in the perceptual outcome. This difficulty of interpretation is one of the major restraints when trying experimentally to prove the manifestations of perceptual set.

Fig. 20.4 Ocean-liner drawing by Street. (Applied and redrawn after Steinfield, G. J., 1967 pp. 505–522.)

Nonspecific Experiences, Attitudes and Perceptual Organization

Around 1950 a research group was active at Princeton, USA, the most prominent members of which were Ames, Ittelson and Kilpatrick. Their basic hypothesis was that perceptual formations are given a "reasonable" structure on the basis of the perceiver's prior experience. In order to verify this hypothesis they designed an extensive series of visual situations in which elements of object perception, nonveridical in themselves, when seen monocularly from a particular angle were organized into meaningful three-dimensional objects. These experimental setups (see e.g. Fig. 20.5), though they are still excellent demonstration devices, did not provide empirical support for Ames' theory.

Fig. 20.5. Illusory three-dimensional objects from Ames' experiments. (From v. Fieandt, 1966 p. 238.)

As the most central result attained by this group we may take the observation that the organism's perceptions are determined on the basis of varying dynamic factors, while static components play a secondary part. In certain situations perception is affected by so many factors that it becomes impossible to predict (see Ames *et al.* 1932).

Perhaps the most prominent representative of later research is Carlson, whose particular area of work has been the relationship between motivation and size constancy (Carlson 1960, 1961). Carlson assumed that one natural consequence of biological adaptation would be the size constancy of the perceptual object (see chapter 13 pp. 367–368). In test situations "over-constancy" sometimes occurs. According to Carlson, over-constancy is correlated with the difficulty of the instructions given to the subject. He believes that this over-constancy is due to the subject's automatic error-correcting drive. In a neutral motivational situation, according to Carlson's later work (1961), the subject's perception is characterized by perfect constancy. A sleep-deprived subject, motivated for a good performance, shows an over-strong constancy effect. According to Carlson, this is due to the fact that the subject's perspectival vision produces the most unambiguous and "economic" way (in Mach's sense) to handle visual information (see chapter 13).

Of the other research workers of the 1960's, we should mention Landauer (1964 a and b), who analyzed the effect of set caused by instructions in a simple experimental situation. He was able to show that the subject may sometimes give "real" and sometimes "projective" estimates of shape and brightness. A similar relationship between the instructions given to the subject and his perception was found by Cautela and Vitro (1964) for autokinetic phenomena (see p. 419). Similarly, in situations involving the perception of actual rotational movement, such motion is experienced more easily if supported by the instructions.

In Ertel's (1968) experiments, the following apparatus was used: in front of the subject, in a frontal parallel position, a wall was set up with a round hole covered by translucent film. The size of the aperture could be regulated. This self-illuminating disc was sometimes described to the subject as a coin; sometimes as a piece of cardboard. Ertel's results were not consistent with those of Bruner and Goodman, who concluded that the phenomenal size and brightness of visual objects in certain cases were determined by their subjective values (see p. 546). In Ertel's investigation, estimates of size consistent with each alternative were gradually established in the experiments.

Landis et al. (1966) carried out two experiments, one with coins and one with cardboard discs of the same size. The size and type of the stimulus objects were varied. Rewarded choices of cardboard discs rendered overestimation of the objects chosen. When asked to judge the variable discs or coins as either "greater" or "smaller" than the standard one, the subjects overestimated big size more often than high value. With large stimuli, coins were overestimated more often than discs of the same size; with small stimulus objects the reverse was true. Furthermore, the results offered no support for the assumption of the part played by need in overestimation, which turns out to be a perceptual problem in its own right.

Levy (1967), like Landauer, showed the influence of verbal instructions on size constancy. The stimulus objects used were squares; the standard was varied in size and held at a fixed distance from the subject. The variable was placed at different distances. One group of subjects was rewarded verbally during the preliminary practice sessions; another group was instructed to make discriminations between physical size and phenomenal size. A third group received both rewards and instructions. The group that made the most veridical size estimations was the one which received both rewards and instructions; rewarding in itself was not sufficient to improve the performance.

Experimentally-elicited selective tuning was investigated by Egeth and Smith (1967). They applied the tachistoscopical method, presenting their subjects with a single critical picture preceded or followed by a set of four other pictures. For some subjects the experiment involved pre- as well as post-imposed instructional pictures.

The subject had to isolate critical elements in pictures presented under several conditions. He was told that the critical element was one of four items displayed before or after the test picture. Sets involving highly similar alternative items as well as those with rather divergent items including a radio, vacuum cleaner, sports car, and a man's shoe were prepared.

The purpose of Egeth and Smith's study was to find out whether a rather crude memory would suffice to discriminate the emphasized critical item in the test picture, or if crude memory alone would be insufficient to get the critical attribute recognized in the "after" condition. Ability to discriminate the critical element among highly dissimilar elements would speak in favour of the impact from crude memory only. The authors predicted (1967, p. 544) that "perceptual selectivity ought to result in less difference in recognition accuracy between similar and dissimilar alternatives when the sets of alternatives are presented before, rather than after, the test picture". The experimental data confirmed this prediction. The average number of correct identifications indicated less difference due to the degree of similarity under the before-after condition than under the after condition.

The authors were able to show that perceptual processes can be selectively tuned. Their main results are summarized under the following points:

(1) The experiment with pre- as well as post-imposed instructional pictures rendered a higher recognition accuracy than the experiments in which the instructional pictures only came later.

(2) A certain amount of interaction can be shown to exist between the temporal conditions of the picture presentation and the similarity of the presented pictures—as predicted on the assumption of a mechanism of perceptual selectivity.

In the studies reported so far, the formation of set has rather axiomatically been referred to the role of "past experience".

Attention has also been drawn upon cases with interesting controversies between autochtonous perceptual factors ("organizing factors", Koffka 1935) and past experience. Kanizsa (1969) has reproduced an excellent collection of "embedded figures". Typical for these figures, already familiar from the contributions of Gottschaldt (1926), is the disappearance of previously familiar line patterns (triangles, squares, diamonds, etc), if the elements of these patterns are "masked" by a homogeneous context of a more global, embedding stimulus pattern. A good example of the point stressed by Kanizsa is the figure by Galli and Zama (Fig. 20.6). One of the edges of a triangle surrounded by a circle disappears if "masking" stimuli are introduced: other strings in the circle drawn equidistant from each other and parallel to that edge.

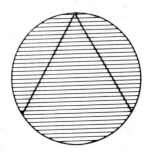

Fig. 20.6 Embedded triangle as devised by Galli and Zama. (From Kanizsa, 1969 p. 31.)

The mechanism of set Since the days of Karl Duncker (1935) many studies have centred on finding *intervening variables* which could account for the modification of the effect of an elsewhere unaffected test stimulus. The crucial question is: "Does the set directly affect the processes of perception or is the result merely a result of memory?" (Murch 1973, p. 307). In Duncker's famous demonstration this question remained unanswered.

From one sheet of dark green paper Duncker cut out two figures: a donkey and a leaf. Each was presented alternately against a dark background and illuminated with red light. The colour of the light source was adjusted precisely complementary to the green of the paper and rendered the surface of the stimulus (leaf, donkey) perfectly grey. When provided with a colour mixer the subjects always used more green to match the leaf than to match the donkey.

According to Murch (1973) both memory and perceptual factors are operative in set, and he gives an extensive and informative survey of several experimental studies dealing with the problem. There are some tasks in the solution of which perceptual factors on their own play a predominant role. On the other hand there are cases in which the mechanism of set may be the result of memory or "encoding strategy".

Harper (1953) tried to control the influence of memory by placing conventionally red objects (heart, apple, lobster) and traditionally neutral objects (oval, triangle, the letter Y) on the front of a colour mixer. An equal proportion of red and yellow on the colour mixer matched the red of the six targets. The subject had to adjust the colour mixture until the red object disappeared by becoming the same colour as the shade of the mixer. In these experiments also the subjects tended to add more red to the matches of the conventionally red objects. Based on his results Harper proposed that set modifies perception. The other alternative which always has to be taken into account, and which was pointed out earlier in this presentation (see p. 530), that *response sets* might actually have been developed during the experiments, has not apparently been fully observed by Harper. It therefore remains an open question whether his conclusion that the subjects really saw the targets as redder is justified. In any case Harper's experimental results were confirmed by Murch and Bashford (Murch 1973) with a slightly modified set-up.

Lawrence and Coles (1954) also found a memory aspect involved in the formation of set. They presented pictures of single familiar objects as test stimuli. Prior to, or following the test stimulus, names of four alternatives for the test stimulus were given. In this respect the procedure resembled that applied by Egeth and Smith (see p. 533). The control group received no verbal labels. Both the before and the after group were superior to the controls.

In a long row of studies a strong emphasis has been laid on the interpretation in favour of memory factors, both in the above mentioned study of Lawrence and Coles (1954), and in the experiments performed among others by Long, Henneman and Garvey (1960), Long, Reid and Henneman (1960), Reid, Henneman and Long (1960). This is the point taken by Haber (1966): the *prior* conditions increase the opportunity of the subject to memorize relevant information, but the *after* conditions also provide a better employment of memory than if no information at all had been available.

In Steinfeld's ocean-liner experiment the story of the sinking ship reduces the number of possibilities to "be held in storage" when carrying on the organization of the figure. Steinfeld (1967) puts forward a compromise: "the set enhances the clarity of the incoming percept and aids the observer's memory in developing that percept" (Murch 1973, p. 309).

Instead of arguing in favour of *either* "initial perception" *or* of memory after the stimulus is gone, Harris and Haber (1963) pointed to the possibility of different "encoding strategies". By encoding, they meant the way the subject transformed perceptions into a verbal description for memory. When presented with tachistosopically flashed stimulus cards displaying figures varying in location, colour and shape, one group of subjects separated the elements on a card into objects on the left and right and remembered them by listing number, colour and shape (two blue circles, one yellow square). The authors called this method the *objects strategy*. On the other hand, the *dimensions strategy* categorized the objects in logical conceptual groups: blue yellow, circle square, two one. When subjects in another experiment were trained to use either one of these strategies the effect of set disappeared for subjects using the objects strategy. The critical attribute which was especially emphasized by the experiments was mostly *encoded first* by subjects using the dimensions strategy, and they improved their accuracy for the critical attributes of the test card.

If short-term visual storage is involved, perceptual isolation should show some decisive effect on the developing structure. In his experiments Forsyth (1970) was able to confirm the first of his two hypotheses: perception isolation prolongs the duration of short-term visual storage. There was not sufficient evidence in favour of the other hypothesis: that perception isolation brings about changes in the cognitive-perceptual structure.

If the subject is instructed to attend to *two aspects* instead of one, how does the performance interrelate with the exposure-duration of the test stimulus? Van der Heijden (1972) has argued in favour of the *subjective duration* as an efficient independent variable in all visual information processing situations. It is a well-known fact (Sperling 1960) that a visual stimulus is followed by a longer lasting iconic duration.

Against Lie and Orszagh (1971), Van der Heijden points out that this subjective duration is sufficiently high to allow successive processing of two stimulus attributes as efficiently as a parallel processing of them. Within the limits of a 4 to 200 milliseconds exposure-time of the stimulus there appears no difference in the respective subjective duration.

Sensory deprivation Motivational factors are also repeatedly touched upon in studies concerning the lack of external stimulation on the perceptual functions of the individual. Murch (1973, p. 327) makes a distinction between *perceptual deprivation* involving perceiving processes under slightly reduced stimulus conditions, e.g. reduction screen viewing (see p. 358), visual Ganzfeld (pp. 314–316), auditory white noise (p. 213), etc, and *sensory deprivation*. The last-mentioned expression denotes conditions which reduce as completely as possible the sensory input to the individual. Prolonged conditions of darkness, silence, lack of tactual,

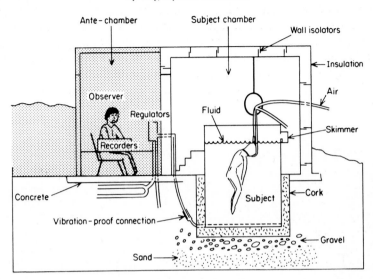

Fig. 20.7 The water-tank deprivation experiment (hydro-hypodynamic experiment after T. Shurley). (From *Proc. 3rd World Congr. Psychiatr.*, 1960.)

gustatory or olfactory sensations are apt to be enlightening in their effects on the perceiving organism. An almost total isolation of sensory input from the external environment can be achieved by immersing the subject in water tank (see Shurley 1960). The basic experimental set up is shown in the schematic drawing, Fig. 20.7. Each subject wore a black-out

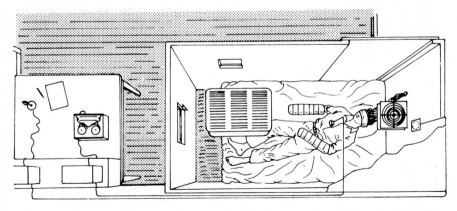

Fig. 20.8 Typical situation in a sensory-deprivation experiment. (From v. Fieandt, 1972 p. 261.)

s

mask to which was attached a breathing-tube. The water-temperature was held constant. More familiar is the second condition Fig. 20.8, developed by Bexton *et al.* (1954). The subject reclines on a soft bed in a sound-proof room with arms encased, and wears translucent goggles which allow only a diffuse dim light to enter the eye bulbs. In a third type of set up designed by Wexler *et al.* (1958) monotonous stimulation was brought about rather than isolation (see Fig. 20.9). The subject was placed in a

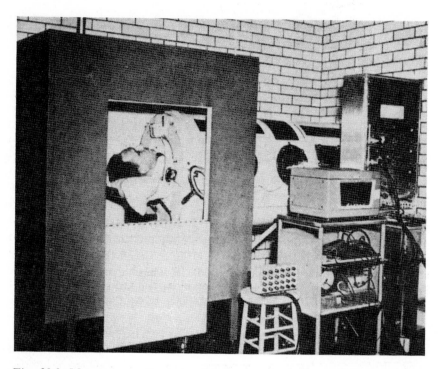

Fig. 20.9 Monotonous stimulation by means of a polio respirator enclosure. (From Murch, 1973 p. 330.)

polio respirator on a soft mattress with arms and legs encased in cylinders, in order to prevent movement and to reduce tactual stimulation.

How long is the period during which subjects can endure sensory deprivation? The various techniques lead to different results. A comparison of some results obtained with the above mentioned methods is shown in Fig. 20.10. As might be expected, the tolerated period is lowest in the water tank situation. Under the bed-confinement design most subjects have been able to tolerate an isolation for 24 hours. However, deprivation periods might occasionally be lengthened up to two weeks in different types of experiments and by varying the set ups.

Typical effects of sensory isolation have been listed by investigators who managed to keep their volunteer subjects in darkness and silence for a period of one week (Zubek *et al.* 1961):

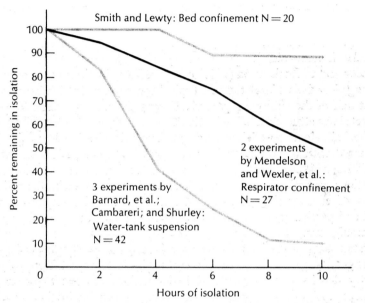

Fig. 20.10 Comparison of some results obtained in the deprivation experiments. (From Murch, 1973 p. 331.)

(1) Visual vigilance: watching the sweeping hand of an electric clock and reporting when the movement of the hand stopped for 0·10 seconds.

(2) Auditory vigilance: when watching the clock, subjects were also asked to indicate any change in the frequency of a constant tone.

(3) Depth perception: aligning a moveable rod with a stationary rod.

(4) Size constancy: adjusting the dimensions of an equilateral triangle located at 15 feet until it appeared equivalent in size to a triangle located at 4 feet.

(5) Reversible figures: reporting the number of apparent changes in a Necker cube.

(6) Perception of colours: description of differentially coloured squares. Each day during the period of isolation the subjects had also to press a key to indicate the estimated duration of an interval between buzzer sounds (1, 3, 5, 15, 30, 60 and 120 minutes, respectively).

The test results compared to those of the control group clearly indicate that isolation brings about reduction in depth perception, reduction in size constancy and less reversals of the Neckar cube. No significant differences could be observed in the two vigilance tasks. Among the time judgments, the experimental subjects underestimated only the 120-minute period (Murch 1973, pp. 329–330).

A special effect of the isolation conditions are the hallucinations often reported by the subjects. Frequently both visual and auditory hallucinations occur (flashes of light, dim unclear shapes, sometimes animal forms and animal or human voices).

According to Zuckerman (1969) complex hallucinations occur only after prolonged periods of isolation. In typical sensory deprivation experiments about half of the subjects report visual sensations. About one fifth of the subjects have structured hallucinations.

The hallucinations elicited during sensory deprivation have also been compared with those reported by psychotics and drug-addicted patients (Zuckerman 1969). Marked differences have been observed. Psychotic sensations are typically auditory, which is seldom the case with the hallucinations of sensory deprived subjects. Drug induced hallucinations are vivid and persistent, while those of deprived persons are generally unclear and ambiguous.

Systematic observations made on workers with monotonous tasks, such as long-distance truck drivers, seem to indicate that after prolonged sensory deprivation imagery and hallucinations are apt to occur very frequently. Like dreaming and day-dreaming these hallucinations provide a "higher level of perceptual activity" which seems to continue their functions despite the absence of contemporary external input to the sensory system.

A thorough investigation of this field has been inhibited by the restricted scientific knowledge so far available of these often unpredicted and strange perceptual events.

Attentional Conditions of Perception

Recently, attentional variables have become a central field of interest when investigating transient and situational determinants of perception. Vigilance, alertness, exploratory activity are modern keywords, all referring to a state of heightened activity of the organism in its function of encoding stimuli. Seminars and symposia have centred on themes like "Attention and Performance". The improvements in electronic registration equipment have contributed to this focus of interest which is clearly in line with appraising physiological variables (e.g. GSR, PV).

In this connection too, one might speak of selectively directed perception or selective attention (see e.g. Swets and Kristofferson 1970). In case of set (pp. 524–526) the selectivity was mostly unconscious, whereas attention involves an active focusing of the perceptual input on certain groups of stimuli—whether deliberately or undeliberately. Egeth conceives attention as a mechanism "which enables organisms to respond selectively to important features of the environment while ignoring features which are of little or no importance". The pioneer in the field of attentive perceptual psychology is Broadbent (1958). His famous "filter hypothesis" is often still invoked to explain the prevailing perceptual focus of interest in different individuals. Because the perceiver's capacity for processing stimuli from the environment is limited, Broadbent stipulated the concept of a selective filter. At some point in the normal perceptual process certain stimuli must be selected and others disregarded. This procedure is described in terms of a "filtering". Broadbent's theory was based mainly upon experiments on selective listening to speech. The single central channel whose capacity is limited is called the "*P*-system". According to Swets and Kristofferson:

inputs that are blocked by the filter at the time of their arrival may enter the P-system later because they remain in a short-term store for a matter of seconds If the filter switches appropriately, the stored representation of an input will enter the P-system. Short term storage, which is interposed between sensory input and the filter, may be refreshed by rehearsal via feedback from the output of the P-system into the short-term store. The theory has other structural components, but the ones mentioned are those relevant to selective attention. (Swets and Kristofferson 1970, p. 341.)

Broadbent's filter model will be further discussed during this and the following chapter.

One method of quantifically testing the effect of attention is by measuring *reaction times* (*RT*) in situations requiring motor performances at the occurrence of some specific stimuli (see Sanders 1970).

The promising and expanding research on sensory evoked brain potentials has provided quite a new system of indicators for changes in vigilance and attention in general (Näätänen 1967, 1975).

If the sequence of experimental and control stimuli is sufficiently predictable and the interval between successive stimuli long enough, it is possible that enhancement of evoked potentials to significant stimuli may reflect the effects of differential preparatory states (Näätänen 1967). Karlin (1970) suggested that reactive resolution of certain slow voltage changes, such as contingent negative variation (CNV) and other so-called "readiness" potentials in anticipation of a relevant stimulus, produce the positive enhancement in evoked potentials. He emphasized that such changes indicate a *non-specific* change in the state of the organism rather than any direct correlate for selectivity of attention.

What kind of stimulus features are "significant", "impressive" or "salient" to the human species? There have been numerous studies during several decades (e.g. Bühler 1930, Kaila 1932, Fantz 1963; a good survey in Bühler 1962) showing the importance of *human face expressions* to babies about six months old. Since the studies by Lorenz it has even been claimed that spontaneous reactions to faces belong among the few "instinctive patterns" so far known to exist in man.

It is known from the experiments of Sackett (1966) that rhesus babies, when raised separately from their species, were able to discriminate between aggressive and non-aggressive expressions in portraits of older rhesus monkeys.

Wilcox and Clayton (1968), using motion pictures, investigated infant visual fixation periods of human faces. The subjects, five months in age, looked at two movies successively showing smiling, grimacing and neutral female faces (moving as well as stationary pictures). A white light source served as the control stimulus. All fixations for face pictures were consistently longer than those for the control stimulus. The moving faces were fixated for a longer time than the stationary faces. No sufficient evidence could be gathered in favour of the statement that moving *faces* were especially attention evoking.

As to the effect of salient features in evoking attention, Lindahl (1968) found that when her subjects were confronted with classification problems which could be solved either by conceptual reasoning or by immediate perceptual learning, they inclined more toward the perceptually loaded situation the more salient the attributes available. When it was rewarding to base responses on easily distinguishable traits of the stimulus display the subjects did so. When that was not rewarding, subjects switched to responses that were logically determined.

The experimental display designed by Lindahl consisted of two parallel inclining chutes, the slopes of which extended forward in the sagittal plane toward a goal line in front of the subject (Fig. 20.11). The degree of inclination could be varied and was indicated to the subject by two ribbons located beside the respective chutes. Balls could be rolled down along the chutes. The subjects were to learn which of the two balls would come first to the goal line. A deductive solution of the task was available as soon as the subject worked out the general principle that the ball with a larger slope/distance ratio should win. An inductive solution would mean memorizing presented instances and generalizing them until the solution could be found.

With understandable verbal stimuli we can refer to a familiar phenomenon, elucidating the perceptual differences caused by attended and unattended messages. In a situation known as the "cocktail-party-phenomenon" everybody engaged in a particular conversation is generally unable to follow other conversations, which represent so-called irrelevant stimuli to the speakers. However, if one's name is mentioned in one of these conversations, one's attention usually shifts in the direction of this single stimulus. A vast amount of experiments demonstrating this effect have been reported in connection with the shadowing technique of investigating selective attention (see Cherry 1961). Two streams of speech are presented

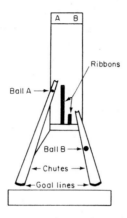

Fig. 20.11 Experimental setup in Lindahl's experiment. (From Lindahl, 1968 p. 209.)

simultaneously, one to each ear. The listener is asked to follow one of the messages (the shadowed message) while rejecting the other one. In Moray's experiment (1959) the subjects noticed brief instructions given to the "rejected ear" more often if the subject's own name preceded the instructions. This effect of one's own name was confirmed also in more recent studies by Oswald et al. (1960) and to some extent by Broadbent and Gregory (1964).

Broadbents filter model has been criticized from several points of view and does not account for all experimental findings. Several other theories have been advanced. It has been suggested by some investigators (e.g. Deutsch and Deutsch 1963) that all stimuli are at first processed perceptually (short-term storage). Selection is said to take place only in connection with the perceiver's responses to the stimuli. Rather than assuming a filter mechanism for incoming stimuli one should conceive of some kind of generating response as a determinant of selective attention. Figure 20.12 gives two parallel schemes, one for the filter model and one for the response model of selective attention. The reader might wish to find out at which points the two models disagree with each other.

Two models of attention seem to be best equipped to deal with prevalent findings (see Murch 1973, p. 316). Broadbent's model has been developed further by Treisman (1968; see also Swets and Kristofferson 1970, p. 347). Unattended elements of a stimulus should also be taken into account. Treisman's model assumes *perceptual analyzers* to be at work on several levels of the sensory input. Analyzers for shapes, forms and colours are supposed to conduct visual inputs, whereas analyzers of intensity, frequency and phase transmit auditory input. The more different the attributes of

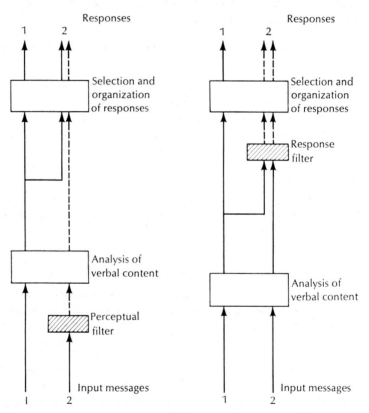

Fig. 20.12 Two parallel models of selective attention. *Left*, perceptual filter model. Prior to an analysis of their verbal content, messages 1 and 2 are differentiated by means of a filter tuned to specific physical characteristics of the message. *Right*, response model. Messages are differentiated after the analysis of verbal content but before responses to them have been organized. In both models dotted lines represent unattended messages, solid lines represent attended messages. (From Murch, 1973 Fig. 8.7 p. 314.)

information entering two separate channels, the easier it is to maintain a strict attention for only one, when the other channel is also occupied (Murch 1973, p. 316).

The other model is developed by Norman (1968). The attention process is here presented in three phases. In the first phase all incoming stimuli are registered and the first level of processing (+ selection) is initiated. The second phase passes these sensory inputs to a short-term storage area. The third phase consists of input-storage within a more permanent (memory) area. The intercorrelation of these phases brings about a response and a final selection of relevant interpretations.

Norman argues that the initial processing in the system depends on the physical characteristics of the signal:

(1) the signal is translated from physical form to physiological representation,
(2) salient features of the signal are selected and forwarded,
(3) the input is directed to the appropriate storage area.

Selective attention as well as selective set provide convincing evidence in favour of the statement that the sensory system receives a much larger amount of stimuli than that perceived and accounted for by the organism. Far from being bound to a detailed correspondence between stimulus and percept, what is focussed upon by the organism in terms of reactions to changes in the environment evidently shows symptoms of some kind of monitoring of the prevalent array of messages. Among the array of ambient potential stimuli the observer can attend only to a few at any given moment.

Evidence Indicating the Role of Motivational Factors

According to Allport (1955), there are six different types of evidence indicating that the individual's personality and motivational factors play a decisive role in shaping his perception:

1. *The needs of the organism seem to affect what is perceived and what is not, and even to lead to completion phenomena in cases of otherwise veridical perception.* This was shown, for example, by Levine and his colleagues (1942), who presented ambiguous figures tachistoscopically to hungry and non-hungry subjects. Those who were hungry perceived the pictures as food objects significantly more often than those who were not. Discrimination learning by dogs has been shown to be most effective when the animals are hungry and expect food; the recognition thresholds are improved for stimuli representing food.
2. *Perception is affected by rewards and punishments.* A perceptual

function which is a condition for satisfaction of a need is more easily triggered; there is a change in recognition thresholds for stimuli which are associated with reward or with punishment.

3. *The recognition of objects from among a large number of stimulus objects depends on their subjective value or valence.* One of Goldstein's sorting tests included, among various tools and other objects, a ripe red apple. This apple was usually recalled first (see also Bruner and McGinnies, 1948).

4. *Bruner and Goodman* (1947)—as mentioned above (p. 532) have been able to show *that the phenomenal size and brightness of visual objects may be determined by subjective values.* Coins may be perceived as larger or smaller, depending on the financial situation of the subject. Negative results, however, have also been obtained, e.g. by Saugstad and Schioldborg (1966) and by Ertel (1963). These differences may be due to different instructions and to reduced experimental conditions (see p. 358). Both Saugstad and Ertel emphasized the part played by the sensory perceptual processes rather than by motivational factors as the explanation for the findings reported.

5. *The way in which our perception is directed and completed depends on personality factors.* A schoolboy sitting in a train sees the young girl sitting opposite as a middle-aged lady, while a young executive notices her sex-appeal, and the shopkeeper's wife sees only her clothes.

6. Freud showed that our *perception is dependent to a great extent on the dynamic processes of our unconscious: suppression, sublimation, rationalization, inhibition* and *regression.* This was recently emphasized by Klein (1951).

If these factors are summed up under the term "set", then the following division can be proposed:

(a) These factors become apparent when we approach perception as an interaction between a number of independent variables.

(b) These factors become apparent when perception is approached in terms of systematic differences between individuals. This approach can be considered as an analysis of perception from the point of view of differential psychology.

21 | Perception and Personality

Theoretical Approaches to the Relationships of Perception and Personality

What we should understand by the term "normality" has in the clinical field been a source of controversy and argumentation. The discussion has been especially accentuated and augmented in terms of the psychoanalytic theory developed by Freud. According to him a person should be regarded healthy if he is able to *love* and to *work*. Among Maslow's criteria of normality the perception of realities plays a predominant role. It has been customary to make a distinction between what is called a *nomothetic* and an *idiographic* description of personality.[1] In some recent studies these two approaches have been too sharply separated. When looking for definitions of mental health, we should not forget that the idiographic as well as the nomothetic approach are needed. This is especially true if we want to do justice to the study of individuals: each person admittedly is a *unique* individual. In all study of the psychology of perception and personality, the idiographic explanation deserves consideration for the very reason that we rely on scientific knowledge as the best way to an understanding, a prediction and a control of phenomena—above a level achieved by way of unaided common sense (Allport 1951). If in matters of mental life we resort to what mere nomothetic probabilities have to tell us we hardly reach the same level of understanding, prediction and control as when looking for the special uniqueness of a single organism.

1. Allport (1951, p. 53) defined this opposition by stating that the nomothetic approach "classifies the experience and contemplates the general principles that emerge", whereas the idiographic is "concerned with the individual happening or single event confronting it".

Mental illness is often reflected in a severe loss of *meaning* in customary life situations. To find meaning is related to perception in our sensorial achievement. This assumption has been confirmed by Wertheimer's (1961) explicit statement that a quality of "requiredness" is inherent in the perceptual situation and even that "the demands and requirements of the situation are objective qualities".

As concerns personality as well as acts of perception we find an all-embracing *isomorphism*, an ultimate unity of rhythms and symmetries, the quantitative laws of our life, of cells and electrical particles.

The finding that individuals are selectively sensitive in their reactions to various types of environmental stimuli has been accounted for by postulation of an interaction existing between perceptual and personality variables (Bruner 1951, Bruner and Postman 1948, Frenkel-Brunswik 1951).

As mentioned above (p. 545) a number of experiments have shown how the past experiences as well as current motives tend to influence the perception of man (Postman *et al.* 1948, Eriksen 1951).

When tachistoscopically presented stimuli are recognized by the subjects, the reaction time of their verbal answers might serve as a measure of the act of *selective perception*. This method of research is rewarding from the psychoanalytic point of view. The projective defence system and frontal attack on perceived threats by the paranoid is directly related to his underlying concern with perverse sexual impulses, primarily bi- or homo-sexual. There is presumably a greater awareness of and sensitivity toward such sexually-connotative stimuli.

Gibson (1966) has strongly stressed the necessity of replacing the sensation-centred approach by a new, information oriented approach. However, the informational components of a perceptual act apparently first have to be linked up with the motivational factors of the perceiving situation in order to be effectively transferred from familiar to new and unusual situations.

Perception may also be used for the gratification of instinctual wishes in scoptophilic activity. In abnormal cases it can lead to *hysterical* disturbances of vision. The degree of perceptual distortion is more severe in dreams and in psychotic sensations, and it shows up as *hallucinations*—perceptual outcomes lacking all counterparts in the actual stimulus patterns. This kind of perceptual function might be utilized both by the id and the superego dynamics of personality.

We know from the findings of sensorial physiology that the *thresholds* of interoceptors in the body cavities are rather high, at least for warmth, coldness and pressure sensed in the "interior" of the organism. The affective states have a good deal of similarity with the interoceptor-sensitivity. They are "massive" rather than "precise". At every moment a good deal of "the inner sensory world" varies through a range falling clearly below the thresholds of recognition, identification and designation of the very state of experience. We probably have a great deal of massive, *sub-threshold* excitation going on within our organism all the time. Relatively little of it takes conscious form.

The sensorial contents provide the raw material for the concluding perceptual experience. As soon as *meaning* is involved in sensation, it is perception instead of sensation proper. In general, perception as a term is reserved for processes that include cortical activity. There are investigators who claim that all sensory experiences are perceptual in nature, whereas others stress the *cognitive* aspects of perception. The last-mentioned almost tend to identify what they call perception with other related phenomena such as learning and thinking. Recognition or becoming aware of an external world is generally regarded as the foremost criterion of what is understood by perception. Lively arguments are still going on concerning the role of innate versus learned factors in perception. Many investigators have devoted most of their attention and energy to problems of *exteroceptive* stimulation. We have much less information concerning stimulation of *interoceptors* inside the organism. Furthermore, Dennis (1951) suggests that perceptual events are modifiable as a result of *cultural* experience, at least indirectly.

Gestalt theory represents a view-point opposite to associationist and empiricist views of perception.

Allport has summarized the main principles of Gestalt thinking as follows:

1. Perceptual experience has a Gestalt quality parallel to the Gestalt configurations within the central nervous system, pre-eminently in the brain, i.e. the configurational qualities of brain processes are isomorphic to those of the perceptual experience which accompany them.
2. The "whole-quality" of the perceptual experience is holistic in nature.
3. Field forces are essential to Gestalt formation.
4. The pattern of stimuli received by the organism from external stimulation does not bear a one-to-one relationship to the perceptual experiences of the organism. Transformations and transpositions may take place which follow certain "laws".
5. The configurations which are perceived, as well as underlying brain processes, tend to follow the general principle of "good form".
6. The organism tends to organize the field and the configuration into combinations, i.e. to give it "structure" according to the known Gestalt laws (Allport 1955, Zubin *et al.* 1965). Thus, wholes are governed by internal rather than external factors (Law of Autonomy).

The information approach of Shannon and Weaver has contributed considerably to our knowledge concerning the Gestalt processes. This theory has shown, for example, that the concept of form is by no means simple and unanalyzable. Gestalt theory has been fruitful but not sufficient in explaining the multiplicity of perception. Many functional constructs of Gestalt psychology, such as those of Köhler and Koffka, are essentially *phenomenological* in nature. Empirical determinants of perception relate to modifications, not origins, of perceptual responses (Wolman 1973).

Lewin's *topological* field theory is concerned only with phenomenological data. Perception plays an important role in this topology, but it is not in essence a theory of perception. However, Lewin has inspired a number of other psychologists to recognize the importance of considering the phenomenological sphere of the human being himself and his way of perceiving things and not only the physical world.

Werner and Wapner (1949) suppose that perception involves the *interaction* between sensory and motor processes. Their theory, known as the *sensory-tonic-field* theory of perception, was touched upon and discussed in a previous chapter (see chapter 12 pp. 332–337). The sensory-tonic-field theory has much in common with the Gestalt theory, but it enlarges the sphere of Gestalt, or the concept of interaction. In order to account for what is perceived in the realm of a single modality, other modalities and cognitive-emotional systems must also be included in the explanation (Werner and Wapner 1952, Wolman 1973).

According to the *probabilistic functionalism* represented by Brunswik, psychology has to focus its description on what the organisms have focused on. The concern of psychology should be the organism's "distal focusing" in its achievement in the environment. Brunswik claims that the organism and the environment are both systems, each with properties of its own. Perception is subsumed in cognition, but it is a more intuitive kind of cognitive process, and it mediates, between the organism and its environment. "Cues" are utilized probabilistically, according to their ultimate validity, expressed as probabilities rather than as certainties. The strategy of the organism is to weight and combine cues so as to derive the likeliest perceptual inference about the distal object. In Brunswik's approach utilization is indexed by determining the *ecological* validities of different cues and ascertaining the organism's weighting of the "cues". Ecological validity is a statistical concept based on the principle of contingency or correlation and requiring the gathering of a representative array of information (Brunswik 1956, Vernon 1970b, Wolman 1973).

Bruner and Postman postulated that the outcomes of perceptual processes are influenced by *needs, motives, predispositions* and *learning effects* of the perceiving individual. Their theory is characterized as *functional*, yet their contribution is best known as *New Look*, a slogan introduced in the 1940's and representing a row of explanatory goals pointed out by some cognition-oriented theorists (Bruner and Postman 1947).

The New Look originally tended to revolutionize the perceptual theory by stressing the role of the perceiver and his personality in the perceptual act. In the days of Weber and Fechner any psychologist who allowed the subject's needs, values, attitudes, or similar *O*-variables to affect their experimental results, would have been considered a poor experimentalist. Nowadays, experiments on the effect of such variables are in the forefront of research in the field of perception. This approach has been called the *directive-state theory* on the ground that it assumes the direction of perceptual experience to be influenced by the said type of *O*-factors or, in the language of psychophysics, by *intervening* variables. As a contribution by Bruner and Postman, the New Look principles of accentuation, fixation vigilance, defence and selectivity should be added to the Gestalt law familiar from previous research.

The *accentuation* effect refers to the effect of value, in the first place to the perceived size of an object. In order to demonstrate the process of selectivity—the "differential tuning" given to perceptual objects by their perceiver—Postman *et al.* (1948) reported an experiment which threw light upon the speed of recognition of different words, presented tachistoscopically. In their discussion of the results, the workers spoke of values as *sensitizers* which could lower or raise perceptual thresholds. This effect was regarded as *perceptual defence*. Recent years have seen a number of works on *affective* or *motivational* factors influencing our perception of objects, pictures and words. People tend to *recognize* more readily those words that refer to their values than those that do not, and to set up defences against stimuli that arouse unpleasant associations. Indeed these phenomena have turned out to be more complex than was originally supposed, and their explanation more controversial (Brown 1961). It is probable that *attitudes* and *values* arouse our *expectations* and sensitize us toward the stimulation by certain cues or make us repress other cues and stimuli.

Klein and his colleagues point out that insufficient attention has been devoted to the *perceiver* in perceptual theory (Klein 1951, Vernon 1970b). According to Klein, perceiving is *adaptive*. The adaptive process reveals the *Anschauung* of the individual—his solution, which reflects his ego control system (Zubin *et al.* 1965).

Klein and Schlesinger (1951) originally termed an additional type of cognitive control "form-bound" v. "form-labile", later termed "tolerance of perceptual ambiguity". The more tolerant show more free imagination in their responses to the Rorschach test; the less tolerant give concrete and constricted responses (Vernon 1970b). Various personality features have been hypothesized which relate to the dimension of cognitive control (see pp. 560–566).

It seems obvious that Klein and his co-workers are more interested in tracing relationships between overt test behaviour (e.g. form ambiguity) and the unconscious personality structures postulated in the Freudian theory. The ego-defences particularly have turned out to be interesting. Klein is less concerned with conscious and explicit motivational trends and he is therefore more clinical in his approach than most other perceptionists.

Dynamic Inner Determinants in Perception

Perceptual Styles

Work on cognitive style can, in many respects, be viewed as the culmination of the effort to bring research on personality and that on perception into a fruitful integration and interaction. The concept of *field dependence-independence* is known from the works of Witkin and his colleagues. They have established that there are characteristic analytic or global perceptual styles which distinguish individuals (Witkin *et al.* 1967). Relationships between perceptual field dependence-independence and patterns of intellectual functioning have also been shown to exist within some specific areas (Goodenough and Karp 1961).

Cohen *et al.* (1963) found that field-dependent individuals, when confronted with threatening situations, were more likely to show maladjusted physiological changes than subjects who were field-independent. Stuart and Bronzaft have examined the relationships between perceptual style, test anxiety and test structure (Stuart and Bronzaft 1970).

Examinations of the differences in perceptual styles have been far too much neglected. Some reference has been made to intolerance of ambiguity. Frenkel-Brunswik (1949) claims that this is a "perceptual and personality" variable: that persons who show rigidity and insistence on definite categories in their perception and thinking tend correspondingly to show authoritarian prejudice and ethnic intolerance, frequently due to insecurity in their own personality make-up. There are also individual differences in ways of viewing personalities. Some are satisfied with describing persons in terms of relatively superficial traits and interests, others look for deeper motivations, perhaps because they have a strong, neurotically based need to make analyses of people. There are variations also in the treatment of cues, some obtaining a more synthetic or global impression, others inferring particular traits from particular impressions or behaviour.

Noteworthy in this connection are also Jung's four types of mental function: thinking, feeling, sensation and intuition, though there is hardly any experimental proof of their operating as consistent styles. The *sensation* type, for example, would perceive literally in terms of concrete actions, and the *intuitive* person tries to perceive the essential nature of other people by way of non-analytic processes. Jung claims that when one type of function is strongly developed in a person, any other type is repressed. Thus it would be possible to predict marked discrepancies in the way different persons perceive a mutual acquaintance, as well as to demonstrate differences among psychologists who interpret personality from different theoretical points of view (Goodstein and Lanyon 1971).

Recent workers on perceptual and other cognitive styles have continually been interested in the effects of motivational and defensive processes on perception, such as the role of conscious and unconscious factors in perception. Several research results indicate that extremely defensive or psychopathological symptoms are associated with a steady and rigid reliance on a certain perceptual-cognitive strategy (Israel 1966, Wolman 1973). Israel suggests that ". . . extreme levelling may exemplify a form of *perceptual defence* involving the dampening of attentional and arousal mechanisms . . .". Levelling refers to "maximal assimilation effects, and memory organizations in which the fine shades of distinctions among individual elements are lost" (Gardner *et al.* 1959).

Influences of Sets in Motivation

We know that the sets have attentional and selective effects on perceptual processes, so that the organism is already "tuned" to react before it actually reacts. Sets can be introduced, for example, through needs and motivation.

Freeman (1948) outlines many of the principles governing set and their applicability to perception. His theory implies that motor adjustments play an important role in perception, especially as regards meaning. Muscular reactions are involved in all perceptual reactions. Motor adjustments, including specific muscular tensions, thus contribute to the final perceptual integration.

The similarity between Freeman's theory and the sensory-tonic-field theory (see pp. 332–337) is obvious.

Another noted theory of set is the *hypothesis* or *expectancy* theory of Bruner. According to him perceiving is always based on an expectancy or "hypothesis" on the part of the individual, who is "tuned" to take into account certain qualities of his environment. In this conviction Bruner comes close to the concept of set. Perception involves a process of inference, as it were, or what he calls categorization based on cues notifying the identity of things in our surroundings (Bruner 1957, Zubin *et al.* 1965). In general, frequency of past experience is equated with familiarity, on the argument that the more familiar with an object we are, the easier we recognize it.

Psychologists have carried out several investigations in order to indicate the effects of *intensity* and *direction* of *attention* on perception. Many experiments show that in certain situations the observer may perceive some aspects of his environment though he is not aware of the perceptual process going on. This phenomenon is called *subliminal perception* (Eriksen 1962, Vernon 1970b, Wolman 1973). During longwinded or prolonged experiment or work, attention might decline and perception in general might become inaccurate and diffuse; this is declared to be due to a loss of vigilance (Buckner and McGrath 1963).

At all events, Heron (1957) offers one explanation that is based on the conception that normal functioning of the brain depends on a continuing *arousal* reaction produced in the *reticular formation*, which in turn depends on constantly varying sensory stimulation. If this variability of sensory input is reduced, for example, in prolonged darkness and silence or diffuse light and noise, the sensory stimuli lose their power and effect on arousal (chapter 20 p. 536). Then the activity of the brain may be impaired and the psychological processes are disturbed. Certain neurophysiological facts support this point of view.

Some results by Davis *et al.* (1961) complete this explanation. They found that "what the brain needs for normal functioning is not quantity or change in sensation per se, but a continuous *meaningful* contact with the outside world". It would seem that what is required for normal functioning of the brain is ongoing and constantly varying meaningful stimulation. When meaning is lacking or reduced for long periods, psychological disturbances will appear.

An increased amount of research has in recent years been devoted to the problem of *attention*, which has been summarized in Broadbent's (1958) work. Broadbent's *filter theory* has been described and evaluated in a previous chapter (see p. 541).

Lindsley (1957) and Samuels (1959) stress that the *ascending reticular activating system* (ARAS) and the related *diffuse thalamocortical projection system* (DTPS) may form a basis or energy source for attention and motivation.

The evoked potential (see p. 541) represents a composite of the many individual neuron action potentials. When a new stimulus is presented, an evoked potential can be recorded from the cortical projection area of its sensory modality.

In a series of studies, summarized in Hernández-Peón (1964), it was observed that evoked potentials elicited by stimuli in one modality are reduced or blocked when the animal's attention is distracted by a stimulus accounted for by some other sense modality. Thus, the click-evoked potential, recorded from the cochlea nucleus in the brain of the cat becomes smaller when the cat gets a sniff of sardines or sees a mouse. This is probably due to the fact that the cat's ears change their positions as the animal orients its body toward the more interesting stimulus (Kaufman 1974, p. 534). This influence of attention is seen in all sensory modalities (Hernández-Peón *et al.* 1956, Brust-Carmona and Hernández-Peón 1959).

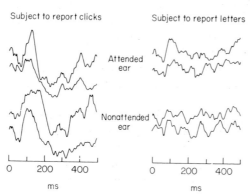

Fig. 21.1 Average brain potentials evoked by sound stimuli from a human scalp under various conditions of attention. (From Harlow, McGaugh, Thompson, 1971 p. 246.)

Using scalp recording and averaging techniques, Garcia-Austt *et al.* (1964) and Spong *et al.* (1965) confirm that the amplitude of the cortical evoked response varies with the extent to which the subject's attention is focused upon the stimulus.

Several writers maintain that all sensory messages are perceptually analyzed at the highest neural level; some researchers, on the other hand, claim that their results demonstrate a neural blockage of "rejected" messages at the lower levels of the primary sensory pathways (Hernández-Peón, *et al.* 1956, Hugelin, *et al.* 1960).

According to Näätänen (1975), there are two major procedural problems generally not satisfactorily solved in these studies.

1. The inability, reliably, to separate from each other the *specific* and *non-specific* physiological changes concomitant with selective attention.

2. Inadequacy of peripheral sensory control possibly inducing contaminating changes already at the level of the proximal stimulus.

The first influential factor originates from, and the importance of the second problem is emphasized by, the temporal stimulus structure of experimental tasks in those studies which allow the subject to predict above the change level the relevant events and, thus, differentially to prepare himself for these in advance (increased non-specific arousal and selective peripheral sensory orientation—the latter often made possible by insufficient control—have probably been among these changes).

The difficulties and inherent limitations of inferring brain events from scalp-recorded evoked-potential data, especially with respect to the important selective-filtering hypothesis, seem to be overwhelming (Horn 1965, Worden 1966).

In general, the processing of sensory information, as reflected in the evoked potential, seems to vary as a function of arousal or attention. Habituation decreases the amplitude of evoked potentials. This change of cortical evoked responses seems to be a reliable finding whilst habituation of peripheral evoked responses is secondary. Such an inhibition is first seen cortically but may involve also lower sensory pathways.

The Influence of Needs, Motives and Values on Perception

Numerous representative experiments indicate that *needs* and *motives* influence perception. McClelland and Atkinson (1948) found that when the time period since eating increased, food-related instrumental words (spoon, fork) became more frequent in the verbal reaction of the subjects whereas ordinary food responses (names of foods) remained unaffected. Similar results were obtained when pictures of the TAT type were used.

Carpenter *et al.* (1956) used the Sentence Completion Test (SCT). They found that *repressers* were slower than *sensitizers* in perceiving words related to sex and aggression. Forrest and Lee (1962) investigated the relation of Murray's need system to perception. Words related to overt needs were perceived more quickly and correctly than unrelated ones. McClelland and Liberman (1949) found that observers with a strong need of achievement (evaluated on the basis of TAT) perceived "achievement related" words more readily.

However, we know from both animal and human experiments that organisms do not always "perceive" in accordance with their needs. Habits or other factors, e.g. structural or stimulus factors might occasionally dominate what we suppose to be "motivated perception".

A great deal of the investigation of motivational effects on perception centres around the topics of *perceptual sensitization, perceptual defence,* and *subception* (related to subliminal perception). The tachistoscope is still one of the main instruments for studying motivational effects on perception, especially when it is a question of examining the effects of need upon thresholds for perceptual recognition (see p. 533).

Postman *et al.* (1948) carried out an experiment which explored the relationship between personal values and the speed of recognition of pre-selected words. The personal value system was defined in terms of individual profiles based on the Allport-Vernon Study of Values. Each of the words used represented one of the six Spranger values. Recognition times and all pre-recognition responses were recorded. This information was compared to the scores of the same subjects on the Allport-Vernon Study of Values. The results indicated that subjects recognized the words representative of their own high values more quickly than other words. The authors spoke of values as "sensitizers" which are able to lower or to raise perceptual thresholds (Zubin *et al.* 1965, Wolman 1973).

McGinnies found that taboo words such as "raped", "penis", etc, were perceived more slowly by all observers than neutral words. Also GSR responses arising before the words were recognized were larger for the taboo than for neutral words. Lazarus and McCleary investigated discrimination without awareness. Their results indicate that at tachistoscopic exposure speeds too rapid for correct recognition, subjects are able to give discriminatory responses as measured by their galvanic skin responses (GSR).

The subception effect has implications not only for perceptual theory, but it may also have relevance in the fields of personality and clinical psychology. The procedure employed by Lazarus and McCleary might be regarded as one possible tool in the study of the perceptual face of different clinical conditions (Wolman 1973).

A very important theoretical approach toward the study of perception within a broader context, stems from theories predominantly concerned with *motivational dynamics*. Generally, these theories are only minimally concerned with the mechanisms which mediate between motivation and perception. Their interest is in the manner in which perception serves motivational requirements. Perceiving is regarded as regulated by the economy of personality. It operates to aid in wish-fulfillment, in the reduction of tension, in reality testing, in ego defence, etc. (Bruner and Krech 1950).

Furthermore, particularly within the clinical field, one may make predictions about the selectivity of perception based upon psychoanalytic principles and, indeed, make predictions about differential and absolute sensitivity. But Freudian theory tells us nothing about the mechanisms which bring about such perceptual changes. Yet, either directly or indirectly, the Freudian view of personality has inspired such suggestive studies as those by Murphy on perceptual autism, by McClelland on need gratification, by Klein on threshold phenomena and by other authors on a host of other topics mostly clinical in nature.

It seems obvious that under certain conditions, size accentuation is a function not of positive value as such but of degree of *personal relevance*.

The problems involved in accentuation as a function of personal relevance still need deeper investigation. The very term "personal relevance" in itself is somewhat difficult to render in operational terms.

A number of experiments indicate that perceptual recognition is the more rapid the more of the stimuli applied are familiar, probable, or congruous with prevailing needs, motives, or values. Similar phenomena can be observed at a more complex level when more "meaningful" or emotionally life-centred stimuli are used.

Emotional Selectivity and Perceptual Defences

Brown (1961) and Minard (1965) define *perceptual defence* as a systematic relationship between the emotionality of a stimulus and the ease of its recognition.

A number of experiments indicate the effect of emotionally charged stimuli upon perception. The Word Association Test experiments carried out by Jung demonstrated that a relationship exists between emotionality and the speed of verbal association. A multitude of, in particular, clinical evidence points to an explanation in terms of a blockage. It is supposed to increase the association time of "emotionally loaded" stimuli. A *defence* against anxiety-charged stimuli is presumably responsible for this pheno-menon. With an increase in the emotionality of stimuli, their recognition may cause anxiety. Therefore the reaction seems to be avoided as long as possible. Bruner and Postman (1947) found that some of their subjects revealed a perceptual defence of this nature over the broad range of "emotionality". An analysis of *"prerecognition"*, i.e. responses of the subject before he has perceived the stimulus word correctly, has thrown additional light on the problem of perceptual defence.

Erdelyi has proposed his own explanation of perceptual defence and vigilance by reinterpreting them in an information-processing framework. He notes that a major premise of the information-processing approach is that the input is sequentially subject to different types of transformations and storages. It would only be natural, therefore, to assume that different selective processes might be operative at different stages of processing (Haber and Herschenson 1973, p. 265).

A second perceptual process is that of *sensitization*. It represents the obverse of perceptual defence—a lowering of thresholds for stimuli with great personal relevance. To this sphere of dynamically motivated perceiving belongs the famous cocktail-party-phenomenon, touched upon in other parts of this presentation (see chapter 20 p. 543). Bruner and Postman observed sensitization especially in situations with dangerous stimulus contents.

In connection with emotionally loaded stimuli, consequently, the two phenomena, perceptual defence and perceptual sensitization, may both be supposed to occur.

McGinnies (1949) found that his subjects, who were college students, reacted with significantly stronger galvanic skin responses during the pre-recognition presentation of the critical, socially taboo words, such as "raped", "whore" and "bitch", than they did before recognition of ordinary neutral words. Furthermore, the subjects displayed significantly higher thresholds of recognition for the critical than for the neutral words. An apparent resistance against the recognition and the utterance of these critical, emotionally charged stimuli, was observed.

McGinnies' result indicates a significant relationship between GSR and word meaning during the prerecognition period. Evidently symbols provided with unconventionally sexual or otherwise socially hazardous, unethically extreme and inconvenient connotations, may evoke fear and anxiety in the perceiver, reflected in these especially conditioned "emotional responses".

Longenecker (1962) found that performance could either be impaired or facilitated according to the degree of anxiety experienced. A light degree of anxiety may facilitate performance, such as perceiving, learning, or motor skills. Under stress auditory perceiving may become more accurate whilst visual perceiving is less accurate.

Several experiments have shown that the simple moods of pleasure and unpleasure may have some effect on perception. Newbigging (1961) indicated that the recognition time was shorter for pleasant words.

Dixon and Haider (1961) found that the word "cancer" produced an effect similar to that of the taboo words. It was concluded that certain words possess inhibitory incentives which might affect the reticular formation, the whole procedure going on below the level of awareness of the perceiver.

Kissin et al. (1957) received a correlation of +0·64 between constrictedness of personality (as assessed from the Rorschach test) and the delay in recognition of taboo words.

Kempler and Wiener (1963) have constructed the *perceptual avoidance theory* in order to describe the view of Allport (1955) and Eriksen (1964), and Osgood et al. (1957). This theory, which assumes the perceptual defence to be a result of learned avoidance of certain perceptual responses, is to some extent similar to the reinforcement explanations of what happens in perceptual defence (Brown 1961, Vernon 1970b, Wolman 1973).

Cable (1969) evaluated the exposure time for neutral words presented after taboo words, nonsense words, and other neutral words, in order to test whether increased recognition thresholds could be found for neutral words following taboo words and for those following nonsense words.

The results indicated significantly higher recognition thresholds for the nonsense-neutral situation. No difference was found between taboo-neutral and neutral-neutral. Also, no differences were found on the basis of the order of presentation or of the response words used. This, according to the author, allows for a re-evaluation of perceptual defence in terms of set.

In some investigations concerning emotional selectivity and perceptual defence, the control has perhaps not been sufficiently valid; for example, the critical words used have appeared less frequently in literature and in conventional speech than in many of the experiments carried out. However, the findings are stimulating. If perceptual defences become clearly established, a very valuable technique will be available for exploring the dynamics of perception.

Effects of Personality Type and Personality Traits on Perception

In his "Körperbau und Charakter" Kretschmer stresses the opposition of the synthetic and the analytic perceptual approach, the cyclothyme type being more synthetic, whereas the schizothyme is supposed to be more analytic. Rorschach again emphasizes the whole versus detail perceiving type in the evaluation of the answers in his test. A corresponding polarity is found in the colour-dominance versus form-dominance in the Rorschach responses. Jaensch postulated a "unity of style" within the frame of each person so that a few simple perception tests would suffice to carry out a universal diagnosis. The spatial perceptions of his synesthetic or S-type are unstable, loosened up, even dissolved. As a contrast to the S-type Jaensch describes the "integrated" or I-type whose basic characteristics are firmness, consistency, and regularity. He claims that these same tendencies become apparent in the perception, imagination and thinking of these two opposite types.

Further developments of psychoanalytic theory formation have been connected with a marked emphasis of personality-centred approaches as opposed to perception-centred explanations. An example can be found in Fenichel's discussion of the *compulsive* character. He deals with the need of being systematic and perfect. This quality often appears as a tendency to "type" and to classify things into categories, which is seen as protection against fear and drive impulses. For instance, deviations from symmetry look intolerable to these persons. If we compare this depth-psychological explanation of the symmetry tendency with the one given by Gestalt psychologists, we get a further illustration of a difference between personality-centred and perception-centred approaches.

The clinically described defensive reaction of compulsive persons known as *isolation* can especially, according to Fenichel, bring about inhibition of perceiving visual "Gestalten" and thus lead to merely additive unstructured compounds of the perceptual material.

The concept of *field dependence—independence* has grown out of works by Witkin and his colleagues (Witkin *et al.* 1962, 1974). Witkin investigated the individual differences in a perceptual task called the rod-and-frame test (RFT). In this test a subject is seated in a completely dark room and is required to adjust the position of a luminous rod to the true vertical. The rod is surrounded by a luminous square frame. The experimenter can independently tilt the positions of the rod and the frame. The subject's score on this task is based on the absolute deviation of his settings from the true vertical under several conditions of body, frame, and rod tilt. Witkin claims that subjects differed considerably in their scores on the RFT.

People differ in the extent to which their perception is analytical. This dimension of individual differences has been called field-dependence— independence. This dimension is according to several studies very similar to dimensions of perceptual functioning (flexibility of closure and spatial decontextualization) identified by other investigators. It is possible that these various terms refer to the same dimension, named in different ways (Witkin *et al.* 1974 p. 58).

Witkin supposes that the basis for performance on this test is the ability to overcome an "embedding context". This ability is one which permits a subject to ignore irrelevant aspects of a situation in order to concentrate on those factors which will make the correct performance possible. Witkin has studied the relationship between scores on the RFT and two other perceptual tasks which are supposed to be measures of the ability to overcome an embedding context—the body-adjustment test (BAT) and the embedded-figure test (EFT). In the BAT the subject's task is to set his chair to the true vertical while the room remains tilted under conditions in which the room and chair are initially oriented in the same or opposite directions.

The EFT is based on a series of figures developed by Gottschaldt. A simple figure is hidden in a complex geometrical figure. The subject's task is to find the simple figure.

The combination score of these three tests is called the *perceptual index*.

Witkin uses the concept of *differentiation*, earlier used by Werner and Lewin, as a basis for his theory. He uses the perceptual index as a measure of differentiation, on the assumption that the differentiated person is able to achieve an analytic perception of his environment and to separate items from the context in which they are embedded. Using the differentiation hypothesis Witkin has considered the interrelation between the perceptual index and defensive behaviour. He assumes that individuals who are relatively undifferentiated tend to resort to primitive defences, such as repression and denial, more often than differentiated individuals. Clinical experience shows that a highly differentiated person is unlikely to use broad *repression* or primitive *denial*. According to the psychoanalytic theory repressions and denials should be used in an undifferentiated way: it seems unlikely that an individual should segregate an item from its context and then go on to repress that very item.

Witkin supposes that highly differentiated persons use more elegant defences such as *intellectualization* and *rationalization*, which involve the ability to differentiate between the elements of a situation. His research results showed a correlation of $+0.61$ between a well-organized versus diffuse defensive structure (assessed by means of projective techniques) and the perceptual index, indicating that relatively undifferentiated persons are likely to have diffuse defensive structures (Witkin *et al.* 1954).

There are also several studies which have dealt with the relationship between scores on the perceptual index and social behaviour. Witkin reports a number of studies which seem to demonstrate that individuals who score low on the perceptual index are more influenced by others and thus field-dependent. They are less able to rely on their own judgment than more differentiated individuals who score high on the index and are more field-independent. Some related studies indicate that there exists an interdependence between scores on the perceptual index and indices of field independence and self-reliance.

Field-dependent people rely on the visual framework, whereas people who rely on their own internal feelings and convictions are field-independent.

The relationship between intelligence and the perceptual index has led Zigler to argue that this index is essentially a non-verbal measure of intelligence (Zigler 1963), and in the first place a measure of spatial ability.

Minard and Mooney (1969) were able to derive a measure of the extent to which the subject's identification of words was influenced by their emotional significance for him. They found a correlation of $+0.41$ for this index with a measure of differentiation based on the tasks defining the perceptual index. This measure of the effect of emotion on perceptual recognition was, according to the results, unrelated to intelligence.

A number of research results indicate sex differences on the perceptual index, males scoring higher on this index than females. The dimension of *ego-closeness—ego-distance* (the ego-close person experiences very restricted autokinetic movement) is orthogonal to Witkin's field dependence—independence dimension (Wolman 1973, Kagan and Kagan 1970).

Schizophrenic patients who hallucinate, and particularly paranoids, tend to be field-dependent.

In general, the field-dependent are, according to Witkin, passive, low in self-esteem, and anxious about their sexual and aggressive impulses, while the field-independent are active, socially independent, able to struggle for mastery and to analyze their perceptual performances.

Already in 1944 Thurstone presented evidence of a perceptual field-independence factor, which he labelled E, as an ability "to manipulate configurations" according to an independent "set" in the observer. Cattell (1969) reports results which support the hypothesis according to which this perceptual tendency is only part of a far broader personality factor of independence.

Witkin and his colleagues have made a valuable contribution to the study concerning the role of personality factors in the individual's perceiving: the investigations of Minard and Mooney as well as those of Cattell represent a significant advance in testing a central concept in the frame of Witkin's theory.

The best-known personality types are the *introvert* and the *extrovert* ones. There does seem to exist a certain correspondence between the introvert personality and an analytic way of perceiving on the one hand, and the extrovert personality and a synthetic perceptual procedure on the other.

What we perceive cannot be explained simply in terms of the isolated aspects of physical objects. Perception involves a continual interaction between the physical properties of objects, the information we receive from our nerves, and our state of mind at the time we receive the information (Haber and Fried 1975).

The Way of Perceiving in Disorders of Personality

Numerous experiments have been carried out in order to study the effects of *anxiety* upon human perception.

Siegman (1956) found that subjects assessed by means of the Taylor Manifest Anxiety Scale as liable to avoid and suppress anxiety, did perceive taboo words more slowly than neutral words.

Greenbaum (1956) showed that high-anxious subjects more readily identified tachistoscopically presented hostile faces than did low-anxious subjects. Anxious people appear to be generally more vulnerable to stimulation, including noxious stimulation.

Howard (1956) indicated that high-anxious subjects tend to judge photographs of people as "exacting", "strict", "cruel" or "malicious".

Spence (1957) praised his subjects when they solved anagrams and shamed them when they failed. He stated that in general the words which had led to failure were subsequently more readily perceived, especially by subjects whose anxiety had been heightened as a consequence of these failures.

Zahn (1960) found that high scorers on the Taylor Manifest Anxiety

Scale (MAS) significantly overestimated the size of pictures associated with failure; low MAS scorers showed a slight tendency toward the opposite direction. No such differences were brought about by pictures connected with successes or with those merely "neutral" in their significance.

Whyman and Moos (1967) found that patients with a high level of anxiety showed greater distortions in their time perception than did the "low-anxiety" patients.

Gardner has expressed doubts about the significance of an inter-relationship between the way of perceiving and the *defence mechanisms*. In addition, Gardner and Moriarty (1968), have stressed the importance of other personality factors—those not assessed by the authors—as influencing the direction and outcome of perception.

Disorders of perception and attention during psychoses are well known. In particular, *schizophrenic* patients frequently report that the world during illness looks somewhat different to them than before. Some of the patients might report peculiar changes in their "body feelings". Parts of their bodies may seem too large or too small, objects around them either coming too close or being too far away. Others remark that the world does not look as it used to, it appears flat, probably colourless.

The most dramatic distortions of perception are called *hallucinations*. These are sensory experiences occuring in the absence of any stimulation from the environment.

Mintz and Alpert (1972) hypothesized that the reason why schizo-phrenics are apt to hallucinate is their impaired perception of reality and their predisposition for a vivid way of imagery.

Precisely this impotence of differentiation between relevant and ir-relevant information is, according to Cash et al. (1972), the trait in schizo-phrenics worthy of explanatory consideration.

Das (1958) pointed out that during *hypnosis* of the patient what can be inhibited by means of *suggestion* remains restricted to what is called perception (a coding and interpretation, as it were, of the sensorial content), whereas the physiological outcome of sensations is left unaffected. Leuba and Lucas (1945) suggested to their subjects three kind of moods—happiness, critical attitude and anxiety—during a state of deep hypnosis. They found that the perception of the pictures presented was influenced by the moods induced. Barber (1961) has observed that if carefully in-structed and motivated, subjects asked to shift their focus of concentration from an ongoing auditory stimulation, tend to react thereafter to auditory stimuli in a way reminiscent of the answers given by "hypnotically deaf" subjects.

Also, within the sphere of *organic brain damages*, perceptual disorders belong to the most prominent symptoms. Nevertheless, wide discrepancies

Fig. 21.2 Series of cat paintings showing successive stages of breakdown in a schizophrenic artist. (From Mental Health special issue 1959, **12**, **2**.)

might be found in the behaviour of two patients with the same lesion in a particular area of their brains. There is always an interaction of the pre-morbid personality with the effects of a brain injury in the observed individual.

Psychological manifestations of damages in the *temporal lobe* include numerous visual, auditory, olfactory and gustatory deviations. Penfield refers to the temporal area of the cortex as the "interpretative" or "per-ceptual" area in order to distinguish it from the motor and sensory areas, which are concerned with less complicated neural processes.

The *parietal* and *occipital* lobes are important areas of the cortex, concerned with sensory-perceptive discriminations. Dysfunction of these areas gives rise to visual, auditory, and language disorders as well as to deviations in the sensory-perceptive estimation of objects and in orientation. Distortions in the perception of body image occur frequently, as well.

However, *subcortical* lesions involving conduction pathways to the cortex may produce the same behavioural changes as the very cortical lesions themselves. This is one of the reasons why efforts at localization have so often been unproductive. Several limitations in psychological techniques add to the complexities and difficulties of diagnostic localiza-tion. Solid neuroanatomical research also becomes difficult because lesions rarely occur in areas which are formally identifiable with certain types of neuroanatomical structures.

The slow and diffuse perceiving ability of deeply *feeble-minded* people indicates what an important role intelligence plays in all perceptual behaviour. The results of Douglas *et al.* (1969) argue against the commonly held notion that perception is a unitary process. Rather, the findings suggested that failures on visual-motor tasks, at least, by mentally retarded (brain-damaged) subjects result primarily from faulty executive or integrative components in the performance situations.

Discussion

At the present time there is no answer to the question "To what extent are the laws of perception laws of perceivers?". The challenge faced by personality-oriented perceptual research is to bridge together two conven-tionally separated fields of psychology: the system that accounts for the general directive state of the organism and the one representing actual perceiving functions (Bruner and Krech 1950, Davison and Neale 1974).

Investigators concerned with the dynamic background of perception are eagerly looking for ever-increasing connections and linkages be-tween perception proper and other areas of personality. The study of per-ception is rendered important for an understanding of human behaviour because of Koffka's (1935) and Adler's (see Gilbert 1970) presuppositions. We live, according to them, in "private worlds of personal perception", which do not necessarily correspond to the "real world" of our environment. Nowadays the body of neurophysiological opinion agrees with Hebb upon his statement that one neural unit stands for a single percept (the reader may consider chapter 3, for control). The patterns of excitation must depend for their origin upon the excitation of specific cells. Yet, as described earlier (pp. 143–144) for example, in accordance with Melzack and Wall (1962), the patterns arise to some extent independent of specific cells and units. Instead these patterns become a kind of design imposed by the synaptic and dendritic micro-structure of the brain. These designs may serve as neurological correlates to what is understood by percepts.

It takes hours to learn to recognize unfamiliar patterns. Nevertheless infants—only a few weeks old—have been shown to correctly estimate the relative size of a figure when it is presented at various distances. In the problem of what is going to be recognized, learning has only a relative role. So far we must give the Gestaltists credit for what they stressed in their nativistic explanation. Inborn neural mechanisms giving rise to imagery and space organization have been shown to exist. Yet the Gestaltists were wrong in their assumption that this would make up the whole story of perception. After them, however, the pendulum (according to Pribram 1971) has swung far in the opposite direction, and there persists a real danger that a whole bevy of interesting phenomena will be neglected because of an exclusive interest in the problem of how we *learn* to recognize.

It is generally agreed upon that motivation and emotion, for example, represent a certain reciprocity between perceiving and action in general. If the variety of perceptual goals sometimes considerably exceeds the extent of actions available to the organism, the latter becomes "interested"—that is, it is motivated to extend its repertory. Whenever failures occur in this attempt, so that the activity is non-reinforced, "frustrated" or interrupted emotional reactions show up, i.e. the coping mechanisms of self-regulation and self-control come into play. Further, on the basis of previous experience, emotion is likely to occur when the probability of reinforcement from action is deemed low. Motivation and emotion, action and passion, being effective and being affective, are the polar mechanisms of man when he perceives more than he can accomplish.

There are "intervening variables" supposed to gear in between the stimulus (S) and the response (R) and modify the process of perception and bring a large element of subjective interpretation to bear on any cognitive-perceptual experience. It is customary to insert an O (for organism) between the S and R to indicate the intervening variables of attitude, set, and previous experience.

Solley and Murphy offer a detailed analysis of the perceptual processes. It lends itself readily to the task of relating cognition to personality. It is in line with the learning models suggested by Miller, and by Pribram. According to Solley and Murphy's analysis, there is in the beginning a state of ongoing expectancy, followed by attention to the new stimulus. Then comes a moment of "trial-and-check" process before the percept is finally apprehended (Gilbert 1970).

Table 21.1 The process of perceiving. (After Solley and Murphy 1960.)

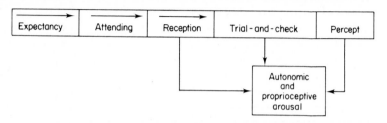

Between reception and perception, and simultaneously with the trial-and-check process, interaction occurs with autonomic and proprioceptive arousal mechanisms. This serves to screen the apprehended stimulus for its affective and sensorimotor connotations before the percept is finally structured and its meanings (with connotations) understood. It is important to note as well, that perception as the impulse to behavioural reaction is constantly subject to cognitive-affective "sets" or canalized motives, and also subject to defence mechanisms which may inhibit or distort both cognition and overt reaction. The whole process of perception and cognition undergoes continuous and cumulative modification in time, as products of learning, canalization of drives, and maturational changes interact or synthesize. These changes affect the total personality, but they are sometimes most easily tapped by their effects on perceptual individuation. Actually, perceptual cues are not merely seen or heard or tasted: they are selectively *attended* to and *interpreted* in the frame of past experience, and so sensitivities are built up from these past associations. Some of this perceptual individuation is *culturally* determined. The perceptual patterns of selective attention and interpretation influence further attitude formation These *dynamic determinants* affect the growth and maturation of the total personality. It is, therefore, not surprising to find the same personality characteristics reflected in verbalized attitudes, in expressive movements and in affective reactions to some significant stimuli. Also the interpretation of events referred to as the organization of visual material by Rorschach, reflect the accomplishment of these common personality dimensions.

22 | Perception of Pictorial Art

Not since the most remote days of antiquity has it been believed that pictorial art should strive to reproduce nature precisely. The great master of the Renaissance, Leonardo da Vinci, belittled mere reproduction of nature. He said, "Art is an inner, spiritual recreation of the presented objects." The transformation is so complete that an artistic representation creates another, new world, superimposed on the regularly perceived world. "Painting is a matter of mind." The spirit of the artist remodels nature. And the French Romantic Delacroix develops this idea further:

Nature is only a dictionary for the artists. Most important is the need for expression. The conscientiousness of most artists only manages to make their art tedious. If it were possible, such people would even paint the back of their pictures just as carefully (quoted in Grünewald 1946).

Following Katz we can briefly summarize the role of the artist. On the one hand, all artists, except for some atypical extremists, use certain technical artistic effects to produce an impression of "reality", but on the other hand, they make their real artistic contribution by a personal, and original reworking of the perceptual material. All the well-known fads, trends, and schools in art have swung back and forth between these limits, between the framework of reality and the artist's own conception of what should be presented. The reference to "outer reality", to physical nature, is almost never completely missing; our natural experience of space provides the raw material for imaginative constructions. Yet even during pictorial art's most realistic periods, as perceptual psychologists could show, a far-

T

reaching "poetic licence" prevailed. The artist does not, for example, reproduce all elements, all colours, shadings, dimensions, and forms of natural perceptual space in a mechanistic, literal manner. He selects and combines: and some of his combinations often look arbitrary. Some of Rubens' and Rembrandt's paintings convincingly show that the directions of light can be represented contrary to nature without disturbing the total unitary effect of the canvas. At the same time as a piece of art must be recognized by the onlooker, the artist can teach us to see in a new way. The stimuli can have a different angle of vision, a change in illumination or whatever, and still be familiar to us. What we can see depends on our past experiences and our future expectations. Recognition obviously demands some anchorage. This anchorage is probably the choice of a code that coincides with the way we are used to seeing things.

A painter can have a vision of his own in his piece of art. After seeing a fresh interpretation of some daily thing we can learn to see it anew. A nice example of this teaching process is the caricaturist that transforms his victim. He can single out characteristic invariants which we have never used for recognition. Thus we learn to focus our attention on these features —and we have learnt a fresh code. After that experience we cannot help thinking of the caricature whenever we meet the victim.

We could obviously claim that visual discovery in art is the thing that makes art interesting. The artist can make us discover new things by changing our interest after having taught us to see in a new way. When art is at its best, it is frequently a source of novel interest (Gombrich 1965).

Scientific investigations of art, whether pictorial or literary, proceed from immediate descriptions of content to an analysis of structure. Structure and dynamics are closely interrelated in the production of art. At any rate, compositional factors can be analyzed separately as in an analysis of the architectonics of a piece of art. Modern perceptual psychology offers useful conceptual tools for such a structural investigation. By comparison with this interest in composition, the evaluation of dynamic content factors is still scientifically in its infancy; it is reminiscent of efforts to interpret responses in a projective test of personality.

It has been said (Arnheim 1943) that elementary features of expression are perceived as directly as you see the colour and the shape of an object. You see kindliness or aggression, determination or hesitation in geometrical curves. Arnheim claims that you should proceed from the expressive qualities of the curves and shapes and show how, by representing any subject matter through such curves and shapes, the same expression is conveyed to whatever you want. He (Arnheim 1949) describes some expressive features that different shapes express. Straight lines, broken by angles, are used in combination with such expressions as excitement, hardness, powerfulness, while curves suggest such adjectives as sad, quiet, lazy, merry. Lines directing upward expressed strength, energy, force, while downward lines expressed weakness, lack of energy, relaxation, depression.

Pickford (1972, pp. 22–27) protests against the importance of experimental psychology in helping us to understand art. He admits that people in general feel beautiful such lines that show unity in direction and movement. Beautiful lines show also continuity, absence of angles and intersection, and a periodical return of the same elements or a certain symmetry. People also, according to Pickford, prefer simple lines and shapes to complex lines and shapes: but he insists that all these findings are of relatively little interest when trying to understand art.

However, Pickford regards as very interesting apparent facts such as the tendency for people to prefer circles and the feeling that curves and circles are beautiful, while angular figures may be seen as ugly (see also Lundholm 1921). Another fact which emerges is the very great influence of mental attitudes, associations and spontaneous interpretations. Pickford is also interested in the significance of movements, that is, the expressive values of different lines. On the whole he thinks it is unlikely that you could show how highly developed works of art must or could be built up and organized with the help of primary facts of aesthetic valuation in relation to elementary visual lines, figures and shapes. Although armed with a thorough knowledge of harmony, form and shape we could not create any masterpiece of art (according to Pickford), since the artistic value lies in the whole and not in the summation of the quality of its parts.

It is likely however that a structural analysis of art can help us analyse and understand art in a more thorough way. It has been shown (Arnheim 1949) that increasing knowledge leads to more differentiated interpretations. Artistic instruction can make people see in a different way by opening their eyes to what is directly perceiveable. (For example: when you have been told to look in a special way at Adam's leg in Michelangelo's famous painting "The Creation of Adam" you will notice a figure of a woman in Adam's upper leg. You have probably never seen her before, but after having this pointed out you cannot help seeing her.)

We can also analyse visual art by studying what motivates people to look at visual art. Structural analysis can probably answer this question. Beauty is possibly one thing that motivates people to look at art.

It has been thought that the perception of the "good figure" is dependent on facts to which the eye can respond (in other words, that a good form appears as a result of organization along lines of figural simplicity, balance and symmetry) without the necessity of prior training, learning or experience (Arnheim 1970).

Lindauer (1970) found that an unaided response to a shape does not spontaneously lead to an awareness of the "good figure". Even here we see the importance of structural analysis of art (see also chapter 12 p. 352). Lindauer noticed that the awareness of "good figure" is facilitated by instruction which focuses attention on the critically relevant aspects of the form. This result implies that guidance can assist aesthetic judgment.

Goude (1972b) has reported similar results. One of his results was that those subjects who had studied the history of art perceived emotional qualities to a greater extent, while the others based their estimates of similarity of pieces of pictorial art primarily upon factors concerning motif and composition.

Some Principles of Artistic Construction and Composition

Generally speaking, every closed figure has its phenomenal centre of gravity. Its location is in most cases a matter of mathematical derivation and calculation—yet what we experience as the figural centre of gravity cannot always be mathematically derived. Metzger (1954) has shown that the centre of gravity may act simultaneously as an anchoring point (*Verankerungspunkt*) and as the focal part (*leitende Stelle*) of a figural pattern.

Within a rectangle the centre of gravity is mostly determined by the crossing of the diagonals. One could also begin from the centres of the sides. If a large rectangle serves as background for a smaller circle, maximum phenomenal equilibrium requires locating the circle at the crossing of the diagonals. Next in order as location yielding phenomenal stability are the corners, while there is an area of minimal equilibrium and stability between the centre (the centre of gravity) and each of the corners. If the smaller, "nearer" figure does not coincide with the centre, it appears restless and unstable—and, as a matter of fact, that is how we are phenomenally informed of the existence of a centre of gravity (Fig. 22.1).

A tendency to maintain equilibrium can be shown to exist in all organisms. Every kind of art, whether classical or modern, takes the demand for equilbrium into account in some way or another. Pictorial art has several means for stabilizing interrelations among elements which would otherwise be too unbalanced as figural Gestalten. If a piece of art is to have a dynamic effect, however, it cannot restrict itself to representing the level of equilibrium characteristic of systems that maintain a completely static state and remain continuously at rest. Not infrequently the impressive effect of a piece of art is due to a state of continuous tension in equilibrium, like a rope stretched by equally strong men pulling at each end (Arnheim 1954, pp. 1–11). Art generally considers the tense relationships in the perceptual organization of the stimulus material; a frequently sought-after ideal is an apparently static state with strong internal tensions. This requirement becomes central, according to Josephson (1955, pp. 72–73), whenever the static representation is intended to indicate motion. The artist tries to condense imaginary successive movement phases into the static configuration of his creation. A momentary "snapshot" posture or attitude of persons pictured in paintings or sculptures produces restless dynamics in the immediate static appearance.

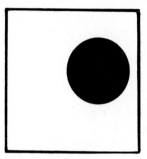

Fig. 22.1 Unstable equilibrium within a figure pattern. (From v. Fieandt, 1972 p. 400.)

A good example is the statue of Paavo Nurmi, by the sculptor Wäinö Aaltonen, in front of the Olympic Stadium in Helsinki. The bold low step of the runner simultaneously represents the backward straining movement of the foot and the powerful forward motion in the athlete's performance. A similar complex of motion has been condensed by Myron in his famous "discus thrower". Actual snapshots would probably never reveal the tremendous variety of simultaneous motor innervations and achievements which are sometimes projected into the positions of artistically represented persons.

A corresponding dynamic ambiguity is probably illustrated by the frequently discussed mysterious smile of the Mona Lisa. The figural compostion of the face presents two competing articulation possibilities, the tension between which provides an apparent yet strained equilibrium. In an artistic masterpiece one can experience the forces which are brought into equilibrium. Thus the configurations of the perceptual world contain more than just immediate sensory experiences. Classical painted landscapes reveal the phenomenal vanishing point of parallels converging in perspective. Arnheim reasonably points out that every visual pattern is actually dynamic. An analysis of the static relations in a stimulus field is not enough if we want to describe this play of mutual interactions. Perceptions of real life situations owe their "meaning" to the tensions produced by the various organizing factors (Arnheim 1954, pp. 21–22).

If the two articulatory tendencies are permitted to affect each other with opposite forces approximately equal in strength, the picture may look disturbing because of its ambiguity. We know of such artistic works, but they have not generally survived very long. What is to be pictured must be placed into an appropriate frame of reference.

Fig. 22.2 Manet: "Déjeuner sur l'herbe." (From v. Fieandt, 1972 p. 401.)

The techniques of anchoring and accentuation can be used in paintings in various ways. If a person in perspective should look closer than the rest of the group, he can be made larger than he should be at that distance, to accentuate his role in the scene (Manet, "Déjeuner sur l'herbe"). A dark region must be enlarged relative to a light one if it is to counterbalance the effect of the latter (Fig. 22.2).

In pictorial composition, equilibrium is achieved by applying the simple principle of the physical lever. Even a small object, if placed far enough from the centre, displaces the centre of gravity proportionately to the distance concerned. In some of Rembrandt's paintings, for example, in "Night Watch" and in "Christ at Emmaus", (Fig. 22.3) the phenomenal centre of gravity clearly differs from the centre of the picture as defined by the physical frame (Schöne 1954). Comparably, Cézanne often made his landscapes asymmetrical by displacing the centre of gravity—painting a conspicuously dominant tree or rock to one side of the figural centre ("Mont Ste-Victoire" and especially "Rocks, Forest of Fontainebleau", Fig. 22.4).

Fig. 22.3 Rembrandt: "Christ at Emmaus." (From v. Fieandt, 1966 p. 340.)

Isolation from the rest of the group increases the gravitational influence. If a full moon is painted in an otherwise empty sky, it gains an accentuation out of all proportion to its size.

Pasto (1964, pp. 14–15) points out that

A good piece of art originates in the space-frame experience of the artist. Man feels secure in the vertical and horizontal biological fields within which he moves. Man is two right angles, i.e., the angle of sight and the vertical axis, and the horizontal on which he prefers to stand and his vertical axis. He prefers also to experience these two right angles as the terminal point of his perceptual movement into distance.

Masterpieces of art are, according to Pasto, successful applications of these simple principles. Pasto's theory gains some evidence from the conclusions of Werner and Wapner which we considered in chapter 12. The STF postulates assume that stimulations, irrespective of modality, are always accompanied by tonus alterations. The various modalities are regarded, at least to some extent, as interchangeable. A visual stimulus, for example, can interfere with a posturally and kinesthetically determined experience of verticality and vice versa. So the artist creates his space frame and projects it about him as a medium within which he expresses himself.

The relation between composition and human expression hence is intensely tied up with the emotional-motor body image . . . Aesthetic and expressive fame has been accorded those artists who have adroitly expressed their images in the perceptual motor language inherent in this concept. (Pasto 1964, pp. 14–15.)

Fig. 22.4 Cézanne: "Mont Ste-Victoire". (From v. Fieandt, 1966 p. 341.)

There are, however, artists who originally are or have become so "visually cerebral" that they are unable to extend or transfer their vertical body image to the surface of the canvas. As a consequence, in their works "no emotional message can be conveyed, only a visual assessment of data . . . , it degenerates into a map, a diagram." Too many surfaces are turned only into decorative devices. Great artists have, according to Pasto, preserved their sensitivity to the tonic tensions in their sensory motor system. The perceiver feels an effortless pleasure in contemplating such a painting. "He walks into the painting; he stands where Rembrandt stood and gazes at the portrait" (Pasto 1964, pp. 18–22).

Pasto considers Michelangelo, Rembrandt, and Pieter Brueghel the Elder the best interpreters of form dynamics in the early modern era. Among more recent artists, he enumerates Cézanne, Seurat, and Picasso. Brueghel's "Hunters in the Snow" reveals the sensitivity of the artist to the requirements of his perceptual-motor organization (Fig. 22.5). Vertical

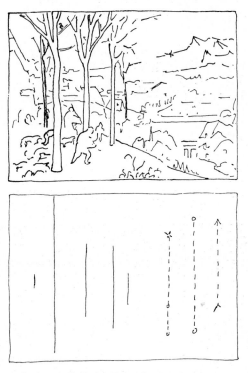

Fig. 22.5 Some vertical parallels in Brueghel's painting (according to Pasto). (From v. Fieandt, 1972 p. 405.)

parallels are quite clear. A pointed rock summit is directly above a pointed house roof, the flying bird is directly over a bush below, another cliff top is over the right-hand support of the bridge, a bird is perched above the bramble bush in the foreground. If one now examines the more obvious horizontals, it can be seen that these parallels, too, function in accord with man's predilection for the cardinal dimensions. But there are also various diagonals sloping to the right, thus completing the partly visible network of lines and making for an even more dynamic composition (Fig. 22.6). In

Fig. 22.6 Brueghel: "Hunters in the Snow". (From v. Fieandt, 1972 p. 407.)

Fig. 22.7 Seurat: "Un dimanche à la Grande-Jatte." (From v. Fieandt, 1972 p. 408.)

Seurat's famous picture "Un dimanche à la Grande-Jatte" we find a replication of Brueghel's sensory-motor construction simplified into a system of cylinders and balls. There is a persistent harmony between vertical and horizontal elements (Fig. 22.7). For the same reason, Picasso's "Still Life with Guitar" deserves consideration, although it is a rather abstract creation of art. Piet Mondrian, among purely abstract painters, can be mentioned as a skillful interpreter of motor form dynamics.

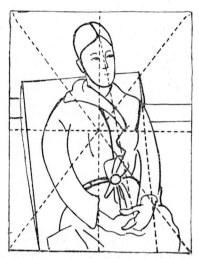

Fig. 22.8 Cézanne: Portrait of his wife (outline). (From v. Fieandt, 1972 p. 410.)

What has been generally pointed out regarding kinesthetic proprioceptive stimulation might serve as a background for investigating visual equilibrium tendencies in relation to the vertical-horzontal coordinates. However, as has been shown in chapters 11 and 12, if there is a conflict between the kinesthetically sensed cardinal dimensions and what is seen as vertical and horizontal in one's own body or in a picture, the visual organization usually, at least for some time, overrides the kinesthetic frame of reference.

Cézanne's portrait of his wife, painted in the years 1888 to 1890, can serve as an example (Fig. 22.8). The viewer is impressed by the apparently restful yet rather powerful dynamics. The tensions are achieved by skilful use of various balanced accents in the composition. The person portrayed appears to be a well-supported configuration, slightly in front of and above the chair cushion (Fig. 22.9). The figural proportions are about 5:4. An oval form surrounds the geometric centre of gravity. The background is divided into two rectangles, the higher of which is farther away. The chair inclines to the left, as does the vertical line of the woman and of the chair (Arnheim 1954, pp. 20–23).

The left-right symmetry of a picture is most interesting from the point of view of composition. Wölfflin was able to show the degree to which well-known paintings become flat and uninteresting if they are replaced by their

Fig. 22.9 Cézanne: Portrait of his wife (complete). (From v. Fieandt, 1972 p. 409.)

mirror images. A good example is provided by Raphael's "Sistine Madonna," with the emphatic figure of Sixtus in the lower left of the picture (Fig. 22.10).

Dessoir, the psychologist of art, points out that "three ways to affect visual organization are available in pictorial art, i.e., linear techniques, brightness gradients and coloration." This list is reminiscent of Katz's previously quoted remark that immediate natural perceptual space contains a rich variety of forms, dimensions, illuminations and colours from which the artist makes his choices—and some of these effects do not fit together simultaneously. The art schools of different ages have been inclined to favour now one, now another of the organizing factors mentioned by Dessoir. One can create hierarchical scales, centration and balance, by working exclusively either with lines, brightness gradients, or with colours. Some modern art critics have gone so far as to maintain that the value of a piece of art is increased if the artist has used only one of these "monistically

Fig. 22.10 Raphael: "Sistine Madonna." (From v. Fieandt, 1966 p. 348.)

conceived" articulatory devices. To avoid evaluative statements, one feels inclined to assume that for organizational reasons a monistically achieved line configuration or colour configuration may appear better differentiated and as a more clearly structured totality than a pattern combined of line, colour, and brightness articulations. It is a future task for careful experimental research to provide us with an answer to this difficult problem.

Real art, as mentioned before, does not imply a registration of all the available stimuli, but rather aims at indicating essential invariances in the sensory flux of variability, and fulfils this aim via sensitive, delicate choices of effects. To grasp essential components in reality we need not, thanks to our inner dynamics, have a painstakingly detailed stimulus pattern. On the contrary, if only hints or indications are presented as dominant in the pattern, a richer and more effective totality can emerge. All perception probably started—from the point of view of biological development—with the mere recognition of vitally significant combinations of figures. Thus a "triangle" is not a late abstracted product, but a complex quality, primordial in its generality and thus preceding later stages of more precise differentiation. Even an infant may perceive indeterminate "dogginess" before he learns to distinguish among various breeds of dogs. A ball in phenomenal space is perceived as complete; we have the impression of a spherical object that doubtless has a "back surface" even though it is turned away from us. The back of the head of a familiar person, the "invisible part of him," has for us the same degree of reality as parts of him which are immediately perceived. When we face this person the back of his neck is an integral part of the visually perceived total object (see earlier statements on amodal perception, chapter 14, p. 396). The laws of optics learnt by painters during the Renaissance rejected previous methods of illustration too sharply. Our immediate world does not generally follow a strict application of optics but appears to follow certain rules of simplicity instead. We have already considered the favouring of a single monistic technique of creation in art. Some of the great masters, when adopting and perfecting a specific method, were actually obeying the *law of simplicity*. This principle has the following implications for the artist's work: *He should not use more artistic effects in his production than he needs for achieving his goals.* Some art historians maintain that Rubens belongs among those who resorted to the simplest methods in their creative work. This means "using the most reasonable system for assuring an ingenious understanding of what is essential in the content." At a certain stage in his development, Titian abandoned the dualism of contours and surface treatment. From that point on, his lines not only serve as contours or as a device for shading, but the entire surface is treated all over in the same uniform and well-balanced manner. The same technique is used to picture brightness differences, volume, and airiness.

A mature artistic creation is characterized by a certain stylistic invariance. It looks as if sky, water, soil, trees, and humans were made of the same substance. A viewer who has, with emotion, seen the bit of nature concerned would not call such a painting a falsification, because it captures what is essential. Thus a great artist keeps creating genuinely new products by simply following his particular system of invariances when representing quite familiar things. E. Kaila wrote in the first chapter of his "Human Knowledge" (translated from the original text in Finnish):

An interesting task would be to follow the search for and realization of invariances in the aesthetic behaviour of human beings. For instance, what is an artistic style? It is a principle of uniform coherent configurations repeating itself throughout a wide variety of material. Artistically speaking, "stylistic" means something which captures an invariance. Clarity, consistency within variability, equilibrium, harmony, beauty, all this is a fulfilment of invariances.

H. Erpf (according to Grünewald 1946), enumerates three relations in the aesthetics of music, employed as devices of organization for rhythmic, dynamic, and balanced patterning. He calls these relations repetition, variation, and contrast. Repetition can really be considered a structural device in all creative art. The act of repeating assures a unifying invariance among all the various elements and components which together constitute a piece of art. On the basis of experimental findings, Eysenck tried to demonstrate that a leading principle even in pictorial art is a consistent unification of the variable elements. *Figural* style rests upon repetitive similarity of single figural elements, while the point of *compositive* style is use of a consistent device in combining elements. *Qualitative* style appears as an attempt to achieve consistent similarity among all the various elements.

The process of differentiation plays a predominant role in all artistic modelling and organization. Where a multitude of forms and figures prevails without any balance or hierarchy among the details, before long we observe nothing but sheer chaos. On the other hand, maximum consistency among the elements brings about a barren totality. Throughout various fields of artistic production we have in recent years witnessed occasional lapses into one or the other of these extremes.

The principle of repetition is most profitably combined with the idea of variation.

Contrast may well be considered an extreme form of variation. The effect of this relation is a sharpening of dualistic tensions between alternative articulation possibilities.

Three-Dimensional Pictorial Space

When we turn to techniques for representing pictorial space, we again encounter artistic expressions which are hardly comprehensible without some knowledge of the cultural and historical background of the various trends in pictorial art. The purpose of the religious art of the Middle Ages —confined as it was to illustrations in religious books and to church decorations—was to exalt the supernatural power of an almighty God.

Therefore, the message of the picture reached the viewer from far above, as though it came from another world, and the human being stood facing this transcendental being, constituting, as it were, one pole of a dualistic relation. The consumers of these artistic productions were considered recipients of a divine proclamation; the picture did not invite them to participate in the scene on an equal footing.

The change produced by the new world picture offered during the Renaissance was most profound. We know that it determined new directions in Western European artistic trends for centuries. To be sure, the Renaissance did not avoid proclamation. What it proclaimed, however, was the eternal divinity of the human being. The essence of this new philosophy was the love of life, the approval of our sensory world image, the search for aesthetic values in the human being himself. It was the mentally and physically proportionate, well-balanced human figure that was emphasized

Fig. 22.11 Superposition impressions in a plane figure. (From v. Fieandt, 1972 p. 414.)

and adored. A new type of divinity was found in the beauty of living organisms and their natural environments. Thus formalism turned into idealistic realism, and art was given the task of revealing the unsophisticated reality of the objects around us. A painting, it seemed, should appear as an immediate continuation of the real environment, as though it wished to invite the viewer to participate in the scene occurring on the canvas. The works of Tintoretto, one of the great masters of the Renaissance, convincingly show us that the picture, including the painted illumination, is presented as if it were located in the viewer's perceptual space.

When we turn to a discussion of three-dimensionality in paintings, we face the problem of depth gradients or depth articulation, an extreme case of which is the differentiation of the picture surface into figures and background. A sheer articulation into figure and ground is, however, almost a limiting case, because most groupings and still lifes are more richly varied. Thus one might perceive a figure on a background, which in turn forms a figure of its own on a wider background, etc. In those cases one appropriately speaks of a gradient of depth. If a homogeneous broad surface is broken up by contours, our perceptual organization seems to prefer super-

Fig. 22.12 Matisse: "Luxe, calme et volupté." (From v. Fieandt, 1972 p. 413.)

position to mere discontinuities in a flat, even surface. In Fig. 22.11 the white field (b) has two borders, an outer and an inner one, so that one could say that *b* has a hole through which the continuous common black background (c) is visible; another possibility would be to experience an inner black spot (a) as a figure on *b*, which in turn would appear as a figure on *c*. However, because of the homogeneity and the similar structure of the black

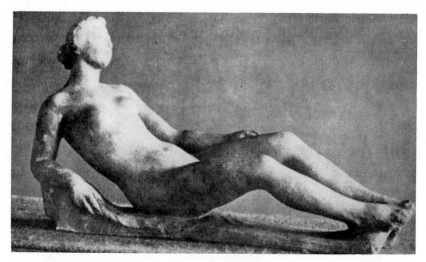

Fig. 22.13 Maillol: "Resting Woman." (From v. Fieandt, 1972 p. 416.)

Fig. 22.14 Moore: "Reclining Figure." (From v. Fieandt, 1972 p. 417.)

fields this second possibility is less popular. Superposition is always based upon the simplest possible alternative of articulation. Only rarely are there more "steps," more overlapping surfaces, than the articulating conditions make unavoidable.

As we know from chapter 11, richly differentiated, detailed, and structured parts of a field are preferentially seen as figures, and stand out from a homogeneous background. Matisse, who belonged among the artists who strove for artistic effects which reduced spatiality on the canvas, favoured ambiguity and therefore painted the background as more richly articulated and structured than his main figures. His nudes, actually the most important perceptual objects in the scene, could appear as huge light openings in a darker, detailed, and elaborated background. Several of Matisse's seashore scenes provide good examples of this kind of artistic effect ("Dance," "Lux, calme et volupté," and "Three bathing girls"—see Fig. 22.12). The nude pinkish-tan female figures and the green meadow are painted in almost complementary colours. In such a composition the unifying factor of figural cohesion and the contrasting colours act in opposite directions, a circumstance which, as we know from the famous Wertheimer-Benussi phenomenon (see inside cover of Osgood's 1953 textbook in experimental psychology), adds to the dynamics of the picture. As a consequence of the gestalt law of closure, a concave borderline gives an impression of approach, withdrawal and passivity.

Sculptures with rounded convex surfaces (Maillol's, for example) show a tendency to expand and rise, while hollow and concave ones (for example, Moore) express a submissive, passive, reclining position and attitude (Fig. 22.13 and 22.14).

Jaensch's Studies in Pictorial Space

E. R. Jaensch in 1911 published his classical experimental work "Über die Wahrnehmung des Raumes" (On the Perception of Space). Jaensch arrived at the following conclusions in his work: none of the so-called empirical depth cues, nor binocular disparity, any more than overlapping of contours or succession, motion parallax, accommodation, convergence, or distribution of shadows, provides a primary stimulus basis for stereovision (see chapter 11, pp. 289–311). They are relatively equal in importance, and act as a kind of releasing stimuli for triggering a central function. According to Jaensch, a common mental process is behind the stereo tendency, a process which is dynamically based on the mobilization of attention.

In his book Jaensch included a detailed chapter on the conditions of space impressions in Renaissance paintings. We know that a photograph, which faithfully reproduces perspective with correct object proportions, seems to distort immediate reality. Nevertheless, in the art schools of the Renaissance, artists were instructed to depict three-dimensional objects purely in terms of a "funnel" space perspective. The use of central perspective in pictures developed among Italian artists in the early days of the Renaissance. Thus Alberti recommended suspending a fine-meshed net vertically between the artist and the model posing for him. Dürer in his

Fig. 22.15 Dürer: "Visiergerät." (From v. Fieandt, 1972 p. 419.)

youth had already become acquainted with this method of preparing pictures on his first trip to Italy. Thereafter he designed his famous *Visiergerät* "Visualization Apparatus" (Fig. 22.15). During his second Italian trip Dürer began to apply "secret perspective", praising the Italians as the real masters of it. Certainly not all of Dürer's works display faultless perspective, but the creations of his mature age have, in this respect, been almost perfectly correct. Clearly, size proportions in these pictures closely

correspond to what we see in photographs. Consider the ridiculous small-
ness of remote buildings or trees in some of his works! The artist's eye was
placed in the plane of the frontal square net, where these perspective
painters of the early Renaissance projected their picture surface (Arnheim
1954, pp. 233–234).

Jaensch raises the question of how it is possible that Dürer and the other
Renaissance masters did not notice this distorting effect of an optically
perfect perspective when they were otherwise so careful and conscientious.
He finds the answer in the conjecture that they very likely noticed the
effect but did not avoid it because it provided them with a welcome device
in their efforts to stress and accentuate the voluminosity and the "life-
approving roundness" of their perceptual objects. If one takes the trouble
to look monocularly at early Renaissance pictures and puts one's eye close to
the canvas, where the artist looked at it with his single open eye, the
striking outcome is an over-emphasized vividness of all the forms in an
almost mysterious manner. In order to understand fully what the artists of
that time wanted to show in their pictures it would thus seem appropriate
to look at them as they did, that is with their observation distance and their
visual angle to the canvas. The early Renaissance masters may have conceived of their products in a sensory way different from that of our
contemporaries.

When considering the emphasis on voluminous space,—conspicuous in
the book of Jaensch—we must observe that Hering was already interested in
"intervening media". He wrote:

The empty space between us and visual objects is experienced differently in
daylight than during the night. Gathering twilight does not appear only on object
surfaces, but descends as it were into the space between viewer and objects,
finally covering all visible things and replacing them in the visual world. If I look
through a tiny hole into a black box it appears filled with darkness. It is impossible
to perceive a dark surface colour on its walls. A shadowed corner in an otherwise
bright room is filled with twilight which is not conceived of as only covering the
wall surfaces, but is experienced as being in that part of space which is contained
by the walls of the corner.

Jaensch (1911, pp. 250–265) points out that the impression of this
"medium" is a psychological event. There are no physical stimuli in the
mass of air which could provide a basis for this peculiar perception.

The experiments by Jaensch aimed at a detailed phenomenal analysis of
the space perceived in a corner. He observed that under several conditions
of illumination the "space medium" impression is not so precisely determined as Hering assumed. Whether or not a "substance" is perceived can
depend on the subject's set.

The results are in several respects relevant for the effects that can be created in pictorial art. They show convincingly, for example, that even a completely empty corner of a room, viewed from a sufficient distance, seems to be filled with a substantial space colour. If the walls of the corners are painted in saturated colours, the "medium" shows up only under quite special "space organizing" conditions (e.g. in the case where the experimenter provides some hints as to the contour formation of imaginary objects, such as strings suspended from the roof in front of the corner). The strength of the medium impression, therefore, is inversely proportional to the distinctness of the wall surfaces. Jaensch proposes that the perceptual set leading to the impression of a medium be labelled "impressionistic vision".

Additional clarification of the described regularities is yielded by Jaensch's striking experiments with glass containers. A prism formed by three vertical strings at different distances from the eye was shown to the subject in certain chromatic solutions (various dissolved anilin dyes and tints were used). The thin strings were suspended from a plywood or cardboard sheet covering the glass basin which contained the liquid. Dim horizontal light illuminated the solution. The cube-shaped container stood at the subject's eye level, and he saw only its front wall through a rectangular opening in a masking screen.

The three subjects gave quite similar results. The liquid appears as a colour which is hard to localize. The impression alternates between what Katz would call film colour and space colour appearances. When viewed through the aperture, the colour of the solution still had something "spatial" about it. The subjects were asked to describe how the part of their visual field framed by the strings looked to them.

Jaensch found these observations useful for a better understanding of the impressionistic art of the end of last century, with regard to the treatment of forms and colours on the canvas and the rendition of the spatial characteristics of the subject. As a consequence of the Renaissance programme, European pictorial art during the first centuries of the modern age was primarily concerned with objects. The goal was to reproduce objects realistically, using precise optical as well as psychological methods to obtain the desired effects. Impressionism was a pioneer movement, paving the way for later growing interest in pure illumination and in the colour characteristics of the pictured subject. An art gallery in Paris in the 1870's opened an exhibition of a new style of painting which differed radically from what was familiar in the then contemporary realism. These paintings displayed "experiences," and the new key word "impression" appeared frequently in the directory of the pictures: "My impression of a cat," "My impression of a flower vase", etc. Since then, no survey of art history can avoid reference to this word. Art historians of the turn of the century probably somewhat over-emphasized the revolutionary influence of impressionism. Muther, writing in the 1890's, went so far as to speak of "these painters' new way of perceiving". "Is this talk of a new way of perceiving to be taken literally?" Jaensch wonders. "Or is this just jargon, a transferred meaning of words actually intended to claim something about a new way of painting." (1911, pp. 244–245. Cf. our remarks on the possibility of *response sets* in chapter 20 p. 530).

The impressionists have admitted that what they aimed at in an unconventional way was the representation of chromatic airiness, of the atmosphere and the regions of air surrounding objects. The main purpose of painting should be an interpretation of this spatial airiness, even at the cost of a successful "thingness" in the picture. We must not forget that the divine, dispassionate and ethereal beauty of Giorgione's and Titian's nudes had already deteriorated in Rubens' and Courbet's nymphs and angels into a realism of protrusive voluminosity. According to the impressionists, when painting a landscape, the artist must "grasp the sentiment of a summer day's burning illumination." No doubt Courbet could depict plasticity, but he was unable to show his human figures in a light, ethereal illumination.

The experiments we cited confirmed that in certain conditions it is as possible to experience an "intervening medium" as it is to discriminate between its colour and that of the environment. A brief glance proved favourable as an economical way to obtain impressionistic experiences. This procedure allows perception of the medium and yields a maximum of chromaticity.

After the first exhibition of impressionist work an indignant critic objected: "Drawing has been completely neglected in these works. One sees a background with red spots instead of flowers. Even faces are indicated only by some hints of colour; they appear as vague splotches of chromaticity." But there were others, for example, contemporaries of Manet, who admitted: "When viewed from further away, the painting comes to life, the air flickers and glows. Nature and men are bathed in a shiny ether" (Jaensch 1911, p. 309). It is noteworthy that the subjects of impressionist painters, viewed as objects, are rather uninteresting and commonplace: a sunny street, a man harvesting, the steel bow of a bridge. If we recall Jaensch's experiments, the objects themselves, for example, within a corner, are not supposed to attract much attention. What the impressionists also try to stress in their pictures is the transient, temporary character of the depicted activity.

It must be admitted that classical artists, who prefer to reproduce a clearly differentiated, striking depth effect, fill their space with pieces of architecture, with stems of trees, and with pillared hallways in order to permit, as Pasto puts it, a promenade in depth. These objects serve the same purpose as do the strings in Jaensch's experiment, providing way stations for our wandering gaze. This solution of the problem, however, simultaneously eliminates the alternative of directly displaying a *coloured spatiality*. This is what some of the impressionists, for example, Monet, working with soft, mild, scattered contours, have so skilfully contributed.

Fig. 22.16 Monet: "Sunrise." (From v. Fieandt, 1966.)

Colours and Illumination in Pictorial Space

Schöne (1954), who studied the handling of pictorial space in Western European art after the Renaissance, has carefully enlarged on Katz's list of appearances of colours. Surface colours can be conceived of in two different ways in Western European painting; they can have, as it were, two different roles.

(1) They can represent the colours of the surfaces shown by the picture and (2) they can be surface colours in themselves, regardless of their

symbolic function, if the picture is considered nothing but a bit of canvas covered with colour. Even without the purpose of depiction, and no matter what the picture represents, a colour brushed on the canvas is a surface colour rather than a film colour. Already the picture frame and the artistic method of painting are conditions for a differentiation of the picture; they prevent the appearance of film colours in the painting. Admittedly, when a surface colour is indicated by the artist in a scene, the colour he puts there is not the original surface colour of the material on which he paints (canvas, a sheet of wood, a plastered bit of a wall, etc.). Nevertheless, it would be wrong to call them film colours; they have the characteristics of surface colours. If a red house happens to stand in the landscape of the picture, the two alternative ways of seeing that red as a surface colour presupposes changes in the set of the onlooker. When viewed through a reduction tube (screening the edges and frame of the picture) or when projected by means of a mirror projector or slide projector on the screen of a dark room, even substantial classical paintings lose their apparently concrete reality; the colours are released from their surface character and the illusion of the pictorial world feels more complete.

In addition we must not forget the considerable dynamic tension which occurs between experiencing a surface colour just as some chromatic material brushed on the canvas, and seeing it as a surface colour which has been perceptually localized precisely where it belongs in the three-dimensional pictorial space of the painting. Phenomenally, and from the point of view of the artist, there is a frontal plane somewhere in the pictorial space, either the background of a portrait, or the front of a landscape or the interior of a room. This experienced plane is the "optical plane". In this optical plane both the surface materially carrying the painting and the illusory pictorial depth become integrated. The surface colours, too, in their double function, are involved in this integrative procedure.

The distinction between "palette value" and "picture value," first made by Bühler, is interesting in this connection (Schöne 1954, p. 243). The first term has to do with the physical, technical qualities which are required by a certain place in the picture. What he called "picture value" can be observed and expressed only in terms of the impression given by the complete composition. Palette value is not identical with what Katz called "reduced colour", although these expressions are conceptually related. The technical use of palette colour is supported by what we know about the object colour constancies familiar from perceptual psychology. We must also distinguish among:

The location of the picture.
The visual field of the onlooker.

Visual space.
Pictorial space.
Pictorial depth.
The pictorial or painted illumination.
The autonomous light (e.g. luminosity) of depicted objects.
The directed pictorial radiation or light flux.

The first serious restriction met by the artist is the two-dimensionality of the canvas surface and the impossibility of using binocular disparity for creating the illusion of depth. Another difficulty is the highly restricted brightness scale of palette values compared to the enormous variations in nature (the extremes of brightness obtainable on a palette are in the ratio of 1 to 60, which must be made to represent natural extreme relations as great as 1 to 800 000).

The following hypothetical experiment was reported by v. Helmholtz in 1896. Let two pictures be suspended under equal illumination. One of them shows Arabs in white clothing on an open plain in the bright light of the burning sun. The other represents a moonlit landscape in which a ribbon of moonlight can be seen on the water behind white-stemmed birches and dark human figures among the trees. Both of the paintings can give rise to the intended experience of brightness gradients and can look entirely veridical, even though we might be quite aware that precisely the same palette value of white was used for the white vestments of the Bedouins as for the ribbon of moonlight on the water. The white which the artist can use may still, even in a strongly illuminated exposition hall, reflect only one twentieth of the intensity of real white cloth surfaces under the Arabian sun. If the painting, reflecting the amount of light it does in the exhibit hall, could be moved to the sunny plains of Arabia the white colour on it would still look deplorably dark. Real moonlight should have only at most one fifth the intensity of sunlight reflected from white fabric.

To surfaces in the moonlit landscape, if they are to be appropriately painted, the artist must give 10 000 times the brightness value they physically would have relative to what actually emanates from the moon. V. Helmholtz' hypothetical experiment reveals the restrictions within which the artist struggles, but also beautifully demonstrates the artistic effects and the freedom available: the best artists cannot be criticized either for slavish realism or for illusionism. They have always had their freedom. This expression refers not only to visual freedom, but also implies a technical and stylistic release from the strict requirements of nature. When Leonardo, in his famous book on art, maintained that painting is nobler than sculpture, he clearly had in mind the greater flexibility of the former despite its numerous restrictions: sculpture is more dependent on the immediate local position than painting; it is determined by the requirements of an appropriate environment. Brightness levels in a painting are dictated by the requirements of the composition; they are system conditioned.

Some Special Features of the Use of Colours in the Middle Ages

Colours in the stained-glass windows of Gothic cathedrals are not surface colours, but rather film colours with a touch of spatiality. Under such conditions a painting has a completely "thingless" appearance, looking like a coloured liquid or fog, or a shapeless colour substance within which events float without having any object characteristics.

The so-called Ottonic era of book illumination (in the tenth and eleventh centuries) applied surface colours in such a way as to cover the pages of the book with a layer of coloured substance. In their function of covering parts of the picture intended to represent objects, these colours are reminiscent of surface colour. Nevertheless, they typically do not have the appearance of surface colours, since no micro-structure is discriminable and our sight seems able to penetrate these decorated portions of the surface of the illuminated page. For that matter, a painting on a parchment page rarely indicated three-dimensional objects. The entire coloured area was imprecisely and vaguely localized relative to the parchment, in a manner not unlike a film colour. When used for the background of the painting, such a colour was detached and independent of any spatial framework. This disconnectedness, however, also characterized the coloured surface in its function of representing the figures. A frontal location perpendicular to the line of sights lifts the figures up from an indeterminate two-dimensional background. Notice that Rubin similarly was aware of the background having a film colour.

It was as characteristic of modern art as of the art of the Middle Ages, that the latent possibility of finishing the colours of the picture into either film or surface colours was inherent in the production. The difference between these major historical periods shows up in the dominant role given to one or the other of these appearances of colours. During the Middle Ages those colouring techniques which resulted in the following appearance were dominant: (1) the film colours should have a luminescent surface, (2) the film colours had to make an immaterial impression.

Typical was the use of gold leaf. Phenomenally, it creates an experience of lustre. Katz described lustre as follows: it ". . . appears only on an object, and . . . is apprehended as a light which does not really belong to the colour of the object." "Lustre light does not lie in the plane of the object to which it belongs, but appears rather either in front of the object or superimposed on it." Both of these localization alternatives make lustrous areas resemble film colours (Katz 1935, p. 24).

The Problem of Directed Illumination in Renaissance and Modern Art

The Renaissance, while emphasizing the voluminosity of objects and the approval of our sensory world, could not confine itself to the representation of flat surfaces which was characteristic of the religious decorations of the Middle Ages. Objects, especially human figures, should appear rounded. This could be achieved, for example, by relinquishing luminous coloured surfaces and by introducing surfaces imagined as receiving unilateral, directed illumination. The distribution of light and shadow on the intended surfaces offered a device for the spatial representation of the three-dimensionality of objects. This technique raised the problem of the assumed location of the light source in the scene on the canvas. It also led to the requirement of visible directed illumination in pictorial space. Either the light source or its effects should be clearly visible on the canvas, so artists were faced with the task of creating an "illumination within the picture". At first this made for considerable technical difficulties (Schöne 1954, pp. 107–143).

Before Caravaggio there had been a few fumbling attempts to let the light in the picture seem to come from outside the canvas. This was seriously attempted for the first time in the fifteenth century. Some of Caravaggio's paintings reveal this technical effort, although he must not be regarded as a Renaissance artist. His treatment of light and shadows does not always correspond appropriately to what one would expect, considering the point from where he let the clearly directed light beam sweep over his figures. (see Fig. 22.17).

Since the time of the early Renaissance it has been customary to paint shiny, bent surfaces, especially armour, which allow for a complex play of light and shadow. This traditional period produced many inconsistent pictures of human figures. The torso might appear flat, in accord with the ideal of the religious art of the Middle Ages, while some of the limbs already clearly show a tendency toward "material" spatiality (Fig. 22.18).

Masters of the Baroque definitely best presented the correspondence between the indicated total illumination and the light-receiving surfaces. Rembrandt sensitively combined both the luminous lustre of golden surfaces and the directedness of illumination in his canvases. Further, he was able to handle a hidden light source in the centre of the picture which produced illumination gradients on the surrounding surfaces, on the faces and clothes of the persons surrounding the light, as can be seen so magnificently in his work "The Conspiracy of Julius Civilis".

Besides brightness gradients, Baroque art used empirically derivable gradients of location of hues. If a painting like "The Night Watch" is analyzed perceptually, it becomes obvious that Rembrandt was aware of the apparent difference in location of "warm" and "cold" hues. He

Fig. 22.17 Caravaggio: "The Calling of Mathew." (From Schöne, 1954 p. 139.)

developed the three-dimensionality of the picture by concentrating yellow and red hues in the centre. Captain Cocq, with his red scarf, stands closest to the focal part of the picture. The centre of gravity is moved slightly to the right by Lieutenant van Ruytenburch, dressed in light yellow. These two central figures are placed on the canvas a bit below the other subjects. Because of the brightness gradient amply employed by Rembrandt, these persons look ready to step out into the space of the observer. This "forward motion" component is supported by clear depth gradients. A considerable crowd of men are following the leaders, and behind this entire large group we see a house wall with a shield on the corner. The transverse spear in the middle of the picture has a particularly strong lever effect. Furthermore, the figures in the focal part of the picture are painted more accurately, while

Fig. 22.18 Witz: "Sabothai and Benaja." (From Schöne, 1954 p. 97.)

precision of detail fades as the sight wanders from the centre toward the edges. The strongly illuminated girl in the left half of the painting also seems to squeeze forward into space. The movement of the boy running in front of the crowd favours the salience of the centre. On the left side of the girl there is a dark musketeer, the colour of whose clothing prevents her from being too obtrusive.

Fig. 22.19 Rembrandt: "The Night Watch." (From v. Fieandt 1966.)

On the opposite side of the picture there are three objects serving the same purpose, that is, the drum, the gun barrel visible behind the lieutenant, and the arm stretching from near the drum toward the gun barrel. These objects create a strong impression of space in the right third of the painting. In the centre we notice the similar function of Captain Cocq's forward thrust hand. All this produces the striking feeling of space in the front centre of the picture, and gives rise to the observer's impression of being able to step into the picture at the same time that the central figures appear to approach him from the canvas. In order further to accentuate depth articulation, Rembrandt spread out efficient dimensional cues at various distances in the pictorial space. Thus, well-illuminated human faces can serve as basic points for successful accommodation and convergence. Because these plates catch the observer's gaze, Rembrandt succeeded in making his painting convincingly three-dimensional.

Like most of Rembrandt's creations, "The Night Watch" too has a mysterious unexpected distribution of light. Sometimes it looks magical or even supernatural. This picture of a club which we have been analyzing contains various kinds of directed illuminations; one part of the radiation enters from outside into pictorial space, but we also suspect a hidden light source somewhere behind the musketeer on the left. In addition to this, some of the faces look luminous. Along with this skilful gradiation of illumination goes a corresponding use of efficient shadow effects, varying in kind as well as in density. The gradual dimming of the shadowed areas has the characteristics of space shadows. On the surfaces of the human figure, as well as on the three-dimensional objects, there are object shadows which emphasize spatial plasticity. Moreover, there are some shadows cast in the picture, especially the superb, famed shadow from the hand of the captain falling on the lieutenant's coat, which creates an efficient articulation. This particular shadow keeps the protruding yellowish surface from getting too far in front of the pictorial space. Of all the many artistic effects used by Rembrandt, his use of brightness gradients may be considered the most efficient. The perceptual analysis presented above, however, indicates that this single effect alone is not responsible for the sensational fame of "The Night Watch", which has persisted for centuries.

Leonardo (quoted in Schöne 1954, pp. 109–110), in his famous book on painting, listed the various forms of indirect light (lume). They are three: (1) diffuse daylight, (2) reflected light and (3) transparent light. In our time three kinds of interrelation between a presumed light source and the illuminated pictorial world have been enumerated:

1. The beam from a light source outside the picture extends into the scene. One can rely on lustres, object shadows, or dim illuminations filled with the shadows cast by narrow light beam (as in Caravaggio, Fig. 22.17).

2. The light source outside the picture provides a soft and mellow diffuse illumination to the entire pictured world. This luminescent space can be achieved by illuminated surfaces bearing carefully controlled chiaroscuro, object shadows, space shadows and cast shadows (as in Rembrandt).

3. The light source appears in the picture.

These varieties have been called modes of appearance of pictorial light. In addition to these one could list the following kinds of light radiation:

1. Natural radiation: daylight, sun, moon.
2. Artificial radiation: campfire, hearth, candle, torch.
3. Sacred radiation: gloria, visionary light, etc.
4. Indeterminate radiation: appears all over in the picture.

With the Renaissance revolution, degrees of brightness gained in importance relative to mere colour surfaces. The shades of chiaroscuro became more common for accentuating differences in illumination. Paint was given an opportunity to demonstrate layered surfaces.

Neo-impressionism is often defined by describing its emphasis on light and motion. More important than the actual objects in such works was the veil of light. It is the artist's task to capture the illumination of a given moment. But this is only one side of the story. The other side is a specific technique aiming at an appropriate physiological fusion of a colour mosaic in the visual organs of the viewer. It was regarded as a requirement for this school that the chromatic spots be as saturated and pure in hue as possible and that they be placed close together on the canvas. This method further required an accurate consideration of simultaneous contrast, of coloured illumination, and of light reflected from surfaces.

The culmination of this trend is represented by the pointillists, above all by Seurat and by the Finnish painter A. W. Finch.

If we look at Seurat's "Un dimanche à la Grande-Jatte", we can easily see that mood and the main illumination are the things of primary interest to the artist (Fig. 22.7). The people on the shore do not move around, nor are they shown in any particular relation to each other or to the outside environment. They are reduced almost to geometrical solids, and their only function is to support the verticals and horizontals needed by the artist in setting up his visual coordinates. Despite this schematism, however, the many single colour spots combine to give an impression of a hazy summer afternoon. The alternation of dark and light forms fits the lazy pace of a Sunday evening.

Many modern painters have been influenced by Seurat's thoughts, by the impressionistic pioneers, and by Cézanne. The impressionistic era includes some of Delacroix's later works and even a few of Cézanne's. This trend in Cézanne's development dates from the time beginning with 1872 when he lived at Auvers. By that time Pissarro, influenced by Delacroix, had started mosaically covering the canvas with pure, saturated unmixed colours. Even the reciprocal neutralization of complementary colours could be achieved if the onlooker viewed the painting from a greater distance. "The House of the Hanged Man" is a good example of a work in which many pure, saturated colours were combined in different nuances.

An essential difference between Cézanne and the impressionists was

u

that he was not primarily interested in illumination. He turned to coloured surfaces and to contrast effects among adjacent parts of the picture in his treatment of surface compositions.

All artistic impressionism, according to Schildt, in addition to the above-mentioned traits, included a new ethical orientation toward life. The artists belonging to this group were rootless and superficial, yet they were also soundly affirmative toward life. In their art they prized existence, intentionally stripped of its former ideology, but containing rich sensual and aesthetic values (Schildt 1947, pp. 87–104).

Paintings of the same landscape by Pissarro and Cézanne show this difference strikingly. Pissarro's picture is vivacious and realistic, while Cézanne's represents the world of an introvert. For him, the subject was only an excuse for a particular pictorial composition. The most distinctive mark of his art was a superb rising above the humdrum search for the expression of life, that is, an elevation from the level of the beauty of nature to the level of pure artistic loveliness.

For the neo-impressionists colour was above all a means for picturesque expression. Admittedly this scenic representative mode was already encountered even in Cézanne's paintings.

The Swede J. Grünewald describes this new school, and the experiences of one of them in Paris, as follows:

He admired Titian, Rembrandt, Raphael, Tintoretto and the other masters. He also went to the Luxembourg galleries and admired the impressionists. He dropped into a studio where he painted living models. He painted apples and towels and in the evening he drew models. Then he again went to Louvre.

But the pulsating life of a capital, the night clubs, the Metro, the cars and the electric lighting sang a new song with a new melody. The solemn air of the Louvre's vast galleries became heavier and more exhausting. He was able to see and experience things completely unfamiliar to the reverent old people on the walls around him. His language was different from theirs. When using their expressions he was unable to describe what was new and important. The clothes of our time did not fit their antique figures, and their dark eyes could not stand the blinding beams of our spotlights. The expressionist felt that he had to create a new language, to clear his palette and to change his brushes. (Grünewald 1946, pp. 43–44).

There has been much argument about Cézanne's colour techniques and about his interest in colour depth effects. Actually, his greatest achievement was a depth-inducing application of degrees of brightness in his paintings. Cézanne was a real master in his use of brightness gradients and contrasts.

The Dutch physiologist Einthoven is the man usually mentioned in connection with colour stereoscopy. He has shown that the optical axis of the eye and the line of sight form an angle subtending 5 degrees. One consequence of this asymmetry is that short-wave bluish radiation and long-wave reddish radiation have different diffusion areas on the retina. In some persons the stronger refraction of bluish light causes the illusion of "warmer" colours being closer than bluish ones. Because of the opposite asymmetry in the eyes of other people, they have a contradictory experience, bluish colours phenomenally appearing closer. Schildt found that the second physiological alternative occurred in 30 per cent of his subjects. We must also not forget that at the distances from which we usually look at paintings, colour stereoscopy hardly has any effect at all. The size of the pupil also affects the degree of the illusion.

We might assume therefore, that colour stereoscopy plays its greatest role, if any, when we look at generally dark paintings, such as Rembrandt's "The Night Watch", which used many other techniques for achieving an illusion of space. Cézanne's pictures are mostly brighter, which would make for a smaller pupillary opening and thus act against colour stereoscopy. Only few surfaces in his works can be discriminated on the basis of brightness differences—as he himself used to point out.

Actually, Cézanne generally strove for two-dimensionality on his canvases. He avoided illusory effects. Therefore, Schildt proposes that one should drop the argument of differential depth effects of various hues when speaking of Cézanne's art (Schildt 1947, pp. 186–190).

Cézanne's art is mainly based on figural organization. His paintings are almost as appealing when reproduced in black and white. It is the brightness gradients in his pictures which contribute to their spatial frame of reference.

Art and Personality Dynamics

So far in this chapter the perception of pictorial art has been analyzed on the basis of the figural organization of visual stimulation. Such an approach may be useful in providing a systematic survey of the structural conditions of pictorial organization, but we must not forget that any isolation of sensory experience from the dynamic totality of personal life is inevitably an abstraction. When perceiving masterpieces of art, it is especially true that "attitudes, evaluations and emotional connotations are generally involved in all sensory activity" (Hartshorne 1934). We would certainly be applying the principles presented in chapter 21 poorly if we were to ignore the emotional tones of the total personality which give perceptual configurations their deeper significance.

Colours may have a great meaning in conveying different emotional tunes which the artist may have experienced when painting his picture.

It has been found out (for example, Wright and Rainwater, 1962) that colours have different connotations. When talking about colours it is important to notice also the meanings of hue, brightness, and saturation.

Wright and Rainwater noticed among others that, "elegance", as experienced by the observer, when judgments were expressed on a semantic differential, seems to be caused by blueness. In other words, the greater the blueness the greater the feeling of elegance. Redness seemed to be the hue change which corresponds with "warmth". The more redness a colour has the more it connotates "warmth".

Although we may like a picture because of its colours, and we may experience some special feelings when looking at special colours, a piece of art is more than colours plus a heap of other qualities.

Affective continua clearly operate in all perceptual enjoyment of pictorial art. The representation of a motif or a subject is not the only thing expected by the observer; the allegorical or symbolic meaning involved in the artistic product may unconsciously affect him even more strongly than the mere representation of a bit of outside reality. Therefore, it is not even necessary for the motif itself to appeal to us, if a picture is to be appealing.

This fact can be demonstrated convincingly if we look at the works of two artists representing exactly the same landscape. One of them might leave us completely cold despite skilful and structurally well-performed composition, coloration, and depth articulation. The other may contain those hidden artistic qualities which appeal directly to a cross-modal emotion evaluation.

Drawings and artistic styles are notably expressive of the person who creates them. His reaction is specific to himself or to his mood in addition to being specific to an object. A painter is usually identifiable with his pictures. A painter can make other people see what he has seen and a person can learn to think in terms of drawings the painter has made (Gibson, 1954, p. 4).

Often it seems that the artist has been able to project something of his own motivation, his wishes, his needs, or his mood into the structure and coloration of the composition and that he has mastered the appropriate means for evoking the corresponding mood in us. It is not even necessary to have a clearly topically organized pictorial world in order to grasp the allegorical meaning intended by the artist. In a way similar to how a poem with an uninteresting motif can appeal to our emotions by affecting what Kretschmer called the "spheric" regions of our consciousness, i.e. physiologically speaking, by causing some "resonance" in the motivation centres of the brainstem, so a good painting can directly approach our personality without our being aware of how it does so (Kretschmer 1952).

The Finnish artist H. O. Mäkelä's landscape called "Spring", is a rather crowded picture, with two faces and a few strokes indicating trees and bushes has nothing strongly reminiscent of spring-time; yet everyone asked about it became aware at first glance of the spirit of spring which speaks to us unmistakably from the canvas. The symbolic meaning detectable in Cézanne's "Blue Landscape", into which he projects something of himself in an unanalyzable manner, probably is much more important than the question of how he succeeded in representing the forest.

This matter of being able to convey the artist's motivation and sentiment to the person looking at the creation is, however, an extremely delicate one. As soon as the artist discovers that he can express himself and his own problems on the canvas, he might feel tempted to neglect the perceptual treatment of space, form and colour in his pictures entirely. Exclusive concentration on one's own emotions and mood generally means avoiding the difficulties of the formal spatial elaboration of the illusory pictorial world.

Pictorial art, however, usually appeals to ordinary "normal" people, whose personality organization might not be as original, unique, or extreme as that of the artist. Man himself is a part of nature, and the immediate beauty inherent in certain creations of nature can appeal to him in the same way as do works of art. If the artist harshly distorts recognizable parts of nature without successfully mediating what is central in his mood and motivation, such a product usually remains unintelligible to the majority of the public.

The works of many modern painters, such as surrealists and abstractionists, are more interesting to the clinical psychologist—insofar as he can "read" the personality dynamics of the creator in the production—than to the ordinary art enjoyer. If the artist is not too radical, most of us can even enjoy slight compulsory repetitions like Mondrian's skilfully composed and balanced patterns or a spontaneous gay interplay of colours and forms in a slightly manic pictorial production. Yet the majority of art lovers are no psychopathologists; what is highly satisfactory to the artist as a release of his tension may sometimes be annoying to his public.

Pasto rightly points out that spontaneous expressions, devoid of all intended motifs or interpretations, like water colours by children or chimpanzees, impress us more than analogous, apparently haphazard, creations by adult artists. This level and this technique is typical and natural for children at a certain age. In chaotic water colour patterns by adults we can usually discern a sophisticated or conscious striving for primitivism, which makes these creations less spontaneous and in a sense less artistic than the genuine spontaneous expressions of children. Except for art critics, most people feel as though they were faced with personality regressions, because many of the extreme modernist work display a disorganization often encountered—as Pasto strikingly shows—in schizo-phrenic art (Pasto 1964).

One of the psychoanalytic explanations of artistic enjoyment maintains that the product should allow for the possibility of identification. People feel happy with a movie if they have been able to identify with the hero. This may be why some kind of space frame, including three-dimensional objects, could be an important condition for a successful painting. Human beings are typically more interested in what they see depicted and in what gives them the opportunity to identify than in the personality of the artist.

Fig. 22.20 Harrold: "The Demon." (From Pickford 1971 p. 109.)

An interesting problem in aesthetic preference is simplicity and complex-ity. When asked to sort several cards of visual complexity (when visual complexity was defined in formal elements of line, direction, shape, size, colour, tone and texture) according to preference, subjects rated visual complexity very high aesthetically (Osborne and Farley, 1970 p. 70).

Barron (1963) suggested that the person who prefers complexity is more likely to be nonconforming, flexible, and creative than the person who prefers simple stimuli.

Perhaps a flexible and nonconforming person can better stand stimuli which are opposite to one another. This might probably explain why some people can see the artistic value of a very ugly picture and some see only the ugliness.

Pickford (1971, p. 108) found three types of responses to an ugly picture "The Demon" by J. W. Harrold (see Fig. 22.20).

(1) Some can tolerate the aggression depicted in it, recognize its aesthetic quality, and like it.

(2) Others find it intolerable, consider it ugly and fail to appreciate its aesthetic value.

(3) A third group can see its aesthetic quality, but at the same time find it repulsive and ugly.

A good piece of pictorial art combines hidden emotional and mood factors with spatially balanced and agreeable pictorial space which is familiar and allows for identification. It fails in its purpose if it acts as a merely correct figural representation or as a releasing stimulus for some drive impulses or appeals to the libido of the enjoyer. Generally speaking, at least with respect to certain sensory channels, there is physiological evidence for the participation of brainstem "arousal centres" in artistic enjoyment. Because of this emotional tuning associated with perceptual activity, our total personality resonates, as it were, along the affective continuum crossing and connecting the separate modalities. This is aptly described in a quotation from v. Hornbostel: "A dancer had a dance, 'The Lily.' Her humanity vanished in the high, waving chalice of her veil, a deep violet faded away in spirals, a dazzling white rose up, expanding indefinitely. The noises of the suburban music hall could not spoil this pure music" (v. Hornbostel 1925, p. 290).

23 | Conclusions and Perspectives

The chief purpose of this text has been to give the reader a *true* picture of the existing knowledge in the field of perception. For that reason we have not tried to represent this *perceptual world* as if it were an ordered and fully consistent system of scientific theories and data. Such a delineation obviously would be a false representation of the state of affairs.

The world of perception, however, is not chaotic. It may be structured and surveyed by means of a few fundamental principles of perceptual functioning which have been exposed and discussed throughout the whole text.

In this concluding chapter we want to reconsider the most important among these principles.

In spite of its long history the psychology of perception still has to struggle with a number of problems, the fundamental nature of which is epistemological. In this book we have not tried to hide the existence of such fundamental problems and there may even be readers who find that our approach is too problem-oriented in this respect. The psychology of perception, however, has to be intimately tied up with epistemology and its basic problems concerning the possibilities of man to achieve an adequate cognition of the external world and of himself within this world by means of his perceptual equipment. In this chapter we therefore want to discuss a few of these problems of knowledge, concentrating on instances where these problems interfere with questions of methodology.

As a third and concluding part of the chapter, we want to point to certain perspectives opening up for the psychology of perception, provided that this field of research still succeeds in attracting an optimal amount of interest and scientific skill among psychologists, and granted that it will be secured a sufficient supply of resources.

Main Principles of Perceptual Functioning: A Review

As mentioned in chapter 10, perceptual psychologists at the end of the last century had great confidence in the so-called *constancy hypothesis*, that is, in the assumption that there always is a constant one-to-one relationship between the elements of a stimulus situation and the elements of the corresponding phenomenal response.

It is easily comprehensible why this doctrine was able to gain such widespread credence. Various sciences in the same epoch, e.g. chemistry, had very clearly demonstrated the fruitfulness of an elementaristic approach, and the empirical investigations of perceptual psychology itself had, so to speak, forced through a development in the same direction. Whenever investigators were confronted with a case where it was not possible to find at once a stable one-to-one relationship between the stimulus basis and the corresponding experience they *had* to go further in their analysis in order to discover the set of true co-varying elements.

The phenomena of illusions, and later on, the phenomena of object invariance (chapter 13) became the most important topics of research just because of the fact that they most obviously contradicted the classical hypothesis of constancy.

It has been very difficult for the psychology of perception to overcome this classical elementarism and arrive at a more adequate understanding. Such a development has now taken place, however. A very important result has been that more and more psychologists have realized that in addition to the factors of physical stimulation a number of other factors play a decisive role. These are factors connected with the perceiver, his personality and social milieu, and which have a decisive influence on the perceptual processes and on their end-results, the percepts (see chapters 20 and 21).

Nevertheless, the hope to find and to characterize regular relations between variables of stimulation and corresponding phenomenal variables has not been given up, but such relations seem to be much more complex by nature than the ones expected during the early prime of psychophysics. In addition, psychologists today have had to acknowledge, mainly as a consequence of the effect of the so-called Gestalt-revolution, that a one-sidedly analytical and elementaristic approach to perception is far from being fruitful, and may even lead to a pre-occupation with phenomena without relevance for an understanding of the perception of daily life.

A more and more pronounced tendency to specify variables of stimulation by means of relating them to the sensorial apparatus of the perceiver is a consequence partly of the expansion of our knowledge concerning sensory physiology, and partly a result of the failure of the classical constancy hypothesis. It seems impossible, however, to choose an adequate degree of stimulus specification without relating this specification to our knowledge of the psychophysiological processes mediating between stimuli and phenomenal responses. Consequently the description of stimuli, in one way or another, is rendered dependent on the reactions of the experimental subject including his phenomenological descriptions of the phenomena on which he is instructed to concentrate. The classical dream of a *pure* psycho-physics, within the scope of which variables belonging to the physical and to the phenomenal pole could be defined in an absolutely independent way before the presumed one-to-one correspondence was to be experimentally demonstrated, thus seems to have failed.

We shall not try to conceal that there still are outstanding scholars hoping to re-establish a pure psycho-physical psychology of perception.

To take an example: Gibson has followed his early professional credo from his book "The Perception of the Visual World" (1950, p. 62). He argues for a return to a psycho-physical way of thinking with empirical as well as theoretical research showing that if one interprets the physical pole (stimuli) not as a mere collection of uncorrelelated elements but as a more or less integrated complex of variables, it is possible in many cases to demonstrate "higher order variables" corresponding strictly to variables of phenomenal experience.

The most well known example of this type of research, is the work done by Gibson and his co-workers concerning gradients of texture and the importance for human space perception of these gradients (chapter 11, pp. 307–311).

The same basic idea led Gibson to construct an "ecological optics" which, better than classical optics, was to assist the psychologist in pointing out and varying relevant variables of stimulation in a new and more lifelike visual perception (chapter 14, p. 387).

Gibson's reformulation of, and carrying on with, a psycho-physical paradigm of research may in a historical perspective be looked upon as an attempt to unify a classical point of view with a consistent gestalt-psychological way of thinking.

To many psychological researchers, the Gibson-approach has the same weakness as Gestalt psychology, namely, a tendency to circularity. If the same aspects that are needed to explain the phenomenal response are "projected" into the physical pole then, of course, the explanation is empty. Such a tendency to circularity cannot be avoided until the description of stimuli has been made fully independent of the phenomenal response. In the case of gradients of texture, it seems to be possible to give this type of higher order variable a mathematical form in order to avoid the disadvantageous circularity.

In our opinion there is no doubt concerning the fruitfulness of the concept of higher order variables. Many empirical results point to the fact that the perceptual equipment of man bases its functioning on complexes of variables rather than on single variables. The degree of veridicality of percepts seems to depend on the way in which invariant relations among aspects of the complexes of stimuli have been implied by these perceptual systems.

Gibson has in addition to this point of view been a very persistent advocate of an opinion which sees the perceptual apparatus of man as composed of a series of "perceptual systems" rather than "senses" in the classical meaning of this word.

What has been named earlier "polymodal interaction" is thereby given a new status as the rule and not the exception. Consequently a *principle of organization* is fully accepted as the most fundamental principle of perceptual functioning.

This point of view is of course no hindrance to a necessary analysis and separation of such organized systems—both with regard to their adequate systems of stimulation and to the corresponding sensory-physiological components—into hierarchically subordinate parts. A pre-condition for such a separation must always be kept in mind, however, namely, that a subordinate part can only be truly understood *in its connection with* other parts of the system.

We here encounter the very intricate part-whole problem of psychology which was discussed and emphasized as early as 1911 by the Danish philosopher and psychologist Høffding in the following words:

La vie psychique et la personnalité ne peuvent se comprendre comme des produits d'éléments donnés antérieurement, par cela que les éléments que nous en connaissons tiennent ce qui leur est propre du fait qu'ils sont des chaînons de la vie psychique (Høffding 1911, p. 14).

One of the most important advantages of the principle of organization, both in respect to the way of reasoning and of experimenting, is the fact that until now this principle has allowed us to specify in the clearest possible way how certain relational features can be preserved in an organized whole in spite of variations and/or replacement of single elements.

Another basic principle of perceptual functioning has—it is to be hoped

—been clarified by the preceding chapters, namely, the concept of *frame of reference*. It was already touched upon by Katz (1911) in his laws of field size, to which we will return. Koffka (1935) paved the way for a more systematic treatment of this principle when speaking of "thing and framework"—the "surrounding frame" being important for the way we perceive a thing. Koffka (1935, p. 177) apparently considered the total, complex stimulus-pattern decisive for what was perceived as a "thing" in Rubin's ambiguous figures—in the same way as are the elements of framing patterns decisive for what is seen in the famous "embedded figures" of Gottschaldt (1926). Yet, it was not until Metzger coined the term *system of reference* (Bezugsystem) in his fundamental text book (1st ed. 1941, 2nd ed. 1954, pp. 131–175) that a careful analysis of this principle was carried out. This very principle later became one of the key concepts in modern social psychology, since Sherif (1958) found it especially applicable in the field of social science.

More recently, Broadbent (1958) and Sarris (1971)—among others—have discussed the effects of frames of reference when stressing what they call the *context* of a stimulus pattern. (For instance the significance of the context in a "phone voice" has been pointed out in our chapter 7 p. 239).

In the present text we encountered this principle of frame of reference when dealing with the problem of *object constancies*. It is a remarkable fact that even if a single square on a slanting surface becomes strongly distorted in its perspective projection—the more distorted, the stronger the inclination of its "background surface"—we are able to perceive a system of *invariant slanted squares* when we receive a rich flux of stimuli representing the total slanted area, e.g. the back of a rocking chair covered by a broader pattern of squares (chapter 13 pp. 359–361). The problem of perceptual invariances has referred to the role played by concomitant, parallel stimulations affecting all responsive sense modalities. This is the "polymodal aspect" of the principle of frame of reference (see chapter 19 p. 519).

In his discussion of colour constancies, Katz touched upon the crucial role of the "framework" in the two laws of field size presented by him (1935, pp. 217–219). Katz states his laws as follows:

If within an area of the visual field which is filled with objects the intensity of the illumination is uniformly reduced, the changed impression thus induced varies with the way in which this area is filled. If only a small section of the external world is seen within it, the colours of the objects are then in essential correspondence with the intensity of retinal excitation and with the illumination perceived in the total visual field. If a large section of the external world is seen within this area (at a correspondingly greater distance), the illumination within it appears reduced, and the colours undergo such changes as they would undergo if the illumination of the whole visual field were reduced.

This consistent relationship between change in illumination impression of part of the visual field and change in its *real* size (i.e., change in its retinal size) or in *apparent* size (retinal size held constant) may be expressed in two laws. These we may term the *first and second law of field size*.

Presumably these laws refer to the *retinal* and the *apparent* size of the field, respectively. The larger the field *actually* is (Law I) or appears to be (Law II) the less likely is a colour to look like a film colour.

However, this principle of frame of reference becomes—as we have seen—even more important for how we perceive *moving objects* and how our visual system carries out its movement analysis (chapter 16). The fact that we see the face of a moving lecturer as a constant object nodding and looking at the audience (chapter 16 p. 412) is due to the totality of concomitant stimuli covering the entire situation. The impression of speed of movement and of direction of moving sound stimuli in the darkness are—as has been pointed out—equally dependent on the complexity of the stimulus situation (chapter 17 p. 469).

To put the essentials of this principle into a statement by Metzger (1954, p. 141): "Any single stimulus is at the same time a stimulus of a system". The older and quite independently evoked "cue"-concept thus gets incorporated in this broader principle of explanation.

The scholar who has had the most significant influence on the development and clarification of the principle of organization, is in our opinion, the late Finnish psychologist and philosopher Kaila. His concept of *invariance* has relevance for all human processes of cognition—from systems of scientific knowledge to the perception of daily life with its very significant stamp of invariance in spite of more or less marked variations in regard to proximal stimulation (chapter 19).

The concept of invariance is not only relevant for a description of the structure of stimuli in experimental situations, but it can also be used to characterize the sort of lawful covariation which can be proved to take place between such complexes of stimuli and corresponding perceptual experiences.

Regular covariation may be thought of as a superior invariant feature of the situation—a perceptual lawfulness.

In accordance with this point of view we do not find that explanations in terms of reductionism which replace psychological explanations by "more basic" physiological laws constitute the only acceptable type of explanatory model. Lawful covariations established in psycho-physical experiments are very important material for theory construction even if data from such experiments are not usable at once as basic data in a reductive theory (chapter 2). Such bodies of data may be useful for the construction of theoretical models in the future and for a period of time they may be the empirical basis of such a model. These data may eventually gain a new life in other theoretical contexts. Data of this sort, which are the results of experiments skilfully carried out in well defined situations, are, so to say, immortal.

Theoretical models of the reductive type are created in a great number of ways, and it is not possible to give some sort of recipe for model construction. The creative researcher himself is often quite unable to specify how he arrived at his theoretical ideas and from where he got the necessary inspiration.

More systematic and goal-oriented efforts to construct adequate theoretical models are becoming more and more common in the field of perception. In this connection a system-analytical approach seems to be very fruitful in asking: what are the necessary and sufficient characteristics of a sensory-physiological system capable of producing such and such an area of perceptual phenomena?

This way of reasoning is by no means a new approach and as an illustration we may use a classical example, namely, the *hypothesis of visual localization* created by v. Helmholtz. His hypothesis was based on a couple of very simple phenomenal findings with subjects suffering from paralysis of various specified groups of extrinsic eye muscles. These findings contradicted earlier theories of localization (e.g. Lotze's theory of local signs, see chapter 11, p. 298). If a subject tried to move his eyes in the direction where the paralysis hindered every factual eye movement he had the impression of the external objects moving in the *same* direction as the intended movements of his gaze.

This finding together with the well known experiments by Mach where he "paralyzed" the eyes of his subjects by pressing a little ball of wax into the corner of the eye, made v. Helmholtz conclude that . . . "wir beurtheilen . . . die Richtung unserer Gesichtslinie weder nach der wirklichen Stellung des Augapfels, noch nach der von ihm abhängigen wirklichen Verlängerung oder Verkürzung der Augenmuskeln" (v. Helmholtz 1867, p. 600).

These two possibilities of explanation being excluded, the only hypothesis left to v. Helmholtz was "dass wir die Richtung der Gesichtslinie nur beurtheilen nach der Willensanstrengung mittels der wir die Stellung der Augen zu ändern suchen" (ibid. p. 601).

This hypothesis has—as is often the case with the ideas of v. Helmholtz— undergone a renaissance in modern models of visual localization, e.g. the "out-flow theory" of Gregory (Gregory and Zangwill, 1963).

It is naturally very difficult to foresee the theoretical development of the psychology of perception in the years to come but it seems obvious that the painstaking work of constructing and testing more or less specialized models will continue with a growing realization of the very complex character of this scientific endeavour. It is to be hoped that this work will increasingly bear fruit in the form of combinations of such models into more extensive theoretical constructions. A general theory of perception including all areas of the human perceptual world is not in sight, however, and the confidence of earlier days in the possibility of formulating deductive theories similar to those of natural science seems now to be on the decline. We are not going to discuss this topic further here but we do want to refer to Dodwell's excellent analyses (Dodwell 1970).

The very obvious differences between various psychological schools in respect to their way of coping with problems in the psychology of perception are, on a closer view, consequences partly of different conceptions regarding the ultimate aim of this field of psychological research, and partly of a disagreement concerning what methods are acceptable as a means of getting valid scientific data.

In our opinion, the chief purpose of this discipline should be to try to understand the perception of man as it functions *in* the very complex situations of daily life. With a modification of the words of Gibson, we want to try to understand "the perceptual *world*" and not only "the perceptual field" of man (Gibson, 1950).

Studies of the way of functioning of sensorial systems are, we think, also very important for perceptual psychology as far as their results throw new light on the highly integrated perceptual processes. We hold the same opinion regarding special studies in the fields of psychophysics.

If one wants to contribute to our knowledge of this perceptual world of daily life it is of no use listening to the well-meant suggestion that when studying perception one has to concentrate on "real-life situations" only. Such situations are—as mentioned above—so complicated in their structure of influencing variables that it is very seldom possible to point out and specify the various variables in a precise way. Some sort of simplification is unavoidable if the researcher has any chance of finding and testing perceptual invariances (laws). In other words, it is necessary that the researcher in the field of perception should have, so to speak, the courage to simplify.

Thus, perceptual psychology is confronted with the old dilemma: on the one hand it has to carry out research in rather simple situations; on the other hand it must be acknowledged that data from such situations are not immediately and necessarily valid with regard to more complex situations. This is the part-whole problem in its perceptual version.

In our view this dilemma can only be solved by founding the invariances of our field of research on the widest possible empirical basis.

At one extreme we have a multitude of systematically structured simple situations—created experimentally or arising in daily life—the influencing variables of which, can be specified with a high degree of exactness; at the other extreme, all the complex daily-life situations where lawful invariances can only with great difficulty be identified as perceptual tendencies.

There seems to exist a widespread misunderstanding that the phenomenological method is only fit for the last mentioned type of research. That, of course, is not the case, for a specification of the phenomenal responses is necessary in all types of experiments in perception—psychologically as well as psycho-physiologically oriented experiments—and if this specification has not been made beforehand it must be made *in* the actual experimental situation on the basis of profound phenomenological analyses.

The simplification of an experimental situation and the ensuing better possibilities of specification leads to a decreasing number of possible responses and additionally to more simple responses in general. This fact has often convinced researchers that such "exact" experiments are not hampered by any problems of communication.

It is very important, however, not to prevent the experimental subjects from expressing themselves in adequate ways because of an exaggerated confidence in simple categories of response (e.g. purely behavioural responses).

If this is not kept in view, one risks being trapped by an experimental "Whorf-effect", in the sense that the simplified categories of expressions influence the perception *in statu nascendi*, the perceptual processes being adapted to the possibilities of expression (Moustgaard, 1975b).

Such problems of communicative identification ought to be taken seriously. One must acknowledge that the effects of types of responses used experimentally (whether these take the form of a verbal description by means of certain fixed categories or of motor performances) must be investigated independently of the experiments actually going on. Only after such investigation can specific types of responses be used in an acceptable way.

It has been quite common to use the concept of *information* in the psychology of perception and we have accepted this terminology, though with some hesitation. It is important, however, to notice that we do not use this word in the strict sense of the theory of information, but in order to stress that we consider the main function of the perceptual equipment of man to be a cognitive function, and especially cognition of the external world.

The neo-cognitivistic approach to perception, of which the use of the term information is a sign, remains in some respects problematic. One of the most dangerous pitfalls of this approach, and the one we most of all want to warn against, is the postulate, made in one way or another, that perception consists essentially of inferences made by a conscious person "a little man, a *homunculus*" within the perceiving person.

In the nineteenth century he was named "mental activity", "sensorium", "will", etc., nowadays "CNS", "cerebral cortex", "higher centres", etc. Regardless of the changing terminology the tendency remains the same. One concentrates on such perceptual variables as may serve as premises for "the little man" in his endeavour to reason out the nature of the outside world, i.e. such variables only as have a direct and clear correlate in consciousness.

By talking about information without specification the researcher prevents himself from making the very important distinction between such situations, on the one hand, where this "information" has no correlates in the awareness of the perceiver (but acts, so to speak, automatically), and such situations, on the other hand, where the information is handled in clear awareness, and where the perceptual functioning may have a resemblance to problem solving.

As an illustrative example of this area of problems we may mention the series of experiments made by Kohler (1951) concerning the capacity of the perceptual systems of man to accommodate to radically changed conditions of stimulation. Here we only want to call attention to two important experimental results which seem to be valid for a broad field of findings from various modalities:

(1) The accommodation to changed conditions of stimulation is possible only if there are some new *invariant structures* of stimuli available for the perceptual system.

(2) During the introductory phases of perception under the changed conditions the stimulus information tends to have clear correlates of awareness which vanish during continued training (see also chapter 11, p. 320).

It would be very important for a fruitful development of our discipline if in the years to come a sterile dispute between its various methodological schools could be replaced by profound discussions concerning the establishment of experimental research into the most basic problems of perceptual investigations—the problems of adequate communication in experimental situations.

A great deal of thought has been devoted to this field of problems but what we still need are experimental projects aiming directly at these problems.

Perspectives

The contribution made by the psychology of perception in our endeavours to define by means of adequate theories the boundaries of human cognition and knowledge—in order to be able to break these boundaries for new scientific conquests—is often much more appreciated than the practical application of the results of this discipline, e.g. in human engineering.

We are not inclined to see a contrast between the interest in the theory of perception and its practical application. Practical perceptual problems, for instance, the serious problem of road safety, may often function as catalyzers of theoretical development. A profound insight into the theoretical structure and epistemological basis of perception is often very important for a fruitful application of the more useful results and for a creative inclusion of new fields of application.

The perceptual equipment of man has undergone a very slow process of development over an immense number of years in the remote past. New evidence concerning prehistoric man indicates that his perceptual equipment was adapted to what might be called "a life on the steppe", and, as could be expected, the later and much shorter epoch has not altered this state of things.

His technical development has, however, during a relatively short period radically changed the stimulating milieu of man. Therefore, the perceptual systems which were adequate in the external milieu of the past are to-day often quite insufficient when exposed to the demands of a modern technological society.

In order to compensate for this shortage, technicians often have to improve existing systems, or even superimpose extra systems of control onto the control of action which the normal perceptual equipment of man is able to perform. For instance, in man-machine systems in space-flight, one may have the impression that the participation of man is very inconvenient to technicians, or even a matter of mere show.

The psychology of perception here has one of its most important tasks in describing as accurately as possible the quality and limits of this perceptual equipment and in warning against cases where the technical milieu is overloading this equipment. In this way the perceptual psychologist becomes something like an advocate of human dignity in these complicated matters.

Seen in the right light the perceptual processes are typical of the integrative functioning of a healthy human being. At the same time these processes are the main conditions of adequate actions in our physical and social environment and expressive of the emotional and cognitive life—actually the total personality of the individual (chapter 21).

For generations differential psychology has based its testing on this fact by using standardized perceptual situations as test situations.

The psychology of perception still wants to contribute to our understanding and knowledge of man in his entirety. In doing this job it will not give up its conquests in the fog of a diffuse global point of view. Through the continuous development of its sub-fields it aims at clearly demonstrating the importance of this discipline *for*, and its place *in*, psychology as a whole.

Such a development will without doubt contribute in a still increasing degree to the emancipation and appreciation of *perceiving man* and his perceptual world.

Bibliography

Abresch, J. and Sarris, V. (1975). Anchor effects in figural aftereffects: A comparative psychological investigation. *Percept. and Mot. Skills* **41**, 791–796.

Adams, O. S. (1955). Stereogram decentration and stereobase as factors influencing the apparent size of stereoscopic pictures. *Am. J. Psychol.* **68**, 54–68.

Adler, F. H. (1965). "Physiology of the Eye. Clinical Application" (4th edn.). Mosby, Saint Louis.

Adrian, E. D. (1912). On the conduction of subnormal disturbances in normal nerves. *J. Physiol.* **45**, 389–412.

Adrian, E. D. (1950). The electrical activity of the mammalian olfactory bulb. *Electroenceph. clin. Neurophysiol.* **2**, 377–388.

Ahrens, R. (1954). Beitrag zur Entwicklung des Physiognomie und Mimikerkennens I–II. *Zs. f. exp. u. angew. Psychol.* **2**, 412–454; 599–633.

Akishige, Y. (Ed.) (1961). "Experimental Researches on the Structure of Perceptual Space, IV". The Faculty of Literature, Kyushu University, Fukuoka, Japan.

Akishige, Y. (Ed.) (1967). "Experimental Researches on the Structure of Perceptual Space". The Faculty of Literature, Kyushu University, Fukuoka, Japan.

Akishige, Y. (1969). Poincaré's problem and the law of conservation of perceptual information. *In.* Järvinen, E. J. *et al.* (Eds) "Contemporary Research in Psychology of Perception in honorem Kai von Fieandt sexegenarii." WSOY, Porvoo.

Allen, D. B. and Rudy, K. P. (1970). Perception of simple figures drawn upon the body surface. *Percept. and Mot. Skills* **30**, 369–370.

Allport, F. (1955). "Theories of Perception and the Concept of Structure." Wiley and Sons, New York.

Allport, G. (1951). "The Use of Personal Documents in Psychological Science." Social Science Research Council, New York.

Alpern, M., Lawrence, M. and Wolsk, D. (1967). "Sensory Processes." Wadsworth, Belmont.

Alrutz, S. (1908). Untersuchungen über die Temperatursinne. *Zs. f. Psychol.* **47**, 161–202.

Al'tman, Ya. A. and Markovich, A. M. (1968). О нейронах – детекторах направления движения источника звука (Neurones-detectors of the direction of movement of a sound source). *Biophysica* **13**, 533–535.

Ames, A. (1951). Visual perception and the rotating trapezoidal window. *Psychol. Monogr.* **65**, No. 324.

Ames, A., Gliddon, G. H. and Ogle, K. N. (1932). Size and shape of ocular images: I. Methods of determination and physiological significance. *Arch. Ophthal.* **7**, 576–597.

Amoore, J. E., Johnston, J. W. Jr. and Rubin, M. (1964). The stereochemical theory of odor. *Sci. Am.* **210**, 42–49.

Andersen, D. C. and Moss, C. A. (1964). The auditory autokinetic effect. *Am. J. Psychol.* **77**, 502–503.

Anderson, N. H. (1974). Algebraic Models in Perception. *In* Carterette, E. C. and Friedman, M. P. (Eds) "Handbook of Perception, Vol. 2." Academic Press, New York and London.

Anderson, N. H. (1975). On the role of context effects in psycho-physical judgment. *Psychol. Rev.* **82**, 462–482.

Anstis, S. M. (1975). What does visual perception tell us about visual coding? *In* Gazzaniga, M. S. and Blakemore, C. (Eds) "Handbook of Psychobiology" Academic Press, New York and London.

Antonitis, J. J. (1969). A new photographic illusion. *Am. J. Psychol.* **82**, 389–391.

Appley, M. H. (Ed.) (1971). "Adaptation Level Theory: A Symposium." Academic Press, New York and London.

Armington, J. C. (1973). Color Vision. *In* Wolman, B. J. (Ed.) "Handbook of General Psychology." Prentice Hall, New Jersey.

Arnheim, R. (1943). Gestalt and art. *J. Aesth. and Art Crit.* **2**, 71–75 and *In* Hogg, J. (Ed.) (1969) "Psychology and the Visual Arts." Penguin Books, Harmondsworth.

Arnheim, R. (1949). The gestalt theory of expression. *Psychol. Rev.* **56**, 156–171 and *In* Hogg, J. (Ed.) (1969) "Psychology and the Visual Arts." Penguin Books, Harmondsworth.

Arnheim, R. (1954). "Art and Visual Perception." University of California Press, Berkeley.

Arnheim, R. (1970). "Visual Thinking." Faber and Faber, London.

Attneave, F. and Benson, B. (1969). Spatial coding of tactual stimulation. *J. Exp. Psychol.* **81**, 216–222.

Attneave, F. and Frost, R. (1969). The discrimination of perceived tridimensional orientation by minimum criteria. *Perception and Psychophys.* **6**, 391–396.

Aubert, H. (1861). Eine scheinbare bedeutende Drehung von Objekten bei Neigung des Kopfes nach rechts oder links. *Virchows Arch.* **20**, 381–393.

Aubert, H. (1865). "Physiologie der Netzhaut." Morgenstern, Breslau.

Baltzer, F. (1923-1924). Beiträge zur Sinnesphysiologie und Psychologie der Webespinnen. *Mitt. Naturf. Ges.*, 163–187 Bern.

Barber, T. X. (1961). Physiological effects of "hypnosis". *Psychol. Bull.* **58**, 390–419.

Barlow, H. B. (1953). Summation and inhibition in the frogs retina. *J. Physiol.* **119**, 69–88.

Barlow, H. B. (1972). Single units and sensation: A neuron doctrine for perceptual psychology. *Perception* **1**, 371–394.

Barlow, H. B. (1975). Visual experience and cortical development. *Nature* **258**, 199–204.

Barlow, H. B., Hill, R. M. and Levick, W. R. (1964). Retinal ganglion cells responding selectively to direction and speed of image motion in the rabbit. *J. Physiol.* **173**, 377–407.

Barlow, H. B. and Levick, W. R. (1965). The mechanism of directionally selective units in rabbit's retina. *J. Physiol.* **178**, 477–504.

Barlow, H. B. and Pettigrew, J. D. (1971). Lack of specificity of neurons in the visual cortex of young kittens. *J. Physiol.* **218**, 98–100.

Barron, F. (1963). "Creativity and Psychological Health". Van Nostrand, Princeton.

Batteau, D. W. (1968). Role of the pinna in localization: Theoretical and physiological consequences. In Derenck, S. and Knight, J. (Eds) "Hearing Mechanisms in Vertebrates." Little Brown, Boston.

Baumeister, M., Wapner, S. and Werner, H. (1967). Method of stimulus presentation and apparent body position under lateral body tilt. Percept. and Mot. Skills 24, 43–50.

Baylor, D. A. and Fuortes, M. G. F. (1970). Electrical responses of single cones in the retina of the turtle. J. Physiol. 207, 77–92.

Baylor, D. A. and O'Bryan, P. M. (1971). Electrical signalling in vertebrate photoreceptors. Federation Proc. 30, 79–83.

Bazett, H. C. (1941). Temperature sense in man. In "Temperature, its Measurement and Control in Science and Industry." Reinhold, New York.

Beck, J. and Gibson, J. J. (1955). The relation of apparent shape to apparent slant in the perception of objects. J. Exp. Psychol. 50, 125–133.

Beebe-Center, J. G. (1931). The variability of affective judgments upon odors. J. Exp. Psychol. 14, 91–93.

Beidler, L. M. (1963). Dynamics of taste cells. In Zotterman, Y. (Ed.) "Olfaction and Taste." Macmillan, New York.

Békésy, G. von (1928). Zur Theorie des Hörens: Die Schwingungsform der Basilarmembran. Physik. Zs. 29, 793–810.

Békésy, G. von (1929). Zur Theorie des Hörens: Über die Bestimmung des einem reinen Tonempfinden entsprechenden Erregungsgebietes der Basilarmembran vermittelst Ermüdungserscheinungen. Physik. Zs. 30, 115–125.

Békésy, G. von (1939). Über die mechanisch-akustischen Vorgönge beim Hären. Acta Oto-Laryngologica 27, 281–296, 388–396.

Békésy, G. von (1957). The ear. In Held, R. and Whitman, R. (Eds) (1971)."Perception: Mechanisms and Models." Sci. Am. Freeman.

Békésy, G. von (1960). "Experiments in Hearing." McGraw-Hill, New York.

Békésy, G. von (1964). Duplexity theory of taste. Science 145, 834–835.

Békésy, G. von (1967). "Sensory Inhibition." Princeton, New Jersey.

Benussi, V. (1912). Stroboskopische Scheinbewegungen und geometrisch-optische Gestalttäuschungen. Arch. Ges. Psychol. 24, 31–62.

Berkeley, G. (1871). An Essay towards a New Theory of Vision (1709). In Fraser, A. C. "The Works of George Berkeley, vol. I." Clarendon Press, Oxford.

Berman, A. L. (1961). Interaction of cortical responses to somatic and auditory stimuli in anterior ectosylvian gyrus of cat. J. Neurophysiol. 24, 608–620.

Bernardin, A. C. and Gruber, H. E. (1957). An auditory autokinetic effect. Am. J. Psychol. 70, 133–134.

Bernstein, A. S., Taylor, D., Austen, B. G., Nathanson, M. and Scarpelli, A. (1971). Orienting response and apparent movement toward or away from the observer. J. Exp. Psychol. 87, 37–45.

Bernstein, I. H. (1970). Can we see and hear at the same time?—Some recent studies of intersensory facilitation of reaction time. Acta Psychol. 33, 21–35.

Bexton, W. H., Heron, W. and Scott, T. H. (1954). Effects of decreased variation in the sensory environment. Canad. J. Psychol. 8, 70–76.

Bilger, R. C. and Melnick, W. (1968). Shifts in masking with time. J. Acoust. Soc. Am. 44, (4), 941–944.

Bischof, N. (1966). Erkenntnistheoretische Grundlagenprobleme der Wahrnehmungspsychologie. In Metzger, W. (Ed.) "Handbuch der Psychologie, Vol. I, Part 1," Hogrefe, Göttingen.

Bishop, P. O., Coombs, J. S. and Henry, G. H. (1971). Interaction effects of visual contours on the discharge frequency of simple striate neurones. *J. Physiol.* **219**, 659–687.

Blake, R. R. and Ramsey, G. V. (Eds) (1951). "Perception: An Approach to Personality." Ronald Press, New York.

Blakemore, C. (1964). Developmental factors in the formation of feature extracting neurons. *In* Schmitt, F. O. and Worden, F. G. (Eds) "The Neurosciences." Third Study Program. MIT Press, Cambridge, Mass.

Blakemore, C. (1974a). Central visual processing. *In* Gazzaniga, M. S. and Blakemore, C. (Eds) "Fundamentals of Psychobiology." Academic Press, New York and London.

Blakemore, C. (1974b). Development of the mammalian visual system. *Brit. Med. Bull.* **30**, 152–156.

Blakemore, C. and Campbell, F. W. (1969). On the existence of neurones in the human visual system selectively sensitive to the orientation and size of retinal images. *J. Physiol.* **203**, 237–260.

Blakemore, C. and Cooper, G. F. (1970). Development of the brain depends on the visual environment. *Nature* **228**, 474–478.

Blakemore, C. and Sutton, P. (1969). Size adaptation: a new after effect. *Science* **166**, 245–247.

Blane, H. T. (1962). Space perception among unilaterally paralyzed children and adolescents. *J. Exp. Psychol.* **63**, 244–247.

Blix, M. (1882–1883). Experimentalla bidrag till lösning af frågan om hudnervernas specifika energi. *Uppsala läkaref örenings f örhandlingar*, **XVIII**, 87–102, 427–440.

Blough, D. S. (1972). Visual psychophysics in animals. *In* Autrum, H., Jung, R., Loewenstein, W. R., MacKay, D. H. and Teuber, H. L. (Eds) "Handbook of Sensory Physiology, Vol. VII/4." Springer, Berlin.

Blough, D. S. and Lipsitt, L. P. (1971). The discriminative control of behaviour. *In* Kling, J. W. and Riggs, L. A. (Eds) "Experimental Psychology." (3rd edn. of Woodworth and Schlosberg). Holt, Rinehart and Winston, New York.

Bonnet, C. (1967). Influence de la vitesse du mouvement et de l'espace parcouru sur l'estimation du temps. *L'Année Psychol.* **67**, 51–60.

Bootzin, R. R. and Natsoulas, T. (1965). Evidence for perceptual defense uncontaminated by response bias. *J. Pers. Soc. Psychol.* **1**, 461–468.

Borg, G., Diamant, H., Ström, L, and Zotterman, Y. (1967). The relation between neural and perceptual intensity: a comparative study on the neural and psychophysical response to taste stimuli. *J. Physiol.* **192**, 13–20.

Borg, G., Diamant, H., Ström, L. and Zotterman, Y. (1968). Neural and psychophysical responses to gustatory stimuli. *In* Kenshalo, D. R. (Ed.) "The Skin Senses." Thomas, Springfield, Ill.

Boring, E. G. (1933). "The Physical Dimensions of Consciousness." Century, New York.

Boring, E. G. (1942). "Sensation and Perception in the History of Experimental Psychology." Appleton Century Crofts, New York.

Boring, E. G. (1950). "A History of Experimental Psychology." 2nd edn. Appleton Century Crofts, New York.

Boring, E. G., Langfield, H. S. and Weld, H. P. (Eds) (1935). "Psychology. A Factual Textbook." Wiley and Sons, New York.

Boring, E. G., Langfield, H. S. and Weld, H. P. (Eds.) (1948). "Foundations of Psychology." Wiley and Sons, New York.

Bosma, J. F. (Ed.) (1967). "Symposium in Oral Sensation and Perception." Thomas, Springfield, Ill.

Bourdon, B. (1902). La perception visuelle de l'espace. Scleicher Frères, Paris.

Bovet, P. (1968). Échelles subjectives de durée obtenues par une méthode de bissection. *L'Année Psychol. Fasc.* **2.** 23–36.

Bowditch, H. P. and Hall, G. S. (1880). Optical illusions of motion. *J. Physiol.* **3,** 297–307.

Bower, T. G. R. (1964). Discrimination of depth in premotor infants. *Psychon. Sci.* **1,** 368.

Bower, T. G. R., Broughton, J. M. and Moore, M. K. (1970). The coordination of visual and tactual input in infants. *Perception and Psychophys.* **8,** 51–53.

Boycott, B. B. (1974). Aspects of the comparative anatomy and physiology of the vertebrate retina. *In* Bellairs, R. and Gray, E. G. (Eds), "Essays on the Nervous System. A Festschrift for Professor J. L. Young." Clarendon Press, Oxford.

Boynton, R. M. (1960). Theory of color vision. *J. Opt. Soc. Am.* **50,** 929–944.

Boynton, R. M. (1971). Color vision. *In* Kling, J. W. and Riggs, L. A. (Eds) "Experimental Psychology" (3rd edn. of Woodworth and Schlosberg). Holt, Rinehart and Winston, New York.

Braunstein, M. L. (1976). "Depth Perception through Motion." School of Social Sciences, Univ. of California, Irvine, Ca.

Breland, K. and Breland, M. (1966). "Animal Behavior." Macmillian, New York.

Brindley, G. S. (1970). "Physiology of the Retina and Visual Pathway." *Monogr. Physiol. Soc.* London.

Broadbent, D. E. (1958). "Perception and Communication." Pergamon Press, New York.

Broadbent, D. E. and Gregory, M. (1963). Division of attention and the decision theory of signal detection. *Proc. Roy. Soc.* **158,** 222–231.

Broadbent, D. E. and Gregory, M. (1964). Stimulus set and response set: The alternation of attention. *Quart. J. Exp. Psychol.* **16,** 309–318.

Broadbent, J. M. (1975). "Wine Tasting." Christie's Wine Publications, London.

Brosgole, L. (1966). "An Analysis of Induced Motion." *Techn. Rep.* Navtradeveen IH–48, U. S. Naval Training Device Center.

Brown, J. F. (1928). Über gesehene Geschwindigkeiten. *Psychol. Forsch.* **10,** 84–101.

Brown, J. F. (1931a). On time perception in visual movement fields. *Psychol. Forsch.* **14,** 233–248.

Brown, J. F. (1931b). The thresholds for visual movement. *Psychol. Forsch.* **14,** 249–268.

Brown, J. F. (1931c). The visual perception of velocity. *Psychol. Forsch.* **14,** 199–232.

Brown, P. K. (1972). Rhodopsin rotates in the visual receptor membrane. *Nature New Biol.* **236,** 39.

Brown, P. K. and Wald, G. (1964). Visual pigments in single rods and cones of the human retina. *Science* **144,** 45–52.

Brown, W. P. (1961). Conceptions of perceptual defence. *Brit. J. Psychol. Monogr. Suppl.* **35,** 1–106.

Bruner, J. S. (1951). Personality dynamics and the process of perceiving. *In* Blake, R. R. and Ramsey, G. V. (Eds) "Perception: An Approach to Personality." Ronald Press, New York.

Bruner, J. S. (1957). On perceptual readiness. *Psychol. Rev.* **64,** 123–152.

Bruner, J. S. and Goodman, C. C. (1947). Value and need as organizing factors in perception. *J. Abnorm. Soc. Psychol.* **42,** 33–44.

Bruner, J. S. and Krech, D. (1950). "Perception and Personality. A Symposium." Duke University Press, Durham.

Bruner, J. S. and Postman, L. (1947). Emotional selectivity in perception and reaction. *J. Pers*. **16**, 69–77.

Bruner, J. S. and Postman, L. (1948). Symbolic value as an organizing factor in perception. *J. Soc. Psychol*. **27**, 203–208.

Brunswik, E. (1929). Zur Entwicklung der Albedowahrnehmung. *Zs. Psychol*. **109**, 40–115.

Brunswik, E. (1934). "Wahrnehmung und Gegenstandswelt. Grundlegung einer Psychologie vom Gegenstand her." Deutiger, Leipzig.

Brunswik, E. (1936). "Psychology in Terms of Objects." Proceedings of the 25 Anniversary Celebration of the Inauguration of Graduate Studies at the University of Southern California. University of Southern California Press, Los Angeles.

Brunswik, E. (1956). "Perception and the Representative Design of Psychological Experiments" (2nd edn.). University of California Press, Berkeley.

Brust-Carmona, H. and Hernández-Peón, R. (1959). "Sensory Transmission in the Spinal Cord during Attention and Tactile Habituation." *Proc. 21st Intern. Congr. Physiol*., Buenos Aires.

Buckner, D. N. and McGrath, J. J. (Eds) (1963). "Vigilance: A Symposium." McGraw-Hill, New York.

Bugelski, B. R. and Alampay, D. A. (1961). The role of frequency in developing perceptual sets. *Canad. J. Psychol*. **15**, 205–211.

Bühler, Ch. (1930). "Sinn und Gestalt." Bericht ü. d. *XI Kongress f. Exp. Psychol*., Berlin.

Bühler, Ch. (1962). "Psychologie im Leben unserer Zeit." Droemersche Verlaganstalt Th. Knaur Nachf., München.

Bühler, Ch. und Hetzer, H. (1928). Das erste Verständnis für Ausdruck im ersten Lebensjahr. *Zs. f. Psychol*. **107**, 50–61.

Bühler, K. (1922). Handbuch der Psychologie. I Teil. Die Struktur der Wahrnehmungen. 1. Heft. Die Erscheinungsweisen der Farben. Fischer, Jena.

Burkamp, W. (1923). Versuche über das Farbenwiedererkennen der Fische. *Zs. f. Sinnesphysiol*. **55**, 133–170.

Burkhardt, D. A. and Whittle, P. (1973). Intensity coding in the frog retina. Quantitative relations between impulse and graded activity. *J. Gen. Physiol*. **61**, 305–322.

Burnett, N. G. and Dallenbach, K. M. (1927). The experience of heat. *Am. J. Psychol*. **38**, 418–431.

Burzlaff, W. (1931). Methodologische Beiträge zum Problem der Farbenkonstanz. *Zs. f. Psychol*. **119**, 177–235.

Butler, R. A. (1971). The monoaural localization of tonal stimuli. *Perception and Psychophys*. **9**, 99–101.

Buytendijk, F. J. (1924). Über die Formwahrnehmung beim Hunde. *Pflügers Arch*. **205**, 4–14.

Buytendijk, F. J. (1948). "Über den Schmerz." Huber, Bern.

Cable, D. (1969). Perceptual defence or set: A re-examination. *Psychon. Sci*. **16**, 331–332.

Campbell, F. W. (1974). The Transmission of Spatial Information through the Visual System. *In* Schmitt, F. O. and Worden, F. G. (Eds) "The Neurosciences." Third Study Program. MIT Press, Cambridge, Mass.

Campbell, F. W. and Kulikowski, J. J. (1966). Orientational selectivity of the human visual system. *J. Physiol*. **187**, 437–445.

Campbell, F. W. and Maffei, L. (1971). The tilt after-effect: A fresh look. *Vis. Res.* **11**, 833–840.

Campbell, F. W. and Maffei, L. (1974). Contrast and spatial frequency. *Sci. Am.* **231**, 106–114.

Campbell, F. W. and Robson, J. (1968). Application of Fourier Analysis to the visibility of gratings. *J. Physiol.* **197**, 551–566.

Cappone, M. K. (1966). The effect of verbal suggestion on the reversal rate of the Ames trapezoidal illusion. *J. Psychol.* **62**, 211–219.

Carhart, R., Tilman, T. W. and Johnson, K. (1967). Release of masking for speech through interaural time delay. *J. Acoust. Soc. Am.* **42**, 124–138.

Carlson, V. R. (1960). Overestimation in size-constancy judgments. *Am. J. Psychol.* **73**, 199–213.

Carlson, V. R. (1961). Effects of sleep deprivation and chlorpromazine on size constancy judgments. *Am. J. Psychol.* **74**, 552–560.

Carlson, V. R. (1962a). Adaptation in the perception of visual velocity. *J. Exp. Psychol.* **64**, 192–197.

Carlson, V. R. (1962b). Size constancy judgments and perceptual compromise. *J. Exp. Psychol.* **63**, 68–73.

Carpenter, P., Wiener, M. and Carpenter, J. (1956). Predictability of perceptual defence behavior. *J. Abnorm. Soc. Psychol.* **52**, 380–383.

Carterette, E. C. and Friedman, M. P. (Eds) (1973, 1974). "Handbook of Perception I–II." Academic Press, New York and London.

Carterette, E. C., Friedman, M. P. and Wyman, M. J. (1966). Feedback and psychophysical variables in signal detection. *J. Acoust. Soc. Am.* **6**, 1051–1055.

Cash, T., Neale, J. and Cromwell, R. L. (1972). Span of apprehension in schizophrenia: Full-report technique. *J. Abnorm. Psychol.* **79**, 322–327.

Cattell, R. B. (1957). "Personality and Motivation. Structure and Measurement." World Book, New York.

Cattell, R. B. (1969). Is field independence an expression of the general personality source trait of independence? *Percept. and Mot. Skills* **28**, 865–866.

Cautela, J. and Vitro, F. (1964). The effect of instruction on the appearance of the autokinetic effect. *J. Psychol.* **58**, 85–88.

Chapanis, A., Garner, W. R. and Morgan, C. T. (1949). "Applied Experimental Psychology." Wiley and Sons, New York.

Charnwood, J. R. B. (1951). "Essay on Binocular Vision." Hatton, London.

Cheng, M. F. (1968). Tactile-kinesthetic perception of length. *Am. J. Psychol.* **81**, 74–82.

Cherry, C. (1961). "On Human Communication." Science Editions, New York.

Chow, K. L. and Nissen, H. W. (1955). Interocular transfer of learning in visually naive and experienced infant chimpanzees. *J. Comp. and Physiol. Psychol.* **48**, 229–237.

Chung, S-H., Raymond, S. A. and Lettvin, J. Y. (1970). Multiple meaning in single visual units. *Brain Behav. Evol.* **3**, 72–101.

Churchill, A. V. (1969). Effects of head movement in visual-kinesthetic localization. *Percept and Mot. Skills.* **28**, 785–786.

Clark, B. and Graybiel, A. (1949). Linear acceleration and deceleration as factors influencing nonvisual orientation during flight. *J. Av. Med.* **20**, 92–101.

Cleland, B. G., Dubin, M. W. and Levick, W. R. (1971). Simultaneous recording of input and output of lateral geniculate neurones. *Nature New Biol.* **231**, 191–192.

Cleland, B. G. and Levick, W. R. (1974). Properties of rarely encountered types of ganglion cells in the cat's retina and an overall classification. *J. Physiol.* **240**, 457–492.

Cohen, A. (1961). Further investigation of the effects of intensity upon the pitch of pure tones. *J. Acoust. Soc. Am.* **33**, 1363–1375.

Cohen, S. I., Silverman, A. J. and Shmavonian, B. M. (1963). Psychological studies in altered sensory environments. *J. Psychosom. Res.* **6**, 259–281.

Cohen, W. (1957). Spatial and textural characteristics of the Ganzfeld. *Am. J. Psychol.* **70**, 403–410.

Coltheart, M. (1969). The influence of haptic size upon visual judgments of absolute distance. *Perception and Psychophys.* **5**, 143–144.

Comalli, P. E. Jr. (1966). Effect of unilateral above-knee amputation on perception of verticality. *Percept. and Mot. Skills* **23**, 91–96.

Coombs, C. H. (1964). "A Theory of Data." Wiley and Sons, New York.

Coren, S. (1969). Brightness contrast as a function of figure-ground relations. *J. Exp. Psychol.* **80**, 517–524.

Cornsweet, T. N. (1971). "Visual Perception." Academic Press, New York and London.

Corsini, D. H. and Pick, H. L. Jr. (1969). The effect of texture on tactually perceived length. *Perception and Psychopys.* **5**, 352–356.

Corso, J. F. (1958). Absolute thresholds for tones of low frequency. *Am. J. Psychol.* **71**, 367–374.

Corso, J. F. (1963). Bone conduction thresholds for sonic and ultrasonic frequencies. *J. Acoust. Soc. Am.* **35**, 1738–1743.

Corso, J. F. (1967). "The Experimental Psychology of Sensory Behavior." Holt, Rinehart and Winston, New York.

Corso, J. F. (1973). Hearing. *In* Wolman, B. J. (Ed.) "Handbook of General Psychology." Prentice-Hall, New Jersey.

Corso, J. F. and Levine, M. (1965). Pitch discrimination at high frequencies by air- and bone-conduction. *Am. J. Psychol.* **78**, 557–566.

Cragg, B. G. (1975). The development of synapses in the visual system of the cat. *J. Comp. Neurol.* **160**, 147–166.

Creed, R. S. (1935). Observations of binocular fusion and rivalry. *J. Physiol.* **84**, 381–392.

Critchley, M. (1965). Acquired anomalies of colour perception of central origin. *Brain* **88**, 711–724.

Cross, J. and Cross, J. (1969). The misperception of rotary motion. *Perception and Psychophys.* **5**, 94–96.

Culver, C. M. (1970). Errors in tactile localization. *Am. J. Psychol.* **83**, 420–427.

Dallenbach, K. M. (1927). The temperature spots and end organs. *Am. J. Psychol.* **39**, 402–427.

Dallenbach, K. M. (1931). A method of marking the skin. *Am. J. Psychol.* **43**, 287.

D'Amato, M. R. (1970). "Experimental Psychology: Methodology, Psychophysics and Learning." McGraw-Hill, New York.

Das, J. P. (1958). The Pavlovian theory of hypnosis: An evaluation. *J. Ment. Sci.* **104**, 82–90.

David, H. A. (1963). "The Method of Paired Comparisons." Griffin, London.

Davis, H. (1963). Discussion (to Beidler 1963). *In* Zotterman, Y. (Ed.) "Olfaction and Taste." Macmillan, New York.

Davis, J. M., McCourt, W. F., Solomon, P. and Courtney, J. (1961). Sensory deprivation: The role of social isolation. *Arch. gen. Psychiatr.* **5**, 84–90.

Davison, G. C. and Neale, J. M. (1974). "Abnormal Psychology. An Experimental Clinical Approach." Wiley and Sons, New York.

Davson, H. (Ed.) (1962). "The Eye: II. The Visual Process." Academic Press, New York and London.

Day, R. H. (1969). "Human Perception." Toppan Printing Co., Hong Kong.

Day, R. H. and Avery, G. C. (1970). Absence of the horizontal-vertical illusion in haptic space. *J. Exp. Psychol.* **83**, 172–173.

Day, R. H. and Power, R. P. (1963). Frequency of apparent reversal of rotary motion in depth as a function of shape and pattern. *Austral. J. Psychol.* **15**, 162–174.

Day, R. H. and Singer, G. (1969). "Issues in the Explanation of Sensory Adaptation and After-Effect." *In* Järvinen, E. J. *et al.* (Eds.) "Contemporary Research in Psychology of Perception in honorem Kai von Fieandt sexegenarii".

Day, R. H. and Strelow, E. (1971). Reduction or disappearance of visual after-effect of movement in the absence of a patterned surround. *Nature* **230**, 55–56.

Day, R. H. and Wade, N. J. (1969). Mechanisms involved in visual orientation constancy. *Psychol. Bull.* **71**, 33–42.

Deatherage, B. H. (1966). Examination of binaural interaction. *J. Acoust. Soc. Am.* **39**, 232–249.

Dennis, W. (1951). Cultural and developmental factors in perception. *In* Blake, R. R. and Ramsey, G. V. (Eds). "Perception: An Approach to Personality." Ronald Press, New York.

DeLorenzo, A. J. (1963). Studies on the ultrastructure and histophysiology of cell membranes, nerve fibers and synaptic junctions in chemo-receptors. *In* Zotterman Y. (Ed.) "Olfaction and Taste." Macmillan, New York.

DeSilva, H. R. (1928). An analysis of the visual perception of movement. *Brit. J. Psychol.*, Gen. Sect. **19**, 268–305.

Deutsch, J. A. (1955). A theory of shape recognition. *Brit. J. Psychol.* **46**, 30–37.

Deutsch, J. A. and Deutsch, D. (1963). Attention: Some theoretical considerations. *Psychol. Rev.* **70**, 80–90.

DeValois, R. L. (1960). Color vision mechanisms in the monkey. *J. Gen. Physiol.* **42**, 2, 115–128.

DeValois, R. L. (1965a). Analysis and coding of color vision in the primate visual system. *In* "Cold Spring Harbor Symposia on Quantitative Biology", Vol. 30.

DeValois, R. L. (1965b). Behavioral and electrophysiological studies of primate vision. *In* Neff, W. D. (Ed.) "Contributions to Sensory Psychology," Vol. 1. Academic Press, New York and London.

DeValois, R. L. (1972). Processing of Intensity and Wavelength Information by the Visual System. Abstract Guide of 20th International Congress of Psychology, Tokyo.

DeValois, R. L., Abramove, I. and Jacobs, G. H. (1966). Analysis of response patterns of LGN cells. *J. Opt. Soc. Am.* **56**, 966–977.

DeWolfe, R. K. S. and Duncan, C. P. (1959). Time estimation as a function of level of behavior of successive tasks. *J. Exp. Psychol.* **58**, 153–158.

Diamant, H., Funakoshi, M., Ström, L. and Zotterman, Y. (1963). Electrophysiological studies on human taste nerves. *In* Zotterman, Y. (Ed.) "Olfaction and Taste." Macmillan, New York.

Ditchburn, R. W. and Ginsborg, B. L. (1953). Involuntary eye movements during fixation. *J. Physiol.* **119**, 1–17.

Dixon, N. F. (1971). "Subliminal Perception: The Nature of a Controversy." McGraw-Hill, New York.

Dixon, N. F. and Haider, M. (1961). Changes in the visual threshold as a function of subliminal stimulation. *Quart. J. Exp. Psychol.* **13**, 229–235.

Dodwell, P. C. (1957). Shape recognition in rats. *Brit. J. Psychol.* **49**, 158.

Dodwell, P. C. (1964). A coupled system for coding and learning in shape discrimination. *Psychol. Rev.* **71**, 148–159.

Dodwell, P. C. (1970). "Visual Pattern Recognition." Holt, Rinehart and Winston, New York.

Dodwell, P. C. and Engel, G. R. (1963). A theory of binocular fusion. *Nature* **198**, 39–40.

Donner, K. O. (1973). Näön fysiologia (Physiology of Vision). *Duodecim* **89**, 883–898.

Douglas, F., Fuller, G. B. and Hawkins, W. F. (1969). Relationship between perception (input) and execution (output). *Percept. and Mot. Skills* **29**, 923–934.

Dowling, J. E. (1970). Organization of vertebrate retinas. *Invest. Ophthal.* **9**, 655–680.

Dowling, J. E. and Boycott, B. B. (1966). Organization of the primate retina: Electron microscopy. *Proc. Roy. Soc.* B, **166**, 80–111.

Dreher, B. (1972). Hypercomplex cells in the cat's striate cortex. *Invest. Ophthal.* **11**, 355–356.

Duke, J. D. (1966). Perception of finger drawings upon the body surface. *J. Gen. Psychol.* **75**, 305–314.

Dulany, D. E., DeValois, R. L., Beardslee, D. C. and Winterbottom, M. R. (1963). "Contributions to Modern Psychology: Selected Readings in General Psychology" (2nd edn.). Oxford University Press, New York.

Duncker, K. (1935). "Zur Psychologie des produktiven Denkens." Springer, Berlin.

Duncker, K. (1938). Induced Motion. *In* Ellis, W. D. (Ed.) "A Source Book of Gestalt Psychology." Routledge and Kegan, London.

Duncker, K. (1945). On problem solving. *Psychol. Monogr.* **58**, No. 270, 1–113.

Duran, P. and Tufenkjian, S. (1969). Tactile-kinesthetic methods for measuring length used by congenitally blind children. *Percept. and Mot. Skills* **28**, 395–400.

Dushkin, D. A. (Ed.) (1970). "Psychology Today: An Introduction." CRM Books, Del Mar.

DuVerney, G. J. (1683). "Traité de l'organe de l'ouie" (Engl. translation of 2. edn. 1748).

Døving, K. B. (1964). Studies on the relation between the frog's electro-olfactogram (EOG) and single unit activity in the olfactory bulb. *Acta Physiol. Scand.* **60**, 150–163.

Døving, K. B. (1965). Studies on the responses of bulbar neurons of the frog to different odour stimuli. *Rev. Laryng. Bordeaux* **86**, 845–854.

Døving, K. B. (1966a). Analysis of odour similarities from electrophysiological data. *Acta Physiol. Scand.* **68**, 404–418

Døving, K. B. (1966b). Electrophysiological Studies on Olfactory Discrimination in the Frog (diss.). From the Department of Physiology, Karolinska Institutet, Stockholm.

Døving, K. B. (1967). Problems in the physiology of olfaction. *In* "Symposia in Foods: The Chemistry and Physiology of Flavors," 52–94. AVI Publishing Co. Oregon State University, 1965. West Port, Connecticut.

Døving, K. B. (1970). Experiments in olfaction. *In* Wolstenholme, G. E. W. and Knight, J. (Eds) "Ciba Foundation Symposium on Taste and Smell in Vertebrates." Churchill, London.

Døving, K. B. (1972). "Introduction to the Physiology of the Olfactory Sense." Proceedings of the 3rd Nordic Aroma Symposium, Helsinki." Nordforsk Committee on Sensory Properties of Food, Hämeenlinna.

Døving, K. B. (1973). Luktesansen. Naturen no. 4, Oslo.

Eccles, J. C. (1973). "The Understanding of the Brain." McGraw-Hill, New York.

Edwards, W. (1954). Autokinetic movement of very large stimuli. *J. Exp. Psychol.* **48**, 493–495.

Egeth, H. E., Kamlet, A. S. and Bell, R. A. (1970). The reversal of classical contrast in temperature perception. *Psychon. Sci.* **19**, 96.

Egeth, H. E. and Smith, E. E. (1967). Perceptual selectivity in a visual recognitive task. (Selective tuning of visual perception.) *J. Exp. Psychol.* **74**, 543–549.

Eisler, H. and Ekman, G. (1959). A mechanism of subjective similarity. *Acta Psychol.* **16**, 1–10.

Ekman, G. (1954). "Similarity analysis of olfaction. A preliminary investigation." *Rep. Psychol. Lab., no. 10*, University of Stockholm.

Ekman, G. (1961). "A methodological note on scales of gustatory intensity." *Rep. Psychol. Lab., no. 98*, University of Stockholm.

Ekman, G. (1962). Measurement of moral judgment: a comparison of scaling methods. *Percept. and Mot. Skills* **15**, 3–9.

Ekman, G. (1972). Psychophysik und psychologische Messmethoden. *In* Meili, R. und Rohracher, H. (Eds) "Lehrbuch der experimentellen Psychologie" (3rd edn.). Huber, Bern.

Ekman, G., Frankenhaeuser, M., Berglund, B. and Waszak, M. (1969). Apparent duration as a function of intensity of vibrotactile stimulation. *Percept. and Mot. Skills* **28**, 151–156.

Ekman, G. and Künnapas, T. (1962). Measurement of aesthetic value by "direct" and "indirect" scaling methods. *Scand. J. Psychol.* **3**, 33–39.

Elfner, L. F. and Delaune, W. R. (1970). Detection of shift in binaural images: A rating method approach. *Perception and Psychophys.* **8**, 158–160.

Elliott, J. (1780). "Philosophical Observations on the Senses of Vision and Hearing, to which are added, A Treatise on Harmonic Sounds and an Essay on Combustion and Animal Heat." J. Johnson, London.

Elliott, J. (1786). "Experiments and Observations on Light and Colours: to which is prefixed the Analogy between Heat and Motion." J. Johnson, London.

Elliott, J. (1787). "A Narrative of the Life and Death of John Elliot. M.D. Containing an Account of the Rise, Progress, and Catastrophe of his Unhappy Passion for Miss Mary Boydell: A Review of his Writings, together with an Apology written by himself, under the Pressure of Expected Condemnation, after his Commitment for attempting to assasinate Miss Boydell." London.

Engelmann, W. (1928). Untersuchungen über die Schallokalisation bei Tieren. *Zs. f. Psychol.* **105**, 317–370.

Engen, T. (1961). Direct scaling of odor intensity. *Rep. Psychol. Lab., No. 106.* University of Stockholm.

Engen, T. (1962). "The psychological similarity of the odors of the aliphatic alcohols." *Rep. Psychol. Lab., No. 127.* University of Stockholm.

Engen, T. (1971a). Psychophysics. I. Discrimination and Detection. *In* Kling, J. W. and Riggs, L. A. (Eds) "Experimental Psychology" (3rd edn. of Woodworth and Schlosberg). Holt, Rinehart and Winston, New York.

Engen, T. (1971b). Psychophysics II. Scaling Methods. *In* Kling, J. W. and Riggs, L. A. (Eds) "Experimental Psychology" (3rd edn. of Woodworth and Schlosberg). Holt, Rinehart and Winston, New York.

Enroth-Cugell, C. and Robson, J. G. (1966). The contrast sensitivity of retinal ganglion cells of the cat. *J. Physiol.* **187**, 517–552.

Enterline, E. G. (1970). Form discrimination: Spatial relationships between a standard and comparison figure. *Percept. and Mot. Skills* **30**, 959–969.

Epstein, W. and Mountford, D. (1963). Judgement of slant in response to an isolated gradient of stimulation. *Percept. and Mot. Skills* **16**, 733–737.

Eriksen, C. W. (1951). Perceptual defence as a function of unacceptable needs. *J. Abnorm. Soc. Psychol.* **46**, 557–564.

Eriksen, C. W. (1962). Figments, fantasies and follies: A search for the subconscious mind. *In* Eriksen, C. W. (Ed.) "Behavior and Awareness." Duke University Press, Durham.

Eriksen, C. W. (1964). Perceptual defence. *In* Hoch, P. H. and Zubin, J. (Eds). "Psychopathology of Perception." Grane and Stratton, New York.

Eriksson, S. (1967). The shape slant invariance hypothesis in static perception. *Scand. J. Psychol.* **8**, 193–208.

Erismann, Th. (1946). Das Werden der Wahrnehmung. Deutscher Psychologenkongress.

Ertel, K. (1968). Wahrnehmung, Wahrnehmungsantwort und Grössenakzentuierung. *Studia Psychologica* **10**, 304-312.

Evans, E. F. (1972). The frequency response and other properties of single fibres in the guinea-pig cochlea nerve. *J. Physiol.* **226**, 263–287.

Evans, E. F. (1974a). Neural Processes for the detection of acoustic patterns and for sound localization. *In* Schmitt, F. O. and Worden, F. G. (Eds) "The Neurosciences." Third Study Program. MIT Press, Cambridge, Mass.

Evans, E. F. (1974b). Normal and abnormal functioning of the cochlea nerve. *In* Bench, R. J., Pye, A. and Pye, J. D. (Eds) "Sound Reception in Animals." Academic Press, New York and London.

Evans, F. J., Gustafson, L. A., O'Connell, D. N., Orne, M. T. and Shor, R. E. (1969). Sleep-induced behavioral response. *J. Nerv. and Ment. Disease* **148**, 467–476.

Ewald, J. R. (1899). Zur Physiologie des Labyrinths: VI. Eine neue Hörtheorie. *Pflügers Archiv.* **76**, 147–188.

Exner, S. (1894). "Entwurf zu einer physiologischen Erklärung der Psychischen Erscheinungen." Deuticke, Leipzig.

Exner, S. (1896). Über autokinetische Empfindungen. *Zs. f. Psychol.* **12**, 313–330.

Fabre, J. H. (1966). The Pine Processionary. *In* Breland, K. and Breland, M. "Animal Behavior." Macmillan, New York.

Falmagne, J. C. (1973). Foundations of Fechnerian psychophysics. *In* Atkinson, R. C., Kranz, P. H., Luce, R. D. and Suppes, P. (Eds) "Contemporary Developments in Mathematical Psychology. Vol. I." Freeman, San Francisco.

Fantz, R. (1963). Pattern vision in newborn infants. *Science* **140**, 296–297.

Fechner, G. (1966). Elemente der Psychophysik. (English translation "Elements of Psychophysics"). Holt, Rinehart and Winston, New York.

Fender, D. H. (1964). Control mechanisms of the eye. *Sci. Am.* **211**, 24–33.

Fernald, R. D. (1971). A neuron model with spatially distributed synaptic input. *Biophys. J.* **11**, 323–340.

Ferrall, S. C. and Dallenbach, K. M. (1930). The analysis and synthesis of burning heat. *Am. J. Psychol.* **42**, 72–82.

Festigner, L., Allyn, M. R. and White, C. W. (1971). The perception of color with achromatic stimulation. *Vis. Res.* **11**, 591–612.

Fieandt, K., von (1938a). "Ein neues Invarianzphänomen der Farbenwahrnehmung." *Ann. Acad. Sci. Fenn.* B **41**, 2. Helsinki.

Fieandt, K., von. (1938b). "Über Sehen von Tiefengebilden bei wechselnder Beleuchtungsrichtung." Rep. Psychol. Inst. University of Helsinki.

Fieandt, K., von. (1949). Das phänomenologische Problem von Licht und Schatten. *Acta Psychol.* **6**, 337–357.

Fieandt, K., von. (1951). Loudness Invariance in Sound Perception. *Acta Psychol. Fennica* I, 9–20. Helsinki.

Fieandt, K., von. (1957). Ein Beitrag zur einheitlichen Wahrnehmungstheorie. *Studium Generale no. 10.*

Fieandt, K., von. (1958). Toward a unitary theory of perception. *Psychol. Rev.* **65**, 375–320.

Fieandt, K., von. (1959). Form perception and modelling of patients without sight. *Confinia Psychiatrica* **2**, 205–213.

Fieandt, K., von. (1962a). Current trends in perceptual psychology. *Psychol. Beiträge* **6**, 651–661.

Fieandt, K., von. (1962b). Erweiterung des Körperschemas im Spiegelbild. *Zs f. Psychol.* **167**, 57–65.

Fieandt, K., von. (1965). The interaction of modalities. *Ars Gratia Hominis* **2**, no. 5. Sacramento State University Press, Sacramento.

Fieandt, K., von. (1966). The World of Perception. The Dorsey Press, Homewood, Illinois. (Finnish edition 1972, WSOY. Helsinki and Porvoo.)

Fieandt, K., von., Ahonen, L. and Järvinen, E. J. (1964a). A scaling method for measuring color constancy. *Scand. J. Psychol.* **5**, 10–16.

Fieandt, K., von., Ahonen, L., Järvinen, E. J. and Lian, A. (1964b). Color experiments with modern sources of illumination. *Percept. and Mot. Skills* **20**, 555–556.

Fieandt, K., von., Järvinen, E. J. and Korkala, P. (1974). Space perception. *In* "Encyclopaedia Britannica" 1974, 378–381ᶠ Helen Hemmingway Benton, Encyclopaedia Britannica, USA.

Fieandt, K., von. and Gibson, J. J. (1959). The sensitivity of the eye to two kinds of continuous transformation of a shadow pattern. *J. Exp. Psychol.* **57**, 344–347.

Fieandt, K., von. and Näätänen, R. (1970). The effect of urbanization on simple and choice reaction time, on movement speed, preferred tempo and time estimation. *Rep. Inst. Psychol. University of Helsinki, no. 3.*

Fieandt, K. von. and Wertheimer, M. (1969). Perception. *Ann. Rev. Psychol.* **20**, 159–192.

Firestone, F. A. (1930). The phase difference and amplitude ratio at the ears due to a source of pure tones. *J. Acoust. Soc. Am.* **2**, 260–268.

Flanagan, J. L. (1962). Computational model for basilar-membrane displacement. *J. Acoust. Soc. Am.* **34**, 1370–1376.

Fletcher, H. (1940). Auditory patterns. *Rev. Mod. Physics* **12**, 47–65.

Fletcher, H. (1953). "Speech and Hearing in Communication." Van Nostrand New York.

Flock, A. (1965). Transducing mechanisms in the lateral line canal organ receptors. *Cold Spring Harbor Symposia* **30**, 133–145.

Flock, H. R. (1962). "Stereokinetic Phenomena" (Translation and comments of Musatti's study of 1924.) Psychology Department, Cornell University.

Flock, H. R. (1964). A possible optical basis for monocular slant perception. *Psychol. Rev.* **71**, 380–391.

Flock, H. R. (1965). Optical texture and linear perspective as stimuli for slant perception. *Psychol. Rev.* **72**, 505–514.

Flock, H. R., Graves, D., Tenney, J. and Stephenson, B. (1967). Slant judgments of single rectangles at a slant. *Psychon. Sci.* **7**, 57–58.

Forrest, D. W. and Lee, S. G. (1962). Mechanisms of defence and readiness in perception and recall. *Psychol. Monogr.* **76**, 4. No. 523.

Forsyth, G. A. (1970). Perceptual isolation effects: Short-term visual storage vs. cognitive-perceptual structure. *Perception and Psychophys.* **7**, 342–344.

Fraisse, P. (1963). "La Psychologie du Temps." Presses Universitaires de France, Paris.

Fraisse, P. (1964). "The Psychology of Time." Eyre and Spottiswoode, London.

Fraisse, P., Sifre, M., Oleron, G. and Zuili, N. (1968). Le rythme veille. Sommeil et l'estimation du temps. Actes du IIIe Symposium, Bel Air 257–265, Masson, Paris.

Fraisse, P. and Voillaume, C. (1969). Conditionnement temporel du rythme alpha et l'estimation du temps. *L'Année Psychol. Fasc.* **1**, 1–12.

François, M. (1927). Contribution à l'etude du sens du temps. La température interne, comme facteur de variation de l'appréciation subjective des durées. *L'Année Psychol.* **28**, 186–204.

Frank, H. (1930). Über den Einfluss inadequater Konvergenz und Akkomodation auf die Sehgrösse. *Psychol. Forsch.* **13**, 135–144.

Frankenhaeuser, M. (1958). Time estimation as affected by barbiturate and metamphetamine. *Rep. Psychol. Lab., University of Stockholm*, **62**.

Frankenhaeuser, M. (1959). "Estimation of Time. An Experimental Study." Almqvist and Wiksell, Uppsala.

Frankenhaeuser, M. and Järpe, G. (1962). Psychophysiological reactions to infusions of a mixture of adrenaline and nor-adrenaline. *Scand. J. Psychol.* **3**, 21–29.

Frankenhaeuser, M. and Post, B. (1966). Objective and subjective performance as influenced by drug-induced variations in activation level. *Scand. J. Psychol.* **7**, 168–178.

Franzén, O. (1969). The dependence of vibrotactile threshold and magnitude functions on stimulation frequency and signal level. A perceptual and neural comparison. *Scand. J. Psychol.* **10**, 289–298.

Franzén, O., Markowitz, J. and Swets, J. A. (1970). Spatially-limited attention to vibrotactile stimulation. *Perception and Psychophys.* **7**, 193–196.

Freeman, G. L. (1948). "The Energetics of Human Behavior." Cornell University Press, Ithaca.

Freeman, R. B. Jr. (1966). Ecological optics and visual slant. *Psychol. Rev.* **72**, 501–504.

Freeman, R. B. Jr. (1967). Contrast interpretation of brightness constancy. *Psychol. Bull.* **67**, 165–187.

Freeman, R. B. Jr. (1968). Perspective determinants of visual size-constancy in binocular and monocular cats. *Am. J. Psychol.* **81**, 67–73.

Freeman, R. B. Jr. and Pasnak, R. (1968). Perspective determinants of the rotating trapezoid illusion. *J. Exp. Psychol.* **76**, 94–101.

Freeman, R. B. Jr. and Pettigrew, J. D. (1973). Alteration of visual cortex from environmental asymmetries. *Nature* **246**, 359–360.

x

Frenkel-Brunswik, E. (1949). Intolerance of ambiguity as an emotional and perceptual personality variable. *J. Pers.* **18**, 108–143.

Frenkel-Brunswik, E. (1951). Personality theory and perception. *In* Blake, R. R. and Ramsey, G. V. (Eds) "Perception: An Approach to Personality." Ronald Press, New York.

Frey, M., von. and Kiesow, F. (1899). Über die Funktion der Tastkörperchen. *Zs. f. Psychol.* **20**, 126–163.

From F, (1959). Apperception: A new approach to a forgotten problem. *Acta Psychol.* **16**, 254–266.

From, F. (1953). Om oplevelsen af andres adfaerd. Nyt Nordisk Forlag, Copenhagen.

From, F. (1971). "Perception of Other People." Columbia University Press, New York and London.

Fry, G. A. (1933). Modulation of the optic nerve current as a basis for color-vision. *Am. J. Psychol.* **45**, 488–494.

Funkenstein, H. H., Nelson, P., Winter, P., Wollberg, Z. and Newman, J. (1971). Unit responses in auditory cortex of awake squirrel monkeys to vocal stimulation. *In* Sachs M. (Ed.) "The Auditory System; a Workshop." National Educational Consultants, Baltimore.

Fuortes, M. G. F. (1971). Generation of responses in receptor. *In* Autrum, H., Jung, R., Loewenstein, W. R., MacKay, D. M. and Teuber, H. L. (Eds) "Handbook of Sensory Physiology," Vol. I, Springer, Berlin·

Galanter, E. (1962). Contemporary psychophysics. *In* Brown, R., Galanter, E., Hess, E. H. and Mandler, G. (Eds) "New Directions in Psychology." Holt, Rinehart and Winston, New York.

Galanter, E. and Messick, S. (1961). The relation between category and magnitude scales of loudness. *Psychol. Rev.* **63**, 149–159.

Galli, P. A. (1932). Über vermittelst verschiedener Sinnesreize erweckte Wahrnehmung von Scheinbewegungen. *Arch. f. d. ges. Psychol.* **85**, 137–180.

Ganchrow, J. R. and Erickson, R. P. (1970). Neural correlates of gustatory intensity and quality. *J. Neurophysiol.* **33**, 768–781.

García-Austt, E., Bogacz, J. and Vanzulli, A. (1964). Effects of attention and inattention upon visual evoked responses. *Electroenceph clin. Neurophysiol.* **17**, 136–143.

Gardner, M. B. (1968). Historical background of the Haas and/or precedence effect. *J. Acoust. Soc. Am.* **43**, 1243–1248.

Gardner, R. W., Holzman, P. S., Klein, G. S., Linton, H. B. and Spence, D. P. (1959). "Cognitive Control: A Study of Individual Consistencies in Cognitive Behavior." *Psychol. Issues I*, Monogr. 4.

Gardner, R. W. and Moriarty, A. (1968). "Personality Development at Preadolescence." University of Washington Press, Seattle.

Garner, W. R. and Creelman, C. D. (1967). Problems and methods of psychological scaling. *In* Helson, H. and Bevan, W. (Eds) "Contemporary Approaches to Psychology." Van Nostrand, Princeton.

Garner, W. R., Hake, H. W. and Eriksen, C. W. (1956). Operationism and the concept of perception. *Psychol. Rev.* **63**, 149–159.

Garner, W. R. and Miller, G. A. (1947). The masked threshold of pure tones as a function of duration. *J. Exp. Psychol.* **33**, 293–303.

Gazzaniga, M. S. and Blakemore, C. (Eds) (1975). "Handbook of Psychobiology." Academic Press, New York and London.

Gelb, A. (1929). Die Farbenkonstanz der Sehdinge. Handb. norm. pathol. Physiol. 12 (I), 594–678.

Gelb, A. (1938). A distortion of "surface contours." *In* Ellis, W. D. (Ed.) "A Source Book of Gestalt Psychology." Routledge and Kegan, London.

Geldard, F. A. (1953). "The Human Senses." Wiley and Sons, New York.

Geldard, F. A. (1972). "The Human Senses." (2nd. edn.) Wiley and Sons, London.

Geldard, F. A. (1974). Punctiform vibratory sensitivity of hair skin. Proceedings of 20th International Congress of Psychology, Tokyo, 327.

Gemelli, I. F. M. A. (1935). Neue Beobachtungen über das Wesen der Wahrnehmung. *Acta Psychol.* **1**, 83–98.

Gengerelli, J. A. (1948). Apparent movement in relation to homonymous and heteronymous stimulation of the cerebral hemispheres. *J. Exp. Psychol.* **38**, 592–599.

Gescheider, G. A., Barton, W. G., Bruce, M. R., Goldenberg, J. H. and Greenspan, M. J. (1969). Effects of simultaneous auditory stimulation on the detection of tactile stimuli. *J. Exp. Psychol.* **81**, 120–125.

Gescheider, G. A. and Niblette, R. K. (1967). Crossmodality masking for touch and hearing. *J. Exp. Psychol.* **74**, 313–320.

Gibson, E. J. (1969). "Principles of Perceptual Learning and Development." Appleton Century Crofts, New York.

Gibson, E. J., Walk, R. D. and Tighe, T. J. (1959). Enchangement and deprivation of visual stimulation during rearing as factors in visual discrimination learning. *J. Comp. Physiol. Psychol.* **52**, 74–81.

Gibson, J. J. (1937). Adaptation with negative after effect. *Psychol. Rev.* **44**, 222–244.

Gibson, J. J. (1950). "The Perception of the Visual World." Houghton Mifflin Co., Cambridge, Mass.

Gibson, J. J. (1954). A theory of pictorial perception. *Aud.-Vis. Comm. Rev.* **1**, 3–23.

Gibson, J. J. (1956). The non-projective aspects of the Rorschach experiment: IV. The Rorschach plots considered as pictures. *J. Soc. Psychol.* **44**, 203–206.

Gibson, J. J. (1959). Perception as a function of stimulation. *In* Koch, S. (Ed.) "Psychology: A Study of a Science, Vol. 1." McGraw-Hill, New York.

Gibson, J. J. (1960). The concept of stimulus in psychology. *Am. Psychol.* **15**, 694–703.

Gibson, J. J. (1962). Observations on active touch. *Psychol. Rev.* **69**, 477–491.

Gibson, J. J. (1966). "The Senses Considered as Perceptual Systems." Houghton Mifflin Co., Boston.

Gibson, J. J. (1969). Further thoughts on the perception of rigid motion. *In* Järvinen, E. J. *et al.* (Eds) "Contemporary Research in Psychology of Perception in honorem Kai von Fieandt sexagenarii." WSOY, Porvoo.

Gibson, J. J., Kaplan, G. A., Reynolds, H. N. Jr. and Wheeler, K. (1969). The change from visible to invisible: A study of optical transitions. *Perception and Psychophys.* **5**, 113–116.

Gilbert, G. M. (1970). "Personality Dynamics: A Biosocial Approach." Harper and Row, New York.

Gilson, R. D. (1969). Vibrotactile masking: Some spatial and temporal aspects. *Perception and Psychophys.* **5**, 176–180.

Glass, D. G. and Singer, J. E. (1972). "Urban Stress: Experiments on Noise and Social Stressors." Academic Press, New York and London.

Glick, J. A. (1968). An experimental analysis of subject-object relationships in perception. *In* Haber, R. N. (Ed.) "Contemporary Theory and Research in Visual Perception." Holt, Rinehart and Winston, New York.

Glick, J. A., Wapner, S. and Werner, H. (1965). Some relations between autokinetic motion and space localization. *Acta Psychol.* **24**, 41–48.

Goethe, J. W., von. (1810). "Zur Farbenlehre." J. G. Cotta, Tübingen.

Gogel, W. C. (1963). The visual perception of size and distance. *Vis. Res.* **3**, 101–120.

Gogel, W. C. and Mertens, H. W. (1966). A method of simulating objects moving in depth. *Percept. and Mot. Skills* **23**, 371–377.

Goldscheider, A. (1909). "Gesammelte Abhandlungen." Thieme, Leipzig.

Goldscheider, A. and Hoefer, P. (1923). Über den Drucksinn. *Pflügers Arch.* **199**, 292–319.

Goldstein, J. L. (1967). Auditory nonlinearity. *J. Acoust. Soc. Am.* **41**, 676– 689.

Goldstein, K. and Gelb, A. (1920). Über den Einfluss des vollständigen Verlustes des optischen Vorstellungsvermögens auf das taktile Erkennen. *Zs. f. Psychol.* **83**, 1–94.

Goldstone, S., Boardman, W. K. and Lhamon, W. T. (1959). Intersensory comparisons of temporal judgments. *J. Exp. Psychol.* **57**, 243–248.

Gombrich, E. H. (1965). "Visual Discovery through Art." Arts Magazine, November 1965 and *In* Hogg, J. (Ed.) (1969) "Psychology and the Visual Arts." Penguin, Harmondsworth.

Goodenough, D. R. and Karp, S. A. (1961). Field dependence and intellectual functioning. *J. Abnorm. Soc. Psychol.* **63**, 241–246.

Goodstein, L. D. and Lanyon, R. I. (Eds) (1971). "Readings in Personality Assessment." Wiley and Sons, New York and London.

Gottschaldt, K. (1926). Über den Einfluss der Erfahrung auf die Wahrnehmung von Figuren. *Psychol. Forsch.* **8**, 261–317.

Goude, G. (1972a). A multidimensional scaling approach to the perception of art. I. *Scand. J. Psychol.* **13**, 258–271.

Goude, G. (1972b). A multidimensional scaling approach to the perception of art. II. *Scand. J. Psychol.* **13**, 272–284.

Gouras, P. (1971). The function of the midget cell system in primate color vision. *Vis. Res.*, Suppl. **3**, 397–410.

Gouras, P. (1974). Opponent-colour cells in different layers of foveal striate cortex. *J. Physiol.* **238**, 583–602.

Graham, C. H. (1950). Behavior, perception and the psychophysical methods. *Psychol. Rev.* **57**, 108–120.

Graham, C. H. (Ed.) (1965). "Vision and Visual Perception." Wiley and Sons, New York.

Granit, R. (1947). "Sensory Mechanisms of the Retina." Oxford University Press, London.

Granit, R. (1955). "Receptors and Sensory Perception." Yale University Press, New Haven.

Granit, R. (1962). The visual pathway. *In* Davson, H. (Ed.) "The Eye. Vol. 2." Academic Press, New York and London.

Granit, R. (1968). The development of retinal neurophysiology. *Science* **160**, 1192–1196.

Granit, R. and Svaetichin, G. (1939). Principles and technique of the electrophysiological analysis of colour perception with the aid of microelectrodes. *Uppsala Läkareförenings Förhandlingar* **65**, 161–177.

Graybiel, A., Clark, B., McCorquodale, H. and Hupp, D. (1946). Role of vestibular nystagmus in the visual perception of moving target in the dark. *Am. J. Psychol.* 59, 259–266.

Green, D. (1958). "Detection of Signals in Noise and the Critical Band Concept." University of Michigan. Techn. Rep. no. 82.

Green, D. M. and Swets, J. A. (1966). "Signal Detection Theory and Psychophysics." Wiley and Sons, New York.

Greenbaum, M. (1956). Manifest anxiety and tachistoscopic recognition of facial photographs. *Percept. and Mot. Skills* 6, 245.

Gregory, R. L. (1972). Cognitive contours. *Nature* 238, 51–52.

Gregory, R. L. and Zangwill, O. L. (1963). The origin of the autokinetic effect. *Quart. J. Exp. Psychol.* 15, 252–261.

Gregson, R. A. M., Mitchell, M. J., Simmonds, M. B. and Wells, E. (1969). Relative olfactory intensity perception as mediated by ratio range category scale responses. *Perception and Psychophys.* 6, 133–136.

Gregson, R. A. M. and Paris, G. L. (1967). Intensity-volume interaction effects in gustatory perception. *Perception and Psychophys.* 2, 483–487.

Gregson, R. A. M. and Russell, P. N. (1965a). "Problems and Results in the Scaling of Intermodal Complex Taste Similarities by D Metrics." Department of Psychology and Sociology. University of Canterbury, New Zealand, Research Project 7.

Gregson, R. A. M. and Russell, P. N. (1965b). Psychophysical power law exponent value for sucrose intensity. *Percept. and Mot. Skills* 20, 294.

Groos, K. (1896). Zum Problem der unbewussten Zeitschätzung. *Zs. f. Psychol.* 9, 321–330.

Gross, C. G., Rocha-Miranda, C. E. and Bender, D. B. (1972). Visual properties of neurons in inferotemporal cortex of the macaque. *J. Neurophysiol.* 35, 96–111.

Grossmann, R. C. and Hattis, B. F. (1967). Oral mucosal sensory innervation and sensory experience. *In* Bosma, J. F. (Ed.) "Symposium on Oral Sensation and Perception." Thomas, Springfield, Ill.

Grünewald, I. (1946). "Henri Matisse." WSOY, Porvoo.

Guilford, J. P. (1954). "Psychometric Methods (2nd edn.)." McGraw-Hill, New York.

Gulliksen, H. (1950). "Theory of Mental Tests." Wiley and Sons, New York.

Gulliksen, H. and Messick, S. (Eds) (1960). "Psychological Scaling: Theory and Applications." Wiley and Sons, New York.

Haber, R. N. (1965). Limited modification of the trapezoidal illusion with experience. *Am. J. Psychol.* 78, 651–655.

Haber, R. N. (1966). Nature of the effect of set on perception. *Psychol. Rev.* 73, 335–351.

Haber, R. N. and Fried, A. H. (1975). "An Introduction to Psychology." Holt, Rinehart and Winston, New York.

Haber, R. N. and Hershenson, M. (1973). "The Psychology of Visual Perception." Holt, Rinehart and Winston, New York.

Hake, H. W. and Myers, A. E. (1969). Familiarity and shape constancy. *J. Exp. Psychol.* 80, 205–214.

Hammond, P. and MacKay, D. M. (1975). Responses of cat visual cortical cells to kinetic contours and static noise. *J. Physiol.* 252, 44–45.

Harper, R. S. (1953). The perceptual modification of colored figures. *Am. J. Psychol.* 66, 86–89.

Harris, C. S. (1965). Perceptual adaptation to inverted, reversed and displaced vision. *Psychol. Rev.* **72**, 419–444.

Harris, C. S. and Haber, R. N. (1963). Selective attention and coding in visual perception. *J. Exp. Psychol.* **65**, 328–333.

Hartline, H. K. (1934). Intensity and duration in the excitation of single photoreceptor units. *J. Cell. Comp. Physiol.* **5**, 229–247.

Hartline, H. K. and Graham, C. H. (1932). Nerve impulses from single receptors in the eye. *J. Cell. Comp. Physiol.* **1**, 277–295.

Hartline, H. K. and Ratliff, F. (1957). Inhibitory interaction of receptor units in the eye of *Limulus*. *J. Gen. Physiol.* **40**, 357–376.

Hartshorne, C. (1934). "The Philosophy and Psychology of Sensation." University of Chicago Press, Chicago.

Hay, J. C. and Sawyer, S. (1969). Position constancy and binocular convergence. *Perception and Psychophys.* **5**, 310–312.

Hazlewood, V. and Singer, G. (1969). Kinesthetic orientation judgements during lateral head, body and trunk tilt. *Perception and Psychophys.* **5**, 141–142.

Head, H. (1920). "Studies in Neurology." Oxford University Press, London.

Heaton, J. M. (1968). "The Eye." Camelot Press, London.

Heidegger, M. (1961). "Sein und Zeit (10. Aufl)." Niemeyer, Tübingen.

Heijden, A. H. C. van der (1972). Note on simultaneous discrimination of visual attributes. *Scand J. Psychol.* **13**, 71–72.

Heinemann, E. G. (1961). Photographic measurement of the retinal image. *Am. J. Psychol.* **74**, 440–445.

Heinitz, W. (1931). Strukturprobleme in primitiver Musik., De Gruyter and Co. M.B.H., Hamburg.

Held, R. and Richards, W. (Eds) (1950–1972). "Perception: Mechanisms and Models. Readings from Scientific American 1950–1972." Freeman, San Francisco.

Helmholtz, H., von. (1863). "Die Lehre von den Tonempfindungen als physiologische Grundlage für die Theorie der Musik." Vieweg, Braunschweig.

Helmholtz, H., von. (1867). "Handbuch der physiologischen Optik." (1. Auflage). Voss, Hamburg.

Helmholtz, H., von. (1896). "Handbuch der physiologischen Optik." (2. Auflage). Voss, Hamburg.

Helmholtz, H., von. (1894). Über den Ursprung der richtigen Deutung unserer Sinneseindrücke. *Ps. Psychol.* **7**, 81–96.

Helson, H. (1964). "Adaptation-level Theory. An Experimental and Systematic Approach to Behavior." Harper and Row, London.

Helson, H. and Bevan, W. (Eds). (1968). "Contemporary Approaches to Psychology" (2. edn.). Van Nostrand, Princeton.

Henning, H. (1924). "Der Geruch." Barth, Leipzig.

Hensel, H. (1952). Physiologie der Thermoreception. *Ergebn. Physiol.* **47**, 166–368.

Hensel, H. (1966). "Allgemeine Sinnesphysiologie. Hautsinne, Geschmack, Geruch." Springer, Berlin.

Hensel, H. (1973). "Cutaneous Thermoreceptors." *In* Autrum, H., Jung, R., Loewenstein, W. R., MacKay, D. H. and Teuber, H. L. (Eds.) "Handbook of Sensory Physiology, Vol. II." Springer, Berlin.

Herget, C. M. and Hardy, J. D. (1942). Spatial summation of heat. *Am. J. Physiol.* **135**, 426–429.

Hering, E. (1861). Der Raumsinn und die Bewegungen des Auges. *In* Hermann, L. (Ed.) "Handbuch der Physiologie, I Theil, III Band." Vogel, Leipzig.

Hering, E. (1920). Grundzüge der Lehre vom Lichtsinn. *In* Graefe and Saemisch (Eds) "Handbuch der gesammten Augenheilkunde, vol. III." Springer, Berlin.

Hering, E. (1964). "Outlines of a Theory of the Light Sense." Harvard University Press, Cambridge, Mass.

Hernández-Peón, R. (1964). Attention, sleep, motivation and behavior. *In* Heath, R. G. (Ed.) "The Role of Pleasure in Behavior." Harper and Row, New York.

Hernández-Peón, R., Guzmán-Florea, C., Alcarez, M. and Fernandez-Guardiola, A. (1957). Sensory transmission in visual pathway during "attention" in unanaesthetized cats. *Acta Neural. Latinoamer.* **3**, 1–8.

Hernández-Peón. R., Scherrer, H. and Jouvet, M. (1956). Modification of electric activity in cochlea nucleus during "attention" in unanaesthetized cats. *Science* **123**, 331–332.

Heron, W. (1957). The pathology of boredom. *Sci. Am.* **196**, 52–56.

Hershberger, W. A. and Urban, D. (1970). Three motion-parallax cues in one-dimensional polar projections of rotation in depth, *J. Exp. Psychol.* **86**, 380–381.

Hess, E. H. (1959). Imprinting. *Science* **130**, 133–141.

Hess, E. H. (1961). Shadows and depth perception. *Sci. Am.* **204**, 139–148.

Hill, J. W. (1971). Processing of tactual and visual point stimuli sequentially presented at high rates. *J. Exp. Psychol.* **88**, 340–348.

Hill, J. W. and Bliss, J. C. (1968). Perception of sequentially presented point stimuli. *Perception and Psychophys.* **4**, 289–295.

Hirsch, H. V. B. and Spinelli, D. N. (1970). Visual experience modifies distribution of horizontally and vertically oriented receptive fields in cats. *Science* **168**, 869–871.

Hirsch, H. V. B. and Spinelli, D. N. (1971). Modification of the distribution of receptive field orientation in cats by selective visual exposure during development. *Exp. Brain Res.* **13**, 509–527.

Hirsh, I. J. and Sherrick, C. E. (1961). Perceived order in different sense modalities. *J. Exp. Psychol.* **62**, 423–432.

Hoagland, H. (1933). The physiological control of judgments of duration. *J. Gen. Psychol.* **9**, 267–287.

Hoagland, H. (1935). "Pacemakers in Relation to Aspects of Behavior." Macmillan, New York.

Hochberg, C. B. and Hochberg, J. E. (1952). Familiar size and the perception of depth. *J. Psychol.* **34**, 107–114.

Hochberg, J. E. (1964). "Perception." Prentice-Hall, Englewood Cliffs, N.J.

Hochberg, J. E. (1971a). Perception: I. Color and shape. *In* Kling, J. W. and Riggs, L. A. (Eds) "Experimental Psychology" (3rd edn. of Woodworth and Schlosberg). Holt, Rinehart and Winston, New York.

Hochberg, J. (1971b). Perception: II. Space and movement. *In* Kling, J. W. and Riggs, L. A. (Eds) "Experimental Psychology" (3rd edn. of Woodworth and Schlosberg). Holt, Rinehart and Winston, New York.

Hoffman, F. B. (1925). "Die Lehre vom Raumsinn des Auges 1–II." Springer, Berlin.

Hoffmann, K-P. (1973). Conduction velocity in pathways from retina to superior colliculus in the cat: A correlation with receptive-field properties. *J. Neurophysiol.* **36**, 409–424.

Hoffmann, K-P. and Stone, J. (1971). Conduction velocity of afferents to cat's visual cortex: A correlation with cortical receptive field properties. *Brain Res.* **32**, 460–466.

Hogg, J. (Ed.) (1969). "Psychology and the Visual Arts." Penguin, Harmondsworth.

Holmes, G. (1945). The organization of the visual cortex in man. *Proc. Roy. Soc.* **132 B**, 348–361.

Holway, A. H. and Hurvich, L. M. (1937). Differential gustatory sensitivity to salt. *Am. J. Psychol.* **49**, 37–48.

Honisett, J. and Oldfield, R. C. (1961). Movement and distortion in visual patterns during prolonged fixation. *Scand. J. Psychol.* **2**, 49–55.

Horn, G. (1965). Physiological and psychological aspects of selective perception. *In* Lehrman, D. S. and Hinde, R. A. (Eds) "Advances in Animal Behavior." Academic Press, New York and London.

Horner, W. G. (1834). On the properties of the daedaleine, a new instrument of optical illusion. *Phil. Mag. 3 : er Ser.* **4**, 36–41.

Hornbostel, E. M., von. (1925). Die Einheit der Sinne. *Zs. f. Musik,* **5**, 290–297.

Hornbostel, E. M., von and Wertheimer, M. (1920). Über die Wahrnehmung der Schallrichtung. Akademie der Wissenschaft am Berlin. Preussiche Sitzungsberichte.

Hornstein, A. D. and Rotter, G. S. (1969). Research methodology in temporal perception. *J. Exp. Psychol.* **79**, 561–564.

Howard, I. P. and Templeton, W. B. (1966). "Human Spatial Orientation." Wiley and Sons, New York.

Howard, R. C. (1956). An Experimental Investigation of Projection Theory. Unpubl. Research, Northwestern University, Evanston, Ill.

Hsia, Y. (1943). Whiteness constancy as a function of differences in illumination. *Arch. Psychol.,* New York, no. 284.

Hubel, D. H. (1963). The visual cortex of the brain. *Sci. Am.* **148**–156.

Hubel, D. H. and Wiesel, T. N. (1959). Receptive fields of single neurones in the cat's striate cortex. *J. Physiol.* **148**, 574–591.

Hubel, D. H. and Wiesel, T. N. (1960). Receptive fields of optic nerve fibres in the spider monkey. *J. Physiol.* **154**, 572–580.

Hubel, D. H. and Wiesel, T. N. (1961). Integrative action in the cat's lateral geniculate body. *J. Physiol.* **155**, 385–398.

Hubel, D. H. and Wiesel, T. N. (1962). Receptive fields, binocular interaction and functional architecture in the cat's visual cortex. *J. Physiol.* **160**, 106–154.

Hubel, D. H. and Wiesel, T. N. (1965). Receptive fields and functional architecture in two nonstriate visual areas (18 and 19) of the cat. *J. Neurophysiol.* **28**, 994–1002.

Hubel, D. H. and Wiesel, T. N. (1967). Cortical and callossal connections concerned with the vertical meridian of visual fields in the cat. *J. Neurophysiol.* **30**, 1561–1573.

Hubel, D. H. and Wiesel, T. N. (1968). Receptive fields and functional architecture of monkey striate cortex. *J. Physiol.* **195**, 215–243.

Hugelin, A., Dumont, S. and Paillas, N. (1960). Tympanic muscles and control of auditory input during arousal. *Science* **131**, 1371–1372.

Humboldt, A., von. (1799, 1800). A letter in two parts, September 1, 1799 and November 17, 1799. *In* Fr. von Zach's monatliche Correspondenz zur Beförderung der Erd- und Himmelskunde, Bd. 1, 1800, 396.

Hurvich, L. M. and Jameson, D. (1955). Some quantitative aspects of an opponent-colors theory: II. Brightness, saturation and hue in normal and dichromatic vision. *J. Opt. Soc. Am.* **45**, 602.

Hurvich, L. M. and Jameson, D. (1957). An opponent-process theory of color vision. *Psychol. Rev.* **64**, 384–404.

Hurvich, L. M. and Jameson, D. (1960). Perceived color, induction effects and opponent response mechanisms. *J. Gen. Physiol.* **43** (suppl.), 63–80.

Hurvich, L. M. and Jameson, D. (1966a). "The Perception of Brightness and Darkness." Allyn and Bacon, Boston.

Hurvich, L. M. and Jameson, D. (1966b). Theorie der Farbwahrnehmung. *In* Thomae, H. (Ed.) "Handbuch der Psychologie." Hogrefe, Göttingen.

Hurvich, L. M. and Jameson, D. (1974). Opponent processes as a model of neural organization. *Am. Psychologist* **29**, 88–102.

Huttenlocher, J. (1967). Discrimination of figure orientation: Effects of relative position. *J. Comp. Physiol. Psychol.* **63**, 359–361.

Høffding, H. (1911). "La pensée humaine. Ses formes et ses problèmes." Felix Alcan, Paris.

Israel, N. R. (1966). Individual differences in GSR orienting response and cognitive control, *J. Exp. Res. Pers.* **1**, 244–248.

Ittelson, W. H. (1951). Size as a cue to distance: Static localization. *Am. J. Psychol.* **64**, 54–67.

Ittelson, W. H. and Kilpatrick, F. P. (1951). Experiments in perception. *Sci. Am.* **181**, 50–55.

Ittelson, W. H. and Kilpatrick, F. P. (1960). "Visual Space Perception." Springer, New York.

Jaensch, E. R. (1911). "Über die Wahrnehmung des Raumes." *Zs. f. Psychol.*, Erg. Bd. **6**.

Jalavisto, E. (1942). Oma ruumiimme havaintomme kohteena (Über die Wahrnehmung des eigenen Körpers). *Duodecim* **58**, 187–209.

Jalavisto, E. (1948). Observations on Arm-Amputees. *Ann. Acad. Sci. Fenn.* A 17. Helsinki

Janet, P. (1903). "Les obsessions et la psychoasthenié." Felix Alcan, Paris.

Jansson, G. and Runeson, S. (1969). Measurement of perceived oscillation. *Perception and Psychophys.* **6**, 27–32.

Jauhiainen, T. (1974). "An Experimental Study of the Auditory Perception of Isolated Bi-Syllable Finnish Words." Inst. Physiol., University of Helsinki.

Jeffress, L. A. and Blodgett, H. C. (1962). Effect of switching earphone channels upon the precision of centering. *J. Acoust. Soc. Am.* **34**, 1275–1277.

Jenkins, R. A. (1961). Perception of pitch, timbre and loudness. *J. Acoust. Soc. Am.* **33**, 1550–1557.

Jenkins, W. L. (1938). Studies in thermal sensitivity: VIII. Analytic evidence against the Alrutz theory. *J. Exp. Psychol.* **23**, 417.

Johansen, M. (1954). "An Introductory Study of Voluminal Form Perception." Nordisk Psykologi's Monograph Series, No. 5, Copenhagen.

Johansen, M. (1957). The experienced continuation of some three-dimensional forms. *Acta Psychol.* **13**, 1–26.

Johansen, M. (1959). "Voluminalfigurale faenomener." Munksgaard, Copenhagen.

Johansson, G. (1950). "Configurations in Event Perception. An Experimental Study". Almqvist and Wiksell, Uppsala.

Johansson, G. (1964). Perception of motion and changing form. A study of visual perception from continuous transformations of a solid angle of light at the eye. *Scand. J. Psychol.* **5**, 181–208.

Johansson, G. (1975). Visual motion perception. *Sci. Amer.*, 76–87.

Johansson, G. and Jansson, G. (1968). Perceived rotary motion from changes in a straight line. *Perception and Psychophys.* **4**, 165–170.

Johnson, D. M. (1972). "A Systematic Introduction to the Psychology of Thinking." Harper and Row, New York.

Jones, P. D. and Holding, D. H. (1975). Extremely long-term persistence of the McCollough effect. *Human Percept. and Perform.* **1**, 323–327.

Josephson, R. (1955). "Konstverkets födelse." Natur och Kultur, Stockholm.

Judd, D. B. (1940). Hue, saturation and lightness of surface colors with chromatic illumination. *J. Res. Nat. Bureau Standards*, **24**, 293–333.

Judd, D. B. (1951). Basic correlates of the visual stimulus. *In* Stevens, S. S. (Ed.) "Handbook of Experimental Psychology." Wiley and Sons, New York.

Judd, D. B. (1960). Appraisal of Land's work on two-primary color projections. *J. Opt. Soc. Am.* **50**, 254–268.

Julész, B. (1960). Binocular depth perception of computer-generated patterns. *Bell System Techn. J.* **39**, 1125–1161.

Julész, B. (1963). Stereopsis and binocular rivalry of contours. *J. Opt. Soc. Am.* **53**, 994–999.

Julész, B. (1964). Binocular depth perception without familiarity cues. *Science* **145**, 356–362.

Jung, R. (1961). Korrelationen von Neuronentätigkeit und Sehen. *In* Jung, R. and Kornhuber, H. (Eds) "Neurophysiologie und Psychophysik des visuellen Systems." Springer, Berlin.

Jung, R. (1967). Neurophysiologie und Psychiatrie. *In* Gruhle, H. W. *et al.* (Eds) "Psychiatrie der Gegenwart," Vol. I/1, Part A. Springer, Berlin.

Jung, R. (1973). Visual perception and neurophysiology. *In* Jung, R. (Ed.) "Handbook of Sensory Physiology," Vol. III/3, Part A. Springer, Berlin.

Junge, K. (1966). "Some Problems of Measurements in Psychophysics." Universitetsforlaget, Oslo.

Järvilehto, T. (1973). Neural coding in the temperature sense. Human reactions to temperature changes as compared with activity in single peripheral cold fibers in the cat. *Ann. Acad. Sci. Fenn.* B **184**, Helsinki.

Järvinen, E. J. (1964). Relative depth localization of chromatic surfaces in alternating incandescent and fluorescent illumination. *In* v. Fieandt, K., Ahonen, L., Järvinen, E. J. and Lian, A. "Color Experiments with Modern Sources of Illumination." *Ann. Acad. Sci. Fenn.* B **134**, 2.

Järvinen, E. J. (1969). "Orthogonal Localization of Visual Objects." *Ann. Acad. Sci. Fenn.* B **165**.

Jørgensen, J. (1941). "Psykologi paa biologisk grundlag." Munksgaard, Copenhagen.

Kagan, J. and Kagan, N. (1970). Individual variation in cognitive processes. *In* Mussen, P. H. (Ed.) "Carmichael's Manual of Child Psychology." Wiley and Sons, New York.

Kaila, E. (1932). "Die Reaktionen des Säuglings auf das menschliche Gesicht." *Ann. Univ. Aboensis.* B **17**, Turku.

Kaila, E. (1939). "Inhimillinen tieto; mitä se on ja mitä se ei ole" (Human Knowledge: What it is and what it is not). Otava, Helsinki.

Kaila, E. (1944). Logik und Psychophysik, Ein Beitrag zur theoretischen *Psychologie*. *Theoria*, **10**, 91–119.

Kaila, E. (1962). "Die Perceptuellen und Konzeptuellen Komponenten der Alltagserfahrung". *Acta Philos. Fennica*, **13**.

Kaneko, A. (1970). Physiological and morphological identification of horizontal, bipolar and amacrine cells in dogfish retina. *J. Physiol.* **207**, 623–633.

Kaneko, A. (1971). Electrical connexions between horizontal cells in the dogfish retina. *J. Physiol.* **213**, 95–105.

Kanizsa, G. (1966). Die Erscheinungsweisen der Farben. *In* Thomae, H. (Ed.) "Handbuch der Psychologie" I, 1. Hogrefe, Göttingen.

Kanizsa, G. (1969). Perception, past experience and the "impossible experiment". *Acta Psychol.* **31**, 66–96.

Kanizsa, G. (1970). Amodale Ergänzung und "Erwartungsfehler" der Gestaltpsychologen. *Psychol. Forsch.* **33**, 325–344.

Kanizsa, G. (1976). Subjective contours. *Sci. Am.*, 48–52.

Karlin, L. (1970). Cognition, preparation and sensory-evoked potentials. *Psychol. Bull.* **73**, 122–136.

Katz, D. (1911). Die Erscheinungsweisen der Farben und ihre Beeinflussung durch die individuelle Erfahrung. *Zs. f. Psychol.*, Erg. Bd. **7**.

Katz, D. (1921). Zur Psychologie des Amputierten und seiner Prothese. *Zs. f. ang. Psychol.*, BHft. **25**.

Katz, D. (1925). Der Aufbau der Tastwelt. *Zs. f. Psychol.*, Erg. Bd. **11**.

Katz, D. (1935). "The World of Colour." Routledge and Kegan, London.

Katz, D. (1944). "Gestaltpsychologie." Schwabe, Basel.

Katz, D. (Ed.) (1951). "Handbuch der Psychologie." Schwabe, Basel.

Katz, R. (1941). "Barnpsykologiska studier." Natur och Kultur, Stockholm.

Kaufman, L. (1965). Some new stereoscopic phenomena and their implications for the theory of stereopsis. *Am. J. Psychol.* **78**, 1–20.

Kaufman, L. (1974). "Sight and Mind." Oxford University Press, London.

Keidel, W. D. (Ed.) (1970). "Kurzgefasstes Lehrbuch der Physiologie." 2. Auflage. Thieme, Stuttgart.

Kempler, B. and Wiener, M. (1963). Personality and perception in the recognition threshold paradigm. *Psychol. Rev.* **31**, 386–393.

Kenshalo, D. R. (1971). The cutaneous senses. *In* Kling, J. W. and Riggs, L. A. (Eds) "Handbook of Experimental Psychology" (3rd edn. of Woodworth and Schlosberg). Holt, Rinehart and Winston, New York.

Kenshalo, D. R. and Nafe, J. P. (1962). A quantitative theory of feeling. *Psychol. Rev.* **69**, 17–33.

Kikuchi, Y. (1957). Objective allocation of sound-image from binaural stimulation. *J. Acoust. Soc. Am.* **29**, 124–128.

Kimura, K. and Beidler, L. M. (1961). Microelectrode study of taste receptors of rat and hamster. *J. Cell. Comp. Physiol.* **58**, 131–140.

Kimura, R. S. (1966). Hairs of the cochlea sensory cells and their attachment to the tectorial membrane. *Acta-Oto-Laryngologica* **61**, 55–72.

Kirmse, W. (1964). Messende Versuche über die Grössenkonstanz bei der optischen Wahrnehmung. *Zs. f. Psychol.* **170**, 224–241.

Kissin, B., Gottesfeld, H. and Dickes, R. (1957). Inhibition and tachistoscopic thresholds for sexually charged words. *J. Psychol.* **43**, 333–339.

Klatt, D. H. and Peterson, G. E. (1966). Reexamination of a model of the cochlea. *J. Acoust. Soc. Am.* **40**, 54–61.

Klein, G. S. (1951). The personal world through perception. *In* Blake, R. R. and Ramsey, G. V. (Eds) "Perception: An Approach to Personality." Ronald Press, New York.

Klein, G. S. and Schlesinger, H. J. (1951). Perceptual attitudes towards instability. I: Prediction of apparent movement experiences from Rorschach responses. *J. Pers.* **19**, 289–302.

Kleint, B. H. (1940). "Versuche über die Wahrnehmung. Beiträge zur Analyse der Gesichtswahrnehmungen." 11 Heft. Herausgegeben von Schumann, F., Barth, Leipzig.

Kling, J. W. and Riggs, L. A. (Eds) (1971). "Experimental Psychology" (Woodworth and Schlosberg's Experimental Psychology, 3rd edn.). Holt, Rinehart and Winston, New York.

Klix, F. (1971). "Information und Verhalten." VEB Deutscher Verlag d. Wissenschaft, Berlin.

Knudsen, F. (1974). "Stereokinese. Et eksperimentalpsykologisk studium af synsoplevede figurbevaegelser." English summary: Stereokinesis. An experimental and phenomenological study of visually perceived depth in shadow projections of rotating objects. Akademisk Forlag, Copenhagen.

Koch, S. (1959). "Psychology: A Study of a Science." Vol. 1. McGraw-Hill, New York.

Koch, S. (1962). "Psychology: A Study of a Science." Vol. 4. McGraw-Hill, New York.

Koelega, H. S. (1970). Extraversion, sex, arousal and olfactory sensitivity. *Acta Psychol.* **34**, 51–66.

Koffka, K. (1935). "Principles of Gestalt Psychology." Routledge and Kegan, London.

Kohler, I. (1951). "Über Aufbau und Wandlungen der Wahrnehmungswelt." Sitzungsberichte, 207, no. 1, Abhandlungen Österreichischer Akademie der Wissenschaften, Wien.

Köhler, W. (1920). "Die physischen Gestalten in Ruhe und im stationären Zustand. Nieweg, Braunschweig.

Kolb, H. (1974). The connections between horizontal cells and photoreceptors in the retina of the cat: Electron microscopy of Golgi preparations. *J.Comp. Neurol.* **155**, 1–14.

Konorski. J. (1967a). "Integrative Activity in the Brain." University of Chicago Press, Chicago.

Konorski, J. (1967b). Some new ideas concerning the physiological mechanisms of perception. *Acta Biol. Exp.* **27**, 147–161.

Korte, A. (1915). Kinematoskopische Untersuchungen. *Zs. f. Psychol.* **72**, 193–296.

Koseleff, P. (1957). Studies in the perception of heaviness I, *Nordisk Psykologi* **9**, 184–194.

Koseleff, P. (1958). Studies in the perception of heaviness II. *Nordisk Psykologi* **10**, 65–86.

Kozaki, A. A. (1963). A further study in the relationship between brightness constancy and contrast. *Japanese Psychol. Res.* **5**, 129–136.

Kozaki, A. A. (1965). The effect of co-existent stimuli on brightness constancy. *Japanese Psychol. Res.* **7**, 138–147.

Krantz, D. H., Luce, R. D., Suppes, P. and Tversky, A. (1971). "Foundations of Measurement." Academic Press, New York and London.

Kretschmer, E. (1951). "Körperbau und Charakter." Springer, Berlin.

Kretschmer, E. (1952) "A Textbook of Medical Psychology" (2nd English edn.) Hogarth Press, London.

Kries, J., von. (1895). Über die Natur gewisser mit den psychischen Vorgängen verknüpfter Gehirnzustände. *Zs. f. Psychol.* **8**, 1–33.

Krus, D. M., Werner, H. and Wapner, S. (1953). Studies in vicariousness: Motor activity and perceived movement. *Am. J. Psychol.* **66**, 603–608.

Kryter, K. D. (1970). "The Effects of Noise on Man." Academic Press, New York and London.

Kuffler, S. W. (1953). Discharge patterns and functional organization of mammalian retina. *J. Neurophysiol.* **16**, 37–68.

Külpe, O. (1893). "Grundriss der Psychologie auf experimenteller Grundlage dargestellt." Engelmann, Leipzig.

Künnapas, T. M. (1957). The vertical-horizontal illusion and the visual field. *J. Exp. Psychol.* **53**, 405–407.

Künnapas, T. M. and Künnapas, U. (1973). On the relation between similarity and ratio estimates. *Psychol. Forsch.* **36**, 257–265.

Land, E. H. (1959a). Color vision and the natural image. Part II. *Proc. Nat. Acad. Sci.* **45**, 636–644.

Land, E. H. (1959b). Experiments in color vision. *Sci. Am.* **200**, 84–99.

Land, E. H. (1967). Retinex theory of color vision. *J. Opt. Soc. Am.* **57**, 1428.

Landauer, A. A. (1964a). The effect of viewing conditions and instructions on shape judgment. *Brit. J. Psychol.* **55**, 49–57.

Landauer, A. A. (1964b). The effect of instructions on the judgment of brightness. *Quart. J. Exp. Psychol.* **16**, 23–29.

Landis, D., Jones, J. M. and Reiter, J. (1966). Two experiments on perceived size of coins. *Percept. and Mot. Skills* **23**, 719–729.

Lashley, K. S. and Russell, J. T. (1934). The mechanisms of vision. XI. A preliminary test of innate organization. *J. Genet. Psychol.* **45**, 136–144.

Lawrence, D. H. and Coles, G. R. (1954). Accuracy of recognition with alternatives before and after the stimulus. *J. Exp. Psychol.* **47**, 208–214.

Leeper, R. (1935). A study of a neglected portion of the field of learning: The development of sensory organization. *J. Genet. Psychol.* **46**, 41–75.

Le Gros Clark, W. E. (1951). The projection of the olfactory epithelium on the olfactory bulb of the rabbit. *J. Neurol. Neurosurg. Psychiatr.* **14**, 1–10.

Lehtovaara, A., Saarinen, P. and Järvinen, E. J. (1966). Psychological studies on twins (11). The psychomotor rhythm: Environmental versus hereditary determination. *Rep. Psych. Inst., University of Helsinki.* 3/1966.

Lester, G. and Morant, R. B. (1969). The role of the felt position of the head in the audiogyral illusion. *Acta Psychol.* **31**, 375–384.

Lettvin, J. Y., Maturana, H. R., McCulloch, W. S. and Pitts, W. H. (1959). What the frog's eye tells the frog's brain. *Proc. Inst. Rad. Engineer* **47**, 1940–1951. Repr. in Gross, C. G. and Zeigler, H. P. (1969). "Readings in Physiological Psychology: Neuropsychology/Sensory Processes." Harper and Row, New York.

Leuba, C. and Lucas, C. (1945). The effects of attitudes on descriptions of pictures. *J. Exp. Psychol.* **35**, 517–524.

Levine, R., Chein, J. and Murphy, G. (1942). The Relation of the intensity of a need to the amount of perceptual distortion: A preliminary report. *J. Psychol.* **13**, 283–294.

Levy, L. H. (1967). The effects of verbal reinforcement and instructions on the attainment of size constancy. *Can. J. Psychol.* **21**, 81–91.

Lewin, K. (1936). "Principles of Topological Psychology." McGraw-Hill, New York.

Lewis, D. (1960). "Quantitative Methods in Psychology." McGraw-Hill, New York.

Lewis, T. (1946). "Pain." Macmillan, New York.

Lian, A. (1969). "Persepsjonspsykologi." Universitetsforlaget, Oslo.

Libermann, A. M., Cooper, F. S., Harris, K. S. and MacNeilage, P. F. (1962). A motor theory of speech perception. *Proc. Speech Communication Seminar*. Royal Institute of Technology, Stockholm.

Licklider, J. C. R. (1959). Three auditory theories. *In* Koch, S. (Ed.) "Psychology: A Study of a Science." Vol. I. Sensory, Perceptual and Physiological Formulations. McGraw-Hill, New York.

Lie, I. (1969a). Psychophysical invariants of achromatic colour vision: I. The multidimensionality of achromatic colour experience. *Scand. J. Psychol.* **10**, 167–175.

Lie, I. (1969b). Psychophysical invariants of achromatic colour vision: III. Colour constancy and its relation to identification of illumination. *Scand. J. Psychol.* **10**, 269–281.

Lie, I. (1969c). Psychophysical invariants of achromatic colour vision: IV. Depth-adjacency and simultaneous contrast. *Scand. J. Psychol.* **10**, 282–286.

Lie, I. and Orszagh, G. (1971). Simultaneous discrimination of visual attributes. *Scand. J. Psychol.* **12**, 128–130.

Liebman, P. A. (1972). Microspectrophotometry of photoreceptors. *In* Autrum, H., Jung, R., Loewenstein, W. R., MacKay, D. M. and Teuber, H. L. (Eds) "Handbook of Sensory Physiology" VII/1, Springer, Berlin.

Lindahl, M.-B. (1968). On transitions from perceptual to conceptual learning. *Scand. J. Psychol.* **9**, 206–214.

Lindauer, M. S. (1970). Effects of clues in perceiving the "good figure". *Percept. and Mot. Skills* **30**, 588.

Lindauer, M. S. and Lindauer, J. G. (1970). Brightness differences and the perception of figure-ground. *J. Exp. Psychol.* **84**, 291–295.

Lindsley, D. B. (1957). The reticular system and perceptual discrimination. *In* Jasper, H. H., Proctor, L. D., Knighton, R. S., Noshay, W. C., and Castello, R. T. (Eds). "Reticular Formation of the Brain." Churchill, London.

Linke, P. (1907). Die stroboskopischen Täuschungen und das Problem des Sehens von Bewegungen. *Psychol. Stud.* **3**, 393–545.

Linschoten, J. (1956). "Strukturanalyse der binokularen Tiefenwahrnehmung." Wolters, Groningen.

Loewenstein, W. R. (1959). The generation of electric activity in a nerve ending. *Ann. N. Y. Acad. Sci.* **81**, 367–387.

Loewenstein, W. R. (1970). Mechano-electric transduction in the Pacinian Corpuscle. Initiation of sensory impulses in mechano-receptors. *In* Autrum, H., Jung, R., Loewenstein, W. R., MacKay, D. M. and Teuber, H. L. (Eds) "Handbook of Sensory Physiology. I." Springer, Berlin.

Long, E. R., Henneman, R. H. and Garvey, W. D. (1960). An experimental analysis of set: The role of sense-modality. *Am. J. Psychol.* **73**, 563–567.

Long, E. R., Reid, L. S. and Henneman, R. H. (1960). An experimental analysis of set: Variables influencing the identification of ambiguous stimulus-objects. *Am. J. Psychol.* **73**, 553–562.

Longenecker, E. D. (1962). Perceptual recognition as a function of anxiety, motivation and the testing situation. *J. Abnorm. Soc. Psychol.* **64**, 215–221.

Lord, F. M. and Novick, M. R. (1968). "Statistical Theories of Mental Test Scores Reading." Addison-Wesley, Mass.

Lowenstein, D. and Roberts, T. D. (1950). The equilibrium function of the otolith organs of the thornback ray (Raja Clavata). *J. Physiol.* **110**, 392–415.

Luce, R. D. (1972). What sort of measurement is psychophysical measurement? *Am. Psychologist* **27**, 39–74.

Luchins, S. A. (1954). The autokinetic effect in central and peripheral vision. *J. Gen. Psychol.* **50**, 39–44.

Lundholm, H. (1921). The affective tone of lines: Experimental researches. *Psychol. Rev.* **28**, 43–60.

Luneburg, R. K. (1950). The metric of binocular visual space. *J. Opt. Soc. Am.* **40**, 627–642.

Löwenstein, O. (1966). "The Senses." Chaucer Press, Suffolk.

Mach, E. (1865). Bemerkungen zur Lehre vom räumlichen Sehen. *Zs. Philos. u. Phil. Krit.* **46**, 1–5.

Mach, E. (1875). "Grundlinien der Lehre von den Bewegungsempfindungen." Engelmann, Leipzig.

Mach, E. (1900). "Analyse der Empfindungen und das Verhältnis des Physischen zum Psychischen." Fischer, Jena.

MacKay, D. N. and McCulloch, W. S. (1952). The limiting information capacity of a neuronal link. *Bull. Math. Biophys.* **14**, 127–135.

Mackworth, J. F. (1970). "Vigilance and Attention: A Signal Detection Approach." Penguin, Harmondsworth.

McBurney, D. H. and Pfaffmann, C. (1963). Gustatory adaptation to saliva and sodium chloride. *J. Exp. Psychol.* **65**, 523–529.

McClelland, D. C. and Atkinson, J. W. (1948). The projective expression of needs, I: The effect of different intensities of the hunger drive on perception. *J. Psychol.* **25**, 205–222.

McClelland, D. C. and Liberman, A. M. (1949). The effect of need for achievement on recognition of need-related words. *J. Pers.* **18**, 236–251.

McCormick, E. J. (1970). "Human-factors Engineering." McGraw-Hill, New York.

McDermott, W. P. (1969). Linear perspective and perceived size. *Perception and Psychophys.* **5**, 33–36.

McDonald, E. T. and Aungst, L. F. (1967). Studies in oral sensorimotor function. *In* Bosma, J. F. (Ed.) "Symposium in Oral Sensation and Perception." Thomas, Springfield, Ill.

McDonald, E. T. and Solomon, B. (1962). Ability of normal children to differentiate textures, weights and forms in the oral cavity. A pilot study. The Pennsylvania State Univ. Unpublished.

McDonald, R. P. (1962). An artifact of the Brunswik ratio. *Am. J. Psychol.* **75**, 152–154.

McGinnies, E. (1949). Emotionality and perceptual defence. *Psychol. Rev.* **56**, 244–260.

McGree, J. M. (1963). The effect of group verbal suggestion and age on the perception of the Ames trapezoidal illusion. *J. Psychol.* **56**, 447–453.

McNichol, D. (1972). "A Primer of Signal Detection Theory." Allen and Unwin, London.

McNichol, D. and Pennington, C. W. (1973). Sensory and decision processes in anchor effects and aftereffects. *J. Exp. Psychol.* **100**, 232–238.

Maffei, L. and Campbell, F. W. (1970). Neurophysiological localization of the vertical and horizontal visual coordinates in man. *Science* **167**, 386–387.

Maffei, L. and Fiorentini, A. (1973). The visual cortex as a spatial frequency analyser. *Vis. Res.* **13**, 1255–1267.

Magaro, P. A. (1970). An hypothesis concerning the relation between drive and size estimation for paranoids and nonparanoids within specific schizophrenic subgroups. *Percept. and Mot. Skills,* **31**, 489–490.

Maltzman, J. and Rastin, D. C. (1965). Effects of individual differences in the orienting reflex on conditioning and complex processes. *J. Exp. Res. Pers.* **1**, 1–16.

Manning, S. A. and Rosenstock, E. H. (1968). "Classical Psychophysics and Scaling." McGraw-Hill, New York.

Marks, L. E. (1974). "Sensory Processes: The New Psychophysics." Academic Press, New York and London.

Marks, W. B., Dobelle, W. H. and McNichol, E. F. (1964). Visual pigments of single primate cones. *Science* **143**, 1181–1183.

Marriott, F. H. C. (1962). Colour vision. *In* Davson, H. (Ed.) "The Eye, Vol. 2., The Visual Process."

Marshall, D. A. (1968). A comparative study of neural coding in gustation. *Physiol. and Beh.* **3**, 1–15.

Maslin, R. H. (1969). Visual motion perception: Experimental modification. *Science* **165**, 819–821.

Massaro, D. W. (1970). Preperceptual auditory images. *J. Exp. Psychol.* **85**, 411–417.

Mathiesen, A. (1931). Apparent movement in auditory perception. *Psychol. Monogr.* **41**, 74–131.

Mayer-Hillebrand, F. (1934). Zur Frage ob nur den willkürlichen oder auch den unwillkürlichen Augenbewegungen eine raumumstimmende Wirkung zukommt. *Zs. f. Psychol.* **133**, 99–134 and 247–305.

Mayhew, J. E. W. and Anstis, S. M. (1972). Movement after-effects contingent on colour intensity and pattern. *Percept. and Psychophys.* **12**, 77–85.

Mefferd, R. B. Jr. and Wieland, B. A. (1967). Perception of depth in rotating objects: 2. Perspective as determinant of stereokinesis. *Percept. and Mot. Skills* **25**, 621–628.

Mefferd, R. B. Jr. and Wieland, B. A. (1969). Influence of eye dominance on the apparent centers of simple horizontal lines. *Percept. and Mot. Skills* **28**, 847–850.

Meisel, P. and Wapner, S. (1969). Interaction of factors affecting space localization. *J. Exp. Psychol.* **79**, 430–437.

Meissner, G. (1859). Untersuchungen über den Tastsinn. *Zs. f. Rationelle Medizin* **7**, 92–118.

Melzack, R. and Wall, P. D. (1962). On the nature of cutaneous sensory mechanisms. *Brain* **85**, 331–356.

Merzenich, M. and Harrington, T. (1969). The sense of flutter-vibration evoked by stimulation of the hairy skin of primates: Comparison of human sensory capacity with the responses of mechanoreceptive afferents innervating the hairy skin of monkeys. *Exp. Brain Res.* **9**, 236–260.

Metzger, W. (1929a). Optische Untersuchungen am Ganzfeld: II. Zur Phäno-menologie des homogenen Ganzfelds. *Psychol. Forsch.* **13**, 6–29.

Metzger, W. (1929b). Optische Untersuchungen am Ganzfeld: III. Die Schwelle für plötzliche Helligkeitsänderungen. *Psychol. Forsch.* **13**, 30–54.

Metzger, W. (1934). Tiefenerscheinungen in optischen Bewegungsfeldern. *Psychol. Forsch.* **20**, 195–260.

Metzger. W. (1954) "Psychologie, die Entwicklung ihrer Grundannahmen seit der Einführung des Experiments." (2. Aufl.) Steinkopf, Frankfurt a. M.

Michon, J. A. (1964). Studies on subjective duration: I. Differential sensitivity in the perception of repeated temporal intervals. *Acta Psychol.* **22**, 441–450.

Michon, J. A. (1965). Studies on subjective duration: II. Subjective time measurement during tasks with different information content. *Acta Psychol.* **24**, 205–212.

Michotte, A. (1954). "La perception de la causalité." Studia Psychologica Edition "Érasme" Paris–Bruxelles.

Michotte, A. (Ed.) (1962). "Causalité, permanence et réalité phénoménales." Publications Universitaires de Louvain.

Michotte, A., Thinès, A. et Crabbé, G. (1967). Les complément amodaux des structures perspectives. *Studia Psychologica.* Edition "Érasme", Paris–Bruxelles.

Mill, J. S. (1858). "A System of Logic, Ratioconative and Inductive." Harper and Bros, New York.

Mill, J. S. (1963). "Philosophy of Scientific Method." Nagel, E. (Ed.) Hafner, New York.

Mills, A. W. (1958). On the minimum audible angle. *J. Acoust. Soc. Am.* **30**, 237–246.

Mills, A. W. (1960). Lateralization of high-frequency tones. *Ann. Rev. Psychol.* **32**, 132–134.

Minard, J. G. (1965). Response-bias interpretation of "perceptual defence". A selective review and an evaluation of recent research. *Psychol. Rev.* **72**, 74–88.

Minard, J. G. and Mooney, W. (1969). Psychological differentation and perceptual defence: Studies of the separation of perception from emotion. *J. Abnorm. Psychol.* **64**, 131–139.

Mintz, S. and Alpert, M. (1972). Imagery vividness, reality testing and schizophrenic hallucinations. *J. Abnorm. Psychol.* **79**, 310–316.

Moed, H. (1964). Constancy and contrast I. *Acta Psychol.* **22**, 272–320.

Moed, H. (1965). Constancy and contrast II. *Acta Psychol.* **24**, 91–166.

Mohrmann, K. (1939). Lautheitskonstanz im Entfernungswechsel. *Zs. f. Psychol.* **145**, 145–199.

Mollon, J. D. (1969). "Temporal Factors in Perception." D. Phil. thesis, University of Oxford.

Mollon, J. D. (1974). After-effects and the brain. *New Scientist* **61**, 479–482.

Mollon, J. D. and Krauskopf, J. (1973). Reaction time as a measure of the temporal response properties of individual colour mechanisms. *Vis. Res.* **13**, 27–40.

Moray, N. (1959). Attention in the dichotic listening: Affective cues and the influence of instructions. *Quart. J. Exp. Psychol.* **11**, 56–60.

Morgan, C. T., Chapanis, A., Cook, J. S. and Lund, M. W. (Eds) (1963). "Human Engineering Guide to Equipment Design." McGraw-Hill, New York.

Mosier, C. I. (1940). Psychophysics and mental test theory: I. Fundamental postulates and elementary theorems. *Psychol. Rev.* **47**, 355–366.

Mosier, C. I. (1941). Psychophysics and mental test theory: II. The constant process. *Psychol. Rev.* **48**, 235–249.

Moskowitz, H. R. (1970). Sweetness and intensity of artificial sweeteners. *Perception and Psychophysics.* **8**, 40–42.

Mountcastle, V. B., Poggio, G. F. and Werner, G. (1963). The relation of thalamic cell response to peripheral stimuli varied over an intensive continuum. *J. Neurophysiol.* **26**, 807–834.

Mountcastle, V. B., La Motte, R. H. and Carli, G. (1972). Detection thresholds for stimuli in humans and monkeys: Comparison with threshold events in mechanoreceptive afferent nerve fibres innervating the monkey hand. *J. Neurophysiol.* **35**, 122–136.

Y

Moustgaard, I. K. (1963). A phenomenological approach to autokinesis. *Scand. J. Psychol.* **4**, 17–22.

Moustgaard, I. K. (1966). Autokinesen som socialpsykologisk instrument. *Nordisk Psykologi* **18**, 375–391.

Moustgaard, I. K. (1967). Autokinesen som differentialpsykologisk instrument. *Nordisk Psykologi* **19**, 141–161.

Moustgaard, I. K. (1969). Autokinese. Studier over bevaegelseoplevelser af autokinetisk natur. English summary: "Autokinesis. A Study of Autokinetic Phenomena of Movement." Nyt Nordisk Forlag—Busck, Copenhagen.

Moustgaard, I. K. (1975a). Perception and tonus. *Scand. J. Psychol.* **16**, 55–64.

Moustgaard, I. K. (1975b). Phenomenological description after the manner of Edgar Rubin. *J. Phenomenol. Psychol.* **6**, 31–61.

Movshon, J. A. (1974). Velocity preferences of simple and complex cells in the cat's striate cortex. *J. Physiol.* **242**, 121–123.

Mozell, M. M. (1966). The spatiotemporal analysis of odorants at the level of the olfactory receptor sheet. *J. Gen. Physiol.* **50**, 25–41.

Mozell, M. M. (1971). The chemical senses II. Olfaction. *In* Kling, J. W. and Riggs, L. A. (Eds) "Experimental Psychology." (3rd edn. of Woodworth and Schlosberg). Holt, Rinehart and Winston, New York.

Munsell Book of Color (1929). Munsell Color Co., Baltimore.

Munsinger, H. and Gummerman, K. (1967). Identification of form in patterns of visual noise. *J. Exp. Psychol.* **75**, 81–87.

Murch, G. M. (1970). Perception of rotary movement. *J. Exp. Psychol.* **86**, 83–85.

Murch, G. M. (1973). "Visual and Auditory Perception." Bobbs-Merrill, New York.

Musatti, C. L. (1924). "Stereokinetic Phenomena." Psychology Department, Cornell University, 1962. (Translation from *Archhivo Italiano di Psicologia*, 1924, **3**, 105–120.)

Müller, G. E. (1930). Über Farbenempfindungen. Psychophysische Untersuchungen. *Zs. f. Psychol.* Erg. Bd. **17, 18**.

Müller, J. (1838). "Handbuch der Physiologie des Menschen." Holscher, Coblenz.

Myers, D. E. (1965). Conversion from spectral to temporal pattern. *Nature* **206**, 918–919.

Mörner, M. (1963). "Voice Register Terminology and Standard Pitch." Speech Transmission Laboratory, Royal Institute of Technology, Report no. 4. Stockholm.

Mörner, M., Franssou, F. and Fant, G. (1964). Voice registers. Speech Transmission Laboratory, Quarterly Progress and Status Report IV, 18–20.

Nadoleczny, M. (1926). "Kurzes Lehrbuch der Sprach- und Stimmheilkunde." Vogel, Leipzig.

Nafe, J. P. (1934). The pressure, pain and temperature senses. *In* Murchison, C. A. (Ed.) "Handbook of General Experimental Psychology." Clark University Press, Worcester.

Nafe, J. P. and Kenshalo, D. R. (1958). Stimulation and neural response. *Am. J. Psychol.* **71**, 199–208.

Nafe, J. P. and Kenshalo, D. R. (1966). Somästhesie. *In* Thomae, H. (Ed.) "Handbuch der Psychologie, I. 1: Halbband." Verlag für Psychologie, Göttingen.

Nafe, J. P. and Wagoner, K. F. (1941). The nature of sensory adaptation. *J. Gen. Psychol.* **25**, 295–321.

Nagel, W. A. (1898). Über das Aubert'sche Phänomen und verwandte Täuschungen über die vertikale Richtung. *Zs. f. Psychol.* **16**, 373–398.

Naka, K.-I. (1972). The horizontal cells. *Vis. Res.* **12**, 573–588.

Nealy, S. M. and Riley, D. A. (1963). Loss and discovery of discrimination of visual depth in dark-reared rats. *Am. J. Psychol.* **76**, 329–332.

Neff, W. D. (Ed.) (1965, 1967). "Contributions to Sensory Physiology. Vols I, II." Academic Press, New York and London.

Neisser, U. (1967). "Cognitive Psychology." Appleton-Century-Crofts, New York.

Neisser, U. (1971). The processes of vision. *In* Atkinson, R. C. (Ed.) "Contemporary Psychology". San Francisco, 124–141.

Nelson, R., Lützow, A. V., Kolb, H. and Gouras, P. (1975). Horizontal cells in cat retina with independent dendritic systems. *Science* **189**, 137–139.

Newbigging, P. L. (1961). The perceptual reintegration of words which differ in connotative meaning. *Can. J. Psychol.* **15**, 133–142.

Newman, J. D. and Wollberg, Z. (1973). Multiple coding of species-specific vocalizations in the auditory cortex of squirrel monkeys. *Brain Res.* **54**, 287–304.

Newman, J. D. and Symmes, D. (1974). Arousal effects on unit responsiveness to vocalizations in squirrel monkeys. *Brain Res.* **78**, 125–138.

Nissen, H. W., Chow, K. L. and Semmes, J. (1951). Effects of restricted opportunity for tactual, kinesthetic and manipulative experience on the behavior of a chimpanzee. *Am. J. Psychol.* **64**, 485–507.

Norman, D. A. (1968). Toward a theory of memory and attention. *Psychol. Rev.* **75**, 522–536.

Näätänen, R. (1967). "Selective Attention and Evoked Potentials." *Ann. Acad. Sci. Fenn.* B **151**, 1.

Näätänen, R. (1975). Selective attention and evoked potentials in humans: A critical review. *Biol. Psychol.* **2**, 237–307.

Näätänen, R. and Summala, H. (1976). "Road-User Behavior and Traffic Accidents." North-Holland Publishing Co., Amsterdam.

O'Connell, R. J. and Mozell, M. M. (1969). Quantitative stimulation of frog olfactory receptors. *J. Neurophysiol.* **32**, 51–63.

Ogawa, H., Sato, M. and Yamashita, S. (1968). Multiple sensitivity of chorda tympani fibres of the rat and hamster to gustatory and thermal stimuli. *J. Physiol.* **199**, 223–240.

Ogawa, H., Satoru, Y. and Sato, M. (1974). Variation in gustatory nerve fiber discharge pattern with change in stimulus concentration and quality. *J. Neurophysiol.* **37**, 443–457.

Ohmura, T. (1961). Experimental studies on brightness constancy: Problems concerning the effects of the conditions of illumination of space and those of serial stimuli. *Bull. Fac. Lit. Kyushu University* **7**, 103–147.

Olson, R. K. and Attneave, F. (1970). What variables produce similarity grouping? *Am. J. Psychol.* **83**, 1–21.

O'Neill, J. J. (1957). Recognition of intelligibility text materials in context and isolation. *J. Speech and Hearing Disab.* **22**, 87–90.

Ono, H. (1969). Apparent distance as a function of familiar size. *J. Exp. Psychol.* **79**, 109–115.

Ornstein, R. E. (1969). "On the Experience of Time." Penguin, London.

Osborne, J. W. and Farley, F. H. (1970). The relationship between aesthetic preference and visual complexity in abstract art. *Psychon. Sci.* **19**, 69–70.

Osgood, C. E. (1953). "Method and Theory in Experimental Psychology." Oxford University Press, New York.

Osgood, C. E., Suci, G. J. and Tannenbaum, P. H. (1957). "The Measurement of Meaning." University of Illinois Press, Urbana.

Österberg, C. A. (1935). Topography of the layer of rods and cones in the human retina. *Acta Ophthalmol.* Suppl. 6.

Ostwald, W. (1921). Die Grundlage der messenden Farblehre. Grossbrother, Berlin.

Oswald, I., Taylor, A. M. and Treisman, M. (1960). Discriminative responses to stimulation during human sleep. *Brain* 83, 440–453.

Ottoson, D. (1956). Analysis of the electrical activity of the olfactory epithelium. *Acta Physiol. Scand.* 35 (suppl. 122), 1–83.

Over, R. (1963). Size- and distance-estimates of a single stimulus under different viewing conditions. *Am. J. Psychol.* 76, 452–457.

Over, R. and Over, J. (1967). Detection and recognition of mirror-image obliques by young children. *J. Comp. and Physiol. Psychol.* 64, 467–470.

Oyster, C. W. (1968). The analysis of image motion by the rabbit retina. *J. Physiol.* 199, 613–635.

Oyster, C. W. and Barlow, H. B. (1967). Direction-selective units in rabbit retina distribution of preferred directions. *Science* 155, 841–842.

Palmer, G. (1786). Théorie de la lumière applicable aux arts et principalement à la peinture. Hardouin and Gattey, Paris.

Parviainen, Kati (1973). Puhe-elimistön rakenne ja sen toiminnan perusteet. Helsingin yliopiston monistesarja. ("The Structure of the Speech Organs and the Principles of their Function." Mimeographed Report Series. University of Helsinki. Manuscript Helsinki.)

Pasto, T. (1964). "The Space-Frame Experience in Art." Barnes and Co., New York.

Pastore, N. (1952). Some remarks on the Ames oscillatory effect. *Psychol. Rev.* 59, 319–323.

Paul, J. (1970). Entwicklungspsychologie und -psychiatrie des Raumbewusstseins bei Kindern und Jugendlichen. *Materia Medica Nordmark* 22.2, 65–70.

Pentti, L. (1955). Auditory localization during rotation of the visual environment. *Rep. Inst. Psychol., University of Helsinki*, no. 2.

Perrot, D. R., Elfner, L. F. and Homick, J. L. (1969). Auditory spatial orientation. *Perception and Psychophys.* 5, 189–192.

Pettigrew, J. D. (1971). The importance of early visual experience for neurons of the developing geniculostriate system. *Investig. Ophthal.* 11, 386–394.

Pettigrew, J. D. and Garey, L. J. (1974). Selective modification of single neuron properties in the visual cortex of kittens. *Brain Res.* 66, 160–164.

Pettigrew, J. D., Olson, C. and Hirsch, H. V. (1974). Cortical effect of selective visual experience: Degeneration or reorganization? *Brain Res.* 51, 345–351.

Pfaff, D. (1968). Effects of temperature and time of day on time judgments. *J. Exp. Psychol.* 76, 419–422.

Pfaffmann, C. (1941). Gustatory afferent impulses. *J. Cell. Comp. Physiol.* 17, 243–258.

Pfaffmann, C. (1948). Studying the senses of taste and smell. *In* Andrews, T. G. (Ed.) "Methods of Psychology." Wiley and Sons, New York.

Pfaffmann, C. (1950). Somesthesis and the chemical senses. *Ann. Rev. Psychol.* 11, 79–94.

Pfaffmann, C. (1951). Taste and smell. *In* Stevens, S. S. (Ed.) "Handbook of Experimental Psychology." Wiley and Sons, New York.

Pfaffmann, C. (1959a). The sense of taste. *In* Field, J., Magoun, H. W. and Hall, V. E. (Eds) "Handbook of Physiology. Neurophysiology I." Am. Physiol. Soc. Washington.

Pfaffmann, C. (1959b). The afferent code for sensory quality. *Am. Psychologist.* **14**, 226–232.

Pfaffmann, C. (1960). The pleasures of sensation. *Psychol. Rev.* **67**, 253–268.

Piaget, J. (1930). "The Child's Conception of Physical Causality." Harcourt Brace, New York.

Piaget, J. (1954). "The Child's Construction of Reality." Basic Books, New York.

Pick, A. D. (1965). Improvement of visual and tactual form discrimination. *J. Exp. Psychol.* **69**, 331–339.

Pick, H. L. Jr., Klein, R. E. and Pick, A. D. (1966). Visual and tactual identification of form orientation. *J. Exp. Child Psychol.* **4**, 391–397.

Pick, H. L. Jr., Hay, J. C. and Martin, R. (1969). Adaptation to split-field wedge prism spectacles. *J. Exp. Psychol.* **80**, 125–132.

Pick, H. L. Jr., Hay, J. C. and Pabst, J. (1963). Kinesthetic Adaptation to Visual Distortion. Paper presented at the meeting of the Midwestern Psychological Association, Chicago, May 1963.

Pickford, R. W. (1951). "Individual Differences in Colour Vision." Macmillan, London.

Pickford, R. W. (1971). The Psychology of ugliness. Conscious and unconscious expressive art. *In* Jakab, I. (Ed.) "Psychiatry and Art 3." Karger, Basel.

Pickford, R. W. (1972). "Psychology and Visual Aesthetics." Hutchinson Educational Ltd., London.

Pierce, A. H. (1901). "Studies in Auditory and Visual Space Perception." Longmans Green, New York.

Pirenne, M. H. (1970). "Optics, Painting and Photography." Cambridge University Press, London.

Polyak, S. L. (1941). "The Retina." University of Chicago Press, Chicago.

Postman, L., Bruner, J. S. and McGinnies, E. (1948). Personal values as selective factors in perception. *J. Abnorm. Soc. Psychol.* **43**, 142–154.

Poulos, D. A. and Lende, R. A. (1970). Response of trigeminal ganglion neurons to thermal stimulation of oral-facial regions. I. Steady-state response. *J. Neurophysiol.* **33**, 508–571.

Poulsen, H. (1972). "Kognitiv struktur". Akademisk Forlag. Copenhagen.

Poulton, E. C. (1968). The new psychophysics: Six models for magnitude estimation. *Psychol. Bull.* **69**, 1–19.

Power, R. P. (1967). Stimulus properties which reduce apparent reversal of rotating rectangular shapes. *J. Exp. Psychol.* **73**, 595–599.

Pratt, C. C. (1930). The spatial character of high and low tones. *J. Exp. Psychol.* **13**, 278–285.

Pribram, K. H. (1971). "Languages of the Brain." Englewood Cliffs., N.Y.

Pribram, K. H. and Kruger, L. (1954). The new neurology and the functions of the "Olfactory Brain". *Annals of the New York Academy of Sciences* **58**, 109–138.

Pritchard, R. M. (1964). Physiological Nystagmus and Vision. *In* Bender, M. B. (Ed.) "The Oculomotor System." Harper and Row, New York.

Pritchard, R. M., Heron, W. and Hebb, D. O. (1960). Visual perception approached by the method of stabilized images. *Can. J. Psychol.* **14**, 67–77.

Proshansky, H. M., Ittelson, W. H., and Rivlin, L. G. (Eds) (1970). "Environmental Psychology: Man and his Setting." McGraw-Hill, New York.

Quinlan, D. (1970). Effects of sight of the body and active locomotion in perceptual adaptation. *J. Exp. Psychol.* **86**, 91–96.

Raaheim, K. (1961). "Problem Solving: A New Approach." Norwegian Universities Press, Bergen.

Rabin, A. J. (Ed.) (1968). "Projective Techniques and Personality Assessment." Springer, New York.

Rahn, C. (1913). The relation of sensation to other categories in contemporary psychology. *Psychol. Monogr.* **16**, Whole No. 67.

Rall, W. (1970). Dendritic neuron theory and dendrodendritic synapses in a simple cortical system. *In* Schmitt, D. O. (Ed.) "The Neurosciences. Second Study Program." Rockefeller University Press, New York.

Ransom, H. H. (1958). Great expectations. *The Texas Quart.* **1**, IV–VIII.

Ranta- Knuuttila, J. (1962). "Amputoitu sotavammainen. (The amputee disabled soldier)." WSOY, Porvoo.

Ratliff, F. (1962). Some interrelations among physics, physiology and psychology in the study of vision. *In* Koch, S. (Ed.) "Psychology: A Study of a Science, vol. 4." McGraw Hill, New York.

Ratliff, F. (1965). "Mach Bands: Quantitative Studies on Neural Networks in the Retina." Holden-Day, New York.

Rausch, E. (1952). "Struktur und Metrik figural-optischer Wahrnehmung." Kramer, Frankfurt a. M.

Reenpää, Y. (1959). "Aufbau der allgemeinen Sinnesphysiologie." Klostermann, Frankfurt a. M.

Reenpää, Y. (1961). "Theorie des Sinneswahrnehmens." *Ann. Acad. Sci. Fenn.* A 5. *Medica* 78. Helsinki.

Reenpää, Y. (1966). Über die Zeit. Darstellung und Kommentar einiger Interpretationen des Zeitlichen in der Philosophie. Über die Zeit in den Naturwissenschaften. *Acta Philosophica Fennica* **19**. Societas Philosophica Fennica, Helsinki.

Reenpää, Y. (1973). Über die Gründe der von Fechner, Tammi und Stevens aufgestellten psychophysischen Formeln. Deren informationstheoretische Deutung. *Ajatus* (Yearbook of the Philosophical Society of Finland), **35**, 108–123.

Reid, L. S., Henneman, R. H. and Long, E. R. (1960). An experimental analysis of set: The effect of categorical restriction. *Am. J. Psychol.* **73**, 568–572.

Renner, M. (1955). Ein Transozeanversuch zum Zeitsinn der Honigbiene. *Naturwissenschaft*, **42**, 540–541.

Renvall, P. (1929). "Theorie des stereo-kinetischen Phänomens." Annales Universitatis Aboensis B X, 1.

Révész, G. (1934). System der optischen und haptischen Raumtäuschungen. *Zs. f. Psychol.* **131**, 296–375.

Révész, G. (1946). "Einführung in die Musikpsychologie." Francke Ag., Bern.

Révész, G. (1950). "Psychology and Art of the Blind." Longmans Green, London.

Révész, G. (1954). "Introduction to the Psychology of Music." Norman, London.

Reynolds, H. N. (1968). Temporal estimation in the perception of occluded motion. *Percept. and Mot. Skills* **26**, 407–416.

Rice, K. K. and Richter, C. P. (1943). Increased sodium chloride and water intake of normal rats treated with desoxycorticosterone acetate. *Endocrinology* **33**, 106–115.

Riesen, A. H., Ramsey, R. L. and Wilson, P. D. (1964). Development of visual acuity in Rhesus monkeys deprived of patterned light during early infancy. *Psychon. Sci.* 1, 33–34.

Riggs, L. A. (1971). Vision *In* Kling J. W. and Riggs, L. A. (Eds) "Experimental Psychology" (3rd. edn. Woodworth and Schlosberg). Holt, Rinehart and Winston, New York.

Robinson, D. W. and Dadson, R. S. (1956). A re-determination of the equal-loudness relations of pure tones. *Brit. J. Appl. Physics.* 7, 166–181.

Robson, J. G. (1975). Receptive fields: Neural representation of the spatial and intensive attributes of the visual image. *In* Carterette, E. C. and Friedman, M. P. (Eds) "Handbook of Perception, V" Academic Press, New York and London.

Rock, I. and Ebenholtz, S. (1959). The relational determination of perceived size. *Psychol. Rev* 66, 387–401.

Roeckelein, J. E. (1968). The effect of set upon length estimation in active touch perception. *Psychon. Sci.* 13, 193–194.

Roelofs, C. O. and van der Waals, H. G. (1935). Veränderung der haptischen und optischen Lokalisation bei optokinetischer Reizung *Zs. f. Psychol.* 136, 5–49.

Roiha, E. (1966). "Johdatus musiikkipsykologiaan." (Introduction to the Psychology of Music.) Gummerus, Jyväskylä.

Rose, D. (1974). The hypercomplex cell classification in the cat's striate cortex. *J. Physiol.* 242, 123–125.

Rose, J. E., Brugge, J. F., Anderson, D. J. and Hind, J. E. (1967). Phase-locked responses to low-frequency tones in single auditory nerve fibres of the squirrel monkey. *J. Neurophysiol.* 30, 769–793.

Rose, J. E., Gross, N. B., Geisler, C. D. and Hind, J. E. (1966). Some neural mechanisms in the inferior colliculus of the cat which may be relevant to the localization of a sound source. *J. Neurophysiol.* 29, 288–314.

Rosenblith, W. (Ed.) (1961). "Sensory Communication." MIT Press, Cambridge, Mass.

Rosner, B. S. (1962). Psychophysics and neurophysiology. *In* Koch, S. (Ed.) "Psychology: A Study of a Science, vol. 4." McGraw-Hill, New York.

Ross, P. L. (1967). Accuracy of judgments of movements in depth from two-dimensional projections. *J. Exp. Psychol.* 75, 217–225.

Royce, J. R., Carran, A. B., Aftanas, M., Lehman, R. S. and Blumenthal, A. (1966). The autokinetic phenomenon. A critical review. *Psychol. Bull.* 65, 243–260.

Royce, J. R., Stayton, W. R. and Kinkade, R. G. (1962). Experimental reduction of autokinetic movement. *Am. J. Psychol.* 75, 221–231.

Royer, F. L. and Garner, W. R. (1970). Perceptual organization of nine-element auditory temporal patterns. *Perception and Psychophys.* 7, 115–120.

Rubin, E. (1915). "Synsoplevede Figurer." Gyldendal, Copenhagen.

Rubin, E. (1920). Vorteile der Zweckbetrachtung für die Erkenntnis. *Zs. f. Psychol.* 85, 210–223.

Rubin, E. (1921). "Visuell wahrgenommene Figuren." Gyldendal, Copenhagen.

Rubin, E. (1927). Visuell wahrgenommene wirkliche Bewegungen. *Zs. f. Psychol.* 103, 384–392.

Rubin, E. (1936). Taste. *Brit. J. Psychol.* 27, 74–85.

Rubin, E. (1947). Om det psykiske og det fysiske. *Tidskrift för psykologi och pedagogik, no.* 1–2. Göteborg.

Rubin, E. (1949). Experimenta Psychologica. Collected Scientific Papers in German, English and French. Munksgaard, Copenhagen.

Rushton, W. A. H. (1961a). Rhodopsin measurement and dark adaptation in a subject deficient in cone vision. *J. Physiol.* **156**, 193–205.

Rushton, W. A. H. (1961b). Peripheral coding in the nervous system. *In* Rosenblith, W. A. (Ed.) "Sensory Communication". MIT Press, Cambridge Mass.

Rushton, W. A. H. (1963). Increment threshold and dark adaptation. *J. Opt. Soc. Am.* **53**, 104–109.

Rushton, W. A. H. (1965). Visual adaptation. *Proc. Roy. Soc. Lond.*, Ser. B. **162**, 20–46.

Rushton, W. A. H. (1972). Pigments and signals in colour vision. *J. Physiol.* **220**, 1–31.

Sackett, G. P. (1966). Monkeys reared in isolation with pictures as visual input: Evidence for an innate releasing mechanism. *Science* **154**, 1468–1473.

Samuels, I. (1959). Reticular mechanisms and behavior. *Psychol. Bull.* **56**, 1–25.

Sanders, A. F. (1970). Some variables affecting the relation between relative stimulus frequency and choice reaction time. *In* Sanders, A. F. (Ed.) "Attention and Performance III." Proceedings of a Symposium on Attention and Performance. North-Holland Publishing Comp., Amsterdam.

Sarbin, T. R. and Chun, K. T. (1967). A logical flaw on an index to suppress response-bias in perceptual defence measures and the application of a proposed improvement. *Austral. J. Psychol.* **19**, 151–157.

Sarris, V. (1967). Adaptation-level theory: Two critical experiments on Helson's weighted average model. *Am. J. Psychol.* **80**, 331–344.

Sarris, V. (1968). Adaptation-level theory: Absolute or relative anchor effectiveness? *Psychon. Sci.* **13**, 307–308.

Sarris, V. (1971). "Wahrnehmung und Urteil. Bezugssystemeffekte in der Psychophysik". Hogrefe, Göttingen.

Sarris, V. (1974). Wahrnehmungsurteile in der Psychophysik: Über einfache Tests zur Untersuchung eines Informations-Integrations-Modelles. *In* Flix, F. and Geissler, H-G. (Eds) "Organismische Informationsverarbeitung: Zeichenerkennung, Begriffsbildung, Problemlösen." Volk und Wissen, Berlin.

Sarris, V. (1976). The relativism of psychophysical judgment: contrast effects as a function of stimulus range and anchor value. *In* Geissler, H. G. and Zabrodin, Yu, M. (Eds.) "Advances in Psychophysics." VEB, Deutscher Verlag d. Wissenschaften, Berlin.

Sarris, V. and Heineken, E. (1976). An experimental test of two mathematical models applied to the size-weight illusion. *J. Exp. Psychol.: Human Perception and Performance* **2**, 295–298.

Sato, M. (1971). Neural coding in taste as seen from recordings from peripheral receptors and nerves. *In* Beidler, L. M. (Ed.) "Handbook of Sensory Physiology," Vol. IV, Part 2. Springer, Berlin.

Saugstad, P. (1958). Availability of functions. A discussion of some theoretical aspects. *Acta Psychol.* **14**, 384–400.

Saugstad, P. (1965). "An Inquiry into the Foundations of Psychology." Universitetsforlaget, Oslo.

Saugstad, P. and Schioldborg, P. (1966). Value and size perception. *Scand. J. Psychol.* **7**, 102–114.

Saunders, J. E. (1968). Adaptation, its effect on apparent brightness and contribution to the phenomenon of brightness constancy. *Vis. Res.* **9**, 451–468.

Savage, S. W. (1970). "The Measurement of Sensation." University of California Press, Berkeley.

Schachtel, E. G. (1959). "Metamorphosis. On the Development of Affect Perception, Attention and Memory." Basic Books, New York.

Schilder, P. (1950). "Image and Appearance of the Human Body." International University Press, New York.

Schildt, G. (1947). "Riktlinjer för en enhetlig psykologisk tolkning av Paul Cézannes personlighet och konst." Schildt, Helsinki.

Schiller, C. H. (1957). "Instinctive Behavior." International University Press, New York.

Scholz, W. (1925). Experimentalle Untersuchungen über die phänomenale Grösse von Raumstrecken, die durch Sukzessivdarbietung zweier Reize begrenzt werden. Psychol. Forsch. 5, 219–272.

Schweizer, G. (1857). Über das Sternschwanken, I. Bulletin de la société impériale des naturalistes de Moscou. 30, 440–457.

Schweizer, G. (1858). Über das Sternschwanken, II. Bulletin de la société impériale des naturalistes de Moscou. 31, 477–500.

Schöne, W. (1954). "Über das Licht in der Malerei." Verlag Gebr. Mann. Berlin.

Segundo, J. P., Moore, G. P., Stensaas, L. J. and Bullock, T. H. (1963). Sensitivity of neurons in Aplysia to temporal pattern of arriving impulses. J. Exp. Biol. 40, 643–667.

Sellin, T. and Wolfgang, M. E. (1964). "The Measurement of Delinquency." Wiley and Sons, New York.

Shelton, R. L., Arndt, W. B. and Hetherington, J. J. (1967). Testing oral stereognosis. In Bosma, J. F. (Ed.) "Symposium on Oral Sensation and Perception." Thomas, Springfield. Ill.

Shephard, R. N. (1964). Circularity in judgments of relative pitch. J. Acoust. Soc. Am. 36, 2346–2453.

Shephard, R. N., Romney, A. K. and Nerlove, S. B. (Eds) (1972). "Multidimensional Scaling: Theory and Applications in the Behavioral Sciences." Vol. 2. Seminar Press, New York and London.

Shepherd, G. M. (1970). The olfactory bulb as a simple cortical system: Experimental analysis and funtional implications. In Schmitt, D. C. (Ed.) "The Neurosciences. Second Study Program." Rockefeller University Press. New York.

Shepherd, G. M. (1972). The neuron doctrine: A revision of functional concepts. Yale J. Biol. Med. 45, 584–599.

Shepherd, G. M. (1974). "The Synaptic Organization of the Brain." Oxford University Press, New York.

Sherif, M. (1935). A study of some social factors in perception. Arch. Psychol. No. 187.

Sherif, M. (1958). Group influences upon the formation of norms and attitudes. In Macoby, E. E., Newcomb, T. M. and Hartley, L. (Eds) "Readings in Social Psychology." Holt, Rinehart and Winston, New York.

Sherif, M. and Sherif, C. W. (1969). "Social Psychology." Harper and Row, New York.

Sherrington, C. S. (1906). "The integrative Action of the Nervous System." Constable, London.

Shibuya, T. and Shibuya, S. (1963). Olfactory epithelium: Unitary responses in the tortoise. Science 140, 495–496.

Shontz, F. C. (1967). Estimation of distances on the body. Percept. and Mot. Skills 24, 1131–1142.

Shurley, J. T. (1960). Profound experimental sensory isolation. *Am. J. Psychol.* **117**, 539–545.

Siegel, R. J. (1965). A replication of the mel scale for pitch. *Am. J. Psychol.* **78**, 615–620.

Siegman, A. W. (1956). Some factors associated with the visual threshold for taboo words. *J. Clin. Psychol.* **12**, 282–286.

Sinclair, D. C. (1967). "Cutaneous Sensation." Oxford University Press, New York.

Sinclair, D. C., Weddell, C. and Wander, E. (1952). Relationship of cutaneous sensibility to neohistology in human pinna. *J. Anat.* **86**, 402–411.

Singer, G. and Day, R. H. (1969). Visual capture of haptically judged depth. *Perception and Psychophys.* **5**, 315–316.

Singer, G., Purcell, A. T. and Austin, M. (1970). The effect of structure and degree of tilt on the tilted room illusion. *Perception and Psychophys.* **7**, 250–252.

Singer, W., Tretter, F. and Cynader, M. (1975). Organization of cat striate cortex: A correlation of receptive-field properties with afferent and efferent connections. *J. Neurophysiol.* **38**, 1080–1098.

Sinha, A. K. P. and Sinha, S. N. (1967). Müller-Lyer illusion in subjects high and low in anxiety. *Percept. and Mot. Skills* **24**, 194.

Sjöberg, L. (1963). An empirical application of a new case of the law of comparative judgment. *Scand, J. Psychol.* **4**, 97–107.

Sjöberg, L. (1965). A study of four methods for scaling paired comparison data. *Scand, J. Psychol.* **6**, 173–185.

Sjöberg, L. (1975). Models of similarity and intensity. *Psychol. Bull.* **82**, 191–206.

Skowbo, D., Timney, B. N., Gentry, T. A. and Morant, R. B. (1975). McCollough effects: Experimental findings and theoretical accounts. *Psychol. Bull.* **82**, 497–510.

Skramlik, E. von (1937). Psychophysiologie der Tastsinne. *Arch. ges. Psychol.* Erg. Bd. **4**. Leipzig.

Sluyters, R. C. van and Blakemore, C. (1973). Experimental creation of unusual neuronal properties in visual cortex of kitten. *Nature* **246**, 506–508.

Smith, D. V. and McBurney, D. H. (1969). Gustatory cross-adaptation: Does single mechanism code salty taste. *J. Exp. Psychol.* **80**, 101–105.

Smith, K. R. (1948). Visual apparent movement in the absence of neural interaction. *Am. J. Psychol.* **61**, 73–78.

Smith, K. U. and Smith, W. K. (1962). "Perception and Motion." Saunders, Philadelphia.

Smith, O. W. (1958). Judgments of size and distance in photographs. *Am. J. Psychol.* **71**, 529–538.

Smith, O. W. and Smith, P. C. (1954). The use of photographs as a basis for behavioral adjustments to space and distance. *Rep. Aud. Vis. Aids Div.*, HRRL, Bolling AFB, Washington DC, 1–51.

Smith, O. W. and Smith, P. C. (1957). Interaction of the effect of cues involved in judgments of curvature. *Am. J. Psychol.* **70**, 361–375.

Sokolov, E. N. (1960). Neuronal modes and the orienting reflex. *In* Brazier, M. A. B. (Ed.) "The Central Nervous System and Behavior." Josiah Macy Jr., New York.

Solley, C. M. and Murphy, G. (1960). "Development of the Perceptual World." Basic Books, New York.

Solonen, K. A. (1962). The phantom phenomenon in amputated Finnish war veterans. *Acta Orthop. Scand.*, Suppl. **54**.

Somervill, J. W. and Sharratt, S. (1970). Retinal size in the visual cliff situation. *Percept. and Mot. Skills* **31**, 903–911.

Sovijärvi, A. (1938). "Die gehaltenen, geflüsterten und gesungenen Vokale und Nasale der Finnischen Sprache, Physiologische physikalische Lautanalysen." *Ann. Acad. Scient. Fenn.* B **44**, 2, Helsinki.

Sovijärvi, A. (1949). Muutamia äänenkäytön perusohjeita ja artikulointimme hoitoharjoituksia (some fundamental advice for articulation improvement exercises). *In* Krohn, E. (Ed.) "Teatteritaide. Gummerus, Jyväskylä."

Sovijärvi, A. (1953). Lauluäänen käyttö ja äänifysiologiset harjoitukset (The singing voice and the soundphysiological training) *In* Kirkko ja Musiikki, Helsinki.

Sovijärvi, A. (1976). Psychological treatment of the singing voice (published in Finnish 1953) (In press).

Spence, D. E. (1957). A new look at vigilance and defence. *J. Abnorm. Soc. Psychol.* **54**, 103–108.

Sperling, G. (1960). The information available in brief visual presentations. *Psychol. Monogr.* **74**, No. 498

Spong, P., Haider, M. and Lindsley, D. B. (1965). Selective attentiveness and cortical evoked responses to visual and auditory stimuli. *Science* **148**, 395–397.

Stavrianos, B. K. (1945). The relation of shape perception to explicit judgments of inclination. *Arch. Psychol.* No. **296**.

Stebbins, W. C. (Ed.) (1970). "Animal Psychophysics: The Design and Conduct of Sensory Experiments." Appleton-Century-Crofts, New York.

Stein, D. G. and Rosen, J. J. (1974). "Basic Structure and Function in the Central Nervous System." Macmillan, New York.

Steinberg, R. H. and Schmidt, R. (1970). Identification of horizontal cells as S-potential generators in the cat retina by intracellular dye injection. *Vis Res.* **10**, 817–820.

Steinfeld, G. J. (1967). Concepts of set and availability and their relation to the reorganization of ambiguous pictorial stimuli. *Psychol. Rev.* **74**, 505–522.

Steinmetz, G., Pryor, G. T. and Stone, H. (1970). Olfactory adaptation and recovery in man as measured by two psychophysical techniques. *Perception and Psychophys.* **8**, 327–330.

Stevens, S. S. (1936). A scale for the measurement of a psychological magnitude: Loudness. *Psychol. Rev.* **43**, 405–416.

Stevens, S. S. (Ed.) (1951). "Handbook of Experimental Psychology." Wiley and Sons, New York.

Stevens, S. S. (1956). The direct estimate of sensory magnitudes: Loudness. *Am. J. Psychol.* **69**, 1–25.

Stevens, S. S. (1959a). Measurement, psychophysics, and utility. *In* Churchman, C. W. and Ratoosh, P. (Eds) "Measurement: Definitions and Theories." Wiley and Sons, New York.

Stevens, S. S. (1959b). Tactile vibration: Dynamics of sensory intensity. *J. Exp. Psychol.* **57**, 210–218.

Stevens, S. S. (1961). The psychophysics of Sensory function. *In* Rosenblith. W. A. (Ed.) "Sensory Communication." Wiley and Sons, New York.

Stevens, S. S. (1966a). Matching functions between loudness and ten other continua. *Perception and Psychophys.* **1**, 5–8.

Stevens, S. S. (1966b). A metric for the social consensus. *Science* **151**, 530–541.

Stevens. S. S. (1972). *Psychophysics and Social Scaling.* General Learning Press, Morristown, N.J.

Stevens, S. S. and Newman, E. B. (1936). The localization of actual sources of sound. *Am. J. Psychol.* **48**, 297–306.

Stevens, S. S., Volkman, J. and Newman, E. B. (1937). A scale for the measurement of the psychological magnitude pitch. *J. Acoust. Soc. Am.* **8**, 185–190.

Stevens, S. S. and Davis, H. (1947). "Hearing. Its Psychology and Physiology." Wiley and Sons, New York.

Stevens, S. S. and Galanter, E. H. (1957). Ratio scales and category scales for a dozen perceptual continua. *J. Exp. Psychol.* **54**, 377–411.

Stewart, E. C. (1959). The Gelb effect. *J. Exp. Psychol.* **57**, 235–242.

Stoebauer, M. K. (1967). The relationship of psychometrically determined personality variables to perception of the Ames trapezoidal illusion. *J. Psychol.* **67**, 90–97.

Stone, H., Oliver, S. and Kloehn, J. (1969). Temperature and pH effects on the relative sweetness of supra-threshold mixtures of dextrose fructose. *Perception and Psychophys.* **5**, 257–260.

Stone, J. (1972). Morphology and physiology of the geniculocortical synapse in the cat: The question of parallel input to the striate cortex. *Investig. Ophthal.* **11**, 338–346.

Stone, J. and Dreher, B. (1973). Projection of X- and Y-cells of the cat's lateral geniculate nucleus to areas 17 and 18 of visual cortex. *J. Neurophysiol.* **36**, 551–567.

Stone, J. and Hoffmann, K-F. (1973). Very slow-conducting ganglion cells in the cat's retina: A major, new functional type? *Brain Res.* **43**, 610–616.

Stratton, G. M. (1897). Upright vision and the retinal image. *Psychol. Rev.* **4**, 182–187.

Stuart, I. R. and Bronzaft, A. L. (1970). Perceptual style, test anxiety and test structure. *Percept. and Mot. Skills* **30**, 823–825.

Sutherland, N. S. (1957). Visual discrimination of orientation and shape by the octopus. *Nature* **179**, 11–13.

Sutherland, N. S. (1961). Figural after-effects and apparent size. *Quart. J. Exp. Psychol.* **13**, 222–228.

Svaetichin, G. (1956). The cone action potential. *Acta Physiol. Scand.* **39**, 17–46.

Svaetichin, G., Krattenmacher, W. and Laufer, M. (1960). Photostimulation of single cones. *J. Gen. Physiol.* **432**, 101–114.

Svaetichin, G. and McNichol, E. F. (1958). Retinal mechanisms for chromatic and achromatic vision. *Ann. N. Y. Acad. Sci.* **74**, 385–404.

Sweet, W. H. (1959). Pain. *In* Field, J., Magoun, H. W. and Hall, V. E. (Eds) "Handbook of Physiology. Neurophysiology I." Am. Phys. Soc., Washington D.C.

Swets, J. A. and Kristofferson, A. B. (1970). Attention. *Ann. Rev. Psychol.* **21**, 339–366.

Takala, M. (1951). "Asymmetries of the Visual Space." *Ann. Acad. Sci. Fenn.* B **72**, 2. Helsinki.

Tapper, D. M. (1964). Cutaneous slowly adapting receptors in the cat. *Science* **143**, 53–54.

Tarow, I. (1969). An application of the T scale of taste. Interaction among the four qualities of taste. *Perception and Psychophys.* **5**, 347–351.

Tasaki, I., Davis, H. and Eldridge, D. H. (1954). Exploration of cochlea potentials in the guinea pig with a microelectrode. *J. Acoust. Soc. Am.* **26**, 765–773.

Teas, D. C. (1962). Lateralization of acoustic transients. *J. Acoust. Soc. Am.* **34**, 1460–1465.

Ternus, J. S. (1926). Experimentelle Untersuchungen über phänomenale Identität. *Psychol. Forsch.* **7**, 81–136.

Teuber, H. I., Battersby, W. S. and Bender, M. B. (1960). "Visual Field Defects after Penetrating Missile Wounds of the Brain." Harvard University Press.

Thomae, H. (Ed.) (1966). "Handbuch der Psychologie. 1. Bd. Allgemeine Psychologie, I. Halbband." Hogrefe, Göttingen.

Thompson, R. F. (1967). "Foundations of Physiological Psychology." Harper and Row, New York.

Thompson, R. F., Smith, H. E. and Bliss, D. (1963). Auditory, somatic sensory and visual response interactions and interrelations in association to primary cortical fields of the cat. *J. Neurophysiol.* **26**, 365–378.

Thor, D. and Crawford, L. (1964). Time perception during two-week confinement: Influence of age, sex, I.Q. and time of day. *Acta Psychol.* **22**, 78–84.

Thurlow, W. R. (1971). Audition. *In* Kling, J. W. and Riggs, L. A. (Eds) "Experimental Psychology" (3rd edn. of Woodworth and Schlosberg). Holt Rinehart, and Winston, New York.

Thurlow, W. R. and Kerr, T. P. (1970). Effect of a moving visual environment on localization of sound. *Am. J. Psychol.* **83**, 112–118.

Thurlow, W. R., Mangels, J. W. and Runge, P. S. (1967). Head movements during sound localization. *J. Acoust. Soc. Am.* **42**, 489–493.

Thurlow, W. R. and Runge, P. S. (1967). Effect of induced head movements during sound localization. *J. Acoust. Soc. Am.* **42**, 480–488.

Thurstone, L. L. (1927). A law of comparative judgment. *Psychol. Rev.* **34**, 273–286.

Thurstone, L. L. (1947). "The Measurement of Values." University Press, Chicago.

Titchener, E. B. (1896). "An Outline of Psychology." Macmillan, New York.

Titchener, E. B. (1901). "Experimental Psychology." Macmillan, New York.

Titchener, E. B. (1908). "Lectures on the Elementary Psychology of Feeling and Attention." Macmillan, New York.

Titchener, E. B. (1915). "A Beginner's Psychology." Macmillan, New York.

Tobias, J. V. and Zerlin, S. (1959). Laterlization threshold as a function of stimulus duration. *J. Acoust. Soc. Am.* **31**, 1591–1594.

Toch, H. H. and Schulte, R. (1961). Readiness to perceive violence as a result of police training. *Brit. J. Psychol.* **52**, 389–393.

Tolkmitt, F. J. (1970). Auditory pattern perception: processing limits and organizational tendencies. *J. Exp. Psychol.* **86**, 171–180.

Tomita, T. (1966). Electrophysiological study of mechanisms subserving color coding in the fish retina. *Cold Spring Harbor Symposia on Quantitative Biology* **30**, 559–566.

Tomita, T. (1970). Electrical activity of vertebrate photo-receptors. *Quart. Rev. Biophys.* **3**, 179–222.

Tonndorf, J. (1958). Harmonic distortion in cochlea models. *J. Acoust. Soc. Am.* **30**, 929–937.

Torgerson, W. S. (1963). "Theory and Method of Scaling." (2nd edn.) Wiley and Sons, New York.

Toshima, Y. (1967). Experimental studies on radial velocity constancy. *In* Akishige, Y. (Ed.) "Experimental Researches on the Structure of the Perceptual Space 6." *Bull. Fac. Lit.* Kyushu University **11**, 1–37.

Toyama, K., Maekawa, K. and Takeda, T. (1973). An analysis of neuronal circuitry for two types of visual cortical neurones classified on the basis of their responses to photic stimuli. *J. Neurophysiol.* **61**, 395–399.

Treisman, A. (1962). Binocular rivalry and stereoscopic depth perception. *Quart. J. Exp. Psychol.* **14**, 23–37.

Treisman, A. M. (1968). Strategies and models of selective attention. Mimeographed. *Inst. Exp. Psychol.* Oxford.

Troland, L. T. (1921). The enigma of color vision. *Am. J. Physiol. Optics* **2**, 23–48.

Tullio, P. (1929). "Some Experiments and Considerations on Experimental Otology and Phonetics." Licinio Cappelli, Bologna.

Ueno, H. (1967). Particular ways of perceiving body in persons who have disease image: From the point of view of body boundary theory. *Tohoku Psychol. Folia* **25**, 91–96.

Uexküll, J. von (1934). "Streifzüge durch die Umwelten von Tieren und Menschen." Springer, Berlin.

Underwood, B. J. (1966). "Experimental Psychology." Appleton-Century-Crofts, New York.

Vernon, M. D. (1970a). "Experiments in Visual Perception." (2nd edn.) Penguin, London.

Vernon, M. D. (1970b). "Perception through Experience." Methuen, Edinburgh.

Verrillo, R. T. (1966). Vibrotactile thresholds for hairy skin. *J. Exp. Psychol.* **72**, 47–50.

Verrillo, R. T. (1968). A duplex mechanism of mechanoreception *In* Kenshalo, D. R. (Ed.) "The Skin Senses." Thomas, Springfield Ill.

Viitamäki, R. O. (1969). Contemporary Approaches to the Dynamics of Perception. *In* Järvinen, E. J. *et al.* (Eds) "Contemporary Research in Psychology of Perception in honorem Kai von Fieandt sexagenarii." WSOY Porvoo.

Virsu, V. (1973). An algorithm for solving some aspects of the relationships between sensory channel systems. *Rep. Psychol. Inst., University of Helsinki* 2/1973.

Virsu, V. and Haapasalo, S. (1973). Relationships between channels for colour and spatial frequency in human vision. *Perception* **2**, 31–40.

Volkelt, H. (1914). Über die Vorstellungen der Tiere. *In* Krueger, F., v. (Ed.) "Arbeiten zur Entwicklungspsychologie, II.".

Voth, A. C. (1941). Individual differences in the autokinetic phenomenon. *J. Exp. Psychol.* **29**, 306–322.

Vroon, P. A. (1970a). Divisibility and retention of psychological time. *Acta Psychol.* **32**, 366–376.

Vroon, P. A. (1970b). Effects of presented and processed information on duration experience. *Acta Psychol.* **34**, 115–121.

Wade, N. J. (1968). Visual orientation during and after lateral head, body and trunk tilt. *Perception and Psychophys.* **3**, 215–219.

Wagner, H. G., MacNichol, E. F. Jr. and Wolbarsht, M. L. (1963). Functional basis for "on"-center and "off"-center receptive fields in the retina. *J. Opt. Soc. Am.* **53**, 66–70.

Wald, G. (1964). The receptors of human color vision. *Science* **145**, 1007–1016.

Wald, G. (1967). Blue blindness in the normal fovea. *J. Opt. Soc. Am.* **57**, 1289–1301.

Wald, G. (1968). Molecular basis of visual excitation. *Science* **162**, 230–239.

Walk, R. D. and Gibson, E. J. (1961). A comparative and analytical study of visual depth perception. *Psychol. Monogr.* **75**, No. 15

Walk, R. D., Gibson, E. J. and Tighe, T. J. (1957). Behavior of light- and dark-reared rats on a visual cliff. *Science* **126**, 80–81.

Wallach, H. (1939). On sound localization. *J. Acoust. Soc. Am.* **10**, 270–274.

Wallach, H. (1940). The role of head movements and vestibular and visual cues in sound localization. *J. Exp. Psychol.* **27**, 339–368.

Wallach, H. (1948). Brightness constancy and the nature of achromatic colors. *J. Exp. Psychol.* **38**, 310–324.

Wallach, H. and Kravitz, J. H. (1965). The measurement of the constancy of visual direction and of its adaptation. *Psychon. Sci.* **2**, 217–218.

Wallach, H., Newman, E. B. and Rosenzweig, M. R. (1949). The precedence effect in sound localization. *Am. J. Psychol.* **52**, 315–336.

Wallach, H. and O'Connell, D. N. (1953). The kinetic depth effect. *J. Exp. Psychol.* **45**, 205–217.

Walls, G. J. (1960). Land! Land! *Psychol. Bull.* **57**, 29–48.

Wapner, S., Werner, H. and Chandler, K. A. (1951). Experiments on sensory-tonic field-theory of perception: I. Effect of extraneous stimulation on the visual perception of verticality. *J. Exp. Psychol.* **42**, 341–345.

Wapner, S., Werner, H. and Morant, R. B. (1951). Experiments on sensory-tonic-field theory of perception: III. Effect of body rotation on the visual perception of verticality. *J. Exp. Psychol.* **42**, 351–357.

Warm, J. S., Clark, J. L. and Foulke, E. (1970). Effects of differential spatial orientation on tactual pattern recognition. *Percept. and Mot. Skills* **31**, 87–94.

Warren, D. H. and Pick, H. L. Jr. (1970). Intermodality relations in localization in blind and sighted people. *Perception and Psychophys.* **8**, 430–432.

Watson, C. S. (1973). Psychophysics. *In* Wolman, B. B. (Ed.) "Handbook of General Psychology." Prentice-Hall, N.J.

Weale, R. A. (1953). Cone-monochromatism. *J. Physiol.* **121**, 548–569.

Weber, E. H. (1834). De pulsu, resorptione, audito et tactu: annotationes anatomicae et physiologicae. 86–92, 132–142, 159–161.

Weddell, G. (1955). Somesthasis and the chemical senses. *Ann. Rev. Psychol.* **6**, 119–136.

Wegel, L. R. and Lane, C. E. (1924). The auditory masking of one pure tone by another and its probable relation to the dynamics of the inner ear. *Phys. Rev.* **23**, 266–285.

Wellek, A. (1934). Die Aufspaltung der Tonhöhe in der Hornbostelschen Gehörspsychologie und die Konstanztheorien von Hornbostel und Krueger. *Zs. f. Musikwissenschaft* **16**, 481–496.

Wellek, A. (1935). Der Raum in der Musik. *Arch. ges. Psychol.* **91**, 395–443.

Weitzmann, E. D., Ross, G. S., Hodos, W. and Galambos, R. (1961). Behavioral method for study of pain in the monkey. *Science* **133**, 37–38.

Werblin, F. S. and Copenhagen, D. R. (1974). Control of retinal sensitivity III. Lateral interactions at the inner plexiform layer. *J. Gen. Physiol.* **63**, 88–100.

Werner, G. and Mountcastle, V. B. (1963). The variability of central neural activity in a sensory system and its implications for the central reflection of sensory events. *J. Neurophysiol.* **26**, 958–977.

Werner, G. and Mountcastle, V. B. (1965). Neural activity in mechanoreceptive cutaneous afferents: Stimulus-response relations, Weber functions, and information transmission. *J. Neurophysiol.* **28**, 359–397.

Werner, G. and Mountcastle, V. B. (1968). Quantitative relations between mechanical stimuli to the skin and neural responses evoked by them. *In* Kenshalo, D. R. (Ed.) "The Skin Senses." Thomas, Springfield, Ill.

Werner, H. (1937). Dynamics in binocular depth perception. *Psychol. Monogr.*, No. **218**.

Werner, H. and Wapner, S. (1949). Sensory-tonic-field theory of perception. *J. Pers.* **18**, 88–107.

Werner, H. and Wapner, S. (1952). Toward a general theory of perception. *Psychol. Rev.* **59**, 324–338.

Wertheimer, M. (1912). Experimentelle Studien über das Sehen von Bewegung. *Zs. f. Psychol.* **61**, 161–265.

Wertheimer, M. (1961). Some problems in the theory of ethics. *In* Henle, M. (Ed.) "Documents in Gestalt Psychology." California University Press, Berkeley.

Wever, E. F. (1949). "Theory of Hearing." Wiley and Sons, New York.

Wexler, D., Mendelson, J., Leiderman, P. H. and Solomon, P. (1958). Sensory deprivation: A technique for studying psychiatric aspects of stress. *Arch. Neurol. and Psychiatr.* **79**, 225–233.

Wheeler, L. (1963). Color-matching responses to red light of varying luminance and purity in complex and simple images. *J. Opt. Soc. Am.* **53**, 978–993.

Wheeler, L. (1965). Modification of induced hue-responses by means of forced matching. *J. Opt. Soc. Am.* **55**, 1020–1023.

Wheeler, L. (1967). Two-component image synthesis: Effects of surround variables. *J. Opt. Soc. Am.* **57**, 1036–1047.

White, B. J. and Mueser, G. E. (1960). Accuracy in reconstructing the arrangements of elements generating kinetic depth displays. *J. Exp. Psychol.* **60**, 1–11.

White, B. W., Saunders, F. A., Scadden, L., Bach-y-Rita, P. and Collins, C. C. (1970). Seeing with the skin. *Perception and Psychophys.* **7**, 23–27.

Whitfield, I. C. and Evans, E. F. (1965). Responses of auditory cortical neurons to stimuli of changing frequency. *J. Neurophysiol.* **28**, 655–672.

Whitsel, B. L., Roppolo, J. R. and Werner, G. (1972). Cortical information processing of stimulus motion of primate skin. *J. Neurophysiol.* **35**, 691–717.

Whittle, P. and Swanston, M. T. (1974). Luminance discrimination of separated flashes: The effect of background luminance and the shape of t.v.i. curves. *Vis. Res.* **14**, 713–719.

Whyman, A. D. and Moos, R. H. (1967). Time perception and anxiety. *Percept. and Mot. Skills* **24**, 567–570.

Wiesel, T. N. and Hubel, D. H. (1965). Extent of recovery from the effects of visual deprivation in kittens. *J. Neurophysiol.* **28**, 1060–1072.

Wiesel, T. N. and Hubel, D. H. (1966). Spatial and chromatic interactions in the lateral geniculate body of the rhesus monkey. *J. Neurophysiol.* **29**, 1115–1156.

Wilcox, W. W. and Clayton, F. L. (1968). Infant visual fixation on motion pictures of the human face. *J. Exp. Child Psychol.* **6**, 22–32.

Wilkening, F., Sarris, V. and Heller, O. (1972). Cnntrast effects in the child's judgment of lifted weight. *Psychon. Sci.* **28**, 207–208.

Willmer, E. N. (1946). "Retinal Structure and Colour Vision." Cambridge University Press, London.

Wilska, A. (1938). "Untersuchungen über das Richtungshören." *Acta Societatis Medicorum Fennicae Duodecim.* Helsinki.

Wilska, A. (1954). On the vibrational sensitivity in different regions of the body surface. *Acta Physiol. Scand.* **31**, 285–289.

Wilson, P. D. and Riesen, A. H. (1966). Visual development in rhesus monkeys neonatally deprived of patterned light. *J. Comp. Psychol.* **61**, 87–95.

Winters, J. J. and Baldwin, D. (1971). Development of two- and three-dimensional size constancy under restricted cue conditions. *J. Exp. Psychol.* **88**, 113–118.

Wishner, J. and Shipley, T. E. Jr. (1954). Direction of autokinetic movement as a test of the "Sensory-Tonic-Field" theory of perception. *J. Pers.* **23**, 99–107.

Witkin, H. A., Dyk, R. B., Faterson, H. F., Goodenough, D. R. and Karp, S. A. (1962, 1974). "Psychological Differentiation." Wiley and Sons, New York.

Witkin, H. A., Goodenough, D. R. and Karp, S. A. (1967). Stability of cognitive style from childhood to young adulthood. *J. Pers. and Soc. Psychol.* **7**, 291–300.

Witkin, H. A., Lewis, H. B. and Herzman, M. (1954). "Personality through Perception." Harper and Bros, New York.

Wohlgemuth, A. (1911). On the after-effect of seen movement. *Brit. J. Psychol.*, Mon. Suppl. No. **1**.

Wolman, B. B. (Ed.) (1973). "Handbook of General Psychology." Prentice Hall, Englewood Cliffs.

Wolsk, D. (1967). The internal environment. *In* Alpern, M., Lawrence, M. and Wolsk, D. (Eds). "Sensory Processes." Wadsworth, Belmont.

Woodworth, R. S. (1938). "Experimental Psychology." Holt, Rinehart and Winston, New York.

Woodworth, R. S. and Schlosberg, H. (1955). "Experimental Psychology." (2nd. rev. edn.). Holt, Rinehart and Winston, New York.

Worden, F. G. (1966). Attention and auditory electrophysiology. *In* Stellar, E. and Sprague, J. M. (Eds) "Progress in Physiological Psychology." Academic Press, New York and London.

Wright, B. and Rainwater, L. (1962). The meanings of colour. *In* Hogg, J. (Ed.) "Psychology and the Visual Arts." Penguin, Harmondsworth.

Wright, M. J. and Ikeda, H. (1974). Processing of spatial and temporal information in the visual system. *In* Schmitt, F. O. and Worden, F. G. (Eds) "The Neurosciences: Third Study Program." MIT Press, Cambridge, Mass.

Yates, J. T. (1974). Chromatic information processing in the foveal projection (area striata) of unanaesthetized primates. *Vis. Res.* **14**, 163–173.

Young, R. W. (1971). A hypothesis to account for a basic distinction between rods and cones. *Vis. Res.* **11**, 1–5.

Young, T. (1801). On the theory of light and colours. A Lecture (read Nov. 12.1801). *In* Peacock, C. (Ed.) "Miscellaneous Works of the Late Thomas Young." 1855. London.

Yoshioka, J. G. (1958). Weber's law in the discrimination of maze distance by the white rat. (1929) *Univ. Calif. Publ. Psychol.* **4**, 155–184. (Cited in Krech, D. and Crutchfield, R. S. "Elements of Psychology", p. 55 Knopf New York).

Zahn, T. P. (1960). Size estimation of pictures associated with success and failure as a function of manifest anxiety. *J. Abnorm. Soc. Psychol.* **61**, 457–462.

Zajonc, R. B. (1962). Response suppression in perceptual defence. *J. Exp. Psychol.* **64**, 206–214.

Zegers, R. T. (1965). The reversal illusion of the Ames trapezoid. *Transact. N.Y. Acad. Sci.* **26**, 377–400.

Zeki, S. M. (1973). Colour coding in rhesus monkey prestriate cortex. *Brain Res.* **53**, 422–427.

Zeki, S. M. (1974). Functional organization of a visual area in the posterior bark of the superior temporal sulcus of the rhesus monkey. *J. Physiol.* **236**, 549–573.

Zelkind, I. and Ulehla, J. (1968). Estimated duration of an auditory signal as a function of its intensity. *Psychon. Sci.* **11**, 185–186.

Zigler, E. (1963). A measure in search of a theory. *Contemp. Psychol.* **8**, 113–135.

Zotterman, Y. (Ed.) (1963). "Olfaction and Taste." Macmillan, New York.

Zotterman Y. (1971). The recording of the electrical response from human taste nerves. *In* Beidler, L. M. (Ed.) "Handbook of Sensory Physiology. Vol. IV, part 2". Springer, Berlin.

Zubek, J. P., Pushkar, D., Sansom, W. and Gowing, J. (1961). Perceptual changes after prolonged sensory isolation. *Canad. J. Psychol.* **15**, 83–100.

Zubin, J., Eron, L. and Schumer, F. (1965). "An Experimental Approach to Projective Techniques." Wiley and Sons, New York.

Zuckerman, M. (1969). Variables affecting deprivation results and hallucinations, reported sensations and images. *In* Zubek, J. P. (Ed.) "Sensory Deprivation: Fifteen Years of Research." Appleton-Century-Crofts, New York.

Zuili, N. and Fraisse, P. (1966). L'estimation du temps en fonctions de la quantité de mouvements effectués dans une tache. Etude génétique. *L'Année Psychol.* **2**, 383–396.

Zwislocki, J. (1960). Theory of temporal auditory summation. *J. Acoust. Soc. Am.* **32**, 1046–1060.

Zwislocki, J. and Feldman, R. S. (1956). Just noticeable difference in dichotic phase. *J. Acoust. Soc. Am.* **28**, 860–864.

Index